THE POLITICAL STAGE

The Political Stage

AMERICAN DRAMA AND THEATER
OF THE GREAT DEPRESSION

MALCOLM GOLDSTEIN

New York
Oxford University Press
1974

To the Memory of
Alan S. Downer

1789740

PREFACE

As THE TITLE SHOULD MAKE CLEAR, this book is intended as a study of one aspect of American dramatic and theatrical art in a particular period. It is, in other words, far from comprehensive in its treatment of the products of our national stage. Two giants of the period, Eugene O'Neill and Thornton Wilder, receive only brief mention in relation to many of their inferiors whose dramatic themes fall within the range of the book. An opening chapter provides comment on the social attitudes of some writers of the nineteen-twenties, and a brief addendum to the final chapter traces into the forties and fifties some of the currents generated by the thirties, but the bulk of the work is a close-focused look at the writers, producers, directors, and actors who helped to give the cultural life of the Great Depression its own special tang.

After the opening chapter, the book is divided into two nearly equal parts. It is a particular date that serves as the dividing point —the conclusion of the season of 1934–35 and the beginning of the season of 1935–36. Each half of the decade had its own air and feel, and to the best of my ability I have tried to communicate my own sense of the differences between them. The change in tone at mid-decade was caused by many factors: the ability of the population to grow used to the discomforts and anxieties of the Depression, a resurgence of optimism caused by New Deal pump-priming measures, the darkening threats of global war emanating from Europe and Asia, and—by no means a minor point—the new Communist party policy, official as of August 1935, seeking an alignment of all liberal and left parties in a "Popular Front" against the common enemy, fascism. Within the two halves of the book, the chapters cover the work of the institutional theaters and independent producers of the decade, and in each chapter the plays of writers offered by and especially associated with the various companies or with the independent stage are reviewed and interpreted. In each half a progression occurs from left to right, with the first chapter in each treating the farthest-left, off-Broadway producing units and the last treating the commercial stage of Broadway. The producing units that spanned the midpoint of the decade are thus taken up in two chapters, and the reflection on their work of national and international social and political developments is, I hope, demonstrated. Inevitably, some repetition occurs, but it is minor; a reader who wishes to go through the two chapters on a particular organization successively should be able to do so without a tiresome sense of *déjà vu*.

In accordance with present-day American practice, I have used the spelling "theater" throughout, except when the word occurs in the titles of books and magazines or as part of a quotation. Thus the reader will find, among other curiosities, both the New Theater League and *New Theatre*, both the Federal Theater Project and *Federal Theatre*.

My sources of information for this book have been varied and abundant. It is a pleasure to acknowledge my great debt to the Theater Collection of the New York Public Library at Lincoln Center, Astor, Lenox, and Tilden Foundations, without whose vast files of typescripts, correspondence, clippings, programs, and shelves of scrapbooks no extended study of the twentieth-century New York stage can be written. I was grateful to find there, in addition to such materials, an extensive collection of mimeographed plays published by the New Theater League and the Federal Theater. From this collection came all the illustrations other than the photographs of the New Dance Company's *Van der Lubbe's Head*, Tamiris and her dancers, and Hallie Flanagan. Other libraries whose special collections I have consulted are those of Princeton, Yale, and Harvard, the

Library of Congress, and the National Archives; for their aid I am grateful. I owe a note of thanks also to the many writers who have preceded me in interpreting the theater and political climate of the nineteen-thirties. In a special category of importance to me were Harold Clurman's *The Fervent Years* and Hallie Flanagan's *Arena*, two essential documents of the intellectual history of the decade, the former a memoir of the Group Theater by one of its three founders and the latter a memoir of the Federal Theater by its National Director. A more recent memoir, John Houseman's *Run-Through*, provided, at virtually the last minute, an account of the Mercury Theater of nearly equal value, along with much else of interest on the Depression stage. The secondary sources and their authors are too numerous to mention in this paragraph but are fully cited in the notes. Two books, however, I wish to acknowledge as being of particular usefulness to me: Irving Howe and Lewis Coser's *The American Communist Party* and Jane De Hart Mathews's *The Federal Theatre, 1935–39.*

Chapter 1 is adapted from my article "The New Playwrights: Theatrical Insurgency in Pre-Depression America," *Theater Survey*, II (1961), 35–53.

I am deeply indebted to Ben Irwin and George Sklar for reading early versions of the chapters on the New Theater League and the Theater Union, respectively. (Neither, I must point out, is responsible for any errors that may have remained uncorrected, or for any errors in comments on the two organizations that may have crept into other chapters.) I wish also to thank Mr. Sklar for the loan of photographs and a typescript of his unpublished play *Merry-Go-Round*, written in collaboration with Albert Maltz, as well as for his patient explanation to me of the political outlook of the Theater Union. Both Mr. Irwin and Mr. Sklar could place historians forever in their debt by writing memoirs of their experiences in the theater of the thirties.

Special thanks for their aid are due the following: Toby Cole, the late John Dos Passos, Lillian Feder, Gilbert W. Kahn (for permission to consult the Otto H. Kahn Papers at Princeton), Armina Marshall (for permission to consult the Theater Guild Papers at Yale), Emanuel Peterfreund, the late Dawn Powell, Harold Rome, Hiram Sherman, and Victor Wolfson (for the gift of a typescript of his play *Bitter Stream*). Still other debts to individuals who thoughtfully replied to my queries on many specific points are recorded in the notes; to list all the illustrious names here would no doubt provide a delightful sop to my vanity, but would also exaggerate the importance of my queries. My greatest personal debt, to my late teacher and friend Alan S. Downer, is recorded in the Dedication.

I wish also to express my gratitude to the American Philosophical Society for a grant in aid, awarded to me many years ago, for preliminary research, and to the John Simon Guggenheim Memorial Foundation for the award of a fellowship for the completion of the book.

MALCOLM GOLDSTEIN

Queens College and the Graduate School, City University of New York

CONTENTS

THE POLITICAL STAGE

1

"NEW" PLAYWRIGHTS AND OTHERS: THE AMERICAN STAGE IN THE NINETEEN-TWENTIES

THE MODERNIST MOVEMENT THAT SWEPT through the stages of Europe in the last quarter of the nineteenth century witnessed the establishment of more international reputations among dramatists than any period since the seventeenth century. By 1900 Ibsen, Strindberg, Zola, Hauptmann, Chekhov, and Shaw had added to the world's store of dramatic masterpieces. A new, unpatronizing forthrightness in the treatment of the working class and the bourgeoisie characterizes much of the work of these writers. But it was not social rebellion that they recommended; primarily their great gift to the theater lay in their determination to explore and describe the human personality with an unexpected candor. In the United States, despite interesting attempts at truth-to-life in the eighteen-nineties and early years of the twentieth century by such writers as James A. Herne, David Belasco, Edward Sheldon, and William Vaughn Moody, it was not until the years immediately following the First World War, when a constellation of new talent emerged, that American dramatists joined the modernist movement in earnest. In consequence, American drama commanded the attention and respect of the international audience as never before. Preeminent among the playwrights of this generation was Eugene O'Neill.

Behind these events was the shattering of serenity caused by the war and the steady growth of respect for psychoanalytic theory. No playwright who considered himself a modernist could still take seriously the prewar belief that the moral lapse of a character had to result in the loss of his life or the lowering of his social status, and audiences, despite some instances of local censorship, shared this view. If any one figure could be described as the writers' principal inspiring force, it was Sigmund Freud, the investigator of the inner life. The ascendancy of the ideas of the social philosopher Karl Marx would come, but not until the following decade, when economic distress was so widespread that social issues necessarily took precedence over personal issues in the playwrights' system of values. For the time being, though social issues were not neglected, it was the problems of the individual in relation to his family or his inner self that appeared to have the strongest theatrical appeal. But if the plays of the twenties on the theme of individual psychology did not prophesy a mass uprising, they were nevertheless astonishing in their encouragement of the liberation of the spirit from conventional taboos. Both Broadway and the off-Broadway stage harbored such dramas. They were realistic works designed to be acted in box sets representing, almost exclusively, the homes of the characters. In Eugene O'Neill's *Anna Christie* (1921), for example, the setting (after Act I) is the barge in which Chris Christophersen and his daughter Anna live; in Sidney Howard's *They Knew What They Wanted* (1924), it is a farmhouse; and in O'Neill's *Strange Interlude* (1928), the settings are dwellings of several kinds and sizes in cities, the suburbs, and the country. Such settings enhanced the personal qualities of the plays by focusing on the characters and keeping a clamorous society, with its numerous stratifications and complaints, out of sight behind the walls. They reflected the mood of a prosperous nation largely satisfied with things as they were, daring enough in its willingness to listen to new ideas about sexual freedom, but ruling out drastic changes in the structure of society.

The happy endings of the best of the new plays were in themselves also indicative of the boom-period optimism of the audience at the same time that they signaled the new freedom felt by the writers. O'Neill's Anna is a former prostitute who in the Victorian age would surely have died before the final curtain (probably of tuberculosis), but in 1921 was allowed to make a love match.[1] Howard's Amy, in *They Knew What They Wanted*, conceives a child in an adulterous episode on her wedding night, but is forgiven by her understanding sixty-year-old husband. At the end, she is happily surrounded, in the combination living and dining room of her husband's farmhouse, by decorative items of her choice—cretonne curtains, lamps with painted shades, and many new pictures. Both of these plays and *Strange Interlude*, the frankest major play of the entire decade, were certified as embodiments of the spirit of the age by the award of the Pulitzer Prize.[2] Without these path-breaking domestic dramas and others such as O'Neill's *Desire Under the Elms* (1924), Arthur Richman's *Ambush* (1921), George Kelly's *Craig's Wife* (1925), and Howard's *The Silver Cord* (1926), the plays of the thirties combining the issue of sexual frustration with social themes would be unimaginable. Clifford Odets, Lillian Hellman, Sidney Kingsley, and many other writers who came to the fore after the Wall Street collapse of 1929 owed more to their immediate predecessors in the theater than perhaps they realized.

But long before the end of the prosperous twenties, voices objecting to the postwar complacency could be heard. So tenacious is the notion that American life in the twenties received its most accurate description in the fiction of F. Scott Fitzgerald that only with difficulty can it be recalled that the age was not a jazz age for everyone. Disapproving comments on capitalist economics could be heard throughout the decade, if one listened closely enough. As early as 1901 the Socialist party had been founded, and in 1919 its farthest Left members began the planning that led eventually to the formation of the Communist party. The anarchistic International Workers of the World (the "Wobblies"), though not so successful as the Socialists or Communists in recruiting members, remained active through the twenties. When A. Mitchell Palmer, Woodrow Wilson's Attorney General, directed raids on meetings of radicals in 1920, the radicals were joined by liberals in voicing complaints. Nor did radicals alone disapprove of discriminatory practices in the professional and business worlds or the verdicts handed down in the much-discussed trials of Tom Mooney and Sacco and Vanzetti.

Reflections against the conservative position on most of these issues

appeared in the drama of the decade—fitfully, but in some very good
plays, on Broadway and off. Among the dramatists of major reputation, those who made the strongest impression as social writers were
O'Neill, with three plays produced off Broadway by the Provincetown
Players, and Elmer Rice, with works on Broadway. Maxwell Anderson, who in the thirties became a leading theatrical spokesman for
the American tradition of rugged individualism, also contributed, as
coauthor, one memorable play to Broadway on an urgent theme,
Gods of the Lightning, and John Howard Lawson, who at the decade's end offered two clamorous radical plays that failed disastrously
in the noncommercial theater, was justly praised for his one good, innovative radical work for the Theater Guild, *Processional.*

In the vanguard as always, O'Neill not only made the boldest
moves forward in drama on psychosexual themes, but in his plays for
the Provincetown group created the decade's strongest dramas on the
black American, *The Emperor Jones* (1920) and *All God's Chillun
Got Wings* (1924), as well as a vivid tragedy of labor, *The Hairy Ape*
(1922). These plays, though requiring antinaturalistic effects and
couched in most scenes in staccato, expressionistic dialogue, are nevertheless intimate, poignant works. They reveal in combination the
writer's understanding of the social inequities under discussion and
his skill in profound, fully rounded characterization: both the social
issue and its psychological effect are sharply illustrated. Brutus Jones,
the black American fugitive from justice who rules an island of blacks
in the Caribbean until threatened with an uprising, is an oafish swag-
gerer, yet a man to pity because of the dehumanizing indignities
forced on him and his race by whites. His flight through the jungle,
highlighted by blood-chilling fantasies and an incessant drumbeat
sounding at the rate of his pulse, ends in a death that is almost noble.
A more sympathetic character, yet one not sentimentalized, is Jim
Harris in *All God's Chillun Got Wings.* Hoping to make his white
wife proud of him, he aspires to a law degree, while she tries to prevent his passing the bar examination and is glad when he fails, lest he
rise to a level of achievement reserved for whites. The isolation of the
couple from society is suggested scenically by the contraction of the
walls of their apartment in the second half of the play, as life closes
in on them. The box set of realistic drama is used to a new purpose,
becoming an enclosure ever more cramping for its paranoid inhabi-

tants. O'Neill's resoundingly expressed indignation distinguishes these plays from the pathetic dramas of life in the South that other, more typical white dramatists offered when attempting to bring the black minority to the stage—for example Paul Green's *In Abraham's Bosom* (1926; a Pulitzer Prize play, also offered by the Provincetown Players) and Du Bose Heyward's *Porgy* (1927), which, though well-intentioned, offered sentimental views of black poverty and withheld all hope of equality.

O'Neill's view in *The Hairy Ape* is as severe as in his black plays: a grim depiction of the indifference of capitalistic society to the workers who keep it going, unlike any Broadway offering of the decade as a revelation of the laborer's sense of his place on the human scale. Yank, the ship's fireman who is also the "ape" of the title, suffers the complete destruction of his pride in his work when the daughter of the chairman of the board of the fleet faints at the sight of him in the stokehole. No mode of revenge on society is possible for him. Even the Wobblies reject him—and reasonably enough, since, misunderstanding their views, he goes to them with an offer to commit acts of violence with their support.

O'Neill did not abandon social and political themes after these early plays, but as his interest in psychology deepened, he wrote less about specific issues in the lives of workers and minority-group members—did not in fact offer the public a work touching on these issues again until 1946 with *The Iceman Cometh*—and wrote more about the broad subject of the relation of economic success to spiritual and sexual fulfillment. This is an issue in *The Great God Brown* (1926) and *Strange Interlude*, among other plays of the twenties, and also in the posthumous *Long Day's Journey into Night*.

Though a less talented writer, Elmer Rice was as much an experimenter with dramatic form as O'Neill, and a more ardent social dramatist. Among the best of his works in almost fifty years of playwriting are the plays on specific social issues viewed from the liberal position. His display-piece of the twenties was *The Adding Machine* (1923), one of the first American plays offered by the Theater Guild, the most prestigious and high-minded commercial producing unit of the decade. Like O'Neill's social tragedies, the play possesses an affinity to the work of the German expressionists in its short scenes, staccato dialogue, and antinaturalistic scenic requirements. To suggest the indifference of employers to their workers, Rice named the white-collar protagonist Mr. Zero and his friends the numbers One through Six. Zero, after a quarter of a century of daily work totaling up figures, is summarily fired and replaced by an adding machine. After another twenty-five years adding figures on a machine in heaven, where he lands after being electrocuted for killing his boss, he returns to earth and another lifetime of the same occupation. "With the great toe of your right foot," he is told,

> you release a lever which focuses a violet ray on the drum. The ray playing upon and through the white mark, falls upon a selenium cell which in turn sets the keys of the adding apparatus in motion. In this way the individual output of each [coal] miner is recorded without any human effort except the slight pressure of the great toe of your right foot (scene vii).

In the hectic, unfeeling twentieth-century world, Zero himself thus becomes the machine. In *Street Scene* (1929) Rice provided a realistic description of life in a New York tenement whose residents are beset by the problems of drink, poverty, and marital infidelity. The building stands for melting-pot America, the families being members of many ethnic groups who learn, rather slowly, how to live together. In one respect it creates an interesting comparison with *All God's Chillun Got Wings:* O'Neill's black protagonist has a sister, Hattie, who is proud of her race and troubled by her brother's marriage to a white woman, just as Sam Kaplan, the sympathetic Jewish undergraduate with the hope of becoming a lawyer, has a sister, Shirley, who is troubled by her brother's fondness for a non-Jewish girl. As schoolteachers, both have chosen one of the most respectable, challenging means of escaping the ghetto open to young women of their time.

The staying power of the plays of O'Neill and Rice is due not only to the writers' craftsmanship, but to their avoidance of specific headline issues in registering complaints against the temper of the period. None of the topical plays of the twenties achieved status as a classic in the American repertory.[3] Maxwell Anderson and Harold Hickerson's *Gods of the Lightning* (1928), on the Sacco-Vanzetti case, was the decade's most forceful play on a specific incident. In the seven-year agony of the immigrant anarchists accused of robbery and murder, ending in their execution in 1927, liberals of all persuasions as well as self-proclaimed leftists found a cause worthy of their passion. In view of the insubstantiality of the evidence on which the convictions were based as well as the seeming prejudice of the courts, it appeared to them that the defendants, who in any event were personally appealing, had been put on trial not for the issues cited at their arrest, but because of their avowed anarchism. Anderson and Hickerson dramatized the arrest and subsequent events realistically, but blunted the edge of the play by the inappropriate use of comic dialogue and the invention of a romance involving the younger of the defendants and the daughter of a Russian anarchist criminal. Though John Gassner was right enough in claiming that the play "is the strongest drama of social protest produced in the nineteen twenties," [4] provided that the observation is intended to refer only to topical drama, it is nevertheless sentimental. Not a popular work, it ran for only 29 performances in a small house, the Little Theater.[5]

More skillfully written, more original in conception, and of greater interest to the historian than *Gods of the Lightning* was John Howard Lawson's *Processional* (1925). Though Lawson offered five plays in the twenties, this was his only work of distinction of the entire decade, and, as it turned out, a play superior to the four that he was to offer during the thirties. Subtitled "A Jazz Symphony of American Life," it is a blast against coal operators, the Ku Klux Klan, yellow journalism, and, in Henry L. Mencken's term, the "booboisie," set to jazz and blues rhythms and played against scenery painted, where appropriate, to suggest the brightly colored backdrops of vaudeville. It was Lawson's intention, as he indicated in the Preface, to borrow for serious drama the colors and sounds of the subliterary stage—"a development, a moulding to my own uses, of the rich vitality of the two-a-day and the musical extravaganza," since only in such theater did he find a "native craftsmanship." The title, which may have been obscure to the audience, he thus explained: "I have endeavored in the present play, to lay the foundations of some sort of native technique, to reflect to some extent the color and excitement of the American processional as it streams about us."

By incorporating elements of popular culture into his work, Lawson moved with one of the currents of American intellectual life of the twenties, as reflected in Gilbert Seldes's *The Seven Lively Arts* (published in 1924), a volume of serious essays on such expressions of the liberated artistic sensibility as the films of Charlie Chaplin and the Keystone Cops, cartoon strips, jazz orchestras and recordings, and musical comedies and revues. In the *Dial,* which Seldes edited, Edmund Wilson also had been writing on many of the same phenomena.[6] In Lawson's comedy-with-music set in a West Virginia coal town, the stage Jew, stage Negro, and other exaggerated comic types from vaudeville and burlesque take part in an action that includes a murder, the off-stage blinding of a labor agitator, and a rally of the Ku Klux Klan, all set against the background of a coal strike. Dynamite Jim Flimmins, the illiterate but likable agitator jailed during the strike, murders one of the soldiers sent to keep order in the mines. Before he is caught and blinded, he sleeps with a jazz-loving flapper named Sadie Cohen, the daughter of the town's Jewish storekeeper. Ultimately, Jim is freed of suspicion of murder because of the lack of evidence against him, the strike is ended by management's concessions to labor, and Sadie, though run down by the Ku Kluxers on suspicion of being generally immoral, is released and given in marriage to Jim, by whom she is six months pregnant. The wedding takes place to the accompaniment of jazz music, and all the characters except the married couple exit dancing up the aisles of the theater. An acrid, consistently entertaining comment on American prejudices and foibles, *Processional,* like *The Adding Machine* before it, enlivened the Theater Guild's schedule of predominantly European "art" dramas of spiritual discontent and unfulfilled sexual desire.

Though hardly a central figure in the theater of the twenties, Lawson was a major contributor, for good or ill, to the expressionistic substratum of the American drama. *Processional* is unique among his early plays in being centered in the proletariat. In *Roger Bloomer* (1923) and *Nirvana* (1926) his major theme was the dehumanizing effect of modern materialism, as manifested in the business boom. As in *The Adding Machine,* workers, moving in unison at their jobs, are no better than mechanical devices, and advertising slogans are a part of everyday speech. But between Rice's protagonist and those of Lawson there is one major difference. Whereas Rice's Mr. Zero suffers from a numbness of the spirit before the curtain goes up, Lawson's characters are still young enough to be sensitive to the spiritual danger confronting the individual in search of wealth. Similar youthful characters, thinly drawn and given to fantasies, appear in such other antimaterialistic plays of the twenties as George S. Kaufman and Marc Connelly's *Beggar on Horseback* (1924), Em Jo Basshe's *Adam Solitaire* (1925), John Dos Passos's *The Garbage Man* (1926; produced at Harvard as *The Moon Is a Gong* in 1925), and Francis Edwards Faragoh's *Pinwheel* (1927). Breaking wholly or partly with realism, the authors wrote sympathetically of youthful innocents trying to find a foothold in a nation in hectic growth.

Kaufman and Connelly, who had already established themselves as purveyors of wise-cracking comedies, slipped back at once into the mainstream of Broadway drama, but Lawson, Basshe, Dos Passos, and Faragoh, along with their friend Michael Gold, continued to experiment. In 1927 they banded together to found the New Playwrights' Theater, one of the most controversial producing organizations in American history, as well as one of the oddest and least successful, and the first professional theatrical company to reflect the values of the radical Left. For all its failures, its awkwardness, and its misjudgment of the public, it was a memorable venture.

Writing in 1931, two years after the founders of the company had called it quits and gone their different ways as professional writers and polemicists, Dos Passos observed,

> One attempt to buck the tide and put on plays dealing with the industrial life around us in a novel experimenting manner, the New Playwrights' Theatre, found no support in the kind of interest and enthusiasm that had kept the Provincetown Players going in the early days, and failed after two [*sic*] seasons. Still, I think it may eventually be remembered as a crude forerunner of a new type of theatre.[7]

In his last point he was quite right; the New Playwrights were remembered by groups that established themselves in the thirties to offer art and politics in combination, but remembered mainly for their mistakes. Backed by a series of grants from the financier Otto H. Kahn, in twenty-four months of feverish activity they produced eight consecutive failures that inspired some of the most acid critical notices of the time. Less disciplined in their theatrical and literary experimentation than the Washington Square Players and the Provincetown Players, two of their forerunners among Greenwich Village groups, they were nevertheless driven, like the directors of those more famous companies, to test the potentialities of new ideas of dramatic art.

More than any other company of the decade, they were fascinated by the new stagecraft of revolutionary Russia and by the notion, brought to them by Lawson, of enriching intellectual drama with borrowings from the subliterary stage. They also were alert to the methods of the German expressionists, which, like the Russians' methods, included mass movements and skeletal scenery, but which by the mid-twenties had lost something of their popularity in Germany itself. Michael Gold, who had been to Russia in the early twenties, had seen some Russian theater, and reports of the constructivist productions of Vsevelod Meyerhold and Alexander Tairov were available in the books of Huntly Carter and Oliver M. Sayler. Moreover, all the writers who were to become the New Playwrights had been much interested in the International Theatrical Exposition held in New York in the late winter and early spring of 1926, at which they had had the opportunity to view designs from both Russia and Germany, as well as from other countries.[8] The methods developed abroad, they believed, would work well in an American theater of a radical slant. They were wrong, as it turned out, but partly, one suspects, because of their own heavyhandedness.

As a group working together, the New Playwrights were alike in looking on the accumulation of wealth as an activity imperiling man's social relations and his sense of personal dignity. They were not professional economists or politicians; nor were they what members of the radical parties and high-income groups alike were accustomed to refer to as the "working class"—that is, the blue-collar labor force— though for a time Gold had had a job as an assistant truck driver.[9] With the exception of Basshe, an eternal bohemian, all had something of the middle class about them. With Dos Passos, it was pride in old Southern ancestry; with Gold, born Itshok Isaac Granich, the vivid memory, later described in *Jews Without Money*, of his childhood in a closely knit Jewish family; with Lawson and Faragoh, perhaps the most revealing of all, the use of middle names. Yet their opposition to majority opinion was not a pose. Gold saw an end to economic and social injustice only in the supremacy of the Communist party, to which he had made a permanent commitment. Lawson, though not yet a Party member, took the same view. Dos Passos, despite his un-willingness to become a member at any time, was in sympathy with the Party's ideas, nevertheless, through a kind of native emotional re-belliousness. Basshe, on the other hand, remained a fence-sitter. He was dismayed, as his plays reveal, by the rapid spread of American materialism, but recommended no drastic means of curbing it. The political allegiance of Faragoh, the least communicative member of the company, is not on public record, but it is clear that he sided with Gold, Lawson, and Dos Passos against Basshe on the political and artistic issue that finally broke up their theater.

For Gold, Lawson, and Dos Passos, the theater that they developed under Kahn's protection represented a second venture in producing. In the spring of 1926, in association with Alexander Artokov (a Rus-sian visitor), the Socialist writer Nathan Fine, and the artists Louis Lozowick and Hugo Gellert, they announced the formation of the Workers' Theater, an amateur troupe that they claimed would be the first theater in America to seek a working-class audience. Scheduled as the opening production was Gold's *Strike!*, a short revolutionary skit of a type later to be well known as agitprop. A note printed with the text of the play in the *New Masses* for July 1926 explains that Gold modeled his piece on others that he had seen performed by groups of workers in Europe.[10] It is a satiric, bitter glimpse into a la-bor-management quarrel ending with the consolidation of the workers into an indomitable, militant mass.

Unfortunately, it is impossible to locate contemporary accounts of the production of *Strike!* or of any other Workers' Theater plays; [11] even the Communist press ignored the company. But reports pub-lished at the end of the decade gave evidence that the movement ini-tiated by the Workers' Theater was then advancing under a dozen small nonprofessional companies in New York.[12] If the Workers' The-atre did nothing more before 1928, it made manifest the missionary ardor of Gold and his colleagues; so much is clear from their choice of *Strike!* for the debut performances, since the play could serve no other purpose than to proselytize the working class. From their point of view, the merit of their second, larger organization was that through it they could work on the sensibilities of a broader audience.

Other early activities of the five writers had created more of a stir. Only Faragoh had a negligible reputation before the founding of the

New Playwrights' Theater, but he could at least boast that in 1926 his translation of Ferenc Molnár's *The Glass Slipper* had been produced by the Theater Guild and that *Pinwheel* was on the schedule of the Neighborhood Playhouse.[13] On the strength of a recommendation from O'Neill, Basshe's *Adam Solitaire* had been produced at the Provincetown.[14] Lawson, Gold, and Dos Passos were very well-known young men-of-letters, and Lawson had achieved distinction in the theater with *Processional*. Between 1917 and 1920 the Provincetown gave three one-act plays by Gold: *Ivan's Return, Down the Airshaft,* and *Money.* The last of these, and the only one to be published, is a tale of five immigrant Jews on the Lower East Side of New York whose concern over money nearly destroys their souls. But it was journalism, not dramaturgy, that was Gold's primary occupation. In his position as editor of the *New Masses,* the literary and sociological magazine designed to follow the Party line, Gold functioned as a universal philosopher who commented on literature, social phenomena, or anything else that interested him, in the light of his studies in Marx. As a steady contributor to whatever sort of periodical, daily, weekly, or monthly, that the Party and its sympathizers could afford to publish he was, until his death in 1967, simply the Communist as Writer. The literary reputation of Dos Passos may have gained nothing from *The Garbage Man,* but it had a firm base in his second and fourth novels, *Three Soldiers* (1921) and *Manhattan Transfer* (1925). Regardless of the difference in quality, the writing of all five authors was uniform enough in theme to account for their decision to form a company where each could display his craftsmanship. Unlike the Workers' Theater, the New Playwrights' Theater was intended to have thoroughly professional standards of production, to attract a wide audience, and to receive as much publicity as the press would grant.

It was Kahn, not the writers, who conceived the notion of founding the company. In 1926 Basshe and Gold came to him separately with requests for private subsidies, and he replied generously with an allowance for Basshe and a plan for the support of a producing unit to be organized by Gold with an initial grant of $15,000, to be followed by other grants. He had seen Basshe's *Adam Solitaire* at the Provincetown and had read two plays by Gold in manuscript.[15] Though the writers expressed the intention of returning the sums Kahn advanced and carried them on their books as loans at five per cent interest, there is no reason to believe that Kahn looked forward to repayment. A man of unusually broad range, he gave as much of himself to the creative and performing arts as to his profession of investment banking. Among his benefactions were gifts, or loans so insecure that they could properly be regarded as gifts, to the Theater Guild, the Provincetown, the Civic Repertory Theater, the Metropolitan Opera Company, and countless individual performers and writers. In 1926 he served as Chairman of the Honorary Committee for the International Theatrical Exposition. In the same year in one of his many public addresses he had expressed the hope for a theater where "Young America" could have its chance.[16] No doubt Gold, Basshe, and their friends were just such young Americans as he had in mind. Neither he nor his beneficiaries could have known that theirs was the last age of large-scale private patronage.

It was also the last age in which a capitalist and a Communist could indulge in camaraderie without suspecting each other's motives. True, the *New Masses* pictured Wall Street bankers as obese know-nothings whose cutaways were draped with dollar signs, but the radicals who congregated in Greenwich Village were not always so narrow-minded as to shun a generous, well-intentioned man because of his economic status. Kahn, for his part, was quite aware that his money was supporting a theater whose goal was the destruction of the system under which he prospered, but that knowledge did not dampen his generosity. It was evident that these men amused him. With Basshe, amiable, stagestruck, and still a boy at twenty-six, he was a father figure, happy to receive reports of the playwright's researches for a play on black Southern life (later produced as *Earth*) along with home-tested recipes for economy dishes. Gold, the one authentic Communist of the group, after the first year of his four-year correspondence with Kahn often signed himself "your class enemy"— on *New Masses* stationery—and addressed Kahn as "the Emperor." But to Kahn, who replied in kind, this brashness was only a pleasant joke. After the stock-market crash of 1929, when the Communist party took a hard line of unremitting contempt for all emblems of entrenched power, a Wall Street Emperor's appointment of a Communist "minister of fine arts," as Kahn often called Gold, would be unthinkable on either side. But in 1927 the revolution seemed not so much a threat as a vague, impractical, and somewhat naïve notion.[17]

Odder than the mock titles, in retrospect, was the site Kahn chose for his first meeting with the writers. On hearing early in January 1927 that Gold was ready to introduce him to the group he had gathered together to form the theater, Kahn replied with an invitation to them to lunch with him at the place where he regularly went for his noonday meal: the Bankers' Club, in the heart of Wall Street. Even in 1927 this was an astonishing enough gesture to give rise to gossip, but it resulted in the loan. To the end, Kahn's relations with his protégés remained very pleasant.[18]

Having their money in hand, the New Playwrights obtained a certificate of incorporation from the State of New York, with themselves as the governing board, and went straight to work.[19] In February they began rehearsals of Lawson's *Loud Speaker* and Basshe's *Earth* and issued a manifesto bluntly headed "The Revolt on Fifty-Second Street," that street being the location of their first playhouse. Written by Basshe in his usual high-pitched style, the manifesto promised "a theatre where the spirit, the movement, the music of the age is carried on, accentuated, amplified, crystalized. . . . In all, a theater which is as drunken, as barbaric, as clangorous as our age, whithal permitting a sense of irony to dull the too sharp edges even when the shades are up." [20] There was not much of a hint in Basshe's words of the political coloration of the plays to come, but his raucous style foreshadowed their frenzied theatricalism. For Basshe, "revolt" seems to have meant only an attack on Broadway's overcautious producers. A season was to pass before the New Playwrights settled in the turbulent territory south of 14th Street, but as the manifesto demonstrates, they were there in spirit from the outset, alongside the Provincetown, the Greenwich Village Theater, the Neighborhood Playhouse, and the Civic Rep—the "art" theaters whose disavowal of the profit motive made it possible for them to take on the antinaturalistic works that were too risky for Broadway. But without admitting it, the New Playwrights differed in one important respect from their off-Broadway rivals. While the other little theaters scheduled musical revues, revivals of standard plays of the past, and examples of Oriental drama as well as the antinaturalistic works for which they were best known, the New Playwrights had no patience with plays lacking immediate social and political application and no great enthusiasm for pictorial beauty.

Under Gold's eye the New Playwrights went on to show the generally skeptical press and public what they had learned from such disparate sources as Karl Marx, the Russian constructivists, and Florenz
Ziegfeld, producer of the *Follies*. Lawson in *Loud Speaker* (1927) and
The International (1928) and Gold in *Hoboken Blues* (1928) put together materials from all these sources; of the company's eight plays,
theirs are the most truculent and aggressive. Only Basshe's *Earth*
(1927) and *The Centuries* (1927) took nothing from Marx. Paul Sifton's *The Belt* (1927) and Upton Sinclair's *Singing Jailbirds* (1928)
embrace the idea of class warfare, but do so primarily in the naturalistic style. Dos Passos's *Airways, Inc.* (1929) is vehemently Marxist,
but naturalistic throughout, apart from occasional flashes of caricature. All closed disappointingly soon, the runs lasting from only 16 to
79 performances.

Loud Speaker, the company's first production, is a rancorous satire
on American politics with too much harshness for comic effect. The
main line of the plot is the successful effort of Harry U. Collins to be
elected governor of New York. Its supporting actions are the neurotic
searchings of Collins's wife and daughter for emotional fulfillment. In
the personality of Collins, an adulterer and clever manipulator of minority-group prejudices, Lawson gave his opinion of the "ruling"
class: it is depraved and malicious, constantly pursuing sex and
power. The electorate is also depraved, because it puts such a man
into office. But it is Collins who dominates the action and deprives
the voters of their common sense. Ultimately Lawson effects poetic
justice by sending the man to death in a fall from the edge of a dais
—so much for American politics—and concludes the play with a
glance at the daughter, who flees as far as China with her lover in the
vain hope of finding contentment. To communicate his vision of
American public and private life, Lawson chose relentlessly abrasive
stage devices. He placed a Negro jazz band in full view of the audience and cued it to underline stage movement with music at frequent
intervals; and if photographs of the production are trustworthy, he or
his director, Harry Wagstaff Gribble, demanded as much posturing
and dancing as normal pacing from his actors. The dances were not
improvised steps, but movements designed by a choreographer, who
was given program credit.[21] For the setting, Mordecai Gorelik designed a symmetrical structure of steps and platforms backed by an
unadorned wall. Plainly carpentered and ugly, this skeletal scenery

combined with the jazz and angular stepping to prevent the audience from losing itself in the plot. Lawson's inspiration more likely than not was Russian, but it is impossible to read his play without calling to mind the theory of distancing the audience from the action that Bertolt Brecht had begun to work out in Germany during the twenties. Seeking a method that would indicate his contempt for the characters and their life style, Lawson ended only by making the audience uncomfortable. This, unfortunately, came to be the usual effect of the New Playwrights' productions. As a token of their unwillingness to conciliate the audience, they adopted Gorelik's design for *Loud Speaker* as their signet. It appeared on their programs, their stationery, and the title pages of the printed versions of their plays.

In *The International* Lawson found new ways to baffle and distress the public. Possibly because he thought the play too complex to entrust to anyone else, he directed it himself. In Production Notes printed with the text, he called for a chorus of sixteen women whose purpose was to combine "jazz treatment with the dignified narrative strophe and antistrophe of Greek drama." Eight members of the chorus were musical-comedy girls of medium height, the other eight "taller women, more dominating, with dignity and character, of the peasant type." In climactic moments the chorus was cued to break into blues songs and go into a dance. The setting, designed by Dos Passos, was a more massive construction than Gorelik's scaffolding for *Loud Speaker:* "Two solid blocks front with a gaping canyon between them, and behind this a thin fourteen foot tower rises to cut off the rear of the stage. . . . The structure might suggest a futurist city, a mountain pile or a rough relief map." For the thin frames that in the earlier play had served to support and comment on a feeble people, the American electorate, these new plans substituted a solid base for the world's revolutionary masses.

No matter how grandiose Lawson's descriptions of the chorus and blocks may be—especially when it is borne in mind that the play was presented on the stage of one of the Village's tiniest theaters, familiarly known as the Cherry Lane but for this production rechristened the New Playwrights' Theater—they were overshadowed by the plot. Its action is at once fantastic and topical, schematic and opaque. Virtually impossible to follow on the printed page, it offers glimpses of an international oil cartel, officials of the Russian government, some

Asian revolutionaries, and the U.S. Marines. Young David Fitch, an American (played by Franchot Tone), takes a stand with the exploited classes in the revolution that follows a war touched off by his own father, a reactionary businessman. A kind of adult Rover Boy, he has numerous adventures, of which the most beneficial to him in his search for meaning in the global upheaval is an affair with a pretty Russian operative named Alise. The girl is an international agitator whose primary purpose in the play is to attract sympathy for her government by such phrases as "I pray to the red flag, that it may pass from nation to nation, held with bloody hands, held high!" (IV). When David dies in her arms at the close of the play, the scene is not so much tragic as morbid, as though the author were describing the fulfillment of a death wish.

The haphazard dramatics of Lawson were rivaled for unpleasantness in Gold's *Hoboken Blues*. This play offered the audience scenes in the lives of Harlem blacks as performed by white actors in blackface. It was three long acts of "revival meetings, horse cars, cake-walk galopades, saloon palaver, cabaret and circus scenes and processionals up and down the aisles," as Brooks Atkinson noted in the *Times,* adding that peanuts and lollipops were tossed to the audience.[22] The play was, to fall back on understatement, hard to take. Since work and happiness are unavailable in Harlem, one ignorant black seeks them in Hoboken, that well-known paradise across the river. On arriving there, he finds the place a dizzying world of jungle foliage, heavy industry, amusement parks, the circus, dollar signs, and advertising posters—the gamut of symbols of American decadence. He soon falls prey to exploiting whites. Exhausted by misadventures, he drops into a sleep that lasts twenty-five years and brings him nightmare images of the country's immorality. Drinking, gambling, and swindling are the norms of behavior. Coming out of his dream, he is still the shuffling "darky" of the first act, and ready to go home to Harlem. The rambling action and the profusion of materials from the subliterary stage resulted in a sorry performance, the shortest in the company's brief history. It was the American dada, an instance of stubborn pride in the ability to shock. But it lacked the sustaining force of a strong intelligence. Somewhere in the furious movement a theme lurked, but few could find it. Difficult to locate even in the quiet of the library, Gold's theme is the advice of a professional agitator to a minority group: shake off your humility and enter the coming battle against the upper economic class. But the insensitivity of his portrayal of blacks—coarse even for the heyday of blackface comedians—leaves his sincerity in doubt.

Gold's aims become clearer if the play is compared to Basshe's two plays for the company, *Earth* and *The Centuries*, both of which illustrate the problems of minority groups. Respectively, the plays describe the slow adjustment of blacks and Jews to life in America. In *Earth* Southern blacks, fifteen years after the Civil War, complete the task of conversion to Christianity from the primitive religion of the African jungle. Their community is their own; whites neither menace it nor enter it from outside. In *The Centuries* Jewish immigrants and their children go through another kind of transition. Impoverished and fearful at first, they gradually learn to live with the perplexing ways of New York—including, to be sure, some labor-management conflicts—and ultimately to make a tolerable home for themselves. Neither play is satisfactory, for *Earth* is written in an almost incomprehensible dialect and does not deal squarely with Southern black poverty, and *The Centuries* is a muddle of farce and pathos, but each affirms the benefits of a free society. Gold, on the other hand, warns in *Hoboken Blues* that the powerful majority in a capitalist society will always exploit the have-not minority, but ends by decrying exploitation for exploitative purposes of his own.

Less exotic in form and language are Sifton's *The Belt*, Sinclair's *Singing Jailbirds*, and Dos Passos's *Airways, Inc.* They are outspoken labor pieces exhibiting such familiar phenomena as ruthless bosses, management spies, and righteously indignant workers.

Sifton, a member of the New Playwrights' board for the second and third seasons, took a political line identical with Lawson and Gold's. His play is a class-conscious defense of labor. The plot, most of which is acted out against a naturalistic setting, concerns the attempt of a group of automotive workers to form a union at their plant. The "Old Man" who owns the company, and who is the perfect image of Henry Ford, is opposed to the union and tries to suppress it. For the time being he succeeds. But at the close of the play the dissident workers destroy the assembly line—the Belt—and promise more disruptive acts for the future.

Though the complaints against management voiced by Sifton were not new to radical literature, he provided novelty with views of the Belt itself, the clanking procession of automobile frames to which the workers adroitly and rhythmically added parts in the fashion of a machine-age ballet. This device was placed behind a scrim that framed the back wall of the setting of a worker's modest home as designed by Dos Passos. The drop for the Belt, as described in Sifton's stage directions, combined impressions of "machinery, middle class luxury, a family group in a car on the 'open road,' à la Satevepost, show and movie posters, corner of a bankbook, gin bottle, church, dollar sign, flag, organized charity, Mother and the Holy Grail" (I, ii)—the familiar symbols again, though reduced in importance by relegation to the background. The Belt as a dynamic expression of American industry brought vitality to the play whenever it was shown, but the rest was forbiddingly disputatious.

No less sentimental in its glorification of labor than *The Belt* was Upton Sinclair's *Singing Jailbirds*. An account of the persecution of an I.W.W. leader reminiscent of the embattled Joe Hill, the play is punctuated with thumping Wobbly tunes that present the working-class ethos as a combination of militancy and innocence. The songs are a protest against the imprisonment of Red Adams, a labor leader who is arrested while organizing a strike of marine transport workers in Southern California. At critical moments the songs sweep over the play to lift Red's spirits as he broods on his misfortunes. Their greatest service is to provide relief from the mystical dialogue between Red and his dead wife, the melancholy phrases of which echo—unconsciously, no doubt—Victorian melodramas of the barroom. Sinclair, like many other inexperienced playwrights writing in behalf of beleaguered labor, relied on lofty rhetoric and muffled hints of pain to elevate his sympathetic characters above the plain-speaking villains. The inevitable death of Red as a result of persecution by management is an event that touches bathos, because the noble figure thus sacrificed in labor's cause is characterized as much by elegant diction as by inherent grace and bravery. The staging was left to Basshe, who did well with it, providing a smooth blend of music and dialogue such as Earl Browne, an outside director, had tried for with *Earth*, but less successfully.[23] The run of *Singing Jailbirds* was the New Playwrights' longest, and the production resulted in a good response to the company's newly announced subscription plan.[24] Nevertheless, it was a failure at the box office. The only New Playwrights work written by a complete outsider, it was backed wholly by Sinclair and friends of his and lost the total investment.[25]

When the New Playwrights closed *Singing Jailbirds* in February 1928 they did not know that they were to offer only one more play. Under the overall supervision of Basshe, they had begun the 1928–29 season with enough confidence to open a bookshop and publish a magazine, *Theatre 29*. But a quarrel centering in the production of Dos Passos's *Airways, Inc.* revealed tensions and animosities that could be ended only by the drastic measure of disbanding. On the evidence, it is clear that the issue was the political slant of the play. Basshe appears to have stood alone in protesting the production.

Dos Passos's play was published (as "A New Playwright's Theatre Production") some months before the opening, but, on the evidence of reviews, was acted as printed. It is a blunt interpretation of the American success dream. Who, Dos Passos asks, might better symbolize America in the boom years than the aviator? Not even the clever stock-market operator could so effectively represent the nation's amazing tempo and soaring economic expansion. *Airways, Inc.* has such a symbol in the person of young Elmer Turner, "holder of the world's speed record for heavily loaded planes who recently captured the altitude record for single passenger planes which he still holds" (II). For an act and a half the plot builds to Elmer's business transaction with a group of promoters who ask him to front a new commercial transport fleet using planes of his own design. Since he stands to benefit financially, he is immensely eager to take part. But within minutes of the conclusion of the deal, he is crippled in a hideous crash, thus losing his value to the company. At the end of the play he is as prosperous as he had hoped to be, but paralyzed for life and ignored by his partners.

Had Dos Passos not let his attention slide away from this material, he might have given the company a success, for Elmer's story, despite the obviousness of its political implications, is exciting. But midway through, *Airways, Inc.* becomes the story of two other characters, Walter Goldberg, a labor leader, and Martha Turner, Elmer's sister. Walter at the beginning of the play is directing a strike of textile workers in the little town where the Turners live, not far from New York. The Chamber of Commerce and the police, his enemies, hope to find an opportunity to silence him, since the strike is certain to be costly to management. Their moment comes during a demonstration of the workers on a sunny afternoon. Elmer, flying overhead and dropping antistrike leaflets prepared by the Chamber of Commerce, is suddenly shot down—it is here that he is crippled—and the police drop the gun into Walter's pocket. Nobody believes Walter is guilty, but as Martha, his fiancée, puts it, "Something vague and bloodthirsty like God, the interests, the bosses, call it what you like" (III, ii) wants to destroy him. The play ends with her anguished reaction to the report of his execution for murder.

Though it could be argued that Walter's story relates to Elmer's under the umbrella of Dos Passos's anticapitalist theme, it could not be maintained that the play proceeds in such a way as to develop the relationship effectively. Once Elmer serves as a means of drawing sympathy to Walter, he becomes merely a complaining figure in the background. Dos Passos's published reflections on the production suggest one possible reason for the shift of emphasis and the awkwardness in which it resulted. In *Most Likely to Succeed*, a novel published in 1954, he glanced back at the New Playwrights' Theater, calling it the Craftsmen's Theater, and showed the company at work on what proves to be its last production. The play, *Shall Be the Human Race*, is closer to *The International* than to *Airways, Inc.*, but the men who argue over it are unmistakably Gold and Basshe. Lew Golton, tough, dark-haired, and devoted to the Party, is, of course, Gold; Eli Soltair (the name echoing *Adam Solitaire*), short, mop-haired, rootless, altogether wild in appearance and speech, is Basshe. Against Soltair's better judgment, Golton invites a Party ideologue to suggest the revisions necessary to bring the play into accord with the current Party line—to "class-angle" it, in Dos Passos's phrase. This results in a deplorable failure, after which the company collapses. Five years later he alluded in print to the production again, this time somewhat less obliquely. Shortly before the opening of the dramatization on which he collaborated with Paul Shyre, of his novel *U.S.A.*, he wrote of the old days while explaining his reluctance to return to the theater. He had lost interest because his experiences of the past had given him "a feeling of the hoplessness of the struggle with organized Communists—with whom I still sympathized in some things—who were busy boring from within." [26] The unexpected emphasis placed on Walter Goldberg may represent a Party-inspired effort to class-angle *Airways, Inc.* Walter is not only a victim of money interests, but a figure closely resembling Albert Weisbord, a one-time Harvard law student who undertook agitational work for the Party in the late twenties and was much admired (and publicized) by the Party's elders for his rhetorical skill.[27] Like Weisbord, the Party's instigator of a long and costly strike of textile workers in Passaic, New Jersey, Walter is young, articulate, well-educated, and assigned specifically to the textile industry. The only difference is that Weisbord lived to tell the story.

Basshe's report to Kahn on the breakup of the company is a sad revelation of his sense of loss, and at the same time a hint of the politicking within the organization. In preliminary paragraphs he tells of the plans he had made in the early winter to strengthen the company's reputation. The production of *Singing Jailbirds* promised a new start. Then:

> Suddenly Dos Passos returned from Europe. [The other directors] rallied around him and made a series of disturbances of one kind or another. They wanted Dos' play to be put on by [Edward] Massey. . . . wanted me to resign . . . Claimed that my idea of Theatre had nothing to do with the New Playwrights' Theatre. . . . I agreed to resign but somehow they got frightened: the organization which I had built up was loyal to me and they were afraid it would not function if I stepped out . . . it all seemed childish but since Dos is such a fine fellow and a better writer than I am I agreed to do whatever was in my power to keep the organization intact. Still they were not satisfied. Wanted me to keep away from rehearsals for fear I might affect the actors and the staff. I agreed. It mattered little to me. *That is all!*
>
> The above tells the story not only of this last production but of the manner in which the theatre was run in the last two years. Now the theatre has gone back to its old status. It isn't worth fighting or even worrying about . . . not with this gang.
>
> But it is a pity . . . a great pity . . . there is need for a theatre like this. . . . Not on the same lines. . . . NOT with those "principles" or "ideals," not with a gang which never worked in the theatre proper in any capacity. . . .[28]

And so the New Playwrights gave up. The cost to Kahn was $53,600.[29]

It was no wonder that the five writers could not keep their company going. They were inventive but undisciplined, ambitious but impatient. The assignment of leadership to Gold created a barrier at the very start, because his perfervid faith in communism put him out of touch with things as they were. Inclined always, as his journalism never failed to show, to overestimate the power of the Party and the intellectuals close to it, he could not realize the difficulty involved in conquering a stage whose favorite philosopher was not Marx, but Freud. The period of Marxist ascendancy would come soon enough, but not until the public had experienced a greater shock to its values than any it had felt before. For that matter, the New Playwrights were never in agreement about the distance they were to travel to the left. A conscientious reader of the press might have become aware of this as early as November 1927. In the *New Masses* for that month Gold begged the public to support the group's works: "All these are mass plays. All of them convey the spirit of workers' revolt." Yet in the *New York Times* of November 6, Aben Kandel, a member of the theater's staff, insisted that "the theory [held by the press] that only plays with a strong radical tendency are welcome is decidedly wrong." [30] In the forties Harold Clurman described a revealing moment of confusion at a rehearsal of the first production. Attending the rehearsal, he discovered that the director, Harry Wagstaff Gribble, had no political opinions at all. "This is a theatre of the Left," Gribble told the actors. "Don't ask me what that means, but let it go at that; it's a theatre of the Left. The play we are going to do is John Howard Lawson's *Loudspeaker* [*sic*]. This play is a farce—has a lot of laughs that we have got to get. Let's get going and get them." [31] And confusion in economics as well as politics sometimes beset them: in April 1927 they went as far as the dress rehearsal of an expensive production of Gold's *Fiesta*, a play about rural Mexico, before discovering that it could not break even at the box office.[32]

Added to all this was the problem of writing and producing for the constructivist stage. Compensating for the thinness of their ideas by supercharged theatricalism, they stunned playgoers more often than they stimulated them. That they lacked control was the burden of most reviews. The *Times's* Brooks Atkinson, for example, complained that in *Loud Speaker* "turgid emotion and gags are all one," and that *The Belt* "boils with anger and sputters in all directions." Stark

Young remarked in the same spirit that the New Playwrights' work was always "a slap in the face." For the staff of the *New Masses*, particularly, the task of reviewing the productions seems to have been a source of grief. Gold's colleagues on the magazine mentioned his and Lawson's wrong-headed experimentalism, Basshe's melodramatics, Sinclair's irrelevancies, but did so as tactfully as they could. "I wait for the play," Genevieve Taggard murmured darkly after the fourth production, "that will have the pride of the age in it." Alexander Woollcott of the *New York World* simply (but memorably) dismissed them as so many "revolting playwrights." [33]

For all these reasons, the New Playwrights took separate paths. On publishing *Jews Without Money* in 1930, Gold thought of printing a dedication to Kahn, but decided against it because the public would not understand their relationship.[34] Lawson and Faragoh went to Hollywood, where they quickly established themselves as screenwriters. After writing one more play, the unproduced *Fortune Heights*, Dos Passos returned to fiction. Basshe picked up odd directing jobs and wrote more of his curious plays on a Guggenheim fellowship for which Kahn recommended him.[35] In one way and another, all would be heard of again in the New York theater, but not as a company. Once the long slide downward of the American economy began in the fall of 1929, the dramatic themes preferred by most of the New Playwrights could get a hearing, provided that the plays embodying them were neither dull nor incomprehensible, and companies large and small emerged to put them on. Even before the dissolution of the New Playwrights, Gold was beginning to discover and report on some of those that would prove to be the most stimulating during the Depression years.

PROLETARIAN THEATER
IN THE EARLY THIRTIES

THE ZANINESS THAT HAD LIGHTLY CONCEALED the tense political purpose of the New Playwrights went out of fashion on the far Left with the close of the twenties. In the last three months of 1929 prices of corporate stocks, senselessly inflated by the optimism of investors and the dubious practices of some business and banking executives, took so steep and rapid a slide that a quick recovery was clearly out of the question. The Great Depression settled in, and though fitfully alleviated after 1935, held on until the thirties reached a flaming end. For a writer like Michael Gold, the collapse of the national economy meant that it was not only a time for seriousness of purpose, but for serious artistic representation of it. With Gold always on hand to offer guidance, "proletarian literature" became a subject of profound, extended, and humorless discussion in the leftist press at the beginning of the thirties and continued to be written about, as well as written, for the first half of the decade.

Such literature, it was argued, provided evidence that intelligence was not the exclusive possession of persons who could boast of a college education or wealth, and it could become an important implement in the development of class consciousness among workers and those who identified with them and fought for their cause. But the term "proletarian literature" was vague. Did it mean *only* literature created by workers in their hours away from the factory, the mine, or

the construction job? If so, was it literature aimed only at other workers? Or was it literature *about* them, but written by professional literary men and intended for consumption by all classes? As the Depression ground on, the body of short and long works described as
proletarian by the Communist press piled ever higher, but not all of
it was written by laborers, and little of it seemed to have been written with a readership of such men and women in mind. The Communist party-sponsored anthology *Proletarian Literature in the United
States,* published in 1935 when the movement was waning rapidly, includes a few works by writers who could be said to be workers—in
particular, the authors of a small group of folk songs—but the bulk of
the volume is made up of pieces by such writers as (among many others) Erskine Caldwell, John Dos Passos, Maxwell Bodenheim, Muriel
Rukeyser, George Sklar, Clifford Odets, and Malcolm Cowley, who
may have supported the idea of revolution for a time, but clearly
were not members of the proletariat. But at its birth, which was presided over by Gold in the late twenties, the movement did in fact appear to be an attempt of workers to speak for and of themselves,
though often through a coat of editorial varnish.

As early as 1927 Gold created space in the *New Masses* for quantities of the verse and prose of scantily educated writers, out of faith in
their ability to express themselves with as much force as literary intellectuals could summon when writing about them. It did not trouble
him that most of them were poor stylists, provided they compensated
for roughness of diction with revolutionary ardor. As the stock market
floundered in 1929 Gold initiated the practice of setting aside a page
of the magazine for reports of "workers' art," and as additional encouragement for the development of such art the magazine established the John Reed Club, a cultural society named for the late Harvard graduate who had witnessed the October Revolution in Russia
and written an account of it in *Ten Days That Shook the World,* and
whose ashes rested in the Kremlin.[1] The original New York club was
soon the model for similar clubs in other cities.

Replies to Gold's requests for news of workers' groups was hearten-
ing. An especially strong response came from theatrical craftsmen,
who reported that for the past year many groups of New York factory
employees had begun to perform militant plays in their off hours.
Led by the Workers Laboratory Theater, about twelve companies

had united in a Workers Dramatic Council and according to the Council's secretary were engaged in a full program of production. From their headquarters in the Workers School in Union Square they promoted classes in play-writing to supplement a meager repertory, and on August 1, 1929, they had filmed "the anti-imperialist demonstration in the Square." [2] They were "mobile" groups—that is, units lacking permanent stages—and because they performed only at meetings and rallies with no thought of attracting outside criticism, they had escaped the notice of the press.

There was nothing fraudulent about these bands of worker-actors. They were exactly what they proclaimed themselves to be: part-time performers willing to give up their leisure for the purpose of jarring other workers into class-consciousness through their plays. For the time being they were content to act for such an audience alone and did not wish to hide the fact that in all their activities they supported the Communist party. If genuine proletarian literature was created anywhere, it was created in these troupes for as long as they remained proletarian.

It was the party's burst of trade-unionist activity in the late twenties that brought the proletarian theatrical societies into being and the crash of the market that kept them alive. With virtually no help from persons with previous experience in the theater,[3] they performed in aid of the Trade Union Unity League (before 1929 the Trade Union Educational League), the International Labor Defense, the Workers International Relief, and the International Workers Order, the organizations set up by the party to build Communist-led unions. Beyond this they had the larger purpose of advancing the revolutionary policy of the party's Third Period, so called because in 1929 the Executive Committee of the Communist International (the Comintern) declared in Moscow that in 1927 the economy of capitalist nations had entered its third stage since the First World War, a period of decline after periods of growth and stabilization. The shattering effect of the Depression on social and political values gave cogency to anticapitalist predictions and bills of complaint. With unemployment figures rapidly rising toward the astoundingly high estimate of eighteen million in 1932,[4] it could not be argued convincingly on any side—least of all on the side of the Hoover administration—that this was a temporary lapse. Taking up the work of recruiting for communism, the proletarian actors at least won an audience. Whether they drew many workers into the party is another question, and one for which no answer has been given by known party members. The importance of the Communist theatrical fronts to the party's work in general was no doubt less than that of the American League Against War and Fascism (established in 1933), but certainly greater than that of such Third Period enterprises as the Labor Sports Union, the Freiheit Chorus, and the International Workers Order Mothers' League. More to the point is the fact that the theaters continued to grow as other fronts came and went. Though the Trade Union Unity League itself ended in complete failure in 1935, the proletarian troupes that had taken a hand in its work went on to dramatize the leftist view of the nation's anxieties through the Depression and into the first years of the Second World War, surviving the drastic dramatic shifts of Comintern policy in 1935, 1939, and 1941.

At its window on Union Square in 1929 the Dramatic Council watched and listened with the party's eyes and ears. The bright note of Village playfulness and spontaneity that had sounded throughout the New Playwrights' dealings with Otto Kahn was now silent. "Class Against Class," the motto of the Trade Union Unity League, might have served for all party activity in the Third Period. With stubbornness born of faith in Stalinism, the American Communists took all social institutions outside the party's sphere to be actively hostile to their program. In the editorials of the *Daily Worker* and the skits of the workers' troupes, William Green of the American Federation of Labor was one of labor's "misleaders"; the Socialist party's Norman Thomas, Morris Hilquit, and Heywood Broun were as wicked as the heads of the two major parties in their indifference to labor's needs; proletarian children were safer in the Young Pioneers, a party organization for youth, than in the Boy Scouts, "an organization of the bosses preparing the children of workers for the next war." [5] Under the same myopic view, the slightest hint of mass action was assumed to be evidence of the workers' power. The Third Period was a time of preparation for the revolution that could begin, so the official line had it, at any moment. On one day in that optimistic time a member of the *Daily Worker* staff, according to Whittaker Chambers, mistook a meeting of needle-trades workers in Union Square for a revolutionary platoon and declared, "It's begun. The masses are storming the Amalgamated Bank." On another day Robert Minor, the *Worker's* editor, dashed about the office in a moment of joy on hearing of a small riot in Midwestern farming country, shouting, "It's the beginning of the American revolution . . . we must play it up *big*." [6] This enlivening faith was no less prevalent in the workers' theatrical troupes during the Third Period; as a play of 1931—it could just as well have been a play of 1929 or 1930—reminded the audience,

> Workers of the World
> In your hands lies the power
> To build and rebuild.
> UNITE AND FIGHT
> CLASS AGAINST CLASS.[7]

The Workers Laboratory Theater—usually shortened to WLT in print—was the acknowledged leader of the new theatrical movement. In 1926 its founders, Albert Prentis, Louis DeSantes, and Florence Rauh, among others, had taken part in the activities of the old Workers Theater and had regrouped after its expiration without the help of Gold, Dos Passos, John Howard Lawson, and Nathan Fine, the writers who had established it. In 1930 a number of energetic newcomers took up the work, among them Alfred Saxe, Harry Elion, Will Lee, and the brothers Jack and Hiam Shapiro.[8] Only the Shapiros, who were metal craftsmen, could make much of a claim to membership in the proletariat, but the entire staff identified with the workers and with the party's revolutionary aims. An almost equally prominent company was the German-speaking Prolet-Buehne ("Proletarian Stage"), that since 1925 had brought short plays to fraternal organizations and in 1928 began to present social plays exclusively. The company was headed by John E. Bonn, an exceptionally able director, and Anne Howe.[9] Both WLT and Prolet-Buehne patterned their programs after the widely reported work of the Russian "Blue Blouses" and similar German troupes of factory employees who with simple props and costumes played at labor gatherings whenever requested and often without invitation. Such troupes had originated in Russia in support of the revolution.[10] "This [kind of theatre]," an anonymous spokesman for WLT announced,

> . . . must be organized in such a manner that dramatic troupes may
> be developed thruout the country; traveling groups may be evolved,
> ready one day to go to strike meetings to cheer up the strikers, just

as ready another day to accompany a demonstration to inspire the
workers; it must be a theatre where the worker may be inspired to
fight for his liberation; a theatre of the class struggle—a theatre of
the workers, by the workers, for the workers.[11]

A theater established for such a purpose could not use densely plotted, allusive material of the sort staged by the New Playwrights, for
the audience from shops and lofts would have neither the patience to
sit through prolonged action nor the learning necessary for grasping
the allusions. What was required was declarative speech to an immediately perceivable point. The sketches created by WLT and Prolet-
Buehne, after the example of the European workers' troupes, consisted of short exchanges of dialogue on current topics. In keeping
with the Third Period disapproval of individualism, many of them
were unsigned works composed by teams of writers. The generic
terms for these rapid-fire little pieces was "agitprop," for "agitation
and propaganda."

In agitprop the proletarian companies found a most useful dramatic
method. For all the simplicity of the pieces in which the form was
first used, it could provide exciting entertainment when taken up by a
troupe with theatrical flair, which WLT and Prolet-Buehne possessed.
Some of the earliest agitprop skits were realistic but crude, but most
were a blend of chanted dialogue and mass-movement in which the
actors, performing in unison, symbolized the working-class solidarity
essential for the overthrow of the bosses. The plots, such as they were,
moved ahead so rapidly that the audience had no opportunity to
think over the anticapitalist allegations it heard. Propaganda does
not thrive on reflection.

Gold's *Strike!*, which, it will be recalled, was the first piece announced for production by the short-lived Workers' Theater, was
probably the first agitprop play to be written, published, or performed in America. It is typical of the form. Its theme, and the theme
of the entire genre, is the eternal fight for supremacy between the
working and "ruling" classes. As characterized by Gold, the exploiters
are fat, hand-rubbing corporate directors who even in a period of
high profits decide to cut the wages of their hard-pressed, unorga-
nized workers by ten per cent. "Give us this our daily cake, our daily
lobsters and champagne, our nightly chorus girls and cabarets," they
chant together in prayer at the beginning of a meeting.[12] But their

jubilation does not last long, for a young "leader" comes to the workers with the message that they must unite and strike for higher wages if they are to live decently. Not only do they strike as a result of his encouragement, but stand together and sing a part of the chorus of the "Internationale"—for Gold, as always, was writing in behalf of his party. The action lasts only about ten minutes, but in that short time the audience is shown that with capable leadership a mass of workers can become an irrepressible force.

As written and performed by WLT and Prolet-Buehne, agitprop sometimes took the form of plotless but extremely ardent çhants for the chorus. These pieces could be as brief as WLT's *Daily Worker,* in which for thirty seconds a chorus of eight actors demanded support for the Party newspaper, or as skillfully rounded as *Scottsboro!,* in which members of Prolet-Buehne detailed the reasons behind, the results of, and the cure for Southern injustice in the case of the nine young black boys unjustly accused of rape in Alabama. A later account of the performance of this piece reveals the skill of John Bonn's well-drilled actors:

Actors in a Prolet-Buehne play might appear from any part of the audience. Veteran labor theatre-goers of 1930–31 still remember how, sitting at a mass meeting, they would be caught up into emotional participation as from half a dozen places around the hall one hatless black-clad player after another would come running forward to start the recitation:

> 1ST PLAYER: Attention!
> 2ND PLAYER: Attention, workers!
> 3RD PLAYER: Friends!
> 4TH PLAYER: Comrades!
> ALL 6: ATTENTION
> 1ST PLAYER: Hear the story—of nine Negro boys—in Scottsboro, Alabama.

Then the players would crouch forward, and in a half-whisper that conveyed all the horror and pathos of the plight of the victims, would chant in unison the refrain that kept recurring throughout the piece:

> In Scottsboro,
> In Scottsboro,
> Murder stalks the streets,
> In Scottsboro,
> In Scottsboro,
> Death haunts the cells.[13]

This work, one of many on the case, treats its subject as a conflict between classes, but presents the situation entirely by means of the chorus. When at the conclusion the actors asked the audience to unite in
demanding that the boys be freed, they themselves, performing as a
chorus, provided an impressive example of what could be accomplished through mass action. In performance *Scottsboro!* and other
sketches of its kind had an affinity to "modern dance," theatrical
dancing in the styles developed by Mary Wigman, Martha Graham,
and, earlier, Ted Shawn, Ruth St. Denis, and Isadora Duncan, in
which the movements of classical ballet are discarded in favor of
movement for the entire body and the dancers do not go up on point.
The staccato phrasing as well as the dancelike movement is also reminiscent of the work of Georg Kaiser, Ernst Toller, and other German
expressionist playwrights.

Important to them as the Scottsboro boys, the underpaid coal miners of Kentucky, and other victims of "the system" may have been, the
Third Period troupes never ignored for long the Party's requirement
that as front organizations they promote Comintern policy. Accordingly, the workers' plays very often included eulogies of the Soviet
Union along with appeals to class consciousness and condemnation of
the AFL "labor fakers." WLT's *Unemployed*, a skit first performed in
the winter of 1930–31, is typical. Before a crowd of jobless, hungry
men, one lone Communist speaks out in opposition to a "Capitalist"
and his two henchmen, a minister and a labor leader (specifically,
William Green). It is the Communist's job to crush these enemies of
labor and to convince the workers on stage and those in the audience
that only his party and the government of the U.S.S.R. offer effective
leadership. His last words, which fuse the individual workers into a
mass of rebels, are in effect a summary of Third Period dogma:

> Yes, I am an agitator—an agitator for the fight against exploitation
> and oppression, an agitator for the freeing of the working class, an ag-
> itator against all misleaders who under the mask of friends of labor
> betray us to our exploiters. Yes, I agitate for the defense of the Soviet
> Union, the only country in the world where there are no more ex-
> ploiters, the only country in the world where the workers are free,
> the only country in the world where the worker rules.[14]

The ending is familiar: consolidation of the unemployed followed by
a chorus of the "Internationale."

1789740

Early in 1931 the heads of WLT made the momentous decision to publish a monthly magazine devoted to proletarian drama and theater. A plain title that could confuse no one as to the contents was chosen—*Workers Theater*.[15] The editors were an elected board of seven WLT members, with Albert Prentis in charge; [16] but in keeping with the ultraleftist policy of ignoring the individual for the benefit of the mass, the editors did not list their names on the masthead. The first number, appearing in April, was a mimeographed (and badly typed) collection of pleas to the workers to organize acting troupes and write plays, descriptions of the aims of WLT, and the sketch *Unemployed*. In the second number WLT was identified as a "section of the Workers International Relief Cultural Activities Department," and in August it was announced that Prolet-Buehne had begun to share the work of editing the magazine. It is likely that this expansion of WLT's operation was related to an event that caused similar stirrings within the membership of the John Reed Clubs. This was the meeting of November 6–15, 1930, in the Ukrainian city of Kharkov of the Second World Plenum of the International Bureau of Revolutionary Literature. In a "Program of Action" handed down to the American delegates ° the suggestion was made that the John Reed Club of New York and the *New Masses* sponsor the publication of pamphlets for the masses and foster the development of agitprop troupes. In June 1931 when the New York club called a convention of workers' cultural groups, WLT and Prolet-Buehne sent representatives, and John Bonn delivered a report on the acting companies.[17] By this time the companies had begun to draw favorable attention, and the magazine, though not able to break out of the original rough format for over a year, added a page or two more each month and enjoyed a good following. In a year's time it began to publish at the rate of a thoussand copies a month.[18]

For the first year *Workers Theater* was a belligerently exclusivist journal whose writers refused any assistance to the cause of labor from sources outside the Party and struck back at all criticism, however well-meant, of production, by workers' troupes. Reviewing I. J.

° Fred Ellis, Michael Gold, William Gropper, Joshua Kunitz, A. B. Magil, Harry Alan Potamkin.

Golden's *Precedent,* a sensible piece of work about the case of Tom
Mooney and Warren Billings, the San Francisco labor martyrs, Sidney Ball dismissed the play on the grounds that it "entirely neglects
the treacherous role played by the AF of L who assisted the bosses
in railroading these militant leaders to jail." When John Dos Passos,
still a sympathetic onlooker, observed without malice in the *New Republic* that Soviet playwrights dramatized "the myth of the leader
killed and the revolutionary masses sweeping on," he drew fire from
Albert Prentis, who took exception to the word "myth" in Dos Passos's critical vocabulary. "We may state," Prentis insisted,

> that this is also one of the "myths" of the American theatre of the
> masses. The struggles of the working class were not confined to Russia
> alone but are world wide and can be successful only if the masses
> carry on even if the leaders go down. For the masses are all-powerful
> and permanent while leaders are powerless and temporary. Therein,
> perhaps, lies the reason why a Workers' Theatre can go on with the
> masses, and Copeau, the Provincetown, the Neighborhood, Piscator
> and the New Playwrights must go down into oblivion, while their
> directors wonder . . . and write silly scenarios in Hollywood.

When Hallie Flanagan, head of the Vassar Experimental Theater,
discussed the performances of the workers' troupes in an article in
Theatre Arts Monthly, Prentis was annoyed that she had found some
faults in their programs:

> She claims we are repetitious—we *are*—though no more so than the
> bourgeois theatre with its bedrooms—we must be repetitious so as to
> impress upon the workers our message of solidarity. She claims we
> are violent—shall we talk of hyacinths and eternal beauty . . . while
> the breadlines lengthen and thousands of men and women will starve
> and freeze this coming winter?

And when Mrs. Flanagan and Margaret Ellen Clifford wrote a play,
Can You Hear Their Voices?, about the hardships of Arkansas farmers,
another reviewer, A. Saks, objected to their opinion that communism should be the last, not the first, resort of the working class in time
of trouble. Equally annoying was the emergence of a Socialist group
that called itself "Workers' Theatre." When the secretary of this band
of seven troupes wrote to protest WLT's use of its name on the maga-

zine, the outraged editors denounced it as the creation of Thomas, Hilquit, and Broun and made it clear that WLT would do as it pleased in the matter of names.[19]

"To impress upon the workers our message of solidarity": Prentis's phrase struck the keynote of the Third Period. Pursuing an all-or-nothing policy, the editors of *Workers Theatre* devoted space to entreaties for votes for the Communist party, to praise for the Trade Union Unity League and downright slander against the American Federation of Labor, to opposition to Japanese militarist drives in China, and to appeals for the defense of Russia. They examined not only every expression of critical judgment in the light of Party ideology, but every production method and acting technique as well. For a year they argued back and forth over the merits of vaudeville, expressionism, and realism, while in practice writing and performing in extremely simple skits. As for acting:

> Portraying characters, a thing that sounds very difficult and high-flown, is really much easier than it seems. It is to be remembered that it is not necessary to portray a particular character but rather a class angle or conception of that character, which should not be difficult for a class-conscious worker. The leading comrade, therefore, must be careful not to force his or her conception of the character upon the actor, but rather the class angle—our angle, through the actor's own person.[20]

By the spring of 1932 proletarian troupes across the country were so numerous that the editors of *Workers Theatre* called for a national conference and "Spartakiade" of agitprop productions to be held in New York in April. Fifty-three troupes based in cities from Massachusetts to California sent delegates, and fourteen, from New York, Newark, Philadelphia, and Chicago, offered plays. This was an extremely strong response from a movement so young. During the conference the delegates voted to form a new association, the League of Workers Theaters, and to affiliate under that name with the International Workers Dramatic Union, a federation of national societies with headquarters in Moscow. The new League then took over the publication of *Workers Theatre* from WLT and Prolet-Buehne.[21]

These events were followed by a slow but quite perceptible change

in the character of the movement. Within three years the workers'
theaters freed themselves of parochialism. The new League learned
that a group with no ties to the Communist party could contribute
importantly to social drama and that even a Broadway producer
might now and then open a play that deserved the attention of the
Left. This more tolerant attitude corresponded to the Comintern's
gradual alteration of policy to allow for a united front with all antifascist parties the world over, a line not proclaimed officially until
August 1935, at the meeting of the Seventh Congress of the International in Moscow, but foreshadowed a full two years earlier. Thus in
1933 the American Communist party made friendly gestures toward
the followers of the independent socialist A. J. Muste, and in 1934 it
began to look peacefully on Norman Thomas and the Socialist party
after years of vilification. In 1935 the Trade Union Unity League,
long ineffectual, was dissolved in belated recognition of the superior
power of the AFL. Having come into being to assist in the party's agitational work, the literary and dramatic fronts reflected the changes
in the line as a matter of course. To be sure, additions to the agitprop
repertory of elementary recitations were not automatically disconscontin-
ued. Myra Kay's *Scottsboro Boy*, for example, was published in
Workers Theatre in mid-1933 ("We wuz clapped in jail;/ We wuz
banged and beat;/ We wuz brought to court/ Befo' dere judgmen'
seat") [22] and Elizabeth England's *Angelo Herndon*, a chant describing a Southern black martyr's trip to prison, was published in pamphlet form by the League as late as 1935. But other kinds of drama
came into favor. Though probably only a few readers were sensitive
enough to detect it, a hint of change was in the air by August 1932.
True to form, *Workers Theatre* for that month carried a lively review
of a Solidarity Day celebration of June 12 for which WLT had produced a show that featured Norman Thomas as Normie the Original
Shaker who shook the blues away in a hula costume composed of
strips of the Socialist *New Leader* and *Forward*, but only a few paragraphs below this intriguing description Alfred Saxe, WLT's most talented director, offered the opinion that George S. Kaufman and Morrie Ryskind's *Of Thee I Sing*, a liberal, Pulitzer Prize-winnning
musical comedy about national politics, was in need of only some
agitprop choruses as substitutes for its song-and-dance routines to
give "a constructive point of view" to its funny byplay.[23] Little by lit-

tle, and possibly at the urging of their superiors in the Party, the magazine's writers were adopting the view that appeals to the mass could be effective even if low-voiced, and that didactic drama could work for social betterment without clamoring for a revolution. The July–August 1933 issue carried this pointed suggestion:

> Members of the League of Workers Theatres must pay serious attention to the problem of the treatment in plays of various labor and political organizations and individuals. The revolutionary theatre must call a halt to the writing and production of plays which indulge in mere name-calling and crude caricaturing of, for example, Norman Thomas, the Socialist Party, and the individuals who lead the American Federation of Labor. . . . This will be an important factor in spreading the influence of the revolutionary theatre.[24]

With their outlook broadened, the leaders of the League were able to recruit many professional theater workers to the movement. In 1932 a band of professionals was organized to produce agitational drama on a nonprofit, self-supporting basis in New York, but outside the Broadway area. Theater Collective, a producing unit set up as a branch of WLT and guided by the designer Mordecai Gorelik and the playwright-director Philip Barber, drew attention fitfully with a revival of Claire and Paul Sifton's *1931—*, a piece the Group Theater had produced on Broadway without success, *Marion Models,* a play about the needle trades by League stalwarts John Bonn and Jack and Olga Shapiro, and Barber's bluntly titled play of unrest among the employees of New York's bargain-store giants, *The Klein-Ohrbach Strike.* In 1934–35 the Collective curtailed its producing activity for want of suitable scripts and opened a studio in which a staff of well-known actors and directors instructed forty young people in the theater arts. Clifford Odets, Morris Carnovsky, Lee Strasberg, Cheryl Crawford, Sanford Meisner, Lewis Leverette, and Mary Virginia Farmer, all from the Group Theater, were members of the faculty.[25] In 1935 it acquired a film unit, Nykino, which was set up by the photographers Paul Strand, Ralph Steiner, and Leo Hurwitz. The name sounded vaguely Russian, but signified nothing more exotic that "New York cinema." The Collective continued in existence through the 1935–36 season. The Theatre Union, which operated on a somewhat larger scale than the Collective, was organized in 1932 for the production of militant, Marxist labor plays, but without the aid of the League or association with the Communist party. Though more successful than the Collective, it was never free of financial worries. With a full-time staff and a sound program of audience organization, it remained alive until the spring of 1937. To the disappointment of the directors of the League, the Theater Union did not become an institutional member; many of its staff held individual memberships, however.[26] The work of this impressive organization, which won favorable reviews from the conservative press as well as from the Left, requires comment in chapters of its own.

Each month the League enrolled bands of part-time actors who were no less dedicated than the professionals of the Collective and the Union. With the issue for July–August 1933, *Workers Theatre* suspended publication, to begin again in January 1934 with another name, *New Theatre*, in recognition of the many member-companies that were not proletarian groups, but groups composed of white-collar workers, "little" and community theater participants, and college students. The renamed magazine was well designed and printed, and ably edited by Harry Elion (later by Herbert Kline).° The change of name was one of the first of many to be made by Party-sponsored dramatic and literary organizations and their publications as the idea of a "Popular Front" of Communist and "progessive" parties grew stronger. The leadership of the League was now assumed by Mark Marvin (National Secretary), Ben Blake, John Bonn, Harry Elion, and Herbert Kline.[27] In January 1935 the League of Workers Theaters became the New Theater League, officially dropped the pro-Soviet slogans that it had tacitly abandoned with the first number of *New Theatre*, and in all its publications called for a "united front against war, fascism, and censorship." By mid-1935, when the Third Period came to the official termination so long anticipated, the League had established a New Theater School under the directorship of John Bonn and could claim as its affiliates companies scattered across the country.†

° The masthead listed among the forty-nine contributing editors many familiar Communist party names, such as Joseph Freeman and Michael Gold, but also many liberal sympathizers, such as Em Jo Basshe, Hallie Flanagan, Sidney Howard, and Lee Strasberg.

† Among them were the Los Angeles Contemporary Theater, the Workers Dramatic Society of Gary, Indiana, the Chicago Blue Blouses, the Washington New

Meanwhile, societies in the arts of the dance and the film traveled an identical route from ultraleftism to Popular Front inclusiveness. As early as 1929 a Spartacus Film League existed, with Em Jo Basshe as one of its prime movers. By 1931 the Workers Film and Photo League was established in New York as "a section of the Union of Worker Photographers of all Lands, whose International Buro is in Berlin." [28] In a "call to action" published in July 1931, the Marxist film critic Harry Alan Potamkin listed thirteen steps to be taken by Film and Photo members, the most important being "encouragement, support and sustenance of the . . . left movie-maker who is demonstrating dramatically and persuasively the disproportions in our present society." Other points had to do with support of Russian films, fights against censorship, the abusive representation of minority groups and "the worker generally" in films, the promotion of "significant" films, and the publication of a magazine, that inevitable symbol of success among front groups.[29] Such a journal, titled *Filmfront,* did appear briefly—from December 1934 to March 1935—but the Film and Photo League found it too expensive to maintain and adopted *New Theatre* as its organ. In keeping with the change in political fashion, the League dropped "Workers" from its name in 1935. As a producer of films, the association was less active in the early thirties than as an exhibitor and a watchdog of Hollywood—understandably, in view of the cost of production. Nevertheless, the members did produce short agitational films and shot documentary reels of the Bonus March on Washington, strikes, riots, and the depressed urban and rural environments. Of particular distinction among the members were Willard Van Dyke, Jay Leyda, Lewis Jacobs, and Ralph Steiner. In 1935 Steiner produced a noteworthy short, *Pie in the Sky,* with Elia Kazan and other Group Theater actors, for Nykino, the Theater Collective film unit which was an affiliate of the Film and Photo League.

One of the most seminal developments in radical art during the decade was the Workers Dance League—later the New Dance League

Theater Group, the New Theater Union of Detroit, the Jack London Players Club of Newark, the New Haven Unity Theater, and in New York, in addition to Theater Collective, the Yiddish-speaking Artef (Arbeiter Theater Ferband), and Theater of Action, as WLT was renamed in the spring of the year. But these were only a few out of scores of affiliates and are listed here because of the frequency with which their names and productions were mentioned in *New Theater.*

—which came into being in 1932 as an affiliation of proletarian dance groups. That the allegedly "highbrow" art of the dance might be useful in the service of leftist causes was taken for granted by many "modern" (as distinguished from balletic) dancers, among them the rising performers and choreographers Anna Sokolow, Sophie Maslow, Miriam Blecher, Jane Dudley, and Helen Tamiris. These young women came to the movement from the schools directed by Hanya Holm, Martha Graham, and Doris Humphrey, who were recognized by leftist apologists as very capable even if not radical. With the New Dance Group, founded in 1932, as perhaps the most expert of the member companies, the parent association included troupes located in most major cities with a total of eight hundred dancers in 1934, according to one (possibly exaggerated) report, and two thousand in 1936, according to another.[30] The titles of works offered in the League's early years are similar to those of WLT and Prolet-Buehne: *Van der Lubbe's Head, Kinder, Küche, Kirche, Scottsboro, For Tom Mooney, Eviction, Hunger, Unemployment, Homeless Girl, Barricades, Parasite, Well Fed, Demagogue, While Waiting for Relief, Letter to a Policeman in Kansas City.* A measure of the dancers' dedication is provided by the announcement for a contest held by the New Dance Group: "The prize will be the entire Little Lenin Library." [31] Who could not be moved by the thought of these young dancers settling down, after a strenuous day at the barre, with a stack of Marxist pamphlets? Slower to fall into the mood of the Popular Front than the acting companies, the dance troupes were sometimes scolded during 1933 and 1934 for a tendency toward "mysticism" and an overuse of agitprop; too often for the taste of Michael Gold, the eternal keeper of standards, they presented a pessimistic, hence insufficiently revolutionary, view of the workers' plight.[32] No wonder that Fanny Brice found them a good source of comic material; in the *Ziegfeld Follies of 1935* the celebrated comedienne put on a set of long underwear and performed an energetic dance called *Rewolt!* Although they were still gesticulating and raising fists against the bosses in the very last months of the Third Period,[33] the dancers became sufficiently deradicalized to grow with the decade and to contribute generously to the American stage long after the Second World War.

As the acting companies edged toward the total abandonment of ultraleftist principles that occurred in August 1935, not only the tone of their magazine, but the content of their plays began to change. "Bourgeois" writers were willing to help the movement along as soon as its leaders showed signs of tolerance for them—and in some instances, well before. Agitprop drama proved to have a strong attraction for those academic and professional playwrights who were stirred by the evidence of misery and social unrest. In the workers' dramas they found a form with which to experiment, and in turn they inspired the workers' groups to further experimentation. Although, as noted earlier, primitive recitations were continually added to the repertory, by 1935 they were overshadowed by pieces that widened the range of agitprop to allow for rounded characters and robust, rather than schematic, dialogue. This was a form of progress that could not have been predicted when the first issue of *Workers Theatre* rolled through the mimeograph machines of Union Square—indeed, would have been contemplated with almost as much outrage as later in the decade many members of the League felt on hearing of the pact between Germany and Russia. But it came to pass, even so. As the Third Period drew to its close, the mutual attraction of the proletarian, amateur League and the middle-class, professional dramatists resulted in the movement of agitational drama from the union halls to Broadway.

The earliest noteworthy variant of agitprop to be contributed to the League's repertory by writers outside the Party and its circles of sympathizers was one that at first was poorly received on the Left: Hallie Flanagan and Margaret Ellen Clifford's *Can You Hear Their Voices?* The writers were teachers of drama at Vassar and Barnard, respectively, who based their play on Whittaker Chambers's story titled "Can You Make Out Their Voices?" published in the *New Masses* for March 1931. Unlike Chambers, who at the time was a member of the Communist party, the playwrights were not radicals, and by *Workers Theatre* standards they did not write a radical play. They were liberals who saw the sporadic uprisings of the Depression's victims as the plain-as-day consequences of the indifference of the federal government. These uprisings *could,* in their opinion, end in revolution under Communist leadership, but need not, provided the government came to the rescue. Despite the heresy of the authors' view—for obviously the belief that the oppressed classes would turn to communism only as the last resort was heretic—*Can You Hear Their Voices?* won the respect of the proletarian actors. With revisions it found a place in the repertory of the workers' theaters soon after word spread of its favorable reception at the Vassar Experimental Theater in May 1931.

The agitprop roots of the play are evident in the class-conscious placement of characters on stage. One side, according to the stage directions, suggests power and security, the other, weakness and poverty. The symbol of power is Congressman Bagehot, an immensely rich politician who is willing to spend a quarter of a million dollars on his daughter's coming-out party, but is quite unconcerned about the needs of the desperately poor farmers whom he represents in Congress. His opposite number is farmer Wardell, who declares that in the absence of government aid and adequate food from the Red Cross the farmers should unite to take both food and money from the relief agencies by force. Bagehot and Wardell, poised on the extreme right and left of the stage respectively, engage in a kind of tug-of-war, with democracy as the fraying rope between them. They are only slightly modified versions of the capitalists and agitators of *Strike!*, *Unemployed,* and other plays of the kind; the chief difference is that each has a real name instead of a label. Like any other agitprop revolutionary, Wardell is a sympathetic character with ideas that must be taken seriously. The fact that he sees life as a struggle between economic classes does not indicate a weakness in him from the authors' view; as matters stand in the congressional district where he lives, his beliefs appear altogether reasonable.

In explaining Wardell's activities the authors went well beyond the elementary proletarian plays. Although they were guilty of special pleading to the extent of creating in Bagehot a fatuously pompous character, giving sentimental diction to the farmers, and prompting the actors at the coming-out party to "remember that they represent the upper classes" (Scene iv), they nevertheless made a strong case for their protagonist. If Wardell is to save the farmers, he has no choice but the Marxist method of consolidation and rebellion, since, despite the signs of despair on all sides, Bagehot refuses to support a national relief bill. Moreover, insofar as the relief measures adopted by the Hoover administration were indeed meager, the argument could be extended beyond Wardell to the farmers across the country who banded together to stand off dispossessing sheriffs and took food where they could find it. Thus Wardell would seem to have reasons enough for placing his sons in the care of Communists in a nearby town as he goes off to prison for inciting a riot.

Had the authors added nothing more to their plot, they might have spared themselves the rebukes of indignant Third Period critics. But the play was intended to be only a warning, not a piece of Marxist propaganda. Altering the prorevolutionary theme of Chambers's story, they made a moderator of Bagehot's daughter Harriet—a play for a woman's college must, after all, have a heroine—who points up her father's folly and, after drinking one glass of champagne too many at her party, attacks her own economic class by declaring, "Well, if we want the country to go Communist, carrying on stampedes like this one . . . is the quickest and surest way to do it" (scene iv). Perhaps it is, insofar as the party provides a brutal contrast to the misery on the other side of the stage. But more to the point, because it is not presented in a tone of alcoholic levity and has no embellishment of undergraduate slang, is a final admonition to be flashed on a screen after the departure of Wardell's sons, at the close of the play: "These boys are symbols of thousands of our people who are turning somewhere for leaders. Will it be to the educated minority? CAN YOU HEAR THEIR VOICES?"

Obviously the play could not serve the purposes of the workers' theaters precisely as written. On hearing that Artef, which produced the play in Yiddish, had introduced some changes in the script, Mrs. Flanagan objected, and no doubt she would have had other occasions to protest, had it been possible to sleuth every production. But Artef went on with the play, after offering a defense:

> Artef is a revolutionary theatre group and to make the play consonant with our ideas and those of our audience, certain changes had to be made. Something like a major operation has been performed upon your pet character, Harriet. To us, Harriet is not the leader of the oppressed, but a typical liberal who wants to help the oppressed lest they help themselves at the expense of the ruling class, her father's class.[34]

Yet this production was damned in *Workers Theatre* on the grounds that it was not revolutionary enough. Within four years, however,

Ben Blake, the League's historian, bestowed the epithet "intrepid" on
Mrs. Flanagan for having written the play. "Like an American fore-
runner in another field," he declared, "it was a shot heard 'round the
world.'" [35]

After the academicians came the poets. The first with substantial
reputations to write plays for the movement were Langston Hughes
and Alfred Kreymborg, who used the form of the mass chant for revolutionary sketches in sophisticated doggerel. Hughes, the best-
known black writer admittedly sympathetic to communism in the
early thirties, provided an agitprop piece titled *Scottsboro Limited* in
which a "Red" chorus speaks for the nine boys against a "mob" chorus that mutters threats on their lives. The mob declares,

> You oughta be through—
> Oughta be through,
> In the white man's land there's no place for you.

But the Reds, rising in the auditorium, counter with

> We'll fight for you, boys,
> We'll fight for you.[36]

The first Scottsboro trial was still in process when the *New Masses*
published the play in November 1931, and Hughes's chief purpose
was to urge support for the International Labor Defense, the Party's
legal apparatus, which was engaged in a vastly publicized struggle
with the National Association for the Advancement of Colored People
for the defense of the boys. Hughes suggested at the conclusion of his
play that "the *Internationale* may be sung and the red flag raised," [37]
the use of the conditional verb implying that the producer must consider how much agitation his audience would tolerate. Kreymborg's
America, America!, published in the *New Masses* for February 1933
and reprinted in *Proletarian Literature in the United States* in 1935,
has no such specific battle to fight as Hughes undertook. In approximately ten minutes' playing time, Kreymborg offers some rhymed
Union Square oratory describing American decadence, supplies an illustration of it in dialogue between a rich boy and girl who play at
sex, and for contrast follows with a passage in which a poor but married couple report on the problems they face:

> What have you got for dinner, Honey?
> *Yesterday's soup—I'm out o' money—*
>   (America, America.)
> What'll we do when the rent comes round?
> *Butter's gone up ten cents a pound.*
> I've been all over—no job in sight.
> *Jim—you were awfully late tonight.*
> Every bone o' mine's done in—
> *Sit down now an' let's begin.*

Though some of the exchanges ring true, the sketch as a whole is slight and perhaps too whimsical for an audience of unemployed workers. Yet its inclusion in the anthology of 1935 is in itself evidence that the literary lights of the Party found it to their taste.[38]

Important as it was to the proletarian troupes to draw upon the work of professional writers for the strengthening of the repertory, they were capable of creating strong works of their own in addition to the banal anti-AFL skits that took up much of their time. If the productions of Prolet-Buehne under the direction of John Bonn would seem, from printed accounts, to be the most gripping of the amateur pieces, the most striking single work of any of the troupes was *Newsboy,* an elaborate agitprop skit of twelve minutes' duration devised under the direction of Alfred Saxe by WLT's "Shock Troupe," an élite group of worker-actors who lived communally. The play is an adaptation of a poem of the same title by V. J. Jerome, the Party's chief spokesman on cultural matters. The two opposing forces essential to every agitprop work are in this instance the Communist press and the right-wing papers. Returning the compliment of the professional writers who expanded agitprop, Saxe and his collaborators borrowed liberally from the commercial stage. The sources on which they drew for short pieces of action were the Siftons' *1931—,* Albert Maltz and George Sklar's *Merry-Go-Round,* a political melodrama of 1932, and the ballets of Kurt Jooss. The rapid cutting technique of the great Russian film director Sergei Eisenstein underlay the swift changes of mood in the play, and there were also fleeting suggestions of the movements of the placard-bearing crowds in *Of Thee I Sing,* which Saxe had mentioned with admiration in *Workers Theatre.*[39] Brief though the play may have been, it was the most ambitious in the WLT repertory. Because the company wished to make a distinction between so elaborate a work and its simple plays of earlier years, its members had begun, in January 1934, to drop the term agitprop and refer to themselves as a "theater of action," a phrase that they adopted formally as a name in 1935.[40]

Unfortunately, the play as originally written now seems to be lost. It is possible, nevertheless, to get a taste of its qualities from a commentary on it by Saxe and a version prepared by Gregory Novikov in 1938 for the American League Against War and Fascism.[41] A contention arises between two newsboys, one employed by the leftist press and the other by the capitalist press; a photograph on the cover of *New Theatre* for June 1934 shows one boy with an arm load of copies of the *New York Daily News* and the other with a paper whose name cannot be identified. The boys fight, a blind woman begs for charity, the street crowd chants "Murder, Rape, Scandal, Suicide." In caricature William Randolph Hearst, Senator Huey Long, and Father Charles E. Coughlin, the "radio priest," make appearances. As in the Siftons' *1931—*, unemployed workers line up at barred factory gates. A black is given the "third degree" by white men determined to punish him for a crime he did not commit. The description Saxe gives of this climactic moment demonstrates the staccato rhythm and split-second timing for which he aimed as both writer and director:

> Action—Negro breaks from a group back stage and runs toward the audience. The position of the figures on the stage all grouped at the back—the figure of the Negro worker at the front of the stage makes it very difficult to change to the next scene which is from *Merry-Go-Round*. Four of the figures must leave the stage—four others who are at the moment class-conscious workers must become thugs. The position of Negro and white workers must be completely reversed. The scene is a third degree. Very well. We will make our transition violent. While the Negro worker has been speaking, those not in the scene shuffle quietly and quickly off. At the same time, the white men turn their back to the audience, and as the Negro finishes a white man grabs him and hurls him back. Crash—the Negro finds himself thrown to the floor into a frame-up scene—the backs of the white men loom ominously and obviously tell the story of the change.[42]

The effect of this action is the conversion of the rightist newsboy, who at last sees the light and abandons his stack of reactionary papers. Nothing has been shown by way of proof that the capitalist press reports inaccurately on the situation of workers or minority groups. But the rapid action of the play, its flashing light and balletic movements—these function as substitutes for evidence.

Proud of his play, Saxe described its content for *New Theatre* readers in terms of Marxist theory. He had conceived it as a series of conflicts that, taken together, illustrate the continuing class struggle. Not only the fight between the newsboys and the scene of the black undergoing the "third degree" were designed for this purpose, but also such incidents as a young man's attempt to pick up a girl and a "gent's" gift of a penny to a blind woman who is obviously his economic inferior. "There is no plot, no relationship as we are acquainted with it in the ordinary theatre . . . ," he wrote. "In *Newsboy* . . . the plot is as follows: to show the truth and strength of the revolutionary press in relationship to the working class and in opposition to this the hypocrisy of the capitalist controlled newspapers." [43] The new phrase "theater of action" could not conceal the fact that this was still agitprop, though of the very best quality.

At the Festival and Conference of Workers' Theaters held in Chicago in April 1934, *Newsboy* took the first prize. Yet a speech delivered by Mark Marvin during the conference hinted that plays of its kind were losing favor: "As in the proletarian novel and short story in this country, there is still too much stylization, too much abstract speech, too little variation in themes, and a too quick development of characters." [44] More severe was an essay published in *New Theatre* for September that included a condemnation of the mass recitation as "sectarian in approach both in content and form"—in other words, possessing appeal for the Party's true believers only. *Newsboy* represented an advance beyond the mass recitation, but it was closer to that form than to the realistic drama toward which these two complaints were leading. With this new line the American Communist party indicated its approval of that mode of literature called "socialist realism," to which Russian writers had first been enjoined to give their attention in 1932.[45]

After the Chicago conference the League took steps to find and present new plays and at the same time to raise money for its magazine by inaugurating a series of New Theater Nights on Sunday evenings at the 14th Street house known as the Civic Repertory Theater.

This building, so named because it had been occupied by Eva Le Gallienne's Civic Repertory company, was now the home of the Theater Union. Here affiliates of the League and sympathetic members of non-League companies were invited to act in mixed bills of short pieces. If a company had acquired a new script, it could offer a trial performance before an audience urged to attend by publicity in *New Theatre,* the *New Masses,* and the *Daily Worker.* Actors came to the Civic Rep from WLT, Theater Collective, the Theater Union, the Group Theater, and many of the smaller troupes of New York and Newark, and companies associated with the Workers Dance League also performed on occasion. The first New Theater Night was held on May 20, 1934. At the second, on June 3, the first performance was given of *Dimitroff,* by Art Smith and Elia Kazan of the Group Theater; parts were taken by members of the cast of Sidney Kingsley's *Men in White,* a Group production.[46] Though rooted in the old tradition, *Dimitroff* is a more realistic play than *Newsboy,* inasmuch as its characters are specific persons and its settings are convincingly atmospheric.

Smith and Kazan wrote *Dimitroff* to promote mass action in the form of political pressure on behalf of the imprisoned German Communists Ernst Thaelmann (the party head in Germany) and Ernst Torgler, alleged conspirators in the Reichstag fire of 1933. The conflict between the Communists who were accused of destroying the building and the Nazis who in the belief of most commentators were the true instigators of the fire fitted conveniently into the basic agitprop pattern of "class against class." But by placing the action in a number of specific locales, Smith and Kazan broke with familiar practice and created the sort of mood that induces an audience to lose itself in the proceedings. The locales are of kinds that within only a very short playing time (twenty minutes or less) and with minimal props and scenery project a sense of menace: an office room used by Hermann Goering, the courtroom where the men are tried, a prison cell, a room in the German embassy in Washington, a dark street corner. For the most part, the language is straightforward and naturalistic, with bombast confined to the speeches of the nazis. But the presence of the proletarian mass, vocal though kept off stage during most of the action, keeps the play within the agitprop frame. The most obvious agitational device is held for the conclusion, when actors

planted in the auditorium call out for the release of the Germans after
the Bulgarians Dimitroff, Popoff, and Taneff are freed:

> DIMITROFF: We have been saved by the world pressure of the
> revolutionary masses. But *Torgler* is still in prison and *Thaelmann* is
> held in chains. We must not falter now. *We must fight fascism with
> undiminished strength and courage. We must free our comrades. Free
> all class war prisoners!!!*
> AUDIENCE: Free all class war prisoners!!
> DIMITROFF: Free *Torgler!*
> AUDIENCE: Free *Torgler!!*
> DIMITROFF: Free *Thaelmann!!*
> AUDIENCE: Free *Thaelmann!!* [47]

Though not, so far as is known, a popular play with the workers'
companies, *Dimitroff* was something new in agitprop, and with its realistic scenes it may be said to have broken ground for what was the
most effective and most popular of all agitprop pieces, Clifford
Odets's *Waiting for Lefty*. Odets, like Smith and Kazan a member of
the Group Theater, delivered the play to the League in the fall of
1934. It was named the winner of a contest held by the association for
the best short play on a labor subject. (Odets was to claim that the
contest was something of a hoax—that he knew nothing about the
taxi strike of February 1934 that was believed to have inspired him
and that he had not designed his play for the contest, but had been
approached by the League staff and asked whether, in view of the
poor quality of the entries, he objected to being given the prize.[48]) It
was his first acted play; his next, *Awake and Sing!*, had already been
scheduled by the Group for the 1934–35 season, but had not yet
opened when *Lefty* took the stage of the Civic Rep on the New Theater Night of January 6, 1935. This performance was to become a legend in the American theater. The audience, moved to frequent bursts
of applause as the play proceeded, rose when it was over and rushed
to the stage in thunderous approval.[49]

This spontaneous show of appreciation and enjoyment was Odets's
reward for writing a moving play of the life of the cab drivers of New
York City, a section of the labor force that seldom elicits a sympathetic word. Fortunate in having a good ear for the New York idiom,
Odets presented the drivers to the audience with a degree of robust

naturalism not to be found in the characters of any earlier agitprop play. As he described it, the construction of the play was intended to resemble a minstrel show, in which one after another the performers stood up and did their acts.[50] While this description makes sense, the play is nevertheless put together in the usual agitprop fashion, with scenes centering on the underdogs followed by passages of dialogue exposing members of the exploiting class and an ending in which the underdogs become organized and militant. The situation serving as a basis for all the scenes is a meeting called by a committee of the drivers' union to ask the rank and file for a strike vote. The play begins on a bare stage where the committee members are seated, as though on the platform of a union hall. These men are in favor of a strike, but the double-dealing head of their union, one Fatt, is opposed. While the members wait for the arrival of their chairman, a radical worker appropriately nicknamed Lefty, five of them in turn act out their reasons for approving the strike. It becomes obvious that the play is a call for concerted action, as is every agitprop play, and by virtue of the intimate and vivid scenes depicting the drivers' unhappiness, a call that the union must answer affirmatively. Two of the scenes are designed as explanations of the characters' positions on the strike: in the "Joe and Edna" scene a driver is browbeaten into supporting it by his wife, who threatens to leave him; in the exceptionally sensitive scene of "The Young Hack and His Girl," a driver is shown to be too poor to marry on his present wages. Three incidents explain why men from other walks of life have taken up hacking: in the scene of "The Young Actor" an out-of-work performer is shown facing the rebuffs of a producer; in the "Intern Episode" a Jewish physician is dismissed from his hospital in an economy drive but knows that he is a victim of anti-Semitism; and in the "Lab Assistant Episode" a young scientist loses his job for refusing to spy on his chief and to take part in the manufacture of poison gas. When each man has told his story, word arrives that Lefty has been found with a bullet through his head. A driver called Agate (played by Elia Kazan in the original production) then demands, and gets, a vote for the strike; he is called Agate because he has a glass eye, but the name suggests his purpose in life—agitation.

Written during Odets's brief period of membership in the Communist party, *Waiting for Lefty* accorded with the party's new literary standards of 1934. Although the episodes are acted on a bare stage, they give the audience an intimate view of the life of the drivers through Odets's lively and sympathetic dialogue. The result is a more realistic play than *Dimitroff* as well as a more effective piece of propaganda, and one in which the audience participated nightly and with tremendous volume. Though delineated with short, swift strokes, the characters are full of life; moreover, as Americans faced with the chief problem of the time—earning a livelihood, rather than winning support for the U.S.S.R. or undercutting the Socialists—they had sure appeal for the American audience. *Lefty*, in fact, had more appeal than any other play written or presented under the auspices of the party, if in the absence of hard statistics one may judge by such indications as the numbers of productions it was given and the warmth and frequency with which it was mentioned in print.[51]

Praise for the party as the agent for correcting all wrongs is present in two scenes of *Lefty*, but not in the form of pro-Soviet sloganeering or the advocation of armed rebellion. The first instance, especially blunt, occurs in the young actor's scene; too "sectarian" for the second half of the decade, it was not printed in the volume of Odets's first six plays published in 1939. At the close of the episode a producer's stenographer offers aid to Phillips, the down-and-out actor, in this high-pressure passage:

> STEN: . . . Want that dollar?
> PHIL: It won't help much.
> STEN: One dollar buys ten loaves of bread, Mister. Or one dollar buys nine loaves of bread and one copy of The Communist Manifesto. Learn while you eat. Read while you run. . . .
> PHIL: Manifesto? What's that? (*Takes dollar*) What is that, what you said. . . . Manifesto?
> STEN: Stop off on your way out—I'll give you a copy. From Genesis to Revelation, Comrade Philips! "And I saw a new earth and a new heaven; for the first earth and the first heaven were passed away; and there was no more sea."
> PHIL: I don't understand that. . . .
> STEN: I'm saying that the meek shall not inherit the earth!
> PHIL: No?
> STEN: The MILITANT! Come out in the light, Comrade.
> BLACKOUT.[52]

The second round of praise is more oblique, though unmistakable. It is a part of Agate's militant harangue at the close of the play:

These slick slobs stand here telling us about bogeymen. That's a new
one for the kids—the reds is bogeymen! But the man who got me
food in 1932, he called me Comrade! The one who picked me up
where I bled—he called me Comrade too! What are we waiting for.
. . . Don't wait for Lefty! He might never come. Every minute—

This continues, after the news that Lefty has been murdered:

Hear it, boys, hear it? Hell, listen to me! Coast to coast! HELLO
AMERICA! HELLO. WE'RE STORMBIRDS OF THE WORK-
ING-CLASS. WORKERS OF THE WORLD. . . . OUR BONES
AND OUR BLOOD! And when we die they'll know what we did to
make a new world! Christ, cut us up to little pieces. We'll die for
what is right! put fruit trees where our ashes are! (*To audience.*)
Well, what's the answer?
  ALL: STRIKE!
  AGATE: LOUDER!
  ALL: STRIKE!
  AGATE and OTHERS on Stage: AGAIN!
  ALL: STRIKE, STRIKE, STRIKE!!!

This joyful ending, it must be said, is not much different from the
ending of Michael Gold's *Strike!*, for which the entire audience is to
stand and sing the *Internationale*—if Gold's hopes are fulfilled. But
the tumultuously enthusiastic reception of *Lefty*, though possibly led
by Party members, went very far beyond a response to Agate's call to
action. As Harold Clurman, one of the Group's directors and a warm
friend of Odets, was later to put it,

When the audience at the end of the play responded to the militant
question . . . with a spontaneous roar of "Strike! Strike!" it was something more than a tribute to the play's effectiveness, more even than
a testimony of the audience's hunger for constructive social action. It
was the birth cry of the thirties. Our youth had found its voice. It
was a call to join the good fight for a greater measure of life in a
world free of economic fear, falsehood, and craven servitude to
stupidity and greed. "Strike!" was *Lefty's* lyric message, not alone
for a few extra pennies of wages or for shorter hours of work, strike
for greater dignity, strike for a bolder humanity, strike for the full
stature of man.[53]

Odets's play proved to be not only the high point in agitprop
drama, but, to glance ahead, the only play supporting communism to

become a part of classic American literature. On March 26, 1935, five weeks after the successful opening of *Awake and Sing!*, the Group brought *Lefty* to Broadway where as part of a double bill it ran for 78 performances. Odets, who had been an actor before turning playwright, played Dr. Benjamin, the last role of his career. The second play was *Till the Day I Die*, a short antinazi piece that Odets wrote hurriedly for the occasion.

One of the reasons for the immediate success of *Lefty*, with both the general public and the League hierarchy, was that in writing it Odets had concentrated on the problems of the middle class. Thus in sitting through the episodes of the play, the Broadway audience could witness the development of militancy in characters with whom they could identify more easily than with the "workers." Since the League, along with all other Party-supported organizations, had begun to try to attract the sympathy of the middle class almost to the point of concealing its political identity, *Lefty* suited its purpose very well, despite Odets's use of the agitprop framework. But it was almost the last play retaining the agitprop structure throughout to get the endorsement of the League. The last of all was Archibald MacLeish's *Panic*, a long agitprop verse tragedy. When John Houseman and the press agent Nathan Zatkin drew together a company, Phoenix Theatre, Inc., to produce this play for three nights on Broadway, the League—by now the New Theater League—and the *New Masses* agreed to sponsor the last performance, which took place on March 16, 1935. Thus *Panic* arrived on Broadway before *Lefty* by not quite two weeks. The work was given a full-scale production with Orson Welles in the principal role, settings by Jo Mielziner, and the movements of the chorus directed by Martha Graham.[54]

It was something new for the League to lend its name, even so briefly, to a Broadway venture, and because MacLeish was the author, it was a step that might even be described as audacious. In what now seems the nadir of Third-Period criticism, Granville Hicks, writing under the high-toned pseudonym of Margaret Wright Mather, had scored MacLeish off in a *New Masses* review of 1934 as a "dirty Nazi," and as late as the week in which *Panic* opened, the *Daily Worker* put him through a catechism in which he was obliged to defend his poetry against the imputation of carrying "Fascist tones."[55] But for all that, and the additional questionable fact that he wrote for

Henry R. Luce's *Fortune,* he was the winner of a Pulitzer Prize and a
favorite with liberals; to put it another way, an association with Mac-
Leish, no matter how tenuous, would confer prestige on the League,
and the League was eager to have it.

The result, however, was generally disappointing. Although Mac-
Leish, making full use of the agitprop conventions, alternated scenes
of the life of the organized bosses with scenes of the bewildered mus-
ing of the demoralized workers and concluded with a call for collective action, his play was not another *Lefty.* He delivered only a
familiar description of the progress of abused workers from confusion
to understanding. Taking his plot from the bank failures of 1932, he
reprimanded the masses for having surrendered control of their affairs
to bankers, the unsympathetic high priests of capitalism. After all the
great banks fail and the most important banker of all (played by the
twenty-two-year-old Welles) commits suicide, the masses in the street
are finally free to create a new civilization of their own design. This
simple plot is overburdened by language too ornate for the characters
who speak it. Experimenting with unrhymed, accentual verse, Mac-
Leish provided lengthy lines with a variable number of syllables for
the principal actors and quite short lines for the street crowds. But
the lines and speeches, whether short or long, are too high-flown to
approximate true expressions of human feelings. In consequence
McGafferty, the tragic protagonist who is the "owner of the country's
principal industries and its greatest bank," is not the clear-cut image
of insensitivity necessary to justify a proletarian take-over, but only a
sententious bumbler. The crowds, deprived of explicitly descriptive
phrases when revealing their unhappiness, seem to lack the intelligence they will need for reshaping the world. It is as though Mac-
Leish had taken the language of the mass chants and tried to elevate
it:

> A WOMAN: Why is it happening? Why is it?
>   A MAN: Price of a woolen blanket!
>   Price of a decent bed!
> A WOMAN: After it all: after everything!
> A WOMAN: Our Father who art Thou in Heaven
>   Forgive us our daily bread!

At a symposium held in the theater after the third performance, V. J.
Jerome publicly reprimanded MacLeish for the weakness of his play.

Though, according to Jerome, MacLeish intended to go on record as a friend of the oppressed masses, his inability to express his sentiments with clarity indicated that unconsciously he identified with the oppressors. In one of the most curious outbursts of Third Period dogmatism (and one of the last), Jerome cited as an example of MacLeish's political confusion the fact that the masses were presented as merely a chorus of the crowd in the street and that their lines had only three stresses, as opposed to five for the bankers.[56]

Despite these strictures against the play that it had briefly promoted, it was too late for the New Theater League to turn back to the tabloid displays of WLT and Prolet-Buehne, and in any event the League had no wish to take such a step. In May the Theater of Action, as WLT was now called, moved uptown, turned professional, and offered its first full-length play, *The Young Go First,* written by George Scudder, Peter Martin, and Charles Friedman.[57] This was an attack on the Civilian Conservation Corps, a New Deal agency in whose program the Left detected a dangerous spirit of militarism. Dissatisfied by the conditions of camp life, a group of CCC boys stages a revolt; at a court martial held to discover their leaders, they form into a sort of football huddle and speak in unison. Ultimately they are separated and sent to other camps, but they vow to continue their protest. Revised in the third week to strengthen the antiwar theme, the play ran for a month.* In August, as though to demonstrate that there were no hard feelings, MacLeish declared in the editorial pages of *New Theatre* that the work of Odets was "better than anything else in New York" and praised the workers' dramatic movement for "its passion, its eloquence, its insolence." [58] Meeting that month in Moscow, the Comintern officially sanctioned the alignment of the party with all liberal, antifascist forces, and the American Communist organizations began at once to make new friendships outside the party.

* In the program the Theater of Action listed the members of its Advisory Council, presumably to show the breadth of its outlook. Among the sixteen members were Earl Browder, Joseph Freeman, and Michael Gold, along with Albert Maltz, Paul Peters, George Sklar, and Charles R. Walker of the Theater Union, and Erskine Caldwell, Moss Hart, and Clifford Odets.

THE THEATER UNION
1933-1935

THE MOST PROFESSIONAL of the new producing units of the thirties dedicated to dramatizing the life of the working man was the Theater Union. The notion of establishing the company was conceived in 1932 by Charles R. Walker, a novelist and scholar in the field of labor economics. Walker and his wife, troubled by the reluctance of major producers to offer plays on current social issues, had in mind a theater of prolabor drama written and performed both for workers and the general public. The darkest year of the Depression was not the happiest of times for instituting new cultural enterprises; a year passed before the Walkers got together enough money to rent a home for their company—the off-Broadway Civic Repertory Theater—and another six months before they opened their first play, in November 1933. By working to develop an audience of labor groups and win the attention of theatrical columnists, and by shrewdly choosing sensational if simplistic plays, the Theater Union kept going until relentless economic pressure killed it off in 1937.

Like the New Playwrights' Theater, to which it was often compared,[1] the Theater Union was governed by an Executive Board of young, politically aware playwrights. Its members included Michael Blankfort, Albert Maltz, Paul Peters, and George Sklar, all in their twenties, and Walker, who turned forty in 1933. In 1934 another young playwright, Victor Wolfson, joined this group. The Board was rounded out with seven other persons: Mrs. Walker; Margaret Larkin, a one-time *New Masses* writer who had served as the secretary of Albert Weisbord in the Passaic textile strike of 1926; Liston M. Oak, a Communist journalist; Samuel Friedman, a writer for the Socialist *New Leader;* Mary Fox, Executive Director of the League for Industrial Democracy, a Socialist organization; Sylvia Fennigston, an actress formerly with the Group Theater; and Eleanor Fitzgerald, formerly Secretary of the Provincetown Players.[2]

With the composition of the Executive Board encompassing the full spectrum of radical opinion from socialism to the "pre-revolutionary" position of Third-Period polemicists, the Board members could rightly say that the company was not rooted in a specific ideology. The manifesto that they often released to the press was kept free of Third-Period jargon:

> 1. We produce plays that deal boldly with the deep-going social conflicts, the economic, emotional, and cultural problems that confront the majority of the people. Our plays speak directly to this majority, whose lives usually are caricatured or ignored on the stage. We do not expect that these plays will fall into accepted social patterns. This is a new kind of professional theatre, based on the interests and hopes of the great mass of working people.
>
> 2. We have established a low price sale so that the masses of people who have been barred by high prices can attend the theatre. A scale of thirty cents to a dollar and a half (no tax), with more than half the seats priced under a dollar, is bringing thousands of people into the theatre who have never seen a professional play, or who have not gone to the theatre for years.
>
> 3. In order to exist we organize our audience through benefit theatre parties and subscribing members.[3]

As a confirmation of their independence, the Executive Board appointed an Advisory Board of still greater breadth. The politics of its members ranged from the middle-of-the-road liberalism of Sidney Howard, one of Broadway's most respected writers, and of Lynn Riggs, author of *Green Grow the Lilacs, Roadside,* and other nonpolitical plays, of Rose McClendon, a gifted black actress and unofficial spokesman for other black performers, and of actor Paul Muni, to the ingrained Stalinism of Joseph Freeman of the editorial staff of the *New Masses,* and of H. W. L. Dana, the foremost popularizer of Soviet drama.[4]

One of the principal problems of the Executive Board, along with finding suitable scripts and the money to get them onto the stage, was the problem of brushing off or diverting the efforts of the Communist party to direct its program. Gratuitous advice from party literary specialists was offered in *New Theatre*, the *Daily Worker*, and the *New Masses* in reviews of Theater Union productions as well as in editorial remarks. The presence of Socialists on the Executive Board and of Howard on the Advisory Board, along with the fact that the company offered salaries to its employees, so offended the ultraleft Theater Collective that its officers asked the party to investigate the Theater Union before it had opened a single production.[5] The success of the company's first two plays brought an end to these specific complaints, but not to the party's urge to meddle. In a particularly intense rejoinder to this interference, Liston M. Oak restated the rationale of the Executive Board a year after the opening of the first play:

> *The Theatre Union is not an agit-prop theatre.* It is a united front theatre organized to produce plays that all honest militant workers and middle-class sympathizers can support; plays that, without compromise on questions of principle, will appeal particularly to unorganized workers who are not yet class conscious. . . . Like other organizations which maintain a united front policy, such as the League Against War and Fascism, we stick to specific and limited tasks, functioning as a threatre, not as a political party.[6]

Displeasure in and resistance to the party's efforts at co-optation did not mean that the writers avoided agitprop devices in all their plays or, indeed, that the protagonists of most of the plays failed to take or recommend radical measures to correct social wrongs. The point of view expressed was that of a young, university-bred generation that found itself in a world so chaotic that only Marxism seemed to provide the instrument necessary for restoring order. Peters had graduated from the University of Wisconsin, Sklar and Maltz had studied as undergraduates at Yale and Columbia respectively and afterward at the Yale School of Drama, and Blankfort had trained in psychology at the University of Pennsylvania and had taught at Bowdoin and Princeton before deciding to turn professional writer.[7] Behind their work lay the youthful desire to part from the circumscribed life of the academy and move out into the "real" world of practical

solutions. It was given voice in a poem of 1934 by Blankfort, "Princeton Revisited," the theme of which is established in the opening
stanza:

> Time was when I and others bore into the night,
> bore into the speckled pages, sank our eyes in them,
> sucked up the canny and most subtle scholarship.
> In those days I walked the college lanes,
> benumbed by beauty and narcotized by quiet.
> I thought. I read. I played with books.
> Pale, old faces, portraits of benign
> and understanding saints were soft with human love.
> Young, overeager concentrated faces intent with good
> and their science and the majesty of learning,
> Stalwart minds, new and old, possessed and passionate,
> stripped and hungry, strained for truth.
> Then I was so much a man.
> But
> This is the time of men.[8]

While refusing to be identified with the party, the members of the
Board made no effort to conceal their Marxist assumptions. The work
of the Theater Union took for granted the existence of class exploitation, as could be expected of any producing unit coming to life in
1932, and in certain plays went further to advance Third-Period doctrine. The most dogmatic of the plays expressed the familiar notions
that war was the result of the plotting of manufacturers, that only
radicals were willing workers for peace and the protection of the oppressed, and that the Soviet Union merited the support of workers
everywhere.

The uniformity of tone and attitude was the result of a process that
the Board described as "collective criticism": when an author had
completed a play, he was expected to submit it to his colleagues for
review and to revise it in the light of their suggestions.[9] The process
was familiar enough to all the playwrights, being essentially the same
as that which those writers who hoped to have works produced on
Broadway under commercial managements had to endure. The only
difference was that the Executive Board of the Theater Union was
larger than most independent producing teams or the boards of most
other institutional theaters, such as the Theater Guild or the Group

Theater. Ironically, Walker, though the founder of the company, was never able to persuade his young colleagues to put on his own play, *Crazy American*. This work had been scheduled for production by the Group Theater for the season of 1932–33, but had been recalled by Walker on the grounds that the Group was neither a commercial theater nor "a real revolutionary theatre." As described by Harold Clurman, the play "was the story of a mercurial, imaginative youth with a genius for inventing. What was he going to do with his talent? The play was a kind of realistic parable of America's quandary in the early thirties." [10]

For the younger members of the Theater Union's Executive Board no such quandary existed. Their talents were put to the formulation of a dramatic appeal for working-class solidarity coupled with an attempt to induce the patrons of Broadway to look sympathetically on working-class needs. Though Blankfort could say, "We are less interested in new 'artistic' merits of our plays than we are in making them true and right for our audience of workers," [11] the company was at pains to preserve a balance between outright calls to revolutionary action and rational investigations of character such as Broadway, in the main, strove for. Despite their emphasis on the requirements and limitations of workers as members of the audience, the directors hoped to attract the regular Broadway playgoers. To that end they sent first-night tickets to the reviewers, took exception in print to unfavorable notices, and quoted favorable ones in their ads. Ignoring, but scarcely blind to, the demonstrations of the unemployed, the Scottsboro case, and the banking crisis, issues dramatized in agitprop sketches, the Theater Union presented tragedies of men of good will defeated in the effort to dislodge entrenched power. This theme, one of the most ancient and hallowed in literary history, allowed the writers to probe into the revolutionary mentality with professional deftness at the same time that it allowed them to stage the class struggle in the form of melodramatic, physical combat for persons not interested in psychology. The results were worth seeing, though strident. To a critic like Michael Gold, turning against his own past in the pattern of behavior typical of the Party devotee, the authors' militancy, conceding nothing to the political center (despite the make-up of the Advisory Board), was evidence of greatness: "The streak of shoddy liberalism that stultified such fellow-travelers' ventures as the New

Playwrights' Theatre is absent from this organization, also the grop-
ing amateurism that hung like a doleful curse over many of the first
workers' theatre groups and blighted their sincere will-to-revolu-
tionary-drama." [12]

To open their first season, the Theater Union's directors chose
Peace on Earth, the joint work of George Sklar and Albert Maltz,
former students of playwriting under George Pierce Baker at Yale.
Their play *Merry-Go-Round,* a drama of corruption in municipal politics, had been produced successfully two seasons before by Michael
Blankfort and Walter Hart, despite a campaign by the government of
New York City to suppress it.[13] *Peace on Earth* describes the transformation of a quiet, middle-class citizen into a political activist who
takes a stand with the workers of his home town in their strike to protest the sale of munitions to foreign powers. Beneath this plot is the
belief that the instinctive response of capitalist society to evidence of
economic distress is the promotion of international war. The antiwar
theme was given cogency by the recent drives of the Japanese in
China and the electoral victory of the nazis in Germany, events that
constituted an obvious threat to world peace. Setting the play a year
or two in the future, the writers envisioned an America moving rapidly to the Right. The distinguishing characteristic of its leaders, who
are represented in the play by several recipients of honorary degrees
at a major university, is that, though they think of themsleves as liberals, they are fascists at heart. They are unwilling to use their power
to restrain the manufacturers of munitions from trading with warring
governments, despite the evidence that as a result of their failure to
act America will be drawn into the fighting. The protagonist, shocked
by the blindness of these supposedly enlightened figures of authority,
abandons his liberalism and seeks a firmer ideology. Answering the
charge that Communists are troublemakers, he declares, "I'm no
Communist and I hold no briefs for Communism. But I know this,
that if you don't make trouble, you keep quiet, and if you keep quiet,
you let things happen—you let war happen" (II, i). Two scenes later
he himself makes so much trouble that the defenders of the status quo
accuse him of murder and, not concerned about the lack of evidence,
hang him.

In the amalgamation of styles that was the Theater Union's solution
to the problem of audience resistance, Sklar and Maltz established

the normality of their tragic hero, Professor Peter Owens, in naturalistic scenes of professorial life and then proceeded to pit him against his class enemies under circumstances almost fantastic. Drawn into the strike by a visiting friend, the placid scholar swiftly grows militant, punctuating every step of his transformation with violence. His human ordinariness is established in the opening scene, which discovers him at home among friends and family. His home is a place of private emotion and self-imposed isolation, as homes usually are in naturalistic drama. Except to fulfill his professional obligations, seldom does he emerge from it to mingle with the people who live beyond its walls. The purpose of this initial scene, iterating as it does the popular misconception of the university professor as a man cut off from the issues of daily life, is to hint that Owens is in need of practical education. Though supposedly an intellectual, he imagines himself to be above the economic and political battle involving the townspeople. Not until a friend leads him from the house to a protest meeting does he begin to understand that the workers are beyond reproach in striking and that he must join them, even at the risk of losing his job.

Once the naturalistic base of Owens's life is revealed, the authors move on to introduce elements borrowed from agitprop technique. The city is a seaport, and on the docks is a kind of chorus of German merchant seamen and striking American longshoremen who unite to dump into the water a cargo of guncotton deceptively labeled as soap. When his friend is killed by a spy of the munitions company for assisting the strikers, Owens rushes to the president of the university to protest the award of an honorary degree to the man who controls the company. By great coincidence, this man, John Andrews, also heads the governing board of the university. Owens must hurry, because in the agonizing compression of the play, the ceremonies at which Andrews will be honored are to take place on the following day. Present with Andrews and the president is a group of other persons also to be honored, including a social worker, a scientist, and a writer, and also with them is a clergyman, the university chaplain. Together, these wielders of power resemble an agitprop chorus of bosses determined to override a chorus of workers. Allegedly persons of generous vision, they have been corrupted by the possession of power. It is an instance of class against class, for they defend Andrews against Owens.

The concluding scenes run on in a hit-or-miss attack on things as they are. Returning to his family, Owens finds his home invaded by the belligerent spirit that seems to be overtaking the nation. Three drunken members of his undergraduate class, in town for a reunion and garbed as cowboys, are terrorizing his daughter. They know of his involvement in the strike and on seeing him they make a half-joking, half-earnest attempt to hang him. As the strikers have suffered, Owens now suffers at the hands of these guardians of established order, the middle-aged, successful alumni of the university. The effect of this incident is to drive him permanently out of his corner and into the world. At commencement he objects to the award of the degree to Andrews and soon is held for the murder of an alumnus shot down during the ensuing uproar by a policeman's stray bullet. Another act follows in which he broods in prison during the hour before his execution. Spotted behind him are war-mongers of many varieties: the group given honorary degrees, cabinet officers, Wall Street workers, and a blues singer who wants a man in a uniform.

At its initial engagement *Peace on Earth* played for 125 performances and later in the season ran another three weeks. The melodramatic plot, entertaining despite its improbabilities, the continuing public uneasiness over foreign militarism, and the company's effort at audience organization turned it into a hit. The production, moreover, was strong, with Robert Keith in the role of Owens, settings by Cleon Throckmorton, and direction by Robert Sinclair, who later staged such successes as Clare Boothe's *The Women* and Philip Barry's *The Philadelphia Story*. Only one other Theater Union play had a longer run—the next production, Paul Peters and George Sklar's *Stevedore*, which opened in April 1934.

With *Stevedore* the company offered its only work on the position of the black in American life, a subject that, despite the efforts of O'Neill, the New Playwrights, and the agitprop troupes, was still of little concern to the professional theater. As bad luck would have it, one of the most absorbing plays on the race issue of the entire decade, John Wexley's *They Shall Not Die*, was opened by the Theater Guild two months before the Theater Union play. This took something of the bloom off the production of *Stevedore* but did not spoil its chance.

As was evident not only in the decision to produce *Stevedore* but in its publicity releases and operational methods, the Theater Union took what was for 1934 a boldly advanced position on race relations. Whereas other managements had doubted the reliability of black actors, the company's staff let it be known that those they employed were dependable—contrary to the usual notion, they were in fact not absent from or late for calls, or otherwise unprofessional—and the white actors got on well with them.[14] Such statements to the press made valuable publicity in an age when integrated casts were a rarity. Only the most exceptionally talented black musical performers, such as the singer Ethel Waters and the dancer Bill "Bojangles" Robinson, had been able to achieve high billing among white stars, and this they had managed only in plotless revues, where they did their turns apart from the whites and with the suggestion that the occasion was sportive, that they were Harlem entertainers, "uptown darkies," brought down to Broadway as a special treat for white audiences. For the rest, the most that blacks could expect of their profession was stardom in an all-black cast. As late as 1935 so well-known a performer as Ethel Waters was unembarrassed to pose as a parody Desdemona for the magazine *Stage*.[15] To its credit, the Theater Union did more than open its stage to black actors; it also opened its auditorium to black playgoers. Whereas other professional managements shunted blacks to the balcony, the Union encouraged them to buy whatever tickets they wished and refused tickets to white organizations whose members objected. No wonder, then, that Bill Robinson was so grateful for the company's sympathy that during a performance of *Stevedore* he jumped out of his seat and leapt to the stage to cheer the embattled black actors on. Apart from the Federal Theater, no other company adopted this policy of integrated seating until the Second World War.[16]

In preparing *Stevedore*, Peters and Sklar refurbished a play about black New Orleans longshoremen that Peters had originally written in the late twenties, scenes of which he had published in the *New Masses* for November 1929 and April 1930 under the title *Wharf Nigger* and *On the Wharf*. Despite its New Orleans setting, the early play was based on his observations of outbreaks of race hatred in St. Louis and

Chicago. With Sklar as collaborator he enlarged its compass to include material on labor unions. As originally written, *Wharf Nigger* would not serve the Theater Union, Peters explained in an interview, "because . . . it dealt with the Negro problem from the race angle rather than from a Marxist approach." [17] Of the whites in *Stevedore*, only the bosses are hostile to blacks; the whites of the laboring class who wish to organize a union are their friends.

Within this Marxist frame of reference Peters and Sklar created a melodrama capable of both gripping and shocking the audience. The dialogue was held at a level that is right for the status of the speakers and lacks the spuriously noble quality of the language of most class-conscious drama when working men are speaking. Lonnie Thompson, the black protagonist, speaks with the gruff tone and uncertain grammar to be expected of a man poorly educated and seldom exposed to verbal eloquence. Accused of raping a white woman, not because he is guilty of the offense, but because he is a member and organizer of the stevedore's union, he expresses his outrage in sharp naturalistic diction: "What right dey got to treat us dat way? Line up, nigger. Step out, nigger. Get back in yo' cage, nigger!" (I, iii). Only in the obligatory scene when he tries to persuade other blacks to stage a fight against lynch-minded policemen and brawlers is his tone forced to an implausibly high elevation, and then only briefly: "The lowest animal in the field will fight fo' its home. And all you can think of doing is running away. And supposing you do run away? Whar you gwine go to?" (III, i). Tension builds speedily from the second scene as with wanton indifference to the truth the white establishment begins stalking Thompson, an "uppity" worker who insists on receiving the exact wages due him for the hours he works on the docks. His destruction is ordained as a necessary move in the eternal game of keeping down the entire black race.

In the end, the white bosses get their man; Lonnie is shot and killed by a member of the mob of goons combing the black inner city to find him. But Peters and Sklar make it clear that something is lost by the whites in this campaign, and something gained by the blacks to offset Lonnie's death. Before Lonnie is hunted down, the white race loses its solidarity, for under the leadership and instruction of Lem Morris, a white union organizer, white dockworkers come to see the necessity of joining with the blacks in a united labor front, recognizing that it is not the blacks who are their class enemy but those whites with power and money. What the blacks gain is, not only the friendship and aid of the working-class whites, but courage. Having made an effort to conceal Lonnie, the entire community is in danger. But with the knowledge that the union is behind them, they prepare to make a stand, though their weapons for the most part are only things that can be thrown: bricks, cobblestones, horseshoes, and lumps of coal. The shooting of Lonnie, like the report of the murder of Lefty in its effect on Odets's cabdrivers, moves them the final step in their evolution as fighters. Yet by themselves they are inadequate to the task of driving off the furious mob. It is only the last-minute arrival of Lem and his union rank-and-file that saves them. The Marxist message, that all underdogs must unite to fight the common enemy, is thus delivered in time to terminate the play in a burst of excitement.

Complaints against this hair-breadth rescue were aired by some of the reviewers for the non-Communist weeklies and dailies. "Those brought up on melodrama may be reminded faintly of the old days when the marines used to get there at the last minute," wrote Joseph Wood Krutch in the *Nation*. But in general the protests were mild, the reviewers having been swept along by the flow of the performance, and pleased, as was Krutch, to see that the intended victims of the white rabble were spared—"at least until after the curtain had fallen." [18] The Communist press was also generally satisfied. Gold, writing in the *New Masses*, poured out a cascade of hyperbole.[19] Six months after the opening, John Howard Lawson voiced a belated objection to the absence in the play, and in *Peace on Earth* and Wexley's *They Shall Not Die* as well, of a clear-cut political line, implying that he would have preferred the inclusion of a favorable reference to communism:

> It is absurd for any writer to attempt to write about the class struggle in *general* terms. The Communist Party is playing a definite role in every strike, in every activity of the working class. Other parties and groups are also playing definite roles. Every worker is intensely concerned with the policies of these parties. In fact his life depends on a correct estimation of these policies.[20]

But this criticism elicited no promise of reform and no expression of chagrin, only Liston M. Oak's uncompromising assertion that the company would continue in its own way.

Maintaining the production standard it had set with *Peace on Earth,* the Theater Union had cast the play well, with Jack Carter in the role of Lonnie and Edna Thomas in the major female role. Their performances and the melodramatic finish drew a warm public response, resulting in the Theater Union's greatest success. After 111 performances, the company took a month's respite and then returned for another 64 performances. After the New York closing, the play went on the road, visiting Philadelphia, Washington, Detroit, and Chicago. In London, with Paul Robeson as Lonnie, the New York success was repeated. When the season was concluded, the Theater Union was able to report that its first two plays had drawn an attendance of 300,000.[21]

In the second season, the Board's choice for the opening play was Friedrich Wolf's *Sailors of Cattaro,* translated from the German by Keene Wallis and adapted by Michael Blankfort. Wolf, a German-Jewish physician and a Communist, was at the time a refugee in Moscow, where, it was reported, his play had been given more than a thousand performances.[22] Several months before the opening, Clifford Odets had rehearsed scenes of the play with Theater Union actors.[23] A somewhat curious choice for an organization hoping to draw the American middle class to the support of workers, the work provided a Marxist view of the unsuccessful mutiny of some six thousand Austrian sailors in the last year of the First World War. Their demands, which could be related only indirectly to the life of the audience, were for the cessation of war, the improvement of poor living and working conditions, the establishment of an eight-hour day in the Austrian state factories, the participation of "the Party" in peace negotiations with Russia, and the release of all political prisoners.

The chief value of *Sailors of Cattaro* to the Theater Union was that it offered yet another plea for the prevention of war and another opportunity to press for a front of all workers in opposition to the ruling class, as represented by the officers of the *Sankt Georg.* Like Peter Owens, the sailors are ordinary family men suddenly precipitated into revolution and in the end defeated and sentenced to die. But Wolf's recommendations went considerably beyond those of Maltz and Sklar. The failure of the rebellion as presented in the play illustrated a political theme new to the professional stage in 1934: the superiority of totalitarianism to democracy. All plays approving of communism had, to be sure, this political line as a subtext, but not before the production of *Sailors of Cattaro* had it been expressed so bluntly in the American theater. If Franz Rasch, the intelligent leader of the *Sankt Georg's* mutinous crew, carries out his somewhat hazardous plan for taking the ship out of Cattaro Bay to a port where it can join with other mutinous ships, he and his men can win their goals. If, however, they wait for aid to come to them, they may be captured by counter-revolutionaries. The sailors' elected council, fearing to risk bombardment by the surrounding loyal crews, votes against the plan, and Rasch democratically accepts their decision. The result is disaster: help does not come, and the officers force the surrender of the rebels and execute their leaders. The implication of this conclusion is that Rasch was unwise to act on his democratic impulse; as leader of the crew, he should have insisted that his plan be carried out. One sailor's cry at the close, "Comrades, next time better!," promises that revolutionaries to come will follow the advice of their leaders.

In view of the steady shift in the ideology of the far Left toward the Popular Front philosophy, *Sailors of Cattaro* was out of date for 1934. It seemed, moreover, to put into question the assertion of Oak in *New Theatre* that the Theater Union functioned "as a theatre, not as a political party"—in other words, that the company did not care to take an exclusively leftist position in any production.[24] But in its second and last piece for the season of 1934–35, the Board chose a play that made no mention of revolutionaries or reds, Albert Maltz's *Black Pit*. Like the three preceding plays it proved to be a melodramatic tragedy designed to further working-class solidarity. But also evident in its design is the author's wish not to offend the middle class, along with an awareness of the new doctrine of socialist realism. Maltz had visited the West Virginia coal fields and had reported on the grimness of the company towns for the *New Masses*.[25] No mention whatever is made in the dialogue of John L. Lewis, who as head of the United Mine Workers was one of the most conspicuous labor executives of the Depression years and by dint of native radicalism, paradoxically coupled with conservatism in politics, had crushed the Communist party's effort to set up the National Miners' Union in opposition to the UMW. Maltz, avoiding offense to either the Left or the center, did not specify the organization needed for saving the miners, but merely pressed the belief that some sort of organization was necessary.

What *Black Pit* offers is a view of the miners' life that propagandizes for unionism within the bounds of indigenous American practice. Maltz's ardor confines itself to the portrayal of a society divided between rich and poor—company officers and the workers who make the daily trip down to the face—and of the unhappiness certain to befall the worker who betrays his class. The deserter, Joe Kovarsky, is offered a job as a company spy by a mine superintendent related to his wife. Though reluctant to take it, he does so because his wife is pregnant and needs medical care. When he betrays the organizers of a strike, he is forced by his brother-in-law, a militant unionist permanently crippled as a result of a mining accident, to leave the fields. With a remorseful look at his wife and child and a few mumbled words about his desire for a "li'l bit of sun" (III,ii), he walks away, a man without friends or calling.

The moving delineation of the conscience-stricken, desperate Kovarsky compensated for the obvious contrivance of the family arrangement whereby Joe becomes a spy. Contemporary reviewers did not object to this plot contrivance or, in the main, to the occasional bathos of the language. But the Communist party press argued one point at length: the propriety of the dramatic use of the worker as villain. In the *Daily Worker* Carl Reeve took issue with Maltz for holding up to view a proletarian traitor without mention of the many loyal members of the working class and their equally loyal wives. Joseph North stressed the same issue in both the *New Masses* and the *Daily Worker*, observing that it was better to give the workers a dramatic protagonist to emulate than one to revile. On the other hand, Jack Stachel, a party official assigned to labor problems, approved of the play for its depiction of the workers' struggle.[26] In the end Reeve and North won the dispute, for in no other militant play of the decade did a dramatist attempt to elicit pity for a traitor to the working class.

The quarrel pointed up an inherent weakness in agitational drama that continued to cause difficulty. The injunction against choosing a villain from the masses put a heavy restriction on the writer of a play, because it prevented him from constructing any kind of conflict other than a battle of classes, pure and simple. Too frequently the fight for supremacy broke down to a physical struggle, as in the first three Theater Union plays, or developed into nothing more than a series of symbolic groupings, as in the Workers Laboratory Theater sketches.

In neither sort of work could the plot transcend muscular physicality to become a coherent discussion of ideas or a nonviolent clash of wills, for the workers when pitted against their bosses could not match them in articulateness without seeming too well-educated to remain in the kind of job they had. If, moreover, a member of another class represented them, as in *Peace on Earth*, he was sure to be outnumbered and overwhelmed by others of his own class. One solution to the problem would have been to present a class conflict in the form of a dispute between the head of a corporation and a high-ranking labor official with the intelligence of Lewis, Walter Reuther, or David Dubinsky, for in such a play articulate discussion would not only be appropriate, but essential to the development of character. Such a conflict was, however, never dramatized by the writers of the thirties, possibly because the class distinctions between the disputants would have been disturbingly vague.

A further limitation of agitational drama is often revealed in the outcome of the events of specific plays. In *Black Pit* Joe's melancholy banishment is tragic, but it does not prevent the strike, and the final scene leads the audience to believe that the workers will win without a prolonged battle. It was possible for Maltz to predict success because the task he gave his fighting miners was reasonably small: unionization, not the routing of a superior armed force with, for better or worse, the law on its side. Though such a play as *Stevedore* is the more exciting theatrically, it is, finally, unconvincing, because, unlike *Black Pit*, it leaves the more thoughtful members of the audience with the nagging question, "What happens tomorrow?" In *Peace on Earth* Maltz and Sklar avoided this problem; the play is a tragedy, and Owens goes to his death. Yet at the close of this play also a suggestion is dropped that a new era of social justice is coming: from off stage is heard the chant of demonstrators, as in agitprop: "Fight with us, Fight against War."

With runs of 95 and 85 performances respectively, neither *Sailors of Cattaro* nor *Black Pit* could be described as a hit. Nevertheless, at the midpoint of the decade, with four plays behind it, the Theatre Union appeared firmly established. Nor were its accomplishments confined to the staging of the four works. In a search for new playwriting talent, the company held a one-act play contest in 1934. The prize went to Philip Stevenson for *God's in His Heaven*, and the play was published under the Theater Union's own imprint. Stevenson offered a look at a new Depression phenomenon: the unemployed youngsters roaming the country in empty freight cars in search of work. Returning home to the Midwest, Jimmy Clark, the son of a factory hand, shocks his hard-up, hard-headed parents by telling them that America is not the golden land of opportunity that they believe it to be—shocks them, but does not quite convince them.[27] The company also founded a dance unit and an acting studio. In the studio actors were trained with experiments in the method of acting developed in Russia by Constantin Stanislavsky, and members of the Board devoted their Saturday mornings to delivering lectures on the "Social Basis of the Theater." To raise money, the company held an annual costume ball, like virtually every other radical organization in New York. To show that they could practice in the real world what they preached on stage, the cast of *Sailors of Cattaro* joined the picket lines at Ohrbach's when the department store's employees went on strike.[28] Did it matter that they were late for the matinee? Not to their committed audience, not on 14th Street. Among the company's wishes, never to be fulfilled, was the development of a permanent acting company and the engaging of a permanent director; the financial outlay for this was beyond its means. Nor was it able to acquire the supply of actable scripts for which it continually searched. At the close of the 1934–1935 season, the Board optimistically described for the press the kinds of works it hoped to offer: a comedy of working-class life, vaudeville and revue material, and plays on the professional classes, farmers, and fascism.[29] But worthy scripts were few; only on fascism was the company able to find a producible work. Members of the Executive Board put together a revue, *Parade,* but it was another organization, the Theater Guild, that produced it.

Members of the Executive Board also participated in the first American Writers' Congress, held in New York in April 1935. This meeting resulted in the formation of the League of American Writers, the Popular Front association designed to replace the old John Reed Clubs. Plans for the Congress were drawn up in the fall of 1934 under the aegis of Alexander Trachtenberg of International Publishers, the publishing house of the Communist party. The "call" for the meeting was signed by seventy-one writers of liberal-to-Left opinion, including Maltz, Peters, and Sklar; other signatories who had written for

the theater were John Dos Passos, Michael Gold, Langston Hughes,
John Howard Lawson, and Claire and Paul Sifton.[30] At the Congress
Maltz reported on the special session of the Playwrights' Commission,
and Blankfort, in collaboration with Nathaniel Buchwald of *New
Theatre,* provided a paper titled "Social Trends in the Drama." The
paper included comment on the achievement and history of the agitational theater in America, ending with remarks on Blankfort's own
company. Though interesting enough as an advertisement, which no
doubt in part they were intended to be, these remarks are interesting
even more as evidence of the continuing search of the revolutionary
theater in America for the perfect means of portraying the class struggle in terms acceptable to the varied individuals comprising the audience. Though the paper ends with a note of apology, it is clear that
Blankfort was not only pleased with the work of the Theater Union
thus far, but expected it to become even better. "In a recent play,
Black Pit," he and Buchwald wrote,

> Albert Maltz has taken a step in another direction from the plays
> which have gone before. This play is important because it indicates a
> different type of selection of material and a different treatment. If, for
> example, plays like *Peace on Earth, Stevedore* and *Waiting for Lefty*
> portray man resisting the onslaughts of capitalism, fighting it head on,
> and conquering it, at least temporarily, *Black Pit* deals with a man
> crushed. Both types of plays reveal the forces of oppression, but the
> former by direct means and the latter, indirectly. Both are equally
> effective propaganda. There is still a further distinguishing character-
> istic. In *Stevedore,* the *actions* of the hero are dramatized; in *Black
> Pit,* not only are the hero's actions but also the inner moral and psy-
> chological conflicts. Put in another way, if *Stevedore* stresses action,
> *Black Pit* stresses character. There is, of course, nothing that excludes
> both character and action entering a play to an equal degree, and, in
> our opinion, there is nothing in the direct or indirect treatment of our
> material which determines the stress. We have yet to produce a revo-
> lutionary play in America which strikes an effective balance between
> inner conflict and outer events, between the drama of the individual
> and the drama of his class.[31]

THE GROUP THEATER
1931-1935

AMONG THE PRODUCING UNITS OF THE Depression, none was longer-lived or more influential than the Group Theater. The company offered its first production in the fall of 1931. In early 1941, when the Depression itself at last was at an end, the Group dwindled out of existence, the only public announcement of its death being a *New York Times* article by one of the founders, Harold Clurman, on the closing of the company's offices.[1] But the vitality of the Group's directors and actors continued as a major source of strength of the American stage in the forties, fifties, and sixties. During its ten years the company mounted twenty-five plays, most of which drew mixed or poor notices and were financial failures, but nevertheless helped to set the confident style and mood of the theater of the thirties.

From the beginning the Group was a Broadway organization. Most of its personnel had been employed in the professional theater before joining the company. It drew much the same audience as other producers, applied to "angels" for backing like the others, frequently sharing production credits with other, better-heeled managements, and sought publicity in the daily newspapers and wide-circulation magazines. With six of its plays promoting Marxism and the majority of the rest susceptible to Marxist interpretation, the Group was never free of an association with the far Left in the mind of the public during the thirties; and later, during the post-World War II red scare, long after the dissolution of the company, the association continued to be made. Yet, despite the presence among the actors of a small "cell" of Communist party members, the Group was maintained as a liberal, not a radical, organization, by the efforts of its directors, Harold Clurman, Lee Strasberg, and Cheryl Crawford (after 1937, Clurman alone). The task of the company as they saw it was "to give voice to the essential moral and social preoccupations of our time." [2] Inasmuch as radical political theories were a current preoccupation, they were heard in Group productions, but, on balance, were not of the first importance to the company as a whole.

The preliminary discussions leading to the formation of the company occurred in 1928, when Clurman and Strasberg, employed by the Theater Guild and the off-Broadway American Laboratory Theater respectively, gathered about them a group of young people who like themselves were troubled by the lack of contemporaneity on the American stage. They were more interested in revolutionizing the stage than in revolutionizing the national political structure. Among them were Sanford Meisner, Morris Carnovsky, and Franchot Tone, all of whom were to become Group stalwarts. In their talks they conceived the notion of a completely self-contained theater with a permanent acting company and a distinct style, as opposed to the Theater Guild's eclecticism, which Clurman deplored. The job of the stage director was to extend beyond the usual duty of wrenching a convincing performance from the actors. He was to be an instructor who developed the actors in their craft even while rehearsing them for a particular play. Greater demands were to be made on the actors than were usual. They were not merely to carry out parts under the director's guidance, assuming the roles and filling the requirements of them as the director saw them, but to study the play with as much diligence as would enable them to understand its implications for the contemporary society. Thus, inevitably, the company's productions would be of plays analyzing the structure and temper of modern society. It was possible that such plays would aim toward altering the structure of society, but primarily their purpose as the Group staged them was illustrational rather than propagandistic.[3]

In Clurman's reminiscences of the early planning sessions with Lee Strasberg in *The Fervent Years*, his invaluable history of the Group, the two young men emerge from the pages with a pleasant, unintentional resemblance to the traditional heroes of youthful fiction who compete successfully with their elders for a place on Broadway or in Hollywood. They were self-confident (but not eccentric); they were idealistic (but not arty). And because practical knowledge of the theater, gained through three years of acting and directing, underlay their schemes, they knew how to get down to work. To interest a potential backer in their talents, they rehearsed two plays, Waldo Frank's *New Year's Eve* and Padraic Colum's *Balloon*, for a period of twenty-three weeks.[4] Though in the end the plays did not carry the would-be producers to Broadway, they at least demonstrated Clurman and Strasberg's sincerity. Characteristically, the young men had avoided the pretentious, gloom-ridden European pieces admired by the Guild and the sleek works of American-made machinery favored by most other Broadway producers. Neither Frank's nor Colum's play is a work of distinction, however, for both are dull in plot and uncomfortably inflated with prose dialogue aspiring to poetry. As views of the emotional problems created by economic expansionism, pressagentry, the new morality, and the metropolitan clutter and bustle, they are so markedly products of the twenties as to bear scant resemblance to the works ultimately staged by the Group Theater.

In 1929 the first substantial opportunity came to many of those who were to found the Group. The board of the Theater Guild asked Clurman, Crawford, and Herbert Biberman, respectively the Guild's play-reader, casting director, and stage manager, to supervise a special production to be offered on Sundays to Guild subscribers. Clurman chose a Soviet play, V. Kirchon and A. Ouspensky's *Red Rust*, and engaged Strasberg and Tone as actors.[5] Five other actors, including Luther Adler and Julian (later Jules, still later John) Garfield, who were to take part in the Group also appeared in it. The play opened on December 17 and ran for 65 performances. It was the Guild's first and only so-called Studio Production.

Clurman, Strasberg, and Crawford did not know at the time of the *Red Rust* production that their association would be continued. In a much later year they were annoyed to find that a history of their activities published in the weekly magazine *Time* included the statement that the first Group offering was a Soviet drama—a piece of misinformation with a slightly sinister connotation.[6] Nevertheless, *Red Rust* foreshadowed the Group's work in some ways. Far from being a piece of Third Period propaganda, it was as critical of Russian life under communism as later the Group's plays were critical of American culture. The plot, which was invented shortly before the introduction of doctrines throttling unsympathetic remarks on the Russian governing élite, is an unfavorable comment on the expanding bureaucracy. Kirchon and Ouspensky offer as an example of the Russian breed of political opportunist a bullying party-member named Tere-khine whose career in brutality is symptomatic of the moral break-down of Russia after the revolution. First, he terrorizes his young wife into preventing the birth of a child he does not want; later he kills her. Eventually he is tricked into a confession and rushed off the scene, presumably to his execution. To Clurman, who chose *Red Rust* only for its novelty as the first Soviet play to reach America, the enthu-siasm shown by Russian sympathizers in the audience was astonishing.[7]

Within a year of the closing of *Red Rust*, the company envisioned by Clurman and Strasberg at last became an actuality. Accepting Cheryl Crawford as the third member in their plans, they recruited actors and spent Friday evenings in lecture sessions with them. These meetings were held from November 1930 through May 1931. Beset, like the rest of the population, with financial problems, the actors took encouragement from their association as a group. So frequently did they refer to themselves as a group that the term eventually be-came the name for their company. Not only did they train together, but they conducted an experiment in collectivist living, sharing quar-ters and food. In exchange for these benefits, they agreed to renounce star billing and to accept lower salaries than they might have re-ceived from other managements. Over the winter months they came to view themselves as a responsible body of citizens who could pro-gress intellectually while rehearsing or playing in intelligent plays.[8]

Two other propositions put forward by Clurman and Strasberg sup-ported the principle of communal growth. Playwrights, recognizing the play as only one of many equally important elements in a produc-tion, were to work closely with the actors, writing and revising ac-cording to the actors' needs. In this there was, of course, nothing new, since actors and directors have always applied pressure to dramatists to write and rewrite as theatrical exigencies require. But the point is more interesting than usual in this instance, because it reveals the directors' intention of working with accessible and, therefore, presumably American authors. Second, the actors were to work with the method developed early in the century by Constantin Stanislavsky at the Moscow Art Theater, a performing technique requiring them to assume the emotional states of the characters they portrayed. The method had been introduced to the American stage in 1924, when Stanislavsky's company visited New York. As early as 1925 Strasberg had studied the method with Maria Ouspenskaya and Richard Boleslavsky, actors from the Moscow company who had stayed on in New York to teach at the American Laboratory Theater. Strasberg then used the method himself in directing amateur productions at a settlement house. He discovered that Stanislavsky's devices, as he understood them, of improvision, exercises in the memory of emotion, and concentration on the offstage life of the characters enabled the actors to relieve their tensions and fulfill their parts as though living them. Interpreting their roles under the directors' guidance, the actors worked toward well-coordinated "ensemble" playing.[9] This technique, which became the most famous element in the total style of Group productions, was helpful to the actors in many of the plays, but, it would appear from reviews, not in all of them.

In the spring of 1931 Clurman, Strasberg, and Crawford informed the Guild of their intention of making up a producing unit with their actor-disciples. With two scripts to rehearse and a gift of a thousand dollars from the Guild and additional funds contributed by admirers and friends, including Maxwell Anderson, they left New York for a summer in Brookfield Center, Connecticut, during which they optimistically prepared for a fall opening despite the lack of backing for a production.[10] This was the first of many summers that the company was to spend in the country in a comfortable pattern of work and relaxation, agreeably set off with the visits paid to them by writers, composers, and other workers in the arts, some only at the outset of a career, some already recognized and successful. In addition to their socializing, ball games, performing, and rehearsals the company also took time for lessons in ballet and modern dance, fencing, singing, and diction.

In the Group's first four seasons, from the fall of 1931 through the spring of 1935, the company introduced ten plays, of which two by

Clifford Odets were presented as a double bill. Four of the productions were financial successes of sufficient magnitude to enable the Group to survive its lean periods. The programs of the first two productions offered in the fall of 1931 carried the phrase "under auspices of the Theater Guild," but early in 1932 the three directors severed the connection with the Guild, which by then was tenuous at most, and, without the Guild's prestige to attract investors, raised money from a variety of miscellaneous sources in the trial-and-error manner of all producers. Friends of friends, successful authors, and the richer members of the Group itself all contributed. Though the directors took out papers of incorporation and issued stock, the Group remained in outlook a noncommercial unit, choosing plays on their merits as analyses of social problems, but "never . . . in anticipation of a 'wow.'" [11] They hoped for, but never obtained, a permanent endowment for salaries and production costs, such as Otto H. Kahn had granted the New Playwrights and is provided by every European state to support at least one company. The directors admitted to themselves that an American company would have to appeal to private individuals for the necessary sum (put by Clurman at $100,000), but they quickly discovered that the rich men who had backed nonprofit theaters in the twenties were no longer rich enough to give their money away. Kahn, who in all probability would have helped them before the crash, could do nothing for them. Consequently, they felt their way along from production to production, often sharing the credits and the returns with independent producers who invested in them. For moral support and (possibly) reflected glory, if not for economic assistance, they established an advisory board during the run of their first play.[12] *

Not surprisingly, the directors were frequently hard put to find answers to practical questions of rent and food for the actors, to say nothing of supplying them with a steady weekly wage. Yet even in the grip of hunger most of the members of the company did not defect to other managers or to Hollywood. When they did go elsewhere for work it was usually with the understanding that they would return to their old companions as soon as they were needed for a new

---

* The members of this board included Maxwell Anderson, Philip Barber, Barrett H. Clark, Waldo Frank, Mordecai Gorelik, Paul Green, Theresa Helburn, Robert Edmond Jones, Ralph Steiner, Alfred Stieglitz, Paul Strand, and Gerald Sykes.

play. What sustained their loyalty was the belief that they were growing as craftsmen by acting and studying together. Linked to this was their respect for the pertinence of the plays in which they appeared together, no matter how brief the runs. Though not even their warmest admirers could declare confidently that their literary judgment was infallible, a few of their choices were, and still are, recognized as good contributions to American drama, and none could be said to lack seriousness of purpose.

The plays of the Group's early years could be described as both somber and optimistic. The lightest of them are tragicomedies whose protagonists are able, because of their superior morality and dignity, to escape the disasters that befall their friends and relations. Paul Green's *The House of Connelly* (1931), Sidney Kingsley's *Men in White* (1933), and Clifford Odets's *Awake and Sing!* (1935) were the company's greatest money-makers in this pattern. Dawn Powell's *Big Night* (1933) and John Howard Lawson's *Gentlewoman* (1934) were failures in the same form. Maxwell Anderson's *Night over Taos* (1932), Lawson's *Success Story* (1932), and Melvin Levy's *Gold Eagle Guy* (1934), tragedies on the theme of lust for wealth and power, failed at the box office, but received some good notices. As exposés of the villains who sacrifice personal integrity for material gain these three plays offered uplifting public sermons in the form of personal history. Like the tragicomedies, what they preached was not the power of grace, as do Shakespeare's tragedies, for example, but the belief that unsocial attitudes are dangerous to the individual. A fourth tragedy, Odets's *Till the Day I Die* (1935), provides in the suicide of the well-meaning Communist hero a message of hope in the agitprop manner; it is the only Group tragedy with a consistently sympathetic protagonist. Falling within the center of this short range were two plays incorporating elements of agitprop: Claire and Paul Sifton's *1931—* and Odets's *Waiting for Lefty*. Mordecai Gorelik, the designer of ten Group productions, was to point out more than once that the theme revealed by most of these plays was the biblical formula, "What shall it profit a man if he gain the whole world and lose his own soul?" This question is in fact at the heart of all Group plays, although it does not always appear to be the dominant issue. While Gorelik was right to add in 1940 that "the Group's lower middle class audience scarcely need the advice not to gain the whole world," since most of them had no hope of gaining more than a modest livelihood, the theme was nevertheless important as a general admonition against moral compromise.[13] Most of the Group's playwrights were content to stop with this admonition rather than to preach the Marxist doctrine that under capitalism the "sellout" is inevitable; with the exception of the work of Odets, the Group's few plays offering that variation on the theme were failures.

Green's *The House of Connelly* indicated the direction the company was to follow for its ten seasons. First conceived as a tragedy, the play was revised by the author at the Group directors' request for an affirmative ending. In making this demand of Green, the Group showed its courage, for the Guild was willing to back the production with ten thousand dollars if the original ending was kept, but only five thousand if not.[14] As revised, the play was a kind of forecast of the social attitude to be expressed by American liberals with the emergence of the New Deal. On the surface it is the story of the struggle for the control of a Southern plantation in the early years of the present century, but beneath this is a plea to the audience to break with traditional social views. As the Connelly farmlands waste under the poor management of young Will Connelly, Patsy Tate, the energetic daughter of a new tenant farmer, conceives of a scheme to make it reflourish. Her plan is to seduce Will, talk him into marriage with her, and as mistress of the house spur him into working the land profitably. Patsy lacks the genteel ways of Will's invalid mother, his proud and touchy sisters, and Will himself, but she is honest, as she proves by revealing her scheme to Will before the marriage takes place.

The lines are drawn between the two social classes, landowners and tenants, when Will's relatives try to persuade him to marry a rich girl with whose money he could pay off the debts on the farm. He prefers, however, to go further into debt for new equipment and with Patsy's help to make the farm pay. Denouncing the family's venality, he determines to marry Patsy. His mother dies of heart failure, his drunken uncle commits suicide, and his sisters flee the house rather than live in it with Patsy in charge, but none of this dismays Will for long. As Green originally designed the plot, the black servants Big Sis and Big Sue, who as a chorus offer comments on the fortunes of the house, strangle Patsy on the night the couple return from their honeymoon, and thus the victory goes to neither the aristocracy nor the middle class but to the land itself, which is to resume the primeval placidity to which it was returning before the arrival of the Tates. But in the Group production the servants were put in their place by a warning from Will to respect Patsy as his wife. Will is able to gain the whole world, or at least as much of it as he desires, because he keeps his soul. He cannot be held guilty for the misfortunes of his relatives, for it was the absurd traditionalism of their class that ruined them.

After a successful début with the *House of Connelly,* the Group completed the season with two plays in which the directors had only slight confidence: the Siftons' *1931—* and Anderson's *Night over Taos.* Aware of at least some of the defects of both, they believed nonetheless that these were plays of a sort that the company ought to stage —plays, that is, with pertinent contemporary themes. The chance of success was a long one, and the Group lost, for neither play held on for more than a week and a half.

Of the two, *1931—* was the more original. *Night over Taos,* written in pompous, overelegant verse, traces the melancholy career of Pablo Montoya, ruler of Taos before the coming of the Yankees, to demonstrate that dictators are eventually destroyed by the atmosphere of brutality that they themselves create. Clurman found the play "bookish, contrived, uninspired," but pressed it on the company as "at any rate, a playable stage piece," for want of any script on which he could report more enthusiastically.[15] Playable it may have been, but not watchable. For the Siftons' play it could at least be claimed that it was the first to include documentary glimpses of the Depression scene. A plot illustrating the sorrow of a young, out-of-work shipping-room hand named Adam is interwoven with scenes in which nameless workers gather at the gates of factories in the vain hope of securing work. These scenes are graphic reports of the spread of unemployment and are offered in support of the conventionally dramatic presentation of Adam's conversion to radical politics. As the play moves on, the crowds of unemployed workers increase in size and vehemence of expression, until at last, singing the "Internationale," they march through the streets, where Adam joins them.

What vigor *1931*—possesses it derives from its plotless agitprop interludes. The story of Adam, though well-intended, is banal, for the Siftons present him as an inarticulate man whose difficulties are immense but whose ability to describe them is severely limited. Employers exploit him, his landlady evicts him, and his girl—"*The* Girl" —becomes pregnant, falls into prostitution, and contracts venereal disease, but Adam suffers these blows in silence broken only by mumbled hints of unhappiness. Concerned chiefly with the effort to convince the audience of the cruelty of capitalism, the Siftons did not make him interesting in his own right. As the Group discovered, Adam could have appeal only for persons whose most immediate problems were similar to his, and these were problems related to poverty. On Broadway, where even in 1931 most of the audience was not worrying about unemployment, the play could not draw. The general critical reaction was that the authors treated their subject sentimentally and were, therefore, dishonest. Thus, Percy Hammond, writing for the New York *Herald-Tribune*, responded with annoyance to the sight of the Siftons' breadline:

> It is a depressing sight and I was melancholy last night as I left the Theatre Mansfield to walk through Broadway to this desk. But on my way I was confused by other long lines of men at the Paramount, the Rialto, and Marcus Loew's. None of them was cold or hungry. They were warmly clothed and they had the price of admission. No symptoms of destitution were present. . . . Well, I'll string along with the Siftons, while asking them to be less violent in their showy and shallow propaganda, and, when they write another super-sob song, to be more on the level.[16]

After this, the Group directors never again offered a play of *strictly* working-class life. An audience for Marxist analyses of direct poverty existed, but it bought only balcony seats, and the company could not sustain itself on such limited patronage. Every night during the twelve performances of the play the cheapest seats sold well while the orchestra was sparsely occupied. Most astonishing to Clurman was the cry of "Long live the Soviet Union" which issued from the balcony on the closing night—to be followed by Franchot Tone's "Hurrah for the United States" from the stage.[17] In this there was a lesson; henceforth, the Group confined itself to plays about those sec-tors of society with which the majority of the Broadway audience could identify. There was, to be sure, the exception of *Waiting for Lefty*, but that play had already generated enough publicity to insure a good run before the Group brought it up from the Civic Rep. Not all of the actors in the company were happy with the directors' seeming indifference to radicalism, however, and as their social awareness developed, many of them devoted their spare hours to teaching classes to members of the Theater Union and Theater Collective, where attention was given only to dramatic treatments of the lives of workers. For their part, the directors looked on this kind of activity with respect; Clurman himself attended the organizational meetings of the companies, and Strasberg taught a course for the Collective.[18] They were not indifferent to the problems the Union and the Collective attempted to air in the theater, but they were not inclined to look at them from the position of the worker. From the show-business standpoint, the directors were justified, for throughout the decade no play, whether Marxist or not, whose cast was made up of only down-and-out characters was able to pay its way, with the exception of Jack Kirkland's dramatization of Erskine Caldwell's *Tobacco Road*, which succeeded not wholly because of its social implications but because of its sensationalism as well.

The actors' strong interest in social, economic, and political matters became evident during the summer of 1932, following the first season, which they spent in Dover Furnace, New York. It was reflected in their enthusiasm for the play chosen to open the second season, John Howard Lawson's *Success Story*, a tragedy in which the protagonist's failure in life is explained in part by his renunciation of Marxist ideals. Clurman had earlier read and rejected the play for the Theater Guild, but after reading two acts of a revised version, he found it to be a good vehicle for the Group. Moreover, he believed Lawson to be "the hope of our theatre." [19] In consequence, the relative brevity of the run—121 performances—was a profound disappointment.

Because the characters, setting, and dialogue of *Success Story* are realistic, the play is at least intelligible and, therefore, very much superior to Lawson's works for the New Playwrights. But the plot is one that was to become increasingly familiar as the Depression ran its course: an ironic rags-to-riches story in which financial success does not bring happiness. Sol Ginsberg, the protagonist, makes the climb from a modest clerical job in an advertising office to the presidency of the company. Once a radical "chock full of Marx and Lenin" (I), he forgets the wisdom of those philosophers as soon as he discovers a means of blackmailing his employer for control of the business. In the last scene, a company secretary who has always loved him becomes so confused by the contradictory currents in his nature that she kills him. She had held onto her revolutionary ideals through the years and had been sustained by them; it is clear that in Lawson's view Sol would have spared her and himself much unhappiness had he done the same. What Clurman had admired in this plot was "a new kind of vividness, in which a hectic poetry was compounded from the slogans of advertisements, the slang of gangsterdom, and echoes of Old Testament music," [20] which some of the reviewers took to be only feverishness. A brusqueness in the dialogue that foreshadows the tough wisecracking of Odets is admirable, but it often gives way to shrillness when Sol attempts to justify his money fixation. It is difficult to believe that a sensitive girl like the secretary could love him. When the company took the play on tour in 1934 they found that with the coming to power of Hitler audiences were moved to indignation by the fact that Lawson's protagonist was an unsympathetic Jew.[21]

The identical problem, along with others, arose when the Group produced for its second and final play of the season Dawn Powell's *Big Night*. Like *Success Story*, this work had first come to Clurman's attention when it was submitted to the Guild; it too was a failure, and with a run of only seven performances the worst failure in the Group's history. A satiric account of a desperate salesman's last-ditch effort to succeed in business by offering his reluctant wife as bait to a client, it required the pacing of farce but was given an overintellectualized staging. After exploring the social implications of the play during several months of rehearsal, the company puzzled not only the audience but the author as well. J. Edward Bromberg, in the role of the lecherous client, insisted that his character's name be changed from Jones to Schwartz, offering the explanation that he felt better as Schwartz. As a result Powell was accused by acquaintances of writing an anti-Semitic play in which a Jewish businessman was exhibited as a drunken boor.[22]

After two seasons of mixed notices but increasing critical regard, the Group took a chance at the beginning of the 1933–34 season on a play that provided a good showcase yet was, in Clurman's opinion, "on the level of a *Saturday Evening Post* story": Sidney Kingley's *Men in White*.[23] The longest running of all Group productions, it stayed on Broadway for 351 performances and won the Pulitzer Prize.

The dissatisfaction with Kingsley's play felt by many of the Group's members and friends both before and after the opening originated in the author's failure to take a strong position on social issues. The action is a romance with melodramatic touches and a setting in a large metropolitan hospital. A young intern, George Ferguson, is engaged to a wealthy girl, Laura Hudson, who loves him, but cannot recognize the importance of his hospital training. She is impatient when his duties require him to break dates with her and resentful of his plan to study with a great Viennese surgeon during their honeymoon abroad. By breaking the engagement, she leaves him open to the advances of a lonely nurse. Predictably, the nurse becomes pregnant; concealing her condition from George, she has an abortion and later dies on the operating table as George performs a hysterectomy in the hope of saving her while Laura looks on. A thin coat of social relevance is applied to all this by the presence of certain symbolic characters: a go-getting businessman who pursues his deals eagerly despite a serious heart condition, a weary Jewish doctor who has spent his years practicing in the tenements, and a society doctor whose ineptness almost causes a patient's death. These figures decorate the surface but do not strengthen the sentimental core. It is, moreover, always clear that George will go on to the training that will bring him eminence in his profession. What is best in Kingsley's writing is not his illustration of a human dilemma, the choice between a comfortable life and public service, but his glorification of modern medical practice. Seizing upon the hints given in Kingsley's directions, Strasberg added to the play's substance by staging in perfect detail the operating-room procedure leading to the hysterectomy.[24] The ritual was acted out in a prolonged pantomime that brought the play into focus by giving evidence of the doctor's earnestness, dedication, and professional competence. The art of acting as a unit that was part of the Group ideal had not yet been so effectively revealed to an audience as in this scene. Imitated in the film version under Richard Boleslavsky's direction, the balletlike movements of washing and donning sterile clothing were borrowed for crucial scenes of countless other films of hospital routine.[25]

Praise for the excellence of their performance did not relieve the troubled feelings that the company had developed over the content of the play; nor was it completely satisfying to them that *Men in White* put money into their usually empty treasury, whereas so far their socially relevant plays had not. They turned to a sterner work, John Howard Lawson's *Gentlewoman.* In this play Lawson once more sermonized on the redemptive power of Marxism. He had meanwhile prospered in his Hollywood career, taking a very active role in the previous year, 1933, in the fight for film industry recognition of the Screen Writers' Guild, and serving as the Guild's first president. But he was always happy to desert the West for visits to the Group's spartan summer camps. Lawson seemed caught in a psychic conflict whose resolution he sought in the process of constructing a script. The protagonist (not the title role) of *Gentlewoman,* is a young writer, Rudy Flannigan, so boorish as to seem deliberately designed to make the task of winning sympathy for Marxism difficult. If, Lawson seems to say through his play, Rudy can emerge through the dialogue and action as a sympathetic man, then his faith in the revolution, which is his only possession and only quality, is a faith to which men may subscribe with profit. He is attracted to a beautiful woman, Gwyn Ballantine, and lives with her after she loses her fortune. At the end of the play she senses that he must be on his own if he is to complete his novel and take his place at the side of the embattled workers. His spiritual health, which has been fading, is restored once Gwyn leaves him, and, gladly giving up the rich foods and cut flowers provided by her aunt's generosity, he departs for Iowa, where he expects to help the farmers in their fight to save their mortgaged farms. The experience shared by the lovers proves beneficial to each, for Rudy is more determined than ever to create a new world, and Gwyn learns to be utterly indifferent to her aunt's money. She is pregnant with Rudy's child, but, loving him more than ever now that she must part from him, she keeps him in ignorance of the fact. In poverty both become full of grace.

With a run of less than two weeks, *Gentlewoman* was yet another costly failure for the Group and supplied fresh evidence that Lawson's talent had become constricted by his radicalism. At the time the play opened, however—on March 22, 1934—he was not yet a member of the Communist party, though obviously a sympathizer. His eventual commitment to the party appears to have been hastened by the harsh review of *Gentlewoman* written for the *New Masses* by his old associate in the New Playwrights' Theater, Mike Gold. Titling his piece "A Bourgeois Hamlet of Our Time," Gold sketchily reviewed Lawson's career, only to conclude that the playwright had no firm political convictions. The heart of the essay consists of two paragraphs:

> Audiences are peculiar. . . . Even when they like a bad or cheap play, it has to have some grain of truth in it. The plays of Lawson are synthetic concoctions: they begin, often with some fundamental truth of character, then dissolve back into the solipsist's world of unreality. Worse, still, they make an impression of insincerity, as if the author were writing to a box office formula.
>
> But Lawson tries to be sincere, I believe; it is no formula with him, but a fixation. Always this single theme of the declassed bourgeois colors every line he writes. Today, however, the declassed bourgeoisie of America are not feeling futile, strangely enough. They are beginning to organize, in one form or another, and are preparing to play a serious political role in American history. They are grim, and completely cured of their Menckenism. The fact that Lawson cannot see this is another of the penalties he plays for a delayed adolescence.[26]

Only one week after the appearance of Gold's review, the magazine carried a reply from Lawson. At this time Lawson was a member of the editorial board; the fact that no time was lost before the appearance of his reply suggests that he saw Gold's attack in advance of publication. "In the first place," he wrote, "I hesitatingly admit the truth of 70 per cent of Mike's attack." He then went on to ponder his position at length, calling himself a "fellow-traveler," to praise Marxist criticism as "the only criticism with which he was in the least concerned," and to express the belief that from the Marxist point of view *Gentlewoman* was a flawed work. In concluding he gave a preview of events to come in his own life: "But Mike's case simmers down to the fact that I ask a *monotonous* question": 'Where do I belong in the warring world of two classes?' I'm sorry the question bores him, but I intend to make my answer clear with due consideration, and with as much clarity and vigor as I possess." [27] Writing a bit later, but not long after the end of the 1933–34 season, he claimed that the early closing had been due to the class prejudices of the newspaper critics, whose psychology, he believed, could be revealed by Marxist analysis to be shaped by economic pressures. Only through the revolutionary theater, he declared, could the stage "develop new integrity, vitality and imagination." [28] These remarks, which show that Gold's criticism was beginning to take effect, appeared in the preface to, not one, but two, failures; the second, *The Pure in Heart*, opened under the management of Richard Aldrich and Alfred de Liagre, Jr., two days before the Group opening. This unfortunate play was in fact a two-time loser; in the previous season the Theater Guild had put it on, only to close it during the out-of-town trial performances. Lawson did not inform his readers that among the hostile newspaper critics of his failures had been one writing for the *Daily Worker:* Melvin Levy, a playwright as well as critic, had joined with the critics of the major papers in finding fault with *Gentlewoman*. In his opinion, Lawson would have done well to learn something about the working class before dramatizing the life of a member of it.[29] Perhaps in response to this suggestion, the playwright soon made two trips to Alabama to investigate the situation of the Scottsboro boys. Before the end of the year, in a *New Theatre* article titled "Straight from the Shoulder," he made it known that he had arrived at a definite point of view. While asserting that a writer need not take a Communist view to create meritorious work, he declared, "As for myself, I do not hesitate to say that it is my aim to present the Communist position, and to do so in the most specific manner." [30]

Thus Lawson was one of the first American writers to perform the act of self-humiliation that with time was to become a ritual for Marxists under pressure from the party. Soon enough he himself was to require it of dissidents in Hollywood. Meanwhile, Clurman gave him an advance royalty of a thousand dollars for still another play. He was shocked, however, to find Lawson meekly receptive to leftist criticism of his work, not only when it pointed to obvious flaws, but when it was directed at qualities that Clurman found "rare and valuable." [31] But in spite of the advance, the Group produced no more plays by Lawson.

When *Gentlewoman* closed, the Group was still benefiting from *Men in White*, which continued through the season. But, as always, the company remained on the edge of crisis. Problems in acting technique troubled some members, for Strasberg's use of Stanislavsky's method had not proved wholly satisfactory. In addition, the deepening radicalization of the actors brought them into occasional disagreement with the directors. For reasons then unforeseen, these problems were to be abated somewhat in the 1934–35 season.

The season opened poorly with Melvin Levy's *Gold Eagle Guy*, a gaudy but ultimately dull account of the rise of a San Francisco shipping magnate, Guy Button, from 1862 to his death in 1906. Though the actors had resented the play because it was not, in Clurman's words, "hotly contemporaneous in subject matter or feeling," [32] they could hardly have failed to note its numerous points of resemblance to Lawson's *Success Story*. Button, like Sol Ginsberg, is an intelligent man who through dishonest means gets control of an important company and enjoys the use of power, not stopping to consider the great harm and hardships he causes others. Both protagonists are difficult men, but often inspire loyalty. Guy's career does not parallel Sol's consistently, however, for his rise is less rapid than Sol's, and his death is accidental. Unlike Sol, who is ready for death when the girl shoots him, Guy is still alert and hopeful of crushing his enemies when he meets death. This occurs in the great earthquake of 1906. The marble pillars in his office are heard, after a blackout, to come crashing down on him—a melodramatic end that represents just, if fortuitous, retribution for his cruel aggressiveness. An incidental but interesting plot detail in both plays is that a Jewish woman (Sarah Glassman in *Success Story* and the actress Adah Isaacs Menken in *Gold Eagle Guy*, both played by Stella Adler, the Group's best-known actress), inspires profound love in a Christian—a defensive gesture, whether unconscious or deliberate, made against anti-Semitism by the two Jewish authors.

Though *Gold Eagle Guy* was not a quick failure, it was a failure nevertheless; after eight weeks it closed. The social themes were too familiar, the plot too predictable, and the production, though colorful, not sound. The Group's preoccupation with Stanislavsky's method as interpreted by Strasberg was beginning to create new problems. An item in the theatrical pages of the *Times* before the opening gave an indication that something out of the way was about to be shown:

> In "Gold Eagle Guy" the Group Theatre hopes to present a beginning of the new technique on which it has been working for four years. The play opens in the year 1862; the directors are working toward a full picture of the period not only in costume and speech but also—and here enters the new technique—in the characteristic

rhythms of the period. So, in "Gold Eagle Guy" the company is working out *gestures and rhythms of movement characteristic of this American period.*[33]

That the staging was too studied was suggested by Joseph Wood
Krutch, who wrote, "One occasionally feels in all the Group's carefully thought-out productions a certain stiffness, as though the art had
not quite learned to conceal itself." [34] The difficulty was to continue.
As the *Times* release noted, the company had worked with the Stanislavsky technique for years; during the preceding summer Stella Adler,
who was Clurman's wife as well as the company's leading actress, had
consulted Stanislavsky himself on how best to use his method and
had held some classes for the company after returning home.[35] Yet
the problem remained for Strasberg, who directed Levy's play and all
earlier Group productions except *Big Night,* to teach the actors to
conceal their cerebrations from the audience.

Cool toward *Gold Eagle Guy,* the actors were warmly in favor of
the plays by Clifford Odets with which the Group closed its fourth
season. After three and a half years of financial sacrifice in the name
of art, they experienced the pleasure of performing in works that not
only brought in some money, but were revolutionary, were at least as
well constructed as any others they had staged, and were written by
one of the group. This was a superb confirmation of their original
principles, for Odets had been in the company since its origin and
had discovered his talent through the Group program of constant
study to relate the theater to other aspects of American life. When he
achieved recognition as an unofficial spokesman of the youth of the
thirties, as distinct a symbol of the decade as F. Scott Fitzgerald had
been of the twenties, the Group secured its place in theatrical history.

Before the production opened, the directors did not realize how
sound a talent they had nurtured. During the run of *Gold Eagle Guy*
Clurman, in the face of objections from Strasberg and Crawford, decided that *Awake and Sing!* should be the next play. The decision
was not based entirely on confidence in Odets's writing, for although
the actors admired the work very much, and Clurman himself liked it,
Strasberg and Crawford had doubts. They were in no position to
cavil, however, for no other good scripts were available, and the company, not for the first time, was on the point of disbanding.[36]

Though the child of prosperous, middle-class parents, Odets had struggled on his own as an actor through the twenties on radio as well as in the theater. For a time he headed his own troupe.[37] Before his success as a Group playwright, he acted in seven of the company's productions, always in minor parts, and also appeared with other Group members in a New Theater Night sketch on February 10, 1935. In 1933, after appearing in five Group productions, he had acted in John Washbourne and Ruth Kennell's *They All Came to Moscow;* this was his last role outside the Group. As an actor he had no distinction. In the first years of their friendship, Clurman found him an odd but interesting young man. He was moody, he spoke in nonsequiturs, and he had a vast love of music. Happier and more secure in the collective life of the Group than he had ever been in the booming twenties, he spent the offstage hours writing, striking chords on the piano, and looking at life in the streets and cafeterias of Greenwich Village. Between the end of the first season and the last day of 1934, he brought Clurman four long plays. The first was crude but promising, and the second was weak. Talent was evident, however, in the third and fourth, *I Got the Blues* (later revised and retitled *Awake and Sing!*) and *Paradise Lost.* In 1934, drifting into the Left political current, Odets began to take an interest in the Theater Collective and the Theater Union and gave permission for *Waiting for Lefty* to be acted for the benefit of the New Theater League. Given his sensitivity, poverty and youth, it was inevitable that he should join the Communist party. His rejection of it, after some eight months, when the party's cultural leaders began to exploit him, was also inevitable.[38]

From the outset of his fame as a dramatist, Odets was judged by his reviewers as a political writer. *Awake and Sing!* was put into rehearsal before the Civic Rep première of *Waiting for Lefty* in January 1935, but did not open until February 19, nine days after the critics had attended a performance of *Lefty* at the Civic Rep by invitation.[39] The volatile agitprop *tour de force* served to publicize Odets and to create an audience for the three-act play, but was not, on the whole, a satisfactory introduction to his talent. Among leftist reviewers it engendered expectations that *Awake and Sing!* did not fulfill, and disappointed not to find the new play as explosive as *Lefty,* they discounted it as unimportant, and flawed.[40] On the other hand, the writers for the nonradical press were disposed to prejudge *Awake and*

Sing! as a Marxist tract, and their reviews, though generally favorable, indicated a mild disapproval of Odet's ardor.[41] Too radical for some tastes and too conservative for others, he became what every young writer hopes to be: controversial. But, all complaints aside, he gave fresh evidence in his new play of the same skills he had revealed in *Lefty:* an excellent ear for colloquial speech and the ability to create and stress phrases that distinguish the personality of each speaker. It was these skills that animated the theme and lifted the plot above the banality of most revolutionary drama, not the blunted but jarring call to action that he saw fit to make room for at the final curtain.

In its plot *Awake and Sing!* was closer to the life of the Broadway audience than *Lefty,* inasmuch as Odets had created characters for it with aspirations to a level of life somewhat above that of his militant taxi-drivers. The Bergers, a Jewish family in the Bronx, are shown struggling in the grip of the Depression not merely to keep alive but to maintain social respectability. Behind the anxieties of the older generation of the family lies something larger and darker than the daily necessities: they are possessed by an immoderate fear that through scandal they will be forced back to the penurious life out of which they have painfully risen. Bessie Berger, the matriarch (played by Stella Adler), has managed over the years by sheer force of will to put a good face to the world. Her peace of mind rests upon the well-being and unsoiled name of the family, whose members are less important to her as individuals than as props for her pride. Married to a weakling, she has long since discovered that she must be both mother and father to her children, and that to fulfill her duties, at least as she interprets them, she must suppress her normal yearnings for an occasional change of scene, a game of cards, or even the affection of the family, lest in the momentary dropping of her guard the Berger children cease to be the cleanest on the block. When she discovers that her unmarried daughter Hennie is pregnant, she pushes her into marriage with a young immigrant who is too innocent to recognize her strategy for what it is, and when she hears that her son Ralph has taken up with a girl, she makes an effort to break up the relationship in order to keep his salary in the family. There is something so intense about her singleminded drive that the simple offer of a cup of tea to the family's one friend becomes a monumental gesture when she delivers it.

Bessie's asperity is a weakness of that dire sort that begets disaster. *Awake and Sing!*, despite its title and the excited shout of Ralph as he casts off Bessie's hold in the final moments, is not a happy play. For the most part, however, the tone is comic, because of the idiomatic peculiarities of the dialogue. Extremely harsh passages as well as mild ones become humorous, as, for example, Bessie's gibe at her father: "Go in your room, Papa. Every job he ever had he lost because he's got a big mouth. He opens his mouth and the whole Bronx could fall in" (I). The tough talk of the hardened racketeer disguises the tender feelings of Moe Axelrod, the family friend, when he ponders his difficult relationship with Hennie: "Don't make me laugh— when I get married! What I think [of] women? Take 'em all, cut 'em in little pieces like a herring in Greek salad. A guy in France had the right idea—dropped his wife in a bathtub fulla acid. (*Whistles*) Sss, down the pipe! Pfft—not even a corset button left!" (I). At other moments Odets allows grim humor to creep into the dialogue by means of oblique remarks that reveal the severe emotional strain of the speakers—thus Moe, again, more disturbed by Hennie's impending marriage than he cares to admit, cries, "What the hell kind of house is this it ain't got an orange!!" (I). Myron, Bessie's husband, complains to himself after a shocking argument between Bessie and her father, "My scalp is impoverished" (II, ii). The oblique remarks caused Odets to be compared with Chekhov, whose plays had been performed in New York within recent memory by the Moscow Art Theater in an acting style similar to the Group's. Clurman, on the other hand, detected traces of Lawson and Sean O'Casey in *Awake and Sing!* and said at the time that Odets knew little of Chekhov.[42] But source hunters should not ignore Odets's first-hand knowledge of the life and language of Jews of Eastern European origin, if they are to understand the Bergers.

In *Awake and Sing!* the language imparts a comically human quality to the characters that prepares the audience to accept them as innately decent people. It is the acquisitive society in which they live that is accountable for their faults. Odets expresses this fundamental Marxist tenet by contrasting the personalities of Bessie and her father, old Jacob. Both see, and deplore, the materialism that determines the tenor of American life, but whereas Jacob wishes to fight it with communism, Bessie has long since made peace with it. Jacob is an aged European Jew who still retains the old-country love of learning. He passes the hours reading Marx and Engels and listening to Caruso records. Especially important to him is a Meyerbeer aria: "From 'L'Africana' . . . a big explorer comes on a new land—'O Paradiso.' From act four this piece. Caruso stands on the ship and looks on a Utopia. You hear? 'Oh paradise! Oh paradise on earth! Oh blue sky, oh fragrant air—'" (I). It was such a paradise that he had hoped to find in America and that he still hopes will come into existence one day. But Bessie, whether born abroad or in America (Odets does not say), is New York-bred and holds her father's tastes and views in contempt. To Ralph, whom he hopes to educate in Marxism, Jacob says, "Go out and fight so life shouldn't be printed on dollar bills" (I). Bessie uses the same image to drive home to Ralph the reason for her hardness: "On the calendar it's a different place, but here without a dollar you don't look the world in the eye. Talk from now to next year—this is life in America" (III). Jacob's speech occurs shortly after the rise of the curtain on the first act, Bessie's shortly before its fall at the end of the play. In between, Jacob kills himself in the hope that with his insurance money his grandson Ralph will be able to carry out his instruction to change the world. But the immediate cause of his suicide is Bessie's cruelty in breaking his phonograph records, an act that crystallizes for the audience the corrupting force of her drive to preserve the family's reputation, for she performs it in a rage after her husband blurts out to Ralph the truth about Hennie's pregnancy.

The last-minute attempt to sentimentalize Bessie is followed by a conclusion to the play that falls between melodrama and agitprop. Hennie decides once and for all to escape her mother's influence by eloping with Moe while Bessie is asleep. In terms of the audience's hopes for the girl, this move is not merely justifiable, but obligatory. But similar hopes for Ralph go unfulfilled. He decides to give Bessie the insurance money and to begin at once to change the world by building up a fighting spirit among the other employees of the warehouse where he works. Coming from a moody, sensitive boy, the decision is unexpected and not altogether convincing, as though Odets had added it at the last minute in order to duplicate the successful call to action of *Lefty*. The incongruity of the situation is enhanced by Ralph's approval of Hennie's elopement, an act which in purport is precisely the opposite of his own plan to fight it out at home.

Whether it was in fact Odets's intention to provide a curtain in the spirit of *Lefty,* or merely to dispel gloom, the ending of *Awake and Sing!* is markedly different from that of *I Got the Blues.* At least in part, the revisions were prompted by Clurman's reaction to the early draft, in which he found the last act "almost masochistically pessimistic." [43] In that version, Ralph gets and keeps the insurance money. Myron discloses that Bessie has a bank account with $4,100 in it, Bessie threatens to leave her family, and, after a police detective arrests Moe for illegal betting transactions, Hennie goes glumly back to her husband. Clearly, this was not an ending for the forward-looking Group; nor was it the sort that was likely to appeal to a Depression audience. Odets was wise to make changes, especially with regard to Bessie and Hennie, for the revelation of Bessie's secret horde is clumsy and melodramatic, and the disruption of the relationship between Hennie and Moe is too sudden to be believed. On the other hand, the development of Ralph as an agitprop Young Leader in the revised play is equally sudden and disturbing.

The box-office response to the play was good, and the Group, taking advantage of the publicity given Odets as the preeminent revolutionary playwright, made the decision to bring *Waiting for Lefty* up from the Civic Rep for a Broadway run. Since it took only an hour to perform, Odets filled the bill with another miniature drama, *Till the Day I Die,* which he wrote in less than a week. The new play was based on *New Masses* pieces by F. C. Weiskopf and Karl Billinger on the nazi terrorist campaign to suppress opposition.[44] On March 26 the Broadway opening took place.

Odets chose his subject well, since of all overseas events of the time the rise of Hitler was clearly the most ominous. It was also a subject not yet interpreted by many playwrights; of the most respected, only two had touched it: S. N. Behrman in *Rain from Heaven* and Elmer Rice in *Judgment Day.* Both had been produced in 1934. The New Theater League had two scripts on the Nazis for off-Broadway circulation, Kazan and Smith's *Dimitroff* and Elvin V. I. Abeles's *One of the Bravest,* but of the latter, also inspired by Weiskopf's *New Masses* piece, there is no record of production.

Not the best or the worst of these plays, *Till the Day I Die* is a high-keyed expression of contempt for the nazis, sharp and frequently funny despite its tragic action, but holding up communism for praise as the only alternative to fascism. Although the plot shows members of the Communist underground at work in Berlin to establish a popular antinazi front, the opinions revealed by the characters remain those of the Third Period: all who are not for communism are automatically fascists, and this includes liberals. Odets had already proved with *Lefty* that the black-and-white characterization of agit-prop could make effective drama if the dialogue and action were bold, but with the new play he was too far away from his subject to repeat his success. His Berliners speak like his New Yorkers in tough, wise-cracking slang, with the result that the play is not quite of this world. When not tough, the characters are very sentimental and inclined to describe visions of the bright world of the future. "I won't ever forget the first time we visited the nursery in Moscow," says the hero to his girl. "Such faces on those children! Future engineers, doctors; when I saw them I understood most deeply what the revolution meant" (scene i).

The fame of the two short plays was nationwide before the end of the season. In New York at a low price-range they drew an audience through the end of the summer. According to Clurman, troupes in some thirty-two cities performed the plays, many of the troupes coming into being expressly for that purpose. Odets counted almost twice that number of productions in the first year. In Los Angeles Will Geer, the director of a production of *Till the Day I Die*, was badly beaten by a band of pronazi thugs. On the non-Communist Left, the Socialist *New Leader* damned *Lefty* as "theatrical hokum," to the extreme discomfort of the editors of the *Daily Worker*, who were on the point of ceasing hostilities against the socialists. In Washington, New Haven, Boston, and other cities, municipal authorities refused to license productions of *Lefty*. By 1939 the New Theater League could count thirty-five censorship actions against the play that it had taken to court. Inevitably, these attempts at suppression added to the play's appeal.[45]

Through the late winter and spring of 1935 the Group's actors and directors were continuously busy, not only with their Broadway productions, but, as had long been their way, with other enterprises. The actors performed *Lefty* on several Sunday evenings in late winter before its Broadway opening, and the performance of February 10, given at the Civic Repertory Theater for the company's own benefit, also included a number of the sketches worked up in the annual summer visits to resorts and adult camps. These included "An Original

Idea of the Gravedigger's Scene from *Hamlet*," with Sanford Meisner and Florence Cooper; songs by Tony Kraber, an actor with a repertory of cowboy tunes; improvisations to the allegretto from Beethoven's "Seventh Symphony," with Odets, J. Edward Bromberg, and Walter Coy; "Operation on Hitler," with Elia Kazan and Tony Kraber; "Red Hamlet," with Robert Lewis; "Stylized Sketch from the Cartoons of Georg Grosz," with unspecified members of the company; and "Lincoln and Grant (with Liberties)," with Bromberg, Carnovsky, and others. This was the first evening on which the critics were invited to *Lefty*.[46] As the Communist party approached the formal establishment of the Popular Front in the spring, its leaders set up new organizations to attract liberals, including members of the Group. In late April, when the American Writers' Congress met to form the League of American Writers, the party's cultural officers offered a position on the Executive Committee to Clurman and a position on the National Council to Odets.[47] Odets's monologue *I Can't Sleep* was delivered by Morris Carnovsky at the Mecca Temple (later the New York City Center) in May on a New Theater Night. This sketch, barely ten minutes long, is composed of the nocturnal thoughts of a middle-class businessman who is troubled by the hunger and unemployment around him as his own fortunes rise. A sketch about a San Francisco strike by Art Smith, a group actor, titled *The Tide Rises*, was also performed. Clearly, the company had developed a remarkable versatility and virtuosity.

But the fame of the Group came perilously close to turning into notoriety in June 1935 as the result of Odets's acceptance of the chairmanship of the American Commission to Investigate Labor and Social Conditions in Cuba. Sponsored by the League of American Writers, this body was composed of fourteen members, each representing a different organization. Among the Communist groups to place delegates on the commission were such old regulars as the International Labor Defense and the International Workers Order, but, to establish the façade of a united front of workers, the commission also included a representative of the International Ladies' Garment Workers Union, whose head, David Dubinsky, was known to be opposed to communism. The members originally planned to offer the chairmanship to Ella Reeve ("Mother") Bloor, the grand old lady of American communism. It was decided, however, that she was too old to make the intended voyage to Cuba, and by default Odets, representing the League of American Writers, was given charge. En route to Cuba he discovered that true control of the commission rested with Conrad Komorowski, the delegate of the All-American Anti-Imperialist League, and that Komorowski and the other experienced campaigners on the commission expected to be arrested as soon as the ship docked.[48] That event took place—the maneuver was a scheme carefully worked out by the Communist party to embarrass not only the Batista-Mendieta regime, but also Jefferson Caffery, the American Ambassador to Cuba. On returning, Odets did not divulge his discovery of the plot to reporters. His comments to the press covered only the hardships the commission had experienced in the Cuban jail; the treatment accorded him and his associates he took to be evidence of the reactionary temper of the Cuban government. "I've been in some exciting plays," he remarked, "and they tell me I've written some exciting scenes. But for a personal experience, this was the most exciting." [49] On reading his observations, no one could have told that the experience brought about his disillusionment with organized communism. Seventeen years later, however, he cited it as one of the causes of his break with the party.[50]

In the years of activity remaining to it, the Group gradually resumed its old policy of steering clear of politics outside the theater, conserving its energy for the effective presentation of pertinent social plays. What had happened so suddenly with the success of Odets was not so much that the company had completed "its progress Leftward," as a writer for *Time* asserted,[51] but that the Left had come to it with the welcoming gestures that were soon to expand into the all-embracing Popular Front policy.

THE THEATER GUILD
1930 - 1935

THE MOST DURABLE OF THE "art" theaters that came into existence in the late teens and twenties, the Theater Guild in its first two decades provided more well-mounted productions of intelligent plays than any other management in New York. The organization was founded late in 1918 and offered its first play in the spring of 1919. Though ultimately, in the forties, its leaders forsook high artistic seriousness under unremitting economic pressure, the Guild remained in existence as a producing company as late as the sixties and, as a nationwide theater subscription society, even beyond.

The Guild was, essentially, a reincarnation of the Washington Square Players, the company founded in 1915 by Edward Goodman, Lawrence Langner, Philip Moeller, Ida Rauh, Helen Westley, and others, to offer examples of modernist drama on which commercial managers could not afford to risk money. This was also the aim of the Provincetown Players, a group founded in the fall of the same year by George Cram Cook, Susan Glaspell, Eugene O'Neill, Wilbur Daniel Steele, Mary Heaton Vorse, and others, who had spent the summer producing new plays at the Wharf Theater in Provincetown, Massachusetts. These two groups, which were friendly rivals, constituted America's entry—a very much belated entry—into the "new" theater movement that had swept over Europe in the eighteen-eighties. Despite the name, the Washington Square group did not perform in

Greenwich Village but in mid-Manhattan, first on East 57th Street, later on West 41st Street. Like the Provincetown in that company's early years, it offered one-act plays for the most part. The principal difference between it and the Provincetown lay in the fact that most of its plays were European, not American. The Provincetown's leaders were interested exclusively in American drama and rightly took pride in having offered O'Neill his first production, after one play he had tendered to the Washington Square Players had been rejected.[1]

The First World War put an end to the Washington Square Players, for with the exception of Langner its male founders entered military service. Most of its leaders retained their passionate interest in experimental theater, however, and in 1918 Langner, Moeller, and Helen Westley, meeting one evening in a restaurant, determined to make a fresh start at developing an art theater, but one that should be completely professional in its operation and should produce "full-length" plays exclusively. They chose the name Theater Guild because of the historical use of the term "guild" to designate craft associations. Joining with them in the original Board of Managers were Lee Simonson, Rollo Peters, Augustin Duncan, and Justus Sheffield. In the second season, with additions and departures, the board consisted of Langner, Moeller, Westley, Simonson, Maurice Wertheim, and Theresa Helburn: respectively a lawyer and occasional playwright, a fledgling director, an actress, a designer, a banker, and a writer attempting to make her way in poetry, drama, and criticism. Simonson, Wertheim, and Helburn had studied with George Pierce Baker at Harvard. For two decades the Guild was guided jointly by these six, with Langner and Helburn gradually emerging as the major voices; for periods in the thirties, the directors Herbert Biberman and Rouben Mamoulian and the actor Alfred Lunt also held places on the Board. Beginning with the 1939–40 season, Langner and Helburn guided the Guild alone, though Wertheim continued as a member of the Board until 1946.[2]

Though a commercial organization wholly owned by the Board, the Theater Guild was seldom rich. Its activities were too multifarious and its plays, for the most part, too unalluring at the box office for continuous prosperity. To insure a financial base, the Board at the outset developed an audience of subscribers, who in each season after the first were offered six plays. In the beginning the subscribers numbered only 135, but by the end of the Guild's first decade the list grew to some 60,000, divided equally between New York and the circuit of other Eastern cities to which, beginning in 1928, the company toured plays. In 1933 the company formed the Theater Guild-American Theater Society for presenting its productions to a nationwide audience, which after the Second World War included over 100,000 subscribers. The Depression made inroads on the subscription list, inevitably, but Guild productions continued to be welcomed across the country. Along with those of Katharine Cornell, in which the actress herself appeared, they were the best mounted road attractions of the thirties. But as beneficial as the subscription system was for the Guild, it created problems, for if a play proved a failure in its out-of-town try-out, another had to be found to complete the season's offerings, or an additional play had to be included in the next season's schedule. Even without the problem of the quick failure, no Guild season was made up entirely of financial successes.[3]

Additional financial burdens included the establishment of a permanent company of actors and a school of theater, and the publication of a magazine. These activities were short-lived. The acting company lasted from the season of 1926–27 to that of 1929–30, the school from 1925 to 1927, and the magazine from 1925 to 1932.[4] Yet another expensive undertaking was the building of the company's own theater, appropriately called the Guild, which opened in 1925. To this theater, in the Broadway area on West 52nd Street, it moved from the Garrick, on West 39th Street, between 5th and 6th Avenues, which the Board had subleased from Otto H. Kahn, who offered the house with the kind suggestion that the Board pay the rent only as often as it could afford to do so. The new home was larger, but not large enough for an adequate profit on productions, and therefore in 1944 the Theater Guild sold the Guild Theater and moved out.[5] Becoming, in time, as much a commercial undertaking as any other Broadway organization with or without ideals, the Guild could not ignore the exigencies of the bankbook if it was to continue. Yet even in the Depression the Board provided some assistance to new talent. Its backing of the Group Theater in 1931 was probably the company's most important service of this sort. In view of the youthful arrogance of Clurman, Strasberg, and Crawford, the Board cannot have helped feeling some misgivings about the matter, but did not withhold aid.[6]

Another service was the establishment of the Bureau of New Plays in the thirties, with the purpose, as the name suggests, to search for new play-writing talent. In 1938 Arthur Miller was the recipient of its prize of $1,250.[7]

The hallmarks of Guild productions were expert performing, scenic designs of noteworthy handsomeness whenever the script at hand did not rule otherwise, and literate dialogue on topics well above the level of the trivial (with the exception, to be sure, of such works as Ferenc Molnár's *The Guardsman* and Sil-Vara's *Caprice,* two vehicles for Alfred Lunt and Lynn Fontanne). Though Philip Moeller was the principal director to the mid-thirties, other directors were occasionally engaged. At one point the Board made a tentative offer to Constantin Stanislavsky to direct a production, only to withdraw the offer when the great Russian made it known that he would require two years of preparation and rehearsal.[8] The Board thought of each production as unique and sought variety for the benefit of its subscribers. But to an insurgent like Harold Clurman, the productions seemed to suffer uniformly from a surfeit of good taste.[9] The same damning tastefulness was also evident in the design of the Guild Theater, with its Italianate arches, pilasters, and tiles on the exterior, tapestries in the lobby, and beamed ceiling in the auditorium.

The Guild was never a doctrinaire institution, and its programs were not intended to reflect the state of the world from a particular social angle. On the other hand, it was not a company whose leaders wished altogether to avoid plays on political and social themes. In each season one or more such plays would appear on the Guild's schedule, along with others of quite different interests. A typical season would include comedy and tragedy, European and American works, and perhaps a revival. To take one season as an example, in 1930–31 the Guild offered S. Tretyakov's *Roar China,* Maxwell Anderson's *Elizabeth the Queen,* Claire and Paul Sifton's *Midnight,* Lynn Riggs's *Green Grow the Lilacs,* Hans Chlumberg's *Miracle at Verdun,* and Bernard Shaw's *Getting Married*—a Soviet agitational drama, a poetic history play, a melodrama, and a folk drama by American writers, a German antiwar fantasy, and a twenty-three-year-old English comedy of manners.

From 1919 through the season of 1929–30, the company offered sixty-two foreign plays to only nineteen American plays, including three "editions" of *The Garrick Gaieties*, a revue with songs by Richard Rodgers and Lorenz Hart, and in the next ten seasons it offered thirty-two American plays to twenty-one from abroad. The relative scanting of home-grown drama on the Board's part in the twenties was not necessarily due to a refusal to credit American writers with talent. In part it was due to the fact that to survive in its early years the company had to rely chiefly on pretested works. It could not afford the out-of-town performances necessary to get the snarls out of new writing.[10] Beginning in the later twenties, when substantial sums began to flow through the box-office windows, American plays appeared with increasing frequency on the seasonal schedules. To the American audience the Guild's European plays were new, unknown quantities, no matter how frequently they had been staged abroad, and through the twenties and thirties the company retained the principle of frequently offering works by unfamiliar authors who employed unusual styles. Gradually, however, the Board became increasingly interested in established authors—including, to be sure, some who had become established through Guild productions. Two writers of particular importance to the Guild in its best years were Bernard Shaw, whose major new plays written after 1920 were first produced in America by the company, and O'Neill, whose new plays from 1928 to 1947 were presented by the Guild. If ever an American company had occasion for self-congratulation, it was the Guild in offering the world première of Shaw's *Saint Joan* in 1923. Among other European writers whose works were staged by the Guild in the twenties were the Čapeks, Georg Kaiser, Ferenc Molnár, Luigi Pirandello, Ernst Toller, and Franz Werfel. It was the directors' boast that in presenting Kaiser's *From Morn to Midnight* (1922) the Guild had been the first American company to produce an expressionist play.[11]

The directors also believed that in producing Elmer Rice's *The Adding Machine* in 1923 the company was the first in America to offer a radical play.[12] This claim is open to question, but Rice's antinaturalistic study of the humdrum life of a white-collar worker could at least be praised as one of the most durable and provocative American plays of the twenties. Lawson's *Processional* (1925) was equally provocative, if less durable. O'Neill's *Marco Millions* (1928), a satire in which the attitudes of a go-getting businessman are grafted onto the personality of Marco Polo, was yet another early example of the company's American plays questioning received social values. But more successful and more typical American works offered by the Guild in its first decade were Sidney Howard's *They Knew What They Wanted* (1924) and *The Silver Cord* (1926) and O'Neill's *Strange Interlude* (1928), works reflecting the postwar freedom in the discussion of sex. Apart from *Saint Joan, Strange Interlude,* O'Neill's most massive play and a compendious showcase for the philosophical and artistic preoccupations of the twenties, represented the Guild's greatest achievement of the decade.

While demonstrating increased interest in American plays during the Depression years, the Guild's board could not, of course, allow European works to be crowded out altogether. The company produced many, though with no great acclaim. Inevitably, its two plays written by Soviet authors attracted the attention of the leftist critics, but were of minor interest otherwise. Kirchon and Ouspensky's *Red Rust* was in a special class as a Guild Studio offering. Tretyakov's *Roar China* was more impressive for Lee Simonson's set of a wharf on the Yangtze than for its plot of the exploitation of the Chinese by white foreigners and the uprisings following an incident of brutality. According to the critic from the *Daily Worker,* the Chinese rebels were not allowed to raise the red flag though the author's script called for them to do so; this, the critic believed, was in keeping with the merely moderate political opinions of the Board.[13] Of the continental plays on social themes, the most interesting was neither of the Soviet plays, but Hans Chlumberg's *Miracle at Verdun* (1931), a work later described as the last German play "to express an emphatic anti-war attitude before the rise of Nazism." [14] The action is made up of events following the resurrection of the dead fighters of the First World War. Called from their graves by God to help prevent a new war, they discover that in fact they are not wanted, because of the social and economic havoc created by their presence. Chlumberg's play was more successful in Europe than on Broadway, where it lasted only 49 performances. Still less successful than *Miracle at Verdun* was Ferdinand Bruckner's *Races* (1934), an antinazi play from Germany about the young in bitter conflict over Hitler's policy of anti-Semitism; when mounted by the Guild, it did not survive its out-of-town tryout.[15]

Many of the Guild's social plays of the thirties by American writers also failed, for the company was no more able than the Group or any other producing unit to fill houses with dull material. In three instances the company chose very mild—and very unsuccessful—plays by authors who provided the Group with works much more corrosive, if equally unsuccessful. The board had held an option of the Siftons' *1931*—, but it was the Group that finally produced the play; the only work by the couple that the Guild staged was *Midnight* (1930), a rather mild melodrama on the theme that the circumstances surrounding cases of murder should be taken into consideration by jurors and prosecutors determining the guilt of a defendant. The Guild's only play of the thirties by John Howard Lawson, *The Pure in Heart*, is less heated than *Success Story* and *Gentlewoman*, but also much duller. Cluttered with characters only partially developed, the familiar plot consists of the unhappy enlightenment of a small-town girl who leaves her home for the glamour of Broadway. In the end she and her criminal lover are shot down by the police. Presumably, both the girl and the gangster were intended as victims of capitalist economy, since only through immoral and criminal acts can they live in Depression-cramped America. On the road in 1932 it was a disaster for the Guild. Dawn Powell's *Jig Saw* (1934), a comedy of manners concerning a mother and daughter in love with the same man, offered an abundance of funny lines, but lacked the bite of *Big Night*. The Guild produced a play by one writer, George O'Neil, in whom the Group was also interested, but whose work the younger organization did not stage. O'Neil completed *American Dream* while summering at the Group camp in 1932,[16] and in the following year the Guild presented the play. An overlong, wordy tragedy, it follows the rise and fall of an American family from 1650 to 1933. The last and longest act suggests that the dream of soaring from rags to riches or from log cabin to White House, the cherished dream of inevitable success for the earnest, hard-working American, is delusive, for the thirty-six-year-old Daniel Pingree, heir to his family's considerable fortune and a would-be radical, unhappy with his wife and possibly a homosexual, decides to kill himself rather than go on living in the decadent environment of his social class.

These plays were as crude as the works of the Guild's favorite social playwrights were smooth. In the early thirties after Eugene O'Neill the most esteemed Guild authors were S. N. Behrman and

Maxwell Anderson. O'Neill's three plays of those years, *Mourning Be-comes Electra* (1931), *Ah, Wilderness!* (1933), and *Days without End* (1934), were not based on social issues, but Behrman and Anderson offered literate discussions of pressing topics of the day and drew en-thusiastic audiences with them. As political thinkers they occupied the same position as the Guild's own board: the middle of the road. Different though they were in the range of their interests and their modes of expression, both Behrman and Anderson were liberals and deft craftsmen. That they could not break through the limits of the well-made play was unfortunate, but it was not a weakness that mat-tered importantly to their audience.

Behrman, urbane, affable, a graduate of Harvard, where he had studied with George Pierce Baker, possessed a personality of a sort that, though unexpected, is by no means rare: a mixture of equal parts of political liberalism and social snobbery. His earliest plays show that he believed the well-made format suitable for conveying intelligent comment on human nature, as indeed it had been with Ibsen, but they ring with chatter about boxes at the opera, expensive resorts, champagne, and well-trained servants, and the first names of their casts are family names. The habit was formed with *The Second Man* (1927), Behrman's first play to be produced and a Guild offering. Its leading feminine character is named Kendall Frayne, and the men are called Clark Storey and Austin Lowe. The elegance of speech of the principal characters of all the plays is nothing less than amazing. "Wistful," "tremulous," "immutable," "indurated," "marginal"—these are some of the adjectives dropped casually into conversations with her friends by Marion Froude, the artist heroine of *Biography*. In his relentlessly chic comedies Behrman created good parts for the most fashionable performers of the age, who were also among the most talented: the Lunts, Ina Claire, Jane Cowl, Ruth Gordon, and Katharine Cornell. Most of his central roles were for women; only in the plays for Alfred Lunt and Lynn Fontanne were the leading male roles made equal or superior to the leading female roles. In Holly-wood, Behrman was one of the chief writers for the most glamorous of screen stars, Greta Garbo.[17]

Clothes, manners, money, and family held an attraction for Behr-man. Yet no less important to him was social decency. This fact was made manifest in his work before the end of the twenties with the

Guild's production of *Meteor* (1929). *The Second Man*, the first of his many plays for the Lunts, is a slight comedy concerning a young writer who is pleasantly outgoing and whose love of the good life is so great that he ignores his talent and an opportunity for romance in favor of an alliance with an acquiescent older woman who can afford to keep him in comfort. In *Meteor*, Behrman's second Guild play (following the unsuccessful *Love Is Like That* in collaboration with Kenyon Nicholson and an adaptation of the novel *Serena Blandish* by "a Lady of Quality," produced by Jed Harris in 1929), the Lunts were given a more ambitious if talkier piece. The protagonist is Raphael Lord, a man of uncertain age and antecedents who has the knack of making money through business dealings on a titanic scale. He claims also to possess second sight and in the early scenes seems to demonstrate it. In projecting this generally unpleasant character, Behrman, in his own words, "tried to depict [him] as an artist of some potentialities vitiated by suppression in early youth into a defensive egomania which by progressive steps was to destroy him as a human being," [18] but also, the play makes clear, to suggest a power-mad personality developed and sustained by the economic boom. Unhappily, the production opened only a few weeks before the market tremors in the fall of 1929. The time was no longer right for Behrman's climactic scene in which Lord by a tremendous effort of will not only escapes the destructive rebuff of fortune that he deserves, but threatens to demolish his enemies.

After the crash, Behrman continued much as before, providing a series of slick but not inconsequential comedies. His first play of the thirties, *Brief Moment* (1931), was not produced by the Guild but by Guthrie McClintic. The romantic plot circles around a young bride, formerly a nightclub singer, who is so impressed by the friends of her patrician husband Roderick Dean that she loses her becoming earthiness and tries to emulate them, almost ruining her marriage in consequence. Only months before the opening the New York papers had reported the wedding of Roger Wolfe Kahn, bandleader and flyer, to the musical comedy performer Hannah Williams, a pairing not unlike that of the play. Since the groom's father was Otto H. Kahn, who had tendered the lease on the Garrick Theater to the Guild, it was tactful of the Guild not to produce the play. Of more interest, on the whole, than the plot was the appearance of Alexander Woollcott in his first stage role as Dean's ironic companion. It was not a performance that the author enjoyed.[19]

Following this play, Behrman resumed his association with the Guild, whose subscribers were, after all, his natural audience insofar as they were beyond average means and above trifling interests, like his characters. Into his Guild plays of the decade he put characters elegant of speech and dress, as always, and an expression of the liberal view of life. The rapacious kind of man represented by Raphael Lord, a man with no love but only a liking for the few people near him, became a recurrent figure in Behrman's successes of the thirties. Arrogant and reactionary, such a man may speak of great schemes undertaken in the name of humanity, but in the end is only feeding his own vanity. Invariably Behrman set him opposite an open-minded, vibrant woman who, having passed first youth, has experienced enough of life to learn tolerance.

In *Biography* (1932), Marion Froude, a freedom-loving, unmarried woman in her thirties, finds herself placed in emotional difficulties once she accepts a magazine offer to write her memoirs. A rather daring bohemian and famous portraitist who paints not only Soviet commissars but American tycoons, she has built a life that promises to do well in print. But no sooner does she decide to accept the offer than she finds herself caught in a struggle between two men: Richard Kurt, the magazine's leftist editor, and Leander Nolan, her first lover, a lawyer planning to run for the Senate with the support of a conservative newspaper magnate. In *Rain from Heaven* (1934) an equally disagreeable situation rises to trouble Lady Lael Wyngate (named Lady Violet Wyngate in the Guild's production). She is a charming Englishwoman of means who, like Marion Froude, has a cosmopolitan outlook and the happy ability to make others share in her enjoyment of life. She is in love with Rand Eldridge, a young American polar explorer and popular hero. Ultimately she is forced by circumstances and her own intelligence to give him up. His brother Hobart has planned to exploit him by holding him up as an idol to the young and through him to attract them to fascism. The events of the play cause Rand to discover that he himself possesses the fascist mentality, in which intolerance and selfishness are combined under the disguise of crusading humanitarianism. In both *Rain from Heaven* and *Biography* the heroines cannot bear the political extremism of the

men in their lives and consequently leave them, protected against
loneliness by their innate independence.

Behrman's style is nowhere more personal than in the scenes in
which Marion Froude and Lael Wyngate defend their liberal, centrist
positions in verbal play with their extremist antagonists. It is impossible for him to risk a colloquialism, let alone a slang word, for the
slightest verbal slip would dash the Olympian comedy to earth. Since
neither Marion nor Lael is the sort of woman who can lose her temper without feeling regret and embarrassment, both must defend their
views as calmly as they can, without the faintest waver of self-control.
In a brief debate with Kurt, her editor, Marion quickly moves
through several states of mind, revealing perplexity, hurt, and resignation in turn, each through understatement.

> KURT: You're one of those tolerant people, aren't you—see the
> best in people?
> MARION: You say that as if tolerance were a crime.
> KURT: Your kind is. It's criminal because it encourages dishon-
> esty, incompetence, weakness and all kinds of knavery. What you call
> tolerance I call sloppy laziness. You're like the book-reviewers who find
> something to praise in every mediocre book.
> MARION: You are a fanatical young man.
> KURT: Having said that you think you dispose of me. Well, so be
> it. I'm disposed of. Now, let's get down to business. (*His manner
> plainly says: "Well, why should I bother to convince you? What im-
> portance can it possibly have what you think of me?" It is not wasted
> on* MARION.)
> MARION: You are also a little patronizing . . .
> KURT: (*pleased*): Am I?
> MARION: However, I don't mind being patronized. That's where
> my tolerance comes in. It even amuses me a little bit. (*Crossing to
> piano seat*) But as I have to change for dinner perhaps you'd
> better . . .
> KURT: Exactly. (I)

Lael reveals her mental discipline in wry, bantering phrases throughout *Rain from Heaven*, as in her exchange with Hobart Eldridge on
the fascist Lord Abercrombie, who Hobart thinks is the hope of England:

> Has he told *you* that too? He believes it. He actually believes it. I
> hate messiahs. Fake ones, charlatan ones I enjoy. It's amusing to

watch them do their stuff. I met Aimee McPherson in New York—
you know, the woman who was lost in the desert—I found her in a
cinema theatre. Now there's the kind of blonde messiah I like. But
sincere ones, zealot ones I can't abide. When they tell you they're the
hope of anything—and they're not faking—they're hopeless. But I'm
not persuaded entirely about Lord Abercrombie. Are you, Mr. Eldridge? Perhaps he practices before a mirror. . . .

    HOBART: In my opinion, Lady Wyngate, he is . . .

    LAEL: I know! But on the side. Pretty good circulation-booster,
isn't he? I haven't quite given him up. He may be—what do they call
it in America—delicious word—a phony! Shall we bet on Lord Abercrombie, Mr. Eldridge? (I)

This language, though unnaturally complex and precise for what is
supposed to be spontaneous comment, serves the purpose of establishing the intellectualism of the heroines and in so doing suggests that
liberalism will prove as tough as the forces of Left and Right. In both
plays this quality of the heroines is supported by their ability to make
close friends of eminent persons, particularly in the arts, many of
whom are products of cultures other than the women's own. Their relationships with such men are not invariably romantic attachments,
but always are close ties of sympathy and understanding. The wom-
en's intellectual friends prove able providers of the means of escape
from intolerable situations. Marion, torn between Kurt's eagerness to
publish her memoirs and Nolan's wish that she suppress them, decides at last to burn the manuscript. Both men leave her, despite their
love for her, knowing that she will go on in her customary bohemian
way. At the last moment Melchior Feydak, an old Viennese friend
employed in Hollywood as a composer, wires that he has a commission for her: to paint the portraits of the winners of the Motion Picture Academy awards. Lael Wyngate's situation at the close is not so
comic. She finds that Rand Eldridge has turned against the German
refugee Hugo Willens who, having had a Jewish great-grandmother,
had left Germany as a victim of the "chromosome hunt." Her relationship with Rand now destroyed, she accepts the affection of Willens.
Willens, an eminent music critic, could make a new home in England
or America, but chooses to return to Germany, presumably as a member of the underground resistance. Though not the militant that Willens now is, Lael is deeply moved by him and says to him as they
part, "I shall live forever and so will you. Our enemies will beat

against us and will find that we have a strength beyond their clamor, beyond their forces" (III). His bravery has armed her.

The bittersweet conclusions of both plays have the ring of truth. That *Rain from Heaven* is somewhat more moving than *Biography* is the difference between 1932 and 1934, a measure of the growing menace of totalitarianism. No matter how much Behrman may have wished to maintain a neutralist position, he could not as a Jew ignore the nazis. In sending Willens back to Germany, he joined the outcry against them. The character, as Behrman acknowledged, is largely based on the personality and career of Alfred Kerr, the eminent German-Jewish drama critic who had long championed the work of Gerhart Hauptmann, only to have Hauptmann turn on him after the nazi take-over.[20] But at the same time that Behrman spoke out against the nazis, he offered a hopeful prediction for the future of liberalism, as is evident in the strength and confidence of the two heroines. His fight for the liberal cause was none the fainter for taking the form of drawing-room comedy and relying on the aid of popular actresses who wore their clothes well—Ina Claire in *Biography* and Jane Cowl in *Rain from Heaven*. Moreover, his approach was the correct one for touching the feelings of the Guild's well-heeled metropolitan audience.

Maxwell Anderson, a prolific author with a following as large as Behrman's, drew upon a deeply rooted traditional American antiauthoritarian philosophy for the themes of his much-praised plays of the thirties. Though he had written dialogue in tough contemporary prose in the twenties, at the beginning of the thirties he turned to the writing of verse drama. In part because he was alone among well-known, established playwrights in attempting verse, in part because he was able with almost all of his plays to draw good plots out of English and American history, he developed, as the decade wore on, a reputation as a dramatic poet equal to that of any American lyric poet then writing. Stinting a natural talent for comedy, Anderson spun out his grave, portentous plays in verse that more often than not was bombastic, dull, and overweighted with nonfunctional images, but that nevertheless pleased audiences. In the early thirties the Theater Guild produced the first, third, and fourth of his verse plays, *Elizabeth the Queen* (1930), *Mary of Scotland* (1933), and *Valley Forge* (1934), as well as a prose comedy, *Both Your Houses* (1933).

Anderson's two Guild plays on English history, respectively starring the Lunts as Elizabeth and Essex and Helen Hayes as Mary Stuart, were stylish productions with settings by Lee Simonson and Robert Edmond Jones that offered the audience the opportunity to escape into the past from the mounting problems of their own time and place. It could at least be said for his *Night over Taos*, which the Group Theater presented in 1932 as the final production of its first season, that despite its faults it was relevant to the age in calling for a change in the social order, although its setting was the Spanish colonial territory of the Southwest.

An amusing satire on the U.S. Congress, *Both Your Houses*, was still more relevant, but, except for its references to poverty, could have been presented with as much success in the twenties. The plot concerns an innocent young man from Nevada who in his first term in Congress takes it upon himself to put an end to the corrupt practices of seasoned members. Appropriately, his name is Alan McClean. ("Serious. Wears mail-order clothes. Reads Thomas Jefferson. He came down to Washington three months ago, and he's spent all his time in the Congressional Library" [I, i]). Old congressional hands name him to the Appropriations Committee on the theory that he will support a graft-loaded omnibus bill in part affecting his own district but will not add to the bill. But McClean, offended by the waste and plunder allowed by the bill, hopes to defeat it in the House by adding to it in committee all the many items ever discussed as possibly being included in it. In the last twist of the plot, the plunderers win after all; since the bill includes something for every state, the House passes it, and it is expected to win in the Senate and to escape a presidential veto. Yet, lest the play end pessimistically, McClean and his fellow committee-men are shown to agree that it cannot be long before public resentment of the misuse of Federal funds catches up with the Government and brings about a change. Anderson's message was mild indeed, but it was enough to give the play an edge and bite lacking in the historical English romances. The comedy was given the Pulitzer Prize in 1933, a gesture that seems justified by the dry wit of the dialogue. In retrospect its plot seems overfamiliar, but chiefly, one suspects, because of subsequent echoes of it in *Mr. Smith Goes to Washington*, Frank Capra's film of 1939.

Anderson was never again to write a prose comedy with a contemporary setting, but after *Mary of Scotland* he turned from English to American history to find a theme that would speak to contemporary preoccupations. *Valley Forge*, less popular than the English plays, is a "costume drama" of the Revolutionary War, seriously intended and, apart from passages of comic relief, solemn and respectful. Anderson's theme, that freedom is worth the hardships required to maintain it, was right for the time, inasmuch as reports from Germany told of what could happen to a nation whose freedom had been lost. George Washington, Anderson's protagonist, is shown in the act of deciding to continue the fight against the British despite the shortage of sup- plies and the lack of interest on the part of certain congressmen. A ro- mantic plot line involving a courageous young woman in love with the general pads out what would otherwise be a very slight play. Ad- ditional padding is provided by a hearty comic soldier named Alcock whose uniform is missing a pair of breeches.

Although Alcock's comic prose is ineptly attached to the sober scenes that make up the main body of the play, it is superior to the dialogue spoken by the principal characters. It has the verve of the language provided by Anderson and Laurence Stallings for Sergeant Quirt and Captain Flagg in *What Price Glory?* (1924), one of the high points of realistic comedy of the twenties. Anderson's verse, though not inferior in *Valley Forge* to the verse of his other plays, is either drab or overagitated. When drab, as in the following passage spoken by Washington, it is prose that has been chopped into lines of approximately equal length:

> The reports before us
> show us we've neither food nor clothes nor arms
> for the maintenance of an army, nor defense
> if we're attacked. In my last letter to Congress
> I told them we must either starve or dissolve
> unless they sent instant aid. (I, iii)

As an illustration of Anderson's huffing style, this passage from the close of the play is typical:

> Gather my troops!
> Have they the strength to come together! Gabriel's triumpet
> might rally that vale of bones! Bring on these spectres

with the wind-fed entrails and mouths that open and speak not
gaping their misery! Summon forth brigades
and companies from the lazarettes they lie in,
cry, "Lazarus arise! On to the field!" (III)

Because of the electicism of the Guild's seasonal programs, neither
Valley Forge nor any other single play could be said to represent the
style and tone of the organization in full. Though not a commercial
hit, Anderson's play had the qualities usually present in Guild productions: high-mindedness and the self-conscious pursuit of art. Less
familiar in both tone and substance were the two works by American
leftists produced by the Guild in the early thirties, John Wexley's
They Shall Not Die (1934) and the revue *Parade* (1935) which was
composed chiefly of sketches by the Theater Union's Paul Peters and
George Sklar. These were unequivocally propagandist works, by comparison with which George O'Neil's *American Dream* with its polite
portrait of a well-to-do revolutionary was only a charade. Their inclusion in the Guild's schedule meant, not that the Board members had
turned radical, but that it had come to their attention that well-writ-
ten agitational drama was powerfully appealing. "It has been willing," they wrote of their organization in 1936, "to produce a communistic play as quickly as an imperialistic play, so long as it was a
good play with a definite idea to project." [21] The Theater Union had
drawn good notices and much attention with its first production,
Maltz and Sklar's *Peace on Earth*, in the fall of 1933, and by 1934 the
League of Workers Theaters had demonstrated its strength through
the success of its magazine and the willingness of the Group and other
companies to perform in its behalf. The message of these events was
that the propaganda play had an artistic potential, and the Guild did
not deny it. In any case, in the past it had had a critical success of its
own with such a play, Lawson's *Processional*. Moreover, it was none
too easy to locate a good American play after the crash that was not
based on a social theme. The two Guild productions were not unusually popular—*Parade*, in fact, was generally disliked—but they gave
the subscribers a taste of something new.

Wexley's *They Shall Not Die*, based on the arrest and trials of the
Scottsboro boys, was the most sensational play of the decade on the
life of black Americans. Its heavy weight of pro-Communist comment

aside, the play was bluntly realistic in its depiction of black wretchedness—more so than any other work given a major production. In writing it, Wexley apparently had two goals in view. He wished not only to make good drama out of the plight of the boys in order to generate sympathy for them, but also to propagandize on behalf of the International Labor Defense, the Communist party's legal apparatus, which had taken over the case from the National Association for the Advancement of Colored People in the second trial. To provide a semblance of fiction, Wexley gave new names to the persons and agencies involved. The ILD became the National Labor Defense; the NAACP, the American Society for the Progress of Colored Persons; Ruby Bates, the white woman allegedly molested who later recanted her testimony, Lucy Wells; and Samuel J. Leibowitz, the principal attorney for the defense, Nathan G. Rubin. These changes provided only the thinnest of veils, however, as presumably Wexley intended.

The dual themes of the play are presented in a weave of three strands of action. Foremost, of course, is the situation of the boys themselves when, ignorant, innocent, and frightened, they are brought to jail and herded behind bars. Wexley makes no effort to sentimentalize them. He is, however, somewhat tender in the treatment of the second of his plot lines, the moral regeneration of Lucy Wells, the prostitute who eventually pities the boys and decides to speak out in their behalf. It is the affection of a traveling salesman that causes the change. To be worthy of his love, she confesses, first to him, later to the court, that she had originally lied about the incident on the train in which the boys were said to have raped her. The third development is the conflict between the ASPCP and the NLD for control of the defense. This issue Wexley treats clumsily and at greater length than the plot as a whole requires. The black ASPCP lawyer, one Treadwell, is shown to lack daring when confronting whites, and the other spokesmen for the agency are Uncle Toms. By contrast the NLD spokesman, Joe Rokoff, is extremely vigorous of speech, and the lawyer Rubin is tough and expert. Wexley boggles at identifying the NLD as a Party mechanism, but comes close:

> RUBIN . . . . : You see, I've been hearing a lot of funny things, all sorts of stories. Well, first . . . that you fellers are . . . are . . . well, regular communists.

ROKOFF (*smiling*): Well . . . ?
　　 RUBIN: Well, are you?
　　ROKOFF: I'm not a member of the party, but there are a great
many things they advocate that I do agree with.
　　RUBIN: For instance?
　　ROKOFF: Well, first, I believe that the best legal defense is the best
political defense. . . . (III, i)

But Wexley's political rhetoric does not ruin the play. The malicious treatment of the boys and the shocking revelations of the courtroom provide extremely strong episodes, and the depiction of Lucy's
life as a prostitute, unusually frank for 1934, is another source of
strength. A stunning *coup de théâtre* ends the proceedings in an agitprop call to action. After Rubin and the state's attorney general make
their summations, the jury retires. A moment passes, and then from
the jury room comes the "sound of loud laughter, raucous and deri-
sive," dashing whatever hope is left that the boys will be saved.
Shocked, Rubin announces that he will go on with the case through
the courts until he wins, "if I have to do it in a wheel chair! . . .
these boys, *they shall not die!*" (III, ii). Unlike Sklar and Peters in
Stevedore, Wexley did not damage the logic of his play by actually
showing a victory for the blacks, but only insisted that it must take
place. Moreover, Rubin's cry was prophetic, for none of the boys was
executed.[22]

Previously no friend of the Guild, Mike Gold found much to praise
in the play and took it as a sign of the Board's social development.
"The working-class," he announced, "has entered that hitherto stuffy
museum of bourgeois decay which was the Theatre Guild." [23] But the
Guild was, of course, no more likely to plant itself firmly on the left
than the Theater Union was likely to turn conservative. Behrman, one
of the organization's best and most popular writers, claimed after the
production closed that he had found in Wexley's plays no conflict but
only "the presentation of an outrage," and that in itself he thought
was not enough to justify the production. He ventured the opinion,
already evident in the plots of his own plays, that playwrights should
remain neutral.[24] Yet *Parade,* the last Guild production of the
1934–35 season, offered additional evidence that revolutionary ideas
were penetrating neutral territory. Opening on May 20, it followed
Odets's *Waiting for Lefty* and MacLeish's *Panic* to Broadway very

shortly before the close of the last season before the Comintern issued the official proclamation of the Popular Front policy. Had plans not been altered, the revue would have included *Newsboy*, the best of the agitprop sketches of the Workers Laboratory Theater. But, after the first tryout performance, which took place in Boston, the piece was dropped.[25]

Intended originally as a Theater Union production, *Parade* might have been better served by a company more in tune with its social convictions than was the Guild. It is not easy to see what promise the Guild found in the material. Whatever the expectations, the result was a disappointingly brief run of 40 performances. The light touch that might have given a lift to the show was lacking. Brooks Atkinson's notice in the New York *Times* suggested that the Guild was too set in its ways for such a novelty: "After all these years it is hard for the Guild to cultivate the antic mood successfully. Although 'Parade' includes several first-rate sketches, it is not precisely joyous." [26] Apart from the pantomimist Jimmy Savo and the comedienne Eve Arden, the cast was not memorable.

Of the twenty-eight items shown in the revue in New York, most were unimaginative blackout skits. Among the subjects spoofed were the idea of the master race, in which under an American Hitler all citizens try to make themselves over as Indians; the college graduate seeking a job in a department store; a princess of imperial Russia capitalizing on her past by giving an illustrated lecture on her flight from the bolsheviks; and the image of the bomb-throwing Communist in league with Moscow, as depicted by right-wing newspapers. An amusing song, "Send for the Militia," written by Marc Blitzstein and sung by Eve Arden, depicted a clubwoman as not so liberal as she chose to think. Part of the lyric runs,

> Send for the Militia, the Army, the Navy
> Quick, bring out the Boy Scouts, and battalions of police,
> The country's on the brink of disaster,
> If there's one thing I insist on, its peace.

For contrast there were songs of love blighted by hard times. A sense of the nagging worry over what the future held was aired in lyrics by Sklar and Peters:

If only I were carefree and my heart were light
I'd go on dancing with you through the night,
But how can I surrender to love and romance,
To music and dance,
When tomorrow is the fear in my heart.

And

Life could be so beautiful,
Life could be so full and free;
There's everything in the world to make it so;
Life could be so beautiful,
Life could be so grand for all;
If just a few didn't own everything,
And most of us nothing at all.[27]

For all their banality, the love songs have a touching simplicity. Neither seems to have stopped the show.

Parade was the Guild's last foray into radicalism. Having lost about $100,000 on the production,[28] the company was not eager to try again. Wisely retreating to its customary liberalism, it then proceeded, in the second half of the decade, to produce its most triumphant plays by social dramatists of the middle ground.

BROADWAY: THE INDEPENDENT STAGE
1930 - 1935

In the aftermath of the stock market collapse of 1929, Broadway producers glumly watched their audience slip away. Writing the preface to his annual volume of "best plays," Burns Mantle, the reviewer of the *New York Daily News*, reported discouragingly on events of the season of 1929–30:

> While the percentage of the failures has been no greater than in former years, they have been quicker failures and less creditable to the profession. Box office receipts have been notably reduced, save in the case of the usual six or seven outstanding hits. Rentals have been reduced. More theatres have gone dark and remained dark than in any other season I can recall.[1]

In part, as Mantle pointed out, the trouble could be blamed on the Hollywood studios, for the new talking pictures were capturing audiences everywhere. Movies not only cost less to see than plays; they offered everything that live performances offered except color, and a few even had that of a sort. Paradoxically, it seemed at the end of the twenties that movie money might assist Broadway to new fortunes, for the Hollywood producers, now in need of intelligent dialogue, were backing plays in order to secure the picture rights.[2] But this proved a wan hope, and after a modest rise in the number of productions in 1929–30 over that of 1928–29, the count fell from 249 at the start of the Depression to 149 in 1933–34, rose to 178 in the next season, and then began a steady decline that continued through the decade.[3]

Nothing could be done to stop the gradual debilitation of the stage. The string of legitimate houses on 42nd Street that had held some of the most spectacular productions of the twenties went over to films early in the thirties. Other houses in the Broadway district (roughly, the area bordered on the east and west by 6th and 8th Avenues and on the north and south by 59th and 39th Streets), were torn down to make way for office buildings or were turned over to movie chains or to the radio networks, competitors ultimately fiercer than the Hollywood studios. Actors, insecure in their profession even in boom times, now were beginning to miss meals. Two charitable organizations came into being to help them: the Actors' Dinner Club, organized by the actress Selena Royle in 1931, and the Stage Relief Fund, organized by the playwright Rachel Crothers in 1932. But this was only temporary assistance. The writers of *Workers Theatre* scoffed at it and called for the radical measure of unemployment insurance.[4] The National Recovery Administration, established in the early days of the New Deal, set up a code for Broadway production, as for all other businesses and industries, under a committee headed by producer William A. Brady.[5] In consequence, the NRA's symbolic Blue Eagle was sported on posters and programs, but the benefits of the code to producers, if they existed at all, were inconspicuous.

In 1933 a few professional actors were put on relief rolls and through the good offices of Actors' Equity gave free performances in New York City. The Civil Works Administration employed actors on relief for free entertainments in 1934; in the spring of the following year, when the CWA was closed out, this work was assumed briefly by the Federal Emergency Relief Agency. Substantial aid to unemployed stage workers was not to come until later in 1935, however, when the Federal Theater Project undertook the great task of re-employing them across the nation by the thousands. Meanwhile the New York actors looked hopefully to Hollywood, where, so they believed, their adeptness with the spoken word would be rewarded. It was true that Hollywood was in grave need of actors who could talk as well as flash their eyes, but so many of them, along with vaudeville performers, singers, and dancers, went out that they were no better off in the West than they had been in the East.[6] The number of pictures produced each year was larger than the number of plays offered on Broadway, but it was never large enough to make use of all the talented stage workers who asked for employment.*

With the collapse of the economy making havoc in their own profession, American playwrights began by 1931 to consider the possibility of taking the Depression itself as a dramatic subject. As the previous chapters have shown, many did write of the problem of poverty. Yet among the major institutional theaters, only the Group offered a sizable body of work dealing with this problem in the first half of the Depression. Among the four productions of the late-starting Theater Union through the spring of 1935, only Maltz and Sklar's *Peace on Earth* and Maltz's *Black Pit* had the economic situation as a major theme, and among the Guild's productions, only *Parade* touched on unemployment and the problems created by it. For the most part, the plays of economic hardship were the work of new writers, the most important exceptions being the Siftons' *1931*—and John Howard Lawson's *Success Story.* Slower to respond to the new national distress were the most popular and successful of the writers who had come to the fore in the prosperous twenties. O'Neill, though a writer of consistently liberal sympathies, never provided a play on the major public issues of the thirties, but Maxwell Anderson, Philip Barry, S. N. Behrman, Sidney Howard, George S. Kaufman, Elmer Rice, and Robert E. Sherwood began to write on unemployment and other social ills before the decade's end, even as did the younger, radicalized writers whose first successes occurred after the crash.

Unlike the playwrights who supplied scripts for the noncommercial organizations, the older writers reflected rather than led general opinion. They exhibited alarm over unemployment, militarism, and totalitarianism, but not until after these problems had developed into

---

* Among the promising stage actors put under Hollywood contracts with, or soon after, the advent of sound, were Joan Blondell, James Cagney, Claudette Colbert, Bette Davis, Paul Muni, Edward G. Robinson, Sylvia Sydney, and Franchot Tone.

widespread concerns. Gradually, however, they added social comment to the substance of their plays, almost as though unwilling to be
thought unaware of recent events. They became public-spirited, less
interested in the problems of the individual, more worried about national distresses. The speed with which they adapted themselves to
the new environment differed with each man, but was not rapid with
any of them. Philip Barry, for example, an author known principally
for comedies of manners, allowed a few words on "hard times" to
creep into *The Animal Kingdom,* his successful comedy of 1931, but
showed no very keen interest in the contemporary social and political climate until the end of the decade, with *The Philadelphia Story*
(1939). George S. Kaufman preceded him with three musical
comedies of more or less political interest—*Of Thee I Sing* (1931),
Let 'Em Eat Cake (1933), and *I'd Rather Be Right* (1937)—one
comedy of manners with the market collapse as its background—
Dinner at Eight (1932)—and a stirring panoramic play on the life of
an immigrant—*The American Way* (1939)—but for the most part he
and his various collaborators offered wise-cracking satires on idiosyncratic personal behavior, as in the twenties. Behrman, Sherwood, and
Rice were the first of the older generation to dramatize the national
state of mind in the Depression, but did so with varying degrees of
conviction and intensity. Among them, none but Rice could be described in the first half of the decade as a progressive writer, according to any definition.

The gift that the playwrights of this generation made to the theater
lay in their ability to discuss all sides of serious issues in dialogue
that argued rather than exhorted. In their plays they reviewed the evidence of social decay without dogmatism and without an attempt to
suggest easy cures. Only Elmer Rice borrowed the agitprop call to
action, but in his plays it became an appeal for a liberal social program, not for class-consciousness. The crisp dialogue that in the
twenties exposed the personal difficulties within the home became a
medium for the treatment of public problems. It is noteworthy that
the older writers were seldom moved to seek new techniques of construction to match what for them was new subject matter. Rice put
aside antinaturalism after the success of *The Adding Machine* (1923),
returned to it in modified form in *The Subway* (1929), and did not
take it up again for another nine years, in *American Landscape.* The

most daring innovator among the old school of playwrights was Sidney Howard, who combined elements of constructivism and epic theater in *Yellow Jack* (1934). It was as though the writers believed that their realistic approach to new issues required a realistic presentation, not the radical techniques of extremists.

The preeminence of the older dramatists was challenged in the early thirties by a cadet corps of newcomers to Broadway whose attitude toward the turbulent Depression environment was by no means as detached as that of their elders. Coming to maturity after the excitement over the new discoveries in psychology had cooled down, they casually assimilated the learning that writers of the twenties had used as subject matter and went on to explore new ideas. For such writers as John Wexley and Lillian Hellman, plot motivation based only on the individual's difficulty of establishing personal relationships seemed shallow and, therefore, inadequate. They wished to analyze the social forces that created killers, perjurers, slanderers, and other antisocial beings. They and the many other playwrights who explored the same vein did not displace the older writers, but by winning sympathy among audiences for their fierce disquisitions on social injustice, they succeeded in sharpening the tone of Broadway drama, so that by the second half of the decade most of the new plays on social themes offered by independent producers were not much less astringent than those presented by the institutional theaters. Had the leftist critics cared to do so, they might have argued that the Hegelian dialectic was observable in the theater from 1930 to 1935 as the older writers, faced by the success of the disputatious new talents, adapted their themes to create a new drama of reasoned protest.

Despite the entry of favorite playwrights into the field, that part of the Broadway audience disposed to attend social plays was comparatively small. This was evident in the financial difficulties of the Group Theater throughout its ten years of work as well as in the histories of the independent producers. Recognizing the reluctance of their customers to face anxieties in the theater at a time when life itself offered seemingly endless economic worries, most of the Broadway managers were hesitant to produce social drama. To check through the summaries by Burns Mantle of plays offered on Broadway from the fall of 1929 to the summer of 1935 is to learn that, excluding Group and Guild productions, fewer than thirty productions out of hundreds treated war, poverty, and the rise of antidemocratic philosophy of the Right and Left as major issues. In 1934 and 1935 the magazine *Stage*, which undertook to exploit the fashionable side of theater-going, offered a series of caricatures in color of first-night audiences at plays presented by Max Gordon, Sam H. Harris, and other well-known producers, and although the faces changed in each picture, the groups were similar in the elegance of their clothing.

The Broadway audience, as these caricatures indicate, did not seem to be greatly worried, if worried at all, about the state of the nation or the world. Though cut-rate, last-minute tickets were available thanks to the enterprising Leblang ticket agency, the standard price of theater seats ranged upward to $3.30 for plays and to $4.40 for musicals, and patrons who could afford such prices for entertainment obviously had no trouble paying for the necessities. Barrett H. Clark in his preface to Albert Bein's *Little Ol' Boy*, a play that had been held by several producers before being staged in 1933, commented with weariness and resignation on the difficulty that authors of worthy plays experienced in securing productions and put the blame on the audience:

> The fact is that any theater system that cannot find a place for such plays is neither wholly alive nor wholly representative; our professional theater in New York (except by a fluke, or by the persistence of such companies as the Guild, The Group Theater and the Theater Union) is by and large an institution serving the well-to-do; it reflects for the most part the attitude of the city man and woman, particularly of the leisure and wealthy class. It is foolish to cry out against it; it is what it is. In failing to offer the public seats at low prices, to bring its wares into some sort of relationship with what *all* classes are doing and thinking, it has become a somewhat remote institution, patronized by the wealthy and idle. So be it.[7]

No matter what economic class an author or producer intended to reach, the casual mention of the scarcity of money was, of course, a part of most plays of the Depression. Though Rachel Crothers, the leading woman playwright of the twenties and early thirties, could exclude any such references from her successful comedies of manners *As Husbands Go* (1931) and *When Ladies Meet* (1932), she was something of an exception. In romantic comedies about persons less high on the social scale than the characters of Crothers and Philip

Barry, financial problems were an important fact of life; they plagued the young couples, for example, in Gertrude Tonkonogy's well-received *Three-Cornered Moon* (1933) and Samuel Ornitz and Vera Caspary's unsuccessful *Geraniums at My Window* (1934). But such problems, seen as only temporary and ultimately defeatable by hard work and cleverness, were no less troublesome in such pre-Depression comedies as, to name only two, Marc Connelly and George S. Kaufman's *To the Ladies* (1922) and Maxwell Anderson's *Saturday's Children* (1927), for household money or money to marry on is always a problem for young lovers, off stage and on, in good times and bad.

Many musicals of the early thirties, though expensive and clearly designed for the well-heeled, referred either in casual comment or in lavish "production numbers" to the new look of American life. George S. Kaufman and Morrie Ryskind could find no more pressing campaign issue for John P. Wintergreen in *Of Thee I Sing* than love—*eros*, not *caritas* or *philadelphia*—in 1931, but two years later the threat of revolution at home and the rise of totalitarianism abroad had received enough publicity to figure in the plot of *Let 'Em Eat Cake*, the sequel. Yet in *Of Thee I Sing* a reflection of one extremely grave manifestation of the Depression appeared in "Who Cares?," one of the best of the many good songs written for the show by George and Ira Gershwin: "Who cares what banks fail in Yonkers, Long as you've got a kiss that conquers." From other musicals and revues came songs that were to become the standard numbers of the Depression. For *Face the Music* (1931), a revue with sketches by Moss Hart, Irving Berlin wrote "Let's Have Another Cup o' Coffee," whose cheerful lyric advised that good times were on the way, and therefore another cup of coffee and another piece of pie were definitely in order. George White's *Music Hall Varieties* (1932) included the memorable comic lament by Herman Hupfeld, "Let's Turn out the Lights and Go to Bed," the last word being changed to "sleep" when the song was performed on radio. From *New Americana* (1932), a revue, came the song by E. Y. Harburg and Jay Gorney whose title became a kind of byword as unemployment figures rose month by month: "Brother, Can You Spare a Dime?" [8] These popular songs helped to create the tone of the period, but were only incidental to the shows in which they were sung. It was not until the latter half of the decade that musicals firmly rooted in the issues and problems of the period were brought to the stage, the exception being the Theater Guild's *Parade*. Meanwhile Broadway continued to enjoy all-black revues, "smart" white revues such as the *Little Shows* with small, therefore inexpensive, casts, and weakly plotted extravaganzas with superb scores by Jerome Kern, Cole Porter, and the team of Richard Rodgers and Lorenz Hart.

As in other periods, virtually all varieties of human aspiration and distress were brought to the stage. Topics engaging the minds of the most talented social writers, whether independent or affiliated with institutional theaters, were the conditions endured by prison inmates, antagonism between the races, the rise of fascism, and the individual's problem of maintaining dignity and self-esteem without harming others. The last proved to be the overriding dramatic topic of the decade. The independent playwrights did not champion the U.S.S.R. and were less inclined to write about labor problems than were the playwrights who wrote in the hope of being produced by the Group, the Theater Union, or the companies of the New Theater League, but they also touched occasionally on conditions of work.

It was to become evident through the thirties that the public, perhaps led on by producers and writers, found in the outlaw a fascinating quality running almost to glamour. Plots demonstrating that prison conditions tended to perpetuate the criminal's antisocial impulses became familiar to both stage and film audiences. In Hollywood it was the Warner Brothers studio in particular that developed this theme, employing as felons, murderers, and racketeers, sometimes as much sinned against as sinning, such charismatic actors as Edward G. Robinson, Paul Muni, James Cagney, George Raft, Humphrey Bogart, and, later, John Garfield. The gangster, whether a product of his environment or a psychological misfit, had a profound appeal to a generation kept from the good life by a lack of cold cash. In such pictures as *Little Caesar* (1930), starring Robinson, and *I Am a Fugitive from a Chain Gang* (1932), starring Muni, as well as in less memorable releases, the outlaw had a kind of allure made up of bravery and gallantry in equal parts. When Cagney was the picture's star, the outlaw also possessed an attractive wise-cracking brashness. The stage had shown a few such characters in the pre-Depression years in such plays as Philip Dunning and George Abbott's *Broadway* (1926) and Maurine Watkins's *Chicago* (1926), but was slow to follow Hollywood's lead in accepting the gangster as an antihero. Usually he was a tragic victim of society.

Typical in reflecting the view that under existing conditions the convict had no chance for rehabilitation was Martin Flavin's *The Criminal Code* (1929). The last impressive prison play of the twenties, it ran on for a few weeks of the new decade. The title has a double meaning: it is the state's legal code under which young Robert Graham is sentenced to a ten-year term for manslaughter, and it is also the convict's code inhibiting Graham from informing on a prisoner who murders another inmate. The State's Attorney who had imprisoned Graham on a rather frail charge befriends him after becoming warden of the prison in which he is serving his sentence—but too late, because Graham has already accepted the convict's code. When Brady sends the captain of the prison guard to release Graham from solitary confinement, Graham stabs the captain with a knife supplied him by the murderer he had refused to betray.

Early in 1930 occurred the opening of a tougher, more successful play of prison life, John Wexley's *The Last Mile*. The title refers to the walk the convicted murderer must take from his cell in the death house to the execution chamber. A tense melodrama, *The Last Mile* is an account of the attempt made by the inmates of the death house to force the prison authorities to release them on the threat of death to two guards, the prison's Principal Keeper, and the Catholic chaplain. Keyed up over the execution of a murderer that has just taken place, "Killer" Mears manages to get a stranglehold on one of the guards and to confiscate his gun and keys. With his fellow prisoners helping him to overcome a second guard, the keeper, and the chaplain, he is ultimately in a position to demand that the warden release all the death-row inhabitants. Having between forty and fifty rounds of ammunition, they put up a good fight. But when the bullets are gone, Mears knows that he has lost and walks out on death row to be shot. The play is as unsentimental as its theme, a plea for the abolition of capital punishment, will allow. The cynical Mears (played by Spencer Tracy) is an unrepentant killer, as, for that matter, are most of the others, and in his last-minute walk into machine-gun fire there is no gallantry, but only the courage to admit defeat and to die as quickly as possible. A tough part convincingly presenting a merciless, thoroughly undeceived man, it was the prototype for later roles

played by Cagney and Raft. Wexley found opportunities throughout
the action for questions on the cause of crime and the just punishment for it; repeatedly, the question is raised of whether law-abiding
society is not all too well avenged for murder by the severe mental
torture that prisoners must endure as they await execution. The racial
question is also raised when a black prisoner, afraid to die but reject-
ing the consolation of religion, speaks with bitter irony on the possibility of an afterlife:

> Don't you all know theah is two Heavens, one foah the white man
> and one foah the black man? Why—if ah could sneak mah way into
> that theah white man's Heaven by accident or somethin'—why youah
> keepahs up theah would say to me—What for you want in this
> Heaven anyhow? Who told you to come heah? Don't you all know
> this ain't youah place? Git ovah in your own niggah Heaven long by
> that theah toilet, you black bastard, before you is sent to niggah hell.
> (II)

Though a failure, Bein's *Little Ol' Boy*, produced by Henry Hammond, contains scenes that offer a more moving plea for the humane
treatment of prisoners than are to be found in Wexley's play. An author always on the fringes of the liberal-to-left institutional theater of
the thirties, Bein attracted attention with three plays that demonstrated his identification with workers and the neglected members of
society. His social sympathy was no doubt prompted by the fact that
he, like the young characters of *Little Ol' Boy*, had served time in a
reformatory. A friend of the members of the Group Theater, Bein was
at times a guest in their summer camps. He hoped that the company
would produce his *Heavenly Express* in its third season. Another of
his plays, *Let Freedom Ring*, an adaptation of Grace Lumpkin's novel
To Make My Bread, was held for a while by the Theater Guild.[9] Both
plays were produced in the second half of the decade, but by other
managements. In *Little Ol' Boy* the reformatory boys are inade-
quately fed and made to suffer harsh physical punishment for infrac-
tions of the school's regulations. For such a daring act as writing a
petition to the state's governor, a boy named Bob Locket is beaten
while straddling iron bars. He and another inmate escape, but are
ambushed by farm boys while hiding in a barn. Locket is killed by a
shot through the stomach, and his friend is captured. The innocent,

frail Locket is a sympathetic character, and his death is the occasion for sadness and the pointing of a moral.

The prison plays were attempts to demonstrate the unhappy truth that society through its law-enforcement agencies and correctional institutions often exacts greater punishment from wrongdoers than is sanctioned by the law. At the same time, the authors wrote with the purpose of exhibiting certain prisoners, if not all, as members of the oppressed masses who had never had a chance to lead respectable, happy lives because of the rigid structure of the society into which they were born.

Similar in theme were the plays depicting the railroading of innocent persons to prison on charges fabricated by those who will benefit from their imprisonment. The best of such plays was, unquestionably, Wexley's *They Shall Not Die*, in which the young blacks are sent to jail and kept there by perfervid white supremacists. Among other plays of the early thirties on this theme, inferior to Wexley's but nevertheless interesting, were two melodramas produced off Broadway at the Provincetown by commercial managers. I. J. Golden's *Precedent* (1931) is a thinly veiled retelling of the case of Tom Mooney, the San Francisco labor martyr convicted on scanty evidence in 1917 of participating in a bomb plot and still in prison at the time of the production. (He was released in 1939.) Maltz and Sklar's *Merry-Go-Round* (1932), the first of their plays to be staged in New York, provided a sensational view of corruption in municipal politics. Ed Martin, a bellhop, witnesses while on duty the fatal shooting of a gangster and is also struck by a bullet, though not fatally. Because the mayor of the city is involved, the district attorney quashes the indictment against the killer, though Ed has identified him. Under mounting public pressure for an investigation, those in power decide to put the blame on Ed himself. After being beaten by the police, he signs a confession. Ultimately, it is decided by the chiefs of the ruling party that he must be hanged in his cell and his death reported as suicide. Later, after the deed is done, the mayor is re-elected, and the politicos meet to congratulate one another. The occasion is darkened for them, however, by the fact that they cannot forget Martin. Thus, in this work, as in their Theater Union plays, the authors drew sympathy for a helpless victim of vested interests. With a run of 48 performances in an out-of-the-way theater, the Provincetown, the play did not do badly.

It was a matter of more than passing interest that the producers experienced difficulty in securing a theater and ran into trouble with municipal authorities.[10]

The treatment of the life of black Americans in Broadway drama of the early thirties took for granted a permanently segregated society. As Vincent Johnson, the black killer of *The Last Mile*, sees the plight of his race, segregation extends even to heaven and hell. Given the opinions, spoken and tacit, revealed by the playwrights, Wexley was right to assign such a view to such a man. Though Broadway managers staged a few plays written to promote sympathy for blacks, they were aware that few of their customers came from the black world. Accordingly, their plays did not reflect the truth about black life so much as the notions about black life held by whites. It was Hollywood, however, not Broadway, that took the slow-moving, superstitious, razor-toting, or obsequious black out of the all-black production, as for example in *Hallelujah* (1929), directed by King Vidor, and placed him in a predominantly white society, as in *Hallelujah, I'm a Bum* (1933), a picture starring Al Jolson as a leader of the unemployed squatting in Central Park with a black sidekick who lovingly runs his finger along his razor's edge when trouble brews. It was also Hollywood that created vehicles for Mae West in which robust black maids served as priestesses to the blond, camp sex goddess. On the other hand, Broadway showed itself to be as insensitive as Hollywood in the early thirties with frequent all-black musical offerings studded with stereotyped characters who confirmed for whites the notion that Harlem was a community of irresponsibles. Many of these productions bore titles that were fated to appear distasteful to later generations: *Change Your Luck* (1930), *Brown Buddies* (1930), *Blackberries of 1932, Shuffle Along of 1932,* and *Hummin' Sam* (1933), "a sepia musical comedy in two gallops," for sufficient example. The occasional use of black performers in the otherwise all-white musical, though providing equal billing for the blacks, could scarcely be considered a major step toward integration, since the material given them emphasized their separateness from the whites. Thus Ethel Waters in *As Thousands Cheer* (1933), a revue with songs by Irving Berlin, had a moving number titled "Supper Time" in which a black

Southern woman ponders the problem of telling her children that their father is the victim of a lynching, but also an ironic number titled "Harlem on My Mind" in which a successful black American singer living in France (obviously suggested by the personality of Josephine Baker, the sensational star of the *Folies Bergères*) declares that she would like to give it all up for a return to her native soil and native ways.[11]

The patronizing attitude of white songwriters toward blacks did not escape the attention of the far Left. One writer for *Workers Theatre* raised the issue in harsh terms:

> If the negro worker feels a little discouraged with the injustice of the capitalist system that imposes its slave conditions upon him even worse than upon the white workers, with discrimination against him on the job if he has one, in the restaurant, hotel, apartment house, movie, theatre and any other bourgeois controlled institution he turns to, that grows with the general worsening of the economic status of the working class, and should he look somewhere for consolation and turn to Broadway "to take in a show" he will find even there a reminder. Suppose he succeeds in getting a seat somewhere in the balcony of "George White's Scandals," providing he can pay the price. Here's the explanation he'll get in the song "That's Why Darkies Were Born":
>
> > Brothers! Sisters! What must be, must be!
> > Though the balance is wrong,
> > Still your faith must be strong,
> > Accept your destiny,
> > Brothers, listen to me:
> > Someone had to pick the cotton,
> > Someone had to plant the corn,
> > Someone had to slave and be able to sing,
> > That's why darkies were born.
>
> The bourgeoisie is very kindhearted. It readily supplies the answer to its weary slaves. It spends millions of dollars to supply the ideological explanation to the exploited and enslaved. "Accept your destiny," is the advice they give to the exploited and oppressed negro. Someone has to do the dirty work so that the rich may enjoy the product of his labor.[12]

The critic, Harry Elion, neglected to say that the writers of the song, Lew Brown and Ray Henderson, were white, and that the performer who sang it, Everett Marshall, was also white.

Despite its great popularity and Pulitzer Prize, Marc Connelly's *The Green Pastures* (1930) was no more likely than the musicals to leave the white playgoer with the sense that the black was his equal in dignity. The play, based on the volume of stories by Roark Bradford titled *Ol' Man Adam an' His Chillun*, is a dramatic version of the Old Testament with the characters played by blacks in a comic black Southern accent. Among its features are a cigar-smoking God, a Gabriel ready and willing to blow his horn, and various plump mammy-angels and sharply dressed, high-stepping black Babylonians. (A stage direction reads, "The costumes are what would be worn at a Negro masquerade to represent the debauchees of Babylon" [II, v]). Never deliberately abrading black sensibilities, Connelly nevertheless failed to break with the notion of the adult black as a creature not to be compared to the adult white—if not downright childish, still not fully mature and dependable. In New York the production held on for 640 performances, and road companies covered the nation.

Less successful works by other well-known authors were in effect equally patronizing in the treatment of the morality of impoverished blacks, despite the authors' good intentions. Paul Green's *Roll Sweet Chariot* (1934), a quickly closing failure, was yet another investigation of black life in the back-country South, in the manner of his own *In Abraham's Bosom* and Em Jo Basshe's *Earth*. Subtitled "A Symphonic Play of the Negro People," it called for a black choir to supply musical accompaniment. Basshe directed the production, with the aid of Stanley Pratt. Du Bose Heyward's *Brass Ankle* (1931), a realistic, well-made play, offered the tragedy of a young Southern woman who discovers after the birth of her second child that she has black blood. Unlike her firstborn, a blond, fair-skinned child, the second has a Negroid appearance. Having nobody to turn to and in any event wishing to save the blond child from ostracism, the woman tricks her husband into believing that she conceived the new baby by a recently deceased black servant. Predictably, the husband is outraged and kills both mother and infant. Though the opening scenes carry the suggestion that Heyward intended to write a hard-hitting tragedy on the evil of segregation, the play ultimately suffers a blunting of its message in the melodramatic ending that implies that segregation is inevitable.

From 1930 to mid-1935 the independent producers were for the most part content to leave unionization and unemployment as dramatic subjects to the new institutional theaters. No unaffiliated author could compete with Odets in expressing for the theatrical audience the feeling of the workingman for and about his work. Among established independent playwrights, only Elmer Rice wrote boldly about labor's attempts to organize, but this was only one of a long list of social topics for him, and it was almost lost in the heavily plotted plays in which he aired it. Playgoers who enjoyed drama of the fight between bosses and workers faced no lack of satisfying plays, but aside from the Group's productions they had to visit off-Broadway houses to see them.

A quick closing was the fate of the most militant labor-management play of the early thirties produced independently: John Wexley's *Steel,* offered in 1931 for only 14 performances. A work imbued with the dogma of Third Period communism, the play is an apology for "reds" and "Bolsheviks" as well as an effort to promote unionization. Wexley develops both issues while presenting the brief career of Joe Raldney, a young worker in Ironton, U.S.A., whose father had also been a steelworker. Harsh events in his father's life convince Joe that a strong radical union is necessary for the protection of the workers. The melodramatic action, including a severe beating for Joe at the hands of a policeman during a strike, tends to confuse personal and political issues. For Broadway, the play was ahead of its time ideologically, but so obviously slanted that, as with the Siftons' *1931—,* it would have been a poor risk in any year.

One sensationally successful play of the decade touching on the quality of the worker's life achieved, for a variety of reasons, not merely a long run but at the time of its closing the longest run in Broadway history. Jack Kirkland's adaptation of Erskine Caldwell's novel of destitute Georgia sharecroppers, *Tobacco Road,* opened on December 4, 1933, and remained for 3182 performances, closing on May 31, 1941. By that date it had surpassed by some 850 performances the previous record play, Anne Nichols's *Abie's Irish Rose.*[13] This success was made all the more remarkable by the fact that the reviews published by the New York papers and the major weekly magazines were equivocal at best, the critics finding it primarily a

coarse, sexually exploitative view of backwoods life with sparse redeeming social content. Typical was the reaction of Brooks Atkinson
in the New York *Times,* who thought the play "one of the grossest episodes ever put on the stage," despite its "spasmodic moments of merciless power," at the same time that he offered high praise to Henry
Hull for his performance as Jeeter Lester, the protagonist.[14] Caldwell
was later to say that, although he and Kirkland were prepared for unfavorable reviews, they did not expect quite such a general rejection.
But Kirkland, rumored to be the actual producer despite nominal
credit given to Anthony Brown, was doggedly determined to put the
play over, and did so with the help of Leblang's cut-rate ticket
agency. After six months of poor attendance, it flowered into a hit.[15]

One factor in the success of the play was the much discussed frank-
ness of language and sexual display. Though never obscene, the language is consistently raw and the action more than usually bold in
the presentation of sexual fumblings. As the years of the run rolled
on, the coarseness of the writing was enhanced in performance, so
that in time *Tobacco Road* was reputed to be downright smutty and
attracted an audience seeking a voyeuristic thrill. Finding it possible
to play the uneducated Georgia illiterates for laughs, actors did so,
and thus added to the vulgarity. In this way the play's life was prolonged, but not without violence to the script as prepared by Kirkland. The play is hardly subtle, but the characters and their way of
life, however crude and permissive, amount to more than contemporary publicity led prospective ticket-buyers to believe. The ultimate
intention of both authors was to show the grinding effect of hopeless
poverty and ignorance on both body and soul.

The spokesman for this theme is Jeeter Lester, the head of his family, but now wizened, old beyond his years, and scarcely capable of
any feeling other than hunger. It is in the one passionate outburst allowed him that he expresses the plight of the sharecropper, a speech
triggered by his hearing that the takeover by the banks of the property on which he and his family have always lived, and that the family formerly owned, is inevitable:

> Praise God, it ain't the way things just happen. It's the rich folks in
> Augusta that's doing it. They don't work none, but they get all the
> money us farmers make. One time I borrowed me three hundred dol-
> lars from a loan company there to grow a crop and when I gave them

interest and payments and every other durn thing they could think of
I didn't make but seven dollars the whole year working every day. By
God, that ain't right, I tell you. God won't stand for such cheating
much longer. He ain't so liking of the rich people as they think He is.
God, He likes the poor. (II)

The authors' method of awakening the audience to the problems
faced by tenant farmers was on the whole more oblique than in this
one heated speech. As the play progresses through cruel revelations
of the life of total poverty, their plea for some kind of assistance for
these neglected natives of the backroads develops urgency. It is evident at curtain-rise in the appearance of Jeeter's dilapidated shack
and quickens as the audience watches the responses, such as they are,
of Jeeter to the actions of his family. His frequent, insensitive references to the hairlip of his daughter Ellie Mae finally bring the girl to
tears, only to his astonishment. He is incapable of wrath or jealousy
on hearing from his wife Ada that he may not be the father of Pearl,
the great beauty of the family. Neither he nor anyone else feels pity
or concern when Grandma Lester, who crawls more often than she
walks, goes off into the bushes to die. The warmest character is Ada,
Jeeter's wife, who reveals her maternal love for Pearl by shielding the
girl from her unwanted husband Lov Bensey and dying as the indi-
rect result of her helping action. So dulled are the feelings of most of
the characters by deprivation that the only stimulus, apart from hunger, to which they can respond strongly is sex. Poverty has taken
away virtually everything else. The play includes many sexual scenes,
but as written they are relevant to the overall depiction of the Lester
family's life. However coarse may be the gropings of Dude, Jeeter's
son, with Sister Bessie Rice, the itinerant preacher, it is understood
that in this region of marginal existence sex offers the only gratifica-
tion.

Leftist critics were drawn to the play, though not unanimous in
praising it. Writing in the *Daily Worker,* Harold Edgar observed that
"the most encouraging thing about 'Tobacco Road' is that it was produced at all on Broadway," but complained that the authors were too
detached from their subject to treat it with complete honesty. But in
the *New Masses,* to which Caldwell himself was a sometime contributor, William Gardner found Jeeter just short of heroic. "Admirable
and loveable human values," Gardner wrote, "are enkindled in his en-

raged defiance of the machinations of a predatory system whose agents have finally overtaken even him. The fact that the defiance is hopeless does not reduce the scale of the portrait." [16] This is heavy praise to heap on a rather lightweight play, but there is no disputing that the authors wished to expose a "system" grievously out of order.

PLAYWRIGHTS

In the early Depression years Elmer Rice, Sidney Howard, Robert E. Sherwood, and Lillian Hellman were the most highly esteemed of the writers committed to protest drama who were not associated with institutional theaters. Since most of their themes were also taken up by many other dramatists, it was clearly not originality of vision that gave them their authority. Rather, it was—setting aside individual characteristics for the moment—unusual psychological insight supported by a respectable craftsmanship. Theirs was a place shared only with Anderson, Behrman, Kaufman, Odets, and O'Neill, among *all* American dramatists of the time: that level of achievement at which an author's every work, whether good or bad, makes news.

Elmer Rice

One of Broadway's most prolific playwrights was the veteran Rice. Only the comedy writer George S. Kaufman offered more works than he between 1930 and 1935. A comparison of the two on the basis of output would be meaningless, however, for Kaufman's plays were not wholly his own but were collaborations with other writers, whereas Rice, after trying collaboration twice in the twenties, worked on his own thereafter. He also served as his own director and producer. None of his plays of the thirties could compare with the best of his earlier work, but because of the range of his interests, the well-defined characters that he often, if not always, drew, and his unfailingly passionate attacks against social injustice, he commanded a hearing. Rice, who styled himself a "leftwing liberal," [17] was also a respected participant in public life as a board-member of the American Civil Liberties Union.

The antimechanistic, libertarian themes that Rice dramatized in such plays of the twenties as *The Adding Machine, The Subway,* and

Street Scene, continued to resound in his work of the thirties. As conditions worsened during the Depression, he became increasingly outspoken in his objections to the drift of American society, at first afraid that not even so determined a reformer as Franklin D. Roosevelt could achieve enough social legislation to save it from collapse.[18] In the crash Rice himself suffered losses, but fortunately his finances were cushioned by the royalties from *Street Scene;* his ability to write workable scripts, while not unfailing, kept him in comfortable circumstances as the thirties wore on. Late in life, reminiscing about the theater of the thirties, he remarked, "You couldn't live in the Depression and not be touched by it. The emphasis in play-writing became more on theme than on character; on social, economic, political themes." [19] In his first two plays of the decade, *The Left Bank* (1931) and *Counsellor-at-Law* (1931), the emphasis is as much on the personal concerns of the characters as on social problems. *We, the People* (1933), *Judgment Day* (1934), and *Between Two Worlds* (1934) have a few well-conceived characters in their large casts, but are more noteworthy for the messages of protest that Rice sounded in them. *Black Sheep,* an inane comedy written in the twenties and pulled from the bottom of the trunk, may be dismissed altogether. The unproduced *Not for Children,* which Rice wrote in the early thirties, may also be forgotten; a dramatic disquisition on dramaturgical methods and the quirks of producers, audiences, and critics, it is amusing in part, but talky and labored.

In neither *The Left Bank* nor *Counsellor-at-Law* did Rice deal directly with the economic and social worries that the crash had brought down on the nation. *The Left Bank* is a romantic intrigue in which American expatriates of slender means reveal their preference for discomfort in Paris to stultification at home. Rice had no axe to grind at the moment; in the play a stockbroker, the kind of figure usually represented as a social menace in the plays of leftist authors, is more tolerable than the bohemian writer whom he visits. With *Counsellor-at-Law* Rice created a social play, but not a discourse on the causes and effects of the Depression. It could have been produced with equal success in the twenties; many of the issues are those that Rice had treated in *Street Scene.* George Simon, the attorney to whom the title alludes, is not, however, Sam Kaplan grown older, but an active, purposeful man who through hard work reaches a high place in his profession. (The role was the last played on the stage by Paul Muni before his departure for Hollywood.) Simon is a liberal who conscientiously defends underdogs, yet also takes the divorce cases of foolish society women. His interest in money-making does not relate to the issues of the Depression. It stems from his memory of past struggles and the generous nature that makes him an easy touch.

The questions raised in *Counsellor-at-Law* have to do principally with the contrast that exists between individuals whose environment allows for emotional and intellectual growth and others who are less advantaged. Simon, a Jew, has a Christian wife—a woman who left her first husband for him. Rice makes it clear that Cora Simon is not happy in her second marriage and in fact has a romantic attachment with Roy Darwin, a man with a background similar to her own. As a practical man of affairs, Simon cannot share their aristocratic disdain for the process of earning the money that, through his generosity, they so casually accept and enjoy. Because of his somewhat questionable tactics in the defense of clients obviously guilty of the crimes with which they are charged, Simon greatly angers another attorney, Francis Clark Baird, whose background is also quite different from his own. Baird would like to have him disbarred. Ultimately, however, both Baird and Cora fail to harm Simon, though in their different ways each does violence to his emotions. Though Simon becomes estranged from Cora, his secretary is standing by to give affection, and Baird ceases to be a problem when Simon discovers that he is a bigamist. Simon may be a not altogether honest attorney, and a blackmailer to boot, but he is more decent than his Anglo-Saxon antagonists.

The "fair play" policy that Rice practiced in *Street Scene* by refusing to allow one ethnic or religious group to appear more virtuous than another remained in force in *Counsellor-at-Law*. To make the moral balance as exact as possible, Rice contrasts Simon with a young Jewish Communist whose personality shows a masochistic strain. Though in a good deal of trouble, he resents Simon's attempt to assist him. "You and I," he says, "have nothing in common. I'm on one side of the class war and you're on the other." In reply to this, Simon shouts, "Don't come around me with any of your goddam half-baked Communistic bull and expect me to fall for it." The young man then cries, "Go ahead. Hit me. Beat me up. I'm used to it. I like it. I'd like to be beaten up by Comrade Simon of the working-class, who sits rolling in wealth and luxury, while millions of his brothers starve" (II, iii). In a curiously uncomprehending review in *Workers Theatre*, Alfred Saxe derided the portrait of Simon as "the same sort of charity giver as Rosenwald, Rockefeller, Morgan, etc., who donate millions to the schools and churches, the millions they have taken from the sweat of the people in 'Street Scene.' " He added,

> The one scene which stands out for its honesty is the bit where the Communist who after being beaten up and thrown into jail, faces the lawyer in his office. When this crook attempts to moralize to a boy who has just been beaten up for having an excellent set of morals, the young boy loses his patience and tells him just what sort of a parasite he really is.[20]

Rice was not to create another such complex, multifaceted character as Simon for years—not, in fact, until *Dream Girl* in 1945. In certain plays, such as *Between Two Worlds*, the paucity of rounded characters is simply the result of a failure of wit, but in others, such as *We, the People* and *Judgment Day*, it is the unfortunate result of the panoramic style, in which so many characters take part in the action that none is explored in depth.

For *We, the People*, Rice wrote over forty speaking parts and added a large number of characters designated "passers-by," creating a cast so huge that only in a deflated economy could it be practical. The play is primarily the chronicle of a middle-class family that is forced to abandon its conservatism and because of economic and social pressures to move toward the non-Communist Left. "Their story," Rice later wrote, "is told against a kaleidoscopic background that shows the industrialist, the banker, the university president, the United States Senator, the high-court judge tacitly united in an alliance for the preservation of the status quo."[21] By main force Rice thrust into the plot so many instances of social injustice that it seemed to include, as one critic observed, "nearly every item of indictment which has occurred to Mr. Rice in the course of a life devoted largely to dissent of one sort or another."[22] Among the playwright's targets are not merely the acutely obvious issues of racial and religious discrimination, but also the curbing of academic freedom, the insensitivity of corporate officers, the brutality of undisciplined policemen, the deportation of aliens on unjustifiable charges, governmental neglect of veterans, and rampant militarism, as well as all the anxieties caused by poverty, including the sexual frustration of a young couple who cannot afford to marry. Writing elliptically, Rice turned from incident to incident in the lives of his characters without obvious transitions, in the manner of a film director cutting his work deliberately to tantalize the audience. In the tenth scene, for example, we see young Allen Davis conscientiously working to liberalize the editorial policy of his college newspaper, and in the following scene we see him living in his parents' home, but only obliquely do we learn that the boy has left the college for good. The staccato rhythm established by this quick cutting is reminiscent of agitprop.

The influence of agitprop is also revealed in the closing scene of the play, which is a mass meeting. The meeting has been called to gather suport for Davis, who is now in prison under a death sentence as the result of a police frame-up. As the speakers take their turns, it is not the boy alone for whom they appeal, but *all* Americans. In a ringing speech, one C. Carter Sloane, a *Mayflower* descendant, concludes the play in a flood of oratory presaging the rhetoric of the New Deal:

> In the name of humanity, ladies and gentleman, in the name of common-sense, what is society for, if not to provide for the safety and well-being of the men and women who compose it? "To promote the general welfare and secure the blessings of liberty"—you'll find it there, set forth in the preamble to the Constitution. Does that mean a denial of the right of assemblage and of free speech? Does that mean millions without employment or the means to provide themselves with food and shelter? We are the people, ladies and gentlemen, we —you and I and every one of us. It is our house: this America. Let us cleanse it and put it in order and make it a decent place for a decent people to live in! (scene xx)

As in *We, the People*, Rice upheld the rights of the needy and unprotected in *Judgment Day*, a courtroom melodrama inspired by the Reichstag fire trials in Germany. Moving the scene to an unnamed country in southeastern Europe, he touched the play with irony by making Germany the national enemy. Otherwise, however, the piece has little to recommend it, apart from the author's good will. A hopeful note is sounded in the end when one member of the five-man panel of judges hearing the case whips out a pistol and kills the dictator, Grigori Vesnic. But the play is curiously lifeless, and the lengthiness of the cast provides an unfortunate deterrent to detailed characterization.

While *Judgment Day* was still running, Rice opened *Between Two Worlds*, a shipboard comedy of manners with a liberal, humanitarian theme. The principal figures, with one major exception, are of the moneyed class, and for the most part sympathetic. Once again the cast is large. Only two characters, a Soviet film director named N. N. Kovolev and a rich American girl named Margaret Bowen, are explored in depth, and the result is a work of diffuse feelings and flimsy episodes. The familiar figures of shipboard plays are on hand: soul-searchers, wastrels, the *nouveaux riches,* amiable drunks, and the ship's patient personnel. Kovolev, returning to Russia after an unsatisfactory stay in Hollywood, is obviously an image of Sergei Eisenstein, whose employment at Paramount Pictures in 1930 had been notoriously disastrous. Rice had visited Russia after the dual success of *The Left Bank* and *Counsellor-at-Law,* and though not sympathetic toward totalitarianism had been an unbiased, even-tempered tourist. Kovolev, as one might expect from a man of Rice's disposition, is a mixture of warm and cool qualities: blunt, even cruel when hearing what he takes to be expressions of the capitalist-imperialist mentality, but affable in personal relationships. As the result of a brief fling with him, Margaret Bowen decides to break her engagement to an American of her own class and to marry a well-to-do but far from complacent advertising executive. Kovolev also touches two other lives significantly. He shocks an expatriate Russian princess by recalling for her the inhumanity of her family's treatment of peasants, and momentarily brightens the life of the much put-upon, intelligent black maid of a spoiled film star. By characterizing Kovolev with an even hand, Rice ended with a play that neither the Right nor the Left could describe as propaganda. As though to focus the attention of the audience on this important role, he assigned it to a star, Joseph Schildkraut, and gave all other roles in the play to less distinguished actors.

Having produced two relatively unsucccessful plays within two weeks, Rice uttered in public a virtriolic judgment against the reviewers who had dismissed his work with, he believed, unprincipled casualness, and announced that he had turned his back on the commercial stage. He drew up plans for the formation of a producing organization to be called Theater Alliance, but this came to nothing.[23] A more consequential step for him was the decision, made in the spring of 1935, to accept a major post with the Federal Theater Project, then forming under the Works Progress Administration, with the overall guidance of Hallie Flanagan of Vassar College.

Sidney Howard

With his psychological dramas centering on family tensions, Sidney Howard had established himself by the end of the twenties as a commentator on marital fidelity, the double-standard, and—less firmly—international politics. The celebrated *They Knew What They Wanted* and *The Silver Cord* created his reputation, and *Lucky Sam McCarver* (1927) and *Ned McCobb's Daughter* (1927) sustained it. At the close of 1929 he was represented on Broadway by *Half Gods*, a comedy of the life of rich New Yorkers; unhappily for him and his producer, Arthur Hopkins, the Wall Street débâcle had made such a play something of an irrelevancy, and after only 17 performances it closed. But Howard was able to extend his career successfully into the thirties with four hit plays before the midpoint of the decade. Most of the work was entertaining, if lacking in originality. *The Late Christopher Bean* (1932) and *Dodsworth* (1934) were adaptations, the former of a comedy by the French playwright Réné Fauchois and the latter of the popular novel of the same name by Sinclair Lewis. In *Christopher Bean*, whose plot Howard transferred from France to New England, the pettiness of the provincial mind is revealed in a conflict between a family and their servant when the family learns that the woman possesses several canvasses produced by a posthumously acclaimed painter, to whom, it turns out, she was secretly married. It is a sentimental work, but was right for the time as an appeal for the protection of the meek and poor against the depredations of people of means. The play *Dodsworth*, like the novel, is a study of the conflicts produced in the minds of middle-aged Americans suddenly exposed to the attractions of Europe. With *Alien Corn* (1933), Howard provided his own plot: the struggle of a young woman pianist for a free intellectual and professional life against the temptation to hold onto the security of a post in a dull Midwestern college. It offered an interesting vehicle for Katharine Cornell, then a leading theatrical attraction both in New York and on the road.

Howard's freshest play of the period was *Yellow Jack* (1934), a work different from the others both in structure and the material of its plot. This play also was not the intellectual property of Howard alone, but was based on a chapter of Paul de Kruif's *Microbe Hunters*, a popular book on the fight waged by scientists against disease, and accordingly de Kruif was credited as Howard's collaborator. It had been the hope of the Group Theater to produce the play, but Howard, dismayed by the Group's string of failures in the spring and fall of 1932, ultimately gave it to Guthrie McClintic, Katharine Cornell's husband, to produce and direct.[24]

The material taken by Howard from *Microbe Hunters* centers in the effort initiated by Walter Reed to find the cause of yellow fever and a vaccine for it. Principally it is the history of the work done in Cuba by Reed's team at the turn of the century. The action is a continuous unfolding of events in a manner that departs from naturalism to a degree unexpected of Howard. The antinaturalistic devices consist of a two-level constructivist set, the flashback, and the employment, reminiscent of Brecht's epic theater practice, of a male quartet of singers to provide transitions between scenes. Although Howard was able to wrench a suspenseful plot out of the book, his play is primarily a loosely connected sequence of scenes adding up to a satisfying combination of melodrama and documentary. To the degree that it is a documentary play, it looks forward to the "living newspapers" that were soon to be shown by the Federal Theater: plays in which leading issues of the day, including, as in *Yellow Jack,* public health, were given life on the stage through the dramatic rendering of pertinent documents.

As developed by Howard, the fight to locate the cause of the disease becomes a fight between dedicated but misunderstood scientists on the one hand, and, on the other, obstructionist conservatives who are fearful of experiment. (The rigid commandant of the Marine Corps Hospital in Cuba, Reed's principal opponent, is given the name of Colonel Tory.) Providing a counterpoint to the deliberations of the scientists is the barracks-room chatter of four Marine Corps privates. They are representative of the entire population, the rank and file who make up America. By emphasizing the role of these enlisted men, Howard placed the play squarely within the current liberal Popular Front view of the ordinary citizen as a man who could be counted on to withstand the international rightist trend. The idea of the melting pot, a concept traditionally honored by American dramatists, was also in Howard's mind, for the four privates are of varied backgrounds: "o'hara is a husky young Irishman of spirit and intelligence, his speech still stiff with the brogue of Galway. brinkerhof is an Ohio Valley boy, gentle, serious, and soft-spoken. busch is a city chap of Jewish extraction and intensity. McClelland, a Southerner, is the sturdy and commonplace member of the group." Comic relief is provided by O'Hara (played by James Stewart), who rattles endless blarney about his ambition to become a physician, and by Busch (played by Sam Levene), who is revolution-minded and intends to spend the money given him for participating in the experiments to buy a partnership in a radical press. In later plays Howard was to continue to demonstrate his sympathy with liberal causes by proclaiming faith in the instinctive honesty of the American people acting in unison, but never again with such success.

Robert E. Sherwood

Though claiming to resent the comparison with Bernard Shaw that critics made on reviewing his first Broadway play, *The Road to Rome* (1927),[25] Robert E. Sherwood was the most Shavian of American playwrights of his time. Principally, if not exclusively, he dealt with persons of high rank, placing them in situations combining romance and the exploitation of power, and ending on a note of exaltation. Exceptions to this pattern among Sherwood's early plays are *The Love Nest* (1927), an adaptation of a Ring Lardner story, and *So This Is New York* (1930), both low in tone for Sherwood. But *The Road to Rome, The Queen's Husband* (1928), and *Reunion in Vienna* (1931) are serious comedies in the Shavian vein, and *Waterloo Bridge* (1930), though its ending is equivocal, recalls Shaw's humanitarianism in its appeal for sympathy for a prostitute. More serious still is *Acropolis* (1933), an indifferent work written with the Theater Guild in mind, but rejected by the Guild's board and produced in London by Paul Hyde Bonner. Set in Periclean Athens, it is an attack on the kind of nationalism whose spokesmen promote war in the questionable interest of glory and unity. Sherwood hits at such superpatriots by showing certain bellicose Athenians in full cry against the construction of the Parthenon, their anger stemming from the belief that the money might be better spent in waging glorious war against Sparta. The plot reflected the playwright's pessimistic view that yet another international conflict was soon to break out in Europe and that it too would serve no good end.

Sherwood had not had a play on Broadway since the Theater Guild production of *Reunion in Vienna* when Gilbert Miller, Leslie Howard, and Arthur Hopkins presented *The Petrified Forest* in 1935, with Howard starring in the central male role. In the interim, however, he had written, in addition to *Acropolis*, a successful film titled *Roman Scandals* (1933), in collaboration with George S. Kaufman. This picture, starring Eddie Cantor, offered a glimpse of the new America in its opening scenes, in which the comedian, a postman, bicycles through the "Hooverville" (a collection of the shanty homes of the dispossessed) on the edge of a town called New Rome. With *The Petrified Forest* Sherwood again, and more profoundly, examined the Depression environment. Though not a proletarian work in any sense, the play is made up of characters who in the main are several rungs below the highly placed figures of Sherwood's previous successes. The setting, dull to look at in contrast to the decors that the author had preferred in the past, offered the audience an unbeautiful view of a combination lunchroom and gas station. Such a setting was a fitting locale for a dramatic study of the new Depression-bred transiency, when young intellectuals were continually touring the country to get a sense of its temper, and when the hitchhiker was taking his place in the national folklore.[26] Sherwood gave the locale of his lunchroom a symbolic value: the place is at "a lonely crossroads in the eastern Arizona desert," [27] near the Petrified Forest, and as the play develops it is evident that the desert stands for the totality of mid-Depression America, a parched, sterile country with scarcely a promise of cooling, regenerative rain.

Into this unpromising locale Sherwood put a large cast of characters contrasting the political attitudes of Left and Right, the intellectual and the physical life, youth and age, rich and poor, and black and white. Representing the rightist, one-hundred-per-cent American attitude is Jason Maple, the owner of the gas station and a veteran of the First World War. He is a devout American Legionnaire. Opposed to him politically is Boze Hertzlinger, an ex-footballer who tends the station. Both men are inane and futile. Standing for native American individualism is Gramp, Jason's father, who remembers the days when Billy the Kid was the scourge of the West. In the person of Gabby Maple, Jason's daughter, Sherwood offers a faint—very faint —hope for the future. But it is not an American future. The girl is of mixed parentage, her mother being a French war bride, and it is to France, where her mother now lives and which she has never seen, that the girl turns in her daydreams of a better life.

Wandering into the play from the desert is the character who carries the major burden of Sherwood's theme: Alan Squier, a penniless, failed novelist who carries with him Carl Gustav Jung's *Modern Man in Search of a Soul*. Squier has no soul, having lost it in a loveless marriage. But in Gabby he begins to find it again. Ultimately he dies in order to leave her his life insurance, so that she can fulfill her fantasy of traveling to France. Contrasted to him is Duke Mantee, a hold-up man and murderer for whom the police are on the look-out. Sherwood's characterization of Mantee is especially strong; the killer represents the bankruptcy of the free-enterprise system—free enterprise exhausting itself in the compulsive acquisition of money that can never be used. Both Squier, the wanderer in the day-bright desert, and Mantee, the night-time fugitive, are described as "condemned." In production the contrast was effectively stressed through the casting of the blond, pale Leslie Howard as the writer and the swarthy Humphrey Bogart as the criminal. In the end Mantee shoots Squier at Squier's request and in turn is shot by the police after terrorizing the Maples, their employees, and a rich couple from Ohio. Only in death, Sherwood appears to be saying, can modern man fulfill himself, for the conditions of his life, at least in America, encourage no expectation of solace, to say nothing of joy. It was not for another three years, when another war was imminent, that Sherwood demanded positive action and in so doing implied that humanity was, after all, worth preserving, even at the cost of global war.

Lillian Hellman

After Clifford Odets, whom she preceded on Broadway by three months, Lillian Hellman was the most highly acclaimed new playwright of the thirties. Her first produced play, *The Children's Hour*

(1934), achieved a run of 691 performances, a figure bettered by only six other productions of the entire decade. She based the play on actual events in the lives of two women of nineteenth-century Scotland that were brought to her attention by Dashiell Hammett.[28] It was produced by Herman Shumlin, as were all the subsequent plays written by Hellman through 1944. The great success of *The Children's Hour* stemmed chiefly from the playwright's ability to weave tough-minded expressions of liberal social attitudes into a suspenseful plot, but also, though to what degree one cannot estimate, to the mention in the play of a taboo subject: lesbianism. In previous years the New York City police had dealt stubbornly and harshly with plays on homosexuality, no matter how treated by the authors. In 1927 Edouard Bourdet's sensitive *The Captive*, on lesbianism, was ordered closed by the courts after a police raid, and the producers of Mae West's scandalous *The Drag*, on male homosexuality, decided to close the play out of town rather than bring it into New York, where a raid and arrests were inevitable.[29] But *The Children's Hour* was allowed to run, presumably because sexual deviation could not be considered its principal issue. It is noteworthy that the screen version, *These Three*, written by Hellman and released by Samuel Goldwyn in 1936, substituted a heterosexual love triangle for the lesbian situation in the original with no loss of integrity.[30]

Central to the play is a less controversial topic: the plight of the open-minded individual when assaulted by a stubborn and powerful conservative force. Hellman herself described the theme as "good and evil." [31] The major figures, Karen Wright and Martha Dobie, are two young college graduates who through years of sacrifice set up a boarding school for girls, only to see it destroyed by a neurotic student who tells her grandmother-guardian that they are involved in a lesbian affair. Though the evidence produced by the child is flimsy, it convinces the old woman. Through her power in the area, she persuades the parents of the other children to remove them from the school. She does not investigate the charge. The trouble with this woman is twofold: she is rich and she is old, a member of a generation used to having its own way, of creating its own truths. The ending of the play reveals the extent of her power. One victim of the lie admits that although nothing overtly erotic has taken place, she in fact feels a romantic yearning for her friend. Her only recourse is suicide. The other young woman loses her fiancé as the result of the scandal. The grandmother, Mrs. Tilford, is appropriately sorry for her actions, but her remorse is quite obviously futile. She will suffer bitterly in her remaining years—thus the playwright takes revenge.

Hellman's study of the tyranny of the aged and wealthy over the young and poor is difficult to witness at moments. Bodily as well as mental suffering is presented on stage in the scene in which Mary Tilford, the neurotic pupil, physically abuses two of the other children. In refusing to hide the suffering, whether mental or physical, from the audience, the author set a pattern that she was to use repeatedly in later plays. Tenderness is meager in *The Children's Hour*. In tone, if not in characterization, it was a world apart from the most celebrated Broadway works of the decade, including those of Clifford Odets, which by comparison could be described as feasts of love. Yet Hellman's implied hope that the young could have their chance without interference from obstructive oldsters was also a major theme of Odets. With this theme both writers reflected the mood of the period, for the government itself under the New Deal leadership had come out strongly on the side of the young, as evidenced in the legislation establishing the Civilian Conservation Corps and the National Youth Administration, which created jobs for unemployed youth. Hellman's inability to encourage the young without chastizing the old revealed an unbecomingly vindictive spirit, but undoubtedly contributed to the appeal of her writing.

In the remaining six years of the decade, Hellman was to offer only two additional plays, but her contribution, despite the overtaut wellmadeness of her plots, resulted in the development of a major Broadway reputation. The undeceived attitude projected in her first play included a no-nonsense detachment from the ways of the past and a confident glance ahead to the time when the sacrifices of the Depression would result in a better-balanced political and social climate. In the second half of the decade this attitude was to seep into the plays of her elders, and the ways of the past were to come under question not only in the work of radical authors, but in that of writers of the middle ground.

THE POPULAR FRONT IN THE
THEATER OF THE FAR LEFT
1935-1942

IN CONCEPTION AND EXECUTION the Popular Front as declared by the Comintern representatives at their meeting in Moscow in August 1935 represented a sharp, all-pervading change in position, leaving high and dry the proponents of proletarian drama and dance as they were known in the first years of the Depression—as indeed the new policy left nothing unaffected in which international communism had taken interest. The very phrase "Popular Front" could be read as a repudiation of the old revolutionary idea of class against class. The new dispensation called for an alliance of liberal-to-left elements in all social and economic classes in a stand against fascism. The alliance was intended to curb the aggressiveness of Germany, and though by performing this function it furthered one of the aims of Soviet foreign policy, at the same time it was attractive to liberals in America and other democratic nations who were outraged and frightened by the growth of rightist strength in Europe. Clearly enough, a confluence of liberal and leftist sentiments had occurred. But organized communism had nevertheless to work at the job of maintaining the appeal of the Popular Front. One necessary step was to guard against the use of the very term "communism" in all but the most central party-sponsored or party-controlled enterprises. For a magazine or a theater troupe to identify itself as Communist would have meant the probable loss to it of those middle-class Democrats or those Socialists who might otherwise have spent money on a copy of the magazine or a ticket for a performance.

Thus the effort of Michael Gold, Michael Blankfort, Joseph Freeman, and other literary men of the Communist party to promote a proletarian literature was invalidated. The official anthology, *Proletarian Literature in the United States,* was obsolescent, and the work of the first American Writers' Congress, which had publicized and celebrated the ties of writers to the working class and had advocated the publication of the anthology, was undermined. When the second Congress met two years later, in 1937, it was necessary for the speakers to express the new viewpoint. Newton Arvin, for example, offered a paper on "The Democratic Tradition in American Letters" which in title and substance called attention to the principle on which the nation was founded, thus easing the qualms of any persons present who might have feared that the Congress was under the thumbs of subscribers to an antidemocratic philosophy. With the same purpose in mind, Freeman provided an essay, not for delivery at the Congress, but to serve as the preface for a published volume of the Congress's papers, in which, glancing back at the past, he declared that a kind of Popular Front had existed for some twenty years: "Significantly, throughout the war and the Twenties, those American writers who called themselves socialist or communist, revolutionary or proletarian, were on fraternal terms with the writers who voiced the protest of the middle class against monopoly capital." In the words of these two writers, Arvin and Freeman, lay the suggestion that the Popular Front was in fact nothing more or less than the new revelation of an old truth. On the other hand, Granville Hicks, while forthrightly pronouncing his hope for the ultimate world-wide victory of communism, described the new policy *as* a new policy:

> We know that it is imperative to build the united front. We know that this can only be done by arousing not only the workers but also large sections of the middle class to an understanding of what they have to lose under fascism, to a realization of the immediacy of the danger, to a recognition of the only possible means of winning a victory. The united front is being built in America, not formally as in France or Spain, but nonetheless solidly. Nothing in this world can be so important as the expediting and strengthening of that work.[1]

The bourgeoisie, it now appeared, might have something of value to contribute after all. Though, as in the instance of MacLeish, non-party writers had been approached in the recent past only tentatively and with obvious skepticism for works in behalf of Communist-supported causes, they were welcome now if only they stood firmly in the liberal camp. MacLeish himself was one of the signers of the "call" to the second Congress and presided at the opening session.[2] Ernest Hemingway, having served as a correspondent at the fighting front in Spain and created the narrative for Joris Ivens's film *The Spanish Earth*, was lionized by the party; at the Congress he offered a paper on "The Writer and the War." [3] The credentials of both men as "progressives," to use the new terminology, were obviously impeccable.

The word "progressive," so frequently appearing in the party press, could be applied to any person or institution taking a position in the vanguard of liberalism but stopping short of advocating revolutionary action. What the American Communist party seemed willing to settle for after the Comintern meeting was the democratic welfare state. It placed candidates on the ballot for high office, including the presidency, but was content with Roosevelt, even urging his third nomination until the signing of the Soviet-German pact. The phrase "Communism Is Twentieth-Century Americanism," invented as an election campaign slogan in 1936 and used throughout the Popular Front era, was a two-edged device. It was, first, part of an effort to spread the belief that Communists were a new breed of pioneers, leading the oppressed to a land of peace and plenty in the tolerant and purposeful mood of the frontier. Second, it represented a subtle effort to persuade Communists themselves to play down their rebelliousness and integrate with the American scene. The middle class, finding Communists to be, not grimy, bearded bomb-throwers, but tidy, good-intentioned citizens like themselves, might develop a sympathetic interest in the party, or, if not going so far, take part in the activities of the liberal-seeming party fronts.

To further both these aims in other ways, the party publications altered their character sufficiently to seem at times quite ordinarily human. Especially was this apparent in the *Daily Worker* and the magazine section of the new *Sunday Worker*. Prizes were offered for authentic old American recipes; the fifieth anniversary of the unveiling of the Statue of Liberty was welcomed with the heading of "Happy Birthday!"; a photograph of Gypsy Rose Lee appeared with the caption "A young lady who proves that the capitalist system is in the last stages of a very beautiful decadence . . ."; and a human interest article about Shirley Temple informed readers that the dimpled darling was a kind of tiny slave of the film industry.[4] By the late spring of 1936, the *Worker* and the theatrical troupes close to the party had been so subjected to the influence of Broadway and the commercial theater by Popular Front tacticians that it was only natural for the paper to add a new Broadway gossip column, "Uptown and Down," to the Sunday edition. Over the months, however, this column became more political than theatrical. On December 1, 1937, in the daily edition, occurred the first appearance of a gossip column that *remained* a gossip column: "Left on Broadway," written by one Manngreen in the breathy, confidential style of Walter Winchell. The Communists, it would seem, were out to prove that they could match the tabloid publishers for banality and the homely wise-guy touch, as in these items:

> Whassamatta with you proof-readers in the Adv. Dep't—is the "Harold D. Rome" listed as the composer of music and lyrics in the *Sing Out the News* at the bottom of the page, the same person as Harold J. Rome in the *Pins and Needles* ad? . . . Morton Minsky, youngest of the burlesque-loving Minsky Brothers, has opened an anti-fascist motion picture theater on Houston Street. The name of the corporation owning the theater is the "Non-Aryan Pictures Corporation"!!! [5]

Some events deserved special mention, such as the marriage in 1938 of the popular character Will Geer to Herta Ware, the granddaughter of Mother Bloor. The paper rose splendidly to the occasion by publicizing the event with the enthusiasm of the commercial press in covering society weddings. Geer had taken part in the New Theater movement in New York and Hollywood, and Ella Reeve Bloor was known far and wide as den mother to the entirety of American communism. The wedding took place in a West Side union hall, which the couple entered to the strains of the "Internationale," their guests and attendants having contributed twenty-five cents each to party causes as an admission charge. Afterward, a reception was held in the new offices of the New Theater League.[6]

In this bonhomous atmosphere an occasional note of exasperation could still be heard now and then on the Left, as in Donald Ogden

Stewart's satiric piece in the leftist magazine *TAC*, "Parable of a Playwright," in which he let fly at a comfortably circumstanced liberal playwright, S. Howard Berman, who, neutral to the end, fails to stand up against a brown-shirted stranger who steals his child's candy, assaults his wife, and sets fire to his house.[7] But the prevailing mood of the period was that described by Malcolm Cowley in 1939, as he reflected on the peaceful air of cameraderie of the *third* Writers' Congress. He looked back in bemusement on the old days of "1932 or 1933 . . . those comic opera days when everybody in New York seemed to be talking about the revolution that would come tomorrow," remembering in particular a moment when one writer, though trying to identify with the people, had felt so little concern for humanity that he let a door slam shut in the face of a pregnant woman.[8] Presumably, progressives of the late thirties did not do such things. The attitude was one of accommodation, at times even of playfulness. "We're Against Fascism & Stuff," ran a personal advertisement in *TAC* in 1938, the advertisers identifying themselves only as "Josef and Gloria." An advertisement of the following year was playfully mysterious: "You are invited to visit a *friendly* Broadway Restaurant & Bar where you will find delicious food—excellent cocktails—low prices and congenial atmosphere. The Broadway spot for *progressive* people."[9]

But it was not only that the Left was consciously seeking a new image, though this was true enough. It was also true that the Left, like the nation as a whole, had been invaded by a new spirit of hopefulness midway in the decade. The setting up of the Popular Front coincided with a major economic upswing attributable to the successful functioning of New Deal policies. The indexes of industrial activity published by the Federal Reserve Board and the *New York Times* showed a decided gain in late 1935, and this continued through 1936.[10] Despite the still distressingly high unemployment figures— eight million in 1936—"there was," as one historian of the New Deal was to put it, "a smell of prosperity in the air."[11] In 1937, a sharp recession occurred, plunging the stock market downward again and causing a new wave of lay-offs, but cruelly acute as this was, it did not destroy the confidence created by the Administration. Not again did the nation sink to the mood of despair and the general listlessness that together haunted Hoover's last years in office. There was still talk of the Depression, and it would continue until the war boom began in the forties, but somehow the country was changed. It was possible, despite thunder echoing from abroad, to plan for the future, to think of taking trips, buying new clothes, seeing the lastest Astaire-Rogers extravaganza. At the decade's close this new confidence was symbolized on a magnificent scale by the great New York World's Fair, which opened on April 30, 1939.

The emergence of the New Theater League in the late spring of 1935 as a many-eyed presence in the field of radical theater was an indication of the evolution of Communist policy from narrow Third-Period dogmatism to an inclusiveness in which tolerance for the once-hated middle class was possible. To please and enlighten a more diverse public than the founders of the Workers Laboratory Theater and Prolet-Buehne had thought of reaching in 1929, the League, as we have seen, had supported such plays as *Waiting for Lefty* and *Panic,* and in its brief involvement with MacLeish's play had nodded, at least, at the non-Communist literary establishment. WLT and Prolet-Buehne had not been able to boast of any well-known personages among their authors, and, because they disapproved of the singling out of individuals for attention, would not have cared for such distinction. Nor, until the success of *Newsboy,* did they have a play of more than minimal intellectual appeal. Theirs was not an intellectual following. Of regularly published authors, only Michael Gold had come forward to champion them at the start, and, welcome as praise from Gold may have been, it could scarcely be described as the backing of the intellectual community.

But the proletarian theater gradually began to push out of its hard shell, as evidenced by the growth of the leftist stage outside New York, the inception of annual contests of performances, the transformation of the League of Workers Theaters to the New Theater League and the substitution for *New* for *Workers* in the title of the magazine, the publication of plays of some length and substance, and the opening of the New Theater School. When the Popular Front policy was officially announced, members of and sympathizers with the American Communist party had available a versatile instrument for forwarding that policy through drama. The Executive Committee of the League conducted its many projects, including the frequently held contests for new plays and the choosing of troupes to introduce them in New Theater Nights, under the guidance of its National Secretary—Mark Marvin as the second half of the decade began; after 1937, Ben Irwin—with the aid of a small, ill-paid staff. League activities were shakily financed, judging from the frequently printed appeals of officials to the affiliates for payment of dues and royalties, but continued more or less steadily through the thirties, surviving even the German-Soviet nonaggression pact of 1939. Though the League found *New Theatre* too costly to publish after the spring of 1937, it managed to get out some kind of magazine through most of the period, including, from the fall of 1936 to the spring of 1938, a scholarly journal called *Theatre Workshop*. The League was, in short, a success. What had begun in the murky days of the Wall Street crash as an amateur enterprise turned into an efficient institution confidently run by industrious professionals.

Though the League was the longest-lived mechanism for the development of the left-wing stage, other noncommercial liberal-to-left organizations also helped to enliven Broadway and Off-Broadway in the late thirties. Apart from those which mounted ambitious productions of "full-length" plays—specifically, the Theater Union, the Actors Repertory Company, the Mercury Theater, the Federal Theater, and the Group—there were two organizations noteworthy for their success with special, nondramatic entertainments: TAC and Labor Stage. TAC—in full, Theater Arts Committee—represented an effort to draw Broadway into leftist causes. Initially, its sole concern was one of the principal public causes of the decade: aid to the Loyalist forces in the Spanish Civil War. (Hollywood had a similarly inspired Motion Picture Artists Committee for Peace and Democracy, usually abbreviated in print to an unpronounceable MPAC.) In New York among those citizens with extra spending money, TAC catered to a taste for satirical cabaret theater of the sort long cherished in Middle Europe. Labor Stage, the theatrical arm of the International Ladies' Garment Workers Union, made its presence felt on Broadway with its hit revue *Pins and Needles*—a hit of such magnitude, in fact, that the company never offered the public another show. Meanwhile modern dancers continued to spread leftist social opinion without benefit of language, and independent film-makers did their part to serve the radical movement.

It might have seemed only natural, given the renewed vigor of the nation in 1935 and 1936, that the beginning of the Popular Front era would be the start of a new period of experimentation in leftist theater. But this was not to be, for the policy of socialist realism, originating in Russia late in 1932 and vigorously pressed on Russian men of letters at the All-Union Congress of Soviet Writers in 1934, forbade it. This artistic principle, which as an official policy still controls the arts in Russia, required the presentation of candid "real life" situations showing a revolutionary society in the process of development. "A Socialist realist," declared the Russian esthetician-bureaucrat A. V. Lunacharsky in 1933, "understands reality as evolution, going on by means of a continuous struggle of contradictions." [12] At the Congress of 1934 socialist realism was described as a concept that

> demands of the artist the truthful historically concrete representation of reality in its evolutionary development. However, the truthfulness and historical concreteness of the artistic representation of reality must be linked with the task of ideological transformation and education of workers in the spirit of socialism.[13]

This rather woolly description did not at first mean that designers were required to create only illusionistic settings, though gradually such settings did become the norm and the candid depiction of things-as-they-are as offered by, for example, the venerable Moscow Art Theater was expected to assist in the task of educating the new revolutionary society. It had a more direct appeal and was certainly less cerebral, hence less difficult to grasp, than the methods of the constructivists, to which the creators of agitprop drama owed so much. In a painting or on a stage, a machine was to look like a machine, not a grouping of cubes and discs, and thus could be impressed on all who saw it its machineliness: its function, its expensiveness, its potential for increasing production. Dramatic characters had to be given names, not abstract designations, and as much scenery was to be used as the producer could afford, thus showing the here-and-now of the situation. The socialist-realists' love of truth may not have extended at all times to the realm of ideas, but they had strong feelings concerning persons and places. What went for Russia went, of course, in the American leftist theater. As originally conceived and staged, agitprop was no longer quite respectable.

Reporting in the *New Masses* after the New Theater League's regional conferences in Chicago and New York in the fall of 1935, Mark Marvin let readers know what to expect of the *new* new theater:

> Such a theatre must present a drama that reflects the immediate personal and collective problems of both the past and present; . . . such a theatre naturally fights along with the masses for an extension of democratic rights, for the right to organize trade-unions, against war, against fascism . . . in brief, for a better, a richer life.

The kind of play offered by this theater, Marvin explained, could not be too sectarian, must not use the language of the political platform. It was to concern itself, not with strikes alone, but with "love, ambition, fear and hope." The "conversion drama," in which an individual or a group is led from inertia to rebellion, had been, in Marvin's word, "over-abused." Moreover, it was of little appeal to some elements of the population that the League now wished to include in the audience, which would be made up of *all* groups opposed to war and fascism. "To conceive of going forward without organizing such basic support irrespective of party, race, and creed would be impossible." To readers of *New Theatre* Marvin reported that the conferees had "pledged themselves to root out the vestiges of sectarianism from our ranks. Too often have our theatres been cut off from the main currents of popular life in their communities." Writing in the spring of 1936, before the League's biennial National Conference, Marvin said:

> The new theatres have now to be divided into two major categories, roughly based on definite social needs: People's Theatres and Labor Theatres. The People's Theatres will answer the need in all cities for community centers supplying social drama and recreation to workers, intellectuals and middle class people. These theatres . . . will become the voice of the most progressive elements in every community.

It was his hope that municipal and state governments would underwrite such theaters and that the American Federation of Labor would back "new and more powerful" labor troupes.[14]

Attempts to explain the change in the technique of the leftist dramatists were made repeatedly from the season of 1935–36 on through the decade. Michael Blankfort in an essay of 1937 titled "The Construction of the Social One-Act Play" offered a collective *mea culpa* for all early agitational playwrights. Their work, he declared, had developed in its peculiar form for the simple reason that they were not yet practiced enough to create drama that did not have to rely on sloganeering and calls to action to make its point: "Social playwrights, new ones as well as old, have increased their command over their craft. They do not have to be crude and oversimple to say what they want to say." And again:

> There is a great past as well as a great future to the conversion play. Society has not slowed down in the last decade. Men are still moving. But hereafter where a playwright *chooses* to deal with conversion material, he will not be awkward and sometimes beyond credulity, and he will deal not with slogans but with human values no less dynamic.[15]

Despite these strictures and imperatives, the new position was not based on the notion that *all* the accomplishments of agitprop were to be wiped out immediately. *Waiting for Lefty* remained the jewel of the League's repertory, and still in favor was the agitprop variant known as the mass chant, which had been developed with stunning expertise by the Prolet-Buehne in such pieces as *Scottsboro!* and *Tempo, Tempo!* Mass chants continued to be added to the repertory from time to time; in the fall of 1936 the League released a new one called *Boycott Hearst,* for example, and as late as 1938 it reprinted another, George Sklar and Paul Peter's *Lynchtown,* which had originally appeared in *New Masses.*[16] Moreover, a much admired play of 1936 promoted by the League, Irwin Shaw's *Bury the Dead,* showed in all aspects, including the plot, a debt to German expressionism, a theatrical style to which socialist realism was antithetic. Yet apart from these works and a few musical pieces, the plays disseminated by the League in the late thirties were preponderantly naturalistic. Though the Young Leader might still enter to organize timorous labor, he now had a name and even a family and a home, and no longer did he take center stage and call for the singing of the "Internationale"—for the reason that the middle class would not have liked it.

The issues attractive to League playwrights in the late thirties remained substantially the same as in the earliest days of proletarian drama after the Crash. There were, however, some signs of change in subject matter. Appeals to vote Communist or to support the Soviet

Union had disappeared before the Comintern meeting of 1935, though praise of "Reds" had not. Now such praise also disappeared. Plays about the position of blacks in American life had in the early thirties been confined, in the main, to the Scottsboro outrage and the plight of Angelo Herndon, the young Atlanta militant, but after 1935 embraced a wider variety of topics. War, threatened or actual, and especially the Spanish Civil War, was the subject of many of the plays. Nazism, not only as a threat to peace but in all its grotesque aspects, was also much on the minds of writers. Passing but sternly critical mention of the House Un-American Activities Committee and its chairman, Martin J. Dies, was made in League plays and other publications as soon as the Committee began to hold hearings in 1938. In this new congressional committee the League saw fascism festering on home grounds.

But the topic most frequently and comprehensively treated by leftist dramatists was labor's right to organize. With the wave of strikes that occurred after the passage of the National Labor Relations Act of 1935 (the so-called "Wagner Act") compelling collective bargaining, vigorous plays on labor unrest entered the League's repertory month after month. Hints that Communists were better equipped to take care of all controversial matters than adherents to any other ideology were blanketed over by language of the Popular Front, in which the term "antifascism" became a favorite euphemism for "procommunism." With the abandonment, long overdue, of the Trade Union Unity League in March 1935, the party initiated an effort to penetrate the American Federation of Labor. Two years later, however, when it became apparent that the Congress of Industrial Organizations offered greater opportunities for exploitation, the party shifted its attention from the AFL to the new organization, and with substantial results. Many, if not most, of the radical plays of the late thirties were written in support of and produced in cooperation with the CIO unions and their locals that had come under party control. Not surprisingly, the party-allied theatrical press and the dramatists themselves maintained a diplomatic silence on one major controversial topic of the era: the spurious Moscow trials of 1936–38 by means of which Stalin was enabled to put his rivals to death.

With the July 1935 issue, designated a "Negro Number," the editors of *New Theatre* proclaimed their interest in black drama and theater. George Sklar began an editorial with the announcement, "It's time we had a Negro Theatre in America." As Sklar knew, black troupes did exist and offered regular performances; among them were seven troupes in the New Theater League, one of which, the Negro People's Theater, was honored with the printing of a photograph from one of its productions on the magazine's cover. For a decade in Cleveland, Ohio, the black Kamaru Theater, its Swahili name meaning "the place of feasting and enjoyment," had drawn audiences of both blacks and whites; its acting company, the Gilpin Players, whose members had named it after the black actor Charles Gilpin, O'Neill's Emperor Jones, had been in existence even longer, but was not affiliated with the League. To the same number of the magazine, Langston Hughes contributed a biting essay titled "Trouble with the Angels," on the abortive walkout in Washington of the actors playing angels in *The Green Pastures* in protest over the theater owner's refusal to sell tickets to blacks. ("Monday in Washington," Hughes wrote. "The opening of that famous white play of Negro life in Heaven. Original New York cast. Songs as only darkies can sing them. Uncle Tom come back as God.") In a final burst of enthusiasm capping the issue, the League announced two contests for black plays held in conjunction with another front group, the National Committee for the Defense of Political Prisoners; one contest was for a play on Angelo Herndon, and the other for a play on the general topic of black life. Herndon himself was to be a judge. There was no mistaking the good faith of the League in its effort to draw blacks into agitational theater on a basis of equality, and this despite the observation of the magazine's film editor, Robert Stebbins: "Granted the Negro's innate sense of rhythm and musical genius . . ." [17]

Yet the League's efforts to seed a crop of stage-worthy black plays ended in disappointment. A one-act play by Odets, *Remember*, on the difficulties of a black family on relief, was performed by the Negro People's Theater on October 19, 1935, under Odets's direction, but dropped completely from sight thereafter, having been neither published nor copyrighted. In the February 1936 issue of *New Theatre*, Herbert Kline, the magazine's editor, announced the results of the recent contests. The Herndon contest elicited only one stageable play, Hughes's *Angelo Herndon Jones*, but this was not wholly successful, having "no spine, no essential line of conflict and development." Though Hughes was given the prize, his play was not published. Similarly, only one play submitted in the second contest was judged ready for production, Bernard Schoenfeld's *Trouble with the Angels*, a dramatization of Hughes's essay with the difference that the angels carry out their strike threat; this play the League added to its repertory.[18]

Kline, attempting to analyze the failure of the contests, was astounded by the entrants' lack of understanding of the subject:

> For the most appalling and discouraging facts about these plays were the confusion, ignorance and inexpertness of the playwrights, most of them whites whose lack of knowledge of Negro life leads them on the one hand into unconsciously chauvinistic presentation of what they evidently regard as the admirable "peculiarities" of the Negro and on the other hand into a "lily white" type of idealization that most Negroes would object to as unrealistic and dehumanizing. (In one play, these two tendencies are combined . . . Angelo Herndon is depicted as breaking into a jig when offstage noises tell him that the I.L.D. is "coming for to carry him home.") [19]

The situation did not greatly alter in the remaining years of the Depression. For all the passion of the thirties for social justice and for all the effort of the American Communist party to assert itself in the black community, League plays dealing with the racial issue were as often as not the work of unpromising authors who never overcame their amateurism or their prudence. But, it could have been claimed, the New Deal politicians also demonstrated unseemly prudence, if not amateurism, on this issue; while the concern of Roosevelt over the limited opportunities available to blacks could not be questioned, it was nevertheless true that under him Congress enacted no civil rights legislation.

White women supplied many of the new plays on blacks. Three were the work of one author, Alice Holdship Ware. With earnestness but a talent unequal to the task, she pressed for the social integration of the races, her best realized characters being women, black or white, who rebel against the idea of segregation. In *Mighty Wind A'Blowin'* a family of dispossessed Arkansas sharecroppers overcomes the barrier of prejudice to share in the meal of a black family. All join together with others equally needy, both black and white, to protect their rights to the land. The event behind the action of the play was the bloody fight between tenants and landowners that had occurred in Arkansas after the organization of the Southern Tenant Farmers' Union in 1934. Though the leadership of the STFU was socialist, the Communists, true to the values of the Popular Front, were prepared to promote a play celebrating its activities—but without mentioning its name. Prominently featured in the play are protest songs adapted from spirituals; black members of the SFTU frequently introduced such songs at meetings, which had something of the flavor of the back country religious gatherings common to both races.[20]

In *Like a Flame* and *Together* Ware dealt with the middle class of both races. A talented black musician in the former believes that the blacks should fend for themselves unaided by whites, but is rebuked by a liberal-minded young Southern woman who insists that his attitude, no less than that of her hostile elderly aunt, is the attitude of a racist. In *Together* the subject is the heartbreak experienced by a black who "passes," as revealed in the person of a young woman whose brother, a black physician, is about to be done out of his property by whites who want it for the expansion of their country club. Elizabeth England's *Take My Stand* shows the formation of an alliance of blacks and whites in the South for the purpose of gaining better wages from their redneck employer. Though daring as a recommendation of concerted bi-racial activity, it is nevertheless a thin work; its greatest distinction rests in the fact that it was the first New Theater League play to be issued as a printed pamphlet.[21] For these unimaginative playwrights, whose work was no better than adequate student writing, the proscription against antinaturalistic construction was no real restriction.

A cleverer writer, though one not greatly gifted with skill in characterization, was A. B. Shiffrin, the author of *Kids Learn Fast*.[22] In this grandguignolesque one-act play set in the slums of the East New York section of Brooklyn, a group of five boys, all around twelve years old, play a cruel and curious game: lynching. In the Popular Front manner, each boy represents a different ethnic group: Poles, Jews, Italians, Irishmen, and what the author designates "pure-blooded Americans." Another neighborhood boy, with whom they often play, is black. He becomes the central figure in their game:

JOE: Hey, wait a minute. Why pick on me?

FREDDIE: (*Pretty disgusted*): Well, for Christ sake, will yuh shut up and lemme finish this? D'yuh want to play or don't cha?

JOE: Sure I wanna play. But why should I be chased?

STAN: Because you're a nigger. And the papers always say the nigger is chased and lynched and everything on account he raped somebody. It don't matter where it is, Mississippi, Tennessee, Georgia, Florida, it makes no difference, it's always the nigger what's chased and everything.

Joe enters the game, with the horrifying result that the boys chase, capture, and hang him, leaving his feet resting on a box. Then, confusing play with reality and goaded by the leader, one of them kicks the box away, and the black boy is strangled to death by the rope. In a minute his mother comes to the scene, looking for him; it is his birthday, she says, and his father has a new bicycle for him.

Subtler, and far wiser in the ways of blacks and of whites in their attitudes toward them, than any other writer to offer plays on racial tensions in the thirties was Langston Hughes. He was also remarkably industrious. During the thirties he offered in the neighborhood of a dozen plays of various types and lengths, beginning with the agit-prop *Scottsboro Limited* in 1931, in addition to volumes of poetry and fiction, an autobiography, essays, and newspaper coverage of the Spanish Civil War. Through the second half of the decade, before and after his stint in Spain, he devoted much of his energy to the theater. His bitter three-act tragedy *Mulatto*, which he wrote in 1930, opened successfully on Broadway in the fall of 1935. For part of the season of 1936–37 he worked with the Kamaru Theater on the production of some six of his plays. In 1938 he founded the Harlem Suitcase Theater for the production of his play-with-music, *Don't You Want To Be Free?*, and in the following year he organized the New Negro Theater in Los Angeles. So gifted a writer was not a man to force his work into a pattern at the urging of political theoreticians. He traveled to Russia in the early thirties, contributed to *New Masses* and *New Theatre*, submitted his *Anglo Herndon Jones* to the League's contest, spoke at the first American Writers' Congress, signed the "call" for the second, and was represented in the anthology *Proletarian Literature in the United States*, but declined to join the Communist party because he saw in party membership a threat to his independence as a writer. His published three-act plays of the late thirties, *Mulatto*, *Little Ham*, and *Emperor of Haiti* (the latter two first produced at the Kamaru by the Gilpin Players), are vivid but straightforward depictions of black experience that fit comfortably within any reasonable definition of socialist realism. Yet Hughes could not be expected to keep to this confining technique, and his three published short plays of the same period represent departures from it.[23]

In two of these, *Limitations of Life*, written in collaboration with Louis Davis, and *Soul Gone Home*, Hughes went beyond realism to fantasy. The former, published in the New Theater League, second volume of *Skits and Sketches*, and described "As performed by the Harlem Suitcase Theatre," is a wry parody of the popular film *Imitation of Life* starring Claudette Colbert. In the film the actress is a successful packager of pancake ingredients put together in accordance with a recipe devised by her faithful black servant, played by Louise Beavers. The principal theme of the picture, as illustrated by the unhappy life of the black woman's daughter, who is light-skinned enough to "pass," is that blacks should humbly accept their burden. In the little play, the tables are turned: the rich woman is a black who speaks with an Oxford accent, and the maid is a blond white girl named Audette who never tires in her efforts to please her mistress. She is burdened, however, with a serious problem: "Lawd, Mammy Weavers," she says, "ma little daughter's tryin' so hard to be colored. She just loves Harlem. She's lyin' out in de backyard all day long tannin' herself, every day, tryin' so hard to be colored."

Soul Gone Home,[24] first performed at the Kamaru, is an equally ironic but far more bitter kind of work in which the corpse of a young black boy berates his mother for taking poor care of him when he was alive. Though she has two trades, selling newspapers and selling her body, in neither could she make enough money to keep him properly fed, with the result that he has died from both tuberculosis and malnutrition. The point of this very brief sketch, in which Hughes's comic sensibility hides just below the surface, is that in the world dominated by whites, blacks cannot be expected to improve either their finances or their morals. Putting on a red hat for her night on the streets after two white men take the corpse off to the undertaker, the mother says, "Tomorrow, Ronnie, I'll buy you some flowers —if I can pick up a dollar tonight. You was a hell of a no-good son, I swear."

Of greater length and complexity than these sketches, though only in one act, *Don't You Want To Be Free?* was also something of a hit, running for 135 performances on weekends at the Harlem Suitcase Theater after its opening on April 21, 1938. On June 10, 1938, Hughes's actors took it to a midtown theater for a New Theater Night, sharing the bill with Ware's *Mighty Wind A' Blowin'*; which was offered by a New Haven company. How the audience responded to the plays as a double bill is unknown, but as printed texts they cannot be compared. Ware's play is no more than a glance through a cabin door at two uninteresting though hard-pressed families, while Hughes's is a well-paced, imaginative treatment, with spirituals, blues, and jazz, of black American history from the days of slavery to the militant thirties. The approach to the material owed something to the successful Living Newspaper Unit of the Federal Theater, in whose productions current issues such as housing or public health were brought to the stage in an interesting combination of documented history and illustrative dramatic action. But Hughes, who directed the play himself, also relied for effects on his memories of productions seen in Moscow at the constructivist theaters of Vsevelod Meyerhold and Nikolai Oklopkov.[25] He used an arena-style stage in two parts connected by a runway, and kept it free of scenery, except for a lynch rope and an auction block. On this bare area he put his characters through panoramic scenes of black miseries and triumphs.

To hold the scenes together Hughes provided a young man who appears as his spokesman in each of the scenes, never growing older. "I am a Negro," he says at the beginning, and adds that he has also been a slave, a worker, a singer, and a victim. What follows to occupy the playing time is impressions of many kinds of black experience: discrimination in a restaurant, harsh treatment from an unfeeling landlord, the expression of affection between a mother and child, the bloody Harlem riots of March 1935. Through all of it, Hughes's ability to transmute ugly truths into art is evident. An especially poignant moment is the song of a mulatto girl:

My old man's a white old man!
My old mother's black!
But if ever I cursed my white old man
I take my curses back.

If ever I cursed my black old mother
And wished she were in hell
I'm sorry for that evil wish
And now I wish her well.

My old man died in a fine old house
My ma died in a shack.
I wonder where I'm gonna die,
Being neither white nor black.

This had been published earlier as "Cross"; it was a poem Hughes was in the habit of using when giving public readings of his work.[26] A different kind of feeling marks the rousing close of the play, when Hughes turns back brazenly to agitprop technique, illustrating the modern political activity of blacks with a woman worker's musical call to action:

Who wants to make Harlem great and fine?
Make New York City a guiding light to shine?
Who wants to lead the workers toward the light?
Then let's get together folks,
And fight, fight, fight!

Though this was not the same as urging the audience to sing the "Internationale," as in *Scottsboro Limited*, it was a more ardent call to action than writers of the day usually allowed themselves, and, as such, a measure of Hughes's independence.

One of the strongest of all plays of the thirties touching on the racial issue, and among the three or four most professional works to enter the repertory of the New Theater League, was Paul Green's *Hymn to the Rising Sun*, a short work appealing for revision of the South's ruthless penal codes. Green, a Southerner, had long since revealed his compassion for members of both races for whom the opportunity to enjoy an ample life was slight or nonexistent. The early milestones of his career included three much praised long plays set wholly or partly in backwaters of the South: *In Abraham's Bosom*, *The House of Connelly*, and, the last of his plays to be produced on Broadway, *Johnny Johnson*, which the Group Theater staged in 1936.

With the exception of Patsy Tate in *The House of Connelly*, the major characters of these plays are individuals who seldom or never possess mastery over their fate. In depicting the helpless state of convicts of both races in *Hymn to the Rising Sun*, Green succeeded, as always, in drawing a sympathetic response from the audience. According to a note in *New Theatre*, in which the play was first published, Green was inspired to write his play on reading the diary of a chain-gang guard, who turned the document over to him in the hope that something could be done to correct the horrifying conditions of the prisoners. Green was also moved to write by a report of two black prisoners who lost their feet on being chained for days in freezing weather; this incident is mentioned in the play.[27]

The dramatic action is brief and graphic. On a day that turns out to be the Fourth of July, the convicts, both black and white, are awakened for work. A white youngster called Bright Boy, new to the prison, and put there on a false charge of murder, is greatly disturbed by the groaning of a black prisoner, called Runt, who is locked inside a metal box, a form of punishment given to him for masturbating. Bright Boy and the others are made to listen to the rant of a sadistic prison officer, the "Captain," on the righteousness of the persons of authority—legislators, ministers, the Daughters of the American Revolution—who run the state and see to it that wrongdoers are made to pay for their offenses. With ponderous irony he reminds them that they are in prison to be purged of the temptation to do wrong and that he never whips any man as much as the law allows. In the bitterness of this scene and a tirade that he delivers before the close of the play lies the evidence that the Captain has been hurt by the system he himself serves, and almost as much as have the prisoners.

But in moments that because of their candid, unsentimental expression of brutality and terror are not easily dismissed from the mind, the total helplessness of the convicts in confrontation with this embodiment of the law makes it impossible to feel even the most patronizing sort of pity for him. Central to the play is the scene in which he heartlessly beats the white boy:

CAPTAIN . . . (*And now he stops behind the* BOY): So you're sick, hah? (*His voice is brittle and steely, a new note in it, and a shiver seems to run the length of the dirty gray-striped line. The* BOY *looks out before him with wide frightened eyes and face the color of ash-tree wood.)*

BOY: Yes sir, yes sir, I'm sick.

CAPTAIN (*now looming above him*): Hum. When a man's sick he's got a fever, ain't he? And when he's got a fever the thermometer says so, don't it. Well, the thermometer says you ain't got no fever. There-fore you ain't sick.

BOY (*in a low agonized pleading*): Please sir, please.

CAPTAIN (*suddenly pulling* [*his whip*] *out of the cuff of his boot and touching the boy on the shoulder*): This way, son.

BOY (*terror-stricken*): But I been doing all right, Cap'n. They ain't been any complaint has they, none you've heard of?

CAPTAIN (*kindly*): This way, son.

(GUARD NUMBER ONE *comes up in front of him and touches him in the stomach with his gun.*)

FIRST GUARD: You heard him.

BOY (*his hands fluttering aimlessly in the air, his breath sucked through his lips with a gasp*): Oh, Lord, have mercy! Mercy!

CAPTAIN: So you're callin' on the Lord? Well, the Lord ain't here. The Lord is far away. In fact you might say this ain't no place for the Lord.

BOY (*whispering*): Cap'n, Cap'n!

CAPTAIN: I know you need medicine, son. That's what we're going to give you. Maybe after that you won't be sick. Maybe you won't talk so much either.

The Captain's medicine is ten fierce blows of the whip, leaving the boy almost too weak for tears. But the boy's part in the action is not yet complete. This being the Fourth, the prison regulations call for the singing of "America" by the prisoners, and the Captain, in a move revealing again the complexity of his nature, asks the boy to lead the song. He does, in a clear voice, and this, with irony that is heavy but not overwrought, is the hymn of the title. In the final action Green turns to Runt, the black prisoner, bent double in his box. It appears that his punishment has killed him, and it is left to a huge black named Pearly Gates to carry the body away to be buried. Runt's death is to be recorded as occurring from natural causes. But the real, indisputable cause is the inability of such whites as the Captain to accept blacks as human beings.

Green's naturalism is the real thing: a style informed by a mature author's notion of the best way to tell his story. It is not a method imposed on him by the fiat of nonliterary authoritarians, any more than it is, with him, the technique chosen by a neophyte learning his craft. His plea, as John Gassner pointed out, is for reform, not revolution,[28] and to that end he created at least three unforgettable images: the terrified boy, his hands fluttering like moths trapped in the globe of a lamp; the dead Runt, bent inside the archaic penal device; and the raging Captain, maddened by years of exposure to social decay. The play was first produced by the "Let Freedom Ring" Company at a New Theater Night on January 12, 1936, under the direction of Joseph Losey. It then became a standard item in the repertory of the New Theater League.

In taking up the problems of American Jews, whose foothold in the national cultural and economic life was jarred by new currents of anti-Semitism generated in nazi Germany and spread by such professional American bigots as Gerald L. K. Smith and William Pelley, the writers and staff of the New Theater League were dealing with a subject closer to them personally than the problems of blacks, for many of them were Jewish. Yet their treatment of the subject was tentative, as though they were afraid that by airing the issue they would exacerbate it. The most heartfelt reference to anti-Semitism in all the League plays is the Dr. Benjamin episode of *Waiting for Lefty*. Other references to Jews abound in the blackout pieces on Germany planned for revue programs and ultimately published by the League in its two *Skits and Sketches* volumes; these, however, were negligible. A three-act play on the horrors faced by Jews in Germany, Claire and Paul Sifton's *Blood on the Moon*, produced in 1936 by the Brooklyn Progressive Players, a League affiliate, ran for three weeks but soon dropped out of sight. Many plays on labor-management disputes and the organization of unions include one or more Jews along with representatives of other component groups in the population—for example, Michael Blankfort's *The Crime*, Ben Bengal's *Plant in the Sun*, and Charles Shillet and I. J. Alexander's *Professional Men*—but whatever qualities the authors may have had in mind as constituting Jewishness is not evident in the characterization.

To add a worthwhile piece on Jewish life to the repertory, the League sponsored a contest for such a play late in 1935. In Popular Front fashion, the contest was held in conjunction with a nonpolitical institution, the 92nd Street Y.M.H.A.,[29] the miniature cultural center

on the Upper East Side that supplied the city with a stage not only
for drama, but for dance recitals, poetry readings, and chamber-music
concerts. The winner was A. B. Shiffrin's *Return at Sunset*. Half-seri-
ous, half-comic, it reveals an inevitable debt to the leading Jewish
dramatist of the moment, Odets. The scene is the kitchen of the apartment somewhere in the city in which a poor Jewish family lives—
poorer even than the Bergers of *Awake and Sing!*, and including, like
that family, a stout-hearted mother, an ineffectual father, a working-
girl daughter, a son awakening to the radical movement, and a
sardonic friend. The dramatic action is virtually nonexistent; the content is comprised of speeches on the hardships of daily life uttered by
the members of the family as they come home late in the afternoon,
each with a mishap to report to the others. The most important of
Shiffrin's points is made by the son Joe, who has had a fight with a
policeman. He got into the fight by trying to help an old woman who,
like himself, was listening to a radical speech and who was kicked in
the stomach by the policeman's horse. In reply to his mother's question, "A Jewish woman?" he gives the right answer: "Jewish, Irish,
what's the difference?"

Weighing even more heavily on the minds of writers, it would appear, than the burden of racial and religious intolerance was the
threat of another World War. To this at least, if not to the discontents
of the black minority, the federal government addressed itself
squarely, though not in a manner satisfactory to all elements of the
population. To Jews, who were well represented in the Roosevelt administration and to whom the president was unreservedly cordial, the
nazi military menace was inseparably linked with the unconcealed
nazi policy of anti-Semitism. If other elements of the population were
less concerned about this problem than the Jews, all had been aware
since the rise of Hitler to power in 1933 that nazi fantasies of glorious
Teutonic strength posed a threat to peace. It was, however, Mussolini
who, equally consumed with territorial ambitions, became the first
European leader of the decade to commit an act of war: the invasion
of Ethiopia, which took place in October 1935. Japan joined with
Germany in an anti-Comintern pact in 1936, and, having been in
Manchuria since 1931, made a further advance into China in 1937.
Still more disturbing to the imagination of the general public and
workers in the arts than these dire international events was the civil

war that erupted in Spain in 1936. Clearly this much bloodshed and rage, bad enough in itself, portended worse. With sufficient cause, war became a major dramatic subject. Plays on wars past, present, and future entered the schedules of institutional and commercial theaters, on Broadway and off. For its part, the New Theater League, though investing most of its energy in plays on labor, made an effort to locate actable pieces on the threats to peace.

Surprisingly little of substance on the nazis or the Italian fascists entered the League's repertory. No more resounding dramatic protest against Hitler came to the fore than Odets's *Till the Day I Die,* which despite its sentimentality was at least a sustained, coherent work. Philip Corbin's *S.S. Liberty,* a minor play, made an appeal for the cessation of arms shipments to Italy; in it, American sailors at Le Havre, discovering that their ship's cargo is made up of French munitions bound for Italy, are incensed enough to strike and are joined in their action by the very scabs hired to work in their place. Many of the blackout pieces in the *Skits and Sketches* volumes provided antifascist thrusts; very popular among them was H. S. Kraft's *The Bishop of Munster,* in which a German Catholic prelate prays for the souls of his countrymen under the nazis.[30] But these were only program-fillers. Despite the paucity of good scripts, the fascist menace was by no means neglected, inasmuch as the depredations of Hitler and Mussolini were mentioned in many plays on all subjects, as well as in *New Theatre* editorials and articles.

The worsening situation in Asia, highlighted for Americans by the Japanese bombing of the gunboat *Panay* on December 12, 1937, received its share of attention in the radical theater, but its remoteness from the United States deprived it of the urgency of events in Europe. The China Aid Society, with the assistance of one of the most vigorous of all Communist front organizations, the American League for Peace and Democracy (before 1937 the American League Against War and Fascism), published a quarterly anthology of sketches, *Contemporary Scene,* on Japan.[31] The contents were primitively executed, resembling in style and quality the "Third Period" sketches published in *Workers Theatre.* In one of the plays, a revue titled *Big Boycott of 1938,* with music by Saul Aarons and lyrics by Aarons, Joe Schmul, and Mike Stratton, appeared a song that, though of no artistic consequence, serves as a reminder of the principal move made by the

American public to demonstrate its disapproval of Japanese aggression: the boycott of silk garments. Sung by a salesgirl, it runs in part,

> Rise and shout, silk is out, let the world know what we're all about
> When we say that our slips won't equip Hirohito with battleships.
> Slap a ban on Japan,
> The Heavenly Son's just an also ran,
> No sheer silken brassière will shame my name.

A short comic opera on the same issue, *Maid in Japan*, with book by Maurice Stoller and music by Elie Siegmeister, was offered at a New Theater Night on February 19, 1939, but dropped quickly from sight. Writing in the *Daily Worker*, John Cambridge observed that the writers barely skirted racial prejudice in their mockery of Japanese customs.[32] On China's civil struggle between the Kuomintang and the Maoists there appeared only one League play: John Wexley's *Running Dogs*. Set at a time before the two mutually unsympathetic parties formed a united front against the Japanese, the play shows the birth of skepticism in the minds of some Kuomintang soldiers who, having been much oppressed by their superiors, hear from a spy the Maoist message of "Land to the peasants! Factories and mines to the toilers and workers! Down with the landlords and exploiters of the poor! Down with . . . !" This was first offered at a New Theater Night on February 6, 1937, by the Theater Union Studio.

It was to the Spanish conflict that playwrights turned in greatest numbers, if not with remarkable artistic success. From the outset of the rightist rebellion against the Republic in July 1936, it appeared that Spain was to become a testing ground for the comparative strengths of democratic and fascist ideologies, and that the struggle would work punishing hardships on the population. The very name itself of the country became evocative of imperiled democracy. As both symbol and fact the war stirred writers to action, not only to decry the situation in its aspects both physical and metaphorical, but, for some, to make the journey—without the approval of the federal government—to Spain and there to serve as fighters or correspondents. In January 1937 enough American fighting men were present in Spain to form the Abraham Lincoln Brigade; by the end of the war in 1939, an estimated three hundred thousand Americans had fought in this and other international units.[33] To the New Theater League it was an occasion for great pride as well as sorrow that the actor John Lenthier, who had participated in radical theater since the days of WLT and Prolet-Buehne, was killed in an early battle. Possibly a graver loss to the League and to theater generally occurred when William Titus, the promising author of a strike play, *Sit-Down!*, and an officer in the Lincoln Brigade, was killed at the battle of Teruel in 1938. Herbert Kline, editor of *New Theatre*, went to Spain in 1937 to cover the war for the *New Masses* and to direct the film *Heart of Spain*.[34] Among the many writers well-known outside radical circles, as well as within them, who made one or more journeys to the war were Hemingway, Hughes, Dos Passos, Lillian Hellman, and Dorothy Parker. As for the American writers who stayed at home, the vast majority outspokenly favored the Loyalist cause. The President of the League of American Writers, Donald Ogden Stewart, sent a form letter in February 1938 to all well-known American writers asking replies to two questions: "Are you for, or are you against Franco and Fascism?" and "Are you for, or are you against the legal government and the people of Republican Spain?" The questions were loaded—perhaps not much, but loaded nevertheless—but they brought a response from about four hundred writers, of whom only six considered themselves neutral and only one took a stand with Franco. Those for the Loyalists included not merely the Communist writers such as John Howard Lawson, Kyle Crichton, Joseph Gollomb, V. J. Jerome, and Earl Browder himself, but such conservatives and centrists as William Faulkner and the playwrights Maxwell Anderson, Edna Ferber, Marc Connelly, Thornton Wilder, and Lynn Riggs.[35]

The Communist view on the war, approved routinely by the New Theater League and the League of American Writers, was that support was necessary for the popular front government of the Spanish Republic, with the understanding that the government should include staunch Communists in important offices. Thus the Russians in Spain, and American Communists taking example from them, excoriated the POUM (Partido Obrero de Unificación Marxista) for its Trotskyite radicalism. In the spring of 1937 the Russian disapproval of the working-class Prime Minister Largo Cabellero, who was slow to move against prominent army radicals and unwilling to accede to Russian military strategies, led to his resignation and replacement by Juan Negrin, who though a nonradical proved more receptive to the notion of Communists in his government and turned to them for support.[36] For Americans, Joseph Freeman summed up the party line at the American Writers' Congress in 1937: "We might as well face the issue frankly. The majority of the Spanish people do not at present want socialism." [37]

The complexity of this internal scramble for control of the Republican government was too much for most of the playwrights, apparently; they did not explore it. The League's plays on war, which add up to only middling dramatic experiences, call for a Republican victory, show the bravery of Loyalist troops, and offer glimpses of American soldiers and their friends and relations at home. One author who cannot have failed to understand the political conflict, the Theater Union's Michael Blankfort, provided in *The Brave and the Blind* a long one-act on the siege of the Alcázar, the Moorish fortress of Toledo.[38] It was first performed on March 21, 1937, by the Rebel Arts Players. The Alcázar was held by the Rebels in the summer of 1936 after the outbreak of fighting and surrounded by Loyalists, who at first made diplomatic gestures to persuade the Rebels to abandon it, but after ten weeks took it by military force. Blankfort's play shows the occupants of the fortress in the last hours of the siege. All social classes are represented, from a landowner down to a prostitute, along with a priest and several military figures. One Colonel Sanchez is a thinly disguised portrait of the rebel Colonel Moscardo whose son was held hostage and shot by the Loyalists, as his father well knew he would be if the fortress was not surrendered.[39] As Blankfort imagines these figures under stress, they are a mixture of stout hearts and cowards and, as was proper to the work of a leftist writer in the age of the Popular Front, many, including the priest, though nominally nationalistic are contemptuous of the antisocial views of Franco.

The international embargo on arms to the Loyalists is the subject of Barbara Corcoran's *The Ostrich*—the bird with its head in the sand being in this case the United States. In Theodore Kaghan's *Hello, Franco,* a company of American soldiers in Spain have some fun and a few touching moments while pretending to speak to the homefolks and rightist leaders on a nonfunctioning field telephone; in

Popular Front fashion, they represent a variety of American regional types. More interesting than these rather wooden works, because briefer and more dynamic, is Ruth Deacon's *Spain: 1937*, an old-fashioned mass chant making good use of such off-stage noises as "a scream; terrific bomb explosion; sobbing . . . frequent bombing; constant rattle of machine guns, and droning of airplanes," and, repeatedly, the Loyalist slogan "Madrid shall be the tomb of fascism."

The League also controlled the rights to translations of two foreign plays on Spain: Bertolt Brecht's *Señora Carrar's Rifles* and Ramón Sender's *The Secret*. Brecht's play, an adaptation of John Millington Synge's *Riders to the Sea*, sketches the radicalization of a woman whose husband had fought in the Asturian revolution of 1934; after her son, a fisherman, is gunned down by the Rebels in his boat, she not only hands over to the Loyalists a supply of rifles hidden by her late husband, but decides to fight on their side herself. Sender, a Spanish Loyalist, wrote of the martyrdom of a leftist political prisoner in Barcelona in 1935, when under a suspicious government, before the ascendancy of Largo Cabellero, tens of thousands of dissidents were jailed.[40]

Not all the radical plays on the Spanish Civil War were issued by the New Theater League or presented under League auspices. The *Young Communist Review*, for instance, was the publisher of Irene Paull's *What Price Spain?* in which Hitler, Mussolini, and Franco plan for the victory to come and the rendering up of Spain's islands to Germany and Italy, while Democracy, looking on, curbs their glee by insisting that they will lose.[41] Written with special flair was Kenneth White's *Who Fights This Battle?*, a pageant on recent Spanish history from the abdication of King Alfonso to the outbreak of the war. After a clever beginning in which revelers call out the names of persons and places associated with Spain ("Picasso . . . Goya . . . Dali . . . the Escorial . . . the Alhambra" and others) and a Spanish dancer does a typical heel-tapping, arm-flinging dance, the play proper begins, revealing the gradual coalescence of liberal and leftist political parties to form a united front. The principal character is the world-famed Dolores Ibarurri, "La Pasionaria" (the Passion Flower), the Asturian Communist deputy to the Cortes who invented the ringing slogan, "It is better to die on your feet than to live on your

knees." Directed by Joseph Losey, and with music composed by Paul
Bowles, *Who Fights This Battle?* was presented for only four performances on September 20 and 21, 1936.[42] *

Because of their topicality, the radical theater's plays on Spain and
China had only limited circulation. When the Second World War
broke out, absorbing all other armed quarrels, these plays fell into the
oblivion for which their artistic limitations had destined them from
the first. A longer-lived play was Irwin Shaw's *Bury the Dead,* which,
since it was written in condemnation of all wars, was suitable for revival all too frequently.[43] It was one of the best publicized and most
frequently performed of all the League plays of the late thirties. Shaw
had intended to enter the play in a contest held by the League in
1936, but was two weeks late in submitting it. But the League's board
was sufficiently impressed with the work to promote and publish it in
the pages of *New Theatre.* The first performance took place on March
14, 1936, in a production given by the Actors Repertory Company,
formerly the "Let Freedom Ring" Company. On April 18, with the
same actors appearing under the auspices of Alex Yokel, a commercial producer, the play went to Broadway.[44] Thus Shaw's pattern of
success resembled that of Odets, and since his play appeared not
more than a year after *Waiting for Lefty,* reporters cited the similari-
ties of the two authors' personal histories. Both were young New
Yorkers of middle-class Jewish background. Shaw, seven years
younger than Odets, was Brooklyn-born and a graduate of Brooklyn
College, and both had become overnight sensations as a result of
plays intended for and publicized by the radical theater. Fittingly
enough, the Group, Odets's company, had offered to produce *Bury
the Dead* on Broadway, but Shaw, impatient for a production, would
not wait until the Group directors could fit it into their schedule.[45] It
could be added that the dialogue of the two plays had much the same
tone and cadence; Odets was beginning to set a fashion in verbal
acidity, and Shaw responded to it.

The central issue of *Bury the Dead* had been employed some five
years earlier, in 1930, by the German playwright Hans Chlumberg in

* The producer was the Theater Committee for the Defense of the Spanish Republic, a typical Popular Front group whose members were George Abbott, Adelaide Bean, Heywood Broun, Angna Enters, Joseph Freeman, Charles Friedman,
John Gassner, Albert Maltz, Sylvia Regan, Muriel Rukeyser, and Herman Shumlin.

Miracle in Verdun. American audiences had had an opportunity to see this play in a Theatre Guild production of 1931; with a run of only 49 performances, however, the Guild could not count the play among its successes. The idea presented by both Chlumberg and Shaw is that the return from the grave of men killed during the war would cause such a collapse of received values that the entire population of the world, including the dead men's own relations, would request them to give up life a second time. There are differences, however; Shaw's play is a long one-act work, not, like Chlumberg's, a full evening's entertainment; his soldiers are victims of a war unnamed, not the First World War; the scenery he requires is skeletal, not detailed; and, whether consciously or otherwise, he took the form of his work from late agitprop drama.

As Shaw sets the scene, the stage is decorated starkly and impressively with a dull-black platform running its length at a height of seven feet. On this are placed some sandbags, evocative of trench warfare. For lighting, a strong spotlight sweeps across the platform at hip height from the right wing. Thus figures in silhouette and chiaroscuro complete the stage picture. At moments this simple technique provides a harrowing spectacle, as, especially, in the scene in which the six dead soldiers rise from behind the platform as from their common grave and confront the army's burial detail and chaplains. If such a scenic plan sorted poorly with the notion of socialist realism, it at least accommodated dialogue that, despite the fantastic events it described, was as candid as Shaw could make it.

In familiar melting-pot style, Shaw chose Americans of varied origins and ages as his six revived corpses. One has an Irish name: Driscoll; one, a German name: Schelling; one, a Jewish name: Levy, though for some arcane reason he is said not to be Jewish. The others are named Morgan, Webster, and Dean, representing, possibly, the all-American Anglo-Saxon majority. The six are of quite different economic, social, and educational backgrounds, but all are privates, for their movement to stop war by refusing to die in it is a common man's movement, not for the officer class or any other class in established control of American destiny. The body of the play is made up of exchanges of dialogue in which each of the soldiers in turn speaks to the woman most important to him. Two are wives, and the others are a girl friend, a mistress, a sister, and a mother; all, whether rich or poor, are curiously conservative, not wanting this disruption of their life patterns. In devoting much of the play to these brief scenes, Shaw reveals his debt to *Waiting for Lefty*, for, like the vignettes in *Lefty*, they provide the moments in which the principal figures of the play explain the purpose behind their action. Also taken from agit-prop is the idea of class struggle; here the haves are the officers, whose business is warfare, and the have-nots are the enlisted men, whose business is to stay above the ground in a peaceful society.

The language, not only of the dialogue between the soldiers and their women, but of the entire play, owes something to Odets. "I used to take a shower every day. Can you imagine?" asks a member of the burial detail. "All right, Mr. Lifebuoy," replies another, "We'll put your picture in the *Saturday Evening Post*—in color!" The sting of Odets may be lacking, but the *intention* of stinging in his manner is there. A longer passage—one of many of the same tone, carries the echo of Odets's sentimentality and fondness for the *non sequitur:*

> JULIA: . . . The worst thing is looking at all the books you piled up at home that you didn't read. They wait there, waiting for your hands to come and open them and . . . Oh, let them bury you, let them bury you. . . . There's nothing left, only crazy people and clothes that'll never be used hanging in the closets . . . Why not?
>
> MORGAN: There are too many books I haven't read, too many places I haven't seen, too many memories I haven't kept long enough. . . . I won't be cheated of them. . . .
>
> JULIA: And me? Darling, me . . . I hate getting drunk. Your name would look so well on a nice simple chunk of marble in a green field. "Walter Morgan, beloved of Julia Blake. . . ." With poppies and daisies and those little purple flowers all around the bottom, and . . . (*She is bent over, almost wailing. There is a flash of a gun in her hand, and she totters, falls*) Now they can put my name on the casualty lists, too. . . . What do they call those purple flowers, darling . . . ? (*Blackout.*)

At the end of the play when the burial detail, having no corpses to inter, files off the stage, the tough-guy touch of Odets is equally apparent, and neatly so, in a piece of stage business: as the last soldier passes a maddened general, he "*deliberately, but without malice, flicks a cigarette butt at him, then follows the others* SOLDIERS *off the stage.*"

Having begun his career with a play so provocative in theme, if not wholly original in format and content, Shaw wrote prolifically through the remaining years of the decade and into the forties, until he left civilian life for service in the Second World War. Successful stories for the *New Yorker* pointed toward the later career he would enjoy as a popular though facile novelist, but he also continued to write plays on crucial issues of the day. A short play, *Second Mortgage*, was added to the repertory of the New Theater League. Of his four long plays of the late thirties, the Group Theater offered three, including, as we will see, one major success.

If the New Theater League could discover no new labor play in the Popular Front era comparable in merit to *Waiting for Lefty*, it was not for a lack of contests and New Theater Nights. In the plays advertised and distributed by the Repertory Department and ultimately acted by one or another of the troupes, virtually every kind of strike situation or workers' grievance was dramatized. The continuing problem of unemployment was also a repeated theme. David Danzig's *Ten Million Others* dealt with men out of work who are unable to obtain relief or medical care. Richard Pack's *Great American Game* told of a baseball team on strike. Others had to do with the manufacture or distribution of munitions, textiles, automobiles, steel, raw materials, and other products in amazing variety, including candy and milk, as in, respectively, Ben Bengal's *Plant in the Sun* and Philip Stevenson's *Road Closed*. True to the doctrine of socialist realism, the writers more often than not showed the growth among workers of the wish to organize for decent conditions with as much verisimilitude of dialogue and scenic design as they and the troupes could provide. Mass chants on labor were written and performed also, as were plays with music, highly original in certain instances. One play of unusual design, Albert Maltz's *Rehearsal*, provided a combination of mass chant and socialist realism: an inadequate actress rehearsing a mass chant on labor with a "progressive" troupe suddenly takes fire when she relates the chant to a strike in the coal and iron industries in which her brother had his back broken by company police. But it is only the format of the work that is novel, for the change of the actress's attitude toward her part is akin to the changes occurring in the protagonists of countless League plays—the conversion from diffident or timid bystander, scab, or self-involved loner, to implacable militant in labor's cause.

The strike, and especially the strike with the objective of securing recognition for the union, was the natural topic of writers attracted to the League, not only because national conditions indicated a need and suggested a public for such plays, but because it was possible for the writers to forward the Popular Front concept by putting men of varied backgrounds in the ranks of the strikers. That management could be moved only by a bold show of unity on labor's part was evident early in the New Deal years, for, though Roosevelt had easily pushed through Congress in his first hundred days in office the National Industrial Recovery Act with its much discussed Section 7(a) giving labor the right to collective bargaining, neither the president nor the act's administrators had put up a fight for unionization under it, leaving corporate officers with the impression that they could ignore it with impunity. In any case, in May 1935 the Supreme Court declared the act unconstitutional. Moreover, when in June of the same year Congress passed the National Labor Relations Act, management began to fight passionately against it, expecting that the Court would declare it unconstitutional also. This did not happen; the Court ruled affirmatively on the constitutionality of the law—but not until April 1937. Meanwhile, blood had been shed in many labor disputes, and, despite the court's ruling, labor still had much organizational work on its hands to the end of the decade.

The New Theater League's staff and writers demonstrated their concern not only by promoting and writing new plays, but by visiting strikebound plants and reporting on the activity of the theatrical unions, including the attempt by a radical faction to take over Equity and a successful strike of New York's striptease artists. Performances of plays by union card-holders—certified members of the working class—the encouragement of which had been the driving force of the League of Workers Theaters in the old days, came less frequently within the purview of tne New Theater League in the late thirties as its directors edged toward emulation of the professional stage. On occasion, however, the League promoted such performances, as in a quadruple bill which it sponsored on June 3 and 4, 1939, of works performed by locals in the grip of the Communist party: *Wholesale Mikado* performed by the United Wholesale and Warehouse Employees, *Labor Pains* by the United Office and Professional Workers, Sidney Schoenwetter's *Lights* by the United Electrical and Radio Workers, and Bernard Dryer's *John Doe* by the Furriers.[46]

Elizabeth England's *Take My Stand* was, as we have noted, unusual for its time in dramatizing black and white solidarity. But the principal issue of the play is the more familiar one of the continuing need of the worker, regardless of color, to develop the courage to demand a fair share of the profits of his labor. Worthier plays, though not great ones, were soon forthcoming from Albert Maltz and Michael Blankfort. Maltz's *Private Hicks*, written in 1935, was the second play to be awarded a New Theater League prize, the contest having been conducted jointly with the American League Against War and Fascism.[47] It was first performed on January 12, 1936, by the "Let Freedom Ring" Company. Blankfort's *The Crime* became the last production of the Theater of Action, which as the Workers Laboratory Theater had helped to initiate the proletarian drama movement. Under the direction of Alfred Saxe and Elia Kazan, it was produced on March 1, 1936.

In these short plays both Maltz and Blankfort dealt with the problem of the divided mind. Neither work is of great merit, but each is noteworthy as an attempt to describe a bitter strike in terms of the new realism, with action proceeding linearly in lifelike settings and dialogue. According to one contemporary commentator, Maltz based *Private Hicks* on the anguished strike of workers at the Electric Auto-Lite Company in Toledo, Ohio, in 1934, during which the Ohio National Guard fought the strikers with arms and tear gas.[48] Maltz's protagonist is a young member of the Guard who is shocked by the order to shoot at strikers and refuses to obey it, remembering that his father in his time had gone on strike and realizing that he himself may have occasion to do the same at some point in the future. Despite the efforts of his commanding officer and a Mata Hari nurse to urge him to knuckle under to officialdom, Hicks decides to face a court-martial rather than fight. In the design of this plot, Maltz dwelt on a worry common to labor and the political Left, which saw in the call-up of the National Guard for strike-breaking a proto-fascist development and in the very existence of the Guard a menace to modern revolutionaries comparable to the truncheon-swinging Cossacks of old Russia. Despite its humdrum socialist realism, *Private Hicks* by virtue of its plot was popular with the League troupes, whereas the less conventional *Rehearsal*, which Maltz offered three years later, was largely ignored.[49]

Blankfort's strike play, though considered a one-act play by the New Theater League, is a relatively long piece made up of nine scenes. The strike depicted takes place in an industry that labor found especially difficult to crack: meat-packing, one of the last of the major industries to be unionized, and far from it when the play was written. The young protagonist, a man named Pete Brolyer, is persuaded by an older, more conservative organizer against his better judgment from taking measures to prevent the importation of scabs and is almost broken by the company. But in the end it appears that despite his vacillation the strikers have not given up. From the audience an actor playing the "real" Pete Brolyer stands and tells the end of the story, stressing as he does so the human ordinariness of union members:

> Honest to God, folks, I hope you never go through what we went through. And when you see pickets, or when you read about us in the papers—try to understand what's happening. Understand that we're men and women—folks just like you—fighting for their lives—cleaning house when it's dirty—building—learning—born to come out on top.

The major industries of automobiles and steel, the unionization of which was of the first importance to the entire labor movement, were taken to task in numerous skits and plays of various lengths published by the League and acted by various affiliates. In 1937 Albert Maltz, in Detroit during the series of sit-down strikes of General Motors, persuaded Contemporary Theater, a local troupe, into dropping *Help Yourself*, a rather mild comedy about a self-promoter by the Viennese writer Paul Vulpius, and got together some sketches with greater impact to be taken by the actors to the plants.[50] In the summer of 1938 the New York office of the League began the practice of sending theater organizers out to steel and mining towns to aid the workers in the development of new troupes. "Perhaps now," said the *Daily Worker's* Manngreen, "our American theatre will be taken out of the hands of the carriage trade and given back to the people who can't afford it." [51]

Possibly the best of the plays on the automobile industry—and the qualifying adverb is necessary because of the fact that not all the plays were published—was William Titus's *Sit-Down!*, first performed in April 1937 under League auspices by a troupe of actors from Brookwood Labor College, a Socialist institution located in Katonah, New York. Fashioned after the Living Newspaper quasi-documentaries, Titus's play is a series of blackout scenes on union activities punctuated with the chants and songs of an on-stage chorus and commentaries on current events delivered over a loud speaker. The union in its progress toward the goal of recognition by management proceeds from triumph to triumph, among which are the refusal of plant-inspectors to side with the company and the revelation, important in swaying the public, that an antiunion judge is a General Motors stockholder.

Related to this play in theme, but not dealing with automobiles, is one of the most attractive of all New Theater League plays, Ben Bengal's *Plant in the Sun*, the winner of a contest held in 1937 for plays on youth. It offers a glimpse of some engaging teen-age boys, the employees of a candy factory, who, having heard of the sit-down strikes in Detroit, decide to hold such a strike when one of their own group is fired. At last a New Theater play had humor: Bengal included some opportunities for the boys to engage in low-comedy clowning even as they reveal their brave determination not to back down when management tries to strong-arm them. The Popular Front device of illustrating an idea by showing its appeal to individuals of varied ethnic backgrounds works well, for the boys, no matter what their origins, are still boys, responding after the way of their age and sex to threats of force, maternal importunings, and the allure of girls. In the end a bloody battle takes place, but with the lights out. When it is over, the entire plant decides to stage a strike.[52]

The sit-down strike was not entirely new when General Motors workers tried it in 1936, but no previous effort of labor simply to take possession of a plant had so strongly held the public interest. Despite the apparent illegality of the sit-down, it worked. General Motors capitulated in less than a month and a half. Titus's and Bengal's plays, in which seriousness of purpose is partly concealed by humor, were among the liveliest in the League's repertory.

As a result of placing new plays with troupes located in New York, the League could be assured of a respectful première presentation, with reviews not only in the *Daily Worker*, but often in the *Times* and other metropolitan dailies. Under Ben Irwin, who became National Secretary in 1937, the New York office of the League became a theatrical producer, choosing the right troupe for each play. Programs and fliers of many New Theater Nights of the late thirties carried the legend "Presented by the New Theater League," though the company performing on the particular occasion was the "Let Freedom Ring" Company, the Brookwood Labor Players, or a lesser affiliate. With the demise in 1936 of the Theater of Action and the Theater Collective and in 1937 of the Theater Union, taking on the role of producer no doubt seemed a particularly urgent duty. It was a kind of task that gave the League something, however faint, of the aspect of a quite ordinary production office. The League was not on or *of* Broadway, but it was as busy with publicity and as much concerned with bookings as any Broadway producer—so much is clear from the organization's press releases. Still another way in which the League began to reveal a touch of Broadway in its soul lay in its new interest in musicals and three-act plays. If, as we have noted, agitprop came to Broadway toward the end of the 1934–35 season with the production of *Lefty* and *Panic*, with these new developments of the late thirties leftist agitational drama began to take on the look of the commercial Broadway product. Its themes, however, remained what they had always been: expressions of the propaganda line of the moment, with the specific problems of trade unions the leading issue. Apart from Stoller and Siegmeister's *Maid in Japan*, all the three-act plays and musicals of the League dealt primarily with the struggle to organize.

The "full-length" plays entering the League's repertory or achieving production on a New Theater Night were very few, since clearly such works with their expensive royalties and rounded parts were beyond the financial and technical resources of amateurs. Nor were these plays of notable artistic value. The first long play advertised in the repertory in the late thirties was Doris Yankauer and Herbert Mayer's *Question Before the House,* a work which originated in the Experimental Theater of Vassar College. Like Flanagan and Clifford's *Can You Hear Their Voices?*, it is concerned with the participation of privileged youth in a political and social struggle—in this instance, an industrial strike. Advertised as the first full-length play to be offered on a New Theater Night was Jerome Brookman and Stedman Coles's *Press Time*, which the League presented on November 27, 1938. A melodrama centered in a steel strike, it has as protagonist a liberal newspaper publisher who decides at great risk to take the strikers' part.[53]

Though no less thin and ephemeral than these contentious expressions of middle-class solidarity with labor, Charles Shillet and I. J. Alexander's *Professional Men* had the distinction of becoming the first and only full-length play to be published under the League's own imprint. In praising the authors and the League alike for their accomplishment, Ben Irwin in a brief introduction declared that it was also the first printed play dealing with the unionization of white-collar workers to be published by *any* organization. And in this he was right, though his tacit praise of the play, which is merely an uncomfortably long melodrama, could be disputed. Concerning the effort of the CIO to organize pharmacists and all other drugstore workers, the play was first performed on June 7, 1939, by members of the Retail Drug Store Employees Union.[54] The authors' message is that unionism is for all classes, not merely such un- or semi-skilled workers as janitors, soda jerks, and tobacco clerks, but even college-bred pharmacists, who consider themselves to be members of a learned profession. To make their point, Shillet and Alexander offered scenes of a strike that takes place after the supervisor of a drug store fights with higher management to protect one of his browbeaten workers who belongs to the CIO local. The owners hope to save the company union and prevent the establishment of a closed shop. Not a sound play, even if taken at the low level of melodramatic conflict between men of good will and invincibly ignorant villains, it differs from the average Popular Front stage work only in its length. "By golly," says a customer to the store's tobacconist after the strike, "I didn't think you had it in you. Just for that I got to celebrate. I'm buying a pipe! . . . Let's see. I'd want one to celebrate winning a strike. Let me have a corn-cob! Good old-fashioned a hundred percent American corn-cob!" (III, iii).

With most of its musical discoveries the League left no mark on the theater. *Maid in Japan* was promptly forgotten, though Elie Siegmeister was to become a well-known, if minor, composer of serious music. Equally unmemorable was *Pink Slips on Parade*, a revue with music principally by Earl Robinson, assembled with the purpose of protesting the wave of firings in the Federal Theater Project following a congressional cut of funds in the fall of 1936. The revue was offered by the League on January 31, 1937, with a cast of Project workers. A cantata titled *Life in a Day of a Secretary*, with book by Alfred Hayes and Jay Williams and music by George Kleinsinger, was produced by the League on June 24, 1939, in a performance by the Flatbush Art Players. This work was the winner of the prize offered by the New York Joint Council of the United Office and Professional Workers, a Communist party stronghold, for a short piece on any phase of the life of office workers.[55] The union got for its money a touching pastiche of solos, duets, and choral passages on the grueling, unfulfilling daily routine of the typical office girl, but not a work destined for repeated performances. One musical work first publicized by the League did, however, outlive the decade: Marc Blitzstein's *The Cradle Will Rock*. The original production of this long one-act piece whose first performance, like that of *Waiting for Lefty*, was fated to pass into the realm of theatrical legend, opened on June 16, 1937. It was an event more important to the history of the Federal Theater and the Mercury Theater than to that of the League and will be recounted in its proper place. But the play was nevertheless a League play, having been awarded the League's major prize for 1937.

Blitzstein was recognized as a serious composer with a penchant for theater before submitting his work to the League and had received praise for his short comic-opera, *Triple Sec*. In *The Cradle Will Rock* he created what was in fact a short opera with references in the music to such popular forms as the blues, jazz (or, more accurately, swing), and the pop ballad. Structurally, the work is related, as the Brecht scholar John Willett has shown, to the didactic chamber operas, many of which were intended for children, that became a part of the annual chamber music festival originated by leading modernist German composers in 1921 and held first at Donaueschingen, later at Baden Baden.[56] Later American works in the tradition of the festival, in addition to *The Cradle Will Rock*, were Aaron Copland's *The Second Hurricane* (1937; an opera for high school students originally directed by Orson Welles), Blitzstein's *I've Got the Tune* (1938) and *No for an Answer* (1941), Kleinsinger's above-mentioned *Life in a Day of a Secretary*, and Leonard Bernstein's *Trouble in Tahiti* (1952)—short works with distinct social messages of varying degrees of urgency.

For Blitzstein, who rarely composed without being mindful of social or political themes, the issue of union organization became in *The Cradle Will Rock* the vehicle for a dryly comic satire on the upper middle class, as well as a poignant plea in behalf of the poor and unprotected. The setting is Steeltown, U.S.A., which is run by the all-important Mr. Mister, with its social tone set by his wife, Mrs. Mister. These two are the parents of a boy and a girl, Brother Mister and Sister Mister. The names of others in the cast refer to their occupations: Editor Daily, Reverend Salvation, Harry Druggist, and on down through the social classes to Larry Foreman, who as an organizer aids in the planting of "onions"—unions—in the land. Blitzstein has in mind, presumably, as the association behind Larry, the Steel Workers Organizing Committee, intrepid men of the CIO who planted the union firmly in U.S. Steel and major "little" steel corporations in the spring of 1937. At the start a comic error occurs when, thinking they are arresting a throng of steelworkers and organizers, the police haul into night court the town's leading figures, who comprise Mr. Mister's Liberty Committee. This granite-hard but foolish group is Blitzstein's travesty of the anti-New Deal American Liberty League, an organization of businessmen established in 1934. As the scenes unfold, the audience is shown how dangerous to true liberty is Mr. Mister's control. The schools, the arts, the church, and the press are all under his thumb, while the leading lights of these institutions over which he holds sway disclose their venality in comic but pointed language. Blitzstein's music moves along with a memorable acidity that is occasionally relieved by melody, as in the prostitute's "Nickel Under Your Heel," the Mister children's "Spoon" and "Honolulu," and Mrs. Mister's "Hard Times."

The relation of the work to the more obvious varieties of agitprop is shown in the language and action of Larry Foreman, Blitzstein's most firmly realized character. A Popular Front protagonist insofar as he is genial, all-American, and propertied, he takes over the work at its conclusion in the familiar fashion of the "Young Leader." With an air of indomitability and much good-natured ebullience, he admits in court, after being worked over by the police, "Now I know what the dirty foreigners feel like." He insists that he and those in his union are as representative of the nation as the Liberty Committee: "We got a committee, too, farmers and city people, doctors, lawyers, newspapermen, even a couple of poets—and one preacher. We're middle class, we all got property—we also got our eyes open" (scene vii). Hearing, toward the close, that despite police threats the workers of Steeltown are on the march, he sings a final song that stops just short of urging revolution:

> That's thunder, that's lightning,
> And it's going to surround you!
> No wonder those stormbirds
> Seem to circle around you . . .
> Well, you can't climb down, and you can't sit still;
> That's a storm that's going to last until
> The final wind blows . . . and when the wind blows . . .
> The cradle will rock.

Commenting on his play in a *Daily Worker* article, Blitzstein observed that it was "only incidentally about unions." More important, he believed, was the view he had revealed of the middle class: "I mean the intellectuals, professionals, small shop-keepers, 'little businessmen' in the America of today." Such people "must sooner or later see that there can be allegiance only to the future, not the past; that the only sound loyalty is the concept of work, and to a principle which makes honest work at least true, good and beautiful." [57] Evidently that principle was to be found in Marxism.

In a second radical work, *I've Got the Tune*, composed for radio and broadcast in 1937, but given theatrical performances in 1938 and 1939, Blitzstein wrote about a man whose profession was the same as his own. Mr. Musiker has composed a tune, but can't find the words to go with it. He listens to the chatter of Madame Arbutis and her guests on Park Avenue and to the rant of the fascist Purple Shirties at their meeting in the woods, but what they say will not fit his music. Nor can he find what he wants on the air, in the movies, in Tin Pan Alley, or in ethnic chants and lullabyes. At last, however, he hears it in the uplifting language of young people marching in a May Day parade.

In 1938 the New York May Day Parade, a traditional annual show of solidarity, included a delegation from the New Theater League, as had others before it. In praise of unionism, on this occasion the League marchers adapted a song from Walt Disney's *Snow White and the Seven Dwarfs:*

It's not so hard—
Get a union card
And whistle while you work! [58]

It was their peak year. True, the League's new experimental quarterly, *Theatre Workshop*, had vanished after the fifth number, and the
old monthly magazine was no more. But the school was doing well
and the repertory was thick with actable plays. Moreover, before the
year was out a new monthly, *New Theatre News*, was to begin publication; though intended only as an information bulletin for the affiliates, not as a general theater journal for the public, it was evidence of
continuing vigor. Unhappily, however, this was also the last full year
of the League's respectability—though, not having the confidence of
Soviet diplomats, the members were in no position to know it.

Concurrently with the broadening of the theatrical activities of Communist and "fellow-traveller" troupes in the Popular Front era, respect for the film as both an art form and a medium of propaganda
flourished on the Left. *New Theatre*, which from the first issue had
devoted ample space to films, was the chief organ of criticism of the
medium as well as the sternest watchdog of the Hollywood film-
making hierarchy. Approximately a third of the contents of every issue was given over to reviews of films by Robert Stebbins,[59] profiles
of directors and performers thought to hold "progressive" views, including men of such dissimilar opinions as John Ford, James Cagney,
and Charlie Chaplin, and attacks on men known *not* to have progressive views, such as Louis B. Mayer and Eddie Cantor, complaints
against censorship and the power over Hollywood exercised by the
Catholic Church, and exposés, comic in some instances, of studio labor practices. Antilabor films, such as *Riff Raff*, a Jean Harlow vehicle
produced by Metro-Goldwyn-Mayer, were the principal targets of
Stebbins's criticism; among other films of which he disapproved were
those glorifying the armed services, such as the same studio's *Ship-
mates Forever*. Imported Russian films received thorough coverage as
a matter of course. Though, as noted above, the League was forced to
suspend publication of the magazine (then titled *New Theatre and
Film*) in 1937, in the following year the magazine *TAC* came into ex-

istence, and Stebbins joined it as film reviewer. Other publications of
the party and organizations close to it also maintained an eager interest in film. Under the signature of Robert Forsythe, the pseudonym of
Kyle Crichton, reviews appeared regularly in the *New Masses;* beginning in April 1936 *Fight Against War and Fascism* also published a
page on film. The *Daily Worker,* striving to lessen its sectarian tone
in the Popular Front era, sought to lure readers with stills and analyses of Hollywood trends. In two noteworthy essays David Platt, the
paper's leading film critic, analyzed Hollywood's attitude toward the
American Indian, inquiring why in westerns the Indian was invariably the villain.[60] It was presumed by the editors of all these publications that their readers, precisely like the readers of the liberal and
conservative press, were enthusiastic film-goers. Though the critics
lionized outspoken liberals and leftists in the film industry, they were
eminently fair to nonpolitical artists, sharing their readers' enjoyment
of Astaire and Rogers, Garbo, Cary Grant, and Katharine Hepburn,
among top performers.

The long-established Film and Photo League, a counterpart to the
New Theater League, continued its work of exhibiting the films and
still photographs of members and commercial films of approved social
content, and operating a school of photography. In 1935 members of
the Film and Photo League and Nykino founded the New Film Alliance for the production, distribution, and exhibition of special films.
A Hollywood-based group, American Labor Films, came into being
in 1936, its membership, according to *New Theatre and Film,* being
made up of "sincere" studio employees who were willing to give up
their spare time to make a film; the result was a twenty-minute picture titled *Millions of Us.*[61]

Paul Strand, Ralph Steiner, and Leo Hurwitz, the best-known of
the radical film-makers, were for a brief time in the middle of the decade the employees of the federal government. (Strand had also made
a film titled *Redes*—"nets"—for the Mexican government on coastal
fishermen, released in the United States as *The Wave* in 1936). The
three photographers were approached in 1935 by Pare Lorentz to
write the script and man the cameras for *The Plow That Broke the
Plains,* a documentary on the Midwestern dust bowl commissioned by
the Resettlement Administration, which was attempting to provide
homes for farm families suffering not only from economic disaster but

from the blows of rampaging nature. They accepted the offer, but found the work uncongenial, for Lorentz thought the political messages of their script too strong and insisted upon alterations. To Peter Ellis, writing in *New Theatre* after the picture was released in 1936, the results were disappointing. Where, he wanted to know, was the sequence described in the original script as follows:

> Great herds are driven in on the range. Countless heads of cattle feed on a sea of grass. Steers grow fat. The cattlemen grow rich. The range is free. More ranchers drive in their herds. The herds increase. Scramble for water rights and control of range, and speculation in cattle. More stock men! Each after what he can get—no responsibility to safeguard the great resources—the grass.[62]

In 1937 Nykino was superseded by Frontier Films, founded by Strand, Hurwitz, John Howard Lawson, Robert Stebbins and others, but without Ralph Steiner, who in the experience of making *The Plow That Broke the Plains* had been put off by his fellow-cameramen's politics. Among the members of the board were Kyle Crichton, Elia Kazan, and Philip Stevenson. Frontier's pictures included *Heart of Spain; The World Today,* a news film begun by Nykino; *Return to Life,* also on Spain; *People of the Cumberland,* on Tennessee coal miners, *China Strikes Back,* and *Native Land,* on civil liberties. Herbert Kline, formerly of *New Theatre,* worked on both the Spanish films and went on to a career as an independent producer with *Crisis,* on the nazi invasion of Czechoslovakia; *Lights Out in Europe,* on the outbreak of the Second World War; and other films in the postwar years. Steiner established a new company, American Documentary Films, with Oscar Serlin and Willard Van Dyke, which in 1939 produced *The City,* on city planning, with a script by Lorentz.[63]

Of the documentary films on Spain, that in which leftist groups and their supporters took greatest interest was *The Spanish Earth,* produced in 1937 by the Dutch Communist documentarian Joris Ivens, with commentary written and spoken by Ernest Hemingway and music, based on traditional Spanish tunes, by Virgil Thomson and Marc Blitzstein. At the time the war erupted, Ivens was at work on a film project of the Rockefeller Foundation in New York, having come to America at the invitation of the New Film Alliance. After observing the work of a colleague, Helen van Dongen, as she pieced together

from newsreel clips a picture called *Spain in Flames,* Ivens conceived
the notion of going to Spain to make an original film, a task that he
thought would be both easier and cheaper to carry out than assem-
bling a film from ready-made material. Archibald MacLeish formed a
company called Contemporary Historians to back Ivens in this project.* Hemingway, who also provided the commentary for *Spain in
Flames,* set out with him to shoot footage of the fighting. The plan
was to show the political events that had taken place since the abdication of King Alfonso, demonstrating that the government and its
fighting force represented a united front of workers, farmers, and intellectuals who wished to right the social injustices perpetrated under
the monarchy. In the scenes of battle, the arms, troops, and advisers
supplied by Germany and Italy were pointedly brought within the
camera's range. Orson Welles, rapidly gaining prominence as a Popular Front culture hero as a result of his work for the Federal Theater
and Mercury Theater, originally recorded Hemingway's commentary,
and his voice was heard in the White House when a print of the film
was screened for President and Mrs. Roosevelt in July 1937. But the
voice seemed wrong to Ivens, and it was decided that Hemingway
himself should record the commentary. In June 1937 both Ivens and
Hemingway addressed the second American Writers' Congress, and
Ivens showed two sequences of his picture. In the following year, to
build up public sympathy for the beleaguered Chinese, Ivens made a
film in China, eventually released as *The 400,000,000.* Backing for this
venture was solicited by Luise Rainer, then the wife of Clifford Odets
and acclaimed for her performance as a Chinese wife and mother in
the film version of Pearl Buck's *The Good Earth.*[64]

Like the New Theater League, the New Dance League curbed its sectarian ardor in the Popular Front years and surrendered to the new
enthusiasm for productions reflecting, not the viewpoint of the working-class revolutionary, but the attitudes comfortable to both the left
and the center of all social classes. Vestiges of the old narrowness

* Among those joining MacLeish in the project were John Dos Passos, Dashiell
Hammett, Lillian Hellman, Ernest Hemingway, Dorothy Parker, and Herman
Shumlin.

were still detectable on occasion—for example, in performances of Sophie Maslow's *Two Songs about Lenin,* Jane Dudley's *Song for Soviet Youth Day,* and Miriam Blecher's *Poland—In the Shop*—but the dancers succeeded in expunging from their work the calisthenic revolutionary gestures that had helped to characterize it in the Third Period. After the Seventh World Congress of the Comintern, Doris Humphrey and Charles Weidman might title a work *With My Red Fires,* but with the intention of suggesting only the intensity of the pursuit of love, not a means of laying waste to capitalist institutions. Such danced depictions of romantic passion appeared frequently on recital programs. Other works incorporated elements of ethnic or regional dances or provided a presentation in dance of social questions of broad appeal; with these the dancers offered a choreographic equivalent of socialist realism. Spain, needless to say, was a popular subject, not only newsworthy, but permitting the use of attractively exotic rhythms and movements; among the dances inspired by the Loyalist cause were Lily Mehlman's *No Pasarán,* Dudley and Maslow's *Women of Spain,* Blecher's *Advance Scout—Lincoln Battalion,* and Martha Graham's *Deep Song* and *Immediate Tragedy (Dance of Dedication).* Neutral, nonpolitical titles were sometimes used for dances on themes of general social relevance, as with Tamiris's *Momentum,* on unemployment, class tensions, the American Legion, and the Black Legion, and Weidman's *Atavisms,* on hysteria at the department store bargain counter, the Stock Exchange, and a benighted place called Lynchtown.

Many of the new dances appealing to the taste for socialist realism reflected the American scene, past as well as present, and proclaimed the fact in their titles. Three short dances devised by Doris Humphrey in 1938, "Death of the Hero," "Dance for the Living," and "Fourth of July," comprised a work entitled *American Holiday.* In 1936 Charles Weidman created *American Saga,* on the legend of Paul Bunyan. Martha Graham, having produced an *American Provincials* in 1934 and a *Frontier—An American Perspective of the Plains* in early 1935, produced an *American Lyric* in 1937 and an *American Document* in 1938. The last-named was a dance history of the nation with suggestions of the minstrel show in its design. The episodes, introduced and concluded by a "Walkaround" for the company, bore the titles "Declaration," "Indian Episode," "Puritan Episode," and "After Piece"—the last being an attempt to elucidate the meaning of Americanism and democracy.

Though her company included Sophie Maslow, Anna Sokolow, Miriam Blecher, and others who as soloists and choreographers were members of the New Dance League and its major New York component, the New Dance Group, Graham herself was never on record as a member of the League. As the content of her work reveals, however, she was as much moved as the League members by the social issues of the Popular Front era—in particular, the defense of American democracy and the deepening threat of war. In the cooperative spirit of the day, she occasionally gave her talents to causes endorsed by the Left. In December 1935, for example, she performed with other dancers in a recital to benefit the International Labor Defense, and in October 1938 she danced *American Document* at a *New Masses* benefit. The union, temporary but poignant, of a dance in praise of American democracy and a magazine championing the Communist party was a high point in Popular Front history.[65]

With the development of an audience for modern dance, criticism in the leftist press became increasingly professional. Though political content often received greater emphasis than form, the time had passed when Mike Gold could admonish the dancers on their politics and expect to be taken seriously. Monthly reviews by Edna Ocko of performances and essays by Ocko and others on trends and personalities in the dance appeared in *New Theatre* and later in *TAC*, which Ocko edited. Among the specific issues of importance to commentators were two concerning nazi Germany: the modern dancers' decision to boycott the 1936 Olympics, held in Berlin; and the regrettable news that Mary Wigman, the internationally renowned teacher of the dance, had made an accommodation with the nazi government. Ocko's criticism of the dancers was far from reverential. In complaining of the murky obscurantism of many emotionally charged dances, she revealed a lingering commitment to Third-Period policy. "Is there no choreographer," she asked in April 1936,

> who can take the courtroom, the jury, the lawyer, the witness stand, and create significant dance theatre? The Scottsboro trial, the Dimitroff trial, the trial of any worker on a frame-up charge, the "trials" of

financial magnates, even the judgments rendered outside of court-
rooms, such as the trial Southern mobs give innocent Negroes—all are
within the province of dancing.[66]

Another sort of complaint, that of the common man in the audience,
was expressed in *TAC* almost three years later by John Latouche in
the form of a dancer's New Year's resolution:

> The first thing I'm going to shelve is
> My dark, dismal dancing chemise;
> No more will I leap with my pelvis
> At an angle of sixty degrees.
> I might even rouge my knees . . .[67]

As a headquarters for the dancers and their troupes, the New
Dance League maintained a school, published a bulletin, and, taking
a cue from the leftist writers, organized a Dance Congress. At this
event, which occurred in May 1936, it was reported that the League's
membership had reached two thousand. In the following year the
League joined with the Dancers' Association and the Dance Guild to
form the American Dance Association, with Tamiris as the first president. Most of the membership of this organization was soon absorbed
into the dance division of the Federal Theater Project, for the development and success of which Tamiris was largely responsible. The
New Dance Group, however, in which Sokolow, Maslow, Dudley,
Mehlman, and Blecher were active, continued its existence, its studio
flourishing as late as the seventies.[68]

In the final years of the Depression, as Broadway began to regain the
allure and flair for which it had been famous before the Crash, the
Theater Arts Committee came into glittering life. However praiseworthy, from the vantage point of the Left, were such major Communist
instruments as the American League Against War and Fascism, the
National Negro Congress, the International Labor Defense, and the
American Student Union for their success in drawing disparate elements of the population into party-sponsored causes, or such lesser
ones as the Friends of the Abraham Lincoln Brigade, the League of
Women Shoppers, or the Jimmy Collins Flying Club for their

steadfastness—however praiseworthy were these and scores of others, something special could be claimed for TAC that these workaday fronts conspicuously lacked. This specialness was glamor. Perhaps the Hollywood Anti-Nazi League and the Motion Picture Artists Committee had a touch of the same quality, but only TAC could summon such celebrities as Mayor Fiorello H. LaGuardia, Ethel Waters, W. C. Handy, and the leading actors of the Group Theater to a dinner to honor Marian Anderson; could dispatch Marc Blitzstein, Lillian Hellman, Artie Shaw, and Tamiris to Washington in the causes of peace and adequate salaries for Federal Theater workers; could bring together Cary Grant, Vera Zorina, John Garfield, Jack Benny, Paul Muni, Sidney Kingsley, Dorothy Parker, and Raymond Massey in behalf of refugee aid; or could persuade Helen Hayes to head a milk fund for Spanish children and could enroll as her assistants Brooks Atkinson, Ben Hecht, Burns Mantle, Clifford Odets, and Orson Welles.[69]

A typical Popular Front organization in the breadth of its base, its optimism, and its energy, TAC was established in the spring of 1937. Its founders were members of the company of John Howard Lawson's *Marching Song*, the last play to be produced by the Theater Union. Their purpose was to find ways of raising money for Republican Spain. At the apartment of Hester Sondergaard plans were drawn up for a Theater People's Rally for Spain, and a permanent association was formed with Sondergaard as the Executive Secretary and the backing of executive and advisory boards.* The original name chosen by Sondergaard and her associates was the Theater Committee to Aid Spanish Democracy. But in the spring of 1938, after a year of activity, the name was changed to Theater Arts Committee and the infinitive phrase concerning aid to Spain was dropped as a sign that the Committee wished to aid in the fight against right-wing forces, not only in Spain, but in all other trouble spots. At that point in its history TAC

---

* The members of these boards included Howard Bay, Adelaide Bean, Robert Benchley, Marc Blitzstein, Morris Carnovsky, Harold Clurman, e. e. cummings, Jane Dudley, Hanns Eisler, Angna Enters, John Garfield, Lillian Hellman, John Houseman, Doris Humphrey, Fred Keating, Lincoln Kirstein, Arthur Kober, John Howard Lawson, Edna Ocko, Herman Shumlin, Lee Simonson, Donald Ogden Stewart and his wife (the former Ella Winter), Paul Strand, Kurt Weill, and Orson Welles, among others. Bean, Enters, and Shumlin, it will be recalled, had served on the short-lived Theater Committee for the Defense of the Spanish Republic.

had grown large. In August 1938 it was able to boast of a membership nearing a thousand "and growing daily," and by November of the same year it was able to muster more than three thousand signatures to a telegram to President Roosevelt requesting that he protest to Hitler against the new wave of German anti-Semitic measures. TAC's leaders declared that the *"most important, most basic issue of the day is the defense of Spain"* still, but at the same time, they took up all the additional causes supported by the older party fronts. That TAC itself was a Party front may not have been apparent to its many famous members and fellow travelers at first, but after August 22, 1939, no one could have been left in doubt about the matter.[70]

The appeal of TAC to the public lay in the enthusiasm and expertise demonstrated by the members as they went about the business of publicizing their work, and in the very nature of the work as well. TAC members did not raise money merely by pleading with the wealthy for contributions, but by giving their best as entertainers and writers. After the first year the organization had film, radio, and dance contingents, as well as a devoted group of Broadway actors willing and able to put in appearances at Madison Square Garden rallies for aid to refugees, at gala all-star benefits for Spain at the Mecca Temple, at summertime frolics on the roof of the Ziegfeld Theater, at Christmas-tree lighting ceremonies in Times Square. For a maximum of $2.20 or as little as fifty-five cents, the "hep" Manhattanite could watch Gypsy Rose Lee do a number called "I'll Bare All for the Dies Committee." For only a quarter he could light a Christmas tree bulb on Broadway in the living presence of the no-longer anathematized Eddie Cantor. Quite obviously, TAC's leaders gave good value for the contributions they collected.[71]

They also gave good publicity to those who lent their names and talents to TAC causes. In July 1938 the organization began the publication of a monthly magazine richly illustrated with photographs of stars and theatrical hopefuls who in behalf of antifascist and civil-libertarian causes were gathered over food and drinks, singing and dancing at rallies, or standing on the steps of Washington-bound planes. Since the causes were not strictly Stalinist, but, on the contrary, lay well within the compass of interests of any liberal, it was easy enough for TAC to draw in hundreds of theater workers with the promise of publicity. In the fall of 1938 TAC opened, as another ser-

vice to members, a Theater Arts Center on West 48th Street to provide a kind of clubhouse for performers, where they could drop in to
read, have a snack, or recover from the fatiguing task of making the
rounds of producers' offices.[72] *

Though jauntier than *New Theatre*, *TAC* magazine was a seriously
intended periodical, logging the activities of the organization and reviewing the new plays, films, dance recitals, and radio programs to
signal out, as *New Theatre* had done, the best work of party members
and other progressive producers and performers. Its tone was primarily breathy and Winchellesque, as though the writers took for granted
an intimacy and mutuality of purpose with their readers. A Hollywood correspondent offered news of the Motion Picture Artists Committee, and reports by Jay Allen, Alvah Bessie, and others filled in the
readers on events at the Spanish front. Because Popular Front
policy-makers wished to encourage the American arts, essays on
swing and jazz also appeared, with a glance at the Bahamas and their
calypso music. *New Theatre*, having been aimed primarily at union
and other working-class theater enthusiasts, and expecting to find few
readers among the fans of Broadway, had not allowed so much suav-
ity and breeziness in its pages. But *TAC*, coming after the suspension
of *New Theatre*, was emblematic of the Popular Front at its most
popular. It sought advertising, not only from other party journals and
fronts, but from custom tailors.

Of all the organization's multifarious activities, the most appealing
of all was Cabaret TAC, an attempt to establish in New York the
kind of political cabaret that had long flourished in Central Europe.
Presumably, one impulse behind the attempt was the arrival in New
York of victims of nazi purges who in Berlin, Vienna, or Prague had
taken part in such performances. Both *New Theatre* and *TAC*, reporting on the European cabarets, built up enthusiasm for this kind of
theater. Also contributing to the enthusiasm was the presence, at last,
of some loose change in the nation's pockets and pocketbooks. On
May 5, 1938, at a nightclub on East 55th Street called Chez Fire-
house, Cabaret TAC made its debut. Manngreen of the *Daily Worker*

---

* Aiding the TAC staff in this new and attractive service was a board of advisers
whose names must have had strong appeal to young hopefuls: Harold Clurman,
Francis Edwards Faragoh, Hallie Flanagan, Will Geer, Martha Graham, Hanya
Holm, Elia Kazan, Sidney Kingsley, Joseph Losey, Lee Strasberg, Sylvia Sydney,
and Margaret Webster.

grew ecstatic over the event: "It's gone and happened. People everywhere in the progressive, audacious and outspoken theatre had talked
about it for so long and given it so much private thought that many
had given up believing it would ever come to pass. But it's here: the
social-minded nightclub, the political cabaret." This was a late-eve-
ning entertainment, beginning at midnight, and none too inexpensive.
Admission was $1.10, with drinks and food extra—a bit steep; as a
New Masses writer observed, "The admission is too high . . . and the
hour too late. Only the plutocracy who don't need to get up for work
in the morning can go." [73] Nevertheless, the Cabaret was a success,
and performances were given intermittently on East 55th Street and
in other Manhattan localities for the better part of two years (some
with a lower admission fee and most at earlier hours).

An improving economy and the liberal political climate of the city
helped Cabaret TAC to achieve its success, but without the writing
and performing talent that went into it, it could not have held its
public so firmly. Under the direction of Adelaide Bean (with the assistance of George Abbott at one dress rehearsal) the Cabaret started
out in high spirits, and successive shows maintained the original liveliness. For the opening, Herman Wouk attacked both serious and
nonserious topics in skits entitled "Berlin Broadcast" and "Gone with
the Movie Rights," Emanuel Eisenberg and Jay Williams offered a
parody of the Federal Theater's Living Newspaper titled "One Third
of a Mitten" that was funny enough to be bought by the Federal
Theater itself for a revue, and Harold Rome offered a song called
"One Big Union for Two" that was later to prove a hit in the revue
Pins and Needles. Other writers for this and later editions included
Max Liebman, Kenneth White, and Earl Robinson. A progressive version of the old German rhyming song "Schnitzelbank" was a favorite
number, with slashing references to the Nazis, the dictatorial Mayor
Hague of Jersey City, Generalissimo Franco, and other enemies to
peace and civil liberty. At the opening night the master of ceremonies
was Fred Keating. On later occasions the job was given to Lief Erick-
son, Donald Ogden Stewart, and—the most popular of all—Hiram
Sherman, a witty young member of the Mercury Theater. Among the
many performers who appeared with these M. C.'s over the months of
the Cabaret's existence were Imogene Coca, Frances Farmer, Joey
Faye, Will Geer, June Havoc, Beatrice Kay, Lionel Stander, and
Charles Weidman.[74]

Music was an important element in the performances, with major hits registered by Beatrice Kay in "Picket-Line Priscilla" and "Mama," both by Saul Aarons and Mike Stratton. After the Munich Conference and the consequent partition of Czechoslovakia, a number introduced with success was Tolbie Sacher and Lewis Allan's "Chamberlain Crawl," whose lyrics in part ran,

> First you bow and then you sit,
>   next you do the Munich split;
> Then you stand with your hand up,
>   Doing the Chamberlain crawl.
> First you pirouette around,
>   then you grovel on the ground;
> It's gemutlich if you bootlick
>   Doing the Chamberlain Crawl.
> It's known in the Wilhemstrasse
>   as "diplomacy—first classe,"
> With a "hip-hooray" and "a let's appease"
>   Let Daladier do his striptease.
> It will turn out all right,
>   British honor still is bright;
> Let us revel with dear Neville,
>   Doing the Chamberlain crawl.[75]

For ballast there were also Earl Robinson's ballads of Joe Hill and Abraham Lincoln, both of which achieved wide popularity, and Kenneth White's "Speak Our Word," with which the audience was reminded by direct address of Nazi brutality and the American citizen's obligation to protest against it:

You've seen Fredric March knock Carole Lombard around. You've seen James Cagney push a grapefruit into a girl's face. You've seen it all in the movies. So you're immune. But you're not immune to the word. There's a living horror in the word "pogrom." And there is living strength in the words of President Roosevelt, "I would not have believed such things could happen in a twentieth century civilization!" [76]

Cabaret TAC's good attendance, favorable reviews, and equally favorable word-of-mouth publicity resulted in a vogue for such entertainment in New York and other cities. Hollywood as a matter of course responded with a revue called *Sticks and Stones,* produced by MPAC in August of 1938. This organization was able to call upon artists better known than most of those who went to work for Cabaret TAC, though not necessarily more talented. For an admission fee of ten dollars, the audience from the well-paid film colony was offered Lionel Stander, Milton Berle, Bert Lahr, Jerry Colonna, and several lesser lights in comic sketches on strikes, dictatorships, and the studio story conference, an old spiritual updated as "Swing Left, Sweet Chariot," Robinson's "Joe Hill," and a new ballad about Spain. In the spring of 1939 the Hollywood Theater Alliance, a group sponsored by, among others, Ira Gershwin, Lillian Hellman, Dashiell Hammet, Langston Hughes, Arthur Kober and Donald Ogden Stewart, launched itself with a revue that included skits on the Dies Committee, Chamberlain, and other menaces of the moment. Early in 1939 in the capital city the Washington Political Cabaret, TAC-patterned and pro-New Deal, offered such numbers as "Girl Meets Boycott" and "Swing into Action." The *New Masses,* proving itself open to Popular Front suggestion and outraged by the outcome of the Munich Conference, tentatively launched the Keynote Theater for a few performances in March 1939, enlisting the writing skills of John Latouche and Sylvia Fine and the performing skills of, among others, Danny Kaye and Irwin Corey for numbers titled "Vultures of Culture," "Down on Downing Street," "Cliveden Keeps Cool," and "Thank God for the Atlantic and Pacific." The magazine also sponsored, on January 11, 1938, an evening of music and dance advertised as *Hitting a New High*—a title taken without blush from the jargon of Wall Street—that included Blitzstein's *I've Got the Tune,* Copland's *The Second Hurricane,* nonoperatic compositions by Alex North, Carlos Chavez, Wallingford Riegger, and Virgil Thompson, songs sung by Mordecai Bauman, and jazz played by Count Basie and his band. The evening was repeated on the 27th with Orson Welles taking part. Recognizing jazz as a major American contribution to music, the *New Masses* next sponsored, on December 23, 1938, at Carnegie Hall, the enthusiastically received concert billed as "Spirituals to Swing" which had been organized by John Hammond, Jr., a leading jazz impresario and enthusiast. On Christmas Eve, 1939, a second "Spirituals to Swing" was given, but this time under the aegis of TAC in its last days of glory.[77]

A somewhat different establishment, but very much a part of Popular Front night life, was Café Society, which opened in Greenwich Village on December 18, 1938, and continued in business for the next twelve years. The name of this small night club alluded with mild mockery to the popular newspaper designation for the habituées of such "smart" midtown cafés as "21," the Stork Club, and El Morocco. The club was developed by its proprietor, Barney Josephson, as an oasis in which whites and blacks could mingle comfortably, not only as entertainers, but as patrons. Though Jack Gilford, Jimmy Savo, and other comedians performed there from time to time, Café Society was famous chiefly as a place in which could be heard the best in Dixieland jazz, boogie-woogie, and folk music. With the aid of John Hammond, Jr., Josephson located and hired some of the most gifted, if not in all instances best known, jazz and folk musicians of the day, including Meade "Lux" Lewis, Albert Ammons, Teddy Wilson, Hazel Scott, Mary Lou Williams, Ida Cox, Josh White, Lena Horne, and Billie Holiday. Of lasting memory was the song of a Southern lynching, "Strange Fruit," by the TAC composer Lewis Allan, which Billie Holiday made inimitably and permanently her own. Josephson's Popular Front social consciousness was evident in his choice of decorative details for the club as well as in his choice of entertainment. Behind the bar was a cartoon in oils by Ad Rheinhardt in which were mockingly depicted several assorted symbols of returning affluence, among them a pink elephant, a champagne bucket, a head throbbing with hangover, and a top-hatted gent with a ring through his nose. In magazine advertisements and on the club's matchbook covers was printed the motto "The Wrong Place for the Right People," a phrase tantalizing in its ambiguity. Was it that Café Society was the wrong place for the "Four Hundred," or was it that it was the right place for the left people? No matter—Right and Left jostled elbows companionably in Josephson's crowded club. In 1940 Josephson opened a second establishment, Café Society Uptown, on east 58th Street, maintaining both clubs until 1950, when McCarthyist pressures so undercut their business that he thought it prudent to sell them.[78]

Still another durable product of the Popular Front cabaret theater was the writing and performing team of Betty Comden and Adolph Green, who in 1938 along with Judy Holliday (then Judith Tuvim), Alvin Hammer, and John Frank formed a group called the Revuers.

Their first stage was the floor of the Village Vanguard, a small night club situated, like Café Society, in Greenwich Village. The Revuers as a group did not reflect a specific political point of view, but in the Popular Front progressive vision of American life they found a frame of reference for their sketches. "Not as political as TAC," correctly observed a Winchellesque reporter for *TAC* magazine, "but as satiric about the right things, the show brings celebrities and scouts about town to huzzah and cheer and wonder how Broadway does without them. But it won't be for long as one says·in Hoboken—they have *quelque chose sur la boule.*" [79] Youthful—with Judy Holliday at fourteen the youngest of all—and exuberant with the liberal Jewish élan of the city, the Revuers offered, among other bits, a parody of *Waiting for Lefty,* a sketch about the Un-American Activities Committee called "Never Say Dies," and a sketch titled "The World's Fair is Unfair" presenting the established tourist attractions of New York on strike against the 1939 World's Fair, with Judy Holliday as the Statue of Liberty. For five years the Revuers continued as an act, performing not only in the Vanguard but on radio and in other night clubs, including the Rainbow Room, the large restaurant on the top of the RCA building which in itself became a symbol of New York's night-time elegance at the close of the Depression.[80]

The non-Communist Left, less active in the theater, as always, than the Stalinists, produced only one major stage work during the late thirties: the revue *Pins and Needles,* which opened on November 27, 1937, at Labor Stage, an intimate house formerly known as the Princess Theater. With music and lyrics by Harold Rome and sketches by Rome, Arthur Arent, Marc Blitzstein, Emanuel Eisenberg, Charles Friedman and Daniel Gregory, the revue was presented by Labor Stage, Inc., the theatrical arm of the International Ladies' Garment Workers Union. At first playing only on weekends and attracting no critics to its opening night, the show swiftly built an audience on word of mouth. With frequent revisions of topical material to fit changing events, and with a move in 1938 to the larger Windsor Theater, the union's experiment in popular entertainment played until June 22, 1940, for 1108 performances, a run topped at the time by only one other musical, Ole Olsen and Chick Johnson's *Hellzapoppin'.* With only a few exceptions, the performers came from the ILGWU's locals; they were cutters, pressers, dressmakers, embroiderers, and makers of white goods, knitgoods, and neckwear—and, like their locals, they were a racially integrated cast. Initially they declined to join the stage unions, but in 1938, under pressure, ten principals joined Actors' Equity and others became members of Chorus Equity.[81]

Under its forward-looking president, David Dubinsky, the ILGWU had set up a Dramatics Department as early as 1934 with the hope of persuading other unions to join with it in a consortium for the sponsorship of a professional theater. At first some of the other garment industry unions expressed interest, but ultimately they withdrew their support. Left alone with its plan, the ILGWU decided in 1935 to found an amateur theater for a city-wide audience and allocated $25,000 for the purpose. Labor Stage, Inc., became the name of the organization. Louis Schaffer was put in charge, and a lease was taken on the Princess Theater. The staff, in addition to Schaffer, included Mark Schweid and William Gilman as coordinators of dramatic productions, Sointu Syrjala as designer, and Benjamin Zemach as instructor in dance.

The early activities of Labor Stage amounted to little compared to its successful mounting of *Pins and Needles*. In 1936 the group announced a new-play contest, and in the following year awarded the prize to Francis Edwards Faragoh's *Sunup to Sundown*, a study of inchoate union activity among tobacco workers. Faragoh's first play since *Pinwheel* in 1926, it was produced by D. A. Doran for a run of only 7 performances. On January 17, 1937, the company opened a revival of John Wexley's *Steel*, newly revised, which played for 50 performances in New York, and then, at the suggestion of Clinton S. Golden of the Steel Workers Organizing Committee, toured to Chicago, Youngstown, and Pittsburgh to further the work of the committee. The tour plans were developed, not by Labor Stage alone, but in collaboration with the New Theater League, the Theater Union, Artef, and the United Mine Workers, who shared with ILGWU in the financial backing.

In a sense, Labor Stage was the victim of its own success. Once *Pins and Needles* was launched and attracting an audience, the company had no time for other works. Its staff planned to follow the revue with Sidney Kingsley's *The Outward Room*, but Kingsley decided against the production, thinking the play too difficult for amateurs. The only other work offered by the organization was George

Kleinsinger and Alfred Hayes's Popular Front cantata, *I Hear America Singing*, based on the poetry of Walt Whitman. This was staged at the ILGWU convention of 1940, but was not presented publicly.

Pins and Needles originated in material written by Rome for performance at Green Mansions, a resort in upstate New york. Through Joseph Losey, Rome met Louis Schaffer, who was looking for songs and sketches suitable for presentation by Labor Stage not only at its public theater but at conventions and meetings. When the ILGWU found the material too light-hearted, Schaffer arranged some studio performances in June 1936, with Rome and Earl Robinson supplying the musical accompaniment at two pianos. After these performances, the union had second thoughts about the material. In the summer of 1937 more studio performances were given, after which the decision was made to open the show to the public in the fall.

In content the revue reflected the mood of the day. Labor was rising, unquestionably, and this fact gave cause for optimism on the Left. But it was a qualified optimism, because the process was slow-going, and few unions had such strength or commanded such respect as the ILGWU. There was, moreover, the threat of dual unionism created by the establishment of the CIO under John L. Lewis. (Dubinsky had taken his union from the AFL to the CIO in 1935, but was to lead it back into the AFL in 1938.) Nor could the ILGWU membership ignore the complications of the international scene, implying as they did that no sooner might the worker get his break than he would be sent off to war. Though the tone of many of the show's numbers was wryly satiric, as was traditional in revue, it was poignant in others suggesting that the life of shop and white-collar workers was still one of stringently limited pleasures. The political messages of the lyrics and sketches were solidly those of the Popular Front, decrying the fascist menace and recommending the solidarity of workers. Despite the presence of Communists in Dubinsky's union, Dubinsky himself was an ardent New Dealer, and it was not to be expected that ultraleftism would show itself in an entertainment for which he bore the ultimate responsibility. But because, in any event, organized communism no longer favored ultraleftism, *Pins and Needles* initially received favorable reviews in the party press, apart from the *Daily Worker* critic's objection, after the first studio performance, to Emanuel Eisenberg's "Mother! Let Freedom Wring," a parody of plays by

Bertolt Brecht and Albert Bein that the paper had supported.[82] The drastic change of the party line in 1939, however, brought about a revised revue and new and different notices, as we will see later.

Despite the merits of the show's comic sketches on such topics as Brecht's epic theater, Congressional interference with the Federal Theater, Odets's uninspired *Paradise Lost*, and Mussolini's encouragement of a population explosion, and the appeal of a *Newsboy*-like dance concerning an immigrant who suffers as an oppressed worker, it was principally Rome's songs that gave *Pins and Needles* its attractiveness. One hit number titled "Nobody Makes a Pass at Me," sung by Millie Weitz of the Dressmakers' Local, demanded sympathy for the working girl who uses the right cosmetics and reads the bestsellers, yet still lacks a love life. Satiric thrusts at the "ruling class" were effectively offered in "It's Not Cricket to Picket," in which a woman of means objects, with rapidly fragmenting language, to strikers picketing with impunity in the streets, and "Doing the Reactionary," a song and dance taught to slumdwellers by a society lady investigating their way of life.[83] In "Chain Store Daisy," sung by Ruth Rubinstein of the Underwear Local, a Vassar graduate bemoaned the fact that, despite the excellence of her education, the only job open to her was a position behind the brassiere and girdle counter at Macy's. "Four Little Angels of Peace," the most political of the hits, provided a jaded view of the pacifist claims of foreign rightist leaders: Hitler, Mussolini, an unnamed Japanese, and, for good measure, Anthony Eden, whose government was attacked as imperialist.

Love songs also had a place in the revue, though none was without its social comment. In one particularly memorable number, "Sing Me a Song with Social Significance," Rome brought off the trick of making fun, not only of love songs, but of the overwrought seriousness of individuals who have no time for them. Another of his love songs took its imagery deftly from the headlines:

> I'm on a campaign to make you mine,
> I'll picket you until you sign,
> In one big union for two.
> No court's injunction can make me stop
> Until your love is all closed shop,
> In one big union for two.

In still other numbers Rome took account of the struggles of young workers to find the time, the money, and the place for the pursuit of love. The best of these, and the only number from *Pins and Needles* to reach the Hit Parade, was the touching "Sunday in the Park," in which the singers bravely maintained that their day off and the place in which they spent it was more satisfactory to them than vacations in the country were to the rich. Possibly more typical of the time, and in its way more moving, was the catchy jitterbug tune "Back to Work," on such an unromantic matter as the successful conclusion of contract negotiations heralding the end of a strike. Mundane as the topic was, Rome caught and demonstrated in his song the workers' pride in having participated in a victorious social action.[84]

The end of the Popular Front era came on August 24, 1939, with the breaking of the news, incredible but undeniable, that in Moscow the foreign secretaries of the U.S.S.R. and Germany had concluded a non-aggression pact. To those Americans who had revered Communist Russia as the ideal society, the treaty was dumbfounding, establishing as it did a Soviet alliance with the political arch enemy and implying Soviet acquiescence in nazi anti-Semitism and territorial ambitions. For party members who, like Mike Gold, had held onto their cards so long and so passionately that they had lost the ability to question Stalin's motives, it was only a matter of time—months, weeks, or days—before they adjusted to the new line, praising Stalin for the "cleverness" of this stroke, which protected Russian boundaries. But for those who, abhorring fascism and sensitive to social ills, had been attracted to the party because of its seemingly firm stand on these issues, the truth was out at last: Communist leaders, in Russia and at home, were willing to surrender any priciple for the furtherance of Soviet foreign policy. Many intellectuals of good will, like Granville Hicks and Malcolm Cowley, left the party. In the press the treaty was referred to scornfully as the "Stalin-Hitler pact." To Jews it may have seemed especially repellent, but they were not alone. With this gesture, Stalin did not kill the party in the United States, but for the time being he deprived it of its prestige, credibility, affluence, and liveliness.

The pact caught both the New Theater League and the Theater Arts Committee unprepared, as it did all other organizations within the party's orbit. But, as with the others, the leaders of both were soon able to subdue whatever emotional violence they may have felt. The League, not having a national publication when the pact was announced, was spared the embarrassment of an ideological about-face between issues. *TAC*, on the other hand, was then appearing at its glossiest and plumpest. The September number had already gone to press by August 24. When issued, it reflected the old line of cold fury against all rightist governments. But with the October issue, the editors, headed by Edna Ocko, had made the necessary adjustment and were ready with an editorial headed "Keep America Out of War." Castigating Chamberlain for his role at Munich and questioning his sincerity in coming to the defense of Poland, the anonymous editorial writer or writers declared of the conflict, "It is *not* a war in defense of democracy, and actors and artists and musicians and their colleagues must firmly resist all attempts to enlist them in a campaign to sell the war to the American people under any such label." [85] Unlike the editors of the *Daily Worker*, the *New Masses*, and the *Communist*, journals obviously linked to the party, the *TAC* staff could not mention Stalin by name or refer to the pact, wishing as they did to preserve the illusion that their journal, though left-wing, was politically independent. But their position was identical with that of their colleagues on the party's central publications: America, they held, must stay out of the war, because her entry on the side of the Allies would pit her, in theory if not in bomb-dropping actuality, against the Russians.

While still hoping to maintain a Popular Front image, *TAC* found it ever harder to do so. The new Popular Front was to consist of all elements in the population opposed to both fascism *and* war. Articles on warmongering newscasters and songwriters filled the pages, and reviews began to have a new tone: not quite, but very nearly, pro-German. Of the British film *Nurse Edith Cavell*, Gordon Sager (replacing Robert Stebbins) observed that it contained "as much pro-British, as much bitter anti-German propaganda as could be packed into ninety-seven minutes." Theater reviews by Eleanor Flexner revealed the same ambiguity—especially the notice of Clare Boothe's antinazi *Margin for Error*. The baldest indication of the die-hards' dilemma to appear in *TAC* was offered by Les Koenig while warming himself for an onslaught against *Beasts of Berlin,* a film on the nazi concentration camps, and *Ninotchka,* Garbo's popular anti-Russian farce. "The world," Koenig noted,

> has rapidly changed since August, 1939, and with its changing, has knocked previous systems of thought into arguments that are deader than the film on the cutting room floor. Where once it was highly desirable to have the screen show the horrors of the Nazi and fascist systems of government, to do so now would be like juggling dynamite. It was considered pro-democratic six months ago to produce *Confessions of a Nazi Spy* or the Soviet film *Professor Mamlock.* Today these pictures would only serve to fan the already anti-German flame of hatred which the Gallup and other public opinion polls reveal exists in the United States.[86]

Various activities of TAC personnel aimed against the Allies in the first winter of the war revealed such steely attachment to the party line that no observer of the Broadway scene could miss it. The Russian invasion of Finland in November 1939 touched and angered American liberals no less than it did American conservatives, and a committee headed by Herbert Hoover sprang into being to raise money for the underpopulated country that had always kept up payments on its debt accrued to America during the First World War. TAC's disapproval of the action in behalf of Finland was heard at once as its members playing in New York and on the road voiced objections to appeals that they give benefit performances and as their leaders issued statements to the press that in their opinion Finland was undemocratic. But these steps were costly. Members both famous and little known resigned *en masse,* and the organization had to change its stationery, giving up the sheets adorned with the names of its illustrious directors of old.[87]

Worse, perhaps, as a sign of loss of support and prestige was the drastic change in the format of *TAC* in January 1940. From an attractively designed, slick-paper publication it shrank to a pedestrian semimonthly newspaper half the size of a tabloid daily. The last number, dated August 1940, was produced by offset from typewritten copy, a sad, shriveled reminder of past glory. On April 14, 1940, Actors' Equity issued a statement forbidding its members to take part in TAC rallies, meetings, and campaigns, and this caused further defections. As exercises in futility, in May the remaining members picketed Robert E. Sherwood's new hit concerning the valorous Finns, *There Shall*

Be No Night, and staged a revival of *Waiting for Lefty* jointly with the New Theater League, in June joined with the moribund League of American Writers to present a symposium "Must We Help Sell the War?," and as late as September gave an antiwar play called *A Piece of Your Mind for Peace.* These activities did not serve to enlarge or preserve the membership, however. In October, marking virtually the last gesture of public awareness of the organization, two Broadway producers, John Golden and Gertrude Macy, put up cards in their offices to notify actors on the rounds that no fascists, Communists, or TAC members need apply for work. But it is doubtful whether, by that time, any remnants existed of what had once been the party's most decorative front.[88]

One target of TAC vituperation during its last months was Labor Stage's Louis Schaffer, who as a socialist bitterly opposed the new line. It was Schaffer who organized the stage division of Hoover's committee. After the signing of the pact, Schaffer began altering the contents of *Pins and Needles* in response to the new international situation, giving the show a pacifist but clearly anti-Stalinist tone. Chamberlain, who after Munich had replaced Eden in "Four Little Angels of Peace," was dropped from the number on September 25, 1939, leaving it with only three angels. But on November 29, for the third "edition" of the show, Chamberlain was brought back and a fifth angel was added—Stalin, much to the horror of the Communist press. At the same time, Schaffer added a new and curious Rome number called "Stay Out, Sammy," in which a mother cautions her young son not to enter a street brawl; clearly this was Labor Stage's plea to Uncle Sam to stay out of the war. In 1940, Schaffer, guided by his own instincts and the views of the large Jewish ILGWU membership, expressed the wish to increase the show's anti-Stalinist content. In this he was opposed, however, by Joseph Schrank, who had contributed skits to the third edition. In what may have been a compromise move, "Stay Out, Sammy" was dropped on June 17, 1940.[89]

Older than TAC, older than Labor Stage, the New Theater League managed to outlast both. Like TAC, it was crippled by the Stalin-Hit-

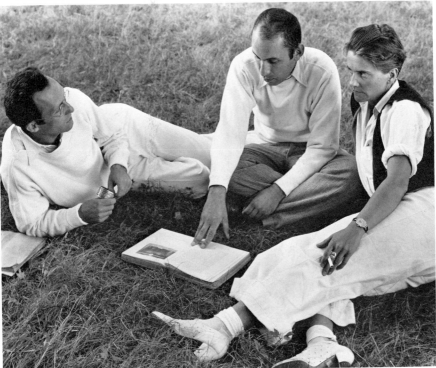

John Dos Passos, *Airways, Inc.* (1929).

Group Theater directors Lee Strasberg, Harold Clurman, and Cheryl Crawford, photographed in 1932 by Ralph Steiner.

Paul Green, *The House of Connelly* (1931); clockwise from left, Eunice Stoddard, Stella Adler, Morris Carnovsky, Mary Morris, Franchot Tone. First production of the Group Theater.

Sidney Kingsley, *Men in White* (1933); operating-room routine as staged by Lee Strasberg.

NEW THEATRE

Harold Clurman, Stella Adler and Clifford Odets working on "Paradise Lost"

JOEL FAITH
ARCHIBALD MacLEISH
JOHN W. GASSNER
DUKE ELLINGTON   DECEMBER 1935 15c

New Theater. Alfredo Valente photograph.

Clifford Odets, *Waiting for Lefty* (1935); Elia Kazan as Agate, with both arms raised.

Clifford Odets, *Golden Boy* (1937); with feet spread, Jules Garfield as Siggie; Luther Adler as Joe Bonaparte, holding violin; at right Frances Farmer as Lorna Moon. Alfredo Valente photograph.

Elmer Rice, *We, the People* (1933); Eleanor Phelps as Helen Davis pleads for her innocent brother's life.

Lillian Hellman, *The Children's Hour* (1934); Anne Revere as Martha Dobie, Katherine Emery as Karen Wright.

Jack Kirkland, *Tobacco Road* (1934); three members of the Lester family: Reneice Rehan as Pearl, Margaret Wycherly as Ada, and Henry Hull as Jeeter.

New Dance Group, *Van der Lubbe's Head* (1934); choreography by Miriam Blecher. Photograph courtesy of George Sklar.

Helen Tamiris and dancers in *How Long Brethren* (1937), choreography by Tamiris; Federal Theater. Dance Collection, New York Public Library at Lincoln Center, Astor, Lenox, and Tilden Foundations.

Paul Peters and George Sklar, *Stevedore* (1934); third from right, Jack Carter as Lonnie Thompson.

Albert Maltz, *Black Pit* (1935); trouble brewing in the West Virginia coal fields.

Sidney Kingsley, *Dead End* (1935); the "Dead End Kids" and, at left, one of their rich neighbors.

Irwin Shaw, *Bury the Dead* (1936); the dead soldiers come out of their grave.

Hallie Flanagan, National Director of the Federal Theater, in a photograph of 1938. Wide World Photos.

Arthur Arent, *One-Third of a Nation* (1938), as staged by the Living Newspaper unit of the Federal Theater in New York City; the spectacular tenement fire at the opening and close of the play.

Sinclair Lewis and John C. Moffitt, *It Can't Happen Here* (1936), as staged by the Suitcase unit of the Federal Theater throughout New York City.

Shakespeare, *Macbeth*, as produced by the Federal Theater's Negro unit in Harlem (1936); the sleepwalking scene with Edna Thomas as Lady Macbeth, Jack Carter (on stairs) as Macbeth.

Shakespeare, *Julius Caesar*, as produced by the Mercury Theater 1937; Orson Welles as Brutus, Joseph Holland as Caesar.

John Steinbeck, *Of Mice and Men* (1937); Broderick Crawford as Lennie, Wallace Ford as George, Claire Luce as Curley's Wife.

The International Ladies' Garment Workers' revue, *Pins and Needles* (1937); "Three Little Angels of Peace": Al Eben as Mussolini, Murray Modick as a Japanese, and Paul Seymour as Hitler.

George S. Kaufman and Moss Hart, *I'd Rather Be Right* (1937); F.D.R. and the Wagner Act: George M. Cohan as President Roosevelt, Jack Reynolds and Sol Black as Hans and Fritz Wagner, Federal Theater Project No. 32468.

Theater Guild Board of Managers, 1927; clockwise from left: Theresa Helburn, Maurice Wertheim, Lee Simonson, Lawrence Langner, Helen Westley, Philip Moeller.

Robert E. Sherwood, *Idiot's Delight* (1936); Alfred Lunt and Lynn Fontanne face the unknown.

Members of the Playwrights' Company: Robert E. Sherwood, S. N. Behrman, Sidney Howard, Maxwell Anderson, Elmer Rice.

Robert E. Sherwood, *Abe Lincoln in Illinois* (1938); Raymond Massey as Lincoln, at close of play, aboard the train for Washington and his first inauguration.

Maxwell Anderson, *Knickerbocker Holiday* (1938); in center, George Watts as Roosevelt, Walter Huston as Pieter Stuyvesant.

At rehearsal of Lillian Hellman's *The Little Foxes* (1939), producer-director Herman Shumlin, playwright Hellman, and star Tallulah Bankhead.

Philip Barry, *The Philadelphia Story* (1939); Tracy Lord and the men in her life: Katharine Hepburn with Frank Fenton, Joseph Cotton, and Van Heflin.

George S. Kaufman and Moss Hart, *The American Way* (1939); the boys come home from the First World War. At left, in black, Florence Eldridge and Fredric March as Irma and Martin Gunther.

ler rapprochement, but not so quickly put out of business. With its school still in existence and its affiliates still to be serviced with new plays, as well as with chestnuts from the repertory, the League held on. Ben Irwin remained at the post of National Secretary, and continuing on hand to assist with publications and the school was Alice Evans, the wife of V. J. Jerome. In Cleveland John E. Bonn set up a second New Theater League School, leaving the New York school, which he had formerly headed, to be directed by Michael Gordon. Beginning early in 1941 the League became decentralized; independent offices were set up in Philadelphia, Chicago, Nashville, and Hollywood, with the New York office functioning as a communications center.[90]

During the pact period, the League maintained close ties with unions known to have a strong Communist membership. Many sent students to the School; among them were the United Federation of Teachers, the Transport Workers Union, the United Office and Professional Workers, and—possibly the most intransigently Stalinist of all—the Furriers.[91] When in June 1940 the League held its biennial convention, dramatic troupes maintained by unions were represented for the first time. Those sending delegates were the New York Cafeteria Employees, the State, County, and Municipal Workers, the Furriers, and—a union which had successfully resisted Communist tactics —the Amalgamated Clothing Workers. At this time the League developed a new attractiveness for black troupes also; the convention was attended by delegates from five of them—four more than ever in the past.

Having suspended *New Theatre News* early in 1939, the League started it up again in November. Mimeographed, apart from two issues produced by photo-offset, the magazine was a rather drab monthly collection of announcements of new repertory items and reports from the affiliates, with only a sprinkling of reviews of Broadway productions to give it life. "Peace . . . it IS wonderful," the editors Ben Irwin and Alice Evans insisted. "Keep America Out of War," "Footlights Across America for Peace," and—a phrase invented by the San Francisco Communist Mike Quin—"The Yanks Are Not Coming" were the new slogans. The July 1940 number carried a "New Theatre Pledge," by the Hollywood screenwriter and novelist Dalton Trumbo which was to be delivered after every performance. "We do not beg for peace like slaves," it read in part, "We do not plead for it like serfs./We command it."

The new additions to the repertory included short plays on unionization and the familiar problems of blacks, a "living newspaper" on the medical profession by Oscar Saul and H. R. Hays, titled *Medicine,* and Earl Robinson and John Latouche's rousing long musical number *Ballad for Americans,* on the religious, ethnic and occupational make-up of the country. But most of the new pieces pressed on the troupes were pacifist plays, all of which were ephemeral. Of particular appeal at the time was the revue *We Beg to Differ,* with sketches by Reuben Shipp and music and lyrics by Reuben Davis and Mel Tolkin, which had been staged in Montreal before coming to the attention of the League. Other revues bore such titles as *Inside America* (with music and lyrics also by Davis and Tolkin), *Peace in Our Time, Before and After,* and *Shake Hands, Brother!* A "peace kit" of various sketches and songs was also available. Among older works, Shaw's *Bury the Dead* was of special value in the promotion of the new line.

A new channel for the New Theater League's energies in the forties was the promotion of folk songs of social protest. In taking up this form of nondramatic entertainment, the League was following in paths opened by TAC and Josephson's Café Society, but proceeding in a way nevertheless its own. In 1940 it published a list of progressive songs, distributed records of Earl Robinson's "Ballad for Americans," "Abe Lincoln," and "Joe Hill," among others, and distributed the sheet music for such antiwar songs as Woody Guthrie's "Why Do You Stand in the Rain?," written for the American Peace Mobilization, and Mike Quin's "The Yanks Are Not Coming." As booking agents for the new, popular group called the Almanac Singers, the League identified itself, not with suavely urbane night-club "acts," but with performers who, though highly professional, projected an air on stage and off of having deliberately chosen purposeful poverty as a way of life, as opposed to show-business affluence and celebrity. The Almanacs, formed in 1941, included at various times Guthrie, Pete Seeger, Lee Hays, Burl Ives, Millard Lampell, Earl Robinson, and Sonny Terry, among others. Like the theater troupes, they followed the isolationist line before the German invasion of Russia. A product of this brief, early period of their organizational life was an antiwar record album titled *Songs for John Doe.* They also recorded a successful album of labor songs titled *Talking Union*. In albums and personal appearances the Almanacs included adaptations of familiar protest material as well as new songs of their composition. Of the latter, some had new words fitted to traditional tunes. Perhaps the most rousing of the songs from these early albums was "Union Maid," with words by Guthrie to the tune of "Redwing." It begins, "There once was a union maid, she never was afraid/ Of goons and ginks and company finks/ And the deputy sheriffs who made the raid." In addition to arranging the appearances of the Almanacs at antiwar rallies, hootenannies, union meetings, and, later, prewar rallies, the New Theater League published *Eight Songs of the Almanacs* in 1941 and *Eleven Songs to Tear Hitler Down* by the Almanacs and others in 1942. These proved to be among the League's best-selling items.[92]

Established writers apart from Shaw from whom the League received help in this difficult time were Marc Blitzstein and the team of George Sklar and Albert Maltz. With *I've Got the Tune* and *The Cradle Will Rock* still in the repertory, Blitzstein supplied a third musical play, *No for an Answer*. The new Party position was reflected in the play, but somewhat obliquely. Deliberately, Blitzstein emphasized issues other than the war: the problems of unemployment, the resentment against immigrants felt and manifested by native Americans— as though to suggest that it was these issues about which the American population should worry, not the problems of Europe. His plot concerns the members of a club of Greek workers who are determined to build a union and press for full employment despite the murder of the club leader's son, a union organizer, and the burning of the club building. The plot also includes a rich young married couple who become interested in the club. The husband, a throwback to the Third-Period outlook, is driven to drink by the conflict between his basic liberalism and the accepted values of his class. Ultimately he betrays the workers, but his wife is steady enough to remain their friend. Graced with some of Blitzstein's most corrosive songs, including, as a reflection of the recent popularity of Cabaret TAC, some amusing pieces staged as cabaret numbers, the play approached the level of *Cradle* but was too bitter to command a following. Three performances were given at Mecca Temple in January 1941, with a cast that included Curt Conway, Hester Sondergaard, Martin Wolfson, and the very young Carol Channing, to whom was assigned the show's cleverest song: "Fraught," written in a parody of Cole Porter's style.* The new work of Maltz and Sklar, *Zero Hour,* was an adaptation of the authors' *Peace on Earth,* which had launched the Theater Union in 1933. Produced by the League, the play opened on May 23, 1941, playing weekends only. The last performance was given on June 21, the night before the German invasion of Russia.[93]

Always busy, the League continued its activities in familiar fields despite the obvious distaste which the public and intellectuals had begun to display toward Communist causes. An attempt to establish a Southern New Theater School in Mena, Arkansas, on the site of Commonwealth College, a radical labor institution founded in 1923, ended in a rout of League operatives and Commonwealth staff by county law-enforcement officials. At the New Theater School in New York, meanwhile, the students, in addition to attending classes, worked on the peace campaign, marched in the annual May Day parade, and made an effort to persuade theater owners to seat blacks in the orchestra. In *New Theatre News,* every production of Broadway and Hollywood touching on the war came under attack. Even Charlie Chaplin, an old friend to the Left, was not spared; his new film *The Great Dictator* was found guilty insofar as it was, in the words of Ben Irwin, "ONLY an indictment of Hitler, of Mussolini," and not of all fascists and reactionaries, wherever they might exist. Lillian Hellman's stern indictment of the nazis, *Watch on the Rhine,* was subjected to similar treatment: "The play becomes cheap, sentimental, full of affected and unnecessary heroics that can contribute very little to genuine anti-fascism but can easily be used by the demogogic 'anti-Nazi' warmongers who represent the people's main enemy today." [94]

When in 1941 yet another change in the line occurred as a result of Hitler's decision to cross the Soviet border, the League quite satisfactorily made the adjustment. Through its mimeographs went the stencils for a collection of prowar sketches, *V for Victory,* and other materials similarly insisting that America join with the Allies in crushing the Axis powers. Though *New Theatre News* stopped with the invasion, the School remained open through the 1941–42 academic year.

---

* Sponsoring this production was a committee consisting of Bennett Cerf, John Hammond, Jr., Lillian Hellman, Lincoln Kirstein, Arthur Kober, James D. Proctor, and Herman Shumlin.

But with the pressure of the draft and the workers' surrender of time free for theater to highly paid overtime work in plants retooled for the war effort, the troupes began to disband. There was nothing for the New Theater League to do but disband with them. In the summer of 1942 Toby Cole, the League's Business Secretary, handed over to the Theater Collection of the New York Public Library the League's collection of scripts and some miscellaneous publicity releases and items of correspondence, and shut the office.[95] Thus, with no public announcement whatever the New Theater ended a decade of dedication. It is a measure of the passion generated by the period's events that with virtually no material gain so much talent should have been given over to the service of a single organization.

THE THEATER UNION
1935 - 1937
AND RELATED COMPANIES

By the fall of 1935 the young writers Michael Blankfort, Albert
Maltz, Paul Peters, George Sklar, and Victor Wolfson, and their older
colleague Charles R. Walker, heads of the Theater Union, had provided the public with four well-mounted productions off Broadway
and had successfully fought the pressure of Communist party officials
to shape their policy. Critical response to the plays, as we noted, had
been generally favorable, and one play, Peters and Sklar's *Stevedore*,
had made a decided hit. Yet only because the company had an iron
determination not to give up could it continue as the most professional of the radical theaters after the midpoint of the Depression.
From the first it had been difficult to locate provocative scripts with
an appeal cutting across lines of education and economic class, and
this problem never lessened. Nor did the burden of financial outlay.
Claiming in January 1936 that some 523,000 tickets had been sold for
the first five plays, the Executive Board nevertheless admitted that at
the end of every season it faced a deficit of $15,000.[1] If, despite an av-
erage attendance of 100,000 for each play, the Theater Union could
not pay its bills, let alone hire a permanent troupe of actors or even
enough extras for convincing crowd scenes, what was to be done? It
was always possible to raise a stopgap sum by holding yet another

dance, in the old New York bohemian-radical tradition of "balls," "carnivals," and "frolics," which the company did in November 1935, or to try to erase the deficit with a public appeal for contributions, which the company made in the winter of 1936 with the aid of Heywood Broun, Lillian Hellman, Sidney Kingsley, John Howard Lawson, and other writers.[2] But the audience was slipping away, much of it to the new, government-subsidized Federal Theater, whose seats were cheaper, though at a top of $1.50 the Theater Union's tickets were priced well below Broadway's.

Hard-pressed as the company was, it nevertheless produced three plays in the second half of the decade. It also took over the failing Broadway production of Albert Bein's *Let Freedom Ring* and gave it a run, with the result that the play's cast was moved to create a producing unit of its own, ultimately known as the Actors Repertory Company.

Six months passed between the closing of Maltz's *Black Pit* at the end of the 1934–35 season and the opening in November 1935 of the Theater Union's fifth play, Bertolt Brecht's *Mother,* based on the novel of the same name by Maxim Gorky. Meanwhile George Sklar and Paul Peters had suffered through the failure of the Theater Guild's production of *Parade,* for which they had written most of the material. For the production of *Mother,* Peters had prepared a new version of Brecht's original script, which had first been staged in Berlin in 1932. On November 15, four days before the opening, the Theater Union held its fund-raising dance, in the advertisements for which the exclamation points streaked by like bullets: "It's going to be different! Dancing! Sideshows! Freaks! Clowns! Games! Casts of all the Shows will attend our County Fair—Stupendous! Astonishing! and above all, Gay!"[3] Thus it seemed that this organization, which in the make-up of its governing body had never been profoundly proletarian, was slipping happily into the mood of the Popular Front. But what the Theater Union gave with the right hand it took away with the left, for *Mother,* as it soon turned out, clanked dismally with the out-dated diction of the Third Period.

Brecht's plot, following Gorky, is set in Tsarist Russia during the decade before the outbreak of the 1917 Revolution. As a dramatic fable, it is simple in the extreme. A peasant woman, Pelagea Vlasova, illiterate as well as conservative in the way of her kind, discovers to

her dismay that her factory-worker son, Pavel, is taking part in a revolutionary movement. When the police come to her living quarters—
merely one room—in search of strike leaflets printed by Pavel and his
friends, she makes no protest though they rip and overturn her furni-
ture. But, scene by scene as passing events bear out Pavel's radical
theories, she herself is drawn into the movement. After a second experience of police brutality, she marches in a May Day parade; when a
worker holding the red flag is shot while marching, she takes up the
flag herself and carries it proudly. She learns to read, propagandizing
her teacher as she does so, and later, emboldened by her new skill,
she is able to preach a simplified version of Marxist economics to all
hearers wherever she finds herself. At the close, though ill, she
marches in the massive demonstrations preceding the Revolution.

As this outline suggests, in offering *Mother* the Theater Union ignored the new leftist politics of accommodation with the bourgeoisie.
Mother could be taken only for an extended agitational drama, complete with the waving of the red flag. Moreover, in staging the play
the company was mindless of the new esthetic of socialist realism.
Though Brecht dramatized the enlightenment and subsequent development of Pelagea with grave attention to detail, his method revealed
not merely a rejection of socialist realism, but hostility toward it. No
matter that the Mother is hit by stones, suffers the news of her son's
death, and is beaten and knocked to the ground—Brecht refused to
treat these events emotionally. Language is for the most part flat, rising occasionally into ironic humor. The technique of many high
points of the action is that of the mass chant, with here and there the
sound of an individual voice for punctuation.

Behind this method was Brecht's intention, well-known in years to
come as a component of his theory of Epic Theater, of preventing the
audience from losing itself in the play and consequently missing the
ideological content. The style of the production was also intended to
assist in the distancing process (the *Verfremdungseffekt,* to use
Brecht's word). To break up the action he called for songs, some of
which were to be sung by a chorus and others by the dramatic characters. Two pianos providing the accompaniment were to be placed
on one side of the acting area, with the chorus on the other. The
Theater Union's director, Victor Wolfson, ignored certain Brechtian
requirements, but met these and others, including an exposed light

grid above the acting area, and over and behind this a screen in which were projected slogans and photographs, along with simple statements amplifying or explaining the content of the scenes. Among the latter were, for example, the words that the Mother attempts to learn: "w-o-r-k-e-r," "e-x-p-l-o-i-t-e-r."

In the view of the Theater Union's Executive Board, the production was sound. The setting was the work of Mordecai Gorelik, the decade's leading designer of leftist drama; the music was composed by Hanns Eisler, and Alex North and Jerome Moross (able theatrical composers themselves) accompanied the singers at the two pianos. The cast, as the reviewers agreed, was satisfactory, though the limits on the company's funds resulted in the assignment of multiple roles to many actors. (Lee J. Cobb and Hester Sondergaard, for example, played four roles each.) But in the view of Brecht, attending rehearsals on his first visit to the United States, the company made a botch of it all. It was a mistake, he believed, to seat the pianists in the darkness rather than in the full view of the audience. It was another mistake that Gorelik had not been allowed to arrange the lighting and grouping of the actors, since these matters pertained to scenic effects. The lighting, in fact, was too naturalistic. The costumes supplied an unwelcome, inappropriate touch of "local color." Moreover, Peters had contrived a damaging rearrangement of the scenes: whereas in the original script the Mother is informed by neighbors of her son's death well before the end of the play and continues her efforts in behalf of the workers with complete presence of mind, in Peters's version she receives the news in the play's penultimate scene and is flattened by it, rising from her sickbed in time to take part in the final demonstration. The pathos introduced by this juxtaposition of events contradicted the cool intellectuality for which Brecht had striven, and he made his feelings clear. To the cast and director he offered his opinion of the production: "Dass ist Scheisse." [4]

The reviewers used politer language, with many, especially those on the Left, finding much to praise, despite the unorthodoxy of theme and method in relation to the new Party line. "Is it possible," Moissaye J. Olgin asked rhetorically in the *Daily Worker's* lavish five-column spread, "to play 'Capital' by Karl Marx on the stage? We think it is." Stanley Burnshaw, writing in the *New Masses*, was equally generous with favorable comments on not only the content but the form.

Yet the Epic Theater style struck many of Brecht's critics as insuffera-
bly patronizing. Objecting to the slides spelling out words in the
Mother's reading lesson, James T. Farrell wrote, "Mother, it seems to
me, might have been a satisfactory play to present to an audience not
yet emerged from illiteracy." Writing in *New Theatre*, John Gassner,
while praising the plot, took the same view: ". . . it is questionable
whether the Theatre Union might not have found a more suitable
play for its audiences, a play whose lesson would be less obvious to
its regular following and more subtly realized for its middle-class
guests." Whitney Bolton, the reviewer for the *Morning Telegraph* (the
horseplayers' daily), headed a damning notice with "Newsreel, Propaganda and Chant; Put 'Em Together, They Spell 'Mother.'" In the
Times, Brooks Atkinson described the play thoughtfully as "techni-
cally interesting, though emotionally tepid." [5]

America, it appeared, was not yet ready for Brecht. Before the
Theater Union plunged in with *Mother*, the American audience had
been offered only three of his works, each a collaboration with Kurt
Weill: *Lindbergh's Flight*, performed in Philadelphia by the Philadelphia Orchestra in 1931; *He Who Says Yes*, produced in New York off
Broadway in 1933; and *The Three-penny Opera*, produced on Broadway (without success) also in 1933. *Mother* was not the play to turn
the tide in Brecht's favor; after only 36 performances, the Theater Union's shortest run, it closed. Mike Gold was unkind enough to hasten
the end by asking in his *Daily Worker* column why the company had
bothered to do the play in the first place. He found it good enough of
its kind, but asked, ". . . does it belong in a pioneer theatre that set
out to explore the virgin continent of American life?" [6]

That Gold should deplore the production of a play about Russia
and the oppression that engendered the revolution, especially when it
was based on a novel by the U.S.S.R.'s foremost man of letters, hinted
at the pervasiveness of the concept of the Popular Front. On the
other hand, it is surprising to find him, in calling for an American
play in the same article, asking that it be "proletarian," for the word
by this time had begun to fade from the critical vocabulary of the
Left. As it happened, the Theater Union's next offering, Bein's *Let
Freedom Ring*, was both American *and* proletarian. A comparatively
close adaptation of Grace Lumpkin's *To Make My Bread*, a novel
published in 1932, the play had as its setting the textile strike that

took place in Gastonia, North Carolina, in 1929. In this bloody uprising, which marked a harsh defeat for labor, the Communist party
played a central role, foolishly hoping to make the strike a starting
point for revolution. With its "pre-revolutionary" attitude taken over
from the novel, Bein's play was ideologically out of date, though not
so much as it would have been one or two years later. Gold liked it,
as did other leftist critics, and the public supported it for 108 performances.

Those performances were not played in a continuous run, however.
Bein himself originally presented the play on Broadway, in association with Jack Goldsmith. The opening took place in November 1935.
Though given a good production with direction by Worthington
Miner and settings by Mordecai Gorelik, the work soon exhausted its
uptown public, and after 29 performances Bein closed it. But by this
time the Theater Union's experiment with Epic Theater had come to
grief, and having a dark house and no new production ready, the
company moved *Let Freedom Ring* downtown. The new engagement
lasted for 79 performances. Bein had hoped from the start for a Theater Union production and had once sent the company a copy of the
script, only to have it rejected on the grounds that it was too long; it
was then that he had turned to Miner and had decided to serve as his
own producer. Before the second opening Gold scolded Bein in print
for failing to promote the play effectively, and Bein, peeved by this
uncomradely attack, replied that the *Daily Worker* had let him down
by not providing adequate publicity. In protest, Gold replied that the
paper had done everything possible short of selling tickets.[7] Gold had
reason on his side: in all, the paper printed six articles about the
play, including the reactions to it of two union organizers and a textile worker.

Bein also wrote a promotional piece for the play. In an article published by the *Times* shortly before the transfer of the production to
14th Street, he observed that as depicted in the play the events in
the lives of his characters, Carolina mountaineers who were forced
off their native soil to work in the cotton mills, constituted the birth
agony of a new working class. This process he described as a "virgin"
field for American playwrights.[8] He was correct insofar as the hill
people had not yet been made the subject of a strike play, but unfair
to imply that *Let Freedom Ring* was especially innovative, since the

first half of the decade had witnessed the production of many plays on militant workers as ignorant and hopeless as his characters, including Maltz's *Black Pit*, produced by the Theater Union itself.

In essence Bein's play is a series of portraits of displaced hill-dwellers who on coming to work in the mills painfully resist management's effort to turn them into industrial slaves. One large family makes up most of the cast: its members are the McClures, the Martins, and Grandpap Kirkland. What had promised to be good life for them—a company-owned house at a reasonable rental and unlimited credit at the company store—turns into a series of horrors. Machines mangle the workers, malnutrition brings on pellagra, a woman is starved into prostitution, wages are frequently cut. The mill hands are like the victims of the ogre in the tale of "Jack and the Beanstalk," for the mill itself is an ogre who threatens to grind their bones to make his bread.

As the play speeds along, it soon becomes clear that the primitive conditions in which the workers live must be corrected, and that young Kirk McClure, a labor organizer long absent from the family circle, will be the one to make the first move. Most of his relations, including his brother John and Grandpap Kirkland, are against the strike effort. Grandpap (played by Will Geer) is the most shrewdly drawn of the characters. An old man bitterly regretting the move of the family to town, he provides the play with a populist emblem, an example of hardy, honest pioneer stock. For the sake of providing a lesson in labor solidarity, he is, however, something of a racist and has to be reminded that "black toilers" also have their rights. The character is a good fiddler and balladeer (as was Geer), and through his talents he livens up the dramatic action. The interruptions for music represented no influence on Bein of the Brechtian theory of distancing, but were merely an attempt to give the play some appealing color. Bein was perhaps justified in that one of the workers killed at Gastonia was the balladeer Ella May Wiggins.

When Kirk is shot by the county sheriff's rabble, John, who had been rising in his work at the mill, takes over as leader, in the familiar pattern of the conversion play. The strike, in John's words, has "only just begun" as the play ends. His determination and strength of character create a surge of expectancy among the other workers that implies a satisfactory conclusion at some later point, in true Third Period spirit. This ending, no matter how encouraging it may have been to Bein's audience, bore no resemblance to the conclusion of events at Gastonia, for there the Party had so stressed the idea of mass action and the unity of the races that the strike was soon imperiled beyond hope. Incensed at the arrival of non-Southerners dispatched by the Party from New York, the law-enforcement agencies and local vigilantes took violent action, with the predictable result of bloodshed on both sides. Sixteen strikers were convicted on charges of conspiracy, felonious assault, and murder. Skipping bail, they got away, leaving the mill hands to take up their jobs again with no improvement of their conditions.[9] But to tell such ugly truths on the radical stage was out of the question. Only Maltz, in *Black Pit*, had shown a betrayal of the proletariat by one of its own and had been chastised for doing so.

Before the closing of *Let Freedom Ring* at the Civic Rep and the mounting of its next regular production, the Theater Union announced a series of Sunday night special programs, on the order of the New Theater Nights, which for the past year had been performed at the Civic Rep. The company gave only one bill, first offering it on February 16, 1936, and repeating it on March 3. It was something of a mixed bag, but with a hard line running through it. The lightest of the entertainments, *Picket Line*, was acted by the Rebel Arts Players, a New Theater League affiliate. It consisted of versions of picket-line oratory as they might be written by Shakespeare, Chekhov, and Noel Coward. A new dance, *Strange American Funeral*, was performed by Anna Sokolow and her company to a score by Elie Siegmeister. The inspiration for this was Michael Gold's poem "A Strange Funeral in Braddock," an impressionistic account of the death and funeral of a steelworker. *Letter to the President*, a song concerning a lynching, with words by Sklar and Peters and music by Jerome Moross, was sung by Juanita Hall and danced by Miriam Blecher. The most sustained work on the bill was John Wexley's *Running Dogs*, on China's internal struggle between the Kuomintang and the followers of Mao-Tse Tung.[10] The play was acted by members of the Theater Union Studio and directed by Anthony Brown, who had made a name for himself as the director of *Tobacco Road* and later would direct John Howard Lawson's *Marching Song* for the Theater Union.

The Theater Union was able to mount only one more play in the 1935–36 season: Victor Wolfson's *Bitter Stream*, an adaptation of the

novel *Fontamara* by Ignazio Silone. The company had had the opportunity to stage Irwin Shaw's *Bury the Dead,* but made the mistake
of turning it down.[11] Wolfson's work, opening at the end of March,
had a run of only 61 performances.

In choosing this particular play, the company could make the claim
that it was the first producing unit to offer New York a work on the
conditions of daily life under Mussolini. Though many political plays
had alluded more or less directly to Italian totalitarianism—one of
them, Robert E. Sherwood's *Idiot's Delight,* opened only a week before *Bitter Stream*—the subject was less urgent to playwrights than
the situation in Germany, which was repeatedly brought to the stage.
It could also be said that in breaking ground with this play the Theater Union was asserting once more its right to determine its own productions in the face of continuing importuning by Gold to hew to a
policy of his devising. He had followed his xenophobic complaint
against *Mother* with a second column devoted to the company in
which he raised an objection to the apparent unwillingness of the
members of the Executive Board to produce works by others than
themselves. Going further, he attempted to impose on the board the
idea of stewardship: "Its directors are only the trustees of the movement, as definitely as if a contract had been signed." These charges
were more than the Board was able to tolerate, and in a firm answer
Maltz declared that the company had put on the best plays available,
that none submitted by outsiders had been worthy of production, and
furthermore that the Theater Union had been established by the
members of its Board, not by the Communist party.[12] Maltz did not
insist that the company's ideology was remote from that of the party.
The content of the plays demonstrated that it was not, though its
Marxist writers were reluctant to adopt the conciliatory tone of the
Popular Front. But on the issue of organizational independence Maltz
was adamant. The production of *Bitter Stream* reconfirmed the determination of the Board not to be cowed by Gold, for the play was not
only the work of one of its members, but had a European setting.

Silone, then a Communist in exile from his native Italy, had published *Fontamara* in 1930. The English translation appeared in 1934.
According to Theater Union publicity releases, Wolfson had happened upon it while visiting his sister's home and had immediately
sensed that it could be turned into a viable play.[13] Though his adap-

tation is close to the novel, it is less absorbing, for he could not invent a dramatic equivalent of Silone's device of an occasional shift of narrators to reveal that the same cherishable simplicity is a quality of all the peasantry. The suspense, the satire, and the ultimate tragedy were worked into the play, but not the sensitivity. The plot outlines the growing restiveness of farmers living near and in the southern Italian village of Fontamara under a government that overtaxes them, seizes their lands, and conscripts their sons. But promising to be worse than these depradations is the threatened diversion of the stream that waters their fields. Like all the other oppressive measures, it is intended to benefit the rich. The farmers' attempted rebellion fails but one of the leaders, Berardo Viola, meets and is impressed with the forcefulness of a young stranger who has aided the protest movement by publishing an underground newspaper. When both are imprisoned and the police attempt to beat out of them the identity of the publisher, Berardo makes up his mind to sacrifice himself in order that the Stranger may go on with his work. Declaring that it was he who had printed the paper, he awaits the inevitable hanging, and the Stranger goes free. In the final scene the farmers are printing their paper on the press left with them by the Stranger.

Though the commercial papers were indifferent to *Bitter Stream,* the leftist press was ready with praise. The *New Masses* editorialized that it was a "Dramatic Necessity"—a play on a subject too long neglected that its readers should see and plug. In the *Daily Worker* Theodore Repard called it the "ruggedest play yet produced by the Theatre Union," and with a tacit reference to *Mother* rejoiced in Wolfson's avoidance of "technical niceties and nifty gags." A calmer report was made in *New Theatre* by John Gassner, who applauded the play but nevertheless found fault with Wolfson's dramatic technique. In Gassner's view, the final scene, in which the peasants are gathered around the printing press, seemed inadequate as a dramatic climax: "The new social theatre sometimes evinces a fondness for leaflets as a dramatic device which I cannot share. Logic is on the side of the leaflets, and they may well play an important role in history, but not all of us find paper on the stage exciting." [14] In other words, Gassner found that the note of hope sounded after Berardo's tragic death did not ring true. The simplicity of Wolfson's (and Silone's) expression of confidence in an ultimate victory for the peasants, it might have been said, was constructed within the same frame of reference as the finale of *Stevedore:* so firm a belief in the righteousness and strength of the gallant oppressed that it blinded the believer to the greater strength of the oppressors.[15]

At the outset of the 1936–1937 season the Theater Union announced that it was moving uptown. The move was dictated by the decision of the owner of the Civic Rep to raze the building and put a parking lot on the land. It was the hope of the Board to produce two plays, John Howard Lawson's *Marching Song* and George Sklar's *Life and Death of an American,* and to enroll ten thousand subscribers for them, with the top price of tickets still a reasonable $1.50. During the season, while trying to raise financial backing, the Board reported other decisions of note affecting the organization's future. To demonstrate that its sympathies toward the working class had not cooled in the move uptown, the Board declared its intention of developing a mobile troupe to perform short plays in union halls. The notion of organizing a permanent acting company was revived but dropped, not only because of the expense involved, but because the existence of such a company might adversely affect the choice of plays. It was then reconsidered, and, ironically, in one of its last announcements, the Board expressed the hope of developing a nucleus of actors.[16] Not surprisingly, the mobile unit, like the acting companies, also remained an unrealized dream.

The plan of producing *two* plays and organizing a large new subscription audience also went unfulfilled. Only one more play was presented by the Theater Union, and this did not reach the stage until February 1937. In offering Lawson's *Marching Song* rather than Sklar's new play, the company for the first time produced a work wholly the creation of an outsider. Lawson had long been a member of the Theater Union's Advisory Board, but had taken no part in the management of the company's affairs. Moreover, he had written the play originally for the Group Theater, whose directors had given him an advance on it.

Since the Group's production of *Gentlewoman* in 1934 and his public announcement through the pages of *New Theatre* and the *New Masses* that he had embraced communism, Lawson had pursued his alternate career of screenwriting and had published the technical and philosophical work, *Theory and Technique of Playwriting,* that was intended to stand as his major statement on both art and life. In this period Lawson received only two screen credits; his brightest Hollywood years were still to come.[17] The book was his greatest literary concern in this period of his life.

A preview of the contents of *Theory and Technique of Playwriting* formed the substance of a paper titled "Technique and the Drama" that Lawson delivered at the American Writers' Congress in 1935, and excerpts appeared in *New Theatre* for June and July 1935 and March 1936. The book itself was published in February 1936. Lawson's premise is that great drama reflects the philosophical and social opinions of its age and that the very shape of a work is controlled by the author's vision of social purpose. No division occurs between form and content, for if the author is uncertain or confused, his uncertainty or confusion will be evident in the shape of his play. The exposition, the ordering of scenes, the climax, and all other elements of dramaturgy will proclaim that he is hesitant or unable to confront his subject squarely, or, on the other hand, will proclaim that he is clearheaded and purposeful if that is the case. In chapters covering each aspect of playwriting, Lawson provides ample evidence of confusion in the minds of his colleagues, drawing it, for example, from Hellman's *The Children's Hour*, Odets's *Awake and Sing!*, and Melvin Levy's *Gold Eagle Guy*, among other recent successes and failures. Yet the book is not an encyclopedia of faulty writing. Lawson is quick with praise for the early plays of O'Neill and reveals respect for a work by two of Broadway's most commercial writers, George S. Kaufman and Moss Hart's *Merrily We Roll Along*. His intention was to offer aid to the would-be Marxist playwright who hoped to shape a perfect dramatic vehicle for political expression.

Unfortunately, the treatise suffers from weaknesses in Lawson's understanding of both theory and technique. In the brief chapter on dramatic conflict, Lawson declares: "The essential character of drama is social conflict in which the conscious will is exerted: persons are pitted against other persons, or individuals against groups, or groups against other groups, or individuals or groups against social or natural forces." [18] Omitted from this list is that vital type of dramatic conflict in which the individual is pitted against himself—against, that is, his own troubled and trouble-making personality—in an effort to achieve the evenness of mind necessary for adjustment to the world around him. For Lawson every conflict, to be dramatically and *socially* valid, had to be external. It was his failure to grasp the validity of the internal struggle as it raged within Alan Squier in Sherwood's *The Petrified Forest* or Nina Evans in O'Neill's *Strange Interlude* that led him ultimately to reject those plays as somewhat antisocial statements; to Lawson, as his comments on these plays demonstrates, confusion in the mind of the protagonist was a reflection of confusion in the mind of the writer. A second serious flaw is evident in the chapter on dialogue. Lawson argued at length for a return to poetic drama—not, to be sure, to blank verse, as in the work of Maxwell Anderson, or to other metrical or accentual forms, but to "language which is incandescent." His plea is for highly imagistic dialogue such as that created in the twenties by Em Jo Basshe, John Dos Passos, and Francis Edwards Faragoh for their lyrical prose depictions of life in the postwar boom. For all their structural errors, Lawson believed that the plays of these writers were "alive." In taking this curious, sentimental glance back at the work of his colleagues in the New Playwrights' Theater, Lawson overlooked their (and his own) tendency to fill the lines with nonfunctional images and symbols of an awkward, embarrassing obviousness. On the other hand, the tough language of *Stevedore* is described by Lawson as being honest and vigorous, but lacking in richness.[19]

With *Marching Song* Lawson put his theory of dramaturgy into practice, arranging a series of scenes to demonstrate that the consolidation of workers into an invincible, monolithic mass was inevitable, as Marx had foretold. Yet no matter how carefully planned and controlled was the development of proletarian fighting morale in the unfolding of the plot, it was an old story. In Brimmerton, an automobile town, some unemployed workers are trying to live in an abandoned factory. They are joined by a married couple, Pete and Jenny Russell. Once an automobile worker, Russell is now blacklisted for taking part in a strike. He and his wife have lost their house, and their belongings are piled in the street. The familiar characters of proletarian drama come on, one by one, to fill up the set and play their inevitable roles in the action. Lucky, the black worker, is on hand as a foil to the (temporarily) bigoted Pete. Bill Anderson, the determined labor leader—not young, but small and awkward—is on hand to encourage the workers to stage a second strike, and to give his life in their cause. Warren Winkle, a paternalistic employer accompanied by his mistress-secretary, is present to thicken the plot by promising Pete to restore his home if he will reveal the identity of the strike organizer. Strike-breaking goons, prompted in their dirty work by an itch to cause pain, enter to play their savage part, which includes the torture and murder of Anderson. The large cast has room for comic relief also; an unemployed drifter is ready to supply it with ironic comments on the state of the nation and the disclosure of his name: Woodrow Wilson Rosenbloom. Given the time, the place, and the characters, the outcome is easily guessed. The workers gain strength through mutual encouragement, and though their troubles do not end with the final curtain, it is nevertheless possible that they will win their strike.

Not only in his choice of characters, but in the design of the action and the patterns of speech did Lawson render up anew the old banalities of workers' drama. The first act ends with a tableau in which all the workers massed in the factory raise their hands in a sign of solidarity, after which lightning streaks through the scene and thunder sounds, as the very heavens portend this to be the start of an action of cosmic magnitude. The accidental slaying of the Russell baby by a policeman's bullet is intended to demonstrate the wantonness of law-enforcement agencies. Language loses its moorings in reality at those moments when Lawson attempts to display his characters' warmest emotions. Though in production the Theater Union excised the most inflated of his phrases, the dialogue retained much language that sorts poorly with the temperament of the speakers. Says Pete Russell, for example, to other workers, with reference to his life with Jenny: "We went courting in the fall of the year. We walked in the deep woods, we rolled in the red leaves like horses in a pasture." (I).[20] Says Mary McGillicuddy, the militant wife of a worker, in conversation with other wives,

> I say its guns we'll be needing. . . . That frightens you, that makes you see; your easy tongues are quiet now. Listen to me, for the pain of what I'm saying is deep in me, tearing me like the bearing of a child. . . . It's not like a bit of gossip when we're hanging out the wash . . . nor the quick talk in the store when we're waiting for a pound of tea. . . . Men die for their homes, don't they? (III).

With the single exception of *Processional,* in all his earlier plays Lawson had focused his attention on the life of the middle class as it is lived at various economic levels from need to affluence. Turning, after twelve years, to look again at the proletariat, Lawson revealed in *Marching Song* that he did not know that class well enough, for all the genuineness of his concern, to write a convincing play about it. In *Processional* he had run less of a risk of self-betrayal because of the antinaturalistic form he had invented for it; the deliberate distortion of character and setting, the jazz music and dancing had carried conviction in a way that the socialist realism of *Marching Song* did not. The hollowness of the new play had been recognized by Clurman on turning it down for the Group Theater. In reply to an attempt on Lawson's part to wring from him an expression of agreement that proletarian plays should be written, Clurman said, "Perhaps. But not by you." [21] After 61 performances *Marching Song* closed. During the run the actors themselves became the producer, taking over for the Theater Union; otherwise the play would have had an earlier closing.[22] The extravagant notices written by reviewers for *New Theatre*, the *New Masses*, and the *Daily Worker* could not offset the tepid reviews in the commercial press, unless perhaps in the mind of the wholly committed author. Not surprisingly, in view of Lawson's fidelity and his position as an editor of the *New Masses*, the play was voted the best of the year by the second American Writers' Congress.[23] It was to be Lawson's last produced play, though not the last he was to write. In 1939, in the midst of his then prosperous Hollywood career, he handed Clurman a new script, *Parlor Magic*, dealing with the middle class. But this also Clurman refused. Later he was to write of it that "the author's point of view was expressed with a carefulness and a propriety the mechanics of which could not be concealed by efforts at a righteously lyric fervor." [24] Precisely the same impression is given by *Marching Song*.

After this production, time ran out on the Theater Union. Hindered, like all privately financed producing units, by the recent recession in its attempts to find backing, the organization also suffered from competition with the Federal Theater which at a top usually of no more than fifty-five cents offered dozens of professional dramas around the city and across the nation. For more radical fare, the productions of the New Theater League and its affiliates were still available at low prices. In August 1937 the Executive Board issued an official announcement of the break-up.[25]

The first of the major institutional theaters of the thirties to dissolve, the Theater Union left behind it a sizable collection of favorable reviews to compensate for its spotty record of financial success. It also went out with a reputation for craftsmanlike, innovative productions. The commissions to Mordecai Gorelik and such other distinguished designers as Cleon Throckmorton and S. Syrjala, the directorial assignments to Robert Sinclair, Jacob Ben-Ami, and Anthony Brown, and the casting of Broadway actors of proven ability—for example, Robert Keith, Jack Carter, Rex Ingram, Tom Powers, Alan Baxter, Albert Van Dekker, and Grover Burgess—set production standards at a new level for the Off-Broadway stage. Young actors whose careers were launched in Theater Union productions included Jules Garfield (*Peace on Earth*), Canada Lee (*Stevedore*), and Lee J. Cobb (*Mother*). How far-reaching was the new force unleashed by the company it is impossible to say, but these facts at least are known: the Theater Guild extended itself into the field of social revue by staging *Parade*, primarily the work of two Theater Union dramatists, Peters and Sklar; the Actors Repertory Company owed its start to the company's rescue of *Let Freedom Ring;* and the Mercury Theater, which came on the scene in 1937, benefited from the Theater Union's spadework in audience organization.[26] It is ironic that the only play produced by the company to become known throughout the world, Brecht's *Mother*, was its greatest failure.

For the young writers who had formed the nucleus of the Executive Board, creative life had scarcely begun. Blankfort, Maltz, and Sklar continued as playwrights, but also set out on rewarding careers as novelists and screenwriters. Wolfson was soon to have a Broadway hit, Peters to become film and book editor for *Life* and drama editor for Twentieth-Century-Fox, and Walker to publish on labor and to teach at Yale. After four difficult years they were entitled to the successes lying ahead.

During the last years of the Theater Union's life and fitfully for a while thereafter, the company assembled by Bein for *Let Freedom Ring* kept in the news. It was evident from the notices for Bein's play that the cast was of more than routine interest, with Will Geer as Grandpap Kirkland revealing an especially sympathetic stage presence. This was not, however, a company of stars; apart from Geer, only two stars emerged from it—Tom Ewell and Shepperd Strudwick—and these two actors did not remain with the company after the closing of *Let Freedom Ring.*° Worthington Miner continued with the company as director. When late in the season of 1935–36 the actors and Miner returned to Broadway with a new play, they chose a new name, the Actors Repertory Company. It was never to become a repertory company, but during its brief life it remained primarily an actors' organization, in contrast with the Theater Union, a playwrights' theater, and the Group Theater, a directors' theater. All of its Broadway work was offered in conjunction with commercial producers.

Yet, like the Theater Union and the Group, the company wished to present only plays relating to the social and political environment. On balance, its Broadway work after *Let Freedom Ring* placed it in the liberal center. A radical splinter group of the actors gathered together for summer tours to mill towns and migratory workers' camps where they performed agitational material. A strain of radicalism was also evident in the bill offered by the company on Sunday nights during the downtown run of *Let Freedom Ring.* Four items were included: Maltz's *Private Hicks*, Paul Green's *Hymn to the Rising Sun* and *Unto Such Glory*, and Elizabeth England's *Angelo Herndon.* As noted in the preceding chapter, the first two were New Theater League plays in the new socialist-realist style. Contrasting with them was the work by England, a mass chant whose blunt propaganda couched in darky dialect might have been written in the earliest days of the League of Workers Theaters, save for its subject. But Green's *Unto Such Glory*, first published in 1927, also provided a contrast. A folk play and in no sense polemical, it gave the actors another opportunity to portray characters from the Carolina hills. In this faintly ribald comedy, Green traced the wily attempt of a revivalist preacher, Brother Simpkins, to seduce the wife of a young mountaineer, and the heroic, successful, effort of the husband to save his home. The range in the tone of the plays from militant to folksy pointed to the parallel paths the actors were to follow in their years together.

° Among the many actors who stayed, in addition to Will Geer, for one or more of the company's Broadway plays were John O'Shaughnessy, later a director of note, Robert Porterfield, founder of the Barter Theater in Abington, Virginia, Paula Bauersmith, Charles Dingle, Rose Keane, Douglas Parkhirst, Erik Walz, and Herta Ware.

The four-part bill was first given on January 12, 1936, and was repeated during the month, with Charles Dingle as the Captain in *Hymn to the Rising Sun* and Geer as Preacher Simpkins in *Unto Such Glory* leading the company in a triumphant performance. Seeing this bill, and having been impressed by *Let Freedom Ring*, Irwin Shaw permitted them to give the première performances of *Bury the Dead* on March 14 and 15. With neither the Theater Union nor the Group available, the new company was then permitted to open the play on Broadway in April for a run, under the joint direction of Miner and Walter Hart, with Alex Yokel as producer. Before making this move, the company adopted its new name. Downtown the actors had coupled Shaw's play with *Over Here*, a one-act recruiting sketch by Walter B. Hare, to which they added jokes to make a parody of patriotic sloganeering. On Broadway they substituted for this a new, original work, *Prelude*, by J. Edward Shugrue and John O'Shaughnessy. This work, largely a product of improvisation, employed a cast of thirty-five actors in a mass protest against the possible outbreak of a new world war. Wishing to couple *Bury the Dead* with a new piece, they had been forced to create one for themselves, because the strike of the Dramatists' Guild then underway had taken all unproduced plays off the market.[27]

Bury the Dead, with a run of 110 performances in two engagements, proved to be the most popular of the few plays the Actors Repertory Company was to offer. It was also the most imaginative. In November 1936 in association with Sidney Harmon, the company presented E. P. Conkle's *200 Were Chosen*, a somber, realistic play with thirty-two roles, which the actors filled with no doubling. The play had first been performed by the Experimental Theater Group of the University of Iowa, where Conkle was a member of the faculty. Harmon, conceiving the idea of producing it in New York, took it to the actors.[28] The lengthiness of the cast could be explained by the fact that it was an academic play—that is, a work designed to exhibit the talents of numerous student actors. Possibly its stodginess could also be blamed on its academic origin. Conkle built his plot on the resettlement, undertaken in 1935 by the Federal Emergency Relief Administration, of some thousand Depression-stricken Midwestern families to the Matanuska Valley of Alaska. In the vanguard were two hundred families, the first group coming from Minnesota. Though

Conkle included some barbed expressions of complaint against governmental sloth and confusion, the result was hardly a stirring work. Its run was a disappointingly brief 35 performances.

Long and diffuse, the play slowly reveals the discontent of the displaced farmers who, having lost their farms in the "States," and having been demoralized by the necessity of accepting relief, find it in no way easy to develop new farms in the far North. It becomes their belief that they were moved only as a vote-getting gesture on the part of those in power in Washington. When ordered to tear down their newly erected log cabins, which do not conform with government specifications, some come to the brink of rebellion. But an epidemic of scarlet fever brings them to their senses by giving them a communal task to fulfill: the building of a hospital. Next will come electricity, and thus the experiment will be saved. Keeping the play in continuous motion are numerous subsidiary actions rising out of sexual frustration and troubled personal relations. The sheer number of events and characters thins to a watery blandness the social relevance inherent in the theme. As John Gassner pointed out in *New Theatre and Film*, the important question of the settlers' ultimate title to their farms is lost in the welter of activity. It is once aired by a rebellious settler, but then dropped altogether from the play.[29]

After this failure a year and a half went by before the Actors Repertory returned to Broadway for a run. A plan to produce Blitzstein's *The Cradle Will Rock* had to be scrapped when the backing proved impossible to raise.[30] When the Mercury Theater offered the play, Will Geer took the part of Mr. Mister. During this period many of the actors in the company were engaged by Broadway managements, and Geer especially was in demand. Those plays in addition to *Cradle* in which he appeared were Melvin Levy's *A House in the Country*, Wexley's *Steel* in the Labor Stage revival, Green's *Unto Such Glory* for the Federal Theater, John Steinbeck's *Of Mice and Men*, and Alfred Hayes and Leon Alexander's *Journeyman*, a dramatization of Erskine Caldwell's novel of the same name. In the last he played the title role and was joined in the cast by O'Shaughnessy and Herta Ware, under the direction of Caldwell and J. Edward Shugrue. When not working, the actors kept themselves busy rehearsing scripts. To cut down on expenses, they made an effort, like the Group Theater, at communal living.[31]

In the spring of 1938 the company appeared on Broadway in what was to be its last play. On this occasion the coproducer was the most prestigious of all those with whom it aligned itself: the Theater Guild. The play, a satirical farce titled *Washington Jitters*, was an adaptation by two members of the company, John Boruff and Walter Hart, of Dalton Trumbo's novel of the same name. Needing a work to add to its schedule in order to fulfill its obligations to subscribers, the Guild's Board of Managers listened to a reading of the play given by the company and decided that it would do. But from the beginning the production was centered in a storm of confusion generated by the Guild. Should a play doctor be brought in to make the piece funnier? Should it—the suggestion of Alfred Lunt—be transformed into a comedy melodrama? Should the title be changed? Should Walter Hart be replaced as director? Should an outsider, Ernest Truex, be added to the cast as the lead? Finally, should the reviewers be kept out of the theater? Except that Miner, who had directed for both companies in the past, joined Hart in the staging and, with the Guild's Philip Moeller, did some rewriting of the script, these questions were ultimately answered in the negative. But their very number boded poorly for the play, as did the fact that the production was in the charge of six persons, three from each company. After three weeks of previews, the press was invited to the performance of May 2, which marked the official opening. What the critics saw did not please them, and in three weeks the play closed.[32]

If in its last play the Theater Union had been too contentious for the Broadway audience, the Actors Repertory Company in its last was too concessive. *Washington Jitters* proved to be a dull and stingless satire on the proliferating New Deal bureaucracy. In the frantic plot a sign-painter named Henry Hogg is mistaken by a radio news commentator for the head of ASP, the Agricultural Survey Program, and almost instantly thrust into national prominence. As a celebrity he sides first with one party, then with the other, until, tiring of the game and losing his self-respect, he reveals the truth about himself. For this act of bravery he is promoted at once as a presidential candidate. With its twenty-nine short scenes, many ending in a blackout, the play has the tempo of farce, but not enough wit to be entertaining. The issues coming under review are the bigness of government that makes such deceptions as Hogg's possible and the venality of the

professional politicos of any and every party. These had received
more attractive treatment in an earlier Guild production, Maxwell
Anderson's *Both Your Houses*.

Reviewed consecutively, the four major works in which the company acted revealed a progression in tone from "pre-revolutionary"
single-mindedness to the seeming levity that marked most entertainments of the Theater Arts Committee, for whose cabarets Will Geer
was occasionally the Master of Ceremonies. *Washington Jitters* had
not only the lightheartedness of the TAC shows, but a debilitating
lightheadedness as well. Though the members of the Actors Repertory
Company never again made a collective appearance, mention of the
company cropped up in the theatrical columns over the next two
years. Two of the original three directors of the Group Theater came
to its aid, Cheryl Crawford with office space and Lee Strasberg with
rehearsal sessions. In the spring of 1939, the company gave a reading
at an art gallery of Dan Garrison's *Boom*, a play of the Oklahoma oil
fields, but nothing followed from this event. In November 1939
O'Shaughnessy inquired of Hallie Flanagan, on behalf of the company, about the rights to the material gathered by the Living Newspaper unit of the defunct Federal Theater for a work to be called
Medicine, but in this he was too late, for the material had already
been taken up by other producers. The last press reports of the Actors
Repertory Company appeared in 1940.[33]

An offshoot of the company made up of those members who were
committed to radical politics, and others of like mind, kept busy on
summer tours and New York benefits during the same span of years.
The guiding figure in this small unit's work was the charismatic Will
Geer. The first tour occurred in the summer of 1936, when, designat-
ing themselves the "Let Freedom Ring" Company, they took scenes
from Bein's militant play to the mill towns in New Jersey and New
England where strikes were underway. Among others in the group in
addition to Geer were Herta Ware and John Lenthier. The patron of
the troupe for this first summer was the United Textile Workers. Assistance was also forthcoming from Labor Stage, Brookwood Labor
College, the New Theater League, and the Actors Repertory Company. Asking a guarantee of $100 per performance and playing, by
the end of the summer season, to an estimated 22,000 customers, the
actors were out to prove that drama could aid in the conquest of fear
and apathy among the workers.[34]

In its later tours the troupe confined itself to short sketches, Geer's "folksay" recitations, and folk songs, and adopted a new name. On April 10, 1937, after the death in the Spanish Civil War of John Lenthier, the actors wrote and sang a ballad in his honor at a memorial service sponsored by the New Theater League at a matinee of *Steel*.[35] Further to honor him, they called their unit the John Lenthier Troupe thereafter. On December 12, 1937, at a benefit for the Newspaper Guild at which another group, the John Ingot Memorial Troupe, gave the première performance of Ben Bengal's *Plant in the Sun*, the Lenthier Troupe gave Ferenc Molnár's *Still Life*, one act of a long work by Sully Lewis, *Freedom of the Press*, and a musical improvisation by Fred Stewart titled *A Town and Country Jig*.

On its tours, the Lenthier Troupe traveled over the Atlantic Seaboard, through Pennsylvania and West Virginia, to Chicago, the South, and at last to California, armed with a repertory of one-act plays, TAC material, and ballads. In the summer of 1938 under the auspices of TAC and the Abraham Lincoln Brigade they raised money for the Brigade. Among the dramatic works they performed were scenes from *Bury the Dead*, Maltz's *Rehearsal* and Em Jo Basshe's antiwar *Snickering Horses*.[36] The folk singers Burl Ives, Tony Kraber, and Woody Guthrie joined the later tours, Ives and Kraber first in 1938 and Guthrie in 1939. Attempting a program in 1939 in which TAC sketches predominated, the troupe found that the material was too sophisticated for its audience, which was then made up of migratory workers, and consequently held a contest for a new play. The prize went to *Middleman* (by an author whose name was never divulged in print), a ten-minute piece about rising prices featuring a pair of pants and explaining the reasons for their high price.[37] Primitive in the extreme, it resembled nothing so much as the earliest sketches of the Workers Laboratory Theater and Prolet-Buehne. With this troupe the radical theater seemed to have come full circle. Between the 1938 and 1939 tours, Geer appeared in a Broadway revue, *Sing Out the News*, by Harold Rome and Charles Friedman, in which slick production values were applied to liberal themes. The contrast with the work of the Lenthier Troupe could scarcely have been more pronounced.[38]

The demand for Geer's services on Broadway at last put an end to the John Lenthier Troupe. On December 11, 1939, he entered the cast of *Tobacco Road* as Jeeter Lester and remained in the part until the play closed on May 31, 1941. During and after this period in his career he still found time to take part in musical benefits for radical causes and institutions, including the Veterans of the Abraham Lincoln Brigade, Commonwealth College, and the *New Masses,* as did Kraber, Ives, Guthrie, and the rising Almanac Singers.[39] To these performers, as to the New Theater League which booked them, it appeared that the new leftist propaganda aims focusing on the war, as well as the traditional one of voicing the plight of the workers, could be served as efficiently by song as by spoken drama.

THE FEDERAL THEATER
1935 - 1939;
THE MERCURY THEATER
1937 - 1939

As THEY SAT ON A TRAIN passing through the slums of Chicago on a day in July 1935, Harry Hopkins, the national head of the Works Progress Administration, turned to Mrs. Hallie Flanagan and suddenly asked, "Can you spend money?" Prompted by the grim view through the windows and the urgent purpose of the trip, the question could not have been more serious. Hopkins had chosen Hallie Flanagan to head the Federal Theater Project, a new arm of his vast work-relief agency, and was accompanying her to Iowa City, where the appointment would be publicly announced. In her position, he explained, she would face the necessity of signing papers authorizing the expenditure of great sums totaling millions, and it would not be easy. Not only would the very fact of committing the government to the expenditures be hard in itself; along with it would come the awareness that, no matter how sensitively she calculated needs and costs, she could count on hearing cries of outrage over her decisions—the cries of those who wanted but did not get the money and also the cries of those who believed it should never have been spent.[1]

The WPA was not the only federal relief agency, and Hopkins and

his lieutenants were not the only New Deal appointees faced with
daily grueling decisions about how best to spend congressional allocations. Older by two years was the Public Works Administration,
headed by Harold Ickes, Secretary of the Interior. Though the two
agencies sounded confusingly alike when referred to, New Deal-style,
by their initials, they were separate and dissimilar undertakings. Year
after year to 1939 Ickes's PWA created large-scale works: schools,
hospitals, municipal buildings, bridges. Though the basic motive for
the establishment of the agency was the employment of idle workers,
Secretary Ickes intended to enrich the nation with structures of permanent value and in the process to aid recovery by pumping into the
lethargic economy the vast amount of capital to pay for them. With
Hopkins the issue of work-relief took on a more personal tone. His
projects would cost money also, but were motivated by the wish to
provide for the speedy re-employment of out-of-work men in jobs for
which they were best suited. His approach led to the creation of such
obviously inessential jobs as leaf-raking and lawn-mowing, but also to
the development of the Federal Arts Projects for the productive employment of writers, musicians, artists, and theater workers. The four
separate projects were joined together as Federal Project Number
One, or Federal One, as it was familiarly known. In 1936 the Historical Records Survey, for the gathering and preservation of documents
of historical importance, became the fifth unit of Federal One; previously it had been a part of the Writers' Project. Of these government enterprises the most conspicuous, and consequently the shortest
lived, was the Federal Theater Project.[2]

Before the era of the WPA, Hopkins had headed other New Deal
relief agencies: the Federal Emergency Relief Administration and the
Civil Works Administration. Under these agencies, the former operating in collaboration with the state governments and the latter operating entirely on Federal funds, the aim was rapid re-employment. Not
always did this lead to the matching of the job and the skill of the
worker, as was to be true of the WPA Arts Projects. But in 1934 an
effort to this end was made when the CWA set up troupes of unemployed theater workers to give free plays and vaudeville and mari-
onette performances in the major cities and the camps of the Civilian
Conservation Corps. As Jacob Baker, Assistant Administrator of the
CWA, put it in 1934, "It has been recognized that when an artist or

musician is hungry he is just as hungry as a bricklayer and has the same right that a bricklayer has to be employed at his own trade. For the first time in our history, the government has become a patron of the arts, officially and quite unashamed." [3] By the thousands New York theater workers inquired about these new jobs, but only a handful were needed. After the disestablishment of the CWA in the spring of 1935, this work was taken over by the FERA, and some of its productions were ultimately inherited by the Federal Theater.[4]

Though having constantly to vie with Ickes for his share of Congressional allocations, Hopkins with the establishment of the WPA had more funds at his disposal for relief than in the days of FERA and CWA. His expansion of the government's theatrical activity added thousands of workers to the few hundred actors and vaudevillians taken on by these agencies. An average of 10,000 were at work on the Project during its four years of existence. These were not only performers, but stagehands, designers, and other theatrical technicians.[5]

Hopkins's choice of Flanagan to head the Federal Theater, though decried by Broadway managers at first, as was, indeed, the entire undertaking, was the result of no snap judgment. He had approached her in 1934 with the suggestion that she consider administering the theater activity of the CWA, only to hear that she had accepted an offer to direct the theater at Dartington Hall in England while on leave from Vassar College. In 1935, having decided against taking the post in England once she had arrived there, she was again available. Hopkins and Hallie Flanagan had been students together at Grinnell College; she had graduated from Grinnell in 1911, one year before him. It was not the personal issue of shared experience of an alma mater that guided Hopkins's decision, however, but the extensive qualifications of Hallie Flanagan for the job at hand.[6] Born Hallie Ferguson, she married her fellow student Murray Flanagan soon after her graduation. On his death in 1919 she went back to Grinnell as a teacher of drama and soon began both to write and to direct plays. Word of her ability in dramatic production reached the ears of Harvard's George Pierce Baker, who asked her to come east as his production assistant in 1923. From Harvard she returned in a year to Grinnell to resume her duties but was soon offered the opportunity to develop a theater at Vassar. In 1926, in her first year at Vassar, she received a Guggenheim Fellowship—the first woman to be so honored —to visit the theaters of Europe and write a book on their productions. This work, *Shifting Scenes of the Modern European Theatre,* was published in 1928. Until her leave in 1934, she continued in her post as director of the Vassar Experimental Theater. It was there in 1931 that with Margaret Ellen Clifford she wrote and produced *Can You Hear Their Voices?*, the early extension of the agitprop formula which was taken up enthusiastically for production by radical, "little," and academic theaters across the land. In 1934 she married Professor Philip H. Davis of Vassar but continued to use her name by her first marriage in her professional activity.

Hallie Flanagan's career had not included work in the commercial theater, but in Hopkins's view her very lack of such experience enhanced her value to such an undertaking as the Federal Theater. This huge enterprise was not intended to return profits to the federal treasury but to return men to work. Whereas the Broadway producer is in the business of making money out of the theater and soon loses his standing with his "angels" if his taste is not supported by the public at the box office, the National Director of the Federal Theater was not obliged to deliver her backers, the United States government, a string of hits. At the outset Hopkins notified Hallie Flanagan that the Federal Theater was not to be viewed as a commercial enterprise: "It's got to be run by a person who isn't interested just in the commercial type of show. I know something about the plays you've been doing for ten years, plays about American life. This is an American job, not just a New York job." [7]

Under the FERA and CWA, admission to theatrical performances was free. Flanagan believed, however, that the Federal Theater as she envisaged it would be capable of mounting productions that audiences would be willing to pay to see, and accordingly asked the WPA for permission to sell tickets. Washington was slow to respond to this idea, but in January 1936 a scheme was worked out authorizing a price scale ranging from ten cents to $1.00, with performances for the underprivileged to remain free. Consequently more than two million dollars was taken in at Federal Theater box offices. This constituted less than five per cent of the total expenditures, however, which came to $46,207,779. [8] The National Director was proud of the fact that her productions did well, on balance, in the way of receipts, but resolutely determined not to let such a consideration guide the tone of the Project. Hopkins had already rejected the proposals for establishing a theater presented to him by Eva Le Gallienne, Katharine Cornell, Edith J. R. Isaacs (editor of *Theatre Arts Monthly*), Frank Gillmore (president of Actors' Equity), and Elmer Rice. When Hopkins reacted unfavorably to Rice's scheme, which would have set up his Theater Alliance with federal backing, Rice gallantly recommended Hallie Flanagan as head of the new government theater.[9]

Rice accepted Hallie Flanagan's invitation to administer the Project in New York City, but apart from the actor-producer Eddie Dowling, who accepted the directorship of the vaudeville and circus units on a national basis, he was the only Broadway figure of major reputation to serve with the Federal Theater. Outside New York, in that three-thousand mile continental sweep that the average New Yorker refers to as "out of town," Project theaters were established in every state in which a sizable body of unemployed theater workers lived. Regional centers were set up in New York, Boston, Chicago, New Orleans, and Los Angeles. Within these regions the local theaters were responsible to the regional directors, who in turn reported to and met periodically with the National Director. In each locality the state or municipal government acted as a sponsor of the units. It was necessary for the heads of local theaters to maintain good working relations with WPA administrators in the various states. Though Hopkins notified the state officials that the Arts Projects were to be directed from Washington by their several leaders, the cooperation of the state officials was not always forthcoming, and instances of censorship at the state level occurred upon occasion.

Hopkins wished, as did Flanagan, to appoint as regional and local directors men and women qualified by prior theater work in their various areas. Thus it came about that E. C. Mabie, who had already drawn up a scheme of regional theater organization for the National Theater Conference of University and Community Theaters, and who headed the theater of the University of Iowa, helped Flanagan plan the organization of the Federal Theater and accepted the directorship of the Midwest. Jasper Deeter, who headed the Hedgerow Theater in Moylan, Pennsylvania, became director for his state; Gilmor Brown, director of the Pasadena Playhouse, became director for the West; Glenn Hughes, director of the University of Washington theater, became director for Seattle; and Frederick Koch, founder and director of the North Carolina Playmakers, became director for the South. Among other appointments of comparable promise was that of Rosamund Gilder, associate editor of *Theatre Arts Monthly*, as head of the Project's Bureau of Research and Publication. Wearying eventually of the swirls of red tape that spun endlessly out of the Washington WPA offices, or aghast over censorship, or, in the instance of Gilmor Brown, dismissed by the state administrator, few of the early administrative appointees were with Federal Theater when it closed in 1939, nor were all of their immediate replacements. But the pattern of choosing the best available regional theater workers for supervisory posts that Hopkins and Flanagan settled on was maintained to the last. In view of the slimness of the authorized annual supervisory salaries, which ranged from $1,200 to $2,500, it was a tribute to Flanagan's impressive powers of persuasion that she was able to assemble so capable a staff. Not always, however, did she get her first choice. The young Broadway producer who she hoped would head the Hartford, Connecticut, project, said, "I want to do it—but how can I manage on $200 a week?" He had failed to understand that it was not $200 a week that he had been offered, but $200 a month.[10]

The actors and other stage workers employed by Federal Theater received substantially less. Unskilled laborers were paid from $21 to $55 monthly. Professionals outside New York City received a maximum monthly wage of $94; for those employed in the city, the maximum was set at $103.40. From 90 to 95 per cent of the total number of workers apart from supervisory staff had to be chosen from the relief rolls; the margin allowed for the hiring of expert nonrelief actors and other workers, though seemingly small, was in fact generous in view of the total number of persons employed on the Project: over 12,000 at the peak in 1936, and, to repeat, averaging about 10,000 per year. When, as a result of cuts in congressional appropriations, orders were received from Washington in June 1937 to reduce the number of employees sharply, most of those not from the relief rolls were dropped. This measure, followed by another cut in December 1938, did not reflect an opinion on the part of anyone in government that the economy had improved in favor of the arts, but, rather, the waning of President Roosevelt's prestige with and power over Congress. The cuts were vigorously protested by strikes and demonstrations of Federal Theater actors and dancers—especially the dancers —and also by the various theatrical and WPA unions representing them.[11]

Whether taken from the relief rolls or borrowed from the ranks of nonrelief performers, as, for example, was Will Geer for Paul Green's *Unto Such Glory* in 1937, all actors given work by the Federal Theater were required to be of professional standing. This was also true of workers in other aspects of theater—the dancers, the stagehands, the designers, the scene painters. Most belonged to unions, though some did not who had worked only in summer theater or, like the dancers, were not yet organized. Federal Theater was not a closed shop, but at the planning stage Flanagan had to consult with, and continued to have to consult with during the Federal Theater's existence, no fewer than fifteen stage unions, one of which, the Associated Actors and Artists of America, represented five separate organizations: Actors' Equity, Chorus Equity, Hebrew Actors, Hebrew Chorus, and the American Federation of Actors (vaudeville performers). In New York the Workers' Alliance, the Communist party-dominated union of relief clients and WPA employees, proceeded to organize the maintenance staffs, guards, timekeepers, and other unaffiliated workers. Its white-collar arm, the City Projects Council, organized the Federal Theater's clerical staff. Though the disturbances created by the unions in response to cuts or alleged grievances were not always easy to deal with, Flanagan recognized the right of workers to membership in protective organizations, not only because it was the policy of the WPA, but out of personal conviction, without which it is unlikely that she could have endured the pressures of her post. Typical of her point of view were the remarks which she made to a meeting of directors in New York during the second year:

> Our study of the human element must include understanding of the rising tide of labor over the whole world today, a knowledge of theatre trade unionism, of unions which already exist and of unions which are just coming into being. There must be in our minds every time we meet with a delegation of workers the knowledge that they are the people for whom the project was made, that they have a right to suggest to us any measures affecting their own welfare. We should learn to *listen* to these delegations, for we can advance in this Federal Theatre only as the 8,000 workers on our project advance with us.[12]

Inevitably, a few incompetent performers succeeded in finding employment with Federal Theater. In New York, Elmer Rice was reluctant to set up audition boards and convinced Hallie Flanagan, who proposed them, to forgo the notion, insisting that "the greatest actor in the world may fall down on an audition." Not foreseeing the problems to come in separating any needy worker from the Project, he believed that incompetents, if hired, could be fired when their lack of ability became obvious. Rice knew that, given the unstable economy of the stage in even the best of times, let alone in the Depression years, and the perennial superabundance of talented actors, unemployment did not necessarily mean inability. But the years of privation had worked havoc with many performers. Flanagan, on writing her memoir of Federal Theater, recalled having seen evidence of the strain they had undergone: the man who on applying for work went mad and beat his head against the wall, the actress who wept at the thought of having her name printed in a Federal Theater program, the musician who apologized for his poor playing because for want of employment in his profession he had been working on a road crew. Valiant efforts were made to use physically handicapped performers in need of relief, such as the flutist in Los Angeles with a lip tremor for whom was composed a motif brief enough for him to play, and the excellent older Seattle actor who when playing always stood near a table or chair because twenty-five years before he had broken both legs in a vaudeville act. Skeptical producers such as John Golden, Eva Le Gallienne, and Brock Pemberton voiced their alarm that the Federal Theater would saturate New York with poorly performed shows by making work for the unemployed, but this did not come to pass.[13]

Nor did the hostility to the idea of Federal Theater expressed by these producers become the prevailing attitude. Behind their remarks lay the fear of competition, and this was confirmed in the agreement of the Federal Theater with the League of New York Theaters, the producers' association, to operate in the city only outside the area bounded by 40th Street on the south, 52nd Street on the north, and the Hudson and East Rivers, though this was soon modified to permit the Project to take over the Biltmore and Ritz Theaters, on West 47th Street and West 48th Streets respectively.[14] But before long the commercial managers, including Lee Shubert of the theatre-owning empire, saw the value of the Federal Theater as renewing public interest in the world of live entertainment. Critics employed by the commercial press held no bias against its productions; among its consistent well-wishers were Brooks Atkinson of the *Times*, the city's most prestigious paper, and Burns Mantle of the *Daily News*, the most popular paper and editorially among the most conservative.

Both these critics served on the Federal Theater Advisory Board, as did Barrett H. Clark, the playwrights Sidney Howard and George Sklar, the producers Herman Shumlin and Maurice Wertheim (of the Theater Guild Board of Managers), the actors Burgess Meredith, Cornelia Otis Skinner, and Blanche Yurka, Helen Hall of the Henry Street Settlement House, Irene Lewisohn of the Neighborhood Playhouse, and Elias M. Sugarman, Editor of *Billboard*. A larger consulting body, the Federal Theater Committee, consisted of these and the producers Cheryl Crawford, Theresa Helburn, and Lee Shubert, the playwrights Marc Connelly, Albert Maltz, and Clifford Odets, Herbert Kline of the New Theater League, Heywood Broun, Jo Mielziner, Martha Graham, and Ralph Steiner. In Los Angeles the Federal Theater benefited from the enthusiastic cooperation of the film colony. On a board set up for screening actors Edward Arnold, Boris Karloff, and Lucille Gleason served, and a production of Hall Johnson's *Run Little Chillun* had as its director the black actor Clarence Muse, a favorite in Frank Capra pictures. The make-up of these various boards supplies only a small part of the evidence of the value placed on the Federal Theater by the most imaginative and respected men and women of creative and interpretive skill, both within and on the periphery of the theatrical profession. Much more evidence was to come in the form of pressure put on the government during Flanagan's last-ditch effort to save the Federal Theater from death by act of Congress in 1939.[15]

On August 27, 1935, Flanagan was sworn in as National Director of the Federal Theater Project, and at the end of the year the New York press was still awaiting the opening of a Federal Theater production. The troupes inherited from the CWA continued to offer free performances, but only in Los Angeles did a new production open in 1935 with a box office and a ticket-seller—and that on December 31. It was not sloth that created the delay but the difficulty of carrying out the procedures necessary under WPA regulations to take on actors and other staff, hire the theaters, and requisition the materials for costumes and scenery. This was, after all, the government's first experiment in large-scale dramatic production—the first of all, if the FERA and CWA shows are set aside—and to determine and refine the method of conducting it was not soon accomplished. To secure a salary for any sort of worker or the money for any nonlabor item, the state directors were required to submit forms in sextuplicate, each copy a color all its own: white, blue, pink, green, yellow, or amber. As Walter Hart, assistant to the head of the production board in New York, was to put it in his letter of resignation of August 13, 1937, "Every time a play is produced by the Federal Theatre a major miracle has been passed. After passing 95 miracles, one begins to tire." [16]

Yet the miracles kept on happening, from coast to coast. In Muskeegee, Oklahoma, the Project operated a theater for the Oklahoma School for the Blind, with blind actors performing for their sighted teachers and friends and their fellow students under a blind director. In Cincinnati, Project actors played to 14,660 victims of a flood of the chronically overflowing Ohio River. In Atlanta a production of Thomas Hall-Rogers's *Altars of Steel* offered the audience the novelty of melodrama, social-message play, and pageantry in one package. In CCC camps up and down the Atlantic seaboard troupers gave a murder mystery that drew in the corpsmen as participants. On Roanoke Island, North Carolina, thousands came to the outdoor production of Paul Green's *The Lost Colony*, which with dramatic action and music presented the saga of the first English settlers in America. At Vassar in the summer of 1937 forty Federal Theater actors, directors, designers, and technicians from seventeen states gathered for six weeks of study and practical theater work. In New York City hundreds of thousands of children attended the Federal Theater circus, complete with all the clowns and other requisite human acts—and, eventually, a female elephant so scrawny that she could truthfully be described as a relief case. On the night of October 27, 1936, Sinclair Lewis and John C. Moffitt's *It Can't Happen Here* opened in twenty-one productions in seventeen cities from Boston to San Francisco. Exclusive of radio programs, which averaged 3000 a year, the Federal Theater offered approximately 1200 productions.[17]

Repeatedly Flanagan stressed her conviction that Federal Theater plays must have something timely to say to the audience. In speeches and articles she made clear her position that the mere pleasant passing of idle hours was not the sole gift of her organization to the public. "The theatre," she wrote in 1935, as the Project got underway, ". . . aside from the rapidly developing left-wing group, has remained curiously oblivious to the changing social order. It is time that the theatre is brought face to face with the great economic problems of the day, of which unemployment is one." In 1938, with some two and a half years of productions good and bad behind her, she wrote, "The play policy of the Federal Theatre is firmly based on the belief that any theatre sponsored by the government of the United States should do no plays of a cheap, vulgar, or out-worn nature, but only such plays as the government can stand behind in a carefully planned program, national in scope, regional in emphasis and American in democratic attitude." In between, in one of many pieces for *Federal Theatre*, the Project's own magazine, she editorialized:

> In [the] attack on injustice, poverty, and despair, so graphically described by President Roosevelt in his Second Inaugural, what part can the Federal Theatre play?
>
> It can make it part of its theatre business to show what is happening to people, all sorts of people, in America today. Not that our plays should be restricted to a study of the one third of our nation which is ill-housed, ill-clad, and ill-nourished, though these millions are so inescapably a part of America today that they are subjects for drama, drama with the militant ring of the Second Inaugural.
>
> Even more potently, perhaps, our plays can concern themselves with conditions back of the conditions described by President Roosevelt.
>
> This, indeed, is happening. Our project playwrights, the characters in their plays, and our playgoers seem to be people not hitherto particularly interested in economic and social conditions, now beginning to study them.

But, though she continued the article with words of praise for some of the Project's new plays with themes relevant to the time, she also took note of its many other kinds of theatrical performance: "The trapeze performer hanging by her heels in the circus, the toe dancer describing an airy arc, the vaudevillian whose inspired ineptitudes console us for our own—all of these are necessary in the many-colored pattern of Federal Theatre. It need not always be Lenin's blood

streaming from the firmament." [18] Here was a word to admonish those
of her supervisors who might in their reforming zeal push too far—as
well as an allusion to Marlowe's *Tragical History of Doctor Faustus,*
one of the Project's greatest hits.

To make the Federal Theater an agency representative of the entire
nation, something more than a pale carbon of the Broadway stage,
was Flanagan's continuing aim. As time went on she was less in
Washington, the original site of her office, than in New York, but she
also spent much time in traveling to the various units of the Project
around the country, listening to problems, interceding with state
WPA administrators, and pondering how to get on to local stages
the quality of their regions. She and her supervisors in all areas
sought the cosponsorship, with the state or municipal government,
of schools, universities, civic groups, clubs, veterans organizations,
trade unions, religious organizations, and private enterprise. Aid
from these various bodies consisted in the sharing of facilities, the
loan of halls for rehearsal space, and the development of good public
relations. The cosponsors in part made up for the Project's lack of
advertising. Washington permitted none, apart from advertisements
in the New York papers on Mondays only, and others in theatrical
magazines, such as *New Theatre* and *TAC.* Contributing to the success of the outlying theaters was the National Service Bureau, with
headquarters in New York, which Flanagan set up in 1937 by combining two previously established offices, the National Play Bureau
and the Play Policy Board. The new Bureau carried on the tasks of
both its predecessors, which were to locate and evaluate old and
new plays. The Bureau staff also arranged for play rentals, published
scripts, and prepared and distributed lists of plays new and old in
many categories—for example, historical, Jewish, labor, religious,
Spanish, Negro, Russian, and children's plays—and sent out scenery,
props, costumes, and actors as well. In consequence of these measures, though mediocre and even poor work was often tendered the
public in small communities with a dearth of talent, and though, inevitably, the New York City units remained the foremost compo-
nents of Federal Theater, the metropolitan centers in all regions
mounted productions that in Flanagan's exacting judgment reflected
credit on the ultimate sponsoring agency—the American people. [19]

In all parts of the country Federal Theater plays were of many types. For each production, no matter who was the author, the program bore the message, "The Federal Theatre Project is part of the WPA program. However, the viewpoint expressed in its productions is not necessarily that of the WPA or any other agency of the government." Over the years fourteen of Shakespeare's plays were produced. Among other premodern dramatists offered were Aristophanes, Plautus, Lope, Molière, Goldsmith, and Sheridan. The major dramatists of the early modern period represented in Federal Theater schedules were Ibsen, Chekhov, Hauptmann, and Wilde. It was a particular point of pride that both Bernard Shaw and O'Neill agreed to let the Project produce cycles of their plays. Shaw, known to be immovably stubborn about royalties, was surprisingly receptive to the Federal Theater's offer which gave him only $50 weekly per production, his reasoning being that with admission at fifty-five cents, usually the top Federal Theater price, the plays were certain to have good runs. The project offered nine of Shaw's plays, including *On the Rocks* in its American première. An outstanding success was the New York production of T. S. Eliot's *Murder in the Cathedral*. Among still other standard and recently established writers produced were John Galsworthy, Synge, Tolstoy, the Čapeks, Thornton Wilder, George S. Kaufman, S. N. Behrman, Maxwell Anderson, Robert E. Sherwood, Clifford Odets, and Elmer Rice. For short periods Los Angeles, Tampa, and New York had companies performing in French, Spanish, and German respectively. New England and New Jersey offered an extensive Italian repertory, and Los Angeles, New York, and other Eastern centers offered some thirty-five plays in Yiddish.[20]

Yet with rare exceptions it was the new American plays that gave the Federal Theater its special tang. In her effort to search out timely, topical plays, the National Director was successful, and the results were well publicized. As she herself noted, productions of the Federal Theater began to have a tone so distinct that productions of the Actors Repertory Company, the Group, and the Guild could be likened to them: "Certain plays opening on Broadway—'200 Were Chosen,' 'Johnny Johnson,' 'But for the Grace of God,' were recognized at once in the terse phrase of *Variety* as being 'down the Federal Theatre's alley.'" [21] Her estimate of the number of plays on social topics produced by the Federal Theater was that it came to less than 10 per cent of the complete list of the Project's productions.[22] But the plays had a potency of which she was not fully aware. If the Project's early undoing could not be blamed wholly on its social plays, certainly the publicity generated by the best of them contributed to it.

Though it was the New York City units of Federal Theater that were the most productive and newsworthy, the outlying units also introduced new topical dramas, as well as many of the new plays previously performed in New York. In a few instances, the regional theaters were visited by companies originating in New York, such as Harlem's Negro unit, which traveled with *Macbeth* and William Du Bois's *Haiti*. Some plays of merit originating in the regional theaters ultimately were acted in New York, and in 1939 an inventive black operetta, *The Swing Mikado*, updating Gilbert and Sullivan, went from Chicago to New York with such success that it inspired commercial imitations and led to the inclusion in Labor Stage's *Pins and Needles* of a sketch called *The Red Mikado*, in which the nazis and American reactionaries were satirized.

In the regional theaters, social protest as represented by new works originating with the Project was mild and confined principally to labor strife. Both Chicago and San Francisco had plays concerning the attitudes of university presidents and students toward local strikes—Howard Koch's *The Lonely Man* and George Savage's *See How They Run*. The disputes reported in the plays are fierce, but both authors took the part of labor without recommending radical solutions. In Koch's play the spokesman for the author's view is a reincarnation of Abraham Lincoln who as a young professor of political economy becomes involved in the strike along with his students.

In Atlanta and Miami Thomas Hall-Rogers's *Altars of Steel* also offered a view of a management-labor confrontation from the middle of the road. The author took pains to make clear that he favored neither the radical take-over of industry nor the labor-crushing devices of reactionary businessmen. A "little steel" company in the South, run by a man of paternalistic instincts, is bought up by the giant of the industry, United Steel, and at once the speed-up and other unfair labor practices are introduced. The result is the death of many workmen in an explosion and the murder of the former owner. Though the play had little to recommend it as literature, it provided the South with a play on its own industry and citizenry, in keeping with Hallie Flanagan's expressed hope that the regional theaters would reflect the atmosphere of their regions. With its scenes of steel workers carrying out the routine of their work in balletic movements, it also provided challenges to the director and designer. The complicated settings, designed to simulate steel in appearance, even to the curtain, were constructed for only $500.[23]

Massachusetts had John Hunter Booth's *Created Equal*, on the development of the idea of democracy in America from 1776 to 1938, the year of the production, with relief workers expressing their confidence in the American way of life, despite the efforts of reactionaries who would constantly compromise and diminish it. More typical of the Federal Theater was Talbot Jennings's *No More Frontier*, first produced in Bridgeport, Connecticut, which, in the fashion of much writing and painting achieved by the various Arts Projects, offered a sweeping view of one region—in this instance the Northwest—and set a story of personal relations against it. Similarly Robert Whitehand's *Precious Land*, produced in San Antonio, dramatized one way of life in the Southwest; in it an Oklahoma farm couple whose property is known to be rich in oil decide against turning it over to the oil industry, despite the promise of wealth, in order to continue their familiar ways on the land dear to them. Other areas of the country were celebrated in such works as Oregon's *Bonneville Dam*, a dance drama created by Project staff members, and North Carolina's *The Lost Colony*.

The Negro units of the outlying theaters introduced several plays, but comparatively little on the theme of the uphill fight of blacks for a place of equality in American society. Theodore Ward's *Big White Fog*, produced in Chicago, was the most noteworthy of these; taking place in 1922, it outlined the dashing of the hope of a middle-class black who has faith in the scheme of Marcus Garvey to create a new black republic in Africa. Los Angeles offered Frank Wells's *John Henry*, a dramatization of the legend of the black construction worker of West Virginia who with his hammer tries to compete against a mechanical steel drill, and dies in the attempt. Seattle produced Theodore Browne's *Natural Man*, on the same legend.

Other regional productions of note were two from Chicago, the musical revue *O Say Can You Sing* by Sid Kuller, Ray Golden, and Phil Charig, and Arnold Sundgaard's *Spirochete*, a Living Newspaper on public health. Though the revue had more than its share of dull sketches, and in the opinion of Hallie Flanagan stooped frequently to vulgarity, it also had a wise premise: the notion that laughing at one-self is sometimes a salubrious exercise. Making fun of the Project, it spoofed the effort of Washington officials, and Federal Theater actors, directors, and supervisors, to create a national institution. "O Say Can You Sing—Dance—or Act?" ran its title song.

> If you can, it's a well-established fact
> That Uncle Sam will take you in . . . (I) [24]

Of new foreign drama on social questions of the thirties, the only major item first performed by a Project theater outside New York was Ernst Toller's *No More Peace*, offered first in Cincinnati, but later given in New York. Toller, then living in exile in America, dramatized in the play the cynical view that even the most ostensibly peace-loving nation in the world could be turned readily into a nation of warmongers. The point is made and proved by Napoleon, who in heaven contrives to make a war between Dunkelstein (a small state lying between France and Germany) and Brazil. Dunkelstein's long-proclaimed love of peace soon turns to love of war, and its leaders begin to suppress the liberties of the citizenry. Of the eighty-one plays introduced by Project theaters that ultimately came under fire in the hearings of congressional committees, this was one. Only one other play first performed in a Project theater outside New York was criticized in the hearings: Booth's *Created Equal*, which earlier came under attack in New Jersey by the actors who were to perform it in that state.[25]

Though the national scope of the Federal Theater was stressed and restressed in Hallie Flanagan's articles and speeches and in the comments of other spokesmen for the Project in *Federal Theatre* and elsewhere, New York inevitably was the vital center of the entire undertaking. As not only the city with the greatest concentration of unemployed theater workers, but also the intellectual capital of the nation, it could hardly have failed to be. Of the funds allocated for the project, 48.97 per cent was spent in New York. Flanagan spent increasingly more of her time there rather than in Washington. In the last two years of the Project, she maintained an office in the city, and thus was able to keep in constant touch with the work of the National

Service Bureau, which administered to the needs of all the outlying units.[26] It was the New York productions that received the bulk of the publicity afforded the Project by the press; national weeklies and monthlies, while generally slighting the regional productions, reviewed the major New York openings as regularly as they reviewed those of commercial managements. The labor agitation which was a constant aspect of life on the Project in New York was another source of Federal Theater publicity emanating from the city, and cruelly self-defeating.

In New York the Project originally set up five major units: the Popular Price Theater under Edward Goodman, for plays in familiar formats by new authors; the Experimental Theater under Virgil Geddes and James Light, for new plays with novel techniques; the Negro Theater under John Houseman and Rose McClendon; the Living Newspaper under Morris Watson; and the Managers' Tryout Theater under Otto Metzger. The last, which was established under the sponsorship of the League of New York Theaters, lasted only a year. Its purpose was to allow commercial managers to test new scripts under Federal Theater auspices. In 1936 another major unit came into being, Project #891, for the production of classical plays, under Houseman and Orson Welles, Houseman having meanwhile turned over the Negro Theater to black supervisors. In addition, a number of smaller units were created under the supervision of Stephen Karnot: a one-act play theater under Em Jo Basshe, a classical unit under George Vivian, a children's unit under Abel Plenn, a Negro Youth Theater under Venzuella Jones; a poetic drama unit under Alfred Kreymborg, a German unit under John E. Bonn, an Anglo-Jewish unit under Boris Thomashevsky, and a Yiddish vaudeville unit. To the directors of these smaller units, Goodman, Geddes, Watson, and Houseman were known as the "Big Four."[27] Without question, their productions were the Project's pacemakers.

Among the productions of all five major units and most of the minor units were plays with content relating to the leading social problems of the thirties. These, however, made up only a fraction of the total number of Project productions: twenty-five, including one-act plays and children's productions, out of some seventy-eight major English-language productions as listed and described in Burns Mantle's *Best Plays* volumes and Flanagan's *Arena*, may be cited as works taking serious issue with traditional social and political institutions.[28] When these are set against the total activity of Federal Theater in the city, including vaudeville, the circus, and marionettes, their importance is indeed slight. The issues taken up in this handful of plays were racial equality, unemployment, trade-unionism, and militarism. Though as late as the seventies each topic remained a matter of public concern, views such as the Project dramatists took of them would in that decade be regarded as moderate, with the exception of those in Oscar Saul and Lou Lantz's *Revolt of the Beavers,* a children's play; Michael Gold and Michael Blankfort's *Battle Hymn;* and the productions of the Living Newspaper unit. Of older plays revived by the project in New York, only Lawson's *Processional* in a revised version, Odets's *Awake and Sing!* (given only in Yiddish), and Kreymborg's *America, America!* could reasonably be said to express a view from the Left. Of hundreds of plays revived by the Project theaters outside New York, only Bein's *Let Freedom Ring,* produced in Detroit alone, and Victor Wolfson's *Excursion,* produced in Atlanta and one other city, could be described as having such a view, and the latter very palely indeed.

Though segregation of the races was not dictated for Federal Theater acting companies in those states where it was not a matter of law, a separate Negro Theater was established in New York, as in ten other cities, including only two in the South: Raleigh and Birmingham. Flanagan's search for the appropriate supervisor for the Negro unit in New York led her to John Houseman, who was not only white but an alien. Houseman was recommended by the distinguished black actress Rose McClendon, around whom he had earlier planned a version of Euripides's *Medea,* and who had played one of the street throng in his production of MacLeish's *Panic.* Houseman had proved his ability to work with black performers with the production in 1934 of the Gertrude Stein-Virgil Thomson opera, *Four Saints in Three Acts.* In the opinion of Rose McClendon, the unit's best interests would be served by the appointment of a white supervisor and white technicians, since blacks had not yet had an opportunity to acquire the requisite skills for those posts. She agreed to join Houseman in heading the unit, but being fatally ill with cancer, left him wholly in charge. Houseman was inspired to ask his young friend Orson Welles, who had been the leading player in MacLeish's *Panic*, to join the unit, and Welles accepted at once. He had been supporting himself in radio work, for which his shimmering mahogony voice put him much in demand; he continued on the air during the decade, while also building a career in legitimate theater. Houseman and Welles proved to be the most dynamic and resourceful producers in the whole of Federal Theater. This was evident to Hallie Flanagan, who recognized them as her "most valuable assets." [29]

Houseman diplomatically secured the good will of three Harlem groups with pronounced opinions on show business and how to conduct it—the veteran performers, the intelligentsia, and the Communists—and set to work in the venerable but crumbling Lafayette Theater. In the short season that he and Welles remained with the unit, they offered four plays: Frank Wilson's *Walk Together Chillun*, Rudolph Fisher's *Conjur' Man Dies* (directed by Joseph Losey), *Macbeth*, and Peter Morrell and J. A. Smith's *Turpentine*.

On the evidence of reviews and Houseman's later comments, these plays, with the exception of *Macbeth*, were mediocre fare. Houseman's two social plays dealt with troubled labor situations exacerbated by racial tension, but the possibilities inherent in the subject, which had been well realized by Peters and Sklar in *Stevedore*, lay partially buried under awkward construction. Wilson, a talented actor who had "created" the title role in Dorothy and Du Bose Heyward's *Porgy*, wrote of the troubles encountered in the North by Georgia blacks imported as laborers because of their willingness to work for lower wages than the resident blacks. Strife erupts between the two groups of blacks, but ultimately they are thrown together in mutual defense against the hostile white community. The coauthors of *Turpentine* devised a more militant play, choosing as their subject black Southern turpentine workers who revolt against the conditions of their work and low wages and succeed in winning their demands. Houseman thought the play worth putting on, though recognizing it as faulty: "[a] routine play of protest, full of leftist clichés . . ." [30]

Neither of these plays nor *Conjur' Man Dies*, a detective story, could compare with the Houseman-Welles *Macbeth* for popular appeal. Set in nineteenth-century Haiti, a far remove from the Scotland of Shakespeare's imagination, the production was given colorful costumes and jungle settings and was enhanced musically by the voodoo rhythms of a troupe of African drummers. Under the direction of Welles, Jack Carter and Edna Thomas as Macbeth and his wife gave highly praised performances in a text that was a somewhat altered and rearranged version of Shakespeare's play, but retained the original language. A vast success, it was a milestone in the careers of both Houseman and Welles. Advance publicity drew a throng of ten thousand toward the theater on opening night. All the major reviewers attended, one having requested in advance that he and his wife be given seats "not next to Negroes," if possible. The critical reception was warm, with the result that the play was popular with blacks and whites equally. After the closing of the production, which ran at the Lafayette from April 9, 1936, through the summer, it went on tour, a proud exhibit of Federal Theater at its most inventive. Yet, pondered by later generations, the reviews and comments of the day suggest that the Negro unit's *Macbeth* was as much a show as a play, and that the voodoo drums and lush visual treats provided a distraction from the language. Was there in this, despite the admiration of Welles and Houseman for their actors and the rapport that they established with them, a stubborn trace of the white man's inability to take the black man seriously? Possibly more insightful than she knew was the observation of Willson Whitman, the early historian of the Federal Theater: "This Macbeth and his lady were wrongheaded children, rather than adults crazed by cupidity." [31]

Leaving the Lafayette to set up their new unit, Project #891, Houseman and Welles turned the Harlem unit over to two black supervisors, J. A. Smith and Carlton Moss. It was Houseman's conviction that blacks on the project had at that point been sufficiently trained to operate the Negro Theater themselves. Under its new management, the Harlem unit offered a program comparable to that devised by Houseman: standard works adapted for black casts, the dance-drama *Bassa Moona* to provide color, and three plays of social content. George MacEntee's *The Case of Philip Lawrence*, though a melodrama built around a murder, offered insight into the troubled minds of Harlem youth in the person of the title character, a young man with a new college degree who cannot find employment commensurate with his ability. Conrad Seiler's *Sweet Land*, a militant labor play produced at the Lafayette by Venzuella Jones's Theater of

Negro Youth, gave the New York audience a view of the all but hopeless conditions of Southern black sharecroppers who, pressed by their white employers, become militant members of the Sharecropper and Tenants' Union. One of the Federal Theater's bluntest labor plays, it depicts a struggle between malevolent white property owners and noble blacks, akin in their two-dimensionality to the characters of the early agitprop sketches. Less militant, and more successful, was William DuBois's *Haiti*, on the uprisings in 1802 of Jean Christophe against the French colonial government. Though possibly intended to put iron into the contemporary black audience, it is as much a drama of domestic intrigue as of the development of a revolutionary consciousness. Given a colorful production with a cast including Rex Ingram and Canada Lee, it was after *Macbeth* the unit's most widely acclaimed play. In Harlem during the run advertisements were to be seen describing it as "better than *Macbeth*." [32]

Wishing to continue the association with Welles that had proved advantageous for them both, Houseman proposed to Hallie Flanagan that he and Welles be permitted to establish a classical unit at the Maxine Elliott Theater on 39th Street, as close to the Broadway area as the Federal Theater's arrangement with the League of New York Theaters would permit at the time. The proposal was accepted, and the two directors chose the WPA number of their unit, Project #891, as its name for want of a better one. In this new unit their task, as before, was to put unemployed workers back to work, but with a difference. The Negro Theater in Harlem had been, and remained, the sole stage operated in New York for black actors; Houseman had had to put on the plays at hand best suited to the talent he had at his disposal, and his choice was limited by his belief that the new plays should be the work of black writers. But with Project #891, he could exercise more exacting judgment, since his was one of several theaters for white actors. As it turned out, the team prepared only three productions for Project #891: *Horse Eats Hat*, an adaptation by Edward Denby of Henri Labiche's farce, *The Italian Straw Hat*; Marlowe's *Doctor Faustus*; and Blitzstein's *The Cradle Will Rock*, a new work, but destined to become a classic of sorts.

As directed by Welles, *Horse Eats Hat* was a bawdy romp of a play, with a cast extended to include dozens of performers, in accordance with the Federal Theater practice of using as many actors as possible. Among the actors introduced to Federal Theater in this production were Hiram Sherman, Joseph Cotton, Arlene Francis, and Paula Laurence. Somewhat disparaged on the grounds of vulgarity, the play nevertheless did well. Better received was *Doctor Faustus*, directed and designed by Welles, and lit by Abe Feder, Federal Theater's lighting wizard, with Welles and Jack Carter, giants in physique and talent, playing against each other as Faustus and Mephistophilis. Like *Macbeth*, this was to be remembered as a major event in the careers of Welles and Houseman, and remembered also as one of Federal Theater's most outstanding productions. But with this success behind them, they chose to ignore the standard repertory and produce Blitzstein's untried *Cradle*. The time was the spring of 1937.

During the run of *Horse Eats Hat*, Blitzstein discussed with Welles the possibility of his directing *The Cradle Will Rock* for the Actors Repertory Company. With that troupe's recognition that the work was beyond their resources, Welles wanted it for the Federal Theater. Houseman heard the score for the first time and liked it. He arranged a dinner party at which Blitzstein played the score for Hallie Flanagan, who enjoyed it and gave permission for a Project #891 production. Meanwhile the play became more topical as the days passed. The Steel Workers Organizing Committee was achieving success in its effort to bring the labor force of "Little" and U.S. Steel into the CIO in late spring, but not without bloodshed. Many strikers were wounded and twelve killed by police near the Chicago plant of Republic Steel on Memorial Day. While these events were taking place in heavy industry, cuts of Project personnel were rumored to be in the offing, and on May 27, two days before the Chicago disaster, members of the Workers' Alliance, the City Projects Council, and the American Federation of Musicians called for a one-day strike on all WPA projects in New York. This did not prevent the cuts from occurring; on June 10 Hallie Flanagan received word from Washington to reduce the New York project by 30 per cent. To do so meant issuing pink slips to 1701 workers.[33]

The Cradle Will Rock was nearing its opening. A preview was scheduled for June 16, and so wide was now the fame of Houseman and Welles that 14,000 tickets had been sold for the expected run. At this point, on June 12, all Federal Arts Projects directors received word that because of cuts no new theatrical production, musical performance, or art gallery could open before July 1. It was clear to Flanagan that this was a new form of censorship; Washington, as she knew, had begun to have some worries about the impending *Cradle*. Though she tried, with the aid of Archibald MacLeish, Virgil Thomson, and others, to persuade WPA officials to allow the production, she could not get a reversal of the original order. Welles, in Washington on June 13 to plead for the production, became convinced that the play could never be performed under WPA auspices, and told David Niles, director of information for the WPA, that if it could not open as planned, he and Houseman would produce it on their own. Niles replied that if they did, the WPA "would no longer be interested in it as a property." [34]

On the following day, Houseman and Welles invited an audience to a run-through of the play to be held that evening. Celebrities of all political persuasions came to observe a talented cast that included Howard Da Silva as Larry Foreman, Will Geer as Mr. Mister, and Hiram Sherman as Junior Mister, and to hear an orchestra of twenty-eight musicians under the baton of Lehman Engel. Though such a performance was not forbidden under the terms of the memorandum received on the 12th, since it could be described as merely a rehearsal, it brought down the wrath of the WPA. The theater building was locked—apart from the ladies' room, which served as the office of Project # 891—and the production staff forbidden the use of scenery, costumes, and props. Still determined to put on their play, Houseman and Welles got word to the holders of preview tickets, mostly left-wing organizations, that the performance scheduled for the 16th would take place, knowing that the stage would be bare and the performers in streetclothes, and knowing too that it would have to be another stage than that of the Maxine Elliott. As they searched for a theater, they received more bad news. The musicians' union required the new management to pay for new rehearsal sessions at Broadway salaries and demanded an increase in the size of the orchestra, and Equity insisted that to perform under the new Houseman-Welles management the actors would have to receive permission from their current employers, the Federal Theater. This, of course, would not be forthcoming. Though not all members of the cast belonged to Equity, the principles did.

Still the team would not give up. Will Geer and Howard Da Silva entertained the ticket-holders gathering on the sidewalk. At the last minute Welles and Houseman learned that the large Venice Theater (later the Century) twenty blocks to the north was available; for hours an entrepreneur who had it at his disposal and was with them in the ladies' room had been trying to catch their ear. Uptown went the producers, the actors (for despite the Equity ruling most had stayed on), Blitzstein, Abe Feder, and several hundred ticket-holders, and a curious but unforgettable performance ensued. With Blitzstein on stage at a tinny piano, and the cast seated among the audience all over the house, the lights went down. Blitzstein set the scene in his speaking voice and began to play. Some of the performers had decided to defy the Equity ruling and sing from their positions in the auditorium; others had not. But as Blitzstein began the prostitute's opening song, Olive Stanton, who had the part, started to sing with him. Others rose up to perform their parts, with Blitzstein doing some eight roles and Hiram Sherman two he had never rehearsed as well as his own of Junior Mister. The performance went on without a hitch. Afterwards, Archibald MacLeish made a speech. So successful was the method of presentation that most subsequent revivals have dispensed with the orchestral score, and almost never has the work been performed with scenery.[35]

This was the end of the association of Houseman and Welles with the Federal Theater. Nor did Project #891 continue without them. In the fall they announced the founding of their own company, the Mercury Theater.

The Managers' Try-Out, the Popular Price, the Experimental, the Poetic, and the One-Act units of the Project in New York offered plays in too great a variety for easy categorization. American plays outnumbered all others, including works from the standard repertory, by approximately two to three. Among the twentieth-century foreign plays were at least six of more than routine interest. These were Valentin Katayev's *Path of Flowers*, a Soviet satire on social parasitism; Friedrich Wolf's *Professor Mamlock,* a tragedy on nazi anti-Semitic measures and their shattering effect on a Jewish physician, his family, and his clinic, with the strong suggestion the most effective counterforce was communism; W. H. Auden's *The Dance of Death,* an expressionistic play on the self-destruction of capitalist society; Toller's antiwar satire, *No More Peace;* Shaw's *On the Rocks,* a satire on conflict among political factions, set in contemporary England; and T. S. Eliot's *Murder in the Cathedral,* a poetic tragedy on the martyrdom of Archbishop Thomas à Becket in 1170. Of these plays, Eliot's was the most enthusiastically received. Opening in March 1936 with the aging actor Harry Irvine as Becket, it provided the Project with its first unquestionable artistic success.

Like most of the celebrated new American plays produced in the thirties by all other managements, those of the Federal Theater revealed their authors' awareness of the new artistic and social attitudes. Hofmann Hays's *Ballad of Davy Crockett* rode the wave of enthusiasm for the American past that swept over the land in the late thirties. Virgil Geddes's domestic drama of the northern Midwest, *Native Ground,* though written at the end of the twenties, provided a response to the new interest in the regional arts, as did Theodore Pratt's *The Big Blow,* set in Florida, with the added importance of an urgent theme: racial intolerance. The old South was glorified in an embarrassingly feeble play, *Jefferson Davis,* by John McGee, the director of the Project's Southern division; produced for a Southern tour at the request of the Daughters of the Confederacy, the play, unhappily, was first unveiled in New York—far from the home of its natural audience.[36] Antiwar plays included Em Jo Basshe's one-act *Snickering Horses,* an attack on the jingoist attitudes of big business, and Samuel J. Warshawsky's *Woman of Destiny,* a glance into the future, when the first woman President averts a war with Japan and, that business taken care of, dashes off to see her grandchild, who is ill with croup. A satire on venality and yellow journalism was offered by Edwin L. and Albert Barker in *American Holiday,* set in a fictional Middletown that was easily recognized as Flemington, New Jersey, when that small town was stormed by sensation seekers during the trial of Bruno Hauptmann for the Lindbergh kidnapping.

In *Sing for Your Supper,* a revue based on the character of Uncle Sam and his decision to go into show business, the big hit was a mus-

ical number by Earl Robinson and John Latouche called "Ballad for
Uncle Sam," on the composite make-up of the "typical" American—
his ethnic origins, his professions, his religions, and his unshakable
faith in democracy. (Retitled "Ballad for Americans" and recorded by
Paul Robeson, it became well known nationally; millions heard it in
1940 when it was played as the theme song of the Republican presidential convention.) In the summer of 1936 was staged Lynn Riggs's
The Cherokee Night, a panoramic play of the corruption suffered by
modern Oklahomans of mixed Indian and white ancestry as they try
to adjust to the predominantly white environment. Under the direction of Madalyn O'Shea, the play was put on at the Provincetown
Playhouse as an exercise by fifty professional theater workers who
were preparing for work in community theater in all five boroughs
of the city.[37] Other productions of the New York units, though uneven
in quality as a group, deserve more extended comment by virtue of
their authors' fame, their greater interest as portraits of the age, or
their political outspokenness.

One of the early successes of the busy first New York season was
Harold A. Clarke and Maxwell Nurnberg's *Chalk Dust* (1936), a sensitive portrayal of the daily life of teachers in a metropolitan high
school. The production stayed on for 51 performances and later was
produced by theaters in ten other localities. Teachers themselves, the
authors described in lavish detail the routine of a profession bound
by strict regulations and supervised by rank-proud petty tyrants
whose conservatism is only insecurity in disguise. Two teachers of
English occupy the center of the action: Allen Rogers, a young man
of twenty-five, and Marian Sherwood, an unmarried woman ten years
his senior. Both are the sort of dedicated teacher to whom the classroom experience means more than family life or material comforts.
Drawn together, they become a major item of discussion for the
school's gossips. Though they are innocent, the rumors about them are
enough to separate them permanently. Deciding that she cannot
marry Rogers because of the age difference, Marian accepts the proposal of an older man of means whom she likes but does not love. In
the moving final scene, however, she changes her mind. After resigning, she returns to her old classroom to pick up some books and becomes so absorbed in a discussion with the students that she does not
go. The scandal meanwhile becomes a lever with which the principal

forces Rogers to accept a transfer to another school. The real reason
for forcing him out is that he has instituted a political discussion club
in which the students talk about subjects that the principal finds dangerous: European militarism and the anti-New Deal decisions of the
Supreme Court. In his last speech of the play, he refutes the principal's charge that a person with his ideas does not belong in the
schools:

> You're wrong, Doctor Harriman. That's just where I do belong.
> You've made me see that. You call me a trouble-maker. I am. I let
> the boys and girls talk about war and peace, strikes and share-crop-
> pers, Communism, Fascism, and Democracy. I intend to go right on
> making that sort of trouble. And I'm not alone, Dr. Harriman. There
> are thousands of teachers throughout the country who are not willing
> to sit around in false security while the world rusts away. We'll go
> right on making trouble—until your whole school system becomes a
> seething cauldron of American Democracy (III, iii).

With this able young teacher Clarke and Nurnberg exemplified a
generation of young people determined to preserve democracy from
dangerous forces on both sides. The same strong feeling pulses
through Orrie Lashin and Milo Hastings's *Class of '29*, a play performed in New York (1936) and eleven other cities. The major characters are four young men who graduated from Harvard with the last
class to whom it seemed that all doors were open. During the Depression all that is changed, and each of the four seeks his salvation in his
own way. Ted Holden, described as an "aristocrat," is trained for
nothing and has spent his entire inheritance, which because of the
Crash did not come to much. Though he limply attempts to sell first
editions that he comes upon in secondhand shops, he is content to
live off his college friends and his girl, who in fact is being kept by a
rich employer. His fate is suicide. Tippy Sayre, trained as a sanitary
engineer, is the most enterprising: he makes his living by washing the
pets of the rich. The solution of Martin Peterson is communism; a
cartoonist, he makes posters for the party, but is not above submitting
cartoons to the *New Yorker*. Ken Holden, an architect, is the most appealing of the four. To him the authors give the play's most passionate speech, an outburst poignant with despair over the world in
which he finds himself:

I'm not the man I was three years ago. People slam doors in my face.
Do you understand? They look at me. They see my clothes, my eyes.
. . . They're antagonized before they speak to me—just as people are
to a beggar. They say "no" before I ask for anything. No, no, no, no.
They say it as if I were asking for charity instead of a job. "Not for
you." "Sorry." "Nothing today."—It makes a beggar out of you! (I, i).

He does find a job, but it is literally bought for him by his father,
who gives the head of a firm $1,200 to be paid out to the young man
in installments as a year's salary.

In Ted's suicide it is possible to see the fatal collapse of a useless
class—more painfully and more vindictively dispatched by the authors than were Madame Ranevskaya and her family by Chekhov in
The Cherry Orchard. But their solution to the problem of the young
and indeed of all others living in a time of blasted hope is not revolutionary. The solution is to *keep going*. Ken, miserable as he is on
hearing the truth about his "job," decides to stay with it anyway; it is
at least something to do and, therefore, a preventive for the malaise
that again threatens him. Tippy, washing a dog on stage, represents
the American enterprising spirit at its best. We see him getting what
he can out of his training—a comedown, no doubt, from the plans of
an engineer, but a way to beat the doldrums and relief. More than in
other Federal Theater plays, Lashin and Hastings got into their work
the feel of the thirties—the harshness and, for many, the cruelty, of
daily life, but along with it the American optimism that could be
dampened but not destroyed.

In a similar vein was a lighter but very popular play of the same
year, Paul Vulpius's Viennese farce *Help Yourself*, adapted for the
American stage by John J. Coman. After the New York opening it was
given in twenty-one other cities. Its message, like that of *Class of '29*,
is that with the untrammeled exercise of initiative one can bring
about a kind of miracle: create a job, get money into circulation,
make things happen. An unemployed young man named Christopher
Stringer walks into a bank where a friend has a job, sits at a desk,
and by writing some letters on the bank's stationery makes a place for
himself at the bank, causes a shut-down factory to be reopened with
jobs for six hundred men, is named general manager of the factory,
and has a proposal of marriage from the bank president's daughter. A
farce, to be sure, and as such not to be taken at face value, it never-

theless had a theme for the time, as expressed by the confident protagonist when it begins to look as though his plan to reopen the factory will go through:

> It's a beginning. It's something new. Life itself always starts
> something new, doesn't it? The sun, the biggest trust in the world,
> breaks down the ice of the world over again each year. The wheat
> kernel develops thousands and thousands of times into the blade.
> Should man be the only one to set himself against the onward motion
> of the world? See what I mean? What would happen, gentlemen, if
> the power above should suddenly say, "This year I won't have any
> spring. I'll wait till better times come along." . . . No, gentlemen!
> We must go on working, as life goes on working. Not figure and pon-
> der, but work. You must pick up the first packing-case you see with a
> shout of *up she goes!* (II).

Such a moderate opinion was not held by all Federal Theater authors. In view of Hallie Flanagan's political sophistication and her
knowledge of recent New York theatrical activity, it is curious that
she should have permitted the staging of *Battle Hymn,* one of whose
authors was Michael Gold, and whose theme is unmistakably revolutionary. On the other hand, the fact that the play was never attacked
by the Federal Theater's congressional enemies may account for the
enthusiasm with which she recalled it in her history of the Project. A
vivid treatment of the life of John Brown, tracing his career from
Ohio to Kansas to Virginia up to the last moment before his fatal raid
on Harper's Ferry, the play had begun some years before as a script
by Gold alone. At his suggestion, it was revised by Michael Blankfort,
who shared the credit with him for it.[38]

The subject may have recommended itself to Gold in 1936 for many
reasons. It was, after all, an important event of the American past
and consequently in keeping with the mood of the Popular Front; in
a promotional piece on the play for the *Daily Worker* signed by
both writers but later maintained by Blankfort to be Gold's alone, the
parallel is drawn between the persecution of Brown and of "our Tom
Mooneys and Vanzettis . . . today, and for almost the same reasons,
and by the same exploiters." [39] The Communist party had another
parallel in mind as well: in this presidential year of 1936, the party,
though gladly settling for Roosevelt, nevertheless had a candidate
of its own in the person of Earl Browder and stressed the fact that he

was a Midwesterner—indeed a native of Kansas. Brown's maniacal
shootings are seen as the result of an unavoidable change in his
outlook and temperament caused by the intransigence of slavers. He is a
convert to a new position, like the protagonists of agitprop plays,
and also like them he is accused of being a general troublemaker, "an
agitator bought by *British gold*" (I, ii). Another borrowing from
agitprop is the nursery-rhyme alliteration in the names of two reactionaries, Banker Buell and Reverend Romney; still another is the
use of a mass-chant prologue before each act, but as a structural device this may have come, not from agitprop, but from the new and very
successful living newspapers.

In the second season of the Project took place the most astonishing
of all the "miracles" that Flanagan and her staff achieved: the multiple simultaneous openings of Sinclair Lewis and John C. Moffitt's *It
Can't Happen Here.* As message-laden a play as *Battle Hymn*, it
looked, not to the past, but to the future—more precisely, to the future as it might grotesquely be if Americans, like the Germans and
Italians, abandoned democracy. Lewis's novel of the same name, on
which the play was based, had been bought for the screen by Metro-
Goldwyn-Mayer on publication, but the studio had dropped plans for
filming it after a script was prepared by Sidney Howard. Lewis believed that the film had been abandoned on orders from Will Hays,
Hollywood's arbiter of controversial subjects. Hays and Lewis B.
Mayer, however, insisted, unconvincingly, that the projected production cost had been prohibitive and that this consideration alone had
governed the studio's decision. It was a decision that drew expressions of satisfaction from the governments of both Germany and Italy.
At the suggestion of William B. Farnsworth, then head of the Federal
Theater Play Bureau, Lewis was asked to turn the novel into a play,
which, also at Farnsworth's suggestion, could not only be produced
nationwide, but with all the openings occurring on the same evening.
With the assistance of Moffitt, a writer for Paramount Pictures, Lewis
went to work on the adaptation. The opening date was set for October 27, 1936, with seventeen cities participating.[40] °

° These included Birmingham, Boston, Bridgeport, Chicago, Cleveland, Denver,
Detroit, Indianapolis, Los Angeles (with two productions, one in Yiddish), Miami,
Newark, New York (with three productions, one in Yiddish), San Francisco, Seattle
(with the city's Negro troupe), Tacoma, Tampa (in Spanish), and Yonkers. Later the
play was acted by troupes in eight other cities.[38]

The simultaneous openings did not come about with the waving of a wand. Confusion over cuts and revisions was rife from coast to coast. To Flanagan's irritation, the New York supervisors requested that their openings be postponed until after the regional theaters had unveiled their productions, thus reducing the status of those productions to that of a massive tryout for New York. This she promptly vetoed. At one point she acted as go-between for Lewis and Moffitt, who were not always on speaking terms. At another, the eve of the opening, she and three of her staff mounted the stage of the Adelphi Theater in New York to repaint and refurnish the poorly executed sets. To do such work on stage and so soon before the opening was in violation of the principles she had taught for many years, but the Adelphi production was the one that would draw the critics who counted. Meanwhile, all the theaters had been warned not to publicize the play with allusions to political powers or figures at home or abroad. Nevertheless, the newspapers pumped out a stream of speculative articles on the content of the play.[41]

Though the productions varied in design, direction, and quality, all offered essentially the same material. At a time described as "very soon—or never," a fascist politician Berzelius ("Buzz") Windrip forms the Corporative party and, after wooing big business on one hand and workers and farmers on the other, is voted into the presidency. The obvious parallel between the Corpos, as the party-members are called, and the nazis and Italian fascists is made more so by the appearance in uniform of Windrip's henchmen and the many scenes in which they brutalize their opponents. In his vulgarity and flatulence Windrip resembles Huey Long, and Pastor Paul Peter Prang, an early supporter of the Corpos, resembles the "radio priest" Father Charles E. Coughlin. (Prang broadcasts, not from Dearborn, however, but from Lewis's familiar Zenith.) Jessup is slow to respond to the Corpo menace as both a newspaperman and a private person. When he does, it is almost too late. The conversion occurs after a series of painful events, including the murder of his son-in-law and the removal from his hands of control of the paper. Joining the underground, he publishes resistance pamphlets in his own home and is caught. At the close of the play, having escaped from a concentration camp, he is residing in Canada, where forces opposed to Windrip have gathered. At the cost of her own life his daughter sends her son across the border to join him. The last, harrowing scene at the border offers a glimmer of hope that eventually the tyrant will fall.

As in Lewis's fiction, the characterization is frequently exaggerated beyond credibility, and too many of the figures are stock types. Among them are Jessup himself and his confidant and friend, the society editor Lorinda Pike—the country editor chockablock with righteous indignation and the mock-comic spinster who decries his few weaknesses. One action of hers all but destroys the play's slowly building suspense. Without telling her, he hides notes for his next pamphlet in a copy of Rabelais, an author of whom she disapproves. When the Corpos on a book-burning drive ask her whether she knows of any "bad" books in his possession she says with a laugh, "I most certainly do," and directs them to the Rabelais. This proves to be a major turning point in the action; as a result of the discovery, Doremus is jailed. Despite its weaknesses, the play was a hit. Altogether, the productions played for a total of 260 weeks, or, as Flanagan noted with justifiable pride, the equivalent of a run of five years.[42]

Following *It Can't Happen Here* into the Adelphi, Barrie and Leona Stavis's *The Sun and I* gave the Federal Theater one of its major successes for 1937. A historical play with a theme relevant to the age woven into the plot, it is a version of the career of the biblical Joseph in Egypt. His life as dramatized by the authors illustrates the folly of the leader who believes that the common good is best served if rule is in the hands of an absolute dictator. Like Hitler, Joseph wishes to build up the strength of his nation regardless of the hardships he may have to work on individuals. Yet at the end, when workers on the Nile revolt against his tyranny, he recognizes his mistake and withdraws into the desert. Sympathetic in his admission of guilt, he looks forward to a later time when a new, humane ruler will come who will teach the people to rule themselves:

> Remember, Time is yet young! Some day a new Joseph will be born who will profit by my mistakes. He will teach the people to put their faith in one another and not in the deceptive powers of rulers, or in the false promises of priests. Understanding and believing, these men will become heroes and will be ready to sacrifice themselves for the future. And when that time comes the gods and their superstitions, the tyrants and their slavery and all things that rob man of his true heritage will vanish for heroes need no gods and no tyrants (III).

Thus prophesying a better form of government to come, this Joseph represents neither the Right nor the Left, despite the criticism of Federal Theater opponents, but the traditional American view of government by and for the people.

This view was also taken by E. P. Conkle in *Prologue to Glory*, a major success of 1938, though the play is only faintly concerned with politics. The only Federal Theater work to be included in one of Burns Mantle's volumes of *Best Plays*, it is a warm, sentimental recreation of Abraham Lincoln's sojourn in New Salem in 1831, when, shopkeeping and studying law, he ran unsuccessfully for the Illinois legislature and had a brief, doomed romance with Ann Rutledge. Apart from references to slavery, only in Lincoln's decision to stand for office—on a mild populist platform—does the play touch on politics. It is primarily a "human interest" drama of the well-balanced, ingratiating personality of a young man destined for greatness. Yet to J. Parnell Thomas, a Republican member of the House Un-American Activities Committee, it offered evidence that the Project was under the thumb of the Communist party. In a newspaper article he was quoted as saying, "The play *Prologue to Glory* deals with Lincoln in his youth and portrays him battling with politicians. This is simply a propaganda play to prove that all politicians are crooked." Amazed by the statement and finding herself on a train with Thomas one day between Washington and New York, Flanagan asked him about it. What had disturbed him in the play was the scene in which Lincoln takes part in a debate on the subject "Resolved: that bees are more valuable than ants," but says, "It seems to me that the subjects for debate b'fore this Forum ought to be alive—subjects for action, useful for living" (I, iv). "That," Thomas told Flanagan, "is Communist talk." [43]

The last of the New York Project's social dramas to be produced, and the last Federal Theater production in New York, was George Sklar's *Life and Death of an American*, which opened on May 19, 1939, and was still running when the Project closed down on June 30. A generally well-received play, it is an episodic account of the short life of Jerry Dorgan (played by Arthur Kennedy), the first child born in the twentieth century. The son of a working-class Irish-American couple, he is deprived of a college education by the death of his father from a lung ailment contracted on the job. A true child of the century, he experiences, and most feelingly, the First World War, the boom, and the bust. Finding work in a steel plant in the thirties, he takes part in a labor demonstration after the company announces a wage slash, and is killed by the bullet of a policeman. In short, Jerry Dorgan in his lifetime and in his death is a victim of all the destructive forces that, according to Marxist opinion, the capitalist system breeds. Though as lively as Sklar's Theater Union plays, *Life and Death of an American* lacks coherence because of the frequent intrusions of a chorus of chanters who introduce and comment on the turns of Jerry's life, demonstrating, as did the chorus of *Battle Hymn*, the influence of the living newspapers.

Apart from the Yiddish version of *Awake and Sing!* and Kreymborg's *America, America!*, only one American play of the recent past given a new production by the Project could reasonably be described as radical: Lawson's *Processional*, the new version of which was presented in 1937 and ran for three months. Lawson's alteration of the original text was extensive, but noticeable chiefly in a reduction of the musical numbers and a change in the characterization of the black workers and the Jewish shopkeeper. Rastus Jelly becomes Joe Green and is no longer the shuffling stage darky but a man of dignified bearing. Jake Psinski retains his name, but speaks in an idiom much different from that of the traditional stage Jew of the original. In plot and theme the work is as it was before: an artful presentation of the class struggle in the coal fields acted out between brave laborers and callous industrialists assisted by the Ku Klux Klan, the militia, and local law-enforcers. Lawson in 1937 was too much the devoted Party enthusiast to allow the potentially divisive caricatures of his 1925 script to stand. Having embraced communism, he had arrived at a position from which he could no longer joke about the minorities, even if the jokes were part of a scheme of ennobling a variety of people's art, the subliterary theater. Nevertheless, the play did not go down well with the Communist press in 1937. Despite the revisions, the *New Masses* reviewer complained of the caricatures, and the *Daily Worker* reviewer bluntly declared, "In 1937 'Processional' is of practically no importance except as a historical exhibit." [44]

Curiously, the work most questionable on political grounds was produced, not by any of the major Project units, but by the Children's Theater: Oscar Saul and Lou Lantz's *The Revolt of the Beavers*, which opened in 1937 and was kept on for a month. A fantasy taking place in the dream of two children of the unemployed, it is an allegory on the theme of mass action scaled to fit the imagination of the young. Visiting Beaverland in their dream, Paul and Mary meet a Beaver-Professor and with him visit the industrial center of the country and watch the beavers at work. These beavers are "sad" because their chief overworks them:

> But the Chief of all the Beavers
> He gets all the bark we make
> All he does is pull the levers
> While we work until we ache. (I)

With the help of the children and the Professor, who loses his professorial timidity, a young beaver leader named Oakleaf sets things straight. Exiled by the chief for having started a Sad Beavers Club, he comes back when sent for by the children and persuades the chief's scabs (the "barkless beavers") to join with the workers in a show of solidarity. Disguised as a polar bear, he tells the chief that he has been sent by the polar bear king to copy the machine whereby the beavers turn bark into the necessities of life. The king wants such a machine in order to manufacture ice cream bricks. Granted permission, he starts to wreck the wheel and rallies the workers and barkless beavers to his side. Massing together, they throw the chief and his gang of toughs out of Beaverland, which then becomes a happy state in which the workers receive the fruits of their labor. A storm of protest rose over the play because the Project's foes read it as an encouragement to revolution. Fourteen hundred free tickets held by the Police Athletic League for distribution to children were sent back. Brooks Atkinson, one of Federal Theater's most sympathetic critics, was among those startled by the inclusion of the work in the Project's bills. "Many children now unschooled in the technique of revolution," he wrote, "now have an opportunity, at government expense, to improve their tender minds. Mother Goose is no longer a rhymed escapist. She has been studying Marx; Jack and Jill lead the class revolution." Children who saw the play were not, according to report, propelled to the Left, but took it only as another theatrical treat. This news, however, did not mollify the opponents of the Project. Nor did Hallie Flanagan herself fail to see the message of the play. Six months before the opening, she wrote to her husband that it was "very class conscious." [45]

For inventive solutions to the problem of how to put the super-abundance of available actors back to work and to get the most out of the limited funds available for other-than-labor costs, no other Federal Theater productions matched the living newspapers. In one of her earliest talks with Hopkins, before receiving the appointment as National Director, Hallie Flanagan suggested the living newspapers for a two-fold purpose: not only as a means of using a great many actors in a single play, but as a means of dramatizing current events. The idea came to her again in discussions with Elmer Rice on what to do with the actors waiting for roles.[46] Her practicality was rewarded with a series of excellently mounted scripts that won the praise of drama critics and drew large, enthusiastic houses but that because of their content raised controversies ultimately damaging to the Project.

The origin of both the term "living newspaper" and the staging methods of the Project's Living Newspaper unit are not wholly clear. As early as March 1933 *Workers Theatre* published a brief playlet by one Isay Murinson titled *O Learned Judge,* on the inequality of the rich and poor in court, with the designation "Sketch for a Living Newspaper." It may be that Hallie Flanagan encountered the term in this instance; she did not credit herself with inventing it and was familiar with the magazine. The narrative method combined historical documents and the latest news flashes with invented dialogue, and brought together real figures of the past and present alongside invented characters, all presided over by the disembodied Voice of the Living Newspaper that rang across the stage by means of a loud-speaker. Projections, films, charts, graphs, the novel use of light, and scenery of both naturalistic and expressionistic varieties were part of the technique. Music, both orchestral and vocal, was used. The combination of all these materials resulted in dramatic offerings of a style unfamiliar to American audiences. In the opinion of Arthur Arent, "editor" of the unit and author of two of its best scripts, the style had no known sources; it evolved from the staff's enjoyment of experimentation coupled with a distaste for repeating their methods from play to play. Flanagan, on the other hand, was ready to acknowledge numerous debts:

Like all so-called new forms the Living Newspaper borrows with fine impartiality from many sources: from Aristophanes, from the *Commedia dell'Arte,* from Shakespearean soliloquy, from the pantomime of Mei Lan Fang. Being a flexible technique and only in its beginning, it still has much to learn from the chorus, the camera, the cartoon. Although it has occasional reference to the *Volksbühne* and the Blue Blouses, to Bragaglia and Meierhold and Eisenstein, it is as American as Walt Disney, the *March of Time,* and the *Congressional Record,* to all of which American institutions it is indebted.

Her own *Can You Hear Their Voices?* she later thought of as the precursor of the living newspapers in "the use of factual material, charts, statistics, loud speakers, and blackouts." Pierre de Rohan, the Project's wry house critic, also offered an opinion: "It is merely a merger of radio programs and topical movie, retaining the worst features of each." [47]

Rice conceived of the notion of asking the Newspaper Guild to sponsor the Living Newspaper unit and put Morris Watson, the Guild's vice president, in charge. Under Watson a staff of unemployed Guild members and playwrights assembled to put the scripts together. With an organization resembling that of an actual newspaper from editor-in-chief down to copyreaders, the members of the unit brought together and sifted the materials pertaining to the general topic of each production. Since living figures appeared in the scripts, a lawyer screened them for libelous details. At first the unit planned to put on a new show every two weeks, concentrating on up-to-the-minute happenings. But, given the time required for the intelligent mounting of a work, it proved impossible to carry out such a program. Instead, the unit chose to create scripts outlining and elucidating current problems, with the introduction to the degree possible of late reports relevant to them. Only once, in 1935, did the unit offer an undifferentiated collection of news events, a review of highlights of the year; it was not a great success. [48]

The productions were central to Flanagan's purpose of providing the audience with intellectually mature theater. In her words, ". . . the Living Newspapers seek to dramatize a new struggle—the search of the average American today for knowledge about his country and his world; to dramatize his struggle to turn the great natural and economic and social forces of our time toward a better life for more people." [49] Yet for all the importance that she attached to them, the Project produced only a few. New York offered five, three of which were mounted in other cities as well. Chicago originated one, which was shown in four other cities, not including New York. Norwalk, Connecticut, had two and Cleveland, one. New York's first living newspaper to be readied, *Ethiopia*, was judged too controversial by Steve Early, Roosevelt's secretary, and WPA officials in Washington, and was not shown. At the time the Project closed, the unit was rehearsing a new production, *Medicine.* John Hunter Booth's *Created Equal*, on the persistence of the American ideals of equality and freedom over the centuries, was in essence a living newspaper, but was not so designated by the Project. In other plays, as noted in the instances of *Battle Hymn* and *Life and Death of an American*, the influence of the living newspaper technique made itself felt. But the record of productions is short—not only because of the difficulty of finding subjects not certain to be forbidden by Washington, but, it seems likely, because of the lengthy periods of preparation required by the elaborate scripts.[50]

The attempt to put *Ethiopia* on the stage was a drama in its own right. The suppression of the play was the first instance of censorship by Washington—but the first of only two, the second being the order indirectly forbidding the opening of *The Cradle Will Rock*. It occurred shortly after an order from the office of the Mayor of Chicago was received by the project in that city suppressing a production of Meyer Levin's *Model Tenement*. A short work, *Ethiopia* was written as a protest against the failure of the democracies to put a stop to Mussolini's African adventure. Intending it to be the first offering of the Federal Theater in New York, Rice and Watson had put much effort into preparing it. The script required actors to impersonate Mussolini, Haile Selassie, Pierre Laval, Sir Samuel Hoare, and Anthony Eden, among other living figures, and was to be climaxed with the voice of President Roosevelt by means of a recording of one of his broadcasts. It was through Watson's effort to secure the recording that Early got wind of the production. Word was sent back to New York by Jacob Baker of the WPA that no living newspaper could include the representation of any foreign head of state or minister or cabinet member without State Department permission, and, inasmuch as approval might be delayed, he believed that no such representations should in fact be made. Flanagan then tried to have the ruling rescinded through the good offices of Mrs. Roosevelt, with the result that Baker came to see a rehearsal of the play and afterward declared that the words of rulers and government officers could be used if the figures themselves were not impersonated on stage. This solution did not satisfy Rice. In Baker's office, Rice offered to resign and was at once handed a letter, previously prepared by Baker, accepting his resignation.[51]

On the day following this tense scene Rice staged a showing of *Ethiopia* for the press which turned out to be its only performance. Rice spoke to the newsmen of his impatience with censorship and told of some of the subjects discussed for the Living Newspaper unit's productions. One was to deal with life in the South and would put some actors on the stage in the guise of Southern senators speaking against a bill prohibiting lynching. It was this speech that put an end to the possibility of opening *Ethiopia* in any form. Worried about the promise of trouble to come that underlay Rice's remarks, Hopkins sent down word barring the play, presumably expecting that this would act as a deterrent to the staging of potentially controversial productions in the future. Flanagan regretted Rice's departure but came to believe that because of his stand the Federal Theater was later spared much pressure from Washington. She appointed Philip Barber, his assistant, as head of the New York project.[52]

Though subjected to hostile criticism by the press and congressional committees, the subsequent living newspapers were not censored by government agencies. *1935*, produced in 1936, could hardly give offense. It offered the audience a series of news items carefully chosen to balance comic and human interest stories with those of political and economic importance, such as the setting up of the National Labor Relations Board under the so-called Wagner Act, the decision of John L. Lewis to bolt the AFL and form the CIO, and the assassination of Huey Long. Flanagan herself objected to the treatment given *Injunction Granted* (1936) by the Living Newspaper staff. Though warned during the rehearsal period by Philip Barber and William Farnsworth that the play, a history of labor's impeded progress toward organization, was politically questionable, she did not take immediate action. At the opening, however, she was disturbed by the slanting of the script, in which she saw a resemblance to the agitprop appeals of old. She objected in particular to a scene showing members of the Workers' Alliance staging a sit-down strike in the chambers of the New Jersey legislature. By letter she complained to Watson and Joseph Losey, the director, but to no avail, for Watson was unwilling to make changes. Four weeks later she wrote again in obvious anger, insisting that she would not have the Federal Theatre "used to further the ends of the Democratic party, the Republican party, or the Communist party." [53]

Her reaction is not difficult to understand as one reads, scene by scene, the increasingly bitter account of labor's struggle as presented in the Project's mimeographed script. Though the New Jersey scene is omitted, others of remarkable tastelessness remain. A particularly savage scene presents a Demagogue, dressed on one side of his body as a capitalist and the other as a worker, who harangues both the well-to-do and the workers on the benefits of a partnership of the two classes. He is followed by John D. Rockefeller, Jr., and Howard Heinz, who speak on precisely the same point. When they conclude, a Clown, who is present through much of the play, offers Rockefeller a dime and Heinz a pickle, after which the two industrialists bow to each other and go off. The last scene, an exaltation of the CIO, offers a parade of representatives of thirteen industrial unions, followed by the appearance of John L. Lewis. "Organized labor in America," he declares, "accepts the challenge of the overlords of steel."

Apart from Chicago's *Spirochete* (1938), Arnold Sundgaard's illuminating history of the attempt to find a test and cure for syphilis, all other major living newspapers dealt with subjects as firmly tied to politics as that of *Injunction Granted*. They were, however, somewhat more moderate in tone. In producing them, the Federal Theater made the case for current New Deal commitments: soil conservation and farm relief, the creation of publicly owned utilities, and the development of public housing.

Triple-A Plowed Under (1936), the collaborative effort of the Living Newspaper staff under Arent's supervision, is a documented history of American agriculture during the Depression, including scenes of the milk strike of 1932, the development of the Farmers' National Relief Conference, the curtailment of farm production under the Agricultural Adjustment Act, and the Supreme Court decision against the processing tax levied on manufacturers under the Act to pay for farm subsidies, through the passage of the Soil Conservation Act, which had occurred shortly before the play opened. With scenes involving the personages who figured in the events and other scenes with fictional figures illustrating the New Deal position on farm price supports, the authors attempted to demonstrate that what is good for farmers is also good for laborers, concluding with a plea to both groups to unite in a Farmer-Labor Party. Among the living personages included in the cast are Secretary of Agriculture Henry A. Wallace, the nine justices of the Supreme Court, and Earl Browder—the last played by a not altogether willing actor.[54] Though the production showed Browder only in silhouette and quoted him only in a mild speech pointing out that the right of the Supreme Court to pass on the constitutionality of laws is not specifically granted in the Constitution, the impersonation itself in a government-sponsored play was strong stuff, and Hallie Flanagan was not soon allowed to forget it.

With a script credited entirely to Arent, *Power* (1937) is a somewhat subtler and a far wittier play. For this work on the high cost of electricity and government steps to combat it, Arent invented the character of an average consumer, Angus K. Buttonkooper, who wanders through the play in search of an education in matters pertaining to electricity and its availability. On behalf of him and the audience whom he represents, the Voice of the Living Newspaper coming over the loudspeakers seeks out information in many forms. Asked to define the term "kilowatt hour," an electrician replies, "The word comes from the Greek, *chilioi*, meaning thousand, and 'watt' meaning watt —*chilioi*—watt or kilowatt. Anything else?" (I, iii). To explain the principle of the holding company, a Man Who Knows orders stagehands to bring on sets of boxes, which he piles up in pyramids to make a simple but clear illustration. But the explanations are only a means of leading to a presentation of facts regarding the comparative prices of privately and publicly owned utilities, arriving finally at the creation of the Tennessee Valley Authority. With song, visual aids, dramatic scenes, and parades, Arent presses for approval of the TVA through the second of the play's two acts, concluding with the future of the undertaking left in the air until the Supreme Court could make a final decision on its constitutionality.[55]

The idea of creating a living newspaper on housing took shape im-

mediately after the opening of *Power*. Present on that occasion, Harry
Hopkins went backstage after the curtain with Flanagan to congratulate the cast. "It's about time that the consumer had a mouthpiece,"
he told them. "I say more plays like *Power* and more power to you."
From the theater the two went on to supper with Langdon Post, the
New York Housing Commissioner, and began to plan the housing
play.[56] The result was *One-Third of a Nation*, Arent's most skillfully
developed living newspaper and also his last. The title was taken
from Roosevelt's second inaugural address, a speech written in the
optimistic mood of the New Deal on the crest:

> I see millions denied education, recreation, and the opportunity to
> better their lot and the lot of their children—I see one-third of a na-
> tion ill-housed, ill-clad, ill-nourished. It is not in despair that I paint
> you that picture. I paint it for you in hope—because the nation,
> seeing and understanding the injustice of it—proposes to paint it out.

Prepared with special reference to housing conditions in New York,
the play opened in January 1938 under the direction of Lem Ward.
During the year it played in nine other cities with the script adapted
to illustrate local conditions. The staging of the first half of it had
been the special project of the Federal Summer Theater at Vassar in
1937.

In New York the curtain rose on a cross section of a slum tenement
over which wisps of smoke began to drift. The smoke soon became
more dense and was followed by flame that trapped one resident on
the fire escape, while crowds watched from below and the wails of si-
rens began to be heard. At the close the scene was repeated. This theatrical wizardry, providing the Federal Theater with one of its most
striking stage pictures, was the work of Howard Bay. For the Vassar
production Bay designed a simpler set in which hanging from flies
were huge depictions of a leaky faucet, a spewing garbage can, a broken toilet seat, a rickety banister, a cockroach, and other symbols of
life in the slums. Both sets, the elaborate one for New York and the
simpler one serving as a model for regional productions, gave vivid
form to the anxiety of the tenement dweller. As in the preceding living newspapers, Arent's text is a combination of documented details
on the history of the subject, clever illustrations of its ramifications,
and a plea for a remedy. Once again the consumer Angus K. Button-

kooper is on hand to represent the audience. He is guided through the history of the city's growth and the accompanying advance in real estate values and rents. Cases of landlord malfeasance are shown through scenes of court trials and human-interest sketches in which immigrant groups suffer disease and corruption of the spirit in unventilated rooms. In a parable illustrating the growth of the city from 1775 to 1850, a Landowner spreads out a grass mat representing his property, which is soon crowded with individuals who lease tiny plots at ever higher prices. The plight of the "little man"— Buttonkooper—is made painfully clear as, hearing of new low-rental housing, he applies for an apartment, only to be told that he is one of 19,000 applicants for 1622 units. Other scenes illustrate the efforts of far-seeing officials to erect public housing and the opposition to their schemes raised by landlords and private builders, though they cannot afford to build apartments that families like the Buttonkoopers can in turn afford to rent.

A call to action concludes the play. Government, the audience is informed, has not been wholly inactive. Congress has passed the Wagner-Steagall Housing Act, despite some opposition, which is illustrated by a re-enactment of senatorial debate. But, summoning Mayor Fiorello H. LaGuardia to the stage, Arent makes it clear that the $526,000,000 allotted by the act for low-cost housing is, in LaGuardia's words, "only a step—a drop in the bucket" (II, v). A homemaker, Buttonkooper's wife, who is more militant than her husband, asks the Voice of the Living Newspaper how much money has been appropriated for the Army and Navy, and learns in reply that for the last four years it was $3,125,000,000. To see that the government spends money where it can be truly helpful, to keep a man alive rather than to kill him, says Mrs. Buttonkooper, the people must protest. "*Can you hear me—you in Washington or Albany or wherever you are!*" she cries. "*Give me a decent place to live in! Give me a home! A home!*" (II, v). Taking once more its familiar role of people's advocate, the Federal Theater in this instance went beyond the president himself, for despite the reference to the ill-housed in the second inaugural and his support of the Wagner-Steagall Act, Roosevelt was not a consistent enthusiast of public housing. Inevitably, the play angered conservative members of Congress who had opposed the act. But apart from an ironic criticism of the play delivered on the floor of the Senate by Josiah W. Bailey of North Carolina and a complaint on quotations from the debate on the bill made by Aubrey Williams, deputy administrator of the WPA, official Washington made no direct protest. In New York, whose needs it so clearly reflected, 217,458 persons came to see it.[57]

Because, as she had earlier demonstrated at Vassar, her concept of theater included dance drama, Flanagan warmly encouraged the development of dance units wherever possible in the Federal Theater. As with spoken drama, New York had an advantage over other centers, since nowhere else was there so large a pool of talent. The New York unit was led at first by Don Oscar Becque. After his resignation in December 1936, Lincoln Kirstein was named his successor, but after one week he also resigned. Thereafter no individual was official head, but the unit nevertheless had a guiding spirit: the gifted, tempestuous Helen Tamiris. Other distinguished choreographers who contributed to Federal Theater dance in New York were Doris Humphrey, Lily Mehlman, Anna Sokolow, and Charles Weidman, who designed the dances for *Sing for Your Supper*. Chicago had Ruth Page and Katharine Dunham. Dance drama was presented in six other localities: Los Angeles, Portland and Timberline Lodge, Oregon, Dallas, Tampa, and Philadelphia. The dancers also took part in musicals and, where needed, in productions of literary drama—for example, in Auden's *The Dance of Death*, in which only dancers appeared on stage, while the dialogue was delivered by actors in the orchestra pit.

American subjects dominated the dance programs, as they did the bills of new plays. Don Oscar Becque's *Young Tramps* (1936), considered by Hallie Flanagan to be the best dance of the Project's first year, brought to the Federal Theater stage that poignant Depression phenomenon, the young boys and girls who, despairing of finding permanent work, took to a life of wandering. Tamiris's *Salut au Monde* (1936) and *How Long Brethren* (1937) were dance interpretations of poems by Walt Whitman and Lawrence Gellert's black *Songs of Protest*, respectively. Ruth Page created for Chicago a striking *Frankie and Johnny* (1938) in which the popular ballad was retold in a scenario by Michael Blankfort to the accompaniment of music by

Jerome Moross. Adding to the long list of dances of the thirties with "American" in the title, Myra Kinch in Los Angeles choreographed *An American Exodus* (1937), on the western expansion of the frontier, and Ruth Page gave Chicago *American Patterns* (1938). The situation in Spain, of all foreign issues the most compelling to dancers of the thirties, was the subject of two dances. Ruth Page and Bentley Stone offered *Guns and Castanets* (1939), a retelling of *Carmen* against a background of the Civil War. Tamiris's *Adelante* consisted of ten scenes of Spanish history as they flow through the mind of an executed Loyalist soldier while he hovers between life and death.[58]

The major field of entertainment into which the Federal Theater did not enter was film. Like many other agencies of the federal government, including divisions of the Labor, Commerce, Interior, Agriculture, and Justice departments,[59] the WPA made films to familiarize the public with its activities, but not with the intention of re-employing idle screen actors and technicians. Though in June 1938 Hallie Flanagan wrote to Hopkins to recommend that the Federal Theater work with the documentary-maker Pare Lorentz on a film to be called *Ecce Homo!*, her proposal was quickly turned down. Hopkins was willing to permit the Federal Theater to offer some assistance, but would not permit it to produce the film.[60] Lorentz's plan for the film, based on his radio script for a Columbia Broadcasting System program aired on May 21, 1938, was to trace the transcontinental wandering of an unemployed man who looks for work in many industrial centers, ending at the Grand Coulee Dam. He began the film later in the year with funds from both the WPA and the PWA, but did not complete it.[61]

The films of Lorentz, the outstanding government film-maker of the thirties, served an end similar to that of the Federal Theater's living newspapers—specifically, to educate the public on steps being taken by the government in its behalf. But the films lacked the stridency of the living newspapers. It was possible to construe them as advertisements for the New Deal, but not as radical propaganda, since they omitted references to obstructionist judges and legislators, as well as to the organizing of labor. From 1936 to 1941 Lorentz made five pictures. Originally a film critic and political columnist, he was em-

ployed in 1935 by the Resettlement Administration to make a short
film on the Midwestern dust bowl showing the abuse of farmland
that, along with severe drought, had created the problem, and the
plight of the region's residents. Written and directed by Lorentz, with
a score by Virgil Thomson, the film was released in 1936 as *The Plow
That Broke the Plains.* Lorentz next wrote, directed, and produced
The River, on the great sweep of the Mississippi River—the commerce on its waters, the industry, agriculture, and civilization along
its banks, and the disastrous floods it created repeatedly. The film
made a plea for soil conservation, like *The Plow,* and showed the benefits in flood control derived from the TVA. Also provided with a
score by Thomson, it was released in 1937 by the Farm Security Administration, as the Resettlement Administration was renamed at the
beginning of the year.[62]

In 1938 under the National Emergency Council, the United States
Film Service was established with Lorentz as its head. The new
agency was intended to service all the filmmaking departments of the
government, but lacked a production budget of its own. Shuffled to
the Office of Education in 1939, it led a hectic life of appealing to
congressional appropriations committees until denied further funding
in 1940. For the Service Lorentz produced three films. *The Fight for
Life,* a feature-length film, directed by Lorentz from a script by him
based on the book of the same name by Paul de Kruif, was undertaken for the Public Health Service. Shot in the Chicago Medical
Center and the slums and streets of the city, with final work in Hollywood, the film showed the dangers faced by the poor and ill-nour-
ished during pregnancy and childbirth. For the Rural Electrification
Administration, Lorentz and the Film Service made *Power and the
Land,* with direction by Joris Ivens and a script by Edwin Locke.
This picture, released in 1940, depicted the welcome changes in the
life of a rural family when the REA gives them power. Finally, for the
Agricultural Adjustment Administration Lorentz undertook *The Land*
in 1939. With direction and script by Robert J. Flaherty, it was completed under Triple-A auspices and released in 1941. Showing the effect of the depression upon agriculture—the erosion of the soil under
drought and overplanting, and the departure of tenants and sharecroppers from the farm—it also included encouraging footage on the
government's program to redeem the land and support farm prices.

The closing down of the United States Film Service in 1940 did not, to be sure, put an end to government film-making. With the peacetime draft in 1940 and the American entry into the Second World War in 1941, the need for training films was immediately felt. If Lorentz's prewar films surpassed all those previously made under government auspices, as the critical acclaim given them on release would suggest, they were at least matched for quality during the war by the *Why We Fight* series of Frank Capra. Lorentz himself, as an officer in the Army Air Corps, made training films during the war.

For the Federal Theater the end came in 1939, four years before the other Arts Projects closed down. More conspicuous than the others because, unlike them, it put the fruit of its labor—the productions—before a mass audience, it brought down on itself the implacable hostility of conservative legislators of both parties. Internal disputes begun by workers on the Project also created problems; objecting to the political content of plays or the alleged radicalism of supervisors and the power of the City Projects Council, the clerical arm of the Workers' Alliance, those workers who belonged to the old-line unions hastened the end.

The Project had scarcely begun to open its playhouses when the attacks began. Early in March 1936 rumbles from the conservative Federal Theater Veterans' League reached the press. In the Senate, Republican James J. Davis of Pennsylvania reported that he had received letters from the League on Communist penetration of the Project and read excerpts from them to his colleagues. Other complaints were aired in Congress in the weeks and months that followed, with particularly bitter lashings by Senator Rush D. Holt of West Virginia. One regrettable result of this unfavorable publicity was the shutting down in 1937 of *Federal Theatre*, the Project's own magazine, which had begun publication in mimeographed form in November 1935 and with the help of a multilith machine donated by the Rockefeller Foundation soon became a colorful, lively report on Project activities. Distributed free of charge within the Project, it was sold for fifteen cents a copy on newsstands and in bookshops, including, to the embarrassment of the WPA staff in Washington, workers' bookshops. The culmination of the various charges made against the

Project was the unfavorable opinion of it expressed in the newspapers in July 1938 by J. Parnell Thomas, a member of the newly formed House Special Committee on Un-American Activities, and before the committee during the summer and fall by disaffected workers.[63]

Flanagan was eager to defend the Federal Theater against the attacks made before the Committee, but was put off by Martin J. Dies, the chairman, until early winter. On December 5 and 6 the Committee heard testimony from Ellen Woodward, director of Women's and Professional Projects for the WPA. It was the wish of Hopkins that she should present the briefs for the Federal Theater and the similarly embattled Writers' Project, rather than their heads, Hallie Flanagan and Harry Alsberg. She spoke strongly in behalf of the Projects but was not allowed to finish.[64] Following her brief appearance on December 6, Flanagan was called.

The questions put to her by the Committee members centered on the alleged propaganda content of Federal Theater plays, the strength of Communist influence on the Project, and her own attitude toward communism. Among the plays criticized were *The Revolt of the Beavers, Injunction Granted, Power,* and *Triple-A Plowed Under* with its unsettling appearance of Earl Browder in silhouette. Questions were raised about the favorable comments on the Russian stage in *Shifting Scenes,* the content of Flanagan's own play *Can You Hear Their Voices?,* and the views expressed in her article "Worker's Theatre Advances" published in *Theatre Arts Monthly* four years before the inception of the Federal Theater. To the question of the number of members of the Workers' Alliance on the Project, she could only reply that she did not know—nor could she know, since union membership was not a condition of work on the Project and was not subject to questioning by the staff. Asked whether she believed that the Federal Theater should be used to convey social, economic, or political ideas, she replied, "I would hesitate on the political." Beyond that, however, she would not be pushed, but, on the contrary, reaffirmed her opinion that a part of the work of the Project should be the production of "plays . . . that do hold a brief for a certain cause in accord with general forward-looking tendencies," as in her estimation did 10 per cent of those the Project had offered.[65] Nor, curiously, did she fail to defend *Injunction Granted,* despite her grave reservations concerning the script and presentation.

Throughout the session Flanagan responded with cool articulateness. Though the transcript suggests a faint touch of exasperation when Representative Joseph Starnes of Alabama noted that she was alleged by a witness before the Committee to be "in sympathy with Communist doctrines" and when Representative Dies attempted to trap her into an admission that she would approve of a play recommending the public ownership of all property, on the whole she maintained a remarkable self-control. At no point did she demonstrate greater aplomb than in the following exchange with Representative Starnes:

> MRS. FLANAGAN: [reading from her *Theatre Arts Monthly* essay]: Unlike any art form existing in America today, the workers' theaters intend to shape the life of this country, socially, politically, and industrially. They intend to remake a social structure without the help of money—and this ambition alone invests their undertaking with a certain Marlowesque madness.
> MR. STARNES: You are quoting from this Marlowe. Is he a Communist?
> MRS. FLANAGAN: I am very sorry. I was quoting from Christopher Marlowe.
> MR. STARNES: Tell us who Marlowe is, so we can get the proper reference, because that is all we want to do.
> MRS. FLANAGAN: Put in the record that he was the greatest dramatist in the period of Shakespeare, immediately preceding Shakespeare.

In her memoirs Flanagan noted that Starnes's questions gave rise to laughter in the Committee room, but that she herself did not laugh. The stakes were too high; eight thousand jobs hung on her response. The hearing continued to the luncheon break, but she was not recalled. Her planned final statement went unheard.[66]

Having been given a mandate by the House to hunt out and expose politically subversive activity, the Dies Committee was undeniably within its rights to investigate the Federal Theater. The shoddiness of the Committee's method was another question altogether. Apart from the rumors that had risen over the influence of the Workers' Alliance as a result of the activity of the Veterans' League, the comments on the political slant of Project plays that appeared in the press would have been sufficient provocation for the hearings in terms of the Committee's authorized task. From the first the improbable behavior of the Committee in allowing friendly witnesses to make preposterous allegations without restraint, coupled with the demonstrable cultural poverty of Thomas and Starnes, created mocking contempt for its work among liberal intellectuals. Most were unable to take it seriously. Yet the Committee had the power to hurt, and exercised it. In the specific case of the Federal Theater, the Committee was unquestionably correct in suspecting that the Workers' Alliance was a Communist-controlled body. Organized by the Socialist party in 1935, it merged in the following year with the Unemployed Councils and A. J. Muste's Unemployed Leagues. The Communists, who came into the new organization from the Unemployed Councils, soon took control. In New York they attracted Project workers who had no other union affiliation, but were prevented by the WPA regulation against the closed shop from organizing all the unaffiliated workers. The white-collar arm of the Alliance, the City Projects Council, was open to the clerical staff, and with this organization was linked the Supervisors' Council, headed by Edward Goodman. Flanagan was probably correct in asserting that the members of the Workers' Alliance were comparatively few in terms of the total payroll, but they were an extremely aggressive contingent. Complaints by non-Alliance personnel that the refusal to join a union—"usually the Workers' Alliance"— could result in the loss of a job were upheld in thirty-seven cases heard in 1937 by the joint appeals board of the Arts Projects. A quarter of a century later Virgil Thomson, still smarting over unpleasant memories of the production of *Injunction Granted,* for which he composed the score, described the Living Newspaper unit as "a communist hotbed." [67]

The suspicion in which the Federal Theater was held by conservatives was continually recharged by the space devoted to it in the radical press. The staff of the New Theater League and its magazine pledged their support to Flanagan even before her appointment was made official. In their view the Federal Theater was a more powerful version of the sort of people's enterprise that for five years they had striven to create. On July 30, 1935, Herbert Kline wrote to the director-designate:

New Theatre magazine and the New Theatre League will do anything and everything that is in our power to see that the theatre people and groups on our side of the fence give you all co-operation possible.

The various drama projects of the CWA and FERA could find no complaint from the left if they had confined themselves to drama instead of to bad propaganda for the status quo. If this theatre project means the revival of good American plays, of popular classics, the occasional production of serious and artistic original plays, we're all for it, and will support it to the best of our ability.[68]

He was as good as his word. Once the Project was underway in New York, every issue of *New Theatre* and *New Theatre and Film* carried an article on Federal Theater—complaints against censorship and the activity of the Veterans' League, announcements of productions to come, and reviews. *TAC*, the *Daily Worker*, and the *New Masses* were also self-appointed guardians of the Project. Not all reviews were lacking in reservations, but the critics and their editors were convinced that the Project was an institution whose instincts, being progressive, deserved all the encouragement they could give.[69]

In view of her powerlessness to stamp out the Workers' Alliance, it is inconceivable that Flanagan could have forestalled the congressional attacks on the Project. Had she kept in the path of the CWA and offered her audience nothing but the classics, Gilbert and Sullivan, modern domestic comedy, and subliterary entertainments, she might have found the forces arrayed against her less massive. But would such a theater have been worth fighting for?

The Dies Committee in itself did not have the ability to shut down the Federal Theater, though the tone of the hearings suggested that the members would have been happy to see it shut. In the report to Congress on the Committee's work filed by Dies on January 3, 1939, the Committee expressed the conviction that "a rather large number" of Project employees were either members of the Communist party or sympathetic to it.[70] In the months that followed, no abatement of the controversy over the Project was permitted by either house, or by the press. Making matters more difficult, the President named Harry Hopkins to the post of Secretary of Commerce in December 1938. His successor as Relief Administrator, Colonel F. C. Harrington, was sympathetic to the Project, but a less forceful spokesman in its behalf than Hopkins. The end was almost in sight.

In March a subcommittee of the House Appropriations Committee sat for hearings on a new relief bill, with Representative Clifton A. Woodrum of Virginia as chairman. In tone and substance the sessions involving the Federal Theater resembled those with the Dies Committee. Obviously unsympathetic with the Project, Woodrum ultimately won his battle to quash it. Though the Senate Appropriations Committee recommended its continuance, the bill that finally passed both houses on June 30, 1939, abolished the Federal Theater as of that day. The remaining arts projects were retained, but were required to turn to local sponsors for one quarter of their total expenditures; under this system they continued to function until 1943.[71]

That evening the Project theaters gave their last performances. There remained the task of making an orderly end to the work of the units; the new act made this possible by providing for the salaries of supervisory staff for the month of July and for the Projects's relief workers through September. One piece of work on hand was the acknowledgment of the support of scores of figures in entertainment and other fields who had risen to the defense of the Project with coast-to-coast broadcasts, newspaper advertisements, telegrams to senators and representatives, and personal appearances in the halls and committee rooms of Congress. Though these forthright supporters of the Project included some of the best known names in America, they lacked the power to overcome the formidable will of Congress.[72] *

In *Arena*, written and published within a year and a half of the closing of the Federal Theater, but a temperate, judicious account of the Project nevertheless, Hallie Flanagan mentions in passing the Mercury Theater with evident regret that the productions of this "offshoot," as she calls it, had not been offered under the banner of the Federal Theater.[73] She was not personally affronted by Houseman and Welles's defiance of the Washington proscription against the opening of *The Cradle Will Rock;* on the contrary, when Houseman

* Among them were the Broadway producers George Abbott, Harold Clurman, Sam. H. Harris, Lawrence Langner, and Lee Shubert; the playwrights Moss Hart, Lillian Hellman, Sidney Howard, George S. Kaufman, and Clifford Odets; the composer Richard Rodgers; the directors Frank Capra, Joseph Mankiewicz, and Orson Welles; the actors Judith Anderson, Jean Arthur, Tallulah Bankhead, James Cagney, Claudette Colbert, Katharine Cornell, Bing Crosby, Bette Davis, Katharine Hepburn, the Marx Brothers, George Murphy and Spencer Tracy; and all major drama critics with the exception of George Jean Nathan.

was forced out, ostensibly under a new ruling which denied WPA posts to aliens, she arranged for him to take over for a year her position as head of Vassar's Experimental Theater. Welles meanwhile had resigned from the Federal Theater.[74] In the voluminous collection of letters and scrapbooks that she bequeathed to the New York Public Library is a scrapbook containing clippings on the Mercury. But it is not realistic to suppose that Houseman and Welles would have remained indefinitely with the Federal Theater without the explosion over *The Cradle.* As a team they were too creative, despite frequent clashes of temperament, not to harbor the wish to go on their own eventually.

Houseman and Welles launched their new theater in the fall of 1937–38 with capital amounting to only $10,500, but plans for a full season based on the production of plays they had considered earlier for Project #891: Ben Jonson's *The Silent Woman,* John Webster's *The Duchess of Malfi,* and Shakespeare's *Julius Caesar.* In addition they announced the intention of producing Bernard Shaw's *Heartbreak House* and an American farce of the 1890's, William Gillette's *Too Much Johnson.* The name of their theater, according to Houseman, came from a magazine they had happened to glance at in Welles's house, presumably the *American Mercury.**

Conceived as a theater primarily for the classics, like Project #891, the Mercury was nevertheless intended by Houseman and Welles to draw the same audience that attended productions of the Federal Theater and the Group and that had patronized the recently dissolved Theater Union. In a manifesto written for the *Daily Worker* Houseman declared that an objective of the new company was "to widen the cultural and social base of the People's Theatre." In his announcement for the *Times,* printed three weeks earlier, he had made the same point, but with somewhat different language and with additional information perhaps not judged suitable for the *Daily Worker:* "We shall produce four or five plays each season. Most of these will be plays of the past—preferably those which seem to have emotional or factual bearing on contemporary life. While a socially un-

---

* Three actors came with them from the Federal Theater: Joseph Cotton, George Duthie, and Hiram Sherman. Among other Project actors who played in Mercury productions over the years were Arlene Francis, Paula Laurence, Grover Burgess (a performer with the Group Theater also), Norman Lloyd, and Frederick Tozere.

conscious theatre would be intolerable, there will be no substitution of social consciousness for drama." To organize the audience, the producers hired Sylvia Regan, who had performed the same task for the Theater Union. To keep this audience, both Houseman and Welles took part in various Popular Front activities. The names of both went onto the letterheads of the New Theater League and TAC as members of the advisory boards of the two organizations. In January 1938 Welles lent his services to the *New Masses* as Master of Ceremonies of the magazine's new Sunday evening musical revue, and in March gave a lecture on "Theatre and the People's Front" to benefit the Workers' Bookshop. (The lecture, which was later printed in the *Daily Worker*, was hardly radical; Welles called upon all theater workers to give the "people" plays about real life, not escapist frivolities.) Equally in the spirit of the Popular Front was their acceptance of financial backing from the publisher of *Time* and his successful playwright wife, Henry R. and Clare Boothe Luce.[76]

In the main the Mercury met the stated aims of Houseman and Welles during its brief life. One modern play was staged: *The Cradle Will Rock* (1938), with the cast now on the stage rather than scattered in the auditorium, but without full orchestra. *The Duchess of Malfi* got no further than a first reading, and nothing came of the plan to stage *The Silent Woman*. *Too Much Johnson* did not survive a week of tryout performances in a summer theater at Stony Creek, Connecticut; in any event, it would have been difficult to justify Gillette's noisy farce in terms of relevant theater, unless much was made of the tendency of the title character to sweat the workers on his Cuban coffee plantation. The plays that made the Mercury's name were *Julius Caesar* (1937), Thomas Dekker's *The Shoemaker's Holiday* (1938), *Heartbreak House* (1938), and Georg Büchner's *Danton's Death* (1938). Though not uniformly well received, these productions brought to Broadway the same showmanship that Welles and Houseman had demonstrated away from it with *Macbeth* and *Doctor Faustus*.

For *Julius Caesar* they painted the floor and back wall of their theater a barn-red, set the stage with blocks and platforms, and, with Jean Rosenthal in charge, illuminated it with columns of light. The lighting carried reminders of the nazi rallies at Nuremburg, and the modern military uniforms and drab street dress served with it to create the ambience of a modern fascist state. Marc Blitzstein's score also served this end; composed for trumpet, horn, percussion, and electric organ, it somehow suggested the cadence of marching storm troopers. Welles, dressed in a dark overcoat, played Brutus to the Cassius of Martin Gabel. With cuts and no intermission, it ran a well-paced hour and forty-nine minutes.[77] A hit, it added to Welles's growing reputation for inventiveness. Yet the conception of the production was not wholly original. Earlier in the year the Federal Theater's Wilmington, Delaware, troupe had staged the play in something of the same manner, with the cast in uniforms and fascist black shirts. Though not seen widely, it was approved by the local audience and by Federal Theater administrators, including Hallie Flanagan, who urged a modern-dress production for New York, only to be denied it when Welles and Houseman were separated from the Project.[78]

Welles cut *The Shoemaker's Holiday* even more extensively, reducing it to a playing time of one hundred and nine minutes. This production was also well received, and went into repertory with *Julius Caesar*. Lacking the presence of Welles in the cast, it could boast an equally fine, though quite different actor: Hiram Sherman, who played Firk, the ebullient workman in the shop of the shoemaker Simon Eyre. Broadway found the bawdry of the play to its liking, and the leftist audience approved of Dekker's egalitarianism, which revealed itself in the marriage of the low-born Rose Oteley to a young army officer well above her in rank. Eleanor Flexner, reviewing the production for the *New Masses*, found the play laden with sentiments for the times: "a passionate democracy of the spirit, a hatred of wars which tear families asunder, reverence for the men who toil with their hands, and an abhorrence for the fetiches [sic] of wealth and position." [79] The antiwar theme was also present in *Heartbreak House,* Shaw's "fantasia in the Russian manner on English themes"; written between 1913 and 1919, it expresses the author's profound dismay over the slackness of the British aristocracy in post-Victorian England that had resulted in a demoralized society and a needless war. It too had contemporary relevance. Yet later in the same year the *New Yorker* reported that, up to the time the play went into rehearsal, Welles had contemplated as an alternative a staging of *Twelfth Night* in a mid-Victorian setting.[80] Despite the appearance of Welles as the ancient

Captain Shotover, the play did only moderately well. Its detailed scenery and extended playing time were not in the Mercury's quickly established tradition.

This tradition was maintained by the radio broadcasts of the company, which began in the summer of 1938 as a series called "First Person Singular"—a title unsubtly indicating that it was Welles's show first and last—then changed its name in the fall to the "Mercury Theater of the Air." With truncated versions of popular favorites and the classics, the program quickly won a following. It immortalized itself on the evening of October 30, 1938, with the broadcast of Howard Koch's version of H. G. Wells's *The War of the Worlds,* so skillfully written and produced as to convince thousands of listeners that an invasion of hostile Martians had landed near Princeton, New Jersey, with the purpose of conquering Earth and destroying the inhabitants. By incorporating in the script the networks' frequently used device of interrupting a broadcast with a critical news item, Koch unwittingly fooled the audience into accepting H. G. Wells's fiction as truth; hearing an orchestra concert interrupted with more and more devastating news, listeners accepted these spurious reports of an invasion as the real thing. Koch compressed into a single hour the landing and fanning out of the Martians, the fall of New York, and much more, including a purported emergency broadcast by the Secretary of the Interior, all of which was accepted as genuine. Living under the threat of a new world war posed by German aggressiveness, a threat that had not been alleviated by the attempts of the French and English to appease Hitler at Munich, many who panicked did so because the reports coming over the air seemed to confirm the fear of havoc they had long been harboring.[81]

Just three nights later, still in the midst of the hubbub created by the broadcast, Houseman and Welles opened Büchner's *Danton's Death.* The notion of putting on this work had come from Martin Gabel, who was ambitious to play Danton. Welles took the relatively minor part of Camille Saint-Just, rather than that of Robespierre, the second major part. He and Gabel were both enthusiastic about the play, perhaps drawn to it because the author, like them, had been a young man in his twenties when writing it (and only twenty-four at the time of his death). During rehearsals it became evident that the production was, in the parlance of Broadway, "in trouble." The trouble began when Marc Blitzstein, who composed a score for the production, and others on the Left became aware of the political implications of the play. Robespierre's persecution of Danton could all too easily be taken as a parallel to Stalin's treatment of Trotsky.[82] On October 20 Manngreen of the *Daily Worker* reported that the play was not an accurate depiction of the past and expressed the hope that it would not open. Four days later, he mentioned it again, in the light of subsequent developments:

> Backstage at the Mercury Theatre . . . a three-cornered discussion in progress. . . . Orson Welles, Marc Blitzstein and John Houseman, all concerned with the production of "Danton's Death." . . . "If it isn't changed, I'll pull out the music," said Blitzstein. . . . "If it's that bad politically, I'll pull out the show," replied Welles. . . . Houseman agreed. So it appears that at the very time we were offering our critical suggestions in last Wednesday's paper the need for correcting the reactionary implications of the play also suggested themselves [*sic*] to the producers.[83]

It was not so simple as that, according to Houseman. Blitzstein suggested that meetings be held with V. J. Jerome to see whether the play could be revised to make it acceptable to the Party. If not, the theater parties arranged by Sylvia Regan with leftist organizations would be canceled; without them the Mercury could not survive. As a result of the meetings, the script was altered, and the Party kept its tickets. But meanwhile the production was ruined; overwork in rehearsals of the revised script and tension resulting from the pressures created by the meetings were responsible for dull notices and an early closing.[84]

With the failure of *Danton's Death* the Mercury as it had been constituted came to an end. No obituary statement by Welles and Houseman appeared in the *Times* such as heads of institutional theaters were wont to offer, but an essay by Atkinson, "In Quest of the Mercury," on the inability of the company to live up to its promise, served the same end.[85] Still the pair continued to use the Mercury name. In midwinter, they collaborated with the Theater Guild in the production of a work hewn by Welles from sections of all of Shakespeare's histories save *King John* and *Henry VIII*. Called *Five Kings*, it was intended as a two-evening performance. Part I covered the plays from *Richard II* through *Henry V*, and Part II, all the *Henry VI* plays and *Richard III*. This production was even more clearly marked for disaster than *Danton's Death*. Suffering from inadequate and ineffectual rehearsal and a balky turntable for its complicated set, Part I opened in Boston in February 1939 to poor reviews. It went on to Washington and Philadelphia, where it closed. Though graced with good performances by Welles as Falstaff and Burgess Meredith as Hal, it was wrong in too many ways to be handily improved. Part II was not even put into rehearsal.[86] In the sixties Welles redeemed the project by making a fine, though unappreciated, film of Part I: *Chimes at Midnight* (also known as *Falstaff*).

Relations between Welles and Houseman suffered as a result of the debacle of *Five Kings* but did not soon come to an end. When Welles accepted an irresistible film offer from the R.K.O. studio, Houseman went to Hollywood with him at his request, along with Joseph Cotten and other Mercury actors. The script of Welles's universally acclaimed first picture, *Citizen Kane*, credited to Welles and the veteran screenwriter Herman J. Mankiewicz, was largely the work of Mankiewicz with assistance from Houseman, though Welles was later to claim that he was the principal writer.[87] The experience gained by both Houseman and Welles in the Federal and Mercury theaters is evident in the film's antinaturalistic lighting and settings, as well as in Welles's willingness to follow Mankiewicz's suggestion that he make a picture based on the life of William Randolph Hearst, a prime target of the liberal-to-left satire throughout the decade of the thirties.

In 1941, for what was to be their last collaboration, Houseman and Welles revived the Mercury name for a production of Richard Wright and Paul Green's *Native Son*, an adaptation of Wright's novel of the same name. The most accomplished black novelist of the day, Wright had formerly been a member of the Communist party and on leaving the party retained a Marxist outlook.[88] In the novel it is the powerful few in control of the shaping of American life who are really to blame for the murder of a white girl committed by Bigger Thomas, the young black protagonist, because it is they who doomed him to the ghetto environment that made him what he is. The girl herself is a wealthy "parlor pink," well-meaning but fatuous and somewhat dissolute. Under an arrangement made by Wright before Houseman acquired the production rights, Green was empowered to add to the original characters and plot as he chose. Wright's service as collaborator was reduced to that of a talking wall. The resultant script was unsatisfactory; among other modifications, Green added a treacly hint of heavenly redemption for Bigger as he awaits execution for the murder. Between them, Wright and Houseman hammered out a new script.[89] It became a hit under Welles's direction, with white actors from the Mercury and blacks from the Federal Theater's Negro unit in the cast, including Canada Lee as Bigger. Thus it happened that this "offshoot," the Mercury, was heard from on Broadway two years after the Federal Theater itself had come to its untimely close. Welles and Houseman went their own ways thereafter.[90]

THE GROUP THEATER
1935-1941

WITH THE DUAL SUCCESSES OF Clifford Odets reflecting credit on the entire company, the Group directors and actors began the second half of the decade with token displays of confidence. This quality, it is true, had rarely been lacking in the company's composite personality, apart from the prolonged period of doldrums that followed the closing of *Big Night* in January 1933 and lasted until the opening of *Men in White* in the fall of that year—the period that Harold Clurman was later to describe as "the winter of our discontent." At that time morale was low not only because of failure to find and stage a play worth the effort, but because of the evidence of continuing economic crisis on every street corner, in every cafeteria. But that was now in the past, and though they would experience lean years again before disbanding, the Group had come through the worst of the Depression. In April 1935, Clurman and Cheryl Crawford felt free to take a five-week trip to Russia for intensive theatergoing. The actors played in *Awake and Sing!* and the double bill of *Waiting for Lefty* and *Till the Day I Die* through July and then went on their first complete nonrehearsing vacation since the founding of their company.[1]

To begin the new season of 1935–36 the Group had two scripts, Nellise Child's *Weep for the Virgins* and Odets's *Paradise Lost*. The first became, in Clurman's words, a "stepchild" of the Group. Though in *The Fervent Years* he accepts the responsibility for the play, ac-

knowledging that he said, "Well, let's do it," to end a session of inde-
cisive debate, it was later remembered by the Group actor Robert
Lewis as a script essentially admired by Cheryl Crawford.[2] A drab
piece of writing on the futile attempt of a lower-class mother, the
wife of a cannery employee in San Diego, to rule the lives of her
three daughters, it played only 9 performances. In a critique for *Partisan Review and Anvil* that appeared two months after the production closed, James T. Farrell described it as "just a mess"; the blunt
phrase might have served as a summary of all the published criticism
of the play.[3] The second of only two works by women produced by
the Group, it was staged by the Group's woman director, Cheryl
Crawford, as was the first, Dawn Powell's *Big Night*. The failure invites speculation on whether so aggressively masculine a company as
the Group could have made the most of the material, an analysis of
four wasted female lives, under the best of conditions, which would
have meant using the talents of a more practiced director. As time
went by, it was the men in the company, apart from Stella Adler, who
stood for the Group in the public awareness—such actors as Carnovsky, Tone, Bromberg, Garfield, Luther Adler, Elia Kazan, and Lee J.
Cobb. Through the late thirties the directors frequently found it necessary to cast actresses from outside the company in leading women's
roles. In *Weep for the Virgins*, for example, though Group regulars
played the three daughters of the household, their mother was played
by an outsider, the veteran Broadway character actress Evelyn Var-
den, in her only Group role.

The Group put this feeble play and the new Odets script into rehearsal simultaneously. In contrast to the company's "stepchild," *Paradise Lost* was a work in which the actors took personal pride. Odets,
lionized by reporters and literary critics through the spring, summer,
and fall, created a steady flow of publicity for the Group as well as
for himself. His public activities at this time demonstrated that he
had begun to regard himself as a major social force. Not only had he
taken part in the ill-fated Cuban expedition in the summer, but, back
on home ground with the new play in rehearsal, he began once again
to participate in "progressive" off-Broadway theater. On October 19
his one-act *Remember*, on relief, was performed with Paul Peters's *Bi-
vouac Alabama;* acted by the Negro People's Theater, it was, according to *New Theatre*, directed by Odets himself. The *New Masses* for

November 19 carried an advertisement announcing that "Clifford Odets will be glad to advise DURING REHEARSALS of First Run Production of any 'Valuable' Play. No charge." In midwinter he served on the panel of judges of the contest sponsored jointly by the New Theater League and the City Projects Council for a play on relief. The same issue of *New Theatre* that carried an announcement of the contest also included a review by Odets of Ben Blake's *The Awakening of the American Theatre*. Meanwhile the Hollywood offers, which had begun in the spring, continued to come in, and for all his devotion to the kind of theater represented by the Group on the one hand and the League on the other—the best professional instrument for the development of forward-looking, "yea-saying" drama, and the amateur troupes borne of radical concern for the working class— Odets was tempted. Metro-Goldwyn-Mayer had mentioned the amazing salary of $3,000 a week; Odets did not accept the offer, but the film company backed *Paradise Lost* with $17,000.[4]

In actuality, *Paradise Lost* proved not to be the major work for which the company had hoped; with only 73 performances, its run was disappointingly brief. Yet it marked something of an advance for Odets insofar as it revealed him moving on in his exploration of American life from the proletariat and lower-middle class to a level of society with greater means and aspirations. The Gordons of *Paradise Lost* are apparently a Jewish family, but, that matter aside, they bear very little resemblance to the Bergers of *Awake and Sing!* Not only do they have a name unrecognizable as Jewish, but they have diction that is free of Yiddish phrases. In these ways Odets stresses their essential Americanness. Of the major Jewish characters, only the repellent Sam Katz, Leo Gordon's partner, is allowed the kind of idiomatic speech that instantly reveals his ethnic background. Another significant difference between the Gordons and the Bergers is that the Gordons do not live in the Bronx. Their home is in a middle-class area of an unidentified city, though probably it is New York, since one character describes it as "the richest city in the world" (I). Wherever they may be, the Gordons do not so much represent an ethnic group as an entire economic class: the once prosperous owners of small businesses who found in the Depression that the America that used to reward the industrious with material comforts and a happy home life no longer existed. It was a paradise, or in their faulty vision seemed to be one, but in the play all that is finished. A home-less character makes the point for Odets near the close:

PAUL: . . . Did you have a business?
LEO: Yes.
PAUL: Like me. You had a sorta little paradise here. Now you lost the paradise. (III)

The title and this exchange more than anything else about the play relate it to *Awake and Sing!*, in which old Jacob's favorite Caruso aria, it will be remembered, is "O Paradiso" from Meyerbeer's *L'Africana*. The immigrant's dream of finding an earthly paradise in the new world is now seen to have become a nightmare of economic and moral bankruptcy. Unemployment, homelessness, and the be-trayal of trust are every man's lot. Yet it is possible, Odets insists, that a new paradise can be created to replace the unstable one of the past.

As he himself described it, Clurman's direction stressed the confu-sion and aimlessness that he found strikingly evident in people around him since his return from Russia. Over there he had been im-pressed by the "sanity" of the people; back in New York he felt that he "was living in a mad world." The uncertainty as to goals that he saw, or thought he saw, he found reflected in *Paradise Lost*.[5] In a *New Theatre* article he described the characters of the play as "a tri-fle 'touched,'" with the exception of the mother, Clara Gordon (an-other role for Stella Adler) and two workers. He offered an explana-tion of their oddness in terms of class distinctions:

Why are the characters in *Paradise Lost* funny? Why are they bewildered, tragic, grotesque, violent as the case may be? They are all looking for reality in a world where nothing is altogether real, where there is something insubstantial and dream-like in the most or-dinary processes of behavior. . . . The world of the ruling class is real in the sense that the rulers know where their interests lie, work hard and fight systematically to protect them against every possible enemy; the world of the working class is real because its struggle is so primi-tive and plain that there is no mistaking or avoiding it. But the mid-dle class carries out the orders of the ruling class with the illusion of complete freedom, and it is sufficiently protected from the terror of material nakedness to believe in transcendental explanations of human woe that keep it "calm" without really satisfying it. There is no enemy in the middle-class world except an intangible "fate"; there is

no fight except with one's own contradictions—and real life (the life
that both the upper and lower classes know in their opposite ways)
enters upon the scene like a fierce, unexplained intruder.[6]

Clurman was given a set of characters who on the printed page do
indeed seem "touched." Quirky, idiosyncratic, and burdened with a
great weight of symbolic significance, the figures in the play are not
always believable. Odets described them as Chekhovian, and so lacking in forward movement that he could not write a well-made play
about them.[7] But the play *is* a conventional well-made play, and
densely plotted. The time covered is three years, during which the
Gordon family descends from a station in life of snug comfort in
which all wants are provided for to a point at which, with money
gone, they are thrown out on the streets with the rest of the nation's
dispossessed, and at the same time thrown back on their inner resources for another kind of comfort: the spiritual happiness of knowing that they are sharing the fate of so many others. That, having
touched bottom both emotionally and financially, the characters
could rise up again emotionally while still lacking shelter and the
means of self-support apparently struck both the author and the
director as a reasonable proposition—perhaps because they knew
that the Group actors were talented enough to give the dialogue conviction. Yet Clurman may not have been so sure. A hint of uncertainty about the characters surfaced ten years later in *The Fervent
Years*. His report on how he interpreted the play to the actors includes a revealing conditional verb: "Nothing was left these people
except their basic sweetness. With this and a little courage to continue life and to learn that their plight was not unique, new hope
might be born and new happiness be achieved." [8]

With bitter irony Odets points out the disparity between the myth
and the reality of the American middle class. Leo Gordon, the father,
unlike Myron Berger, is the true head of the family, but he is nevertheless a man who lives in a cloud, not wholly mindful of the way the
world around him is drifting. Aware of the threat to civilization
posed by the nazis, he makes his wife give away a canary because it
is German, but he has no knowledge of the unpleasant working conditions of his employees until a shop delegation comes to see him
with a grievance. Nor is he aware that his partner Sam Katz is a thief

who for years has been cheating him. So far, so good—Leo makes a suitable representative of the liberal middle class seen from the Marxist viewpoint. But Odets burdens the play with self-conscious cleverness by revealing that the business owned by Gordon and Katz is a shop that manufactures women's handbags, emblems of a capitalist society that have no utility in a depression. Other symbols of comparably obvious irony emerge as the action proceeds.

The symbolic significance of many characters as capitalist types is presented with astonishing simplicity. In particular is this true of Julie, the younger son of the Gordon family. A one-time bank clerk now slowly dying of sleeping sickness, he spends his days making paper profits on the stock market. Ben, the elder son, an Olympic track medalist, is a popular idol. But because of a bad heart he can no longer take part in athletics, and furthermore he has no job. In the Depression the American dream fails him, and he turns to gangsterism with help from his closest friend, a small-time hood called Kewpie, and is almost immediately killed in a holdup. Odets introduces into the play with Ben and Kewpie two examples of a kind of dramatic figure becoming increasingly familiar on both stage and screen as the Depression dragged on: the gangster as laissez-faire extremist, or, put another way, the fascist as gangster. Sam Katz is also a crook, but one who works independently. A man who preys on his partner, abuses his workers, and would like to hire a professional arsonist to set fire to his business for the insurance money, Katz is a conscienceless marauder—but he is also impotent. Though in public he torments his frightened wife by asserting to all hearers that she is sterile, it is his own physical failure that is the cause of their childlessness. With these characters, the dying and the childless, Odets blazons the message that capitalism is through.

The first act takes place on Armistice Day, and this also is ironic, since a war is still going on. To Odets the struggle for security is in reality a class war, and he implores the members of the middle class to see it as such and identify their interests with those of the workers, in keeping with the correct Popular Front ideology. Leo is at ease with the harassed workers who call on him and has a faithful friend in the man employed to tend the furnace in his apartment building, who also plays chess with his son Julie. This man, named Pike, is of old American stock—not of a Mayflower family, but one that "came

over on the next ferry" (I). Holding to the new line with its stress on
the American revolutionary heritage, Odets gives Pike the play's
toughest, most radical lines on the failure of the American dream:

> Yes, first American ancestors and me. The circle's complete. Running
> away, stealing away to stick the ostrich head in sand. Living on a
> boat as night watchman, tied to shore, not here or there! The Ameri-
> can jitters! Idealism! (*Punches himself violently.*) There's for idealism!
> For those blue-gutted Yankee Doodle bastards are making other wars
> while we sleep. And if we remain silent while they make this war, we
> are the guilty ones. For we are the people, and the people is the gov-
> ernment, and tear them down from their high places if they dast do
> what they did in 1914 to '18. (*Slowly sits tremblingly.*) (I)

The overwrought symbolism may not be so far amiss in the theater,
especially in a taut, well-paced production, as in the library, where
the reader, proceeding at his own speed, can pause to linger over it.
But the visionary ending of the play is surely no more reasonable on
stage than in the printed text, for here Odets suddenly leaps beyond
normal human experience into a transcendental frenzy. At pains during the first two acts to show a change in Leo's outlook from short-
sighted complacency to open-eyed awareness of evil, in the last act
Odets gives him such strength that he expects, like Ralph in *Awake
and Sing!*, to make a new world. But the optimism of his view of the
future is unconvincing. We learn at the rise of the curtain on the
third act that the business has failed, and the family has been dispossessed. Julie's illness is now near its inevitable end. It is with a voice
too feeble to be heard by the audience that he speaks. (Clara, his
mother, must make him repeat his words before she understands his
message that United Aircraft is an active stock.) Yet at the final curtain Leo all at once, and quite inexplicably, finds hope. "My darling,"
he tells Clara,

> we must have only one regret—that life is so short! That we must die
> so soon. . . . Yes, I want to see that new world. I want to kiss all
> those future men and women. What is all this talk of bankrupts, fail-
> ures, hatred. . . . They won't know what that means. Oh, yes, I tell
> you the whole world is for men to possess. Heartbreak and terror are
> not the heritage of mankind! The world is beautiful. No fruit tree
> wears a lock and key. Men will sing at their work, men will love.

Ohhh, darling, the world is in its morning . . . and *no man fights alone!* (CLARA *slowly comes down to her husband and kisses him. With real feeling. Every one in the room,* LEO *included, is deeply moved by this vision of the future.* LEO *says*): Let us have air . . . Open the windows. (*As he crosses to the windows a short fanfare is heard without.*)

In this fashion the play ends, with Leo and Clara going off, presumably to join the homeless proletariat. But from what source does Leo get this new optimism? Has it practical meaning, or is it merely a spasmodic, irrational reaction to the surrounding gloom? And what is their future?

Flawed though it is, the play has virtues. One consists in the character of Clara Gordon, whose positive personality compensates for much slack dialogue among the other figures. A model of character-defining language, as well as a restatement of one of the play's themes, is her telling of the tale of Moses and the golden calf to the dying Julie at the start of the third act: "Well," it runs in part,

Moses stayed on the mountain forty days and forty nights. They got frightened at the bottom. Everybody was very nervous. "Where's Moses?" Nobody knew what happened. What did those fools do? They put all the gold pieces together, all the jewelry, and melted them, and made a baby cow of gold. Well, believe me, when God saw that he was very, very mad.

Another character skillfully developed is Kewpie. Odets subtly suggests that this minor monster feels a homosexual attraction for Ben and that he asserts his manliness by sleeping with Ben's wife. In addition, the play has a store of treasurable comic lines. Says the fiancé of the Gordon daughter about the timorous Mrs. Katz, "She sneaks around like a Chinaman in the movies" (I). But these assets were not substantial enough to turn the play into a hit.

Predictably, the notices in the commercial newspapers and magazines were poor. With equal predictability the leftist press was generous with space for this play by a now respected playwright that "progressives" could call one of their own. But the Party was not sure how to deal with it. The reviews came in two waves, a set of stout approvals followed by another set damning the work, principally on ideological grounds.

In the *Daily Worker* for December 13, the Theater Union's Michael Blankfort commented favorably on the play in all its aspects, apart from the "abnormality" of the two families. In the same month Robert Forsythe wrote enthusiastically in the *New Masses*, "The theme is the impact of the depression on the middle class. It is a subject of transcendent importance in these times, and it has been treated by Odets with the utmost honesty." A long and careful review by John Gassner in *New Theatre* included a few complaints, but on the whole was an expression of delight; "one of the most thoughtful and moving plays of the American theatre" Gassner called it.[9]

But the second wave of reviews canceled out this praise. Most appeared in February. Jay Gerlando told *Daily Worker* readers that Odets failed to grasp the problems of middle-class life, and Clara Bagley in the *Sunday Worker* found the play's Marxism "bad" and the characters "wooden." James T. Farrell damned the play along with *Weep for the Virgins* in *Partisan Review and Anvil,* and in a review unkindly headed " 'Paradise Lost': An Obituary," Stanley Burnshaw in the *New Masses* chastised Odets for showing the middle class in a state of decay when in fact it was engaged in a struggle to survive, and could win the struggle by making an alliance with the proletariat. Finally in July *New Theatre* reversed itself in an essay titled "The Case of the Group Theatre," by Norman Stevens, taking the group directors to task for failing to make their organization into a Marxist theater and "a really democratic collective." Stevens found Odets guilty of writing unrealistically about the middle class by picturing it "reaching social awareness only through its own annihilation"—the same complaint that Burnshaw had voiced. Continuing, the critic disparaged the conversion that ends the play as a "romantic gesture of 'leftism.' " His point, put another way, was that this conclusion was an objectionable carry-over from the drama of the "pre-revolutionary" period.[10]

Precisely what was behind this shift of opinion on the play is not known. Possibly it was nothing more than what on the surface it appears to be: a deepening editorial awareness of the implications of the Popular Front. Possibly it was a concerted effort to bring Odets back under Party discipline. Stevens alone seemed on the trail of bigger game: his essay was evidently an attempt to strengthen the position of the few Party members within the Group acting company.[11]

Meanwhile, a moderate success was in the making for a play that the Group had turned down: Maxwell Anderson's *Winterset*. To do it the company would have been required by Anderson to cast an outsider, Burgess Meredith, in the principal male role, but it was not so much this demand that put Clurman and the Group actors off the play as Anderson's poetic diction, which took the life out of his modern subject, the aftermath of the Sacco-Vanzetti case. The company also missed out on a play it would have liked to do, *Bury the Dead*, because of Shaw's impatience to have it staged without delay. When the opportunity arose, in the spring, the Group had already contracted to produce Erwin Piscator and Lena Goldschmidt's *The Case of Clyde Griffiths*, an adaptation of Theodore Dreiser's *An American Tragedy*, and was not able to take on other work. These were two strokes of bad luck in a season that the company had begun optimistically.[12]

The Group agreed to stage the Piscator-Goldschmidt adaptation at the behest of Milton Shubert, who had seen it at Jasper Deeter's Hedgerow Theater. Shubert's money paid for the production. This was the second version of the novel to reach Broadway; the first, by Patrick Kearney, with Dreiser's original title, had been staged in the season of 1926–27. Unlike Kearney's straightforward "well-made adaptation, the new version was in the Epic Theater manner that Piscator had developed in Berlin during the twenties, anticipating and influencing Brecht's epic style. It thus came about that twice in the same season New Yorkers had an opportunity to taste this antinaturalistic form, for Brecht's *Mother* had been offered by the Theater Union four months before the March opening of *The Case of Clyde Griffiths*. In place of the slides and songs that Brecht had employed for pedagogical devices, Piscator introduced a new character, the Speaker, whose function it was to interpret the events of the play from the Marxist viewpoint. As in the novel, Clyde is society's child, killing the factory girl he has impregnated in order to be free to marry his rich fiancée, and doing this because a capitalistic world had from the beginning of his life made him aspire to wealth and material comforts. At critical points in the play the action is stopped so that the Speaker, rising in the orchestra, may pronounce on it. Under Lee Strasberg's direction this provided interesting visual effects, but these were, for most reviewers, overwhelmed by the device of the

Speaker himself, whose commentary on the peril of economic ambition and the responsibility of society for the downfall of Clyde was as
painfully obvious in its didacticism as Brecht's devices in *Mother*.
Even the critic who covered the play for the *Daily Worker* found him
something of a nuisance.[13]

The closing of *Clyde Griffiths* after only 19 performances provided
yet another indication that the Group directors and actors were at the
mercy of playwrights. Like the Theater Union they faced in every
season the unsolvable problem of how to locate good scripts. In February, a month before the *Griffiths* opening, Clurman wrote an eager
letter to writers' agents declaring that the Group was not interested
in propaganda plays only, contrary to popular report, but would like
to receive scripts of wide variety. Included in his letter was a list of
plays that the Group would have considered for production: *Journey's
End, First Lady, Russet Mantle, Winterset, The Petrified Forest, The
Road to Rome, Pride and Prejudice, The Children's Hour, The Jest,*
and *Dinner at Eight.* The inclusion of *Winterset* in the list lessens its
credibility somewhat; though the Group had *considered* the play, it
had rejected it. But the letter nevertheless bespoke a heartfelt need. If
no scripts of unquestionable merit were available, what was the company to do except produce the best at hand? Thus the Group had
produced the Piscator adaptation of Dreiser, yet another propaganda
play. Its failure provoked the directors into issuing a second letter
elucidating their position on social drama. This was addressed directly to the press. Written by Clurman at Strasberg's suggestion, and
signed by Crawford, the letter pointed out that the company had offered works by writers representing a variety of views, not all of
which were radical. But the desired end of inhibiting jaded reviewers
from dismissing Group productions as only additional querulous reports from the Left, or of convincing them that the Group was not essentially a radical association, was not so easily achieved. Nor could
the two letters fail to harm the Group's reputation with the left itself,
as was demonstrated when Norman Stevens cited them disapprov-
ingly in his essay "The Case of the Group Theatre." Later Clurman
described the second letter as "a prime example of collective bun-
gling in both the tactical and the ideological sphere." Yet it cleared
the air, at least to the extent that the company was thereafter able to
see the folly of presenting works so rigidly doctrinaire. The Group

continued to find Marxism a vendible commodity, but only as served up in the rich plots of Odets.[14]

By the season's end Odets, despite the unexciting showing of *Paradise Lost,* had demonstrated himself to be the one playwright to whom the Group could confidently turn for the justification of its existence, as well as for material aid. It was clear to the Group members that Odets, for his part, looked to it for his own justification, as well as for companionship and a home base. When *Clyde Griffiths* closed, the company performed in a radio play on Sarah Bernhardt by Odets, Kazan, Art Smith, and Roman Bohnen for some ready money. The play was banal, and radio in the actors' view was a distraction from their "real" work in the theater, but the performance kept them going. Then, having no other script at hand, they toured in their most dependable property, *Awake and Sing!* The playwright himself had left for Hollywood during the run of *Paradise Lost.* There he signed with Paramount and went to work on his first picture, *The General Died at Dawn.* But his thoughts remained with the Group; he began a new play and, prodded by Clurman, had a draft completed by the start of the new season. Despite his willingness to accept Hollywood's cash and his romantic attachment to and eventual marriage with the Academy Award-winning actress Luise Rainer, he was not "lost" to Hollywood. On the contrary, he remained a source both of plays and the money to finance them and to meet the company payroll.[15]

The new Odets play was one of four that the Group expected to put into production during the 1936–37 season. Titled *The Silent Partner,* it was an agitational play in which legitimate labor leaders try, unsuccessfully, to establish a union in a company that uses every known trick to keep it out, including the setting up of a company union and the hiring of spies, *agents provocateurs,* and thugs. Woven into the plot is a love triangle involving two brothers, both union leaders, who are in love with the same girl. The conflict is decided in favor of the younger, tougher of the two men when the elder brother is slain. This "Young Leader" and the girl provide an Odetsian note of optimism at the close; in Clurman's words, they are " a new Adam and Eve from whom a better world will arise." [16] Crowded with characters expressing maternal, humanitarian, and sexual love, alongside and contrasting with others guilty of a sadistic and murderous antisocialism—some fifty characters in all—the play seldom focuses on any figure long enough to build interest in him, apart, possibly, from Gracie, the kindly but ineffectual company president, and Mrs. Lovelace, the mother of the two leaders of the strike.[17] Recognizing its faults, Clurman asked for revisions on reading the script at the end of the summer of 1936.[18]

On September 2, *The General Died at Dawn* opened in New York to indifferent reviews. A melodrama set in contemporary China and pitting Gary Cooper as an American soldier of fortune against Akim Tamiroff as an oppressive war lord, the film had as its basis a novel by Charles G. Booth. Says O'Hara about his antagonist, "A certain honorable tootsie roll named Yang thinks he has a right to control the lives of thousands of poor Chinese." The melodramatic action, with love interest supplied by Madelaine Carroll, was put to social purpose, as this speech suggests. This was apparent to Robert Stebbins, writing for *New Theatre*, but not to all leftist reviewers, though many nevertheless enjoyed the film. "On the debit side," wrote Perry McAllister in the *Sunday Worker*, "I would place the sometimes too obvious attempts to appeal to Mr. Odets' left-wing following with dialogue about oppressed people and making the world safe for democracy which has nothing to do with the case. The real villain, Imperialism, never shows his face." [19]

Another of the new plays on which the Group counted for its season was Lawson's *Marching Song*—also about militant labor, also diffuse, and ultimately rejected. The company's decision against staging the play was vindicated by the brevity of the Theater Union's run with it later in the season. Still another work for which the Group had hopes was a script by George O'Neil. This too was unsatisfactory. There remained Paul Green's *Johnny Johnson*, an antiwar satire with music by Kurt Weill.

The company's wish to make use of Weill's talent was the moving force behind the planning, writing, and staging of the play. Having fled Germany in 1933, Weill came to the United States in 1935, after stops in France and England, with a contract to provide the music for a production by Max Reinhardt of Franz Werfel's Old Testament pageant, *The Eternal Road*. Not yet so well-known to the American public as he was to become in the forties as a Broadway composer and after his death in 1950 when his German works were revived, Weill had a small following of enthusiasts of his score for *The Three-*

penny Opera, though the work itself ran for only 12 performances when first staged in New York in 1933. Among the admirers of the score were the members of the Group. Having come to know Weill, they asked him to write a musical play. He consented, proposing an American dramatic counterpart to Jaroslav Hašek's *The Good Soldier Schweik*. With Brecht as one of the adapters, a stage version of this popular Czech war novel had been produced by Piscator in Berlin in 1928. Clurman mentioned the subject to Paul Green, whose interest in musical theater was soon to take him into a new phase of his career as the author of librettos for *The Lost Colony* (1937) and other symphonic dramas. Green, a veteran of the First World War, warmed to the project, and with Cheryl Crawford as co-ordinator, the playwright and composer created *Johnny Johnson*.[20]

The play relates to *Schweik* only insofar as its background is the First World War and its protagonist is a private soldier who baffles (for a time) his superiors. Whereas Hašek's soldier only seems naïve in order to beguile others, Johnny is a genuinely simple man. In a promotional piece written for the *Daily Worker* when the play was on the point of closing, Strasberg noted, "We meant to do an American folk legend, full of the humors of old vaudeville and the provincial family album, sharpened with poetic comments on the madness of contemporary life. We felt that fantasy, extravagance, and dramatic music were intrinsic to such an exciting and ambitious experiment."[21] The description suits the play, for Green's characters are caricatures of country people and pompous grandees (military brass hats and medical "specialists") of the sort familiar in turn-of-the-century stock farce. The actions are equally improbable. The result was the only group play that turned away from naturalism in *all* its elements: plot, characterization, structure, language, and spectacle.

Green's point in the play is that Johnny, the ordinary man who abhors war and tries to stop it, is wiser and better balanced than the allegedly sagacious persons who declare and wage war and send him to a sanitarium for his pacifism. His conception of the origin of warfare is not the Marxist view that its cause is the capitalist-imperialist desire to reap a profit from armaments and conquer territories in order to develop new markets, but the humanitarian view that war is caused by government and military leaders so obsessed with the idea of national honor that they are indifferent to life itself. At their council meeting, Green's leaders are pleased to think about the numbers who have died, and will die in the next offensive. Says the French Premier,

> If England gives her hundred thousand dead,
> La Belle France, my native France,
> Can give her hundred thousand so the same. (II, v)

Johnny is shown at the outset to be a great admirer of Woodrow Wilson for his stand on keeping America out of the war. A tombstone carver by trade, Johnny has carved a monument to peace that is unveiled on the bicentennial of the founding of his home town. His name itself, though it confers upon him an Everyman quality, is a kind of joke, as is his profession. But his earnestness in opposing war is not a joke, and he finds it hard to believe that those citizens who at the unveiling speak out for peace can suddenly favor war when word comes that it has been declared. Yet he is momentarily taken in by Wilson's assertion that this is "a war to end war," and enlists, leaving behind his fiancée Minny Belle Tompkins. Overseas, in a company that includes Privates Goldberger, O'Day, and Svenson, in Popular Front fashion, among others, he tries to encourage the restoration of peace by sending back to his countrymen a young German sniper whom he was sent on a mission to find and kill, presenting the sniper with a packet of Wilson's speeches for peace to distribute behind the German lines. Himself wounded and hospitalized, he conceives the bright idea of blowing laughing gas in the faces of the Allied High Command as they meet behind the lines in France, in the full expectation that in their merriment they will end the war. The plan almost works, but when the effect of the gas wears off and the officers recall that they have signed and given to Johnny an order to cancel the new offensive, they search him out and have him arrested. After ten years in an insane asylum, whose chief psychiatrist appears to be a little mad himself, he is released. At the close, some ten or fifteen years later still, we see him as a street-peddler of children's toys. Minny Belle is, and has long since been, married to his old rival for her love.

The play's most arresting scene is, possibly, the final one, in which Johnny tells Minny Belle's little son that he has no toy soldiers for sale. But there are others of interest in which Green relies less on sentiment for effect than on startling stage images. Among them is the scene in which three cannon raise themselves over the edge of the trench where Johnny's company is sleeping, then, pushing their muzzles out over the soldiers, sing a bitter lullabye of death. Equally bitter is Green's use in the same act of a great, black wooden sculpture of Christ as the hiding place of the German sniper. Some laughs are derived from Johnny's engaging rural directness, especially in the first act, and broad comedy is extracted from the cavortings of the gas-intoxicated generals. But, in what is his least characteristic work, Green is not wholly successful in his effort to integrate comedy and pathos. Though scene by scene the play has more to praise than to damn, the shifts in mood are frequently strained.

The music is Weill in transition from the scores based on hot jazz that made him famous in Germany to the lush scores of his later Broadway musicals, such as *Lady in the Dark* (1940) and *One Touch of Venus* (1943). In their wry tunefulness, many of the songs were reminiscent of the songs of the German plays, but Weill also managed an engaging parody of Western music in the "Cowboy Song" and a haunting American-style pop melody in "Johnny's Song," also known as "To Love You and to Lose You." No outsiders were brought in for the production; regular members of the Group sang the songs. Actors first and singers second, they would have delighted Brecht with their lack of musical sophistication.[22]

Beset by troubles in rehearsals and previews, and put on in a house more properly suited for lavish musical comedies, the play did not prosper. After 68 performances it closed, despite a press campaign to keep it going. Though he included it in his annual *Best Plays* volume, Burns Mantle noted, "But in neither direction nor casting had the Group lived up to previously acquired standards. The amateur spirit was a little too strongly in evidence."[23] Later in the season Federal Theater units in both Boston and Los Angeles staged the work. Werfel's *The Eternal Road*, with Weill's second score of the season, proved to be more popular; thanks to Reinhardt's spectacular staging, it ran for 153 performances.

With no other scripts available, Clurman meanwhile persuaded Strasberg and Crawford that the company should proceed with *The Silent Partner*, though Odets had done nothing to improve it. But during rehersals Clurman reconsidered. Noting that the production

would cost $40,000 if allowed to open, he agreed to continue if Odets
wished it, but made it clear that he preferred to abandon the play.
Odets reluctantly consented.[24] There was nothing to be done now but
call it quits for the season. In a piece for the *New York Times* Clurman emphatically denied the current rumor that the company was
disbanding permanently.[25] Meanwhile, the actors sought other work,
some making their first trek to Hollywood. In the fall of 1937 the
Group did reassemble in New York, but on a new organizational
basis with Clurman as sole director.

This change had been in the making for a year. In the summer of
1936 Clurman drew up a new plan for the company in which the actors were to have a voice in its projects through a committee elected
by themselves, with the leadership in the hands of a single director
rather than a triumvirate. To take over this new post he proposed
himself.[26] Involving ultimate responsibility for the maintenance of the
entire company, it was a position requiring courage in abundance.
Both Strasberg and Crawford approved of the new order, which was
put into effect during the summer. After the closing of *Johnny Johnson*, the actors drew up an analysis of the three directors' personalities and talents that, while not wholly favorable to any of the three,
was kinder to Clurman than to the others. Of Crawford, for example,
the actors declared, "She never stops trying to impress people with
her own importance, the work she is doing, how what other people
receive credit for doing is really her work." [27] The leftist press, meanwhile, continued to apply pressure on the directors to advance the
cause of "democracy" by granting still greater authority to the actors,
and to sharpen the political content of its plays.[28] Relations between
Clurman and Strasberg were now seriously strained; between the
lines of *The Fervent Years* it is evident that this situation had been
developing since the rehearsals of *Gold Eagle Guy*, when elements of
Strasberg's direction struck Clurman as unsatisfactory deviations from
Stanislavsky's method, and when Clurman heard from Crawford that
Strasberg believed the actors were losing confidence in him for not
yet having directed a play himself. In April, the sum of these pressures became intolerable to both Crawford and Strasberg. Crawford
sent in a letter of resignation, and Strasberg followed, citing as his
reason his belief that the actors had destroyed the leadership.[29]

Clurman was to continue as the Group's only director until the last

production was mounted under the company's banner in the 1940–
41 season. A new non-profit-making corporation was established. Its
officers were Clurman, Odets, and the Group Theater Council, consisting of Roman Bohnen, Luther Adler, and Elia Kazan. In no other
way was the Group changed. Its standards remained the same, as did
its sense of purpose. Actors came and went as the seasons passed.
Stella Adler, though married to Clurman and proud of the Group's
achievements, did not act with the company again after her appearance in *Paradise Lost,* apart from some radio broadcasts. A most serious loss occurred during the run of Odets's *Golden Boy* when Jules
Garfield left for Hollywood; there, renamed John, he quickly became
a popular star. To offset this defection was the rise of Kazan as both
an actor and a director. Robert Lewis, a young actor with the Group
from the beginning, also received encouragement as a director. In
1937 Lewis set up a Group Theater training school for actors; though
it lasted only a year, it benefited the company with a modest financial
return and the development of some acting recruits.[30]

As always, the members of the company continued to participate in
political life, lending their names and presences to all the Popular
Front causes. The programs for *Golden Boy* informed the audience
that the leading actress, Frances Farmer, wore stockings of lisle; to
wear silk would have signified acquiescence in the Japanese invasion
of China. In 1938 the company gave a party and a benefit performance for the Lincoln Brigade, and in the following year gave a
party for the Committee of 56, a Hollywood-based organization seeking a total boycott of Germany. TAC, of course, commanded their attention; many took part in TAC cabarets. Garfield was a member of
the TAC Executive Board, and Clurman and Carnovsky of the Advisory Council. Kazan and Odets were also members of the National
Advisory Council of the New Theater League (as were Crawford and
Strasberg). Odets signed the call for the second American Writers'
Congress in 1937. In these ways the Group members expressed a
youthful confidence that had not been eroded by seven years of hard
times. Off stage and on, in the roles they chose in both life and the
theater, they remained optimistic. As Clurman recalled in *The Fervent Years,* one of the TAC sketches that reflected their outlook with
particular effectiveness (it is one of only two TAC items to which he
refers specifically) was Emanuel Eisenberg and Jay Williams's *Our*

Borrowed Substance, a parody of Thornton Wilder's *Our Town,* Paul
Vincent Carroll's *Shadow and Substance,* and Paul Osborn's *On Borrowed Time,* plays revealing a "preoccupation with death and other-
worldliness." Defeatism was not for the Group.[31]

The company's first production under the new régime proved to be
the most popular of all its plays, Clifford Odets's *Golden Boy.* Like
most Group plays it is an exploration of the sell-out, but differing
from most in its tragic ending. Joe Bonaparte, the protagonist, does
indeed gain the whole world, or at least as much of it as he desires,
and loses not only his soul but his life. Unlike Ralph Berger, he goes
too far and stays too long. On the threshold of manhood he must decide whether to continue to study the violin, his first love, in preparation for a concert career, or become a prizefighter. His choice is boxing, since the fight ring offers the better chance of financial success.
On the eve of his twenty-first birthday he explains his decision:

> Every birthday I ever had I sat around. Now'sa time for standing.
> Poppa, I have to tell you—I don't like myself, past, present and fu-
> ture. Do you know there are men who have wonderful things from
> life? Do you think they're better than me? Do you think I like this
> feeling of no possessions? . . . You don't know what it means to sit
> around here and watch the months go ticking by! Do you think that's
> a life for a boy my age? Tomorrow's my birthday! I change my life!
> (I, ii)

The drama is sturdily constructed, but the structure rests on a weak
foundation. Boxing, Odets's metaphor for the battle for material
wealth, is intensely brutal; the art of the violin, his metaphor for
spiritual values, is utterly delicate. That one man might excel in both
fields is not so easy to believe as Odets seems to think. The doubly
talented Joe Bonaparte is a bit like the young women encountered occasionally in tabloid newspapers who divide their time between law-
school courses and the burlesque stage. But this painful pursuit of
metaphor is not the whole play. Though intending, as in the earlier
plays, to expose the flaws in American society, Odets shows himself in
possession of a newly heightened curiosity about the problems of the
individual. It is not only the desire for money that goads Joe Bonaparte to the fight ring, but the desire to make up for the indignities he
suffered in childhood and youth because of his odd name and strab-

ismic eyes. In his adulthood the old taunts remain in his mind, and he fights to work off the hostility they induce. Ralph Berger had unhappy birthdays also and never got the black and white shoes for which he longed, but the kind of wound from unhappy personal relations whose scar Joe still bears was never inflicted on Ralph. Nor is the miserably unhappy Sam Katz, who like Joe has a physical problem, and in fact a much worse one than Joe's, as rounded a character. Moreover, though Katz's social malevolence is related to his impotence, it is not the direct result of it; Odets uses Katz's infirmity principally to assure us that his breed of predator is doomed. Joe is something new in the Odets parade of characters: a figure whose personality has been determined by social and psychological forces of equal weight.

The stages of Joe's self-destructive course are marked in undeniably poignant scenes. It is not only that he is a disappointment to his father, as well as to his brother, a CIO organizer, but that he steals his manager's mistress, making the play a tale of traducers traduced, is content to let a gangster buy into his management, rejoices in breaking a hand in the ring, since this makes a concert career impossible for him at last, and kills another fighter in a match—a black fighter nicknamed the Chocolate Drop. This shattering, sobering event leads inevitably to his own death as both a release from the unhappiness that clings to him like a fighter's robe, and as a means of atonement. Driving off into the night with the girl whom his manager is supposed to marry within the week, Joe crashes his high-powered car into a tree, and both are killed. Is it suicide, or is it an accident? Odets does not say; but no matter which, it is inevitable, a judgment passed by the author on a man who too willingly accepts the conditions of a brutal system.

To the manager's pre-empted mistress, Lorna Moon, the self-styled "tramp from Newark" (I, i) Odets gives some of his most insightful lines. She is the first of three proletarian girls glorified by him in his last plays for the Group. Though older than Joe, she is still young. She is also hard, and her hardness is not superficial. Yet not only does she understand Joe's drive, but she recognizes the dangers of it. Early in the play she says to him, "You're a miserable creature. You want your arm in *gelt* up to the elbow. You'll take fame so people won't laugh or scorn your face. You'd give your soul for those things. But every time you turn your back your little soul kicks you in the teeth. It don't give in so easy" (I, iv). With Joe's brother Frank, proud and happy as a worker for the CIO, she shares the duty of spokesman for the author. In the play's penultimate scene she has the kind of visionary speech given to Ralph Berger and Leo Gordon, when, to Joe's bitter question of what's left for him, she replies,

> No, *we're* left! Two together! We have each other! Somewhere there must be happy boys and girls who can teach us the way of life! We'll find some city where poverty's no shame—where music is no crime! —where there's no war in the streets—where a man is glad to be him- self, to live and make his woman herself!" (III, ii)

But for Joe and her, unlike Ralph and Leo, it is too late. Both have waited far too long to escape the trap.

Odets's social vision is revealed not only in Joe's mistaken, "cock- eyed" notion that happiness can be equated with money, the poor showing he makes when contrasted with his morally correct brother, and his cruel death. Messages are packed into other actions and as- pects of character. Mr. Bonaparte, Joe's old father, and his elderly friend Carp are small businessmen, the one a fruitpeddler and the other a candy-store proprietor, and, though obviously not rich, they are content with what they have and happy to talk about music and philosophy. They are a kind of intellectual united front against the depravity of money-mindedness represented by virtually all the other characters, with Frank the most notable exception. They are also a united front of another kind, for Bonaparte is an Italian and Carp is a Jew, as is Bonaparte's son-in-law, Siggie. By surrounding the Italian family with likable Jews, Odets makes an oblique attack on anti-Sem- itism while reminding the audience that good-hearted men, no matter what their superficial differences, must unite to combat their common enemies. The gangster Eddie Fuseli, another Italian, is the foremost representative of the kind of force such men are up against. Behind Fuseli's predatory tactics is the fact that he is homosexual, a condi- tion implying a detachment from society. By imposing this difficulty upon him, Odets may intend to imply, as he did with Katz, that the laissez-faire capitalist is doomed to extinction, since Fuseli is no more likely to reproduce himself than is Katz. The conflicts of personality and ideology were enhanced in the Group's production by the scenic designs of Mordecai Gorelik, who devised a diamond-shaped ground plan based on the boxing ring. In each scene the characters could approach each other from opposite corners, like fighters squaring off.[32]

Odets's own intellectual battle left its impress on the play. This battle he had lost: he had gone to Hollywood. Out of his experience and education as a screen writer he acquired some details of construction useful in the making of *Golden Boy:* the vision of the play into numerous short scenes—twelve in all—to provide a logical basis for a shift in tone, and the "fadeout" to replace the "curtain" or "blackout" as a device for ending them. It is also possible that the milieu of the fight game suggested itself to Odets during his immersion in film, since boxing pictures were a Hollywood staple of the decade; among those that had recently drawn well were *The Prizefighter and the Lady*, with Myrna Loy and Max Baer (1933); *Cain and Mabel*, with Clark Gable and Marion Davies (1936); and *Kid Galahad*, with Bette Davis (1937). Of greater consequence to the play, because it seeped into every nuance of characterization, was Odets's uneasiness of conscience for having given in to the temptation of Hollywood gold—"gelt," to borrow Lorna's word. Is it possible to read the play without seeing Joe's decision in the light of the playwright's? Clurman in commenting on Odets's agonizing over the Hollywood offers observed, "For Odets at this time Hollywood was Sin." While writing *The Fervent Years* after the break-up of the Group, he mentioned this description to Odets with a laugh, only to be answered, "What are you laughing about? It is." [33]

After his first venture to the West, Odets told a *Daily Worker* reporter that he had tried to make his scripts socially relevant. But the effort was not a complete justification of his taking up screen-writing, since it was not completely successful: "Well, I got away with some stuff in 'The General Died at Dawn' and in the other two scripts I did —'The River Is Blue' and 'Gettysburg.' But they've been careful with me. They go over my stuff with a fine tooth comb. It's difficult to do anything with social significance." [34] To subdue his feeling of guilt, he rushed to the assistance of the Group, sending back part of his salary and writing *Golden Boy* to provide a treasury for the company, and, during the run of the play, writing another with the thought that the actors could use it for special performances. This work, titled *The Law of Flight*, centered in the crushing of radical labor in Cuba; unfortunately, the Group found it necessary to turn it down.[35] Odets's gestures on behalf of the Group were generous, but if the content of his plays may be taken as an indication, they did not have the wished-for personal result of assuaging his guilt. The moral problem of the sell-out remained his major theme.

On the other hand, *Golden Boy* fulfilled Odets's hope of providing a cushion for the Group. With 250 performances, its Broadway run was second only to that of *Men in White* among the company's productions. A second company under Stella Adler's direction played in California. With the exception of Frances Farmer, who had "created" the part of Lorna, the Broadway cast went to England for a limited engagement in the summer of 1938, and on returning made a national tour. These ventures were lucrative. The London run with non-Group actors directed by Stella Adler which followed the original company's departure was a disappointment, as was the American tour of a non-Group company which played towns the Group actors had missed.[36] But, despite these let-downs, the Group had reason to be grateful to Odets, and he in turn had reason to be pleased with his achievement. Yet he was not especially so. To an interviewer he declared some twenty-five years later that he could not wholly conquer his distaste for the play as a potboiler: "As a matter of fact, I always held *Golden Boy* a little in contempt for that reason, knowing how the seed had been fertilized. And it was maybe three years later that I saw that the play had more quality than I gave it credit for." [37]

The Group offered New York only one more play in the 1937–38 season, Robert Ardrey's *Casey Jones,* on the wash-up of a devoted railroad engineer at the age of fifty, when his health and eyesight begin to fail him. Despite the work of Kazan in his first Group assignment as a director, a superb set of Jones's locomotive by Gorelik, and the presence in the cast of Charles Bickford (in the title part), Van Heflin, and Howard Da Silva—non-Group actors—the play was not a success. After 25 performances it closed. This was the second blow of the season to Ardrey. During the Group's run, his *How to Get Tough About It,* which Guthrie McClintic produced, closed after 23 performances.

The season of 1938–39, thanks in part to the profits from *Golden Boy,* was the most ambitious in the Group's history. A plan to attract sponsors for a package of four plays fell through, even though the

Group's terms were generous, but the company nevertheless offered four plays, raising the money for them one by one as in the past. In addition it held a new-play contest; the prize went to Ramon Naya for *Mexican Mural*, and special mention was given Tennessee Williams for three one-act plays collectively titled *The American Blues*.[38]

The first of the season's four plays was Odets's *Rocket to the Moon*, which was given its first performance only a year and three weeks after *Golden Boy*. With a run of 131 performances, the play made a good, but not brilliant, showing. A sensitive portrayal of the frustrations of the middle class at the outset of middle age, when no new mysteries of life remain to be unfolded and nothing seems to lie ahead except more, perhaps much more, ground like that already crossed, the work is among Odets's most poignant. Characteristically, it ends in questionable logic, but not with the claptrap flourish of *Paradise Lost*.

No earlier play by Odets is farther removed from social or political problems, whether specific as in *Waiting for Lefty* or general as in *Golden Boy*. In directing it, Clurman hit upon the phrase "finding love" to describe the "main action" (Stanislavsky's term for "theme").[39] Despite some references to the economic situation, including the hysterical outburst of one of the minor characters on his financial problems and his decision to sell his blood to pay his bills, the search for love is indeed the principal motivation of the major characters. The protagonist Ben Stark is a dentist—a member of a profession that in the mind of the public stands at the dead center of bourgeois life. A meek man who has the habit of giving in to his sometimes unpleasant wife, Belle, he decides not to accept a loan from his father-in-law, Mr. Prince, that would enable him to change and vastly improve his practice, because she wishes him not to. She cannot bear her father, and in her view it is better to remain in straitened circumstances than to accept his offer. Yet she resents the absence of cash on hand. Their marriage is further troubled by the fact that they are childless; once they had a son, but he died at birth, and they cannot have another child. Thus, partly by Belle's choice, they live in a state of suspended animation, letting their love for one another show only rarely, and usually by indirection. To the antic and cynical but kindly Prince, Odets gives the language that sums up Ben's life:

A life where every day is Monday. There used to be a week-end, but now it's always Monday. Awnings up, awnings down, coat on, coat off, sweat in summer, freeze in winter—a movie, a bridge game, an auto ride to Peekskill. Gas is twenty cents a gallon, worry about the bills, write a budget—the maid is too expensive—you bought a pair of shoes *last* month. You're old, you're getting old—she's old. Yesterday you didn't look in my face. Tomorrow you forgot I'm here. Two aspirin pills are good for headaches. The world is getting . . . so dull, let me sleep, let me sleep! You sneeze, you have a cold. No, that was last month. No, it's now. Which is now and which is then? Benny . . . you used to be a clever boy! (I)

Through the window of Stark's ordinary waiting room, where all the action takes place, can be seen the back of the Hotel Algiers, a name that suggests exotic sexuality. "What must go on in those rooms at night . . . ," says Prince (I). As an image and idea the place contrasts with the tidiness and constraint of Ben's life: his office and his endless days of quiet desperation. The plot is contructed around his brief affair with his receptionist, Cleo Singer, a very young girl who makes up for the drabness of her own life by inventing glamourous but transparent fantasies of a background of wealth. Prince, a self-made man of considerable means, is attracted to her, believes he would like to marry her, and in a frenzy of lust challenges his son-in-law to keep him from her: "Remember, Dr. Benny, I want what I want! There are seven fundamental words in life, and one of these is love, and I didn't have it! And another one is love, and I don't have it! *And the third of these is love, and I shall have it!*" (III). Ben is forced by Prince to choose between Cleo and Belle, and his choice, in keeping with the personality that he reveals from the start, is Belle, to whom he can return with sensitivity quickened by his fling with Cleo.

But it is Cleo, not Ben, who carries the burden of the play's message. Not by the author's random choice is her surname Singer. Though she could have the wealthy Prince and possibly could make an arrangement with a Hollywood choreographer, Willy Wax, who has been chasing her, she opts for love, keeping her soul her own. To Prince and Stark she cries,

Yes, if there's roads, I'll take them. I'll go up all those roads till I find what I want. I want a love that uses me, that needs me. Don't you think there's a world of joyful men and women? Must all men live afraid to laugh and sing? Can't we sing at work and love our work? It's getting late to play at life; I want to *live* it. Something has to feel real for me, more than both of you. You see? I don't ask for much. . . . (III)

But what she wants represents, in her words, "a whole full world, with all the trimmings!"

Odets's sudden placement of the girl in center stage skews the play somewhat, and her equally sudden display of bravery and maturity is inconsistent with the flighty personality that she reveals earlier. Yet her vision of an ideal future and the possibility of her realizing it are more reasonable than Ralph Berger's and Leo Gordon's. We can only applaud her and wish her well.

During the run of *Rocket to the Moon* the company decided to revive *Awake and Sing!* and split the weeks between performances of the two works. With Stella Adler unwilling to resume her part of Bessie and Garfield busy in Hollywood, it was impossible to reassemble the entire original cast. Most members of it were on hand, however. Stella Adler's sister Julia filled in as Bessie, and Alfred Ryder took Garfield's old role of Ralph. Ultimately *Rocket to the Moon* was withdrawn, and *Awake* played on alone for a total of 45 performances. Once more the value of Odets to the Group—and to the American stage as a whole—became evident.

Odets's growing importance made itself known in the Group's second new play of the season, insofar as the author, Irwin Shaw, owed a recognizable debt to him. For the production of this work, *The Gentle People*, the Group imported two Hollywood stars, Franchot Tone, who had not acted with the Group since its second season, and Sylvia Sydney, who was new to the company, and featured their names in the advertisements along with that of Sam Jaffe, another recruit to the company. This departure from standard Group practice resulted in a run of 141 performances, ten more than *Rocket* played. It did not augur well for the peace of the company, since it left some of the old hands wondering whether the stars were being paid on a higher scale than was usual with the Group, in keeping with their Hollywood fame. In fact, they were not, but had come to the Group to benefit their art.[40]

Shaw subtitled his play "A Brooklyn fable" and in a prefatory note to the printed text wrote, "This play is a fairy tale with a moral. In it

justice triumphs and the meek prove victorious over arrogant and violent men. The author does not pretend that this is the case in real
life." The comment restates in an unfortunately simplistic manner the
serious theme of the play—that a united front against fascism was im-
perative. Yet the play has something of the quality of a fairy tale insofar as it is incredible. Two aging men, the gentle people of the title,
kill a gangster and dump his body into Sheepshead Bay with impunity and without regret. These two old friends, a Jew named Jonah
Goodman and a man of Greek descent named Philip Anagnos, form a
united front against the gangster, who makes them pay him five dollars a week "protection" money on the motorboat in which they fish
four nights a week. They had saved $190 toward the purchase of a
cabin boat in which to escape their dull Brooklyn life and fish in the
Gulf Stream, but when Goff, the gangster, hears about this from Goodman's daughter, he demands the money in addition to the weekly five
dollars. It is this demand that makes them decide to murder him, putting an end to his threats and insolence. Linked to fascism in the play's
subtext is the problem of anti-Semitism. Like Odets in *Golden Boy*,
Shaw obliquely appeals for an end to it by bringing to the stage a
firm friendship between a Jew and a Christian. It is not for nothing
that Jonah's surname is Goodman—a familiar and unremarkable Jewish name, but in this instance given an allegorical value. The menacing Goff, interestingly, is of old Yankee stock and boasts that his family has lived in New Hampshire for two hundred and thirty years.
That he is a racketeer defines him as a symbol of fascism; that he is a
racketeer of native American stock links him to Hitler's Germans be-
mused with pride in their supposed Nordic superiority. "Read the
history books," he says. "The big guys are the tough ones. We are
not all made out of the same material. There are superior people and
there are inferior people. No harm meant, Goodman" (III, iii).

   The Gentle People is absurdly improbable at its climax, in which
the two old friends, having lured Goff, a nonswimmer, into their boat,
hit him over the head and show just enough nervousness to preserve
their respectability. Yet the play has some attractions, not the least of
which are the echoes of Odets. The most wittily constructed scene,
Odetsian in its use of Yiddishisms for robust irony, takes place in a
Turkish bath. As Goodman and Anagnos, towels around their mid-
dles, plot the murder of Goff, a fat, bankrupt Jewish businessman

(played by Lee J. Cobb) getting a massage complains in counterpoint to the world at large:

> What is government? It is an invention of Wall Street. Government is a knife at the throat of the ordinary man. Rub harder! . . . The modern man is a size 12 foot in a size 8 shoe. Massage the spine. . . . Naked I came into the world and naked I will go out of the world. The banks will have my clothes. . . . A quarter. Most people think a quarter is nothing. For a quarter a banker would dump you in the ocean. In front of your mother. (*The two old men eye each other uneasily*)." (III, i)

Like this scene, the scenes on the water, with the boat docked at Coney Island or stalled in the Bay, offered visual surprises. All were well designed by Boris Aronson. Yet sentimentality hangs over the play like a towel damp from the steam bath, depriving the antifascist message of its vitality. The Group company did not like the play. Predictably, however, the matinée ladies did.[41]

The Group's third and fourth new plays of the season were somewhat special productions, "experimental" in the sense in which the term is lamely used in the theater to designate works that for some reason do not fall within an organization's usual range. Both were presented in April 1939, when the season was hastening to its end.

Neither play benefited the Group financially, but the first, William Saroyan's *My Heart's in the Highlands,* provided it with another *succès d'estime.* Clurman was determined to be the first to offer a play by Saroyan, known then only as a writer of short fiction. He did so over the objections of some of the company to the lack of theatricalism in the work, and despite a new financial crisis caused by the loss of $17,000 in a box-office embezzlement.[42] Originally scheduled for only five performances, the production was taken up by the Theater Guild for its subscription audience after receiving generally favorable notices. The two organizations were reunited—temporarily—for the first time since the Group broke with its parent in 1932.

The play was an experiment for the Group because of its brevity and plotlessness. Set in 1914 at the outbreak of the First World War, it is an anecdote concerning a poor, unrecognized poet, his son, and an ancient, daft actor who plays the bugle beautifully and is a refugee from an old people's home. Wandering to the poet's house in search of something to eat, the actor plays his horn while the neighbors listen rapturously and bring food. At the close he dies, and the poet, unable to pay his rent, takes to the road with his son and mother-in-law. The boy utters Saroyan's message in the last line of the dialogue: "I'm not mentioning any names, Pa, but something's wrong somewhere." In a better world, the author wishes to say, the talented would not go hungry, and the energy and money spent on warfare would be put to constructive use. Yet the complaint is very mild. The villain, society, is in the distant background; all the characters brought on stage are kindly, including the grocer to whom the poet is in debt, the young man from the old people's home who comes in search of the actor, and the real-estate agent who evicts the poet. It is difficult to believe that with so many good-natured individuals surrounding him the poet and his family will suffer, and thus the message is lost. What is left, in the end, is a play without conflict that serves principally to remind the audience that, like the rest of us, the most high-minded creatures cannot manage for long without food.

In a promotional piece for the *Times* Saroyan wrote, "I am convinced that there is no place in the world like America. There never has been such a place, there never has been such a fine people, and any of us who does not try to do something about it, or make something of it, is a failure as an artist and as an American—no matter what we do, and no matter how well it happens to be received." With this guileless, uncritical language, Saroyan, like many other young writers who emerged in the late thirties, showed himself to be a child of the Popular Front, though strikingly nonpolitical. His outlook was a worry to Michael Gold, who grumbled that the play should be subtitled "My Art's in the Highlands." [43]

Though a play of more pertinent social implication, Shaw's *Quiet City*, the second "experimental" play, did not appeal to the Group audience. Taking as his protagonist a Jewish department-store president who has changed his name from Mellinkhoff to Mellon and embraced Christianity, Shaw proceeds to illustrate the debased social and personal values of the upper-middle class. After a series of visions which link Mellon's religious quandary with unfair labor practices, he not only returns to the faith of his fathers but determines to correct working conditions in his store. Experimental only in its departures from naturalism, the play was a rehash of familiar themes, and mud-

dled in the treatment of Mellon. The Group staged the play in fulfillment of a promise to Shaw, but gave only two performances on successive Sunday evenings.

Chiefly because of the contributions of Odets, which gave the
Group's well-drilled cadre of actors the roles that suited them per-
fectly, the seasons of 1937–38 and 1938–39 marked the company's
highest level of achievement. But losses on the Shaw and Saroyan
plays drained the treasury dry. To make ends meet in the spring of
1939, the company turned to radio work again, appearing on Kate
Smith's program in scenes from past productions and the Bernhardt
script. But in the new season of 1939–40 it was necessary to begin at
the beginning again in the matter of economics. Moreover, the old
problem remained of finding actable scripts with a viewpoint corre-
sponding to the Group's own viewpoint—still somewhat to the left of
liberalism, but not so much so as to alienate the Broadway audience.
Odets's revised version of *The Silent Partner* would not do. A new
play by Irwin Shaw on the Depression-induced moral corruption of
the middle class also would not do. To make matters much worse,
Clurman had turned down Saroyan's *The Time of Your Life*, which
eventually proved to be the author's most durable work in any medium. From the esthetic, if not the economic, standpoint, this was a
greater mistake than turning down Anderson's *Winterset*. Yet another
problem arose when the company pondered a classical revival: no
backing at all could be found for a projected presentation of Chekhov's *The Three Sisters*. These troubles came to a head in the summer
of 1939, which the company spent at a camp in Smithtown, Long Island. Not until the end of summer did the company secure a work-
manlike script: Robert Ardrey's *Thunder Rock*.[44]

To pull the company together for this play was no easy task. In the
Preface to his *Plays of Three Decades* Ardrey wrote some
twenty-eight years later that Clurman, who was scheduled to direct,
underwent a nervous breakdown in 1939—an event on which Clurman himself remained silent in *The Fervent Years*. It was necessary
for Kazan to take over the direction, though both Ardrey and Kazan
thought Clurman more suited to it. Ardrey also believed that the
Communist faction in the Group had never forgiven Kazan for breaking with the Party, though this had taken place years before, in 1936.
There were still more problems. The play, which dealt with the out-

break of the Second World War, an event clearly in the offing in the summer of 1939, was completed shortly before the signing of the Stalin-Hitler pact, and this required, according to Ardrey, "a line or two" to be put into the third act.[45] More troublesome was the actors' distaste for the play, despite the fact that as revised the script accorded with the new line. Eventually, Clurman convinced the actors that the play was "entirely appropriate for our theatre"; moreover, it was the only script available.[46] While steering clear of the Party and its wrangling, its gross simplifications of international politics, and its equally gross rationalizations, neither Clurman, Kazan, nor Ardrey, it thus would seem, disputed the isolationist view as it was then urged by the extremes of both Left and Right.

The setting of the play is a lighthouse on the tiny island of Thunder Rock in Lake Michigan on the eve of the Second World War. The keeper of the light is a young but cynical exnewspaperman, David Charleston, who, after covering the Civil War in Spain, left it with the conclusion that, man's lust for power being what it is, society's problems are beyond solving. Therefore, he chooses the isolation of Thunder Rock and its tower. It is, quite obviously, his ivory tower of retreat from the dilemmas of modern life, and his conscienceless seclusion in it is highlighted when Ardrey contrasts him with his old friend Streeter, a pilot who is resigning his job with the Lighthouse Service to fly for the Chinese in their struggle against the invading Japanese. Charleston confides to Streeter that he is not quite alone in the lighthouse: he has peopled it in his imagination with the captain and passengers of a ship that sank off the rock in 1849. In the published versions of this play, these characters, who are Europeans in flight from oppression, persuade Charleston to change his mind. Realizing, when he informs them of the current state of the world, that they should have stayed at home and worked to correct the conditions from which they fled instead of taking the easy way out, they pull him out of his isolation. In the third act, having been judged by the Lighthouse Service to be too good for his job because of his single-mindedness, he is required to leave Thunder Rock. But, before departing, he renounces his pessimism to Streeter, who, dead after only one month in China, visits him in his imagination: "We'll win, Street. It's the one inevitability. Now or later, today or in a thousand years—we'll smash this thing. . . . I'd like to be in on the kill, myself; I'm in favor of doing it now." [47]

But these were not the words of the Group production. In the Group promptbook on file in the New York Public Library Theater Collection, a speech recognizably interpolated into the original typescript allows Charleston to regain his humanity, but not to side with the interventionists:

> America's going to war . . . No . . . she's got a bigger job than war. Peace. Peace in the face of war, that's the job, and she can do it. . . . Don't force the world to go our way, force won't work. Show them, show them that our way's best. Do the things we've always done, every man to his peace time job. But go to work with a new responsibility. We've got to show others what Freedom means, freedom of speech, freedom of conscience. A nation at peace can put men to work at better jobs than destruction. A people at peace can have butter to eat and the luxury of justice. America's got one high obligation: to preserve the last peace on earth. That's our job, Street, and we can do it. . . . Thanks for coming by.

To this Streeter replies, "Charlie, I wish I was alive."

Though the play found some supporters and won a Playwrights' Company prize as the season's most promising new work, it was not a success. After 23 performances the Group withdrew it. It was not the isolationist slant that killed it; this was an issue that did not figure importantly in the notices. The production sank under the weight of Ardrey's verbose dialogue and undramatic action. In the following year, however, with the isolationist material excluded, the play became a hit in blitz-shaken London.

The second and final production of the season, and the Group's penultimate play, was Odets's *Night Music*, directed by a recovered Harold Clurman. With a run of only 20 performances, it was the most emphatic failure of Odets's entire career. Yet the play has charm, comparable to that of a very serious child in whose utterances insight and naïveté alternate in an attractive rhythm. This is the quality of its central figure, who, though in his twenties, is still a child. Clurman rightly described the play as "continuously entertaining." [48] Though the whimsicality of the dialogue and action drew comparisons with Saroyan from the reviewers,[49] the play is more pointed, more determinedly didactic than any of Saroyan's works. The validity of Odets's message, however, is subject to question; like Ardrey in *Thunder Rock* he wrote in favor of non-intervention. The greatest structural weakness is a cast overcrowded with minor characters who slacken

the pace of the action. As with *Golden Boy* the influence of Hollywood is evident in the division of the play into numerous scenes—
once more, twelve of them—and the fade-outs in which they end.
The inclusion of many difficult exteriors among them, and especially
the World's Fair and La Guardia Airport sets, also suggests the Hollywood influence; for the Group's production they were designed by
Mordecai Gorelik, on his eleventh and last commission from the company. Still another movie effect was the use of an incidental score,
which Hanns Eisler composed.

In Hollywood fashion, Odets lets his principal characters "meet
cute." The audience does not see the event, but hears about it. Steve
Takis, a minor employee of a Hollywood studio, is being held by the
New York police, because one of a pair of monkeys he had come East
to pick up for the studio slipped away from him on a street corner
and stole the locket of a girl. This girl, Fay Tucker, is an actress in a
play about to close. Hearing her scream on the street out of fright, a
police detective, A. L. (for Abraham Lincoln) Rosenberger, pulled the
boy in. The romantic consequences of this meeting are predictable,
but Odets makes a slight though hardly original switch on the usual
boy-meets-girl formula by giving the girl the role of the aggressor.
Sympathetic and wise, she contrasts interestingly with the boy, who is
truculent and brash. At the same time, however, he is one of Odets's
most ingratiating characters. Like most young men in the Odets corpus, he is poor and uncertain about the future, but, more than any of
the others apart from Joe Bonaparte, he is driven by unhappy memories as much as by poverty. He has good reason to worry about his
job, having delayed the transport of the monkeys to California because of his arrest; but equally powerful among his griefs is the memory of the early death of his revered mother. Whenever the immediate worries grow fierce, he thinks of her. Homeless, friendless, and
motherless, he is lucky to have Fay to make up for his lacks. But the
need to remain self-sufficient, ingrained into him by years of proletarian tough breaks, inhibits him from showing affection. The couple
spend their first night together on a bench in Central Park and their
second in, of all places, the Hotel Algiers. The tenderness of the love
story is kept within reasonable bounds by comic lines in Odets's two
familiar manners, the wise-cracking and the idiomatic. Says Rosenberger's brother-in-law to Fay's father about the Algiers, "A kangaroo

wouldn't live here" (II, ii). To Fay, Rosenberger puts the stately ques-tion, "Would it be a disturbing factor to you if I smoked a cigar?" (I, v).

The isolationist theme enters when Steve begins to consider enlist-ing in the army, for no better reason than its guarantee of economic security, though he can never forget that his father was killed in the First World War—the "third gold star in Massachusetts" (I, v). Odets wastes no subtlety on Steve's notion and the folly of it; it is not merely a question of joining the army, but of "joining the war" (III, ii), though the year is 1939. He gives up this notion, as the audience expects he will, even though the studio fires him. It is the kindly Ro-senberger, his concern for the future not at all lessened by the knowl-edge that he is dying of cancer, who becomes Odets's spokesman. Protecting and shadowing the couple over the weekend as they go from the hotel to Central Park and the World's Fair, he sees them for the last time at La Guardia Airport, where he speaks his piece:

> I'm tired, Takis. . . . Three days I watched you fighting shadows, so young, so strong in the heart. I'll tell you both a secret: no old man can rest if you don't use your health to fight, to conquer disease and poverty, dirt and ignorance. Go back to the city, boy and girl, sweet and sour. . . . You had the wisdom and foresight to be born in the twentieth century. Go, go with love and health—your wonderful country never needed you more. . . . (III, ii)

The argument is convincing to Steve, though he has no job in view. Jubilantly, the three characters go off arm in arm, while, according to the final stage direction, *"Overhead the planes are zooming and sing-ing."* As in *Awake and Sing!, Paradise Lost,* and *Rocket to the Moon,* Odets settles for exultation in place of hard facts.

Belief in the courage, steadfastness, and practicality of youth such as Rosenberger voices was basic to the Odetsian credo. But the more comprehensive article of faith that every social ill can be rooted out by energetic men of good will had been expressed in all the Group plays, not those by Odets alone. Now in 1940, with the long-feared war underway in Europe, unemployment at home still a weary fact of life, and their theater no more secure than it had been in 1931, the company had reasons for discouragement. Tension had been develop-ing to a dangerous degree among the actors, manifesting itself in an

overindulgence in criticism of the plays, the productions, and one another's performances. After the closing of *Night Music,* with everyone
involved in the production angry over the failure, the collapse was
both inevitable and imminent. The best and the most that Clurman
could do for the actors was to function as an independent producer,
using only those members of the old company who could fill parts in
two scripts that he had acquired. The actors met this news with
disbelief when he presented it to them in the summer of 1940, and
angry words followed.[50]

He produced one of the plays, Irwin Shaw's *Retreat to Pleasure,*
which opened in December 1940, for a run of 23 performances, barely
carrying the Group banner into 1941. Only three old company hands
were in the cast: Art Smith, Dorothy Patten, and Ruth Nelson, all in
minor roles. The play wanly describes the mood of a young man who
knows that it is only a matter of time until the United States enters
the war, and he therefore seizes whatever pleasures are immediately
available. He pursues a young girl down the Eastern Seaboard to
Florida in the hope of persuading her to marry him, but on gaining
her consent decides perversely that he can enjoy himself all the more
without her. After screaming with rage for a few seconds, she agrees
that he is right to remain in single-blessedness for the time being. Because of the playwright's attitude of resignation over America's eventual entry into the war, it is a reasonable assumption that the comedy
would not have won the approval of the entire Group company, had
they been asked to vote on it. As for Clurman, his own position on
the war changed after the fall of France in 1940, when he not only
began to advocate American aid to the Allies but quarrelled with
those who opposed it.[51]

With the early closing of *Retreat to Pleasure* the Group Theater, or
what was left of it, quietly vanished from the Broadway arena. Clurman abandoned his second script, an adaptation by Victor Wolfson of
Erskine Caldwell's *Trouble in July.* Plans formed by Odets to take
over the Group office with Strasberg for the production of his latest
script, *Clash by Night,* fell through; in December 1941 the play was
presented by Billy Rose under Strasberg's direction, with only two
Group members, Lee J. Cobb and Art Smith, in the cast. No formal
announcement of the dissolution of the company was given to the actors. Nor was the public apprised officially of the breakup until May

18, 1941, when Clurman published an article in the *New York Times* on the closing of the Group offices. Clurman cited, as the reason for the wasting away of the organization after ten years, the difficulty of sustaining on Broadway a unit that was not show-business-oriented. With a subsidy, it could be done, but none was available, and he no longer wished to keep the Group going on the old basis of scratching for the money for each production.[52] One can scarcely blame him.

On the other hand, the ultimate defeat of the Group cannot be explained on the ground of Broadway economics alone. Nor can it be explained as the consequence of the failure of Clurman and the Group Council to put control of the company into the hands of the actors, for, no matter how accomplished they were in their art, the actors were not producers.[53] Yet leftist critics continued to believe that the company's leaders' position on this issue was the one true damaging factor, as was evident in an anonymous *New Theatre News* review of *Retreat to Pleasure:*

> Our hope is that out of the mistakes, the opportunism, and the genuine tragedy created by the Group Theatre's executives, there will come a new and genuinely progressive theatre in New York that will learn from the example of Mr. Clurman and his associates and proceed to create a professional people's theatre.[54]

The problem was not so simple. The most convincing late criticism of the Group and analysis of its problems was offered in October 1940 by John Gassner, an old champion of the company, in *Theatre Arts Monthly*. Gassner complained that the Group's search for actable social plays had led to the staging of "weighty but foggy dramas," among which were *Gold Eagle Guy, Weep for the Virgins, Casey Jones, Thunder Rock,* and *Night Music.* He also believed that in its plays and productions it had shown too little imagination—that is, had cared too much for realistic drama—had made the mistake of not reviving the classics (though, as we have noted, the company tried to produce *The Three Sisters* but could not for want of backing), and had devoted too much of its attention to the "little man" and the young girl. One of Gassner's most telling points had to do with the Group's insistence on "finding social significance in everything it touched" and the fact that the company's style of acting often had a destructive effect on the expression of those significances:

When the actors perform certain movements or scenes slowly and
with high seriousness, they do not actually convey any meanings that
the playwright has failed to precipitate completely in his script.
Moreover, any such emphases may labor the point unnecessarily, re-
tarding its tempo and giving it a lumbering pretentiousness such as
prevailed in a frequently beautiful play and production like *Night
Music*. Lightness of touch, in fact, has not been one of the Group's
virtues.

To this Gassner added an observation that, though perhaps painful to
the actors, needed to be made: it was possible, he thought, that the
company assembled by the Lunts for touring in their Theater Guild
hits was superior to the Group.[55] In short, the actors had grown pe-
dantic, doctrinaire, and parochial. They had been together too long.

But to say that in its last years the Group became an instrument
out of tune is not to deny its great achievement. No company of the
thirties dedicated exclusively to a program of social drama produced
so many works or garnered so much praise as did the Group. Nor did
any other company nurture a playwright so talented as Odets,
unquestionably the foremost American dramatist to emerge in the
decade. Nor did any other unit (as Gassner knew, despite his praise
of the Lunts) assemble so many capable actors during the decade or
command such loyalty. No matter how beset was the company by
personal, technical, or intellectual problems, its courage and artistry
put it in a class by itself.

The later careers of the members of the Group compensated for
their years of sacrifice. Each of the three original directors became a
leader of the profession—Clurman as a director and critic, Crawford
as a producer, and Strasberg as a teacher of acting and an occasional
director. Kazan and Lewis also established major reputations as
directors, and Stella Adler and Sanford Meisner as teachers of drama.
The list of regular members of the acting company who proceeded to
stardom or to fame as character actors is too long to cite.* Through
the Actors Studio, founded by Kazan, Lewis, and Crawford in 1947
and joined by Strasberg in 1949, the technique of acting developed by
Stanislavsky and extended and refined by the Group became avail-

* Among them were Luther Adler, J. Edward Bromberg, Morris Carnovsky, Lee
J. Cobb, Russell Collins, John Garfield, and Franchot Tone.

able to a new generation of American actors and directors, with the result that the influence of the Group, strong while the company was in existence, grew even stronger in the fifties and sixties and could be felt at least as late as the seventies.

11

THE THEATER GUILD
1935-1940

WHEN IN 1959 HAROLD CLURMAN, the Theater Guild's most rebellious son, edited a collection titled *Famous American Plays of the 1930's,* he included as three out of his five selections S. N. Behrman's *End of Summer,* Robert E. Sherwood's *Idiot's Delight,* and William Saroyan's *The Time of Your Life*—all produced by the Guild in the second half of the decade. Such a contribution to the American repertory in itself would insure any producing unit a place in all the histories. But the contribution of the Guild over the decades of its long life included two, three, or perhaps even four times as many distinguished American plays. Yet season by season the company's failures outnumbered its successes, until at last, discouraged by too many early closings and disappointed subscribers, as the thirties inched to their conclusion the Guild began a long period of decline that ended in the forties with the transformation from "art theater" to opportunist commercial show shop. It was a sad transformation, but no less inevitable than sad, since no company could hope to keep itself alive in the midst of a turgid economy on the proceeds of novel, "experimental" productions.

Other problems apart from the caution of the ticket-buyers were the difficulty of finding intelligent scripts of any artistic stamp or ideological persuasion—a difficulty also faced by all other managements— and the tensions that threatened the good relations among the members of the Guild's Board of Managers. After moving to Hollywood in 1935 for a year's tenure as producer at Columbia Pictures, Theresa Helburn returned for good to the Guild. Helen Westley, Lee Simonson, and Philip Moeller went periodically to Hollywood in these years, and Westley became a leading character actress in films. Simonson was frequently peeved when outside designers were called in to work on plays that he wished to design, and Wertheim, whose chief function as a member of the Board was to look after the Guild's finances, was irritated when in the season of 1935–36 Langner and Helburn approached a Paramount Pictures executive concerning backing for four productions without consulting him. Gradually Langner and Helburn assumed control until, in 1939, they were in complete charge of Guild productions.[1]

Of especially grave significance for the future of the Guild was the decision made in the 1937–38 season by S. N. Behrman, Maxwell Anderson, Sidney Howard, and Robert E. Sherwood, the Guild's most dependable American dramatists, along with Elmer Rice, to found the Playwrights' Company for the production of their plays. Provoking this move was the writers' resentment of the Guild's stubbornness over script revisions and casting—matters that, to be sure, are potential causes of hard feelings between all playwrights and managements. Sherwood, it appears, was particularly troubled by these matters. But also in question were the subsidiary rights to the plays, including the lucrative film rights; by serving as their own producers, the dramatists would no longer be obliged to share them with the Guild. Langner was so troubled by this vast defection from the list of reliable Guild authors that he told the agent Harold Freedman, who represented all the members of the new company save Rice, that the Playwrights might as well take over the Guild's subscription list. Despite Langner's sense of betrayal, relations between the two organizations were satisfactory. Because Behrman and Sherwood frequently shaped their plays to the talents of Alfred Lunt and Lynn Fontanne, who remained loyal to the Guild, it was possible in many instances for the Guild to participate in the Playwrights' offerings as joint producer. Though the Board found one play, Philip Barry's *The Philadelphia Story*, that outran most of the Playwrights' works, it could not discover a new author who could be as successful as they were in attracting the public.[2]

Usually unable to find enough viable plays for the annual schedule of six productions, the Board ultimately hit upon the expedient of offering other managements' productions to their subscribers. Not only was the Group Theater's production of Saroyan's *My Heart's in the Highlands* offered by the Guild under such an arrangement, but also Herman Shumlin's production of Thornton Wilder's *The Merchant of Yonkers*. Many other plays were staged jointly by the Guild and other producers, either because, as with the Sherwood and Behrman plays for the Lunts, the Guild had first call on the stars of the play, or one of the two managements, the Guild or its temporary partner, had the play but lacked the necessary funds. As noted in preceding chapters, in this way the Guild joined forces with the Actors Repertory Company and the Welles-Houseman team. Others with whom it shared billing were Charles B. Cochran, John C. Wilson, Lee Ephraim, Sidney Harmon, Eddie Dowling, and Gilbert Miller. In still other instances silent partners put up substantial backing for Guild plays, as did the Shubert brothers with Ben Hecht's *To Quito and Back* and Billy Rose with Ernest Hemingway's *The Fifth Column,* as adapted by Benjamin Glazer.[3] Thus the creative ferment that had characterized the Guild in 1919 was gradually eroded.

Though continuing with the "menu" system of tendering the subscribers a taste of this and slice of that each season, with a schedule made up of perhaps a historical tragedy, a comedy of manners with a contemporary setting, a new European import, and a revival with the Lunts, the Guild became a leading producer of new drama touching upon contemporary social, political, and economic preoccupations. The frequency with which the Guild began to offer opulently designed well-made trifles starring film personalities doubtless rendered suspect its pretensions to seriousness, but it was nevertheless true that more than half of the twenty-nine works presented by the Guild from the fall of 1935 to the spring of 1940 dealt with serious issues then confronting the American populace. On the political spectrum, the plays clustered at the center, with a few—a very few—inching slightly toward the left.

No such daring a departure from familiar realistic dramaturgy as Elmer Rice's *The Adding Machine* or John Howard Lawson's *Processional* appeared on a Guild schedule during the late thirties—unless George and Ira Gershwin's *Porgy and Bess,* a musical with operatic ambitions, could be described as daring—but the Guild ventured into the proletarian scene for the third time in the decade, following Wexley's *They Shall Not Die* and *Parade*, with Leopold Atlas's *But for the Grace of God* (1937). Also about children, as was Wexley's suspenseful, poignant melodrama, the play has as its protagonist a teenage slum boy who commits armed robbery and murder in a misguided effort to supply his wretched family with money for the basic necessities. The Guild's most radical play of the period, though hardly revolutionary, it made a plea for a more equitable distribution of wealth. John Haynes Holmes and Reginald Lawrence's *If This Be Treason* (1935) offered an antiwar tract in which a newly elected pacifist President of the United States who is burdened with a bellicose Congress abruptly ends a war with Japan by the novel expedient of traveling to that country to make a personal appeal to the premier. A combination comedy of manners and social message play was offered in Julius and Philip Epstein's *And Stars Remain* (1936). At some moments imitating Behrman, at other moments imitating Noël Coward, the authors took up the plight of a wealthy young woman of conservative family who decides to marry a liberal lawyer, the political enemy of her grandfather. The most vital character who drifts through the plot is a young sophisticate who affects liberal opinions for their value as conversational gambits. Cannily, with the use of very faint pressure, he blackmails the conservative grandfather, who is in charge of public works in the state of New York, into restoring cuts in the works program. Though demonstrations of the unemployed are said to be taking place in the street, they do not intrude on the comfortable characters. Essentially the play is a tepid love story with its social comment confined to arch observations on unemployment as the problem is viewed from a nineteenth-storey apartment. Ben Hecht's *To Quito and Back* (1937), inspired by the struggle between the political Left and Right that wracked Ecuador in the mid-thirties, gave the subscribers a look at armed rebellion, though with ideological issues subordinate through much of the action to the love affair of two Americans on the spot. Unfortunately, these plays, well-meaning though their authors undoubtedly were, did not have the strength to withstand the competition on Broadway. Moreover, all had the patchy quality that suggests heavy but hasty rewriting. Each closed quickly after playing to the subscribers.

With works by the authors who ultimately formed the Playwrights' Company the Guild had better luck, though not a record of consistent success. Anderson and Howard contributed one each to the Guild's programs in the late thirties, Behrman and Sherwood two each. As before, their value to the Guild as revealed in the best of these plays consisted of more than the ability to command the attention of the audience with credible actions and equally credible characters to a degree not in the gift of the authors of *And Stars Remain, But for the Grace of God, To Quito and Back,* and *If This Be Treason.* Also as before, their plays were inportant to the Guild insofar as they gave the audience an intellectual stimulus in the form of social comment without leading them in unfamiliar, hence alarming, directions. In commenting on domestic affairs, the authors were resolute only about illustrating problems; seldom did they recommend solutions. With foreign affairs they could, without fear of losing the audience, take a firmer stand and express abhorrence of the fascist dictators and deplore acts of armed aggression. Expressing dismay about the quality of daily life in their time and, unlike the radical writers who had gone to Marx for the answers, admitting to doubt about the future, they were the perfect playwrights to present to an audience of relative affluence for whom the old certainties had long since been exploded.

Neither Anderson's nor Howard's Guild play was a success, though Anderson did at least achieve five weeks of performances beyond those necessary to accommodate the Guild's subscribers. When the Guild opened *The Masque of Kings* in February 1937, Anderson already had two plays running: *The Wingless Victory* and *High Tor,* the latter in the following month being declared the winner of the Drama Critics' Award. The Guild's play was the most opulent of the three, as well as the most political. The setting is the court of the Emperor Franz Joseph of Austria-Hungary and the hunting lodge at Mayerling of his son, Crown Prince Rudolph. The love affair between Rudolph and Mary Vetsera which ended in the mysterious death of the two at Mayerling is a frame on which Anderson drapes ideas of liberty and revolution.[4] In revolt against the rule of his father, Rudolph joins with rebels who wish to depose the Emperor and institute reforms that would result in turning the Empire into a democracy. Though Rudolph has the opportunity to depose and imprison his father and ascend the throne himself, he is deflected from his purpose by the arguments of the Emperor, who makes him realize that to overthrow the tyranny to which he objects he would be obliged to impose a new tyranny of his own making. Abashed and suddenly cynical, Rudolph backs down. His suicide at Mayerling is an admission of both his folly and his despair—folly in thinking that he could accomplish his ends without violence, and despair on recognizing that truth. The dialogue of the long second-act confrontation scene, in which Franz Joseph wins from his son admission upon admission that to conquer his enemies he would have to execute or imprison many and establish censorship of the press, is clamorous with reminders of the aftermath of the Russian Revolution, Europe's most recent armed uprising, and the news then spreading from Moscow of the trials of Stalin's old rivals.

As Anderson turned to the past for comment on the present scene, so Howard in *The Ghost of Yankee Doodle* dramatized a current anxiety by looking into the future. Set in a Western city "eighteen months after the commencement of the next world war," the play has as its prime mover a Hearst-like publisher named James Madison Clevenger who is on the lookout for an international incident that he can exploit as a means of ending American neutrality. In the plot he is pitted against a well-to-do family who publish a liberal newspaper and own a tool-and-die factory, the profits of which are used to finance the paper. Clevenger finds his incident when the French sink an American naval vessel. Though an end to American neutrality would mean prosperity for the factory and a secure future for the paper, the Garrison family—the very name suggesting well-guarded isolation—is shocked by Clevenger's effort. He himself is so much by habit and inclination the yellow journalist that when his own son is killed in a plane crash while hastening to Europe to enter the fight, he can think only of how to use the death for prowar propaganda. The issues of labor agitation and academic freedom also come under discussion, but only with the result of deflecting attention from the major theme, which is the necessity of preserving neutrality so that democracy may flourish. A "younger generation" romance, very often a concomitant of Guild productions, further weakens the play. It was Howard's fourth, and poorest, for the organization. As had become its practice, the Guild bolstered the "production values" by casting a famous actress—Ethel Barrymore—in a leading role, but this gesture was not sufficient to compensate for Howard's overwrought script.

Less self-consciously literary than Anderson and less polemical than Howard was S. N. Behrman. The first of his Guild plays of the late thirties was *End of Summer* (1936), with Ina Claire, one of his favorite actresses, in the leading role of Leonie Frothingham, a woman of independent means but many emotional dependencies. The most poignant of Behrman's plays, it is resonant with his deepening sense that the familiar world of graceful social conventions—good manners and good talk—was withering away at a speed that could not be controlled, its decay caused by forces that he could only dimly comprehend and certainly could not master. Like that of most of his plays, its setting is a drawing room in the home of a person of means. Into Leonie's comfortable summer house in Maine come ten characters, not one of whom, regardless of age or occupation, lacks the ability to express himself with the utmost clarity and incisiveness. Among these remarkably articulate figures are not only two undergraduates passionately devoted to the salvation of society through radical means, but the admittedly unintellectual Leonie and her aged mother, who is afflicted with a fatal illness. It is as though Behrman dreaded, above all else that might result from social change, the loss of rational conversation in which no side of an important issue is left unexamined or undescribed by all whom it concerns. The conversation is appropriately wise, and though the characters may be too well-spoken to be true, they are a pleasure to overhear.

The play begins in the spring of the year, passes through the summer, and in the last act slips into autumn. During this passage of time, a golden age for Leonie, the kind of life lived by such families as the Frothinghams is seen drawing to its end like the year itself, and she herself is on the brink of middle age—at the end of the summer of her life. A bittersweet melancholy drifts through the play as she sees disappearing from her life all the mainstays that supported it. Her estranged husband, Sam, announces that he wants a divorce in order to marry another woman. Her mother, on whose father's oil fields the family fortune rests, dies in the early fall, the death marking the end of an era. Her daughter, Paula, leaves to follow a young radical admirer back to New York. In addition, her two distinguished house guests of the summer prove to be charlatans. The Russian émigré, Count Mirsky, who has come to the house in Maine to work on a biography of his famous father, writes not a word, and has written none. The psychiatrist, a charming healer of the troubled souls of the rich, pursues her with feigned amorousness out of snobbery and a wish to have access to her money. His cunning is masked by a disarming outspokenness about his love of wealth, but Paula, seeing through the mask, exposes him ruthlessly. Like Hitler and Mussolini, he is an upstart; somewhat awkwardly, Behrman has him identify with the fascist dictators in a speech addressed to Paula:

> When I hear the chatter of your friends, it makes me sick. While they and their kind prate of co-operative commonwealths, the strong man takes power, and rides over their backs—which is all their backs are fit for. Never has the opportunity for the individual career been so exalted, so infinite in its scope, so horizontal. House-painters and minor journalists become dictators of great nations. . . . Imagine what a really clever man could do!" (III)

These disappointments to Leonie notwithstanding, the close of the play flickers with a ray of hope for her. Left alone for a moment with young Dennis McCarthy, the closest friend of Paula's fiancé, she decides to put money into the radical magazine that both young men have long dreamed of founding. "It would emancipate you, Leonie," he tells her. "It would be a perpetual dedication to Youth—to the hope of the world." Their last exchange before the final curtain calls for a rueful smile:

> LEONIE: I suppose if it's really successful—it'll result in my losing everything I have—
> DENNIS: It'll be taken from you anyway. You'll only be anticipating the inevitable.
> LEONIE: Why—how clever of me!
> DENNIS: Not only clever but grateful.
> LEONIE: Will you leave me just a little to live on—?
> DENNIS: Don't worry about that—come the Revolution—you'll have a friend in high office.

Thus Behrman alleviates Leonie's plight somewhat. But the passage does not fundamentally alter the prospect of a social climate less warming than that of the past, and Behrman, in middle age like his heroine, awaited the coming changes with perplexity.

Behrman followed up this well-received play with another—an adaptation of Jean Giraudoux's *Amphitryon 38* (1937) for the Lunts. In this, his third play for the couple, Behrman, by way of the original author, gave theatergoers an escape from the contemporary world to a classical antiquity of intelligent, physically attractive characters and risqué situations, but with the purpose of leading them back to a modern problem, the threat of international war. On this subject the characters sermonize for three acts with acid wit. Unfortunately, he could not instill the same sparkle into *Wine of Choice* (1938), his last Guild play of the decade. Langner later wrote of it, "I believe that we produced this play largely because I had once told Sam's play representative, Harold Freedman, that no matter what Sam wrote, he could rewrite is so brilliantly during rehearsal that it would ultimately emerge as a good play." [5] Though it is impossible to point to specific evidence of rewriting in the script as published, the play seems indeed labored, and to no purpose.

Written in the familiar Behrman pattern, *Wine of Choice* is an economical, one-set play with a small cast made up principally of well-to-do liberals and their hangers-on. Doctrinally or professionally, all have counterparts in the author's earlier social comedies, apart from the actress in the clumsily contrived central role. Two unoriginal themes intertwine in the plot: the artist's dilemma of the choice between love and career, and the fact that a liberal, though rich and self-indulgent, may be a more decent human being than a communist, though poor and self-denying. The actress is wooed by the rich young man who for a whim produces a film that will turn her into a star overnight, and also by a well-born senator of liberal views. Not loving either, though liking both well enough, she remains single. It is the senator who is Behrman's exemplar of the enlightened plutocracy; as was recognized by reviewers and admitted by Behrman in a prefatory note to the play, this character had as a prototype the liberal Republican Senator Bronson Cutting of New Mexico, a supporter of the New Deal. The communist is a young writer of proletarian fiction who, it is discovered, made a point of establishing a friendship with the senator merely in the hope of pushing him farther to the Left. Behrman's own social and humanist views, a politics of personal relations, find expression in the senator's furious verbal attack on the novelist toward the close of the play:

You are locked deep in the cold fastnesses of theory—on that surface nothing can take hold, nothing can take root, nothing can flower— neither love nor friendship nor affection. I see how people like you can condemn to death their best friends—because equally well you can condemn yourselves to lovelessness, to abnegation, to death. (III)

Presiding over these antagonistic personalities is a fussy male mother hen named Binkie Niebuhr, a role entrusted to Alexander Woollcott in the Guild's production. In part a reflection of Woollcott's acid personality, the character is primarily a synthesis of Behrman himself and Rudolph Kommer, the financial aide of Max Reinhardt whom Behrman was to memorialize in *The Burning Glass*, his novel of 1967. The setting is a guest cottage of an estate on Long Island—intimate, yet redolent of wealth and upper Bohemianism, and therefore typical of the author. Yet, largely because of the muddled viewpoint of the actress and the woodenness of the other characters, the comedy is devoid of Behrman's usual appeal. Its messages are lost in the air.

Of all the Guild dramatists of the thirties, only one, apart from the temporarily silent O'Neill, had a more solid claim to consideration as a dramatist of serious intention than Behrman. This was Robert E. Sherwood, who in *Idiot's Delight* (1936) constructed the most intelligent drama of the thirties on international politics. It was his only Guild play of the second half of the decade. Late in the season of 1939–40 his *There Shall Be No Night* opened as a joint presentation with the Playwrights' Company, with Guild participation permitted by the Playwrights to secure the services of Lunt and Fontanne, for whom Sherwood wrote the play. Between these two plays he adapted Jacques Deval's *Tovarich* for production by Gilbert Miller and launched the Playwrights with his spectacularly successful *Abe Lincoln in Illinois*. Not only were these years of well-rewarded productivity for Sherwood, but years of intellectual evolution, in which he turned from the pessimism that underlay and controlled the melodramatic action of *The Petrified Forest* to a new and bold confidence in a future in which America might be willing to take a stand with the European democracies in the Second World War.

The new Sherwood is in evidence in *Idiot's Delight*, if perhaps difficult to spot at a glance. The title, referring to a particularly difficult game of solitaire which in the play is described as God's sole occupation, is in itself pessimistic. At the close of the play Sherwood offers an awesome, apocalyptic vision of a world bent on self-destruction, which bears out the suggestion of God's remoteness from the world. Yet the theme of the play as a whole is that things might be otherwise, that war could be averted if the "little people," a phrase Sherwood himself uses, took courageous action against their self-aggrandizing leaders. Sherwood saw this work as in part optimistic, "a compound of blank pessimism and desperate optimism," as he later put it.[6] Harry Van, an American song-and-dance man, is his spokesman. On the first day of a new world war, Van in conversation with a German scientist offers Sherwood's message of confidence:

> I've remained an optimist because I'm essentially a student of human nature. You dissect corpses and rats and similar unpleasant things. Well—it has been my job to dissect suckers! I've probed into the souls of some of the God-damnedest specimens. And what have I found? Now, don't sneer at me, Doctor—but above everything else I've found faith. Faith in peace on earth and good will to men—and faith that "Muma," "Muma" the three-legged girl, really has got three legs. All my life, Doctor, I've been selling phony goods to people of meager intelligence and great faith. You'd think that would make me contemptuous of the human race, wouldn't you? But—on the contrary —it has given *me* Faith. It has made me sure that no matter how much the meek may be bulldozed or gypped they *will* eventually inherit the earth. (I)

But despite the faith in humanity's staying power that he expressed in Van's speech, Sherwood perched his drama on an Italian Alpine peak called Monte Gabriele, a name which honors D'Annunzio, we are told, but also brings to mind the angel Gabriel and the threat of the last trump. Ironically, the precise locale is designed for vacationing: a ski resort. Gathered together in it on this fateful day are tourists representing all the major nations of the West. Italy is the power that sets off the conflagration, though inevitably all the others join in. Located near an Italian airfield, the hotel is in a danger zone. Among the guests are a British honeymoon couple, the Cherrys, who have just been married in Florence; a radical Frenchman, Quillery, on his way home from a labor conference in Zagreb; a German scientist, Dr. Waldersee, en route to Geneva, where he intends to devote himself to cancer research. These are relatively minor characters, though all have an effect on the unfolding plot. Those with more influential roles

are Achille Weber, one of Europe's foremost munitions manufacturers, who travels on a French passport; his mistress, a mysterious Russian named Irene, who has a League of Nations passport issued to her
as a stateless person; and Harry Van, who is working the European
nightclub circuit with a troupe of six girls billed as "les Blondes."
Only Irene and Van—characters invented for and played by Lunt
and Fontanne—stay behind when the first train goes through for Geneva after the war commences.

The minor figures function as melancholy reminders of the suscepti-
bility of much, if not most, of mankind to the allure of patriotic appeals. Though all think of themselves as internationalists, they hasten
back to their respective countries once the fighting starts. Even Waldersee sets aside his plans to search out a cure for cancer and returns
to his nazi masters in Germany, and the radical Quillery at once
strives to form a united front with the English couple. Thus does
Sherwood lash out against the hypocrisy and duplicity of both Right
and Left, whose self-publicized humanitarianism is transparently
false. But these characters are in fact as much to be pitied as condemned; each is nothing more than a willing, brain-washed victim of
his government. To Weber, who as a manufacturer of weapons is the
happy partner of government in warfare, Irene pours out Sherwood's
tortured description of the horror that must be averted, with the English couple as her example of the victims of his irresponsibility:

That young English couple, for instance. I was watching them during
dinner, sitting there, close together, holding hands, and rubbing their
knees together under the table. And I saw him in his nice, smart,
British uniform, shooting a little pistol at a huge tank. And the tank
rolls over him. And his fine strong body, that was so full of the capacity for ecstacy, is a mass of mashed flesh and bones—a smear of purple blood—like a stepped-on snail. But before the moment of death,
he consoles himself by thinking, "Thank God *she* is safe! She is bearing the child I gave her, and he will live to see a better world." . . .
But I know where she is. She is lying in a cellar that has been
wrecked by an air raid, and her firm young breasts are all mixed up
with the bowels of a dismembered policeman, and the embryo from
her womb is splattered against the face of a dead bishop. This is the
kind of thought with which I amuse myself, Achille. And it makes me
so proud to think that I am so close to you—who make all this possible." (II, ii)

The speech was written at the suggestion of Lynn Fontanne, after Langner observed at a rehearsal that the play was too light in tone for its import.[7] Not only does it stiffen the entire plot and create sympathy for Irene, but it also provides a vent for the audience's hatred of Weber. No more dramatically effective antiwar outburst was heard during the decade. But Weber has a telling rejoinder which at once expresses his ingrained cynicism and the playwright's blunt advice to the governed to have a new look at their governors:

> And who are the greater criminals—those who sell the instruments of death, or those who buy them, and use them? You know there is no logical reply to that. But all these little people—like your new friends [the Cherrys]—all of them consider me an arch-villain because I furnish them with what they want, which is the illusion of power. That is what they vote for in their frightened governments—what they cheer for on their national holidays—what they glorify in their anthems, and their monuments, and their waving flags! . . . I assure you, Irene—for such little people the deadliest weapons are the most merciful. (II, ii)

Near the close Sherwood permits Irene to echo, sadly, the last line, by way of suggesting that in a world made uninhabitable by the conflicting ambitions of the great, what Weber says is true.

The starring roles of Van and Irene provide the voices for Sherwood's contrapuntal notes of hopefulness and despair at the same time that they give the audience a romantic plot line to follow. The roles made new demands on the actors who played them: Lunt was required to sing a song and do a tap number with his troupe, and Fontanne spoke with a Russian accent throughout. When Van and Irene are together on stage, the atmosphere vibrates with the possibility of sex, and two teasing questions are raised: was or was not Irene herself a performer in the twenties, and did she or did she not once spend the night with Van in the Governor Bryan Hotel in Omaha? But at the close the romantic byplay gives way to seriousness, though it is a seriousness ironically expressed. Alone in the hotel, since Weber makes it impossible for Irene to leave and Harry will not go without her, the couple face the bombardment with the bravery of despair, singing "Onward, Christian Soldiers" to a jazz beat. Awaiting the mercy of Weber's deadliest weapons, they make no effort in their own behalf. Led on by the playwright to expect a romantic ending, the audience finds itself listening to the sounds of all-out war.

The Guild's second antiwar play in two years, *Idiot's Delight* had a ring of intellectual honesty that Holmes and Lawrence had denied *If This Be Treason* through the simplicity of their solution to the threat of war. But Sherwood's reviewers, though inclined to admire the work as a whole, were troubled by the romantic and comic moments. "You'd think," Sherwood wrote in his diary, "it was a crime to state unpleasant truths in an entertaining way." [8] Consolation came in the form of the Pulitzer Prize.

Sherwood also received the Pulitzer Prize for his next two plays. With these he completed the about-face begun in *Idiot's Delight*, for both, like that play, bespeak confidence in democracy, yet both go the further step of recommending, by implication or direct statement, that democracy must be preserved even if the cost is war. In *Abe Lincoln in Illinois* (1938) he dramatized the early career of Lincoln to point a moral for his own day concerning slavery; just as it was necessary for the abolitionists to stand firm in the nineteenth century regardless of the risk to peace, so was it necessary, Sherwood implied, for the leaders of the democracies to resist the spread of totalitarianism in the twentieth, though in doing so they might be forced to take up arms. This work will be viewed more closely in the next chapter. After the threatened war became a reality and the Russians, not to be entirely outdone by the Germans strove to increase their territory by invading Finland, Sherwood wrote *There Shall Be No Night* and with it provided Broadway with the first major drama on the new conflict.

Sherwood, at the request of Lawrence Langner had agreed in the fall of 1939 to refurbish *Acropolis*, his antiwar play of 1933 that still had not been produced in America. But his new manuscript, originally titled *Revelation*, then retitled *There Shall Be No Night*, was something altogether different. It was not set in ancient Greece, like *Acropolis*, but in contemporary Finland and illustrated the courage of the Finns under Russian attack. The initial impulse to write the play came to Sherwood on listening to a radio broadcast from Helsinki made by William L. White on Christmas Day, 1939; in his Preface to the play he acknowledged that from this broadcast he received most of his information on the Russian invasion. With the sentiment of the American public overwhelmingly favoring the Finns, the subject had a vast theatrical audience awaiting a competent treatment. Immediately before receiving Sherwood's script, the Lunts gave a week of performances of *The Taming of the Shrew* for Finnish relief. On reading the script, they were at once impressed and, though having only recently completed a transcontinental tour with a repertory of three comedies, they postponed the rest they had planned and at once put the play into rehearsal.[9]

Though the war did not last out the rehearsal period, the emotion that it had generated turned the play into a major hit on its opening in April 1940. With the stars in the roles of a Finnish scientist and his American-born wife and members of their touring company in other important parts, *There Shall Be No Night* ran in New York for 181 performances and in the season of 1940–41 began a tour of forty-two cities. In 1943 the Lunts courageously took the play to England, where it also was well received. The script was, however, not entirely the same abroad, for with the Russians then joined with the Allies in the fight against Hitler, Sherwood changed the locale to Greece, with Italy the aggressor nation. In all, the Lunts acted some 1600 performances of the play.[10] During the original run Sherwood, having awakened to new purposefulness as a dramatist, went to work for the common good outside the theater as a member of the Committee to Defend America by Aiding the Allies, which William Allen White chaired. For the Committee he wrote a full-page advertisement, headed "Stop Hitler Now," that took up the entire last page of the *New York Times* on June 10, 1940.

In *There Shall Be No Night* Sherwood mirrored the American confusion over the shifting events of the summer and fall of 1939 by putting forward a spokesman for each of several aspects of the international scene, as though one character alone could not deliver a full exposition of it. He has, nevertheless, a central character, and a strong one, in Dr. Valkonen, a scientist who after devoting his career to an investigation of the causes of insanity suddenly finds himself in the middle of the madness of war. In his last scene, after which his death is reported, Valkonen feelingly reveals his belief that the power of the intellect will eventually overcome the bestiality in man's nature that is the cause of war—that, in other words, the process of evolution has not concluded, and, contrary to the opinion of those who believe that civilization is dying, the best is yet to come for humanity.

His wife stands in the play as an example to all Americans; the valor that she displays after the death of her husband and son, demonstrated by her determination to fight off the Russians herself with a rifle, is a lesson in courage and a reproach to isolationists. The cast also includes a young American who had planned to declare himself a conscientious objector if America should go to war, but who was moved to take part in Finland's struggle, and another young American who had put his faith in the U.S.S.R., only to suffer a great betrayal. Sherwood's harshest expression of contempt for the Russians is voiced, not by a Finn or any of the several Americans who appear in the play, but by a German diplomat, who declares,

> All the little communist cells, in labor movements, youth movements, in all nations—they are now working for *us*, although they may not know it. Communism is a good laxative to loosen the bowels of democracy. When it has served that purpose, it will disappear down the sewer with the excrement that must be purged. (scene iii)

With this passage Sherwood implicates the American Communists in the nazi outrages for their support of both the Stalin-Hitler pact and the invasion.

Sherwood's work was effective in keeping alive American sympathy for the Finns, as the record of its New York run and transcontinental tour testifies. But, despite the intensity of honest concern that underlies it, *There Shall Be No Night* was a play for the moment, not for all time. It was destined to seem both overlong and garrulous once the Second World War had slipped into history. Of Sherwood's successful plays, it is the only one to fail the test of time. Unhappily, it was his last well-received play; the two that followed it, *The Rugged Path* (1945) and *Small War on Murray Hill* (1957), were short-lived. Successes of another kind came his way, however; during the war he was entrusted with the overseas directorship of the Office of War Information, and after it he won a fourth Pulitzer Prize with the biography *Roosevelt and Hopkins*, published in 1948.

Popular as were Sherwood's and most of Behrman's plays, neither of the two writers nor any other writer of the thirties achieved so long a run for the Guild as did Philip Barry with *The Philadelphia Story*. With 417 performances on Broadway, it nimbly outdistanced the runner-up among Guild's plays, *Idiot's Delight*, which played 300 performances. The comedy became available at a moment when the Guild's finances were dangerously low as a result of the failure of Stefan Zweig's *Jeremiah* and the unfortunate episode of Welles's *Five Kings*. For the time being, it saved the company. Barry had seen and admired Katharine Hepburn in the 1938 film of his play *Holiday* and tailored the script to her special talent. Without a stage hit to his credit since *The Animal Kingdom* in 1932 and denied membership in the Playwrights' Company because the founders suspected that he was unsuited by temperament to co-operative ventures, Barry was also at a low point.[11] Similarly in eclipse was Hepburn, who with other film stars of equal magnitude ° had been publicly described as "poison at the box office" by the president of the Independent Theater Owners of America. To her the play was especially beneficial. Her appearance in the role of Tracy Lord in New York and on the road and in the film version of 1940 not only restored her popularity, but set her on the way to becoming a living legend.

Barry's comedy was the product of an era's end. Despite the continuing, nagging problem of unemployment, the rebelliousness of the thirties had so cooled by the spring of 1939, when *The Philadelphia Story* opened, that audiences could relish without guilt Hepburn's uppity role: a well-born heiress who on the day she is to marry a self-made man of lowly origins decides instead to marry a young man of social background and economic status identical with her own to whom she had been married previously. The play was not, to be sure, intended as a piece of elitist propaganda, but, like the comedies of Behrman, as a plea for tolerance of the rich on the part of those who have less. It lacks, however, Behrman's habitually firm references to social iniquities and the dangers of political extremism. Such references are present, but are mild indeed. "With the rich and mighty, always a little patience" is a proverb repeated in the dialogue. The heroine and her family, along with her former husband, are shown to be hearty, loving, and egalitarian in outlook. It is tactfully suggested, moreover, that their wealth, while not of so massive an amount as to establish them in the Rockefeller bracket, is something of a curse, since it brings them unwelcome publicity.

Set off against these affable aristocrats are Tracy's fiancé and a re-

° Edward Arnold, Fred Astaire, Joan Crawford, Marlene Dietrich, Kay Francis, and Mae West.

porter from a publishing house akin to Time, Inc. The fiancé is a fatuous social climber who idealizes Tracy to a degree that she finds intolerable; he is the sort of parvenu who with slight encouragement
could turn fascist overnight. The reporter is a liberal to whom the
folkways of the rich are not so much offensive as amusing. The faint
class antagonism that develops between him and Tracy as each ac-
cuses the other of possessing social prejudices swiftly turns to sex-
antagonism, which is followed, not by a seduction, but by mild intoxica-
tion and a swim in the nude. Both participants are humbled by the
experience and its aftermath. Tracy, suffering from a hangover, is
able to forgive her former husband his own bouts with the bottle and
accepts his humanity as she must accept her own. His intelligent response to the news of this escapade, which he tries to conceal from
the fiancé, forces a conversion upon the reporter, who near the close
voices the explicit moral point of the proceedings: "Well, you see, I've
made a funny discovery: that in spite of the fact that someone's up
from the bottom, he may be quite a heel. And even though someone
else is born to the purple, he may still be quite a guy" (III).

That *The Philadelphia Story* had greater drawing power than any
of Behrman's plays with a similar background and an equally sympathetic view of the rich was due not only to the changing mood of the
decade's close and the gentleness of Barry's social statement. Barry
provided a constant surface play of wit and a cast whose central roles
were youthful, as opposed to Behrman's less shallow but intermittent
humor and his middle-aged heroines. In truth, the piece is no
more than a story of love in idleness with an undercurrent of sensual-
ity and an overlay of democratic mottoes, the whole calculated to
please a comfortable audience. But to say so much (or so little) is not
to deny its charm or the value of works of its kind to a well-balanced
theater. Its success was as much deserved as was the failure of, say,
the turgid *But for the Grace of God*, whose author, despite his sincerity, could not accommodate his urgent theme with cogent dialogue.

In the decade's last season, only six weeks before the opening of
There Shall Be No Night, the Guild opened a belated play about the
Spanish Civil War, Ernest Hemingway's *The Fifth Column*. Written
in 1937 while Hemingway was in Spain, the play is a somber, nondra-
matic portrayal of Loyalist fighters and supporters behind the lines in
Madrid, centering on an American engaged in Loyalist counteres-

pionage. The title phrase, which became a popular term for subversion during the Second World War, originated in a Rebel boast that in the battle for Madrid four military columns were marching on the city while a fifth column composed of sympathizers was inside and ready to join in the attack. Philip Rawlings, the American, is helping to ferret out the sympathizers, but is almost diverted from his purpose by a long-legged female American war correspondent. In the end, though he thinks briefly of fleeing Spain with her for the rich, full life of a well-heeled loafer in France, he is soon revolted by the thought and decides to stay where he is.

As originally written by Hemingway and published in 1938, the play suffered from a lack of conflict and a weakness bordering on insipidity in the major female character—the latter a fault common to the author's novels. (According to Hemingway's biographer, this character, Dorothy Bridges, a young, blond correspondent with a cultivated voice, was drawn after Martha Gellhorn, who became Hemingway's third wife.) In essence the play, in both the published and acted versions, is a candid report on a fighter mightily wearied by war; as such it bears a resemblance to three of Hemingway's novels: *A Farewell to Arms, For Whom the Bell Tolls,* and *Across the River and into the Trees.* Like the novels, it is full of minor native characters who impart both humor and pathos. The play was first optioned for Broadway by Austin Parker, but Parker died before he could get it on. When Langner and Helburn picked up the rights for the Guild in 1939, they did so only with the intention of having the script revised before going into production. Since Hemingway himself was not available, they engaged the screenwriter Benjamin Glazer to make the adaptation, which would be produced subject to Hemingway's approval. Clifford Odets also had a look at the script on behalf of the Guild. Ultimately Hemingway, not pleased with Glazer's draft, revised the revisions.[12]

The script resulting from this effort was not remarkably different from the original, and not markedly better. The major changes consist in a rearrangement of the scenes into a somewhat tauter whole, the inclusion of what amounts to the rape of Dorothy by Philip during a bombardment of Madrid, and the bestowal upon Dorothy of a new and worthy purpose for being in Spain. It is not mere junketing as financed by a popular magazine that takes her there, but the search for a younger brother who is fighting on the Loyalist side. Though Hemingway's appreciation of the valor of the Loyalists shines through, the script is never stirring. It is a foregone conclusion that Philip will not be diverted from his work for the Seguridad by a pretty face and (eventually) willing body. Probably it was true, as Hemingway protested by letter to Langner after the opening, that he was too intelligent and too good a writer to be reworked by Glazer, but in view of the tentativeness of the original script, he had small cause for complaint.[13]

The Guild's production was directed by Lee Strasberg, and the cast included two former Group actors: Franchot Tone as Philip Rawlings and Lee J. Cobb as Max, a German-born member of the Seguridad. It was to have a third, Frances Farmer as Dorothy, but the actress quit the production abruptly during the preliminary tour and was replaced by Katharine Locke. Hemingway, who regretted Farmer's departure, suspected that Odets or perhaps the Communist party had put her up to it, presumably because of his well-known resistance to party dogmatism and the fact that the play, coming after the signing of the Stalin-Hitler pact and the outbreak of the Second World War, could be construed as propaganda for American intervention. The play did not cast slurs on the party, but its kindness in that respect was not sufficient reason to give joy to party members. Lee J. Cobb, for example, was disturbed by his role, though he played it well and was admired in it. Why was he troubled? Because "with the European war, and the rapid shifts of international affairs, a strange thing has happened: the anti-fascist fighter for Loyalist Spain becomes a recruiting sergeant for the present imperialist murder campaigns." One of the very few managements to produce a play on the war in Spain, and the only professional institutional theater to do so, the Guild was unlucky in its timing. The new international alignment undercut the play's validity for both the Left and the liberal center.[14]

The two works which with *The Fifth Column* and *There Shall Be No Night* the Guild rounded out its last season of the decade were products of the antic imagination of William Saroyan: *The Time of Your Life* and *Love's Old Sweet Song*. The actor-producer Eddie Dowling brought both works to the Guild and received credit in the billing as the associate producer. *The Time of Your Life*, which opened in October 1939, became the company's last play of the thirties. As the winner of both the New York Drama Critics' Award and the Pulitzer Prize, it proved an eminently satisfactory piece with which to draw the curtain on the decade.

Saroyan's much-discussed self-esteem, coupled with his irreverence for conventional dramatic structure, made him an author less receptive than most to the Guild's practice of riding herd on its authors during rehearsals and trial performances. Langner and Helburn persisted as usual, but not with equal results to the two plays. With *The Time of Your Life* the system worked, though painfully. In New Haven, where the play gave its first performance, the Group Theater director Robert Lewis was replaced by Dowling, the Group actor Martin Ritt was replaced by Gene Kelly in a minor role (though the Group actors Curt Conway, Grover Burgess, and Will Lee were retained), and the settings of Boris Aronson, a favorite Group designer, were replaced by settings designed by Watson Barratt. The producers successfully resisted the entreaty of Saroyan regarding the staging of a scene in the room of the prostitute Kitty Duvall recommended by George Jean Nathan. Had it been altered, the prostitute's bed would have been set up temporarily (and unaccountably) in the barroom in which all other scenes of the play occur! With *Love's Old Sweet Song*, however, they did not find Saroyan so tractable. Though initially he was willing to accede to their request that the action be divided into two acts rather than the original three, he later refused it firmly, on the advice of Nathan. The result, in the opinion of Langner and Helburn, was a missed opportunity to build up suspense in a sagging script.[15]

Talented Saroyan was beyond question, but insecure despite his bluster, as his reliance on Nathan demonstrated, and unwilling or unable to admit the necessity of developing and resolving a dramatic conflict. The season of 1939–40 proved to be his climactic year in the theater. Though he wrote intermittently for the stage in later years and secured a good run of 120 performances for *The Beautiful People* in 1941, the sole theatrical hit of his career was *The Time of Your Life*, which ran for 181 performances in its first season and 32 in a return engagement, and enjoyed a well-attended tour. Alone among Saroyan's plays, it has achieved the status of an American classic.

The work is imbued with the spirit of the Popular Front. In Saroyan's view it is the courage and integrity of the "little man" who loves America above all else that will preserve democracy. Saroyan attempts to touch on all contemporary liberal concerns. Not only does he celebrate democracy with scenes of good fellowship, and not only does he recall with praise the courageous frontier spirit that won the West, but he also packs in references to labor unrest and racial antagonism. The result is a collection of the literary motifs of the period. The San Francisco waterfront saloon that forms the setting becomes, not a microcosm, but a resort to which spokesmen for all social classes hurry to find warmth at a moment in time made chilling by the inevitability of war. The keynote of the play is sounded by one of the barflies—improbably an Arab—who repeatedly offers his analysis of the contemporary scene: "No foundation. All the way down the line."

It is the war that is the cause of the confusion and chaos. As Saroyan himself remarked in the Preface to the collection of his first three plays, it casts its shadow over the entire action of *The Time of Your Life*.[16] It is always in the background as a threat to the companionable way of life of the characters, and frequently in the foreground. Joe, the protagonist, sends his henchman Tom to buy "the biggest Rand-McNally map of the nations of Europe they've got," so that he can "read the names of some European towns and rivers and valleys and mountains" (II); when he asks for a gun as well, the association of the two objects suggests that he wishes to objectify the distant fighting in his mind's eye. In a curiously painful, effective fashion, Saroyan also projects the threat of war through the character of Harry, a young would-be comedian, whose patter always culminates in doom-ridden images: "A fat guy bumps his stomach into the face of an old lady. They were in a hurry. Fat and old. *They bumped.* Boom. I don't know. It may mean war. *War.* Germany. England. Russia. I don't know for sure . . . waaaar" (I). And again, "I go out and buy a morning paper. Thursday, the twelfth. Maybe the headline's about *me.* I take a quick look. *No. The headline is not about me.* It's about Hitler. Seven thousand miles away. I'm here. Who the hell is Hitler? Who's behind the eight-ball? I turn around. *Everybody's behind the eight-ball!*" (II).

The nation as perceived by Saroyan is a vast brotherhood, a Whitmanesque gathering of souls rejoicing in the democratic spirit. Near

the close of the first act he inserts a long stage description that reads
in part,

> The atmosphere is now one of warm, natural, American ease; every
> man innocent and good; each doing what he believes he should do,
> or what he must do. There is deep American naïveté and faith in the
> behavior of each person. No one is competing with anyone else. No
> one hates anyone else. Every man is living, and letting live. Each
> man is following his destiny as he feels it should be followed; or is
> abandoning it as he feels it must, by now, be abandoned; or is forget-
> ting it for the moment as he feels he should forget it. Although every-
> one is dead serious, there is unmistakable smiling and humor in the
> scene; a sense of the human body and spirit emerging from the
> world-imposed state of stress and fearfulness, fear and awkwardness,
> to the more natural state of casualness and grace.

But this comradely, calmly blissful atmosphere is disturbed by the en-
trance of the menacing figure of a vice squad operative named Blick.
The personification of fascism, he must be dispatched if the mood is
to endure.

A few of the characters are foolish, but only Blick is a menace. He
threatens the gold-hearted Kitty with arrest and beats up Wesley, the
young black who plays piano in the bar. The principle of live-and-
let-live that guides the actions of all the others in the play is unknown to him. It requires two attempts on his life to kill him. The
first is made by Joe, the somewhat mysterious figure who dominates
the action. A benevolent capitalist who made money when young and
now likes to spend it on others, he has no antipathy toward anyone,
apart from Blick. "I'm with everybody," he says. "One at a time" (II).
He is at ease with Krupp the cop and McCarthy the longshoreman,
who are at ease with each other, and is profoundly touched by the
unhappiness of Kitty, with whom his henchman Tom is in love. With
the revolver bought for him by Tom, Joe takes a shot at Blick. But
the gun misfires. The execution is carried out instead by a nameless
old bluffer listed in the cast as Kit Carson who until this moment in
the action spends all his time telling tall stories of the past. In him
the old American spirit of rugged individualism is personified, and
he kills the fascist thug with a pearl-handled revolver—offstage—
making the world of the bar harmonious, as by fighting Hitler the nation could take part in the restoration of moral order to the world. It

is only a second before this necessary violence that from a pinball machine, played fanatically by one of the characters through all three acts, an American flag pops up and when pushed down pops up again. Until the occurrence of this conclusive shooting of Blick, the destruction of the dog in the manger, the work is a vaudeville made up of individual turns as each character comes forward to express the peculiarities of his social class. The shooting is the point to which all else leads. Like Sherwood, Saroyan had arrived, after the pacifism of *My Heart's in the Highlands,* at the belief that if the violence of war was necessary for the preservation of American values, it was justified.

In *Love's Old Sweet Song* Saroyan uttered yet another declaration of belief in American benevolence. The play has two settings in the city of Bakersfield, California: the exterior of the home of Ann Hamilton, a middle-aged spinster of native American stock, and the living room of a family of Greek origin, but named Americanos. Sentimentally, but with some redeeming comic touches, Saroyan details the improbable meeting and mutual attraction of the spinster and a voluble carnival pitchman who sells a panacea called Dr. Greatheart's Five-Star Multi-Purpose Indian Remedy, but whose real stock in trade is the power of suggestion, as with all such salesmen. Intruding into the life of Ann Hamilton at the same time as the pitchman is a vast family of Okies, the Yearlings, who camp on the lawn of her house, soon begin to ransack it, and ultimately burn it down. They are accompanied by a photographer and a novelist who are recording their wanderings. This is an old story to the Yearlings, who get so much publicity that they seldom have a chance to sleep. Outrageously creating a parody of Steinbeck's *Grapes of Wrath* family, Saroyan puts these words into the mouth of Leona, the mother of the clan, who altogether number sixteen ravenous public charges: "We don't want nothing from nobody—hardly. Food. A place to sleep. A roof over our heads. Clothing. A little land to walk around in. Cows. Chickens. A radio. A car. Something like that. We aim to shift for ourselves, the same as ever" (I). But in Saroyan's land of love even the Yearlings can become tamed and purposeful citizens.

Contrary to the impression created by Leona's speech and the piracy committed on stage by the family, Saroyan's opinion is that the Yearlings are not inherently vile, but have been spoiled by publicity.

As the photographer says, reprimanding the oversympathetic writer, "They've got the stubbornness and fertility of weeds. And they're not common either. . . . For all we know one of these kids is a genius. . . . On the other hand they may all be idiots. But how do we know the world isn't supposed to be inhabited by idiots, instead of silly people who want to get everything organized—like you?" (I). No one has yet found the right approach to this kind of family. Not surprisingly, Saroyan's own approach is a bland and soothing kindness that ignores the larger question of economics. No matter how scarce jobs may be for others like them, *this* family will be given jobs, for the pitchman intends to take all the Yearling children on the road with him and Ann in his medicine show. He announces this intention at the end of the play in the Americanos home, where the young son of the family, a telegraph boy, gathers up all the characters in the hope of making peace among them. In this setting, the residence of foreigners who have found contentment in America, the innate good will of all, the native-born and the naturalized citizens alike, comes smilingly to the surface and, as in *The Time of Your Life*, the future seems secure. Unhappily this whimsical statement of confidence in all things American drew few customers at the box office: it was principally the Guild's subscribers who heard Saroyan's message.

Pushing out of the thirties with Saroyan, Hemingway, and Sherwood, the Guild entered the new decade with none of its old problems solved, apart from the replacement of the Board of Managers with the Langner-Helburn team. It was still no less difficult to locate intelligent, well-constructed plays in sufficient number and variety to create a well-attended schedule. Langner and Helburn continued the practice of presenting works jointly with the Playwrights' Company and other managements, but had to be content with only a share of the profits. The old adventurous spirit of the Guild as originally constructed was quite gone before the Second World War came to an end but showed itself fitfully during the war years. The Guild tried to introduce Tennessee Williams to Broadway with *Battle of Angels* (1940) but unhappily watched the play flounder and fail in Boston during the preliminary tour. Another interesting, though undoubtedly deserved, failure was Philip Barry's expressionistic political allegory, *Liberty Jones* (1941). Other noteworthy novelties of the war years were the adaptation by Clifford Odets of Konstantin Simonov's *The Russian People* (1942), directed by Harold Clurman, a production of *Othello* (1943) with the black actor Paul Robeson in the title role, and the musical play *Oklahoma!* (1943), adapted by Richard Rodgers and Oscar Hammerstein II from Lynn Riggs's *Green Grow the Lilacs*, which the Guild had produced in 1931. In its own way, each made a pertinent comment on the period: Simonov's play by making possible a glimpse into the home life of the distant ally; *Othello* by demonstrating that a large audience was ready for the abolition of the old taboo against scenes of passion between a black and a white, at least in a play bearing the dignity of a classic; and *Oklahoma!* by appealing to the wartime nostalgia for the serene bucolic past and catering to the continuing delight in Americana as fostered by the Popular Front in its prime. This attractive work proved not only the Guild's most successful production of all time, but, with 2327 performances, the longest running musical in Broadway history until 1961, when the record was broken by Alan Jay Lerner and Frederick Lowe's *My Fair Lady*. In 1960 it was estimated that for every $1,500 invested in *Oklahoma!*, the return was $50,000.[17]

Secure at last, the Guild followed this musical with other musicals of less distinction and originality, and followed *Othello* with other revivals. The preparation of radio and television scripts for, respectively, the Theater Guild of the Air and the United States Steel Hour and the development of the American Shakespeare Festival Theater in Stratford, Connecticut, were new, postwar interests that competed for the attention of Langner and Helburn with the New York stage. With the exception of O'Neill's *The Iceman Cometh* and *A Moon for the Misbegotten*, produced in the season of 1946–47 (the latter on tour only), no major new plays came to light, and apart from William Inge, whose *Come Back, Little Sheba* (1950) and *Picnic* (1953) were Guild offerings, no new author of more than momentary interest was discovered. After the death of Helburn in 1959 and Langner in 1962, the Guild continued to function under the supervision of Armina Marshall (Mrs. Lawrence Langner), and Philip Langner, her son, but with ever less vitality as a Broadway institution. Its last production was offered in 1968: *Darling of the Day*, a musical comedy with book by Nunnally Johnson and songs by E. Y. Harburg

and Jule Styne. Thereafter, the Guild operated only as a road subscription service, its wares being the productions of other managements.

The Theater Guild's long retreat from its place in the vanguard to
a safe position among the ultracommercial managements was the unavoidable result of the aging process as well as of the scarcity of
scripts. After some twenty years of searching for the works that might
last, how could the mortals who guided the organization not feel the
winter in their bones and opt for security? Deplorable as was the
eventual lowering of standards, moreover, it could not cancel the record of the Guild's past achievements, which included the development of an audience for the new drama of Europe in the twenties and
the presentation of at least five of the most durable American plays of
the thirties: *Mourning Becomes Electra, End of Summer, Idiot's Delight, The Philadelphia Story,* and *The Time of Your Life.*

BROADWAY:
THE INDEPENDENT STAGE
1935-1940

THEMES

With slight justification for it at the box office, the second half of the Depression decade witnessed a renewed vitality on Broadway, a second wind after the flattening blow of 1929 and a consequent diminishment of the audience's interest in live drama. It was not that the boom returned to Broadway; talkies and the radio had made it unlikely that the theater would ever again command an audience as great as that of the twenties and earlier, and the financial reality of the thirties—the grave difficulty of raising money for productions—compounded the problem, with the result that fewer plays were mounted season by season. From a total of eighty-nine openings of new plays on Broadway, exclusive of Federal Theater productions, in 1935–36, the scores declined to a total of sixty in 1939–40. Nevertheless, the chronicler Burns Mantle declared at the end of the season of 1935–36 that

> this theatrical season has been the most exciting and the most satisfying of any New York has enjoyed since the years that preceded the crash of '29. I see no particular reason why we should stop at '29. Ex-

cept in the matter of those statistics that boast the number of plays produced it would be possible to go back even farther without coming upon a record of plays more satisfying or more worthy of enthusiastic endorsement.[1]

The satisfaction that Mantle felt while reflecting on the year just past was in part a function of the new, temporary upswing of the economy that for a year and a half fostered a national expectation of the return of prosperity. Yet in the seasons to come, with no improvement in employment figures, a new slump in the stock market, and a decline in the Federal Reserve Board's Index of Industrial Production, Mantle and other critics could still take heart. The art of the play was on the ascendant. Despite the silence of O'Neill during the entire five-year span, the number of contributions to the standard American repertory—that is, the number of new plays that later generations would find worthy of revival—had never been so large.

Backing for productions came in generous amounts from Hollywood in the mid-thirties, to the extent that in the 1935–36 season a reported 25 per cent of the new plays had the support of the studios. In return Hollywood expected to receive the screen rights to the scripts on favorable terms. But a fight waged by the Dramatists' Guild for the lion's share of money from sales to Hollywood had the double result of uniting the Broadway producers, already organized as the League of New York Theaters, in opposition to the playwrights' effort, and of cooling the studio heads' enthusiasm for backing productions. By the end of the decade, the Dramatists settled for 60 per cent of the proceeds from sales to Hollywood, after first demanding 80 percent.[2]

Still Hollywood scouted events on Broadway, buying scripts if not backing them, offering fat contracts to writers, and stealing actors away from producers. Bob Hope, Martha Scott, J. Edward Bromberg, John Garfield, Helen Westley, Margo, and the half dozen adolescents known as the "Dead End Kids" were among the performers who moved West late in the decade. A few well-known producers also made the trip to California, but for brief stays only; among those who tried it were George Abbott, Harold Clurman, Max Gordon, and Theresa Helburn. In their purchase of scripts the studios showed a commendable catholicity, filming not only weighty works like Sherwood's *Idiot's Delight* and *Abe Lincoln in Illinois*, Odets's *Golden*

Boy, Arent's *One-Third of a Nation,* and Wilder's *Our Town,* but Ole Olsen and Chick Johnson's vaudevillesque extravaganza, *Hellzapoppin,* and Clare Boothe's wise-cracking comedy of manners, *The Women.*

Passed over, however, were George S. Kaufman and Moss Hart's antifascist *The American Way* and all plays having to do with race relations, anti-Semitism, and the Spanish Civil War. Indeed, the timidity of Hollywood was great enough to cause the watering down of most films of plays on presumed controversial subjects. Esperanto replaced Italian in *Idiot's Delight,* and the original names of the young New York Jews of Arthur Kober's *Having Wonderful Time,* set in a modest Catskills resort, were replaced by others with an Anglo-Saxon sound, since in the wake of Hitler's rise Hollywood put anti-Semitism itself on the controversial list. The Hollywood producers' self-imposed code of censorship, toughened as a result of protests from the Catholic Legion of Decency in 1934, caused other dilutions. The code's strictures against promiscuity and the showing of domestic arrangements unhallowed by marriage resulted in revisions of the original texts of, among other plays, *Golden Boy,* Mark Reed's *Yes, My Darling Daughter,* Barry's *The Philadelphia Story,* and Kirkland's *Tobacco Road.*

For lack of broad appeal, plays not necessarily controversial but lacking romance, heroism, or an abundance of laugh lines were also routinely passed over as poor film prospects; those neglected on such grounds were such well-received plays as Behrman's *End of Summer* and Odets's *Rocket to the Moon.* In the same interest—a good response at the box office—a happy ending was given to *Our Town* (with the author's blessing),[3] allowing the young heroine to remain alive. But, despite its penchant for half measures and its lack of daring with respect to crucial political and social issues, Hollywood on balance was not disrespectful of the Broadway properties it lavishly purchased. The film versions of *Idiot's Delight, Golden Boy,* and *The Philadelphia Story,* though somewhat altered from the originals, were good screen renderings, and of special value were Samuel Goldwyn's productions of Hellman's *The Children's Hour* (*These Three*) and *The Little Foxes* and Sidney Kingsley's *Dead End,* all directed by William Wyler, and Frank Capra's version of the Kaufman-Hart success, *You Can't Take It With You.*

The dramatists were not the only contributors to the theater to engage in militant tactics. Dissident members of Actors' Equity formed
a bloc called the Actors' Forum in the spring of 1935 and put up a
fight for improved conditions for junior members of the parent association as well as for unemployment insurance, old-age pensions, and
rehearsal pay. Of their demands, the only one to be adopted in 1935
was that for rehearsal pay, which thereafter was guaranteed by the
agreement of the union with the League of New York Theaters. But
by the decade's end Equity, continually prodded by young militants,
abolished the differential in minimum salaries between junior and senior members and increased the minimum weekly pay to the still
modest figure of $40.00.[4] The previously unorganized treasurers,
house managers, and agents also founded an association before the
decade's end, leaving only directors and choreographers without a
bargaining body.[5] Despite the increased pressure put on management
by the theatrical trade and craft associations, ticket prices remained
stable, with a top of $4.40 for musical comedies and a top of $3.30 for
nonmusical productions, and cheaper, cut-rate tickets available for
bargain-hunters at many box offices. Not until the Second World War
and the postwar boom, with the occurrence of sharply increased demands from the unions, did ticket prices begin their perilous ascent
toward a point of diminishing returns.

Though the most pointed of the new plays on pressing contemporary themes were offered by the institutional theaters, with the Group
Theater taking the lead, the independent producers had access to the
scripts of many established social dramatists. Lillian Hellman continued to entrust her plays to Herman Shumlin after his successful production of *The Children's Hour;* Sidney Kingsley, despite the success
of the Group's staging of *Men in White,* let Norman Bel Geddes produce one play and produced his two others of the period himself;
Maxwell Anderson gave, as we have seen, one script to the Theater
Guild and offered another to the Group, but was principally produced by Guthrie McClintic before joining with Behrman, Howard,
Rice, and Sherwood to form the Playwrights' Company; Kaufman and
Hart put their expensive (and only fleetingly "social") works into the
generous hands of Sam H. Harris; and each of the satiric comedies of
Clare Boothe had a producer of its own. The list is, if not endless, ex-
tensive. With backers to woo, the independents of necessity—and

doubtless in many instances out of personal preference—chose scripts with broad appeal.

In both form and content the impact of the liberal-to-left institutional theaters on the mainstream stage was less discernible at this time than in the earlier years of the Depression. Two ambitious productions of the independent managers stand out in retrospect as importations to Broadway of the liberal-to-left look and outlook: Charles Friedman and Harold Rome's *Sing Out the News* (1938), and Oscar Saul and H. R. Hays's *Medicine Show* (1940). In mounting the Rome and Friedman revue, Max Gordon attempted to recreate the spirit of the ILGWU's *Pins and Needles*. In his cast were such favorites of TAC audiences as Will Geer, Rex Ingram, Philip Loeb, and Hiram Sherman. Rome's songs and the sketches dealt inoffensively with such topics as a national political convention ("I Married a Republican"), the difference in the romantic attitudes of the rich and poor ("Just an Ordinary Guy"), the doubtful future of Harlem youth ("One of These Fine Days"), the night life of the rich ("Café Society"), the taunting of a liberal-minded boy by children of the right and left "A Liberal Education"), and the expensive enjoyments of Roosevelt-hating millionaires at Palm Beach ("Sing Ho for Private Enterprise"). Though George S. Kaufman and Moss Hart, who produced the show along with Max Gordon, received no billing as writers, the sketches have a gloss that is unmistakably theirs.[6] The show veered closest to the half-comic poignancy of *Pins and Needles* in a love song by Rome that took its imagery from the economic climate: "My Heart is Unemployed."

Medicine Show, which lasted only 35 performances, was a direct inheritance from the Federal Theater: a reworking of a living newspaper prepared for the Project on the high cost of medical care, with a recommendation for federal legislation to offset it. These productions aside, the effect of the institutional theaters on the independents was limited to the loan—often the permanent loan—of actors, designers, and directors. In the matter of influences, the tide, as we have noted, went in the other direction in this period, with the New Theater League, under the generous dispensation of Popular Front politics, evidencing ever more respect for Broadway's methods of producing and publicizing its wares.

Plays dealing with the most serious or unpleasant aspects of labor-management relations were left, in the main, to the League and the Theater Union. Broadway sheltered few tragedies of working-class life. The calamitous consequences of unfair labor tactics on the part of management during a strike were dramatized by Lillian Hellman in *Days to Come* (1936), but the play, awkward in its plot contrivances and shrill in its characterizations, met monolithic public and critical disapproval. Closing after 7 performances, it was to stand as the flattest failure of the author's career in the theater. Francis Edwards Faragoh's *Sunup to Sundown* (1938), the ILGWU's prize play, concerned an unsuccessful uprising of tobacco-plantation workers, also lasted a mere 7 performances in a production offered by D. A. Doran. James Hagan's *Mid-West* (1936) offered a view of farm-labor agitation from the Right; couched in dialogue as dull as the parched land it described, it too disappeared quickly. Of slightly greater interest was the conservative labor play, *Tide Rising* (1937), by George Brewer, Jr. Set in a factory town, the play has as protagonist a druggist, Jim Cogswell, whose son David returns from New York out of a job and with a new wife at his side. It is this young woman, Ruth, who is the play's menace. An outsider—in fact, a Slavic type— she helps the local mill workers to organize and encourages them to demand a closed shop. Incensed, the factory owner imports scabs and machine-gun-carrying deputies. As Brewer sees the situation, it is the seemingly excessive demands of labor that produce the dangerous reaction in businessmen leading to violence. Jim Cogswell is made acting sheriff and in that position arrests both the mill owner and Ruth and dismisses the scabs. For taking Ruth under custody, he becomes a target for the fury of her followers, who wreck his drugstore and kill his son. At the close Ruth, being free to leave town, does so, expressing the intention of continuing her career in agitation. Attacked as a piece of fascist propaganda by the New Theater League, whose officers hoped to drive it off the stage, *Tide Rising* hung on for four weeks, perhaps a longer stay than it deserved in view of its stridency and thin characterizations. Having failed to close the play promptly, the League next attempted to discourage the Dramatists' Play Service from publishing it, and in this also failed. That their onslaught against Brewer and his ineffectual drama was in harsh contradiction to its avowed opposition to censorship seems to have been ignored by its staff.[7]

Broadway's most competently written labor play of the late thirties was John Steinbeck's *Of Mice and Men* (1937). Following his strike novel, *In Dubious Battle*, within a year, the play confirmed the impression of Steinbeck given by the novel: that he was a warmly sympathetic observer of the life of the manual laborer, and especially talented in communicating a sense of the laborer's emotional side. The play (Steinbeck's first, and originally designed as a novel) does not treat a strike situation. Its matter is the inability of many willing workers to put down roots and establish a secure routine of life. Not hoboes who love the road and refuse to work, the characters are vagrant laborers who move from job to job as the breaks decree. It is not hard times alone that create the tragic resolution of the play. Beyond the difficulty of finding work that George and Lennie, the dual protagonists, face is a special problem of their own. Locked in a dependency relationship that neither can break, the intelligent George and the muddle-brained Lennie travel and work together, holding agricultural jobs until fired or hounded out because of Lennie's half-wittedness and his propensity for stroking soft living things until, involuntarily, he kills them. Steinbeck makes it clear that theirs is not a homosexual relationship; nor is it a blood relationship, though George is in the habit of describing Lennie as his cousin when speaking with prospective employers. It is the simple need for companionship that keeps them together. Says George, soothing Lennie with a much-repeated speech: "Guys like us that work on ranches is the loneliest guys in the world. They ain't got no family. They don't belong no place. They come to a ranch and work up a stake and then they go into town and blow their stake. And then the first thing you know they're poundin' their tail on some other ranch. They ain't got nothin' to look ahead to . . . with us it ain't like that" (I, i). These two mismatched wanderers do have a plan: to get together enough money for some ranchland, a house, and some rabbits for Lennie to tend. As the audience knows, it is a fantasy never to be realized, for the pattern of their lives has long been fixed. The job that they seek and get at the outset of the play is their last.

Steinbeck builds suspensefully toward the climactic scene in which Lennie for the last time in his life strokes and kills. At the opening of the play it is dead mice found along the roadside that he fondles. Next it is a newborn puppy. Finally it is the wife (unnamed) of Curley, the

ranchowner's son. The looming inevitability of this scene renders it
shockingly grotesque in the event. Yet Steinbeck is cautious to prevent the play from sweeping into sheer gothic sensationalism. The
stroke that snaps the neck of Curley's wife blasts the fantasy of a
quiet home that had given a sense of direction to both the vagrants.
The penalty for Lennie's act is of course severe: George himself does
away with him to spare him the agony of a shooting by Curley and is
left in danger of being found out at the final curtain. Steinbeck is reluctant to point a moral by directly linking the defeat of the pair to
the national economic situation; rather than do so, he is content to
create a situation in which the dual protagonists are victims of their
own skewed psychological structures. Yet darting through their story
are insights into the worker's life—his pride in his job and his modest
physical and material satisfactions—which had special force during
the Depression, when the job itself and consequently the satisfactions
were hard to get.

The same economic anxieties that clutch at Lennie and George
figure in the design of most Depression plays, no matter what the social status of the characters is. In the wildest of the many farces produced and directed by George Abbott the problem of how to pay the
grocer and the landlord slipped in, giving a peculiar manic intensity
to Samuel and Bella Spewack's *Boy Meets Girl* (1935), John Monks,
Jr., and Fred F. Finklehoff's *Brother Rat* (1936), and John Murray
and Allen Boretz's *Room Service* (1937). Respectively in these plays
Hollywood underlings, Virginia Military Institute cadets, and impe-
cunious Broadway producers feel the chill of financial insecurity that
cannot always be diverted by their ability to invent wisecracks and
practical jokes. The plight of youth in search of employment and the
promise of economic stability, taken up in all these farces, was also
examined in a variety of less hectic comedies. Two hits, Kober's *Having Wonderful Time* (1936), and Mark Reed's *Yes, My Darling
Daughter* (1937), explored the notion that in a world devoid of security an adulterous relationship might provide a reasonable alternative
to marriage. Neither author actually condoned the idea, however, and
in both plays the young women in question retain their virginity at
the final curtain. Lynn Riggs in *Russet Mantle* (1936) and Elmer Rice
in *Two on an Island* (1940) treated this still touchy issue more forthrightly, if less comically. Riggs's protagonist, who wishes to be a

writer, must decide whether to accept a sinecure on a Southwestern ranch or go off to explore the "real" world of hunger and violence. He makes the correct decision—the decision to go—and for companionship has the liberated girl, now pregnant, with whom he has had a clandestine relationship for the better part of a year. Rice's male lead, also a writer, sets up an apartment with a would-be actress, a girl who had arrived in New York to live on the same day as he. When they begin to have some luck, they make the decision to marry, at which time the girl announces that she is pregnant.

In *Excursion* (1937), a comedy somewhat more imaginative, though hardly more profound than those just mentioned, Victor Wolfson, late of the board of the Theater Union, set some dozen and a half work-weary New Yorkers afloat on a boat, the *Happiness*, for a Sunday outing on the water between Manhattan and Coney Island. It is supposedly the last time out for the old tub, and the captain, Obadiah Rich, decides with the blessing of his passengers not to take her back into port, but to head out for warm seas and an unpopulated island. But, as the audience knows, society is too well structured to permit such a deviation from the routine of life, however beneficial it might be to the participants. Something must occur to prevent Obadiah from carrying out his plan, and it does. The crew of a Coast Guard dory comes aboard, subdues the officers and the passengers and takes the boat back to the city. It had only been circling in the fog anyway, thanks to a navigator with one drink too many under his belt.

This framework provides the means whereby Wolfson calls attention to the squalor of modern metropolitan existence with its choked subways and tenements, its ill-paying jobs, and its ethnic prejudices. The most engaging of Wolfson's exhibits is Lollie Popps, a salesgirl from Gimbel's who, Cinderella-like, embarks on a romance with Richard Pitman, the son of the owner of the boat. But of nearly equal interest is Lee Pitman, Richard's sister, a self-styled radical who has read her Marx. Wolfson slyly contrasts her with an unpublished writer, Aikens, who, though also claiming to be a radical, has not read Marx and who, while leading some of the passengers in the "Internationale," makes a slip in the words. When Lee begins to speculate on the ideal society that the passengers will establish on the island of their destination, Aikens is struck with alarm to realize that since there will be no "masses," he will be deprived of his customary

literary subject. Can this inept but earnest would-be proletarian commentator be a travesty of writers Wolfson had encountered around
theaters in his time?

It is only a faint spoof of communism that Wolfson allows himself,
not an attack on it in its literary form or any other. At the close a
mild revolutionary message is voiced by the Captain as the ship
steams back to the city: "Take the courage and the vision back there
with you. Fight for the things y' want back there, like y' fought for
your faraway island last night. Be men an' women armed with love
an' wonder, mates, an' make y' life a glowin' thing. Will y' do that?"
(III, iii). One distinct result of his own initiative is already known:
Pitman, pleased by the publicity that Obadiah's adventure receives,
decides to keep the *Happiness* afloat for another season.

Those who fought for what they wanted without concern for their
fellow men—criminals who deliberately broke the law for gain—
continued to the end of the decade to arouse the curiosity of playwrights, who regarded them with a double vision. Out of the career
of the racketeer, who would not stop even at murder if the stakes
were high, it was always possible to fashion a parable of the capitalist
who willfully abrogates the civil rights of others weaker than himself.
It was also possible to show the criminal as a man as much sinned
against as sinning—a person impelled toward crime by a society that
never gave him a chance to earn an honest living. But by mid-decade
Hollywood had projected the life of the gangster with such verve,
and consequently had so attracted the public to crime films, that
Broadway could offer only faint competition. The violent action required by plots set in gangland, including breakneck automobile
chases, chases on foot across rooftops, the fall of plugged bodies from
high places, prison breaks, and other spectacular scenes without number, all edited for speed with rapid cross-cutting—this was matter
that the stage could not provide. Of the studios, it was Warner Brothers that, as at the start of the decade, made the most memorable
crime films, many of which were set in New York. With a high degree
of skill the studio's cameramen and editors succeeded in getting on
black and white film the gritty look of the metropolis. In the early
years of the decade Warner's amassed an impressive roster of tough-
guy stars, including James Cagney, Edward G. Robinson, Paul Muni,

and George Raft; later in the decade the studio added John Garfield and Humphrey Bogart from Broadway.

Possibly no other Broadway gangster projected such chilling malice as Eddie Fuseli, the homosexual takeover racketeer of Odets's *Golden Boy*.[8] Other dramatic explorations of the criminal psyche were less fascinating in their viciousness. In one well-received gangster melodrama, James Warwick's *Blind Alley* (1935), a clever psychologist held captive by a gunman trips up the wits of his captor so skillfully that the man kills himself. It was primarily as a thriller that Warwick's play attracted the public. No less an authority than Warden Lewis E. Lawes of Sing Sing contributed a play, *Chalked Out* (1937), in which the audience was introduced to the facts of prison life and the malign influence that the penal system all too often has upon the incarcerated criminal when in fact it is intended to rehabilitate him. This, however, was a quickly closing production. The playwrights of major reputation apart from Odets who constructed plots on crime and its practitioners that rose above the level of suspense drama were Sidney Kingsley and Maxwell Anderson.

Kingsley's *Dead End* (1935), his first play since *Men in White*, was quickly established as a hit and ran on Broadway for 687 performances, after which it had a second wave of popularity as a film, with a screenplay adapted by Lillian Hellman. To remind the audience of the sharp contrast between the very rich and very poor that is a part of city life, Kingsley chose as his setting a point on New York's East River where a large new apartment house of the luxury class has as its neighbor a decaying tenement building along whose fire escapes the weekly wash is draped. The juxtaposition of wealth and poverty, it is clear in the text, is a relatively new condition of the street (perhaps East 53rd Street, the location of River House, one of Manhattan's most prestigious addresses). In the not distant past it was a district of the poor only, but now in Kingsley's play the rich live there as well, and with no apparent concern over the fate of those they have displaced. Designed with close-focus realism by Norman Bel Geddes, the setting included every expected detail of the urban environment: the grit, the grimy stains, the refuse, the concrete, even (in a downstage tank) the East River for neighborhood adolescents to swim in. (Appropriately enough, the playhouse in which this

spectacle appeared was the Belasco, the theater named for and once
owned by David Belasco, the American master of stage realism.)

The divided nature of the street is further represented by the cast
of characters, where in numerous instances the members of the upper
and lower economic classes exist in parallel. Opposed to the adolescent river rats and street urchins—the famous "Dead End Kids"—is a
rich boy who lives in the East River Terrace. Opposed to Drina, a
working girl now on strike whose brother is the leader of the gang, is
Kay, an attractive, well-groomed young woman who is kept in the
same apartment house by a rich businessman named Hilton. An unemployed architect, crippled by rickets and hence nicknamed
Gimpty, is the opposite number to Hilton; born in the slums, and still
living in them, he would be a rival with Hilton for Kay if it were possible for him to support her. The killer "Baby-Face" Martin, a product of the neighborhood, holds the center of Kingsley's crowded stage
only intermittently, taking his turn with the other characters, but his
presence in the play gives it both its suspense and its social message.
Wanted for murder, he is eventually shot by the police, who are
tipped off to his whereabouts by Gimpty. Overhearing Martin advis-
ing the "Kids" on how to conduct a skirmish with another gang, and
knowing, because of the example of Martin himself, how life in the
slums twists minds as well as bodies, Gimpty wants this malign influence out of the way. Before the event Martin, apparently sensing that
he is doomed, seeks out the two women who matter in his life, his
mother (acted in both play and film by Marjorie Main), and a neighborhood girl named Francey. In both meetings, which are disasters
for Martin, Kingsley finds the opportunity to comment with special
ferocity on the harrowing existence of the slums. Mrs. Martin, bone
weary and slovenly, rejects her son with a slap and a torrent of verbal
abuse: "Baby-face! Baby-face! I remember . . . *She begins to sob,
clutching her stomach.* In here . . . in here! Kickin'! That's where yuh
come from. God! I ought to be cut open here fer givin' yuh life . . .
murderer!!!" (II). Francey, to Martin's amazement, is now a common
whore. She too offers a rejection, but of another kind: he may kiss
her, but not on the lips, because of the sore there. Thus has the environment corrupted these women in both body and soul. They are to
be pitied. Martin, on the other hand, is not, having gone beyond the
stage of social victim to that of social menace. The bullets that pin

him to the asphalt extinguish a life that, were it to be protected, would only add to the savagery of a place already infernal.

It is Kingsley's antisentimental treatment of slum dwellers that gives the play its strength, whether he is dealing with criminals or those who abide by the law. His delineation of the boys is no exception. Despite the filth they live in, including the highly unsalubrious East River in which they swim, there is a liberated spirit about them that by contrast renders the pampered existence of the rich boy claustrophobic. But at the same time their rawness of speech and gesture, their street-bred shrewdness, and their indurated cynicism are causes for dismay. The moneyed classes, denying them the decent public housing that Gimpty wants to build, are condemning them to a life of crime, and condemning themselves as the victims. At the close, when Tommy is in trouble with the police over an incident for which he is not wholly to blame, Gimpty decides to hire a lawyer with the money he is to receive for informing on Martin. Without this financial windfall, the slums would claim another lost soul. With bitter irony, Kingsley reinforces the idea of environmental entrapment with an aural image. Temporarily leaderless because Tommy is in custody, the other boys seek comfort in song: "If I had de wings of a angel. Ovuh dese prison walls I wud fly . . . Straight tuh de yahms a my muddah. Ta da da, da da . . . Da . . . da . . . da . . . dum." This is the traditional ballad known as "The Prisoner's Song"; the boys who sing it are not so free as they seem.

Anderson's *Winterset* (1935) is also set along the river, and in production benefited from the designs of Jo Mielziner, who, on the evidence of photographs, brilliantly met the playwright's requirement of a huge span of a bridge to jut out from the back wall of the stage and to lead out at stage left. Under this structure huddled a cast of waifs and strays, criminals and their pursuers. A drama of the aftermath of the trials of Sacco and Vanzetti, the play is a series of portentous actions dwarfed by the gigantic scenery. Returning after seven years to this subject, which he had treated with Harold Hickerson in *Gods of the Lightning*, Anderson chose as his protagonist the seventeen-year-old Mio Romagna, whose father Bartolomeo (representing Vanzetti) had been convicted and executed for a murder that the boy knows he did not commit. He is now in New York on the track of new evidence, having been spurred on by the comments on the case pub-

lished by a Midwestern professor. His search leads him to the base-
ment apartment of the ancient Rabbi Esdras and his children Garth
and Mariamne. Also led there by the newspaper accounts of the professor's findings are Judge Gaunt, who presided at the Romagna trial,
and the real murderer, Trock Estrella, and his henchman Shadow.
The stage is thus prepared for a double action: the unfolding of Anderson's thoughts on the theme of justice and the playing out of a revenge plot.

Yet despite the careful preparation, Anderson dismissed his opportunity of creating a stunning piece of entertainment and aimed for
something beyond his reach: a modern poetic tragedy. For the first
time employing his peculiarly flat blank verse in a contemporary setting, he created for each member of the cast a series of images floating listlessly above the level of the action. The credibility of the
teenage Mio, for example, and the poignancy of his search for the
means of making a posthumous clearance of his father's name, is
tossed to the winds in his declaration of love for Mariamne:

> Enduring love,
> of gods and worms, what mockery!—And yet
> I have blood enough in my veins. It goes like music,
> singing, because you're here. My body turns
> as if you were the sun, and warm. This men called love
> in happier times, before the Freudians taught us
> to blame it on the glands, Only go in
> before you breathe too much of my atmosphere
> and catch death from me. (I, iii)

In addition to creating a difficulty with his literary style, Anderson
ends with a philosophical puzzle. Questions of the interaction of law
and human feeling abound in the play and constitute its theme. Old
Esdras, a realist to the point of cynicism, tries to impress upon his son
the belief that the young man should not, now that Romagna is in his
grave, notify the police that Trock was the murderer, though he witnessed the killing himself. To Garth's insistent cry of guilt over Romagna's execution, Esdras replies, "Yet till it's known you bear no
guilt at all/ unless you wish" (I, ii). Judge Gaunt, maddened by years
of hearing his decision questioned and knowing that it was unjust,
defends himself by saying that it was better to let the execution of

Romagna occur than to admit new evidence that would reverse the decision and confuse the public. One expects that these points of view will be cast into glaring contempt by Mio's quest for the truth, and that this will happen whether he succeeds or fails. But Anderson, trying for a tragically grand statement on the contradictions, paradoxes, and improbabilities of which human existence is constructed, permits Mio to abandon the idea of revenge in order to spare Garth, the brother of his beloved Mariamne, and then has him shot down by Trock, who does not know of his decision. The wanton killer, as desolate of fellow-feeling as is Martin in *Dead End,* has become, improbably, an instrument of fate and is allowed to go free. The morality of the piece is saved only by the audience's knowledge that in six months Trock will die of tuberculosis.

The second appearance of the gangster in Anderson's plays of the thirties occurred in *Key Largo* (1939). As in *Winterset,* the gangster —in this instance a small-time racketeer named Murillo—is pitted against a man bent on a quest. It is a journey into self that preoccupies King McCloud, the protagonist, as he searches out the families of the American troops whom he left to defend, without him, a hilltop during the Spanish Civil War. This incident comprises a lengthy prologue. Knowing that the position is defenseless, and having grown cynical about the merit of the Loyalist posture, he attempts to encourage his men to leave with him rather than face certain death, but convinces none of them, since in their view they should make a stand against fascism even when death is certain, as an affirmation of democracy, of life itself. McCloud's departure from the hill is, at worst, questionable, not an out-and-out craven act. But it soon appears, when he visits the family of Victor d'Alcala, the member of his company whom he most respected, that McCloud has more to repent than leaving the hill. To d'Alcala's father and sister at their home in the Florida keys he confesses that on being captured by the Rebels he decided to fight alongside them rather than be killed by them. In the end, in an action more clear-cut in its meaning than the conclusion of *Winterset,* he has an opportunity to redeem himself. It is known by the Key Largo sheriff, whom Murillo has bought, that the racketeer has murdered a man for sleeping with one of the girls in his entourage. The sheriff decides to put the blame on McCloud. Though McCloud could be freed by allowing two Seminole Indians to be accused in his place, he will not accept freedom on such terms. Knowing that Murillo's henchman Hunk is quick on the trigger, he shoots and fells Murillo with the expectation that Hunk will shoot him in turn, thus releasing him from the incubus of doubt and guilt that he has borne since the incident in Spain.

Though as usual with Anderson's writing the play is all but stifled by nonfunctional images, it is frequently exciting as action drama.[9] Yet its social and political message could not be overlooked. Murillo is all the fascists that McCloud had fled or knuckled under to in Spain; it is no coincidence that his name is that of the well-known Spanish painter. In standing up to him in the fatal confrontation, McCloud expresses Anderson's conviction that American democracy must be saved at any cost, including the cost of one's own life.

This was a message that Americans were growing accustomed to hearing from their writers as the decade ended. But democracy as the Broadway playwrights and their patrons understood it had its limits. It did not extend to blacks. The idea that black citizens might have professional and economic aspirations and might resent the daily reminders of their inferior status was one to which they remained largely indifferent. The Broadway record of the second half of the decade, like that of the first, is almost strikingly devoid of plays created out of a conviction that the black population was worthy of social equality or capable of benefiting from equality of opportunity. Producers and playwrights inched toward a more sensitive exposition of the conditions of black life, but made no recommendations or prognostications. Two plays about Southern blacks became hits, one the work of a black and the other of two white collaborators. Most theatrical opportunities granted to black actors were confined, as before, to servants' roles, usually delineated broadly for easy, condescending laughs.

In his first Broadway play, *Mulatto* (1935), Langston Hughes scored a hit that ran for 373 performances. In the leading feminine role Rose McClendon played Cora Lewis, the black housekeeper-mistress of a plantation owner, Thomas Norwood, and mother of five children by him. Hughes portrays Cora as a women whose sensibilities are so blunted by the environment that guileful compliance has become her way of life. Yet she is capable of keen feeling and is torn between a lingering fondness for Norwood and concern for her children. Norwood can never bring himself to acknowledge them, though on occasion he reveals a flash of pleasure in their presence. It is Robert, the title character, who becomes the play's tragic protagonist. Resentful that his father will not allow him to continue his formal education, he insists on being recognized as a Norwood, arousing his father's fury in consequence. When Norwood threatens to shoot him, he strangles the old man. To escape a lynching, he shoots himself— with his mother's knowledge and subtle urging. On the printed page, these actions have a dignified pathos as Hughes analyzes the cruel dilemma facing the Southern child of mixed parentage. This was altered in production, however. With Hughes out of the country, the producer, Martin Jones, revised the script to include the violation of Sally, one of the daughters of Cora and Norwood, by the overseer of the plantation.[10] Presumably he was motivated by the assumption that the white audience required this touch of sensationalism to sit through a play on black folkways.

Still more sensational was Dorothy and Du Bose Heyward's *Mamba's Daughters* (1939), a shallow melodrama of maternal love, in which Ethel Waters achieved renown as a dramatic actress. Hagar, the Waters role, and Mamba, her mother, are determined that Lissa, Hagar's daughter, shall have all the fame that her superb singing voice can secure for her, no matter what sacrifices they must make to bring this about. When after years of deprivation Hagar finds that the blackmail threats of Lissa's seducer and the father of her stillborn child are imperiling the girl's career, she strangles him without hesitation and calmly prepares to accept the consequences. As in *Porgy* and its musical transformation, *Porgy and Bess,* the Heywards showed that they harbored cordial feelings for their black characters but lacked sharp insight into black despair. The play consists of, and only of, stereotyped characterizations with views of pious churchgoers and high-living sinners set off against each other, and such familiar actions as a frenzied, tumultuous church service of a black evangelical sect, a knifing, a drunken seduction, and reports of marital infidelity. Onlookers only, the Heywards remained within the old tradition of white dramatists undertaking to portray the black world, a tradition of sympathy mixed with patronization and ultimate skepticism on the overriding issue of racial equality.

Depictions of blacks in the customary role of servant ran the gamut from comic, popeyed absurdity to dignified, long-suffering stalwart-ness, with the former predominating. Donald and Rheba, the comic unmarried servant couple in the wildly undisciplined Vanderhof household of Kaufman and Hart's *You Can't Take It with You*, are described by their employer's daughter as "awfully cute together. Sort of like Porgy and Bess" (I). Like Clementine, Linda Esterbrook's maid in Behrman's *No Time for Comedy*, they have achieved status as trusted, long-time employees and consequently can comment ironi-cally on household affairs without reprimand. Cleota, the maid in James Thurber and Elliott Nugent's *The Male Animal*, is a stage darky in the same mold, and oddly out of place in a comedy with a liberal, antiauthoritarian theme. Still other privileged servants are the comic George and Maimie in Clare Boothe's *Kiss the Boys Good-Bye*, a couple set off in plot and theme against the vapid Southern belle Cindy Lou Bethany, who is angling for the role of Velvet O'Toole in a soon-to-be filmed Civil War spectacle. Maimie, very sharp of tongue, possesses a degree of affection for the Deep South, where she was born, but balks at the thought of returning there with Cindy Lou: "Ah've been thinking—ah'm mighty homesick to see Gawja. But ah doan want to work there no mo'. . . . Mah feet jes' won't stand it" (III, ii). To George, Boothe gives the play's most vivid moment. An actor of sorts, he presents himself as the only possible candidate for Romeo opposite Cindy Lou as Juliet when the girl, wishing to dem-onstrate her talent to the film producer who she hopes will hire her, chooses to perform the balcony scene. As the dialogue progresses, her wish to do well is in sharp conflict with her anxiety that George as a lusty lover will get too close to her chaste body.

Foremost among those authors whose black characters possessed dignity were Lillian Hellman and John Steinbeck. Hellman's vigor-ous, kindly Addie and Cal in *The Little Foxes*, house servants of the predatory Regina Giddens, lack the touches of caricature usually lav-ished upon such workers. They are presented with a respectable real-ism, as might be expected of an author who as a child in the South had been tended by a cherished black nurse.[11] Steinbeck in *Of Mice and Men* included in his cast a crippled black stable worker nick-named Crooks who out of a bone-deep loneliness expresses, to the moronic Lennie, the terrible sense of rejection experienced by his race:

You got George. You know he's comin' back. S'pose you didn't have
nobody. S'pose you couldn't go in the bunkhouse and play rummy,
'cause you was black. How would you like that? S'pose you had to set
out here and read books. Sure, you could play horseshoes until it got
dark, but then you got to read books. Books ain't no good. A guy
needs somebody . . . to be near him. (*His tone whines.*) A guy goes
nuts if he ain't got nobody. Don't make no difference who it is as long
as he's with you. I tell you a guy gets too lonely, he gets sick. (II, ii)

Black performers who could sing and dance continued to find occasional openings in revues and musicals. Ethel Waters, undoubtedly
the pre-eminent black musical performer of the decade, costarred
with Beatrice Lillie in the Howard Dietz-Arthur Schwartz revue *At
Home Abroad* (1935). Among her numbers was "Hottentot Potentate,"
in which she appeared as the Empress Jones. Josephine Baker came
back from Paris to sing and dance in the *Ziegfeld Follies of 1936*.
The popularity of all-black shows began to fade by the end of the decade, though not to vanish. The most publicized of the period were
rival versions of Gilbert and Sullivan's *Mikado*. The Chicago Federal
Theater's famous updated *Swing Mikado* was brought to New York in
March 1939 under the auspices of the Project, though Hallie Flanagan had been of the opinion that one or another of the commercial offers for the show should be accepted.[12] Later in the same month Michael Todd opened *The Hot Mikado* with Bill Robinson in the cast.
Two months after Todd's opening, the Project turned *The Swing Mikado* over to a commercial firm, the Marolin Corporation, headed by
Bernard Ulrich and Marvin Ericson. But Todd's splashier production
won the customers, and under its new management *The Swing Mikado* played for only three weeks. An updated version by Gilbert
Seldes and Erik Charell of Shakespeare's *A Midsummer Night's
Dream*, newly titled *Swingin' the Dream* (1939) foundered after 13
performances. It was more memorable as an experiment in integrated
casting than as a novel rendering of the comedy: the courtiers and
young lovers were played by white performers, while the fairies and
artisans were played by blacks, including Maxine Sullivan as Titania,
Louis Armstrong as Bottom, and Butterfly McQueen as Puck. In the
Richard Rodgers-Lorenz Hart success, *Babes in Arms* (1937), among
the talented young performers making up a cast of show-business
hopefuls were two blacks, the Nicholas Brothers, who were given

their own specialty number. Destined to have a shorter life than the other hits of the show, it was titled "All Dark People (Are Light on Their Feet)." An integrated cast was also employed for the Rome-Friedman *Sing Out the News*, though each race had its own scenes. The production was memorable for one of its black numbers, the song "Franklin D. Roosevelt Jones," in which a black family and its friends sang joyously of a newly born child named for the President. Deserving more attention than it got was a second black number, "One of These Fine Days," the song of a young Harlem boy seated on a wharf and pondering his future, which perhaps lies over the sea. Rome, always a poignant melodist when constructing songs for the young and vulnerable, touchingly defined the tentative, uncertain outlook of the boy through both words and music.

Turning toward Europe, the independent producers and playwrights saw in wars both threatened and actual a subject that, despite the intervening stretch of the Atlantic, was not far from home. Each season brought its quota of war plays, with the desperation of the writers, like that of the public, worsening as the inevitability of a new global war became increasingly evident. There were, however, few successes on this theme, apart from those presented by the institutional theaters, with Irwin Shaw's *Bury the Dead* and Sherwood's Theater Guild hits the most notable. But Shaw and other well-known writers were not always capable of holding the audience with dramas on the horrors of war. Shaw's *Siege* (1937), on the bravery of the Spanish Loyalists, lasted for only 6 performances. Other rapid failures were Sidney Howard's *Paths of Glory* (1935), adapted from the novel of the same name by Humphrey Cobb, and Sidney Kingsley's *Ten Million Ghosts* (1936), plays about the First World War in which that conflict was recalled in order to caution the public against allowing a second to occur. Poorly written, indifferently received dramas of the nazi menace were provided by Oliver H. P. Garrett in *Waltz in Goose Step* (1938), Burnet Hershey in *Brown Danube* (1939), and Dorothy Thompson and Fritz Kortner in *Another Sun* (1940). The only play of the hit class to put nazis on stage was Clare Boothe's *Margin for Error*, in which the German consul to an American city was shot, stabbed, and poisoned. Opening in November 1939, after the outbreak of war, it ran for 264 performances.

If worthy plays on the international situation were scarce, this did not, of course, mean that playwrights or producers were unconcerned. Their concern manifested itself in another way. A cult of nostalgia sprung up among them, as among the public, and Broadway made room for a quantity of plays on specific events of the American past, as well as others on American legends and folklore. Like all such cults, it came into being as a revulsion from the harsh contemporary scene. Encouraged by enthusiasts of the Popular Front, the new fondness for all things American revealed a nation moved by the totalitarian advance overseas to look back to more hopeful times.

Sherwood's *Abe Lincoln in Illinois* was, to be sure, the most firmly constructed of the Broadway plays on American history, but only one of many extolling figures of the past, real or legendary. Peter Stuyvesant and his fellow Dutch settlers in New Amsterdam comprised the cast of Maxwell Anderson's *Knickerbocker Holiday* (1938), set to music by Kurt Weill, and Arnold Sundgaard and Marc Connelly introduced the peripatetic Johnny Appleseed to the stage in *Everywhere I Roam* (1938). Jesse James, romantically portrayed as another Robin Hood, was the hero of E. B. Ginty's *Missouri Legend* (1938). Harriet Beecher Stowe made a spectral appearance in Elmer Rice's *American Landscape* (1938), a morality play with a contemporary setting. Robert Ardrey's *Casey Jones* (1938) and Roark Bradford's *John Henry* (1940) brought two legendary figures to the Broadway stage—both very briefly. Delving into a lesser vein, Albert Bein mined the folklore of hobo life in *Heavenly Express* (1940), a play set in the present in which the legendary Overland Kid, a kind of Angel of Death who travels by rail, calls unhappy creatures aboard a ghostly train bound for Paradise. With some half dozen former Group Theater actors in the cast, including Garfield as the Overland Kid, and with staging by Robert Lewis and settings by Boris Aronson, this play had the look and sound of a Group production. In fact, however, the producer was Kermit Bloomgarden, formerly the Group's business manager. The script had been held by the Group but was offered by Bloomgarden at the suggestion of Harold Clurman.[13] It closed after 20 performances.

The prolific Anderson also turned to the American past for three additional works of the late thirties. In *The Wingless Victory* the scene is Salem, Massachusetts, in 1800. In *High Tor* it is a hill overlooking the Hudson River in the present, but among the characters are spectral Dutchmen from Henry Hudson's day. *The Star-Wagon,* a fantasy about the inventors of a time-machine, begins and ends in the recent past, but stretches back to 1902 in its central scenes, recreating the tone of small-town life in that period of relative calm. As we will see in a moment, all three plays and *Knickerbocker Holiday* were reaffirmations of Anderson's commitment to the principle of resistance to conformist pressures.

Similarly providing a look back into turn-of-the-century life in small-town America was Thornton Wilder's metaphysical *Our Town* (1938). Though Wilder did not create the play as a vehicle for socio-political ideas, but as a speculation on man's eternal problem of living life fully during the brief time allowed him, it benefited from the climate that created an audience for timely drama with a "period" setting. Produced without scenery, the play took on the flavors of its time and place—1901 in Grover's Corners, New Hampshire—through costumes and dialogue. On the bare stage, the actions projected a universal significance; it was not the inhabitants of Grover's Corners alone whose ways and whose destiny Wilder described, but the entire race of man. As the "Stage Manager," Wilder's master of ceremonies, explains, each of the three acts has its own title: "The Daily Life," "Love and Marriage," and "Death." This was remote from the topical concerns of the politically inclined dramatists of the decade, and for that reason the play was parodied, it will be recalled, in Emanuel Eisenberg and Jay Williams's TAC sketch, "Our Borrowed Substance." Yet one of the reasons for the durability of Wilder's tragedy, possibly the most frequently acted American play of all time, is that in constructing it he made no effort to address a specific contemporary issue.

American small town life was also celebrated by George S. Kaufman and Moss Hart in the most ambitious of their eight collaborations, *The American Way* (1939), though this was by no means the only aspect of the American mystique to which the authors turned their attention in the play. With deliberate irony, they build the play around the career of an immigrant from Germany, one Martin Gunther, who soon after his arrival in America in the nineties begins to prosper as a cabinet maker in the town of Mapleton, Ohio, thanks to the confidence of the local banker, Samuel Brockton. As the years pass, he builds a fortune, only to lose it after the crash in a futile move to help Brockton save the bank during a run on its deposits. In the next-to-last scene, Gunther, proud of his American citizenry and spiritually content if still not restored to a position of wealth, is killed in a picnic grove by a mob of brown-shirted bundists whose meeting he had attended only in order to speak out against them.

A play blatant in its sentimentality, *The American Way* nevertheless is a mint of professional showmanship as practiced by Kaufman and Hart. At their best in the early scenes, they created through a few brief pieces of action and snatches of dialogue the small-town past as it existed, if not in their memory, at least in their imagination. In the lavishly equipped Center Theater, owned by the Rockefellers, and with a cast of over two hundred actors lavishly laid on by Sam H. Harris, at the Rockefellers' expense, they commanded a town square with church, bank, post office, courthouse, hotel, newspaper office, barber shop and dry-goods, drug, and cigar stores—the entire architecture of the official and mercantile center of the community. With a few words on the weather, a citizen's plans for a game of whist, some juvenile high jinks over a woman's outlandish hat, the mention of an obsolete brand of cigars (Lillian Russell), a phrase of an old tune, and comment on the McKinley-Bryan campaign of 1896, an era is recreated. Soon it grows dark, and a political rally commences with a torch-light parade. This was expensive, to be sure; the production cost of the play was reported to run to $250,000, a large sum for 1939.[14] Yet the writing itself was economical as a curt selection of images calculated to summon longings for a faded era. In no more than ten minutes Kaufman and Hart presented the audience with sights and sounds that composed the atmosphere of a free and open society, against which the images suggestive of what might come to pass, should Germany dominate the world, resounded and flashed before the play was over.

One late play of the Depression seasons that also delineated the Americanization of an immigrant family was Sylvia Regan's *Morning Star* (1940), which starred Molly Picon, the Yiddish theater favorite. The author had previously made her living performing promotional tasks for the Theater Union and the Mercury Theater.[15] The play was produced by George Kondolf, formerly the New York director of the Federal Theater. As sentimental as *The American Way*, but less entertaining, the action unfolds the life of Becky Felderman, a Jewish

matriarch on the Lower East Side who while organizing and directing her family with a firm hand is uncomfortably aware of the damaging effect of American materialism on the spirit. Over the twenty
years from 1910 to 1931 she grows in fortitude as she learns both how
to concede to and how to resist the pressures that would turn her into
an average American. Proud of the fact that her son was killed in the
First World War, and proud of her high school diploma, she is bitterly ashamed of her daughter Sadie's labor-bating business tactics.
She is best described as a benign Bessie Berger, showing the world a
face that is strong but not hostile. The hostility is left to Sadie, whose
determination to succeed in the garment business without giving an
inch to the unions is in no way tempered by the recollection that her
own sister was killed in the Triangle Shirtwaist factory fire of 1911,
which took the lives of one hundred forty-six garment workers.[16] Not
a consequential play, *Morning Star* serves, nevertheless, as a reminder
of the strength of the influence of Odets on his contemporaries in the
social theater.

A nostalgic glance back at historical and pastoral America, as well
as a quizzical squint at current social mores and institutions, provided substance for new enterprises in dance theater that burgeoned
in the middle and late thirties. The American Ballet and its offshoot,
the Ballet Caravan, came into being on paper in 1933, when Lincoln
Kirstein and Edward M. M. Warburg determined that the nation
should have a traditional ballet troupe of its own, comparable to, or
surpassing, the European descendants of Sergei Diaghilev's Ballets
Russes. It was their plan that the company should have a first-rate
school of ballet as well. Their choice for the post of director was one
of the preeminent heirs of the Diaghilev tradition, George Balanchine, then leading the Ballets 1933 in Paris. The new company made
its New York debut in March 1935. Though most of the early dances
devised for it by Balanchine were abstract works in nondescript costumes and were set to European music, the initial bill in New York
included one work with an American theme and setting: *Alma Mater*,
a spoof of undergraduate life with music by Kay Swift and costumes
by John Held, Jr. It was for the Ballet Caravan, a touring company
organized by Kirstein in 1936 and composed of members of the American Ballet Company, that a repertory of dances on American themes
employing traditional techniques, as opposed to the methods of mod-

ern dance, was first devised by American choreographers to the music of American composers. Among the works were *Pocahontas* (1936), with choreography by Lew Christensen and music by Elliott Carter; *Yankee Clipper* (1937), with choreography by Eugene Loring and music by Paul Bowles; *Filling Station* (1938), with choreography by Christensen and music by Virgil Thomson; and *Billy the Kid* (1938), with choreography by Loring and music by Aaron Copland. *Filling Station*, which depicted the events of one evening at a highway gas stop, included among the characters such familiar emblems of the time as a gun-wielding gangster and two young, slightly drunk, irresponsible members of the upper middle class. In 1953 this work entered the repertory of the New York City Ballet, the successor, both artistically and administratively, of the American Ballet. Loring's *Billy the Kid*, on the life and death of the prime desperado of the pioneer Wild West, became a staple of the international dance repertory.[17]

Colonel W. de Basil's Ballet Russe de Monte Carlo, the most popular troupe to perform in America during the thirties, also experimented with American subjects, though not with pronounced success. In not all instances were the music and choreography created by Americans. The company's *Union Pacific*, a dance on the development of the transcontinental railroad with libretto by Archibald Mac-Leish and music by Nicolas Nabakov, had its first performance in 1934 and was repeated during the decade. In 1939 the company offered *Ghost Town*, a ballet on the old West, with music and libretto by Richard Rodgers. One of its most conspicuous successes was *Rodeo* (1942), with choreography by Agnes de Mille and music by Copland, in which an ungainly but loving cowgirl gets her man despite strong competition from the ranch-owner's daughter The Ballet Theater, which under the patronage of Lucia Chase offered its debut performances in 1940 and developed a wide-ranging repertory, included among its earliest works *The Great American Goof* (1940), with a scenario by William Saroyan on a gullible, naïve, but decent young American, choreography by Eugene Loring, and music by Henry Brant, and *Fancy Free* (1944), with choreography by Jerome Robbins about three sailors on a pass, and music by Leonard Bernstein.

These attempts at the Americanization of classical dancing, with settings and themes strongly, if obliquely, influenced by Popular Front nostalgia, were to flower spectacularly during the war years, when Broadway became interested. The freshness of Agnes de Mille's choregraphy for *Rodeo* resulted in her commission to design the dances for the Theater Guild's *Oklahoma!* and established her as the leading musical-comedy choreographer of the forties. *On the Town* (1945), with book by Betty Comden and Adolph Green, choreography by Jerome Robbins, and music by Leonard Bernstein, was an adaptation and extension of *Fancy Free*. Both musicals were carry-overs into the new decade of the Popular Front admiration of American vistas and sentimental regard for the ordinary, "little" man—the former in the past and on the plains of the Southwest, the latter in the present and amid the skyscraper canyons of Manhattan.

PLAYWRIGHTS

The noninstitutional stage uncovered no new playwrights of unquestionable importance to the history of American literature in the late thirties. Wilder, it is true, had not been represented on Broadway with an original play before *Our Town,* but his translations of André Obey's *Lucrece* and Ibsen's *A Doll's House* had been produced in 1932 and 1937 respectively, his *The Trumpet Shall Sound* had been produced off-Broadway in 1927, and he had published volumes of one-act plays in 1928 and 1931. Of writers introduced by independent producers in the 1935–40 seasons, who received both popular and critical approval, only John Steinbeck, Clare Boothe, and the team of James Thurber and Elliott Nugent contributed plays of durable quality, and Steinbeck alone among them risked a Broadway opening in later years. With the exception of these dramatists and Saroyan, all of whom had distinguished themselves as writers before turning to the stage, it was the seasoned professionals, not novices, who provided the plays that in subsequent decades would be judged worthy of revival.

The Playwrights' Company

Though only Anderson averaged better than one play per season from the fall of 1935 to the spring of 1940, all five writers who in 1938 formed the Playwrights' Company were among Broadway's busiest. Together during these years they offered, under their own aegis or through the offices of the Guild or independent producers, a total of twenty plays, with thirteen scoring runs of more than 100 performances, the number that then justified the designation of "hit." With their extremes of liberalism and conservatism represented by Rice and Anderson respectively, the members of the fellowship were not separated by vast ideological differences. All opposed totalitarianism of both right and left, at the same time that they were eager for, or in the case of Behrman, ready to accept, reforms in the quality of American life. Nor were they far apart stylistically. All five remained in the tradition of the realistic well-made play, with only Rice and Anderson venturing outside the tradition to include elements of fantasy. Anderson's much-vaunted poetry was the element of their collective corpus that was the most uncharacteristic of the era. The best among them as a constructor of plot and character and composer of economical yet accurate language was Sherwood. The author seemingly least interested in the opinion of posterity, if the modest scope of his subject matter may serve as a basis for judgment, was Behrman, though only a foolhardy critic would describe him as the least talented.

Sidney Howard alone among the five writers was never represented on Broadway with a Playwrights' Company production. His accidental death in 1939 occurred before his last play, *Madame, Will You Walk?*, had received a final polishing. In an effort to gather some cash for Howard's widow, the Playwrights staged the play, with George M. Cohan as a devil incarnate who tempts a rich, rather reclusive young woman out of her doldrums. But according to Rice, the partners were hampered in their attempts to revise the script by Mrs. Howard, who resented any tinkering with her late husband's prose.[18] The production failed on the road, but the play was revived off-Broadway with moderate success in 1953 as the first production of the Phoenix Theater. Apart from its fantasy element, the presence in the cast of the Prince of Darkness, the play is familiar in substance— merely the old story of an independent but discontented young woman who is liberated in spirit after a night of romance.

The reliable mainstay of the Playwrights' Company was Anderson, who summoned his creative resources with such speed that no season passed without at least one new work from his pen. In the season of

1936 he was the author of three plays running simultaneously: *The Wingless Victory, High Tor,* and *The Masque of Kings.* The respect that he had developed with his English histories at the beginning of the thirties held firmly through the decade and beyond and was bolstered by the award of the New York Drama Critics' Circle in successive years for *Winterset* and *High Tor.* An increasing interest in the American present is evident in the plays of the late thirties, though in the forties he was to return to the past and civilizations abroad in certain works, such as *Journey to Jerusalem* (1940), *Joan of Lorraine* (1946), *Anne of the Thousand Days* (1948), and *Barefoot in Athens* (1951).

When treating the public to a display of his substantial comic gift, Anderson was at his best. No play of his of the late thirties has the cutting edge of *Both Your Houses,* but sparks occasionally fly out of the dialogue of *High Tor, The Star-Wagon,* and *Knickerbocker Holiday.* Among the determined individualists serving as his protagonists are several whom he characterizes with ingratiating comic touches. Van Van Dorn in *High Tor* and Stephen Minch in *The Star-Wagon* (1937), both played by Burgess Meredith, who also played Mio in *Winterset,* are two of Anderson's most convincing creations: cranks of a sort, but laudable ones whose independence harbors a contempt for conformity. Both are characterized by dialogue clipped and wry; the humor is understated but prickly. Minch's lifelong friend and fellow worker Hanus Wicks is more broadly conceived: an idiosyncratic bumpkin in the long line of descent from Jonathan, the proud Yankee of Royall Tyler's *The Contrast.* Brom Broeck, the young male lead of *Knickerbocker Holiday* (1938), is another man of independent spirit conceived in comic terms, though in this work, a musical comedy, he is only one caricature among many. Wooing posterity as a "serious" writer, Anderson too frequently ignored his gift for comic invention and filled the stage with tragic aphorists, the Mios, Rudolphs, and McClouds who, ironically, became the cause of his posthumous decline in reputation.

Yet increasingly strong in his work, whatever may be his stylistic lapses, was his sense of a call to stiffen the public's resistance to those social and political forces that he regarded as malign. Both business and governemnt he deemed suspect; the bigger they grew, the more dangerous to the individual's welfare they became. Anderson's strong-

est statement of this view occurs in *Winterset* when he allows Judge
Gaunt to condemn himself before Mio by explaining why he let Romagna die though he knew the man was innocent:

> Suppose it known,
> but there are things a judge must not believe
> though they should head and fester underneath
> and press in on his brain. Justice once rendered
> in a clear burst of anger, righteously,
> upon a very common laborer,
> confessed an anarchist, the verdict found
> and the precise machinery of law
> invoked to know him guilty—think what furor
> would rock the state if the court then flatly said:
> all this was lies—must be reversed? It's better,
> as any judge can tell you, in such cases,
> holding the common good to be worth more
> than small injustice, to let the record stand,
> let one man die. (II)

But in this play Anderson does no more than decry the existence of
an arm of government that blatantly abuses its power; as we have
seen, he does not show his protagonist, Mio, taking the action necessary to correct the abuse.

In *High Tor* business, as represented by a trap-rock company, puts
pressure on twenty-three-year-old Van Van Dorn to sell his mountain-
top property above the Hudson, out of which the rock is to be
dug, leaving a hollow palisade above the river. Art J. Biggs of the
company and the dishonest Judge Shimmerhorn, who is related to
several of Biggs's partners, are the figures who visit Van Dorn on his
property to make the offer, none too covertly threatening to use spurious legal means of relieving him of it if he will not sell. Business
and government are in a conspiracy to deprive the independent citizen of what is rightfully his, having designed a maze of legal maneu-
vers and jargon to confuse and defeat him. No ordinary victim, however, Van Dorn gets the upper hand. Yet he decides after all to sell,
facing the fact that the mountain is already scarred by a road, a
trail, a railroad line, and even a quarry like the one under contempla-
tion. It is too late for High Tor, and he will be better off by moving
West, where the land is still open. Meanwhile he drives a hard bargain.

In *The Wingless Victory* another sort of oppression is the subject. To Salem, Massachusetts, in 1800 the trader Nathaniel McQueston returns from the orient with a dark-skinned wife—a Malay princess named Opparre (played by Katharine Cornell). Held in suspicion by the citizens of the town because of her race and knowing that her presence is an endless source of trouble for her husband despite his love for her, the proud, exotic woman kills herself and her children. It is her only way out, since she can neither change the color of her skin nor adjust herself to the customs of Salem. A parallel with the contemporary racial malaise is implied.

In subsequent plays by Anderson, apart from the ideologically confused Rudolph of *The Masque of Kings* the foes or sufferers from injustice and dehumanizing conformity do not give in. McCloud in *Key Largo,* having abandoned principle in Spain, regains it in Florida and is willing to die in defense of the Seminoles trapped by the gambler and sheriff. In *The Star-Wagon* Minch, inventing a time machine with his friend Hanus, takes a trip back through the thirty-five years of his adult life and discovers that had he exercised the options for wealth available to him, he would have been a man far less content than he presently is, despite the fewness of the creature comforts he can afford. Being too good to lose, and possessing company secrets, he is offered a raise by the chemical concern for which he works as an intuitive, untrained inventive genius. But, skeptical of the honesty of those who control the company (and with good reason, since, for one thing, they will not sanction the mass-production of indestructible rubber tires made according to his formula), he will not accept a partnership. With his winning of the right to be his own boss, free of the obligation to take orders, this meek man inherits the earth. But independence on the job and a reasonable salary of two hundred a week are all that Anderson will allow him. More, and his soul would be imperiled.

Knickerbocker Holiday (1938), his first work to be offered by the Playwrights' Company, revealed Anderson in the new role of musical-comedy lyricist, but one who cautioned, as of old, against encroachments upon the freedom of the individual. The setting is old New Amsterdam, adapted from the conception of Washington Irving in the *Knickerbocker History of New York,* but with a contemporary relevance. Pieter Stuyvesant, taking over the rule of the colony with great gusto, was intended by Anderson to suggest America's own head of state in the thirties, and the parallel was supported by the very fact of Roosevelt's Dutch lineage. Anderson's colleagues in the company were at pains to persuade him to remove from the script some of his strokes against the New Deal.[19] Yet the play remained a series of stern rebukes at those who favored big government. Anderson's disapproval of any meddling by government with the natural course of man's affairs, no matter how well-meaning, is made clear not only in the play itself, but in his Preface to the printed text:

> It is not an accident that Germany, the first paternalistic state in Europe, should be governed now by an uncontrollable dictator; not an accident that Russia, adopting a centrally administered economy for humanitarian reasons, should arrive at a tyranny bloodier and more absolute than that of the Czars. Men who are fed by their government will soon be driven down to the status of slaves or cattle.

As the counterpart of Roosevelt, Stuyvesant verges toward the extreme of despotism. He is a rather chilling reflection of Anderson's disapproval of the welfare state. An outright dictator, he sings with ominous obviousness in praise of "strength through joy" and "the regimented life" (I). But to mute the sting of the play somewhat, Anderson invented a New Amsterdam councilman actually named Roosevelt who, though unusually dense even for a stage Dutchman, is also stubbornly honest.

As the play proceeds, Stuyvesant interferes with both the public and private concerns of the citizenry, attempting to steal away the fiancée of Brom Broeck, New Amsterdam's most fiercely independent citizen, abrogating the laws against selling spirits and firearms to the Indians, and threatening to create inflation by raising wages and profits. There would be no end to his political chicanery and fiscal folly if Brom and the usually compliant councilmen did not take a stand. But they do, and in this Anderson reveals an abiding confidence in American individualism—despite the aberrant regard of the contemporary public for the New Deal. This confidence is musically expressed in the portentous patter song, "How Can You Tell an American?," sung in the first act by Brom in a duet with Washington Irving, a witness to the dramatic action. The second chorus, which is reprised at the conclusion, builds to an ardent climax of optimism:

It isn't that he's black or white,
It isn't that he works with tools,
It's only that it takes away his appetite
To live by a book of rules.
Yes, it's just that he hates and he damns all the features
Of any mortal man set above his fellow creatures,
And he'll hate the undertaker when at last he dies
If he hears a note of arrogance above him where he lies;
He does his own living, he does his own dying,
Does his loving, does his hating, does his multiplying,
Without the supervision of a governmental plan—
And that's an American! (I)

Behrman, reluctant at first to join the Playwrights,[20] supplied the company with only one play before the end of the decade and broke with it in 1945 to return to the Theater Guild. In *No Time for Comedy* (1939) he designed a mock-serious investigation of the problem of a witty comic writer who believes that the time is wrong for the kind of stage fare for which he is famous. Though on the surface Behrman was unlike the hard-drinking, flirtatious, dashing dramatist, Gaylord Esterbrook, it is impossible to read the play without concluding that Esterbrook's problem was also his own. How, Behrman asks, is the comic author to keep his self-respect when the world is in need of profound literary analyses of disturbing events and he is not endowed by nature to supply them? The back-handed answer, obvious enough from the start, is that the world also needs the civilizing effect of comedy. Esterbrook's mad decision to write a murky antiwar play under the "inspiration" of a self-important woman with money and a cellolike voice, to marry her (provided both can get divorces from their current mates), and to honeymoon with her in war-torn Spain, threatens to tumble his reputation as a sane and trenchant writer of comedy of manners. Fortunately, his actress-wife, the star of his last three comedies, helps him to revive his good sense at the final curtain. Instead of pursuing Melpomene, he will write a comedy on why he ought to write comedy, and call it *No Time for Comedy*.

Though it provided box-office success for the Playwrights with the popular Katharine Cornell as Linda Esterbrook (and coproducer) and rising star Laurence Olivier as the dramatist, the play was Behrman's most trivial comedy of the thirties, despite the validity of its basic premise. It is not the befuddled playwright who has the best lines, but the actress, who is yet another of Behrman's stellar feminine roles. Sliding away from his theme, Behrman gives equal weight to the problem of the wife, who must find the arguments that will persuade her husband to follow the natural line of his gift, as well as to stay by her side. The result is domestic comedy. Curiously, the play is also flawed by the presence of an awkward caricature—the only such figure in Behrman's entire repertory—a stage darky named Clementine who is the star's personal maid. All that may be said in favor of the part is that she provides Behrman with the opportunity for a few pleasant moments of self-ridicule. These occur when the name of a young Englishman, Makepiece Lovell, is spoken in her presence. The very mention of it, absurd but typical of Behrman's taste in names, sends her into uncontrollable laughter.

Unlike Behrman, Rice was happy among the Playwrights from the start, regaining the enthusiasm for theater that had been dimmed by the critical onslaught against *Judgment Day* and his unfortunate brush with Jacob Baker of the WPA. He directed the company's first play, Sherwood's *Abe Lincoln in Illinois*, and wrote and directed its third, *American Landscape* (1938). In a promotional essay for the *New York Times*, which was also a brief résumé of his career, Rice commented on his moral and intellectual purpose in writing the play, a purpose that he made clear was more important to him than making money with it. It was to express "an affirmation of the American tradition of liberty and the American way of life." [21] His method, which was to mingle the living members of an American family with the ghosts of their ancestors, who include Moll Flanders and Harriet Beecher Stowe, proved cumbersome, and the play in consequence earned Rice another set of mediocre notices.

Rice's plot was the typical response of a liberal author to the new enthusiasm for the American scene. For generations the Dale family, of solid Yankee stock, has owned and operated a shoe factory in Dalesford, Connecticut, but now, faced with the demands of his workers for recognition of their union, Captain Frank Dale, the aged head of the family, wishes to sell out to a larger organization. What is more, he is thinking of selling the family home to one Klaus Stillgebauer, the head of a pronazi German-American association. It is a foregone conclusion that he will do neither; Rice's plot is an explanation of the reasons for Dale's change of mind and the consequences of the change. Poised against Stillgebauer is the ghost of Captain Heinrich Kleinschmidt, a German refugee of 1848, who speaks up for the integrity of the German people, as opposed to their new masters, and along with other spectral visitors and the living Dales he exposes the contempt for humanity lurking beneath the high-minded phrases of the "new" Germany. A delegation of workers from the plant and solid citizens from the town make an equally strong appeal to Dale concerning their future. In Popular Front fashion it is made up of an Irishman, a Jew, a black, a French-Canadian, and a Finn. As they plead with him to keep the property and plant and appeal with equal force for recognition of the rights of labor, the play turns into an argument for the preservation of American freedoms and a reaffirmation of the promises of the Declaration of Independence. The Dale holdings thus become a miniature America beleaguered by reactionary forces. Dale is so moved by the vision of freedom endangered that he suffers a fatal stroke. However, he does not die before making a new will that assures the preservation of both the business and the property for the benefit of his workers and family. By this means the Dale tradition of liberty and tolerance—the American tradition—will be preserved.

Rice also added a contemporary comedy, *Two on an Island*, to the Playwrights' schedule as the decade closed. Though this work was put into rehearsal in the fall of 1939 for an opening in January 1940, curiously it contains no mention of the war. So much the pacifist that he could not bring himself to sign Sherwood's appeal for immediate intervention,[22] Rice was too appalled by the prospect of a second global holocaust to take immediate notice of it in his writing. Yet the play is studded with references to the Depression. First and foremost a love story in which two out-of-towners meet and marry in New York after their paths have crossed randomly for two years, it is also the story of the fight for employment that few of the young men and women of the thirties could avoid. Since the boy and the girl—with classic simplicity named John and Mary—hope to make careers in play-writing and acting respectively, their plight is crueler than that of many others. Throughout the action Rice's social consciousness manifests itself in ironic comments on the local scene. Says a sightseeing guide to his customers, "Now, on these streets where you see those empty lots there used to be a shantytown, dwelling places constructed out of wooden boxes and gasoline cans by the unemployed." To a question about what happened to them he answers, "The police cleared them out. They made a bad impression on out-of-town folks driving up from the Holland Tunnel" (scene ii).

Though tart and occasionally touching, *Two on an Island* was not a milestone in the history of the Playwrights' Company. It was Robert E. Sherwood who gave the company its chief critical and financial success in the first years. Both *Abe Lincoln in Illinois* (1938) and *There Shall Be No Night* (1940) won the Pulitzer Prize. With only one play of the late thirties did Sherwood have a producer other than the Playwrights or the Theater Guild: his adaptation of Jacques Deval's *Tovarich* (1936). In this sentimental comedy a White Russian grand duchess and her noble husband, employed as domestic servants in Paris, decide after much soul-searching to turn over to a Commissar of the U.S.S.R. the great sum of almost four billion francs that is in their keeping. Entrusted them during the Revolution by the tsar himself, the money is to be spent only for the good of Mother Russia. Though expressing doubt at every step of the way, the loyal couple allow themselves to be persuaded that the new Russian rulers will use the money appropriately, for the ultimate good of the Russian people. Intended, like much of Sherwood's work, for the Lunts,[23] but not played by them, the adaptation was presented in London and New York by Gilbert Miller.

With a run of 472 performances, *Abe Lincoln in Illinois* gave the Playwrights an excellent foundation on which to build the company. Sherwood's study of Lincoln's early years sprang from an affection for his subject that manifested itself in unlabored praise rising toward a moving climax in the presidential campaign of 1860. The sincerity of the writing was well matched by the performance of the Canadian-born Raymond Massey in the title role, which he repeated for the film version in 1940. In scope of characterization, Sherwood went beyond all earlier American biographical plays, though the work of an English writer on the same figure, John Drinkwater's *Abraham Lincoln* (1920), had set a high standard for him to emulate.[24] But *Abe Lincoln in Illinois* was more than biography. The playwright, dropping his pacifism at last, exploited Lincoln's stand against slavery to advocate that the audience of 1938 take an equally firm stand on the side of democracy, then demonstrably threatened by foreign militarism and racism. In passing, he also recommended that the audience support organized labor in its massive drive for recognition.

Compared with E. P. Conkle's *Prologue to Glory* of the previous season, Sherwood's play proves intellectually livelier as well as more profound. It also covers more of Lincoln's life. Whereas Conkle confines his attention to Lincoln's New Salem years, Sherwood dwells on this period in only the first of his three acts, proceeding from it to cover the entire twenty-one-year period from 1840, the year of Lincoln's first meeting with Mary Todd, to 1861, when he left Springfield to be inaugurated president. Sherwood's principal source was Carl Sandburg's *Abraham Lincoln: The Prairie Years*, which according to his biographer he read repeatedly from the time of its publication in 1926 to 1936, when he began to compose the play.[25] But Sherwood's own growing fear for the preservation of American democracy was an interior source of equal importance, guiding his hand in the selection of phrases from Lincoln's speeches for inclusion in the dialogue. As he pointed out in notes to his text, the sustained speeches delivered by Lincoln the Senatorial candidate in debate with Stephen A. Douglas and by Lincoln the newly elected president are made up of elements of speeches made by Lincoln on several occasions. Douglas's remarks in the debate are likewise taken from several of his speeches delivered over the years, but to them is added the charge, never made by him, that Lincoln, though concerned over black slavery, was not sufficiently cognizant of the "slavery" of laborers sweating under cruel conditions and, therefore, striking in both Massachusetts and Illinois.[26] To this Lincoln offers a shrewd rebuttal; the white workers, he observes, have the power to take matters into their own hands when severely pressed by their employers, whereas the slaves do not. In the second lengthy speech, delivered at the Springfield railroad station while standing aboard the train that will take him to Washington for his inauguration, Lincoln faces the threat of war and boldly hints that the Union must be preserved at any cost:

> We gained democracy, and now there is the question whether it is fit to survive. Perhaps we have come to the dreadful day of awakening, and the dream is ended. If so, I am afraid it must be ended forever, I cannot believe that ever again will men have the opportunity we have had. Perhaps we should admit that, and concede that our ideals of liberty and equality are decadent and doomed. . . . And yet—

(*Suddenly he speaks with quiet but urgent authority*)—let us believe that it is not true! Let us live to prove that we can cultivate the natural world that is about us, and the intellectual and moral world that is within us, so that we may secure an individual, social and political prosperity, whose course shall be forward, and which, while the earth endures, shall not pass away.(III, xii)

With this rhetoric Sherwood, having both enlightened and moved the audience by alternating glimpses of Lincoln the politician with others of Lincoln the harassed or perplexed private person, offered a valedictory tingling in its revelation of the high purpose and gallantry of the speaker.

Lillian Hellman

After the members of the Playwrights Company, the noninstitutional theater's most respected author of the late thirties was Lillian Hellman, who was also one of the newest. Frugal with her talent and inclined to view the drama as, in her phrase, "a second-rate form," [27] she offered only two plays in the period: *Days to Come* (1936) and *The Little Foxes* (1939). Compensating for the failure of the former, *The Little Foxes,* independent Broadway's stiffest complaint against laissez-faire capitalism, was destined to be the most admired of all her works. In both plays Hellman continued in the way that she had set upon in *The Children's Hour,* inflicting a large measure of physical and mental suffering upon the characters with only faint regard for poetic justice. A generation before the concept became modish, she had devised a theater of cruelty and found an audience for it.

For *Days to Come* Hellman chose a labor situation fraught with the possibility of violence: an effort on the part of industrial management to end a walkout by hiring professional strikebreakers. The company, located in Ohio, has a record of good labor relations, but is unwilling to allow its workers to organize. Though only with misgivings, the Rodman family, owners of the company, give in to the suggestion of their lawyer that the strikebreakers be called in. Violence soon erupts, first between two goons brought in to control the strikers, with murder the result, and then in an attack on the strikers and their families, with more killings ensuing. Ultimately the company is the victor, but the Rodman family is so torn with remorse that the victory is worthless. After struggling mightily through pages of plot to analyze

the personal side of labor-management relations, Hellman falls back
on a melodramatic intrigue for the climax, allowing the dénouement
to hinge on an attempt to frame the organizer Whalen on a charge of
murder. Suspense, not ideology, becomes the major matter of the
play. Yet even on the level of melodrama the play fails, since in view
of the humanitarian temperament of the Rodmans, it is clear that
Whalen will be exonerated without a struggle.

The Little Foxes, animated by the bravura performance of Tallulah
Bankhead in the central role of Regina Giddens, was a resounding hit
both in New York and on the road, as it was later (1941) on film with
Bette Davis in the Bankhead part. Set in 1900 in the deep South, it is a
gothic story of a rapacious family, consisting of Regina and her two
brothers, Ben and Oscar Hubbard. The Hubbards and Regina have
wealth enough for comfort, but not for luxury, which they profoundly
covet. The money passion in itself is sufficient to mark them as damn-
able in Hellman's view, and she wastes no time on inventing any mit-
igating virtues for them. Yet she provides a fleeting indication of a
psychological reason for their greed: having been snubbed all their
lives by the genteel families of the district because of their father's
sharp financial dealings, they desire money as a kind of vindication,
as well as for the things it can buy. A means of getting it comes to
hand: as cotton growers, they are able to interest a Chicago firm in
opening a mill in their town, in return for concessions that they can
secure from the state for cheap water power and for their ability to
provide extremely cheap black labor. But it is necessary for the family to put up $225,000, and on this detail the plot turns.

It is in pursuit of the money that the unholy siblings reveal their
astonishing hostility toward their fellow men. Though Regina's husband, the banker Horace Giddens, could complete the sum by putting
in the railroad bonds that he owns, he refuses on the grounds that the
new company would heartlessly exploit the local blacks. Not only are
his wife and brothers-in-law indifferent to this danger, but they are
equally indifferent to the laws against embezzlement and indifferent
to Horace's declining health. Though Hellman again relies on a melodramatic intrigue, it is the major characters who devise it in this instance, and it is in keeping with their egregious personalities. Horace,
discovering the theft of the bonds from his safe-deposit box, which
has been carried out by his nephew Leo, decides not to make a scene,

since he knows that the bonds will eventually be replaced. In Hellman's most painful scene, Regina coolly lets him die of a heart attack when to save his life she need only fetch his medicine from another room. Then, armed with her knowledge of the theft and her conviction that in a trial at law her testimony regarding it would be believed despite concrete evidence that the bonds were stolen rather than lent, she blackmails her brothers into giving her a controlling share of stock in the new corporation. At long last she has what she had been looking for: the opportunity to begin a new life as a very rich woman. As before, Hellman attempts to demonstrate that in the process of amassing wealth the individual goes through the parallel process of decivilizing himself—of losing ground as a human being and falling into the way of the jungle. Moreover, the promise of contentment is not fulfilled, for at the close Regina is entirely alone, having alienated her daughter Alexandra, the one remaining person from whom, had she been less egocentric, she might have derived some comfort. Like Amelia Tilford and Andrew Rodman, Regina at the close, speaking with her daughter, tries to make up for her offenses of the past, only to be rebuffed.

In her literary attack on predators Hellman was uncompromisingly severe. She was also severe in her adamant refusal to allow *The Little Foxes* to play a benefit for Finnish relief during the Russian invasion. That the Russians were also predators she could not see; on the contrary, the fact that they were invading Finland had the curious result of turning the Finns into fascists, in her eyes. Herman Shumlin, her producer, took a similar stand; though all other hits on Broadway gave benefits for the Finns, only his productions, *The Little Foxes* and Thurber and Nugent's *The Male Animal*, did not, along with Oscar Serlin's production of Howard Lindsay and Russell Crouse's *Life with Father*. The protests of Tallulah Bankhead were to no avail, and a backstage quarrel quickly brewed.[28]

George S. Kaufman

If any such conflict in ideologies ever troubled the mind of George S. Kaufman, they left no record in the press. Moving from play to play with the agility and steadiness of an assembly-line worker, Kaufman lit up Broadway with fifteen works during the Depression, but was only seldom interested in creating drama out of the news of the

day. Rarely did he write alone, without the assistance of a collaborator, and not once did he do so during the seasons of 1935–40. But of
the seven plays of which he was part author during that period, six
were firm hits, as also were Steinbeck's *Of Mice and Men* under his
direction, the Marx Brothers' film *A Night at the Opera*, on whose
screenplay he worked, and his production, with Max Gordon and
Moss Hart, of the Rome-Friedman *Sing Out the News.* The single
failure was *The Fabulous Invalid* (1938), a swooping, superficial review of the American theater from the 1890's to the time of the play,
concluding with the appearance of a young man very much like
Orson Welles, who with his own band of actors hopes to rejuvenate
the stage. Moss Hart was Kaufman's principal collaborator during the
decade; together they offered eight plays. In the second half of the
decade they wrote only three plays apart from one another. Hart provided the script for *Jubilee,* a Cole Porter musical about royalty on
holiday. Kaufman in collaboration with Katharine Dayton, columnist for the Washington *Post,* wrote *First Lady* (1935), a comedy of
manners concerning a woman who wishes to see her husband elected
to the presidency, and with Edna Ferber wrote *Stage Door* (1936), a
romantic play on the dreams and disappointments and triumphs of
young actresses in New York. A tart dash of typical Kaufmanesque
satire in the latter involves a young radical playwright resembling
Clifford Odets. "Romance is for babies!" he declares (I, i). "I write
about *today!* I want to tear the heart out of the rotten carcass they
call life, and hold it up bleeding for all the world to see!" But in II,
ii, a few weeks later, with a hit on Broadway and a Hollywood offer
of $2,000 a week, he is a changed man. Calling on his girl at her theat-
rical boarding house, he comes garbed in top hat and tails.

   The American Way, with its brief scene of a bank panic and the
horrifying murder of Martin Gunther at the hands of bundist thugs,
was the strongest statement on recent and current events that Kaufman and Hart allowed themselves. In other works of the decade they
referred to Depression phenomena, but without committing themselves to a stand on any issue. Their Pulitzer-Prize winning *You Can't
Take It With You* (1936), the most popular of their works in their
own day and the single play by which as a team they are most likely
to be remembered, offers a pleasantly perfumed version of the Depression atmosphere. On an annual unearned income of between three

and four thousand dollars, the large ménage of Grandpa Martin Van-derhof maintains itself in a house near Columbia University, with only one member of the family, a forthright girl named Alice, actually holding down a steady job. A little money comes in from the sale of candy and fireworks made on the premises. It is a house of free ex-pression. One female character practices ballet when not stirring a pot of sweets in the kitchen, and her husband spends most of his time playing the xylophone and setting up quotations from Trotsky on a printing press as exercises in typography. A third member of the fam-ily writes plays because eight years in the past a typewriter was de-livered to the house by mistake. To the Depression audience, such a carefree life could only seem enviable, showing as it did a collection of human beings who, if they worked at all, did so for fun. Virtually plotless, the play is complicated only by the despair of Alice on real-izing that her zany family has nothing in common with the rich, stodgy parents of her fiancé Tony Kirby. In Act III all works out as it should. The pomposity of the senior Kirbys is exploded in a fren-zied evening of exposure to the family. The central, normative role of the young girl bent on making her own way in the world was in itself emblematic of the age. In the year following *Stage Door*, Reed's *Yes, My Darling Daughter*, and Kober's *Having Wonderful Time* pre-sented more such girls to a receptive audience.[29]

In *I'd Rather Be Right* (1937) Kaufman and Hart turned to politi-cal satire in the form of musical comedy. In this work, as in the Kauf-man-Ryskind *Of Thee I Sing* and *Let 'Em Eat Cake*, the central figure was the president of the United States. But there was a major difference. Whereas Kaufman and Ryskind had invented a fictional president, John P. Wintergreen, in *I'd Rather Be Right* the president was Franklin D. Roosevelt. To keep a safe distance from reality, the authors brought Roosevelt into the play as only a figure in a dream. But he was there nevertheless, and as played by George M. Cohan gave a good account of himself as a song-and-dance man. A crisis in contemporary economics accounts for his presence. A young couple, Phil Barker and Peggy Jones, sitting on a rock in Central Park at twi-light on the Fourth of July, sadly decide to postpone their marriage because Phil is not to have the promotion and raise that he had ex-pected. Nor will he have them until his employers can plan on in-creased profits, and this depends on the ability of the president to

balance the budget. The president, strolling through the park on his
way to broadcast a fireside chat (in July), listens to their story and offers what comfort he can. With songs by Richard Rodgers and Lorenz
Hart, with dancing, and pungent dialogue, Roosevelt, his cabinet,
and the Supreme Court justices review the current economic situation
and New Deal legislation. It is with the "nine old men," concerning
whom Roosevelt had recently experienced his greatest political set-
back, that Kaufman and Hart amused themselves the most gleefully.
Sticking their heads out from behind trees and bushes every time
Roosevelt conceives a bright idea about fiscal stability, the justices
declare his ideas unconstitutional. (In reality the Supreme Court so
frequently declared New Deal legislation unconstitutional that Roosevelt earlier in the year had put forward, unsuccessfully, a plan to add
to it younger, presumably more liberal members.) Also popping out
from behind trees and bushes are nine young girls, whom the justices
are in the habit of visiting for "a little constitutional fun" (I). Shortly
before the final curtain the justices pronounce the Constitution itself
unconstitutional. Somewhat invidiously, the Federal Theater is also
lampooned on the familiar ground of its cost. A little number called
"Spring in Vienna" that one of the troupes performs for the president
is reported to have cost $675,000—a project that "we just did on a
shoestring" (I). Later when the president asks an aide to bring him
the Wagner Act—that is, the National Labor Relations Act of 1935—
out come a duo of German acrobats: indeed the Wagner Act, "Hans
and Fritz Wagner—Federal Theatre troupe No. 34268" (II).

     With so much byplay, the president does not come up with an an-
swer to the immediate problem of the budget, though he promises to
do so eventually. His fireside chat, reassuring the public on the future
of America, includes the authors' only serious comment of the play,
and it is brief:

> We've come through a lot of troubles since that first Fourth of July.
> We fought for our freedom, we fought among ourselves, we've had
> bad Presidents and good Presidents; we've had panics and depres-
> sions and floods and strikes and wars. But it seems there's something
> in this country—a sort of spirit that holds us all together—that always
> sees us through. And we mustn't ever lose that. Just remember, folks,
> that even though things are a little wrong right now, we've got a
> chance to make 'em right, because at least this is a country where

you can come and *talk* about what's wrong. And there aren't many
left like that nowadays. You know something? It doesn't matter
whether *I'm* President or anybody else is, and it never has mattered.
That's not important. There's only one thing that really matters in
this country, or ever will. . . . You! (II)

The content of this simplistic speech, in no way a parody of Roosevelt's style, became the theme of the authors' next hit, *The American
Way*. As social dramatists Kaufman and Hart had gone as far as
their temperaments would allow. In the work which followed in the
fall of 1939, *The Man Who Came to Dinner*, with its lack of references
to the economy, its parade of celebrities, and its setting in an upper-
middle-class Midwestern home, we are philosophically as well as
chronologically on the threshold of the forties.

Kaufman's successes, and especially those written with Hart,
gave rise to a "school of Kaufman" made up of writers with a talent
for caricature and satiric dialogue. This became particularly evident
in the forties when, after *George Washington Slept Here* (1940), the
collaboration broke up and Jerome Chodorov, Joseph Fields, and
Ruth Gordon leapt to the fore with slender works whose plots were
bedecked with dazzling idiosyncratic characters. Kaufman and Hart
themselves directed the plays of these writers.

Clare Boothe

But in the thirties Kaufmanesque comedies were already available,
including several that offered more pointed comments on the social
and political scene than Kaufman cared to venture. Clare Boothe
(married to Henry R. Luce since 1935, but not yet using her married
name in her professional life), was the author of three wisecracking
analyses of the life of the rich, famous, and powerful that drew enthusiastic houses between 1936 and 1940. Like Kaufman and Hart she
devised simple plots and tough language and only rarely allowed for
the expression of human warmth. Though much of her satire is limited to quick thrusts at hypocrisy and pretension, in her last play of
the decade she dealt forcefully with an issue of undeniable weight:
the nazi theory of race.

For *The Women* (1936), her second Broadway play (after the unsuccessful *Abide with Me* in 1935), Boothe drew upon her knowledge

of the fashionable world of Park Avenue for a comic exposé of the folkways of the rich. The action involves a youngish society matron, Mary Haines, affable enough but dull, who loses her husband to a calculating shopgirl in the first act and wins him back in the third. This plot supplies a frame into which Boothe sets vignettes of Mary and her friends. Only women appear; men are much talked about, but remain off stage. Though Boothe knew intimately the social types of whom she wrote, she chose to fix on their special qualities of self-love and vulgarity. Of the major characters, only Mary and Nancy Blake, a writer, are presented candidly; Nancy, with an outsize share of the play's best lines, is the voice of the author commenting acidly on the foibles of her friends. The other characters are pampered women whose grievances are as nothing when compared to the acute deprivations of those in daily attendance upon their wishes. Through-out the play is heard a fusillade of observations on this theme of self-indulgence in outbursts from servants, salesgirls, a gymnastics instruc-tress, and a nurse, sometimes with mild irony, but sometimes with savagery. That in the midst of national poverty so many rich women could still maintain their habitual wasteful existence with only a slight, superficial regard for the price of anything was in itself a tell-ing point for Boothe.

It was Boothe's practice to introduce the printed texts of her plays with hints to the reader regarding her aims. With *The Women* she ex-plained that her subject was not the entire sex, as some reviewers had thought, but merely one social class. With *Kiss the Boys Good-Bye* (1938) she began by announcing,

> This play was meant to be an allegory about Fascism in America. But everywhere it has been taken for a parody of Hollywood's search for Scarlett O'Hara. As such it has had a good measure of succcess with the public, far less with the critics—and none at all with myself, its author. For once again I have quite missed my target.

With a plot inspired by David O. Selznick's much publicized (but le-gitimate) search for the perfect actress to portray the heroine of *Gone with the Wind,* Boothe strove for a deeper significance and did not quite achieve it, though the signs of a valiant effort are evident in the writing. Cindy Lou Bethany is brought north from her native Georgia for a home-office screen test that, if successful, will make her the leading contender for the part of Velvet O'Toole. Taken to the Westport, Connecticut, home of the editor of a weekly magazine on the order of the *New Yorker*, she meets the producer of the film, Herbert Z. Harner, the magazine's publisher, and a left-leaning columnist (an obvious counterpart to Heywood Broun). A bird-brained young thing, ostensibly she is no match for these intellectuals, who are capable of brittle invective that she cannot imitate and that incorporates their attitudes toward, not only literature and the art of acting, but Marxism, the New Deal, and the rise of Hitler. Yet, despite her intellectual limitations, in a sense she has her way with them. The conservative, the liberal, and the leftist—that is, the publisher, the editor, and the columnist—possessed as they are with preconceived notions of democracy and the forces that menace it, fail to see that her flirtatious mellifluousness thinly covers a supreme selfishness, and that her inherited notions of racial purity are as dangerous as Hitler's. She is in search of the best possible life for herself, and she finds it. On hand for the Westport weekend is the matrimonial catch of the year, "Top" Rumson, a rich, young sportsman scarcely more intelligent than she, and before the final curtain she snaps him up, though it means turning down the part of Velvet. If ultimately this does not come off clearly as an allegory on the problem of fascism, the reason is that Cindy Lou does not *know* what her political position is and, therefore, cannot express it or even hint at it with enough openness to make it alarming. But this is not Boothe's only error. It may be asked why, in a play intended to decry the Southern racial attitude, she included in her cast the comic pair of stage-darky house servants, Maimie and George. The latter, it turns out, is a one-time member of the Federal Theater. "Ah's called de Harlem Guilgood," he modestly says (II, ii).

In her last play of the decade, and the last Broadway production of her career, *Margin for Error* (1939), Boothe brought the fascist menace to the stage in the presence of a member of the German diplomatic corps. Kurt Baumer is the German consul in an unnamed city that might be New York, except for a disclaimer buried in the dialogue.[30] Its mayor has detailed a Jewish policeman, Moe Finkelstein, to guard the consulate, taking a cue from La Guardia, who assigned only Jewish policemen to guard the German consulate in New York in 1938. The irony in the situation is not humorous in itself, but is made so by the personality of the policeman, a young man still in his twenties, who is himself capable of mildly ironic speech. A rather slack mystery melodrama on the surface, the play has as its subtext the contention and contrast between Baumer and Finkelstein (played respectively by Otto Preminger and Sam Levene), the most detestable and most sympathetic of all Boothe's dramatic characters. Exploiting his power, Baumer takes money from Americans on the pretense of getting their imprisoned relations out of Germany and intimidates his wife with threats against her Czech father, his male secretary with the revelation of the fact that the man had a Jewish grandmother, and the leader of the German-American bund with the threat of "liquidation." Throughout the first half, during which these threats and exposures occur, Finkelstein maintains a running commentary on the virtues of American democracy and the folly of Hitler. Ready to fight Baumer and all other Germans when the time comes, Finkelstein nevertheless fulfills the obligations of his assignment with good will. A true believer in America, he realizes that in a democracy even a nazi has his rights. Mercifully, Baumer is murdered at the end of the first of the play's two acts. Since each character present had good reason to wish him dead, all are under suspicion. By shooting and stabbing, two bona fide attempts are made on his life; but before they are made, Baumer is already dead from having drunk, by accident, a glass of poisoned whiskey that he had prepared for the secretary. For Boothe, as doubtless for her audience, Baumer was a surrogate for Hitler. One attempt at murdering him was not enough. The curtain line, though it comes from the heart, draws a laugh. To the Irish Captain of the homicide squad, Finkelstein reports on the triplicate murder. Asks the Captain, "Well, the son of a bitch—Did it kill him?"

James Thurber, Elliott Nugent

In contrast with Boothe's acerbic comedies of life as it is conducted in the upper strata of social, intellectual, and political life, James Thurber and Elliott Nugent's *The Male Animal* makes a bland showing. In structure and the nature of its central situation, the economic insecurity of a young married couple, it was not new. But into the plot of this domestic comedy, which opened in January 1940, the authors inserted an issue new to the period: the intimidation of liberals by ultraconservatives flaunting the shibboleth of "Americanism." At

Midwestern University—unmistakably Ohio State University, from which Thurber and Nugent graduated in 1920—a young associate professor of English, Thomas Turner, intends to read to his class the famous letter of Vanzetti, written after sentencing, on the victory awaiting him and Sacco after death. It is erroneously reported in the campus literary magazine that he has already read the letter to the class, and with this confusion the plot complications begin.

It matters not in the least, so far as his job security is concerned, that Turner does not admire the letter as the product of an avowed anarchist, but only as an example of instinctual compositional style, and that for the same reason he intends to use letters by Abraham Lincoln and General Sherman. What should he do—read the letter to his class and face an irate board of trustees, or deny that he intends to read it? In the first act, when the subject arises, he tells the know-nothing trustee Ed Keller, "I believe that a college should be concerned with ideas, but all ideas." To this Keller replies, "No, sir! That's the *trouble* . . . too damn many ideas floating around. . . . You put ideas of any kind into young people's heads, and the first thing you know, they start believing them." In the third act, when the issue is forced, Turner tells his sympathetic dean,

> Don't you see: this isn't about Vanzetti; this is about us! If I can't teach this letter today, tomorrow none of us will be able to teach anything except what Mr. Keller here and the legislature permit us to teach. Can't you see what that leads to—what it has led to in other places? We're holding the last fortress of free thought, and if we surrender to prejudice and dictation, we're cowards!

Turner's decision meets the joyful approval of his wife and preserves his home life, but will cost him his job. It is a small price for the intellectual liberation that he experiences, and, in any event, the authors, wishing to avoid a sour ending, drop the suggestion that from the publicity that will follow the firing, offers of new posts are sure to come his way.

Though primarily a play about domestic contentment, with Turner's passionate last-act outburst implying a defense of his home and manliness as well as his freedom of speech, the play in retrospect seems more than the sum of its parts. Turner, the man who will not give in, was a fitting representative of the democratic tradition at the moment in time when the European democracies were suffering under threat of a totalitarian onslaught. Moreover, theater workers, as well as other concerned citizens, had already witnessed the assault on constitutional guarantees made by congressional committees during the hearings on the Federal Theater, when hearsay was allowed to pass as evidence and answers were demanded to loaded questions devised by prejudiced investigators. The play was also prophetic, for more such incidents were to follow in the forties. When in the postwar years, beginning in 1947, the inquiries of the Un-American Activities Committee into show business resumed, and on a much broader scale than in 1938, it was as though the Committee wished to wipe out the theatrical achievement of an entire decade, along with the livelihood of those who had created it. That it could not succeed in the destruction on which it seemed bent was owing to the American tradition of respect for the rights of the individual, including the right to dissent from majority opinion, that the playwrights of the thirties had so repeatedly dramatized.

The form, substance, and intensity of imaginative literature has little to do with figures on the calendar, if anything at all. The rounding out of the thirties did not signal a sweeping change in the content of American drama. The major issue before every American at the start of the forties was, of course, the war, but the welling up of passion that it caused in isolationists and interventionists alike had begun, not with the outbreak of shooting in September 1939, but long before. For some it had commenced with the debacle of the Munich conference; for others, with the Spanish Civil War; for still others, with the Italian invasion of Ethiopia or other military and diplomatic depredations even further back in time. Linked to the war were issues both political and economic: whether the United States did or did not have an obligation to join with the Allies in the struggle for European democracy, or whether it was or was not more practical for the United States to ignore the fighting abroad and invest revenue and manpower solely in pump-priming expenditures to raise the national standard of living. Interventionists also found a cause in Germany's virulent anti-Semitism, which had instilled fears within American Jewish circles and overlapping liberal and leftist circles since the beginning of Hitler's rise.

In the two years preceding the attack on Pearl Harbor, Broadway

offered numerous musicals and domestic comedies that had no relation whatever to the drama being enacted on European battlefields
and in European skies. Audiences could see Bert Lahr as a men's
room attendant who dreamed that he was Louis XIV of France, with
Ethel Merman as his mistress, in the Cole Porter musical, *Du Barry
Was a Lady*. They could also see Gertrude Lawrence as the indeci-
sive editor of a fashion magazine desperately attempting to choose
between two designs for the magazine's cover, in Moss Hart's *Lady in
the Dark*, an opulent musical with a score by Kurt Weill. Among the
big nonmusical hits set in the present but lacking relevance to the
war were Rose Franken's *Claudia*, on the growing up of a young
wife; Kaufman and Hart's *George Washington Slept Here*, on the difficulty of renovating a house in the country; Joseph Kesselring's *Ar-
senic and Old Lace*, on the art of murder as practiced by two comically crazy old ladies; Jerome Chodorov and Joseph Field's *My Sister
Eileen* and *Junior Miss* on, respectively, the problems faced by
Midwestern girls ambitious for a career in New York and the problem
of adjusting to adolescence as experienced by New York girls of the
middle class. But these escapist plays represented only one aspect of
the Broadway output.

In the work of concerned playwrights the war and its extension into
the lives of Americans received coverage from an early date. Boothe's
Margin for Error and Sherwood's *There Shall Be No Night*, two of
the earliest works on aspects of the war by Broadway veterans, were
followed by others in the next season. In Elmer Rice's antinazi melodrama, *Flight to the West*, which opened in December 1940, a confrontation of the fascist and democratic mentalities occurs on a Pan
American clipper en route from Lisbon to New York. One of the lines
of the plot stresses the alliance in sympathy, if not yet in arms, between Britain and the United States. Lillian Hellman's *Watch on the
Rhine*, opening in April 1941, offered the audience a suspense plot in
which a German-born antinazi agent returns briefly to the United
States from Europe with his wife and children before setting off again
for Germany and the underground fight. Maxwell Anderson in *Candle
in the Wind*, which opened in October 1941, also unfolded a melodramatic antinazi plot. Set in Occupied France, the play details the determination of an American woman to aid in the escape of her French
lover from a German military prison, though it costs her her own

freedom. Her final speech, hurled at the German commandant, sums up the playwright's argument: "In the history of the world there have been many wars between men and beasts. And the beasts have always lost, and men have won." In the season of 1941–42 appeared three plays by lesser playwrights allowing a share of humanity to the Germans: Norman Krasna's *The Man with Blond Hair*, Fritz Rotter and Allen Vincent's *Letters to Lucerne*, and John Steinbeck's *The Moon Is Down*. All were doomed by this issue to short runs. Of more than routine interest, though also a failure at the box office, was Howard Koch and John Huston's *In Time to Come*, a psychological study of Woodrow Wilson and his dashed hope of a peace kept secure by American membership in the League of Nations, which obliquely made a plea for the restoration of democracy in Europe.

With the rapid deployment of American troops to combat areas after Pearl Harbor, playwrights found that they had a striking new subject. A surprisingly small number of war plays took place in the actual fighting zones, however. Fewer than ten plays by American writers about American troops overseas were staged before the end of the 1944–45 season (the last of the war), though imports from England and Russia added to the number on the general subject of battlefield experience. Only two of the ten achieved long runs, and both were the work of established writers: *The Eve of Saint Mark* by Maxwell Anderson and *Winged Victory* by Moss Hart. Hart's colorful play tracing the military career of three young men aspiring to pilot's wings was written at the request of the Army Air Force and cast with servicemen on special leave. For all the wartime combat plays and those produced in the immediate postwar years, the theme was essentially the same: a plea for respect for the American fighting man as a crusader against antidemocratic forces, coupled with the hope that the liberal, antitotalitarian principles instilled in Americans by the war would continue strong in peacetime. The same theme, which by extension was a plea for an end to intolerance, underlay such disparate works as Sidney Kingsley's *The Patriots*, on the contention between Thomas Jefferson and Alexander Hamilton; S. N. Behrman and Franz Werfel's *Jacobowsky and the Colonel*, on an anti-Semitic Polish colonel's growing respect for a canny Jew as the two make their way through Occupied France; and Edward Chodorov's *Common Ground*, on the decision of a civilian troupe of American entertainers captured in Italy to go to their death rather than perform for the enemy. In *Decision* Chodorov warned against the continuing presence on the home front of native-born fascists. James Gow and Arnaud d'Usseau in the well-received *Tomorrow the World* appealingly dramatized the awakening to an understanding of democracy experienced by a German-born adolescent steeped in the nazi racist belief. The grave distinction between American democracy and the German and Italian versions of fascism was also the topic of Hellman's *The Searching Wind*, in which the author employed flashbacks to chastise the shapers of American diplomacy for adopting a policy of appeasement when the opposite was necessary to curb Hitler and Mussolini.

The dignity and high purpose of these various plays notwithstanding, none was destined for survival in the postwar theater. Out of all the plays of the war years, the total contribution to the standard repertory consisted of only five: the Rodgers-Hammerstein musicals, *Oklahoma!* and *Carousel*, Mary Chase's *Harvey*, a comedy of the fantasy life of an alcoholic, Tennessee Williams's *The Glass Menagerie*, and Thornton Wilder's *The Skin of Our Teeth*. Williams's play touches on the war, but only fleetingly. Wilder, in his antinaturalistic expression of faith in the durability of the human race, deals with war only in the last act of three, and it is not so much *the* war as all war, man's most violent means of acting on his compulsion for self-destruction.

In the first postwar season, 1945–46, the appeal for national unity underlay three plays on the aspirations and rights of blacks: James Gow and Arnaud d'Usseau's *Deep Are the Roots*, Robert Ardrey's *Jeb*, and Maxine Wood's *On Whitman Avenue*. All dealt with the new issue of the returning black serviceman who is faced with the old prejudices and made to question the principles of the country for which he has risked his life. Also in the same season Arthur Laurents's *Home of the Brave* poignantly but optimistically treated a young Jew's troubled reaction to an outburst of anti-Semitism on the battlefield.

Though, as was inevitable, the preeminence of the dramatists who had first made their mark in the twenties and thirties was challenged after the war by writers who had come of age during the Depression, the passing of prominence from one generation to another did not at first bring about an abandonment of the realistic, well-made social-message play. Not only were the new works on minority rights in the form of the well-made play, but in the same familiar mold were such successful postwar pieces as Garson Kanin's *Born Yesterday* (1945) and Arthur Miller's *All My Sons* (1947), respectively a comedy and a tragedy on the familiar question, "What shall it profit a man if he gain the whole world and lose his own soul?" Yet before the end of the war with the arrival on Broadway of Tennessee Williams's *The Glass Menagerie* in March 1945, a somewhat, if not wholly, new dramatic form was revealed that soon proved popular with writers.

Williams, while creating characters who, though rather special, were recognizable human types, developed his play by means of anti-naturalistic stage devices. Through a back-lighted gauze curtain the vision of the audience passed from the exterior of a dwelling to its interior, and as the play progressed alterations in the lighting altered the mood of the action, while music underscored an occasional gesture or passage of dialogue. The result was a subtly introspective play, externalizing the inner life of the characters. It revealed an exceptionally sophisticated talent. Yet Williams's first Broadway plays (setting aside *You Touched Me!*, his adaptation, with Donald Windham, of a story by D. H. Lawrence, produced in 1945), also revealed that the playwright had not passed through the Depression without feeling its mark in his own way. In the Production Notes printed with *The Glass Menagerie,* the work is described as a "memory play," and the time remembered is the nineteen-thirties. The Depression ambience is palpable throughout the play as Amanda Wingfield executes her small-scale strategies for keeping her creditors at bay and making a show of security for the benefit of her introverted daughter. The cast is small, but in its relationships it bears a close resemblance to the larger Berger family of Odets's *Awake and Sing!,* since it too includes a matriarch with a daughter whom she is eager to marry off and a stubborn, restless son. For *A Streetcar Named Desire* (1947) Williams chose a contemporary setting, but seemed still to be affected by the literary class-consciousness of the thirties in his delineation of the outré, haughty Blanche DuBois and her ultimate debasement.

When Arthur Miller adopted the same dramatic technique for *Death of a Salesman* in 1948, the combination of naturalistic and anti-naturalistic elements received a powerful endorsement. Both writers continued to employ it, though Miller abandoned it for *The Crucible* (1953), *Incident at Vichy* (1964), and *The Price* (1968). Other writers to take it up were Truman Capote in *The Grass Harp* (1952), Arthur Laurents in *A Clearing in the Woods* (1957), and Paddy Chayefsky in *The Tenth Man* (1959). Even the master of sharp-focus realism of the thirties, Odets, tried it in his last play, *The Flowering Peach* (1954); the play is not set in the present or recent past, however, but in biblical times, and the characters—Noah and his family—have the Yiddish accent of the twentieth-century Bergers.

As memories of the Depression faded in the glow of the postwar economic gloom, both Williams and Miller became increasingly bent as writers on exploring the inner life of the individual. Neither of them abandoned social issues, to be sure, but set them at the periphery of the action, rather than at the center, as, for example, with Williams's treatment of racism in *Sweet Bird of Youth* (1959) and Miller's treatment of American immigration restrictions in *A View from the Bridge* (1955). The same was true of their followers, though by no means all of the psychological dramatists of the boom years adopted their antinaturalistic devices or did so for every play. Among the most notable of the new psychological plays consistent in their naturalism were Laurents's *The Time of the Cuckoo* (1952), N. Richard Nash's *The Rainmaker* (1954), and Michael V. Gazzo's *A Hatful of Rain* (1955). The cast of these works were studded with performers trained or retrained at the Actors Studio, the center for the development of talent in acting, directing, and playwriting established in 1947 by former members of the Group Theater. Central to the work of the Studio was Stanislavsky's method of acting as interpreted by Lee Strasberg—"the Method," as it became known not only to its practitioners, but to the public. In the Eisenhower years Broadway was the haven of introspective players in introspective plays.

To an extent that, for better or worse, can never be measured, the shift away from social-message drama to plays of the secret self had another cause in addition to the increasing remoteness of the memory of hard times and the artistic influence of Williams. With Cold-War politics fostering a recrudescence of conservatism, social protest in the arts became politically suspect as the forties drew to a close. When in the fall of 1947 the House Un-American Activities Committee, then under the chairmanship of J. Parnell Thomas, initiated an investigation of alleged Communist party infiltration of Hollywood, it set off an alarmist movement that soon touched all branches of show business. Of the ten balky, "unfriendly" directors and writers subpoenaed for the first round of hearings and unwilling to discuss their politics, two had figured prominently in the theater of the thirties: John Howard Lawson and Albert Maltz. With the refusal of the film industry to contest either the methods of the Committee in questioning witnesses, which had not altered since the uproar over the Federal Arts Projects, or the practicality of the hearings as a means of combating subversion, the Committee went on to pursue its quarry not only among Hollywood employees, but persons working in the broadcasting industry and on the legitimate stage.

With the vigorous entry of Senator Joseph R. McCarthy into the fray, the method of blackening a reputation through unfounded allegations and veiled hints came to be called "McCarthyism." Though not so frequently as HUAC, McCarthy's subcommittee of the Senate Internal Security Committee also questioned show-business figures, including the popular Judy Holliday. Blacklists of uncooperative witnesses were soon established by both the film and broadcasting industries, though never acknowledged. Threats of the boycotts of products by store-owners and consumers put fear into the hearts of radio and television sponsors that an individual suspected of being subversive might be employed on their programs. A potent document aiding in the development of the broadcasting blacklist was *Red Channels,* a publication of 1950 issued by a group called American Business Consultants. This was a book-length list of 151 persons in broadcasting alleged to have belonged to or supported politically suspect organizations. Those who could not or would not clear themselves of the charges soon became unemployable.

The Committee-room manner of the scores of individuals subpoenaed by HUAC and the Senate Internal Security subcommittee varied greatly, as became evident when Congress published records of the hearings. It ranged from the aplomb of Elia Kazan, who reported on his own period of membership in the Communist party and identified other members of the party faction in the Group Theater, to the quiet tenseness of Gale Sondergaard, the near-hysteria of Jack Gilford and Lionel Stander, and the comicality of Will Geer, who were not cooperative. Geer, seeming to pity Representative Bernard W. Kearney for having to investigate un-American activities rather than being free to look into the causes of the high cost of living, remarked, "We all of us have to appear in a turkey once in a while." [31] Of the many writers questioned, two of the most prestigious, Lillian Hellman and Arthur Miller, refused to reveal the names of those they knew to be or suspected of being party members. Among the writers who cooperated were Michael Blankfort and Clifford Odets, both of whom were enjoying well-paid careers as screenwriters when subpoenaed in 1952. Odets seemed to offer a parable of his situation in *The Flowering Peach* when at the close, after the landing of the Ark on Ararat, Noah, decides to make his home with his obsessively material-minded eldest son, Shem. "Why?" he rhetorically asks. "It's more comfortable" (scene 9).

The sorry episode of McCarthyism, which lasted through the fifties, did not, of course, wipe out the memory of the achievement of the putative one-time Marxists of the theater. The record of their work remained, though victims of the blacklist suffered a devastating loss of income and one actor, Philip Loeb, who committed suicide in 1955, was presumed to have ended his life of despondency over the cessation of his television career. The published plays of blacklisted writers continued to be available in libraries, and the films that they and other blacklisted Hollywood employees had helped to create continued to be unreeled on late-night television, with no removal of their names from the credits. For those figures of marketable talent, such as Kazan and Odets, who had given way under pressure from HUAC, professional life went on as before. Broadway, moreover, did not maintain a blacklist. To the extent that their abilities were needed, writers and performers unable to get work in the broadcasting and film industries were welcome in the legitimate theater. Meanwhile, for those major theatrical figures such as Clurman, Strasberg, and Crawford, who had associated with party members, but were known to have held with the liberal center and, therefore, were never subpoenaed, professional life also remained active. Thus, despite the replacement of hard times by affluence and the about-face in the national political philosophy from liberal to conservative, no true break with the past was allowed to occur, and the hard-won skills of the thirties lent vitality to the stage, not only of the forties, but of the fifties and early sixties. That the influence of the theater of the thirties should start to fade at last in the late sixties was only natural, as young writers and directors born after the Depression began an intense search for fresh, unexpected forms of expression. But that is another story.

The following abbreviations are used in the notes:

DW: *Daily Worker*
ETJ: *Educational Theatre Journal*
FT: *Federal Theatre*
HUAC: *House Un-American Activities Committee*
N: *Nation*
NM: *New Masses*
NR: *New Republic*
NT: *New Theatre*
NTF: *New Theatre and Film*
NTN: *New Theatre News*
NY: *New Yorker*
NYPL-TC: *New York Public Library Theatre Collection*
NYT: *New York Times*
TA: *Theatre Arts; Theatre Arts Monthly*
SW: *Sunday Worker*
WT: *Workers Theatre*

NOTES

CHAPTER 1

1. It is well known, however, that O'Neill intended the ending of his play to be less promising of a happy future than it appears to be in the theater. In a letter to the Dramatic Editor, *NYT*, Dec. 18, 1921, Sec. 6, p. 1, he maintained that his characters were merely pausing before heading into an uncertain, not necessarily comfortable life.

2. According to the will of Joseph Pulitzer, who endowed the prizes, each winning play was to "best represent the educational value and power of the stage in raising the standard of good morals, good taste, and good manners," but in 1928 the Advisory Board of the Columbia University School of Journalism, which awards the prizes, dropped the stipulation on manners, taste, and morals.

3. However, Sophie Treadwell's *Machinal* (1928), an expressionistic treatment of the Ruth Snyder-Judd Grey murder case, has survived in college productions and an off-Broadway revival of 1960.

4. John Gassner, ed., *Twenty-Five Best Plays of the Modern American Theater*, Early Series (New York, 1949), p. 530.

5. Unless otherwise indicated, all lengths of runs throughout are taken from the annual *Best Plays* volumes, ed. Burns Mantle. Important exceptions are the runs of the New Playwrights' Theater, which are taken from the end-of-season statistics provided by *NYT*. For the New Playwrights' runs, the authors' correspondence with their patron, Otto H. Kahn, suggests that *NYT* is the more trustworthy of the two sources. Generally the sources do agree, but only Mantle provides statistics on plays running a second season or more.

6. Gathered by Wilson in *The Shores of Light* (New York, 1952).

7. John Dos Passos, "The American Theater: 1930–31," *NR*, April 1, 1931, p. 171.

8. See Huntly Carter, *The New Theatre and Cinema of Soviet Russia* (London, 1924) and Oliver M. Sayler, *The Russian Theatre Under the Revolution* (Boston, 1920). Gold reported on his trip in "Theatre and Revolution," *N*, Nov. 11, 1925, pp. 19–21. Lawson much later remarked that he and the other New Playwrights had been impressed by the International Theatrical Exposition; see Mardi Valgemae, "Civil War Among the Expressionists: John Howard Lawson and the *Pinwheel* Controversy," *ETJ*, Mar. 1968, p. 10.

9. Helen Deutsch and Stella Hanau, *The Provincetown: A Story of the Theatre* (New York, 1931), p. 42.

10. Michael Gold, "Strike!," *NM*, July 1926, pp. 19–21.

11. Ben Blake, the early historian of the militant drama of the thirties, refers to this group as the Workers' Drama League and attributes to it a production of Karl Wittfogel's *The Biggest Boob in the World*. See Ben Blake, *The Awakening of the American Theatre* (New York, 1935), pp. 10–11.

12. "Workers Art," *NM*, Oct. 1929, p. 29.

13. Where it opened on February 3, 1927, to mixed reviews. Not satisfied with this production, the New Playwrights wanted to restage and produce it themselves, but could not afford to; see letter, Dos Passos and Lawson to Kahn, April 22, 1927, in Otto H. Kahn Papers, Princeton University Library.

14. Deutsch and Hanau, *The Provincetown*, p. 139.

15. Letters, Basshe to Kahn, Jan. 5, 1926; Kahn to Basshe, Jan. 6, 1926; Gold to Kahn, c. Dec. 1, 1926; Kahn to Gold, Dec. 2, 1926; Gold to Kahn, Jan. 3, Jan. 5, 1927, in Kahn Papers, Princeton.

16. Otto H. Kahn, *Of Many Things* (New York, 1926), p. 100.

17. Letters, Basshe to Kahn, April–Aug. 1927; Kahn to Gold, Jan. 14, 1927; exchanges between the "Class Enemy" and the "Emperor," Gold and Kahn, letters 1927–1929, *passim*, in Kahn Papers, Princeton.

18. Letters, Gold to Kahn, June 16, 1928; July 16, 1929. Dos Passos was not at the famous luncheon; see letter, Gold and Basshe to Kahn, April 22, 1927, in Kahn Papers, Princeton.

19. The certificate lists as directors Lawson, Gold, Faragoh, Basshe, and one Julia Cohn, but not Dos Passos, who was out of the country; Kahn Papers, Princeton. Dos Passos did, however, become a member of the company's board and was listed on the stationery and in programs. In the second season Paul Sifton was made a member of the board, and the writer Aben Kandel, the director Edward Massey, and the attorney Philip Wittenberg became associate directors.

20. Basshe, "The Revolt on Fifty-Second Street," *NYT*, Feb. 27, 1927, Sec. 7, p. 4.

21. The choreographer was Leonard Sillman, later well-known as the producer of the *New Faces* revues on Broadway.

22. Atkinson, "The Play," *NYT*, Feb. 18, 1928, p. 10. The play was published in *The American Caravan*, ed. Van Wyck Brooks et al. (New York,

1927), pp. 548–626. From the stage directions, it appears that Gold originally intended all the parts, including white characters, to be acted by blacks.

23. Dos Passos, "Did the New Playwrights Fail?" *NM*, Aug. 1929, p. 13.

24. Letter, Basshe to Kahn, March 6, 1929, in Kahn Papers, Princeton.

25. Sinclair, letter to the Editor, *NR*, Feb. 13, 1929, p. 167.

26. Dos Passos, "Looking Back on 'U.S.A.,'" *NYT*, Oct. 25, 1959, Sec. 2, p. 5. In *The Best Times* (New York, 1966), his memoir, Dos Passos passes very briefly over the New Playwrights' Theater, but mentions (p. 198), the "wearing daily struggle" of contending with adherents to the ˈparty line.

27. Irving Howe and Lewis Coser, *The American Communist Party*, (Boston, 1957), pp. 240–41.

28. Basshe to Kahn, March 6, 1929, in Kahn Papers, Princeton.

29. A financial statement of the New Playwrights' Theater as of April 23, 1928, lists a series of seven loans totaling to this amount. The last item is a loan of $5,600 dated Dec. 30, 1927. No other loans were ever recorded. On May 10, 1928, Kahn offered another $5,000, but this was not accepted. Financial statements in Kahn Papers, Princeton.

30. Gold, "A New Masses Theatre," *NM*, Nov. 1927, p. 23; Kandel, letter to the Drama Editor, *NYT*, Nov. 6, 1927, Sec. 9, p. 4.

31. Clurman, *The Fervent Years: The Story of the Group Theatre and the Thirties* (New York, 1945), p. 16.

32. Dos Passos, Lawson, and Faragoh to Kahn, April 22, 1927, in Kahn Papers, Princeton. *Fiesta* was presented by the Provincetown in 1929.

33. Atkinson, "The Play," *NYT*, March 3, 1927, p. 27; "The Play," *NYT*, Oct. 20, 1927, p. 33; Young, "Playwrights and Causes," *NR*, Dec. 27, 1927, pp. 139–40; Taggard, "Life Is a Welter," *NM*, Jan. 1928, p. 27; Bernard Smith, "Machines and Mobs," *NM*, March 1928, p. 27; Lewis Rogers, "Singing Jailbirds," *NM*, Jan. 1929, p. 15; Woollcott, cited by Clurman, *The Fervent Years*, p. 19.

34. Gold to Kahn, c. Oct. 31, 1929, in Kahn Papers, Princeton.

35. Kahn to Basshe, Nov. 21, 1928, in Kahn Papers, Princeton.

CHAPTER 2

1. Michael Gold, "A New Program for Writers," *NM*, Jan. 1930, p. 21.

2. "Workers' Art," *NM*, Oct. 1929, p. 29. Almost invariably front organizations omitted the apostrophe to denote the possessive or were inconsistent in using it.

3. Blake, *The Awakening of the American Theatre*, p. 20.

4. Frances Perkins, *The Roosevelt I Knew* (New York, 1946), p. 182.

5. Quoted from *DW* in Irving Howe and Lewis Coser, *The American Communist Party*, p. 190.

6. Whittaker Chambers, *Witness* (New York, 1952), p. 256.

7. Will Lee, "Mr. Box, Mr. Fox, and Mr. Nox," *WT*, Nov. 1931, p. 20.

8. Blake, *The Awakening of the American Theatre*, p. 20.

9. *Ibid.*, p. 18.

10. See Huntly Carter, *The New Spirit in the Russian Theatre, 1917–1928* (New York, 1929), pp. 204, 260–61.

11. "Dedication," *WT*, April 1931, p. 3.

12. Michael Gold, *120 Million* (New York, 1929), p. 173.

13. Blake, *The Awakening of the American Theatre*, p. 16. The passage quoted by Blake differs somewhat from the translation published in *WT*, April 1932, pp. 14–17. For the chant *Daily Worker*, see *WT*, July 1931, p. 18.

14. *WT*, April 1931, p. 15.

15. The staff of the magazine was divided over the question of whether or not to put an apostrophe after *Workers*. *Usually* they omitted it.

16. Blake, *The Awakening of the American Theatre*, p. 21.

17. "The Charkhov Converence of Revolutionary Writers," *NM*, Feb. 1931, p. 7; John E. Bonn, "Workers Theatre," *WT*, Aug. 1931, pp. 1–2; Sept. 1931, pp. 3–5; H. Shapiro, "Report of the Cultural Convention," *WT*, Aug. 1931, pp. 7–8.

18. Blake, *The Awakening of the American Theatre*, p. 24.

19. Sidney Ball, "Review of *Precedent*," *WT*, May 1931, pp. 5b–6b. A. Prentis, "Dos Passos on the Theatre," *WT*, June 1931, p. 10; A. Prentis, "Our Theatre is Born," *WT*, Dec. 1931, pp. 5–6; A. Saks, "Can You Hear Their Voices?," *WT*, Jan. 1932, p. 3; "Correspondence," *WT*, Feb. 1932, pp. 36–37.

20. H. Shapiro, "Training the Actor for the Proletarian Theatre," *WT*, July 1931, p. 3.

21. Blake, *The Awakening of the American Theatre*, pp. 24–26; John E. Bonn, "Dram Buro Report," *WT*, May 1932, p. 7.

22. *WT*, May–June 1933, p. 18.

23. "Look! Look! Look!," *WT*, Aug. 1932, pp. 4–6; Saxe, "A Play with Propaganda," *ibid.*, pp. 7–8.

24. "A Caution on Repertory," *WT*, July–Aug. 1933, p. 13.

25. Rose Beigel, "Well, Here They Are . . . ," *WT*, Jan.–Feb. 1933, p. 2; Nathaniel Buchwald, "Marion Models, Inc.," *NT*, July–Aug. 1934, pp. 11, 30; Jack Shapiro, "Theatre Collective," *NT*, Oct. 1934, p. 15; "Shifting Scenes," *NT*, Feb. 1935, p. 27.

26. Blake, *The Awakening of the American Theatre*, p. 60.

27. An undated mimeographed pamphlet titled "Facts about the New Theatre League" in NYPL-TC, probably published in late 1935, lists seventeen members of the League's National Executive Board, of whom these five seem to have been the most active. Among the others were John Howard Lawson, Ann Howe, and Molly Day Thacher, the wife of Elia Kazan.

28. "Workers' Art," *NM*, July 1931, p. 22.

29. Potamkin, "Film and Photo Call to Action," *WT*, July 1931, pp. 5–7.

30. Edna Ocko, "The Revolutionary Dance Movement," *NM*, June 12,

1934, p. 27; Louise Redfield, "A Survey of the New Dance League," *The Proceedings of the National Congress and Festival 1936* (New York, 1936), p. 75.

31. Ann Burlak, "Dance Notes," *NT*, Nov. 1934, p. 29.

32. A. Prentis, "Towards the Revolutionary Dance. The New Dance Group Holds Its First Anniversary Recital," *WT*, May–June 1933, p. 11; Gold, "Change the World," *DW*, June 14, 1934, p. 5; Edna Ocko, "Reply to Michael Gold," *NT*, July–Aug. 1934, p. 28.

33. John Martin, "The Dance: To the N[ew] D[ance] L[eague]," *NYT*, June 16, 1935, Sec. 10, p. 4.

34. Quoted in Hollie Flanagan, *Dynamo* (New York, 1943), pp. 109–10.

35. A. Saks, "*Can You Hear Their Voices?*," *WT*, Jan. 1932, pp. 2–5; Blake, pp. 29, 31.

36. Hughes, "Scottsboro Limited," *NM*, Nov. 1931, p. 19.

37. *Ibid.*, p. 21.

38. Also included in the anthology were Odets's *Waiting for Lefty* and excerpts from Albert Maltz's *Black Pit*, Paul Peters and George Sklar's *Stevedore*, and John Wexley's *They Shall Not Die*.

39. Richard Pack, "Shock Troupe in Action," *NT*, Nov. 1934, pp. 13, 33; Peter Martin, "Montage," *NT*, March 1934, pp. 8–10; Saxe, "Newsboy—from Script to Performance," *NT*, July–Aug. 1934, pp. 12–13, 29; Saxe, "A Play with Propaganda," *WT*, Aug. 1932, p. 7. Martin, who sees the influence of the Jooss Ballet, does not refer to specific works by Kurt Jooss, but presumably had in mind *The Big City*. See A. V. Coton, *The New Ballet: Kurt Jooss and His Work* (London, 1946), pp. 40–45.

40. See "International Workers' Theatre Olympiad," *NT*, April 1934, p. 15.

41. Mimeograph copy in NYPL-TC. This version promotes the sale of *Fight Against War and Fascism*.

42. Saxe, "Newsboy—from Script to Performance," p. 29.

43. *Ibid.*, pp. 12–13.

44. Marvin, "Workers Theatre Marches," *NM*, May 8, 1934, p. 29.

45. Stephen Karnot, "From a Director's Notebook," *NT*, Sept. 1934, p. 13; Max Eastman, *Artists in Uniform* (New York, 1934), pp. 15–16.

46. Editorial, *NT*, June 1934, pp. 3–4.

47. Smith and Kazan, "Dimitroff," *NT*, July–Aug. 1934, p. 24.

48. HUAC, Hearings, *Communist Infiltration of the Hollywood Motion Picture Industry*, Part 6 (Washington, 1952), pp. 3483–484.

49. Harold Clurman, *The Fervent Years*, pp. 147–48.

50. Odets, "Waiting for Lefty," *NT*, Feb. 1935, p. 20.

51. By Odets's count, *Lefty* played simultaneously in some sixty American cities in 1935. See Odets, "America Is Waiting for Lefty" [letter], *International Literature*, No. 9, 1935, p. 107.

52. Odets, "Waiting for Lefty," *NT*, Feb. 1935, p. 18.

53. Clurman, *The Fervent Years*, p. 148.

54. For an extended account of the work behind this production, see John Houseman, *Run-Through* (New York, 1972), pp. 147–64. Houseman and Zatkin's Phoenix Theater is not to be confused with the long-lived producing unit of the same name founded by T. Edward Hambleton and Norris Houghton in 1953.

55. "Mather," Review of MacLeish, *Poems, 1924–33*, *NM*, Jan. 16, 1934; Edwin Rolfe, "An Interview with Archibald MacLeish," *DW*, March 15, 1935, p. 5. Hicks identified himself as the reviewer in a letter to the present writer of Feb. 27, 1961.

56. Jerome, "Archibald MacLeish's *Panic*," *NM*, April 2, 1935, pp. 43–44.

57. I have been unable to find a copy of this play. See Nathaniel Buchwald, " 'The Real McCoy,' Says Critic of Thrilling CCC Camp Play," *DW*, March 31, 1935, p. 5; Herbert Kline, "The Young Go First," *NT*, July 1935, p. 30.

58. MacLeish, "Theatre Against War and Facism," *NT*, Aug. 1935, p. 3.

CHAPTER 3

1. Michael Gold, "Stevedore," *NM*, May 1, 1934, p. 28; Mordecai Gorelik, *New Theatres for Old* (New York, 1940), p. 403. This chapter and Chapter VIII, also on the Theater Union, were read in draft by George Sklar, who not only saved me from errors, but added to the knowledge of the company that I had gathered from other sources. As a source of information he is identified in the notes as "GS."

2. Paul Peters, "A Birthday on Fourteenth Street," *DW*, Dec. 2, 1935, p. 5; GS.

3. Quoted in Blake, *The Awakening of the American Theatre*, p. 35.

4. Peters, "A Birthday on Fourteenth Street." Among the other members were John Dos Passos, John Howard Lawson, Elmer Rice, Edmund Wilson, Mary Heaton Vorse, Morrie Ryskind, and Lewis Mumford.

5. Charles R. Walker, "Theatre on the Left," *N*, June 24, 1939, p. 730.

6. Oak, "Theatre Union Replies," *NT*, Nov. 1934, p. 12. This was in response to John Howard Lawson, "Straight from the Shoulder," in the same number of *NT*, pp. 11–12. It should be pointed out that in fact the League Against War and Fascism had strong ties to the Party.

7. Paul Peters was the pseudonym of Harbor Allen. In the late twenties Allen was a staff member of the *New Masses*. In Dec. 1926 the magazine published his talented one-act atheist play, *Mr. God Is Not In*, intended, according to a note, for the "Workers' Theatre." I have not been able to discover whether it was produced.

8. *NM*, March 6, 1934, p. 20.

9. "Collective Drama at the Civic Repertory Theatre," *Brooklyn Eagle*, March 29, 1936, p. 17. Years later Michael Blankfort in a section of his novel *A Time to Live* (New York, 1943), pp. 58–73, gave the impression that outside—that is, Communist party—advice was occasionally sought on script revisions; according to Sklar, however, neither he, Maltz, nor Peters ever did this (GS).

10. Sklar in conversation with the present writer; Clurman, *The Fervent Years*, p. 83. Peters and Walker collaborated on a play about the veterans' Bonus March on Washington of 1932, a fragment of which was published as "Get That Bonus," *NM*, Dec. 1932, pp. 22–23.

11. Blankfort, "Behind the Scenes of 'Stevedore,'" *DW*, April 27, 1934, p. 5.

12. Gold, "Stevedore."

13. On this attempt, see "A Playgoer's Afterthoughts," *Stage*, June 1932, pp. 5–8.

14. Sklar, "Negro Actors in the Theatre Union Play, 'Stevedore,'" *DW*, May 9, 1934, p. 5.

15. "Desdemona Waters," *Stage*, Nov. 1934, p. 25.

16. Sklar, "Negro Actors . . ."; Blankfort, "Facing the New Audience," *NT*, Nov. 1934, p. 25. According to Sklar, in conversation with the present writer, Robinson's exuberant gesture was planned in advance.

17. Sender Garlin, "Paul Peters—Revolutionary Playwright—an Interview," *DW*, May 15, 1934, p. 5.

18. Krutch, "Drama," *N*, May 2, 1934, p. 516.

19. Gold, "Stevedore."

20. Lawson, "Straight from the Shoulder," p. 12.

21. Oak, "Theatre Union Replies."

22. Michael Blankfort, Foreword, Wolf, *The Sailors of Cattaro*, trans. Wallis and adapted by Blankfort (New York, 1935), p. v. The article "The" in the title seems to have been used only in this printed version.

23. Molly Day Thacher, "Revolutionary Staging for Revolutionary Plays," *NT*, July–Aug. 1934, p. 26.

24. Oak, "Theatre Union Replies."

25. Maltz, "Man on a Road," *NM*, Jan. 8, 1935, pp. 19–21. Two months after the opening he published "Dramatists in the Coalfields," *NM*, May 14, 1935, pp. 27–28.

26. Reeve, "Despicable Role of a Scab," *DW*, March 23, 1935, p. 7; North, "Theatre Union's 'Black Pit,'" *NM*, April 2, 1935, p. 43; Stachel, "On the Theatre Union's Black Pit," *DW*, April 29, 1935, p. 5; North, "Joseph North Answers Jack Stachel on 'Black Pit,'" *DW*, April 30, 1935, p. 5.

27. The play was never produced by the Theater Union, but was acted by the Theater Collective on New Theater Night bills of February 3 and 24, 1935.

28. Emery Northup, "Meet the Theatre Union," *NT*, Feb. 1934, pp. 8–10; Molly Day Thacher, "Revolutionary Staging for Revolutionary Plays," *NT*, July–Aug. 1934, p. 26; "Strength in the Theatre Union," *NYT*, Dec. 9, 1934, Sec. 10, p. 2; "Actors Arrested in Store Picketing," *NYT*, Feb. 10, 1935, p. 17.

29. Margaret Larkin, "Theatre Union—Its Tasks and Problems," *DW*, May 15, 1935, p. 5.

30. *American Writers' Congress*, ed. Henry Hart (New York, 1935), pp. 11–12, 180.

31. Blankfort and Buchwald, "Social Trends in Modern Drama," *American Writers' Congress*, pp. 133–34.

CHAPTER 4

1. Clurman, "Group Theatre's Future, *NYT*, May 18, 1941, Sec. 9, pp. 1–2.

2. Clurman, "The Group Theatre Speaks for Itself," *NYT*, Dec. 13, 1931, Sec. 8, p. 2.

3. Clurman, *The Fervent Years*, pp. 22–23, 33–36. Any account of the Group Theater must depend heavily on Clurman's memoir, a full report of the company's activities. Few details in the present chapter are taken from other sources, for Clurman omits nothing of importance.

4. *Ibid.*, pp. 22–24.

5. *Ibid.*, pp. 26–28.

6. "Theatre," *Time*, April 8, 1935, pp. 48–49.

7. Clurman, *The Fervent Years*, p. 27.

8. *Ibid.*, pp. 31–38.

9. *Ibid.*, pp. 11, 35, 42–45.

10. *Ibid.*, p. 38; Robert Lewis interview, Columbia University Oral History Project.

11. Clurman, *The Fervent Years*, p. 111.

12. Clurman, *ibid.*, pp. 64, 79–82; "Name Advisory Board," *NYT*, Oct. 29, 1931, p. 26.

13. Clurman, *The Fervent Years*, p. 35; Gorelik, *New Theatres for Old* (New York, 1940), p. 243.

14. Clurman, *The Fervent Years*, pp. 47–48, 55. Another Guild stipulation for full backing was that the parts to be played by Mary Morris and Morris Carnovsky be given to other actors.

15. *Ibid.*, p. 77.

16. Group Theater Scrapbooks, NYPL-TC.

17. Clurman, *The Fervent Years*, pp. 71–72.

18. *Ibid.*, pp. 106–7, 155.

19. *Ibid.*, pp. 84, 91–93.

20. *Ibid.*, p. 98.

21. *Ibid.*, p. 141.

22. Letter, Dawn Powell to the present writer, Sept. 20, 1959.

23. Clurman, *The Fervent Years*, p. 129. Not all the profits went to the company from this substantial hit, however, for the Group produced it in association with Sidney Harmon and James R. Ullman, who owned the production rights, and Lee Shubert, who had shown it to the Group directors on their behalf and acted as a silent partner.

24. *Ibid.*, p. 125.

25. Not the least of these was the Marx Brothers' *A Day at the Races*

(1937), in which the comedians make elaborate preparations for an operation on Margaret Dumont.

26. *NM*, April 10, 1934, pp. 28–29.

27. Lawson, " 'Inner Conflict' and Proletarian Art," *NM*, April 17, 1934, pp. 29–30.

28. Lawson, *With a Reckless Preface* (New York, 1934), pp. viii–ix.

29. Levy, "The World of the Theatre," *DW*, March 28, 1934, p. 4.

30. Lawson, "Straight from the Shoulder," *NT*, Nov. 1934, p. 12; Lawson, "Biographical Notes," *Zeitschrift für Anglistik und Amerikanistik*, Heft 1 (1956), p. 74.

31. Clurman, *The Fervent Years*, pp. 133–34. See also Clurman, "Foreword: A Preface to John Howard Lawson," Lawson, *With a Reckless Preface*, pp. xix–xxv, in which Clurman writes of Lawson as "the most promising playwright in America."

32. Clurman, *The Fervent Years*, p. 135.

33. "The Group Theatre Returns to the Country," *NYT*, Sept. 9, 1934, Sec. 9, p. 1 (italics added).

34. Krutch, "Drama," *N*, Dec. 12, 1934, p. 694.

35. Clurman, *The Fervent Years*, pp. 138–39.

36. *Ibid.*, pp. 143–45.

37. John McCarten, "Revolution's Number One Boy," *NY*, Jan. 22, 1938, pp. 23–24.

38. Clurman, *The Fervent Years*, pp. 104, 131, 144; Molly Day Thacher, "Revolutionary Staging for Revolutionary Plays," *NT*, July–Aug. 1934, p. 26; HUAC, Hearings, *Communist Infiltration of the Hollywood Motion Picture Industry*, Part 6 (Washington, 1952), pp. 3462–472.

39. *Awake and Sing!* had previously been optioned by the producer Frank Merlin, who was unable to raise money for the production; Edith J. R. Isaacs, "Clifford Odets," *TA*, April 1939, pp. 257–58.

40. Nathaniel Buchwald, "World of the Theatre," *DW*, Feb. 20, 1935, p. 5; Michael Blankfort, "The Theatre," *NM*, March 5, 1935, p. 28.

41. Joseph Wood Krutch, "Awake and Sing," *N*, March 13, 1935, p. 314; Stark Young, "Awake and Whistle at Least," *NR*, March 13, 1935, p. 134.

42. Clurman, *The Fervent Years*, pp. 149–50; Introduction, *Awake and Sing!*, Odets, *Six Plays* (New York, 1939), p. 421.

43. Clurman, *The Fervent Years*, pp. 127–28. A typescript of *I Got the Blues* is on file at the Library of Congress.

44. Clurman, *The Fervent Years*, p. 152. Weiskopf's story was published in the *NM* column "Voices from Germany," Nov. 6, 1934, p. 13; it was part of a longer work, *Those Who Are Stronger*. Billinger's "In the Nazis' Torture House" appeared in *NM*, Jan. 1, 1935, p. 20. On Odets's use of Billinger see Gerald Weales, *Clifford Odets: Playwright* (New York, 1971), pp. 85–86.

45. Clurman, *The Fervent Years*, p. 156; Odets, "America Is Waiting for Lefty," *International Literature*, No. 9, 1935, p. 107; Helen Sheridan,

"New Leader Attack on 'Waiting for Lefty,'" *DW*, March 27, 1935, p. 5; Manngreen, "Left on Broadway," *DW*, Jan. 2, 1939, p. 7.

46. "Group Theatre Night" (advertisement), *NM*, Feb. 5, 1935, inside back cover; Clurman, *The Fervent Years*, p. 148.

47. *American Writers' Congress*, ed. Hart, p. 188.

48. Odets, "What Happened to Us in Cuba," *NM*, July 16, 1935, pp. 9–10; Odets, "Machine Gun Reception," Carlton Beals and Clifford Odets, *Rifle Fire in Cuba* (New York, 1935), pp. 11–29; HUAC, Hearings, *Communist Infiltration of the Hollywood Motion Picture Industry*, Part 6, p. 3469.

49. "Theatre," *Time*, April 8, 1935, p. 49.

50. HUAC, Hearings, *Communist Infiltration of the Hollywood Motion Picture Industry*.

51. "Theatre," *Time*, April 8, 1935, p. 49.

CHAPTER 5

1. Lawrence Langner, *The Magic Curtain* (New York, 1951), pp. 90–104; Louis Sheaffer, *O'Neill, Son and Playwright* (Boston, 1968), pp. 343–46.

2. Information in this and the following paragraph is taken from Langner, *passim*, and Theresa Helburn, *A Wayward Quest* (Boston, 1960), *passim*. Neither volume of memoirs is wholly satisfactory, but Langner's is the more specific and trustworthy. Writing while recuperating from a heart attack, and with an aide, Helburn is vague and frequently inaccurate.

3. Walter Prichard Eaton, *The Theatre Guild: The First Ten Years* (New York, 1929), pp. 3–4; Langner, pp. 261–62. For a list of Guild productions see Norman Nadel, *A Pictorial History of the Theatre Guild* (New York, 1969), pp. 278–87.

4. Langner, *The Magic Curtain*, pp. 212–17, 224–25.

5. *Ibid.*, pp. 211–13; Helburn, *A Wayward Quest*, pp. 197–99.

6. That the Guild's Board of Managers needed a generous endowment of patience in dealing with these insurgents is evident in Helburn, *A Wayward Quest*, pp. 218–25.

7. Robert Hogan, *Arthur Miller* (Minneapolis, 1964), p. 7.

8. Helburn, *A Wayward Quest*, p. 214.

9. Clurman, *The Fervent Years*, pp. 25–26.

10. Helburn, *A Wayward Quest*, pp. 98–99.

11. *The Theatre Guild Anthology* (New York, 1936), Introduction, p. xi.

12. *Ibid.*

13. Myra Page, "'Roar China'—a Stinging Anti-Imperialist Play," *DW*, Nov. 15, 1930, p. 4.

14. H. F. Garten, *Modern German Drama* (London, 1959), pp. 181–82.

15. These were the most radical of the Guild's European plays, but not the only ones to air political, economic, and social questions. Among the others, the most noteworthy were Shaw's *The Apple Cart, Too True to Be*

Good, and *The Simpleton of the Unexpected Isles,* and Denis Johnston's *The Moon in the Golden River.*

16. Clurman, *The Fervent Years,* p. 94.

17. Behrman received screen credits for work on the following Garbo pictures: *Queen Christina* (1933), *Anna Karenina* (1935), *Conquest* (1937), *Two-Faced Woman* (1941).

18. Behrman, *Three Plays* (New York, 1934), p. 113.

19. Behrman, *People in a Diary* (Boston, 1972), pp. 121–26.

20. Behrman, *Rain from Heaven* (New York, 1934), Prefatory Note, pp. 7–13.

21. *The Theatre Guild Anthology,* Introduction, p. ix.

22. On Feb. 15, 1934, six days before the opening of *They Shall Not Die,* occurred the opening of another play on the Scottsboro case, Dennis Donoghue's *Legal Murder.* The play was presented by A. J. Allen Productions and ran only 8 performances.

23. Gold, "Change the World," *DW,* April 11, 1934, p. 5.

24. Behrman, Gilbert Seldes, Max Eastman, "Why the Propaganda Play?," *Stage,* Dec. 1934, p. 16.

25. Edwin F. Melvin, "Darkness for Next Week on Boston Stages," undated clipping from Boston *Transcript* in Harvard University Theater Collection.

26. Atkinson, "The Play," *NYT,* May 21, 1935, p. 22.

27. Included in the typescripts of material from *Parade* in NYPL-TC and the Theater Guild Papers, Yale University Library. Sketches from *Parade* were published in *NT,* June 1935, pp. 5–9, and in *Skits and Sketches* (New York, 1938), pp. 74–88 (a New Theater League publication).

28. Langner, *The Magic Curtain,* p. 263.

CHAPTER 6

1. Mantle, ed. *The Best Plays of 1929–30* (New York, 1930), p. vi.

2. *Ibid.,* p. v.

3. From the annual seasonal statistics of *NYT.*

4. "Actors' Dining Club Opens to Capacity," *NYT,* Dec. 8, 1931, p. 36; "Stage Relief Drive Will Begin Tuesday," *NYT,* Dec. 8, 1932, p. 25; B. Reines, "The Breadline Comes to Broadway," *WT,* Feb. 1932, pp. 10–12.

5. "Code for Clothing Sets 40-Hour Week," *NYT,* July 23, p. 5.

6. For a look at the new "gold rush" from the viewpoint of Broadway insiders, see the first of the collaborations of George S. Kaufman and Moss Hart, *Once in a Lifetime* (1930).

7. Clark, Foreword, Bein, *Little Ol' Boy* (New York, 1935), pp. x–xi.

8. Gorney later remembered that Harburg did not invent the title, but got the phrase from a young man who addressed the question to him in Central Park. Jay Gorney interview, Columbia Oral History Project.

9. Clark, Foreword, Bein, *Little Ol' Boy,* pp. ix, xi; Clurman, *The Fervent Years,* pp. 93–94.

10. See above, p. 429, note 13.

11. In 1969 the title "Harlem on My Mind" was borrowed by the Metropolitan Museum of Art for the name of a photographic survey of the New York ghetto. When black militants, recalling the substance of the song, voiced their disapproval (and went on to disapprove of the exhibition in general), the Museum's staff was taken by surprise.

12. H. Elion, "The Negro on Broadway," *WT*, Nov. 1931, p. 1.

13. After the closing, *NYT* editorialized that the common denominator of the two plays, and the reason for their great popularity, was that both were plays of home and family life; "Topics of the Times," *NYT*, June 3, 1941, p. 20.

14. Atkinson, "The Play," *NYT*, Dec. 5, 1933, p. 31. See also Robert Benchley, "The Theatre," *NY*, Dec. 30, 1933, pp. 30–31; Joseph Wood Krutch, "Drama," *N*, Dec. 20, 1933, p. 718.

15. Caldwell, Introduction, Kirkland, *Tobacco Road* (New York, 1952), unpaged; Burns Mantle, ed., *The Best Plays of 1933–34* (New York, 1934), p. 8; "Tobacco Road Retires Tonight Undefeated . . . ," *NYT*, May 31, 1941, p. 13.

16. Edgar, "The World of the Theatre," *DW*, Jan. 15, 1934, p. 5; Gardner, "The Theatre," *NM*, Jan. 30, 1934, p. 28.

17. Rice, *Minority Report* (New York, 1963), p. 337.

18. *Ibid.*, p. 326.

19. Murray Schumach, "Dean of Playwrights," *NYT*, Nov. 23, 1958, Sec. 2, p. 3.

20. Saxe, "A Play with Propaganda and Three Without," *WT*, Aug. 1932, p. 8.

21. Rice, *Minority Report*, p. 328.

22. Krutch, *The American Drama Since 1918*, rev. ed. (New York, 1957), p. 248.

23. Rice, *Minority Report*, pp. 340–41, 348–49.

24. Clurman, *The Fervent Years*, pp. 108–10.

25. Sherwood, *The Road to Rome* (New York, 1928), Preface, pp. xxxix–xli.

26. Clurman, *The Fervent Years*, p. 83, notes "From 1931 to 1935 all America's younger writers were going on bus and motor trips through the country." Possibly the most enjoyable appearance of the hitchhiker in dramatic art occurred in Frank Capra's film *It Happened One Night* (1934).

27. Sherwood, *The Petrified Forest* (New York, 1935), production data, unpaged.

28. John Phillips, Anne Hollander, "Lillian Hellman; An Interview," *Paris Review*, Winter–Spring 1965, p. 70.

29. "Raided Shows Play to Crowded Houses," *NYT*, Feb. 13, 1927, p. 1, 20; " 'Captive' Immoral, Mahoney Decides," *NYT*, March 9, 1927, p. 27.

30. Under Hollywood's exacting production code of the thirties, Goldwyn was not allowed to use the original title for the film or to advertise that

it was based on the play. See Frank S. Nugent, "These Three, Those Five," *NYT*, March 22, 1936, Sec. 11, p. 3; Richard Griffith, *Samuel Goldwyn: The Producer and His Films* (New York, 1956), pp. 28–29.

31. Hellman, *Four Plays* (New York, 1942), Introduction, p. ix.

CHAPTER 7

1. *The Writer in a Changing World*, ed. Henry Hart (New York, 1937), pp. 20–21, 34–43, 185.

2. *Ibid.*, pp. 195–96, 199.

3. *Ibid.*, pp. 69–73.

4. Annette Castle, "The Truth about Shirley Temple, *SW*, March 15, 1936, Sec. 2, p. 1; *DW*, Sept. 24, 1936, p. 7 (Gypsy Rose Lee); "Happy Birthday!," *DW*, Oct. 28, 1936, p. 1.

5. *DW*, Oct. 7, 1938, p. 7.

6. Ben Compton, "Grandpap Takes a Bride," *DW*, Oct. 14, 1938, p. 7; Hiram Sherman (an usher at the wedding), in conversation with the present writer Ben Irwin, letter to the present writer, June 10, 1972.

7. *TAC*, Aug. 1938, p. 4.

8. Cowley, "Notes on a Writers' Congress," *NR*, June 21, 1939, p. 192.

9. *TAC*, July 1938, p. 9; May 1939, p. 29.

10. Frederick Lewis Allen, *Since Yesterday* (New York, 1940), pp. 222–23; Cabell Phillips, *From the Crash to the Blitz: 1929–1939* (New York, 1969), p. 482.

11. William E. Leuchtenberg, *Franklin D. Roosevelt and the New Deal* (New York, 1963), p. 194.

12. Lunacharsky, "Problems of the Soviet Theatre," *International Literature*, No. 3, 1933, p. 89.

13. Quoted in Abram Tertz, *Socialist Realism*, trans. George Dennis (New York, 1960), p. 24.

14. Marvin, "Organizing an American People's Theatre," *NM*, Nov. 12, 1935, p. 27; "An American People's Theatre," *NT*, Dec. 1935, pp. 24–25; "The New Theatre Conference," *NT*, April 1936, p. 11.

15. In *The One-Act Play Today*, ed. William Kozlenko (New York, 1938), pp. 85–86.

16. "Shifting Scenes," *NT*, Sept. 1936, p. 24; *Skits and Sketches* (New York, 1938), pp. 65–67.

17. *NT*, July 1935, pp. 1, 7–8, 9, 32.

18. "New Plays by Odets and Peters," *NT*, Dec., 1935, p. 4; Kline, "Drama of Negro Life," *NT*, Feb. 1936, pp. 26–27.

19. Kline, "Drama of Negro Life," *NT*, Feb. 1936, p. 27.

20. Leuchtenberg, *Franklin D. Roosevelt . . .* , p. 138; R. Serge Denisoff, *Great Day Coming; Folk Music and the American Left* (Urbana, 1971), pp. 34–35.

21. England, *Take My Stand* (New York, 1935), p. 2.

22. According to an editorial, "Kids Learn Fast," *NT*, Nov. 1936,

p. 4, the play was to be performed by "the younger members of the *Dead End* Company." I have not been able to ascertain whether this occurred. The play was published in the same number of the journal.

23. James A. Emanuel, *Langston Hughes* (New York, 1967), p. 67; Webster Smalley, ed., Langston Hughes, *Five Plays* (Bloomington, 1963), Introduction, pp. x–xi; Hughes, *I Wonder As I Wander* (New York, 1964), pp. 121–22; Darwin T. Turner, ed., *Black Drama in America* (New York, 1971), p. 49.

24. Emanuel, *Langston Hughes*, p. 38.

25. Hughes, *I Wonder As I Wander*, p. 200.

26. *Ibid.*, p. 59.

27. "Backstage," *NT*, Jan. 1936, p. 46.

28. Gassner, "The One-Act Play in the Revolutionary Theatre," *The One-Act Play Today*, ed. Kozlenko, p. 273.

29. Shiffrin, *Return at Sunset* (New York, 1937), p. 2.

30. Toby Cole (Business Secretary of the New Theater League), in conversation with the present writer, on the popularity of Kraft's monologue.

31. This quarterly apparently existed for two numbers only, in 1938. It was edited by Albert Prentis, who had served on the editorial board of *Workers Theatre*. I have seen only the second number, in NYPL-TC.

32. Cambridge, " 'Maid in Japan' Breaks New Ground in Progressive Theatre," *DW*, Feb. 21, 1939, p. 7.

33. F. Jay Taylor, *The United States and the Spanish Civil War* (New York, 1956), p. 103. The question of the extent to which the International Brigades, including the Lincoln Brigade, were manned by communists has never been answered conclusively. "Most of them were not Communists . . . ," says Gabriel Jackson in *The Spanish Republic and the Civil War 1931–1939* (Princeton, 1965), p. 338. But according to Alfred H. Landis, *The Abraham Lincoln Brigade* (New York, 1967), p. xiv, control over the Brigades was exercised by communists. The Communist press and the theatrical organizations close to the Party gave hearty, unqualified support to the Lincoln Brigade. On the role of American communist fighters in the war, see Alvah Bessie, ed., *The Heart of Spain* (New York, 1952), "Editor's Preface," p. vii. This book, an anthology of writing on the war, was published by the Veterans of the Abraham Lincoln Brigade.

34. Kline, "Killed in Action," *NM*, April 20, 1937, p. 19; Ben Irwin, "Resurgence of the New Theatre," *Theatre Workshop*, April–June 1938, pp. 106–7; Titus, "So Certain I Die," *TAC*, Oct. 1938, pp. 11, 16–17. Kline also worked, as a consultant, on a second Spanish film, *Return to Life*.

35. *Writers Take Sides* (New York, 1938), *passim*. The only neutralist of distinction was E. E. Cummings. The lone Franco supporter was Gertrude Atherton.

36. Jackson, *The Spanish Republic* . . . , pp. 368–74, 452–53.

37. *The Writer in a Changing World*, ed. Hart, p. 237.

38. In the play Blankfort chose not to name the fortress. He did name it, however, in his 1940 novel of the same title.

39. Jackson, *The Spanish Republic* . . . , pp. 272–73.

40. Brecht's play, trans. Keene Wallis, was published in *Theatre Workshop*, April–June 1936, pp. 30–50; Sender's, translator not named, was published in *One-Act-Play Magazine*, Nov. 1937, pp. 612–16.

41. Feb. 1937, pp. 12–13.

42. A typescript of this play, retitled *The Spanish Play*, and a flier on the production, are in NYPL-TC. Losey believes that it may have been the first American play to be produced in the round; see Tom Milne, *Losey on Losey* (New York, 1968), p. 98. On the committee, see Albert Bein, "First Play on Struggle in Spain," *DW*, Sept. 18, 1936, p. 7.

43. Its popularity has not always been pleasing to Shaw. Faced with requests to produce it after the outbreak of the Korean War, Shaw decided to withhold the play, on the grounds that productions might contribute to communist causes. Shaw, "Irwin Shaw Withdraws Peace Play," *NYT*, Aug. 20, 1950, Sec. 2, p. 1.

44. "The New Theatres Meet," *NT*, May 1936, p. 4. On the New Theater Night performances at the Civic Rep (March 14 and 15, 1936), the play was presented with a spoofing piece of the First World War, Walter B. Hare's *Over Here*. Uptown under Yokel's management it was presented with J. Edward Shugrue and John O'Shaugnessy's *Prelude*, in which crippled veterans of the First World War recalled their experiences at the front. See Actors Repertory Company Scrapbooks, NYPL-TC.

45. Clurman, *The Fervent Years*, p. 171; "Irwin Shaw Withdraws Peace Play"; Shaw clippings file, NYPL-TC.

46. Del, "Burlesque Strike," *NT*, Oct. 1935, p. 15; "Trade Union Notes," *NT*, Nov. 1935, p. 30; "Trade Union Notes," *NT*, Feb. 1936, p. 34; "With the Stage Unions," *NT*, Dec. 1935, p. 37; "With the Stage Unions," *NT*, Jan. 1936, p. 45; Richard Pack, "The Equity Elections," *NT*, May 1936, pp. 5, 37; Herbert Kline, "Union Smashing—Hollywood Style," *NT*, June 1936, pp. 25–26; "Competition of Trade-Union Theatre Groups," *DW*, May 30, 1939, p. 7.

47. *NT*, Nov. 1935, p. 20.

48. Gassner, "The One-Act Play in the Revolutionary Theatre," p. 267; on the strike, see also Leuchtenberg, *Franklin D. Roosevelt* . . . , p. 112.

49. Unlike *Private Hicks*, *Rehearsal* was not a prizewinner. Nor does it seem to have been frequently performed.

50. Ben Irwin, "Resurgence of the New Theatre," p. 105.

51. "Left on Broadway," *DW*, July 28, 1938, p. 7.

52. In conversation with the present writer, George Sklar and Miriam Blecher (Mrs. Sklar) recalled their astonishment on finding in this play, for once in a League production, something to laugh at.

53. To benefit the Newspaper Guild Emergency Fund, the League presented on April 5, 1936, a short play on a similar subject, Richard Rohman's *Power of the Press*.

54. "Trade Union Groups Active in Theatricals," *DW*, May 27, 1939, p. 7.

55. "Fun, Frolic by WPAers," *DW*, Jan. 15, 1937, p. 7; Charles E. Dexter, "New Theatre League Revue Satirizes Life in the W.P.A.," *DW*, Feb. 2, 1937, p. 7; Manngreen, "Left on Broadway," *DW*, Aug. 6, 1938, p. 7; John Cambridge, "New Cantata Performed by Flatbush Arts Group," *DW*, June 27, 1939, p. 7.

56. Willett, *The Theatre of Bertolt Brecht* (London, 1959), pp. 126, 142. Among the contributions to the festival, or works inspired by it, were Paul Hindemith's *There and Back*, Kurt Weill's *"Little" Mahagonny* and *He Who Says Yes*, and Weill and Hindemith's *Baden Didactic Piece* and *Lindbergh's Flight*, all composed, with the exception of the first, to the words of Brecht.

57. Blitzstein, "Author of 'The Cradle' Discusses Broadway Hit," *DW*, Jan. 3, 1937, p. 7.

58. "Theatre Artists to Parade on May Day," *DW*, April 28, 1938, p. 7.

59. This was the pseudonym of Sidney Meyers, who later directed, wrote, and produced the successful documentary, *The Quiet One* (1949); see Paul Rotha, *Documentary Film* (3rd ed., London, 1963), p. 323.

60. Platt, "The American Indian in Films," *DW*, May 18, 1938, p. 7; May 19, 1938, p. 7.

61. "The New Film Alliance," *NT*, Sept. 1935, p. 29; "Labor Films for America," *NT*, Sept. 1936, p. 3. See also Nykino clippings file, NYPL-TC.

62. Ellis, "The Plow That Broke the Plains," *NT*, July 1936, pp. 18–19; Robert L. Snyder, *Pare Lorentz and the Documentary Film* (Norman, 1968), pp. 29–31.

63. "Films for Progressives Is New Company's Plan," *DW*, April 6, 1937, p. 7; "Liberal News Reel, Frankly Propaganda," *Variety*, April 21, 1937, p. 27. According to these articles, Steiner was a member of the company; but see Snyder, p. 31; Lewis Jacobs, *The Rise of the American Film* (New York, 1939), p. 495.

64. Joris Ivens, *The Camera and I* (New York, 1969), pp. 103–38; Carlos Baker, *Ernest Hemingway: A Life Story* (New York, 1968), pp. 305–15, 621; *The Writer in a Changing World*, ed. Hart, pp. 206–207.

65. Marcia Minor, "Graham Interprets Democracy," *DW*, Oct. 7, 1938, p. 7.

66. Ocko, "Dance Reviews," *NT*, April 1936, p. 37.

67. Latouche, "New Year's Resolutions," *TAC*, Jan. 1939, p. 8.

68. *Report of the Annual Conference of the New Dance League, New York City, May 22, 1936;* M.C., "New Dance League," *Dance Observer*, June–July 1937, p. 66; Margaret Lloyd, *The Borzoi Book of Modern Dance* (New York, 1949), p. 143.

69. These activities were reported month by month in the magazine *TAC*.

70. "A Call from the Theatre Arts Committee," *Theatre Workshop*, April–June 1938, pp. 58–59; Milton Metzer, "TAC Has Stirred Screen, Stage and Radio Stars . . . ," *DW*, April 3, 1939, p. 7; "Editorial Statement," *TAC*, Nov. 1938, p. 12; editorial notes, *TAC*, Jan. 1939, p. 3; for TAC boards, see letterheads, TAC clippings file, NYPL-TC.

71. Manngreen, "Left on Broadway," *DW*, Dec. 7, 1938, p. 7; Samuel Chaiken, "Impressive Ceremonies Mark Lighting of Christmas Trees," *DW*, Dec. 23, 1938, p. 7.

72. These activities were duly reported in *TAC*. See also miscellaneous clippings in TAC file, NYPL-TC.

73. *DW*, May 16, 1938, p. 7; Milton Meltzer, "Political Night Life," *NM*, May 31, 1938, p. 30.

74. Programs and miscellaneous clippings, TAC file, NYPL-TC.

75. *TAC*, Jan. 1939, pp. 14–15.

76. In the New Theater League publication *Skits and Sketches, Second Collection* (New York, 1939), p. 7.

77. Alfred Davis, "The Merry-Go-Round," *DW*, Jan, 29, 1938; Les Koenig, "Hollywood," *TAC*, Oct. 1938, p. 8; "TAC Cabaret One Year Old This Month . . . ," *TAC*, May 1939, pp. 16–17; Koenig, "Hollywood Bites Dog," *TAC*, June 1939, p. 16; "New Masses Presents Keynote Players," *DW*, March 3, 1939, p. 7; "Wit, Song, Dance at Variety Night," *DW*, March 3, 1939, p. 7; advertisements, *NM*, Jan. 11, 1938, p. 26; *TAC*, Dec. 1938, p. 28; *TAC*, Dec. 1939, p. 2.

78. Whitney Balliett, "Night Clubs," *NY*, Oct. 9, 1971, pp. 65–92; "TAC Cabaret One Year Old This Month . . . ," *TAC*, May 1939, pp. 16–17.

79. "TAC Cabaret. . . ."

80. Balliett, "Night Clubs," p. 60; *A Party with Betty Comden and Adolph Green*, Capitol record album WAO 1197, notes; Comden and Green interview, Columbia Oral History Project; clippings, Revuers file, NYPL-TC.

81. The material in this and the three following paragraphs is taken primarily from David Alan Rush, *A History and Evaluation of the ILGWU Labor Stage Production of Pins and Needles, 1937–1940*, unpublished M.A. thesis, U. of Iowa. I am grateful to Harold Rome for lending me this thesis and for granting me an interview. On the 1937 tour, see also Richard Pack, "Road Show—CIO Style," *NTF*, April 1937, pp. 31, 42.

82. Ben Irwin, "The A.F.L. Theatre Presents," *DW*, June 17, 1936, p. 7.

83. The programs of the show identified each performer with his local.

84. Most of the *Pins and Needles* songs may be heard on Columbia record album os 2210.

85. *TAC*, Oct. 1939, p. 3.

86. Sager, "Movies," *TAC*, Oct. 1939, p. 29; Flexner, "Theatre," Dec. 1939, p. 9; Koenig, Dec. 1939, p. 18.

87. Louis Schaffer, *Stalin's Fifth Column on Broadway* (New York, 1940), pp. 6–9; "TAC Replies to Equity Action," *DW*, April 13, 1940, p. 7.

88. "Old 'Lefty' Comes Back to Aid Strike," *DW*, May 15, 1940, p. 7; "TAC Offers Anti-War Play Wednesday," *DW*, Sept. 15, 1940, p. 7; "Two Producers Ban Theatre Arts Group," *NYT*, Oct. 23, 1940, p. 26.

89. Schaffer, *Stalin's Fifth Column . . .* , Rush, *A History and Evaluation . . .* , p. 99 (on Schrank). Rush provides a guide to the changes made in the revue during its run.

90. Except where indicated, the source of information on the last years of the New Theater League is *NTN*.

91. Alice Evans, "AFL and CIO Unity at New Theatre School," *DW*, Oct. 8, 1940, p. 7.

92 On this phase of the League's activity, Toby Cole in conversation with the present writer.

93. Ralph Warner, " 'No for an Answer' a True People's Opera," *DW*, Jan. 7, 1941, p. 7; Blitzstein, *No for an Answer*, original cast album, Theme Records, TALP 103; "Stage Notes," *DW*, April 26, 1941, p. 7; advertisement, *DW*, June 21, 1941, p. 7. A Philadelphia production of *Zero Hour* played from May 1 to June 14, 1941.

94. Irwin, "Editorial," *NTN*, Nov. 1940, p. 2; Alice Evans, "Bits of Broadway," *NTN*, May 1941, unpaged.

95. Toby Cole in conversation with the present writer.

CHAPTER 8

1. "Thus the Union Figures," *NYT*, Jan. 26, 1936, Sec. 10, p. 3; Margaret Larkin, "Theatre Union—Its Tasks and Problems," *DW*, May 15, 1935, p. 5; Michael Gold, "Change the World," *DW*, Dec. 30, 1935, p. 7. This chapter, like Chapter III, was read in draft by George Sklar; information added from his comments is identified in the notes by "GS."

2. Clipping, source unidentified, in Theater Union Scrapbooks, NYPL-TC.

3. *NT*, Nov. 1935, p. 35.

4. Brecht, "Criticism of the New York Production of *Die Mutter*," *Brecht on Theatre*, trans. John Willett (London 1964), pp. 81–84 (written for, but never published by, *NM*); on Brecht's presence at rehearsals, Sklar in conversation with the present writer. A typescript of the Peters translation is on file at NYPL-TC.

5. Olgin, "Mother: The Theatre Union's New Play," *DW*, Nov. 22, 1935, p. 5; Burnshaw, "The Theatre Union Produces 'Mother,' " *NM*, Dec. 3, 1935, pp. 27–28; Farrell, "Theatre Chronicle," *Partisan Review and Anvil*, Feb. 1936, p. 29; Gassner, "The Play's the Thing," *NT*, Dec. 1935, p. 13; Bolton, clipping, Theater Union Scrapbooks, NYPL-TC; Atkinson, "The Play," *NYT*, Nov. 20, 1935, p. 26.

6. Gold, "Change the World," *DW*, Dec. 6, 1935, p. 9. On Brecht productions in America, see Martin Esslin, *Brecht: The Man and His Work* (New York, 1960), pp. 337–48.

7. Worthington Miner, "Actors' Repertory Company," *NYT*, Nov. 15, 1936, Sec. 10, p. 3; Margaret Larkin, Letter to Drama Editor, *NYT*, Nov. 22, 1936, Sec. 10, p. 3; Gold, "Change the World," *DW*, Dec. 5, 1935, p. 7; Dec. 10, 1935, p. 7.

8. Bein, "Of 'Let Freedom Ring,' " *NYT*, Dec. 1, 1935, Sec. 11, p. 6.

9. Howe and Coser, *The American Communist Party*, pp. 258–61.

10. "Theatre Union Gives Act of Wexley Play," *NYT*, Feb. 17, 1936, p. 21; miscellaneous clippings, Theater Union file, NYPL-TC; GS.

11. GS.

12. Gold, "Change the World," *DW*, Dec. 11, 1935, p. 5; Dec. 30, 1935, p. 7; Dec. 31, 1935, p. 7.

13. " 'Bitter Stream' Introduces Victor Wolfson as Playwright," *New York Post*, undated clipping, Theater Union Scrapbooks NYPL-TC.

14. "Dramatic Necessity," *NM*, April 28, 1936, p. 5; Repard, "A Play of Fascist Italy," *DW*, April 3, 1936, p. 7; Gassner, "Perspectives—Past and Present," *NT*, May 1936, p. 11.

15. On May 3, 1936, the cast of *Bitter Stream* acted in Joseph Samuelson and William Hauptmann's *From Little Acorns* at a New Theater Night, under the direction of Albert Van Dekker. The play, dealing with the conflict between a conservative father who is unemployed and his radical son, had won the second prize in a contest held jointly by the New Theater League and the City Projects Council for a one-act work on unemployment; Ben Irwin, "Ten Million Others," *NT*, June 1936, pp. 29–30.

16. GS (on the reason for the move); "Up from Union Square," *NYT*, Aug. 30, 1936, Sec. 9, p. 1; "Uptown? Yes, Upstage? No," *DW*, Oct. 8, 1936, p. 7; Margaret Larkin, "On Becoming Acclimated to Broadway," *DW*, Nov. 24, 1936, p. 7; "Theatre Union's Project," *NYT*, Feb. 7, 1937, Sec. 10, p. 2.

17. For Lawson's screen credits, see John Cogley, *Report on Blacklisting* (New York, 1955), I, 243–45.

18. Lawson, *Theory and Technique of Playwriting* (New York, 1936), p. 163.

19. *Ibid.*, pp. 287–91.

20. Originally the speech was more extravagant. See Lawson, *Marching Song* (New York, 1937), pp. 35–36.

21. Clurman, *The Fervent Years*, p. 187.

22. " 'Marching Song' Cast Enters the Lists as Producer," *New York Telegram*, April 10, 1937, Theatre Union Scrapbooks, NYPL-TC.

23. *The Writer in a Changing World*, ed. Hart, p. 255.

24. Clurman, *The Fervent Years*, p. 244.

25. "Gossip of the Rialto," *NYT*, Aug. 29, 1937, Sec. 10, p. 1.

26. Sylvia Regan, in charge of promotion for the Theater Union, took the same post with the Mercury; Houseman, *Run-Through*, p. 292.

27. Miner, "Actors' Repertory Company." In setting up the name of the company, printers were afflicted with confusion over the use of the apostrophe with "Actors." The company itself omitted the apostrophe, because, according to John O'Shaughnessy in conversation with the present writer, its members somehow thought that to do so would emphasize their concept of the company as one designed by and for actors.

28. Miner, "Actors' Repertory Company."

29. Gassner, "The Diluted Theatre," *NTF*, March 1937, pp. 30–31. In actuality the government offered the farmsites on favorable terms. The settlers had thirty years in which to pay off their federal loans for the land, and interest was low; Clarence C. Hulley, "Historical Survey of the Matan-

uska Valley Settlement in Alaska," *Alaska and its History*, ed. Morgan B. Sherwood (Seattle, 1967), pp. 409–28.

30. John O'Shaughnessy in conversation with the present writer.

31. Helen Ormsbee, "An Acting Group with the Jitters," *New York Herald-Tribune*, May 1, 1938, Sec. 6, p. 2.

32. Roy S. Waldau, *Vintage Years of the Theatre Guild: 1928–1939* (Cleveland, 1972), pp. 300–301; Ormsbee, "An Acting Group. . . ."

33. "Actors Rep Co. Reorg: Film Financing," *Variety*, Nov. 9, 1938, p. 55; "Gossip of the Rialto," *NYT*, March 10, 1940, Sec. 9, p. 1; "News and Gossip of the Times Square Area," *NYT*, Sept. 29, 1940, Sec. 9, p. 1; John O'Shaughnessy in conversation with the present writer; Will Geer, letter to the present writer, July 1972.

34. " 'Let Freedom Ring' Tour," *NT*, Aug. 1936, p. 5; Lawrence Spitz, " 'Let Freedom Ring' on Tour," *NT*, Nov. 1936, pp. 24–25.

35. Flier, John Lenthier Troupe clippings file, NYPL-TC.

36. Herta Ware, "Through the South with a Drama Group," *SW*, Aug. 14, 1938, p. 12; Ben Burns, "Will Green Laughs Last," *DW*, May 3, 1939, p. 7; Theodore Strauss, "Road Presents: W. Geer," *NYT*, Jan. 21, 1940, Sec. 9, pp. 1–2; Geer, letter to the present writer, July 1972.

37. "The John Lenthier Troupe on Tour," *NTN*, Dec. 1939, pp. 12–15. This article incorporates the script of *Middleman*.

38. In this period he also appeared in a film, Pare Lorentz's *The Fight for Life*.

39. R. Serge Denisoff, *Great Day Coming*, pp. 74–75.

CHAPTER 9

1. Hallie Flanagan, *Arena* (New York, 1940), p. 26.

2. William E. Leuchtenberg, *Franklin D. Roosevelt and the New Deal*, pp. 125–28, 133–34; Robert E. Sherwood, *Roosevelt and Hopkins: An Intimate History* (New York, 1948), pp. 68–71; William F. McDonald, *Federal Relief Administration and the Arts* (Columbus, 1969), p. 214.

3. Leuchtenberg, *Franklin D. Roosevelt* . . . , pp. 120–23; Baker, "Work Relief: The Program Widens," in *The New Deal*, ed. Carl N. Degler (Chicago, 1970), p. 159.

4. Jack Pulaski, "The Year in Legit," *Variety*, Jan. 1, 1935, p. 134; Flanagan, *Arena*, p. 79. In a curious slip, Pulaski refers to the CCC as the "Civilian Concentration Camps."

5. Flanagan, *Arena*, p. 436.

6. Information in this and the following paragraph is based on Flanagan, *Arena*, pp. 3–16 and Jane De Hart Mathews, *The Federal Theatre, 1935–1939: Plays, Relief and Politics* (Princeton, 1967), pp. 11–22.

7. Flanagan, *Arena*, p. 20.

8. *Ibid.*, pp. 35, 434–36. The federal tax of 10 per cent was added to the price of tickets. In some instances the top price charged was $1.65; Flanagan, *What Was Federal Theatre?* (New York, 1940), p. 3. Los Ange-

les opened a box office on December 31, 1935, before the national admission scale was arranged. See below, p. 249.

9. Mathews, *The Federal Theatre*, pp. 11–12; Rice, *The Living Theatre* (New York, 1959), pp. 149–53.

10. Mathews, *The Federal Theatre*, pp. 39–40, 57–58; Flanagan, *Arena*, pp. 41–43, 135–36, 225, 286–88.

11. Flanagan, *Arena*, pp. 34, 184–89, 202, 314, 435; Mathews, pp. 41, 103, 120, 245–46. In the beginning, to help the Arts Projects get underway, Hopkins granted them an allowance of 25 per cent nonrelief workers. This was cut to 10 per cent in September 1936.

12. Flanagan, *Arena*, pp. 35–36, 55–56; Flanagan, "Talk at the Meeting of the Regional Staff, New York City, August 19, 1937," p. 11, typescript in Hallie Flanagan Papers, NYPL-TC.

13. Flanagan, *Arena*, pp. 40–41, 52–54, 82, 282, 308–9.

14. "WPA Productions Scheduled by Rice," *NYT*, Dec. 17, 1935, p. 30; "WPA Will Lease 2 More Theatres," *NYT*, Dec. 31, 1935, p. 10.

15. Membership in both bodies apparently changed over the years. With the exception of Meredith, the names listed are taken from undated lists in the Flanagan Papers, NYPL-TC. In 1937 Meredith was head of the Advisory Committee; see Flanagan, *Arena*, pp. 284–85, 316–17; Robert Holcomb, "The Federal Theatre in Los Angeles," *California Historical Quarterly*, June 1962, p. 140.

16. Mathews, *The Federal Theatre*, p. 58; Flanagan, *Arena*, pp. 32, 276–77; Hart to Flanagan, in Flanagan Papers, NYPL-TC.

17. Anthony Buttita, "There Were No Elephants on Relief," *FT*, I, no. 6, unpaged; John W. Dunn, "Oklahoma's Federal Theatre for the Blind," *FT*, II, no. 1, pp. 10, 28; "Entertaining Flood sufferers," *FT*, II, no. 4, pp. 13–14; "CCC Mystery in 189 Camps," *FT*, II, no. 5, unpaged; Pierre de Rohan, *First Federal Theatre Summer Theatre: A Report* (New York, n.d.), p. 5; Flanagan, *Arena*, pp. 110–11, 115–29, 396, 432.

18. Flanagan, "Federal Theatre Project," *TA*, Nov. 9, 1935, p. 868; Flanagan, "Theatre and Geography," *American Magazine of Art*, Aug. 1938, p. 466; Flanagan, "Not in Despair," *FT*, II, no. 4, pp. 5, 28.

19. Flanagan, *Arena*, pp. 261–67.

20. All Project plays and the cities where they were first produced are listed in *Arena*, pp. 377–436.

21. Flanagan, "Not in Despair," *FT*, II, no. 4, p. 5.

22. Flanagan, *Arena*, p. 361.

23. *Ibid.*, p. 88.

24. *Ibid.*, pp. 138–39; Kuller, Golden, and Charig, *O Say Can You Sing*, typescript in Federal Theater Records, National Archives, Washington, D.C.

25. Flanagan, *Arena*, pp. 254–55, 432–34.

26. McDonald, p. 282; Flanagan, *Arena*, pp. 266–67.

27. Flanagan, *Arena*, pp. 60, 194.

28. Mantle's lists of Project plays are incomplete, but his capsule comments on many plays are more informative than those offered by Flanagan in *Arena*. For the number of performances of New York productions, the annual tables of the New York *Times* are the only source of complete information.

29. Flanagan, *Arena*, pp. 62–63; Houseman, *Run-Through*, pp. 129, 175–79, 184–85; Flanagan to Harry Hopkins, Jan. 28, 1938, quoted in Mathews, *The Federal Theatre*, p. 165 ("assets").

30. Philip Stevenson, "Turpentine Workers," *NT*, Aug. 1936, p. 18; Houseman, *Run-Through*, p. 205.

31. Houseman, *Run-Through*, pp. 185, 189–204 (Houseman reveals that the inspiration for this production came from Welles's wife); Brooks Atkinson, "The Play," *NYT*, April 15, 1936, p. 25; Wells's *Macbeth* promptbook, NYPL-TC; Whitman, *Bread and Circuses: A Study of Federal Theatre* (New York, 1937), p. 43.

32. Flanagan, "Introduction," *Federal Theatre Plays: Prologue to Glory, One-Third of a Nation, Haiti*, ed. Pierre de Rohan (New York, 1938), p. x.

33. Leuchtenberg, *Franklin D. Roosevelt . . .* , pp. 240–41; Flanagan, *Arena*, pp. 201–3; Houseman, *Run-Through*, pp. 246–55.

34. Flanagan, *ibid.*, Houseman, *ibid.*

35. This description of the opening of *The Cradle Will Rock* is based on those of four who participated in it: Houseman, *Run-Through*, pp. 255–79; Blitzstein, *Marc Blitzstein Discusses His Musical Compositions*, Spoken Arts record 717; Howard Da Silva, album notes for *The Cradle Will Rock*, M-G-M record E-4289-20C; Archibald MacLeish, Introduction, Blitzstein, *The Cradle Will Rock* (New York, 1937), pp. 9–11.

36. Flanagan, *Arena*, p. 69.

37. *Ibid.*, p. 79.

38. HUAC, Hearings, *Communist Infiltration of the Hollywood Motion Picture Industry*, Part 7 (Washington, 1952), p. 2343 (testimony of Michael Blankfort).

39. Gold and Blankfort, "About 'Battle Hymn,'" *DW*, June 6, 1936, p. 7; HUAC (testimony of Michael Blankfort), *ibid.*

40. "Lewis Says Hays Bans Film of Book," *NYT*, Feb. 16, 1936, pp. 3, 35; "Berlin and Rome Hail 'Ban' on Lewis Film," *NYT*, Feb. 17, p. 21; "Denies Film Was Banned," *NYT*, Feb. 20, 1936, p. 15; David Platt, "The Case of 'It Can't Happen Here,'" *DW*, May 13, 1936, p. 7; Mark Schorer, *Sinclair Lewis: An American Life* (New York, 1961), pp. 623–24; Flanagan, *Arena*, p. 116.

41. Flanagan, *Arena*, pp. 117–23.

42. *Ibid.*, p. 129.

43. *Ibid.*, p. 173. In 1949 Thomas was convicted of defrauding the government and was sentenced to a prison term.

44. Donald Nash, "Sights and Sounds," *NM*, Oct. 26, 1937, p. 28; Judith Reed, "Lawson's Play Belongs in the Past," *DW*, Oct. 20, 1937, p. 7.

45. Atkinson, "*The Revolt of the Beavers*, or Mother Goose Marx, Under

WPA Auspices," *NYT*, May 21, 1937, p. 19; Mathews, *The Federal Theatre,* pp. 116–17; Flanagan to Philip Davis, Nov. 8, 1936, in Flanagan Papers, NYPL-TC.

46. Flanagan, *Arena,* 20, 64–65. Rice much later (1967) observed that in his recollection the idea of developing a Living Newspaper unit came out of discussions that he held with Morris Watson, who became its head; see Dan Isaac, Introduction, Arthur Arent, *Ethiopia, ETJ,* March 1968, p. 16.

47. Murinson, *WT,* March 1933, p. 10; Arent, "The Technique of the Living Newspaper," *TA,* Nov. 1938, p. 821; Flanagan, Introduction, *Federal Theatre Plays: Triple-A Plowed Under, Power, Spirochete,* ed. Pierre de Rohan (New York, 1938), p. xi; Flanagan, *Dynamo* (New York, 1943), p. 107.

48. Flanagan, *Arena,* pp. 65, 71; "Editing the Living Newspaper," *FT,* April 1936, pp. 16–17; Mathews, *The Federal Theatre,* pp. 62–64.

49. Flanagan, Address to the American Federation of Arts Meeting in Washington, D.C., May 12, 1937, quoted in Mathews, *The Federal Theatre,* p. 143.

50. At various times living newspapers were planned for the states of Iowa and Washington and the cities of Denver and Newark, but were never mounted. The material prepared for *Medicine* was used for the Philadelphia New Theater's production of the same name in 1940 and in another form was produced as *Medicine Show* on Broadway by Carly Wharton and Martin Gabel in the same year, with Oscar Saul and H. R. Hays credited as writers. For a history of the Living Newspaper technique, see Douglas McDermott, "The Living Newspaper as a Dramatic Form," *Modern Drama,* May 1965, pp. 82–94.

51. Flanagan, *Arena,* pp. 65–66, 135–36; Mathews, *The Federal Theatre,* pp. 63–66; Isaac, pp. 16–18.

52. "Politics Charged to WPA by Rice," *NYT,* Jan. 25, 1936, p. 7; Mathews, pp. 67–68; Flanagan, *Arena,* p. 67. The New York project was frequently reorganized. In March 1937 William Farnsworth, Hallie Flanagan's deputy director, was made administrator of the New York project, with Barber in charge of the producing units. In August of the same year, Farnsworth resigned and was replaced by George Kondolf, who held the post until the Federal Theater was closed down.

53. Flanagan, *Arena,* pp. 72–73. According to Mathews, p. 113, the scenes to which Flanagan objected were toned down during the run.

54. William H. Humphrey, "I Play Earl Browder—Communist," *Equity,* April 1936, p. 4.

55. The Supreme Court never ruled on the act creating the Tennessee Valley Authority, but in decisions on cases relating to the TVA heard in 1936 and 1939 left no reasonable doubt that the act was constitutional; see C. Herman Pritchett, *The Tennessee Valley Authority: A Study in Public Administration* (Chapel Hill, 1943), pp. 60–65.

56. Flanagan, *Arena,* p. 185; Mathews, *The Federal Theatre,* pp. 114–115.

57. Leuchtenberg, *Franklin D. Roosevelt* . . . , pp. 135–36; Flanagan, *Arena*, pp. 217–21.

58. Flanagan, *Arena*, pp. 141–42, 283; John Martin, "The Dance: 'Adelante,'" *NYT*, April 30, 1938, Sec. 11, p. 6; *The Dance and WPA, Extracts from "Dance,"* ed. Paul Milton, pp. 35–36, typescript, NYPL Dance Collection; Marian Roet, *The Dance Project of the Works Progress Administration Federal Theatre*, M.A. thesis (unpub.), New York University, 1949, p. 13.

59. Snyder, *Pare Lorentz and the Documentary Film*, pp. 9–12.

60. Flanagan to Hopkins, June 9, 1938; Hopkins to Flanagan, June 27, 1938; in Flanagan Papers, NYPL-TC.

61. Snyder, *Pare Lorentz* . . . , p. 83. In 1941 Lorentz undertook to turn this project into a feature-length film for RKO, but this venture also fell through; see Houseman, *Run-Through*, pp. 484–85.

62. This and the following paragraph are based largely on Snyder, *Pare Lorentz* . . . , pp. 82–95, *passim;* U.S. Film Service, *The Plow that Broke the Plains* (Washington, 1938); Pare Lorentz, *The River* (New York, 1938), Pare Lorentz, *The Fight for Life*, in *Twenty Best Film Plays*, ed. John Gassner and Dudley Nichols (New York, 1943), pp. 1081–1112; and the author's viewings of the films, On the making of *Power and the Land* and *The Land*, respectively, see Ivens, *The Camera and I*, pp. 187–206, and Richard Griffith, *The World of Robert Flaherty* (Westport, 1970), pp. 139–43.

63. "30 Police on Guard as WPA Show Opens," *NYT*, March 15, 1936, p. 27; "WPA's Next Drama Already Held 'Red,'" *NYT*, March 17, 1936, p. 20; "Insists WPA Cash Aids Communism," *NYT*, April 27, 1936, p. 19; "Fraud v. Fraud," *Time*, March 23, 1936, p. 21; Flanagan, *Arena*, pp. /203–5; "Theatre Project Faces an Inquiry," *NYT*, July 27, 1938, p. 19.

64. Flanagan, Arena, pp. 335–41; HUAC, *Investigation of Un-American Propaganda Activities in the United States* (Washington, 1938), IV, 2729–830, 2837–838.

65. *Ibid.*, IV, 2871, 2876.

66. *Ibid.*, IV, 2857; Flanagan, *Arena*, p. 342.

67. Sidney Lens, *Left, Right and Center: Conflicting Forces in American Labor* (Hinsdale, 1947), pp. 258–59; Bernard Karsh and Phillip L. Garman, "The Impact of the Political Left," *Labor and the New Deal*, eds. Milton Derber and Edwin Young (Madison, 1955), pp. 88–97; Flanagan, *Arena*, pp. 56–57; "Union Bias Found on WPA Projects," *NYT*, Feb. 14, 1938, p. 20; Thomson, *Virgil Thomson* (New York, 1967), p. 277.

68. In Flanagan Papers, NYPL-TC.

69. For a sampling of equivocal or unfavorable reviews, see Michael Haas, "'1935' and 'The Dance of Death,'" *DW*, May 23, 1936, p. 7; Judith Reed, "Lawson's Play Belongs to the Past," *DW*, Oct. 20, 1937, p. 7; Alexander Taylor, "Sights and Sounds," *NM*, March 9, 1937, p. 29 (on *Power*); John Cambridge, "Negro Dream of Haiti," *DW*, March 5, 1938, p. 9; Philip Stevenson, "Turpentine Workers," *NT*, Aug. 1938, p. 18.

70. *Report of the Special Committee on Un-American Activities—Pursuant to H. Res. 282*, 75th Cong., 4th Sess. (Washington, 1939), p. 31.

71. Sub-Committee of the Committee on Appropriations, *Investigation and Study of the Works Progress Administration under House Resolution 130* (Washington, 1939), pp. 189–207.

72. "Acknowledgments . . . of Letters Urging Continuance of Project (June–July)," in Flanagan Papers, NYPL-TC.

73. Pp. 245, 260.

74. Houseman, *Run-Through*, pp. 279–81.

75. *Ibid.*, pp. 243, 285–91.

76. Houseman, "Again—a People's Theatre, the Mercury Takes a Bow," *DW*, Sept. 18, 1938, p. 7; Welles and Houseman, "Plan for a New Theatre," *NYT*, Aug. 29, 1937, Sec. 10, p. 1; Alfred Davis, "The Merry-Go-Round," *DW*, Jan. 29, 1938, p. 7; "Culture and the People's Front," *DW*, Feb. 18, 1938, p. 7; Welles, "Theatre and the People's Front," *DW*, April 15, 1938, p. 9; Houseman, *Run-Through*, pp. 292, 304–5.

77. *Ibid.*, pp. 298–312.

78. Flanagan, *Arena*, pp. 258–60.

79. Flexner, "Quicksilver at the Mercury," *NM*, Jan. 18, 1938, p. 28.

80. Russell Maloney, "This Ageless Soul," *NY*, Oct. 8, 1938, p. 22.

81. The sociological import of the broadcast has frequently been analyzed in print. See Hadley Cantril, *The Invasion from Mars* (Princeton, 1940), and Howard Koch, *The Panic Broadcast: Portrait of an Event* (Boston, 1970). Both volumes include the script of the broadcast.

82. Houseman, *Run-Through*, p. 384.

83. *DW*, Oct. 20, 1938, p. 7; Oct. 24, 1938, p. 7.

84. Houseman, *Run-Through*, pp. 384–85.

85. Dec. 18, 1938, Sec. 10, pp. 1, 3.

86. Houseman, *Run-Through*, pp. 416, 428; Lawrence Langner, *The Magic Curtain*, pp. 269–73.

87. On the authorship of *Citizen Kane*, see Houseman, *Run-Through*, pp. 447–61, and Pauline Kael, "Raising Kane," *The Citizen Kane Book* (Boston, 1971), pp. 3–84 *passim*.

88. Wright discusses his break with the Party and his consequently troubled experiences with the Federal Theater and Writers' projects in *The God That Failed*, ed. Richard Crossman (New York, 1950), pp. 150–62.

89. Houseman, *Run-Through*, pp. 461–67, 471–72; William Brasmer and Dominick Corolo, eds., *Black Drama: An Anthology* (Columbus, 1970), p. 71. The text of the play published in 1941 is Green's version. For a sense of the stage version, see the condensation by Burns Mantle, ed., *The Best Plays of 1940–41* (New York, 1941), pp. 29–63.

90. Welles kept the Mercury name in use long afterward in connection with independent film and stage productions. None, however, had any relation to the original company; nor was Houseman associated with him in them.

CHAPTER 10

1. Clurman, *The Fervent Years*, pp. 112, 159–60, 164.

2. *Ibid.*, p. 164; Robert Lewis in conversation with the present writer.

3. Farrell, "Theatre Chronicle," *Partisan Review and Anvil*, Feb. 1936, p. 29.

4. "New Plays by Odets and Peters," *NT*, Dec. 1935, p. 4; *NM*, Nov. 19, 1935, p. 27; "A $75 Contest for Relief Plays," *NT*, Jan. 1936, p. 39; Odets, "The Awakening of the American Theatre," *NT*, Jan. 1936, pp. 5, 43; Clurman, *The Fervent Years*, pp. 154, 166; Odets, "How a Playwright Triumphs," *Harper's*, Sept. 1966, pp. 70–73 (Odets remembered the M-G-M offer as $4000 a week, not the $3000 reported by Clurman; on p. 67 he uses "yea-saying" to describe the kind of play sought by Clurman and Strasberg for the company).

5. Clurman, *The Fervent Years*, p. 166.

6. Clurman, "Interpretation and Characterization," *NT*, Jan. 1936, p. 21.

7. Odets, "Some Problems of the Modern Dramatist," *NYT*, Dec. 15, 1935, Sec. 11, p. 3.

8. Clurman, *The Fervent Years*, p. 166.

9. Blankfort, "Clifford Odets Writes a Tragedy of the Middle Class," *DW*, Dec. 13, 1935, p. 7; Forsythe, "Paradise Lost," *NM*, Dec. 24, 1935, pp. 28–29; Gassner, " 'Paradise Lost' and the Theatre of Frustration," *NT*, Jan. 1936, pp. 8–10.

10. Gerlando, "Odets and the Middle Class," *DW*, Feb. 7, 1936, p. 7; Bagley, "The New Play," *SW*, Feb. 16, 1936, p. 6; Farrell, pp. 28–29; Burnshaw, *NM*, Feb. 11, 1936, p. 28; Stevens, *NT*, July 1936, p. 5, 26–27.

11. Gerald Weales, *Clifford Odets: Playwright*, p. 103, suggests that Odets may have brought the wrath of the Party down on himself by resigning from it after the first set of notices appeared. This is a possibility, but there is no good reason to doubt that Odets remained in the Party later than the "middle of 1935," the vague date he gave the House Un-American Activities Committee. See HUAC, *Hearings, Communist Infiltration of the Hollywood Motion Picture Industry*, Part 6 (Washington, 1952), p. 3456.

12. Clurman, *The Fervent Years*, pp. 157, 171, 174.

13. *Ibid.*, p. 174; Gorelik, *New Theatres for Old*, p. 433; John W. Gassner, "Drama Versus Melodrama," *NT*, April 1936, pp. 8–10; Theodore Repard, "Most Significant Play in N.Y.," *DW*, March 17, 1936, p. 7. A typescript of the play is on file at NYPL-TC.

14. Howard Barnes, "The Playbill," New York *Herald-Tribune*, Feb. 16, 1936—in Group Theater Scrapbooks, NYPL-TC. Clurman, *The Fervent Years*, pp. 175–76; Stevens, p. 5. See also John Anderson, "Group Theatre's Communist Disavowal," New York *Journal*, April 22, 1936; Whitney Bolton, "The Stage Today," *Morning Telegraph*, April 22, 1936; John Mason Brown, "What the Group and What Its Playwrights Think," New York *Post*, April 17, 1936—in Group Theater Scrapbooks, NYPL-TC.

15. Clurman, *The Fervent Years*, pp. 177–78; Odets, "How a Playwright Triumphs," pp. 70, 73. A draft of *Sarah Bernhardt* is on file at the Copyright Division of the Library of Congress, where it was entered in 1934. Odets was the second of three Group Theater members to marry Hollywood star actresses. His marriage to Luise Rainer in 1937 was preceded by Franchot Tone's to Joan Crawford in 1935 and Luther Adler's to Sylvia Sydney in 1939. Each ended in divorce.

16. Clurman, *The Fervent Years*, p. 186. A version of the play is on file at the Copyright Division of the Library of Congress. One scene was published in *NTF*, March 1937, pp. 5–9; the play was never published in its entirety.

17. I may have reached this opinion only because of the impression made on me by William Prince and Estelle Parsons in the roles in the staged reading of the play given at the Actors Studio in April 1971, in the first public performances of the play.

18. Odets, "How a Playwright Triumphs," p. 73.

19. Stebbins, "Film Miscellany," *NT*, Oct. 1936, p. 18; McCallister, *SW*, Sept. 12, 1936, p. 12. The line of dialogue is quoted in Sidney Kaufman, "Odets's First Film," *NM*, July 28, 1936, p. 12; the review, published before the release of the film, is generally favorable.

20. Clurman, *The Fervent Years*, pp. 183–84.

21. Strasberg, "Showing the Movie Screen a Certain Trick or Two," *DW*, Jan. 5, 1937, p. 7.

22. The songs as orchestrated by Weill may be heard on M-G-M record E3447.

23. Mantle, *The Best Plays of 1936–37* (New York, 1937), p. 96.

24. Clurman, *The Fervent Years*, pp. 191–92; Odets, "How a Playwright Triumphs," p. 73. Clurman and Odets disagree as to how long rehearsals proceeded before the cancellation. According to Clurman, it was "about three weeks"; according to Odets, "three or four days."

25. Clurman, "The Group Halts, but only to Think it Over," *NYT*, Jan. 17, 1937, Sec. 10, p. 1.

26. Clurman, *The Fervent Years*, p. 183.

27. *Ibid.*, pp. 193–96.

28. Ben Compton, "Facts and the Group Theatre," *SW*. Jan. 10, 1937, p. 12; Jan. 17, 1937, p. 13; "Editorials," *NTF*, March 1937, pp. 50–51.

29. Clurman, *The Fervent Years*, p. 204.

30. *Ibid.*, pp. 206, 208, 212; Robert Lewis interview, Columbia Oral History Project.

31. James Conway, "Broadway Uncensored," *SW*, Feb. 13, 1938, p. 10; advertisements, *DW*, Dec. 6, 1938, and May 8, 1939, p. 7; "Party for Hollywood's 'Committee of 56,' " *DW*, Jan. 28, 1939, p. 7; *The Writer in a Changing World*, ed. Hart, p. 196; TAC and New Theatre League letterheads in NYPL-TC; Clurman, *The Fervent Years*, pp. 214–15. Clurman does not give the name of the Eisenberg-Williams sketch. It was published in *TAC*, Dec. 1938, pp. 14–15.

32. Gorelik, "I Design for the Group Theatre," *TA*, March 1939, p. 186.

33. Clurman, "Clifford Odets," *NYT*, Aug. 25, 1963, Sec. 2, p. 1.

34. Ben Burns, "Odets on Broadway and Hollywood," *DW*, Aug. 23, 1937, p. 7. Heavily revised by John Howard Lawson, *The River Is Blue* was filmed and released as *Blockade; Gettsburg* was never produced.

35. Clurman, *The Fervent Years*, pp. 219–20; a draft of this play under the title *The Cuban Play* is on file at the Copyright Division of the Library of Congress.

36. *Ibid.*, pp. 228, 232.

37. Michael J. Mendelsohn, "Odets at Center Stage," *TA*, May 1963, p. 19.

38. "News of the Stage," *NYT*, March 21, 1939, p. 26.

39. Gorelik, *New Theatres for Old*, p. 169.

40. Clurman, *The Fervent Years*, p. 238.

41. *Ibid.*, pp. 239–40.

42. *Ibid.*, pp. 248–49.

43. Saroyan, "Another Heart's in the Highlands," *NYT*, April 23, 1939, Sec. 10, p. 1 (in revised form the passage is incorporated into the Introduction to the printed text of the play); Gold, "Change the World," *DW*, May 9, 1938, p. 7.

44. Clurman, *The Fervent Years*, pp. 251–59.

45. Ardrey, *Plays of Three Decades* (New York, 1968), pp. 20–21.

46. Clurman, *The Fervent Years*, p. 259.

47. This passage appears in both the English and American wartime-published versions (1940 and 1941 respectively). In *Plays of Three Decades*, Streeter does not appear in the third act, and Charleston is not so bloody minded. Neither, however, does he favor nonintervention.

48. *The Fervent Years*, p. 261.

49. Brooks Atkinson, "The Play," *NYT*, Feb. 23, 1940, p. 18; Richard Watts, Jr., "The Theatre," *New York Herald-Tribune*," March 3, 1940, in Group Theater Scrapbooks, NYPL-TC.

50. Clurman, *The Fervent Years*, pp. 264–78 *passim*.

51. *Ibid.*, pp. 270–71.

52. Clurman, "Group Theatre's Future," *NYT*, May 18, 1941, Sec. 9, pp. 1–2.

53. In later years only Kazan, of former Group actors, took up theatrical production. In 1947 with Clurman, Walter Fried, and Herbert Harris, he produced Arthur Miller's *All My Sons*, and he was a member of the board of the Repertory Theater of Lincoln Center during the first two seasons, 1963–64 and 1964–65. In 1940 Kazan and Robert Lewis planned a Dollar Top Theater, but the project proved impractical.

54. "Two Productions—Two Directions," *NTN*, Jan. 1941, p. 5.

55. Gassner, "The Group Theatre," *TA*, Oct. 1940, pp. 733–35.

CHAPTER 11

1. Langner, *The Magic Curtain,* pp. 336–37; Helburn, *A Wayward Quest,* pp. 301–2; Roy S. Waldau, *Vintage Years of the Theatre Guild,* pp. 223–24, 334. See also Simonson's letter of Dec. 1, 1937, to the Board, in Waldau, pp. 495–97.

2. Langner, p. 268; Rice, *Minority Report,* pp. 374–75; S. N. Behrman, *People in a Diary* (Boston, 1972), pp. 212–17; John Mason Brown, *The Worlds of Robert E. Sherwood: Mirror to His Times* (New York, 1965), pp. 372–75.

3. Waldau, pp. 253, 358 (on silent partners).

4. In September of this same year occurred the American release of the French film, *Mayerling,* on the Rudolph-Vetsera affair, directed by Anatole Litvak and starring Charles Boyer and Danielle Darrieux.

5. Langner, *The Magic Curtain,* p. 266.

6. Sherwood, *There Shall Be No Night* (New York, 1940), Preface, p. xxii. See also Sherwood, *Idiot's Delight* (New York, 1936), Postscript, pp. 189–90.

7. Langner, *The Magic Curtain,* p. 265.

8. Quoted in Brown, *The Worlds of Robert E. Sherwood: Mirror to His Times,* p. 341.

9. Langner, *The Magic Curtain,* pp. 327–28; Sherwood, *There Shall Be No Night,* Preface, p. xxx; Maurice Zolotow, *Stagestruck: The Romance of Alfred Lunt and Lynn Fontanne* (New York, 1965), p. 227.

10. Zolotow, *Stagestruck,* p. 243.

11. Rice, *Minority Report,* p. 375.

12. Carlos Baker, *Hemingway: A Life Story,* pp. 321, 329, 338; Theresa Helburn to Odets, March 13, 1940, letter in Theater Guild Papers, Yale University Library.

13. Hemingway to Langner, received March 19, 1940, in Theater Guild Papers, Yale.

14. Hemingway to Langer, *loc. cit.;* Alice Evans, editorial, *NTN,* May 1940, p. 1.

15. Langner, *The Magic Curtain,* pp. 321–26; Helburn, *A Wayward Quest,* pp. 249–50.

16. *Three Plays* (New York, 1940), Preface, p. 1.

17. Helburn, *A Wayward Quest,* p. 290.

CHAPTER 12

1. Mantle, ed., *The Best Plays of 1935–36* (New York, 1936), p. 3.

2. Jack Pulaski, "The Year in Legit," *Variety,* Jan. 1, 1935, p. 210; Pulaski, "Year in the Legitimate," *Variety,* Jan. 6, 1937, p. 209.

3. "Our Town—from Stage to Screen," *TA,* Nov. 1940, p. 824.

4. "Actor's Forum," *NT,* March 1935, p. 29; Pulaski, "The Year in Legit," *Variety,* Jan. 1936, p. 210; Pulaski, "Year in the Legitimate," *Vari-*

ety, Jan. 5, 1938, p. 191; Pulaski, "The Legit in 1938," _Variety_, Jan. 4, 1939, p. 187; Pulaski, "Legit's Comeback," _Variety_, Jan. 3, 1940, p. 147.

5. This they achieved in 1962.

6. According to Rome, in conversation with the present writer, Kaufman and Hart did work on the sketches, but preferred to leave their names off them.

7. Brewer, _Tide Rising_ (New York, 1937). "A Note from the Author," pp. 5–10; "Editorials," _NTF_, March 1937, p. 51.

8. Kazan, who played the part, was also recruited by Warners as an actor. He appeared in films for the company in 1940 and 1941, but not as a gangster.

9. As such, with its ideational content greatly reduced, it was filmed by Warners in 1948 with Humphrey Bogart as McCloud and Edward G. Robinson as his antagonist, renamed Rocco. The McCloud of the Playwrights' Company production was Paul Muni.

10. Webster Smalley, ed., _Five Plays by Langston Hughes_, Introduction, p. x.

11. See Hellman, _An Unfinished Woman_ (Boston, 1969), pp. 10–15.

12. Flanagan, _Arena_, p. 146.

13. Clurman, _The Fervent Years_, p. 260.

14. Mantle, ed., _The Best Plays of 1938–39_ (New York, 1939), p. 145.

15. Houseman, _Run-Through_, p. 292.

16. Leon Stein, _The Triangle Fire_ (Philadelphia, 1962), p. 109.

17. The information in this and the following paragraph is taken from Anatole Chujoy, _The New York City Ballet_ (New York, 1953), pp. 18–22, 75–79, 365–72; George Amberg, _Ballet in America_ (New York, 1949), pp. 47–49, 55–56, 96–98, 169; Walter Terry, _Ballet: A New Guide to the Liveliest Art_ (New York, 1959), pp. 151–52, 162–63, 250–52, 311–12.

18. Rice, _Minority Report_, p. 390.

19. _Ibid._, p. 380.

20. Behrman, _People in a Diary_, pp. 212–17.

21. Rice, "Apologia Pro Vita Sua," _NYT_, Dec. 25, 1938, Sec. 9, p. 5.

22. Rice, _Minority Report_, pp. 391–92.

23. John Mason Brown, _The Worlds of Robert E. Sherwood: Mirror to His Times_, p. 325.

24. Sherwood had seen the play and admired it in 1920; Brown, p. 368.

25. Brown, _The Worlds of Robert E. Sherwood_. . . .

26. Sherwood, _Abe Lincoln in Illinois_ (New York, 1939), "The Substance of _Abe Lincoln_ . . . ," pp. 231, 246.

27. Hellman, _Four Plays_ (New York, 1942), Introduction, p. x.

28. Tallulah Bankhead, _Tallulah_ (New York, 1952), pp. 241–44; "Benefits for Finns Stir Theatre Row," _NYT_, Jan. 19, 1940, p. 21; "Sees Finnish Aid Imperiling Peace," _NYT_, Jan. 21, 1940, p. 27; Margaret Case Harriman, "Miss Lily of New Orleans," _NY_, Nov. 8, 1941, p. 24.

29. In Hollywood it was the kind of character that became the screen image of Jean Arthur, the working girl *par excellence* of Depression films and the inevitable choice for the role of Alice in Frank Capra's film of the play.

30. Luce, in his Introduction to the printed text (New York, 1940), p. vii, was under the impression that the city was in fact New York.

31. HUAC, Hearings, *Communist Infiltration of the Hollywood Motion Picture Industry*, Part 1 (Washington, 1951), p. 190.

INDEX